AF756016

MATLAB – A UBIQUITOUS TOOL FOR THE PRACTICAL ENGINEER

Edited by **Clara M. Ionescu**

MATLAB – A Ubiquitous Tool for the Practical Engineer
Edited by Clara M. Ionescu

Published by InTech
Janeza Trdine 9, 51000 Rijeka, Croatia

Copyright © 2011 InTech
All chapters are distributed under the Creative Commons Attribution 3.0 license, which allows users to download, copy and build upon published articles even for commercial purposes, as long as the author and publisher are properly credited, which ensures maximum dissemination and a wider impact of our publications. After this work has been published by InTech, authors have the right to republish it, in whole or part, in any publication of which they are the author, and to make other personal use of the work. Any republication, referencing or personal use of the work must explicitly identify the original source.

As for readers, this license allows users to download, copy and build upon published chapters even for commercial purposes, as long as the author and publisher are properly credited, which ensures maximum dissemination and a wider impact of our publications.

Notice
Statements and opinions expressed in the chapters are these of the individual contributors and not necessarily those of the editors or publisher. No responsibility is accepted for the accuracy of information contained in the published chapters. The publisher assumes no responsibility for any damage or injury to persons or property arising out of the use of any materials, instructions, methods or ideas contained in the book.

Publishing Process Manager Davor Vidic

Technical Editor Teodora Smiljanic

Cover Designer InTech Design Team

Additional hard copies can be obtained from orders@intechopen.com

MATLAB – A Ubiquitous Tool for the Practical Engineer, Edited by Clara M. Ionescu
p. cm.
ISBN 978-953-307-907-3

We are IntechOpen, the world's leading publisher of Open Access books

Built by scientists, for scientists

4,000+
Open access books available

116,000+
International authors and editors

120M+
Downloads

151
Countries delivered to

Our authors are among the
Top 1%
most cited scientists

12.2%
Contributors from top 500 universities

CLARIVATE ANALYTICS BOOK CITATION INDEX INDEXED

WEB OF SCIENCE™

Selection of our books indexed in the Book Citation Index
in Web of Science™ Core Collection (BKCI)

Interested in publishing with us?
Contact book.department@intechopen.com

Numbers displayed above are based on latest data collected.
For more information visit www.intechopen.com

For EU product safety concerns:
IN TECH d.o.o., Prolaz Marije Krucifikse Kozulić 3, 51000 Rijeka, Croatia,
info@intechopen.com or visit our website at intechopen.com.

Meet the editor

Dr. Clara M. Ionescu was born in 1979, Cimpulung, Romania. She received the M.Sc. degree in industrial informatics and automation from "Dunarea de Jos" University, Galati, Romania, in 2003. She obtained the Ph.D. degree at Ghent University, Gent, Belgium in 2009, on identification of human respiratory system by means of fractional order models. Currently, she holds a post-doctoral grant in the same university, funded by the Flanders Research Foundation (FWO), one of the most prestigious scientific organizations in Belgium. Her expertise involves modeling, identification and control in both technical and non-technical areas, all developed within the MATLAB framework. She is co-lecturer at Ghent University for the courses 'Modelling and Control of Dynamical Systems' and 'Computer Control of Industrial Processes', where students are instructed by means of MATLAB. She has more than 100 peer-reviewed publications in journals, conferences and books, being actively involved in promoting the concept of fractality in biological systems and their applications to medicine.

Contents

Preface

A well-known statement says that the PID controller is the "bread and butter" of the control engineer. This is indeed true, from a scientific standpoint. However, nowadays, in the era of computer science, when the paper and pencil have been replaced by the keyboard and the display of computers, one may equally say that MATLAB is the "bread" in the above statement. MATLAB has became a de facto tool for the modern system engineer. The present book is written for both engineering students, as well as for practicing engineers. The wide range of applications in which MATLAB is the working framework, shows that it is a powerful, comprehensive and easy-to-use environment for performing technical computations.

The book includes various excellent applications in which MATLAB is employed. Most of the authors are well skilled in working with MATLAB for their educational, scientific or engineering purposes, as in:

- applied mathematics,
- data acquisition and communication issues for real-life experiments and hardware-in-the-loop connections,
- communication protocols with MATLAB (Serial Interface, OPC, Ethernet functions, Real Time Workshop)
- embedded systems (C++, S-functions) ,
- image processing and data archiving
- control systems and algorithms.

This book is in fact a collection of results from a wide range of users, including engineers, scientists, computer experts and applied mathematicians. The diversity of results and applications suggests that a wide range of readers will benefit from its content.

It is clear that MATLAB has opened a fascinating new world of possibilities. The contributions presented in this book serve as a proof that MATLAB is a useful tool to address many challenging problems.

I would also like to add a few personal words on the concept of open access publishing. Although not yet fully matured and not yet fully accepted by the scientific community, the open access database offered by InTech is a great opportunity for researchers to communicate their work in a rapid and broadly accessible manner. I do believe that an open access to science and technology is the key of staying alert in this continuously changing scientific environment and keep the pace with the progress available all over the world.

Finally, I would like to thank the publishing department of InTech for the excellent support and guidance in the development of this book, which is in fact a collection of contributions bearing MATLAB as the interwoven feature.

Dr. ir. Clara M. Ionescu
Faculty of Engineering and Architecture
Ghent University,
Belgium

Part 1

Applied Mathematics

1

Effect of the Guess Function & Continuation Method on the Run Time of MATLAB BVP Solvers

Fikri Serdar Gökhan
Gazikent University, Faculty of Engineering and Architecture, Department of Electrical and Electronic Engineering, Gaziantep Turkey

1. Introduction

The MATLAB computing environment is a package used extensively throughout industry, research and education by users of a complete range in proficiency. MATLAB provides then an ideal platform to introduce such an item of Boundary Value Problem (BVP) software and indeed, Kierzenka and Shampine (Kierzenka & Shampine, 2001) developed the core BVP Ordinary Differential Equation (ODE) software bvp4c to solve a large class of two-point boundary value problems of the form;

$$y'(x) = f(x, y(x), p) \tag{1}$$

$$g(x_L, x_R, y(x_L), y(x_R), p) = 0 \tag{2}$$

where f is continuous and Lipschitz function in y and p is a vector of unknown parameters. Their view was that a user solving a BVP of form (1) in MATLAB would be most interested in the graphical representation of a solution, and as such a solver with a MIRK4-based Simpson Method would be appropriate for graphical accuracy.

If information is specified at more than one point the problem (1) becomes a Boundary Value Problem. The most common types of BVP are those for which information given at precisely two points. These are known as two-point boundary value problems.

The MATLAB BVP solver of bvp4c is introduced as a Residual control based, adaptive mesh solver. An adaptive mesh solver is an alternative approach to that of a uniform mesh, which would specify a uniform grid of data points x_i over the interval $[x_i, x_{i+1}]$ and solve accordingly. The adaptive solver will adjust the mesh points at each stage in the iterative procedure, distributing them to points where they are most needed. This can lead to obvious advantages in terms of computational and storage costs as well as allowing control over the grid resolution. The concept of a residual is the cornerstone of the bvp4c framework; being responsible for both errors control and mesh selection (Hale, 2006).

The most difficult part for the solution of BVPs is to provide an initial estimation to the solution. In order to direct the solver for the solution of interest, it is necessary to assist the solver by informing it with a guess. Not only for the computation of the solution of interest but also whether any solution is achieved or not depends strongly on the initial guess. Therefore, depending of the guess function, BVPs may have no solution or a single solution, or multiple solutions. Moreover, the quality of the initial guess can be critical to the solver performance, which reduces or augments the run time. However, coming up with a sufficiently good guess can be the most challenging part of solving a BVP. Certainly, the user should apply the knowledge of the problem's physical origin (MATLAB Documentation).

In MATLAB, when solving BVPs the user must provide a guess to assist the solver in computing the desired solution (Kierzenka & Shampine, 2001). MATLAB BVP solvers call for users to provide guesses for the mesh and solution. Although MATLAB BVP solvers take an unusual approach to the control of error in case of having poor guesses for the mesh and solution, especially for the nonlinear BVP, a good guess is necessary to obtain convergence (Shampine *et al.*, 2003).

Whatever intuitive guess values/functions are imposed, eventually the BVP solver fails for some parameters or for some lengths. If any guess values works for the range of length, the rest of the length may be extended using *continuation*. The method of continuation exploits the fact that the solution obtained for one input will serve as the initial guess for the next value tried. In case of any difficulty in finding a guess for the interval of interest, generally it will be easier to solve the problem on a shorter interval. Then the solution of the sequence of BVPs on the shorter interval will be used as a guess for the next section. With modest increases in the interval, this will continue until the interval of interest is spanned (Shampine *et al.*, 2003).

The cost of the continuation method is the increased run time. How the guess value good is, the less computation time it takes with the continuation method. This is due the fact that, the remaining length depends of the convergence length (based on the guess value) which its higher value reduces the computation time.

2. Initial setup

The first step in solving a problem is defining it in a way the software can understand. The bvp4c framework uses a number of subfunctions which make it as simple as possible for the user to enter the ODE function, initial data and parameters for a given problem. By way of the following example we see exactly how a problem is supplied and solved by bvp4c. For the evaluation of the guess value /function, the steady-state Brillouin equation is exploited. The coupled ODEs for the evolution of the intensities of pump I_p and Stokes I_s can be written as (Agrawal, 2001),

$$\frac{dIp}{dz} = -g_B I_P I_S - \alpha I_p \tag{3}$$

$$\frac{dIs}{dz} = -g_B I_P I_S + \alpha I_S \tag{4}$$

where $0 \le z \le L$ is the propagation distance along the optical fiber of the total length L, α is the fiber loss coefficient, g_B is the Brillouin gain coefficient, respectively. Here, it is assumed that, Stokes wave is launched from the rear end of the fiber. Then the known values of the input pump power $I_p(0)$ and the Stokes wave power I_s (L) are referred as the boundary values.

The first task is to define the ODEs in MATLAB as a function to return these equations. Similarly the user then rewrites the boundary conditions to correspond to this form of the problem. We may code the ODEs for scalar evaluation and boundary conditions, respectively as,

```
function dydx = bvpode(x,y)
global alpha_s gb K

dydx =   [ -gb *y(1)*y(2)-alpha_s*y(1)
           -gb *y(1)*y(2)+alpha_s*y(2) ];

------------------------------------------------------------

function res = bvpbc(ya,yb)
 global Ip0 IsL

 res = [ya(1)- Ip0
        yb(2)- IsL ];
```

The next step is to create an initial guess for the form of the solution using a specific MATLAB subroutine called bvpinit . The user passes a vector x and an initial guess on this mesh in the form bvpinit (x, Yinit), which is then converted into a structure useable by bvp4c. Aside from a sensible guess being necessary for a convergent solution the mesh vector passed to bvpinit will also define the boundary points of the problem, i.e. x_L = x[1] and x_R = x[end].
The initial guess for the solution may take one of two forms. One option is a vector where Yinit(i) is a constant guess for the i-th component y(i,:) of the solution at all the mesh points in x. The other is as a function of a scalar x, for example bvpinit(x,@yfun) where for any x in [a, b], yfun(x) returns a guess for the solution y(x). It must be pointed out that even when a function is supplied that approximates the solution everywhere in the interval; the solver uses its values only on the initial mesh. The guess can be coded as a function of a scalar x as,

```
function v = guess(x)

global alpha_s L gb k Pp0 PsL Aeff
a=alpha_s*L;
k=gb/Aeff*Pp0*L;
epsilon=PsL/Pp0;
kappa=-log(gb/Aeff*PsL*L);
T=log(kappa*(1-kappa/k));
c0=-(PsL + PsL*k - 1)/((PsL*k^2)/2 + 1);
A=c0./(1-(1-c0).*exp(-c0*k.*x));
B=c0*(1-c0)./(exp(c0*k.*x)-1+c0);
w=(A.^(exp(-a))).*exp(-a.*x);
u=(B.*exp(a.*(x-1)));

v=[w*Pp0; u*Pp0];
```

The next subroutine to look at is bvpset, that specifies which options bvp4c should be use in solving it. The function is called options = bvpset('name1',value1,...) and since MATLAB documentation gives an in depth account of each of the options only a brief outline of those notable is given here (Hale, 2006).

```
options = []; % default
%options = bvpset('Stats','on','RelTol',1e-5,'abstol',1e-4);
%options = bvpset(options,'Vectorized','on');
%options = bvpset(options,'FJacobian',@odeJac);
%options = bvpset(options,'BCJacobian',@bcJac);
```

RelTol - Relative tolerance for the residual [positive scalar 1e-3]
The computed solution *S*(x) is the exact solution of S′(x) = F(*x*, *S(x)*) + *res*(x). On each subinterval of the mesh, component i of the residual must satisfy norm

$$norm\left(\frac{res(i)}{\max(abs(F(i)),\ AbsTol(i)/RelTol)}\right) \le RelTol$$

AbsTol - Absolute tolerance for the residual [positive scalar or vector 1e-6]
Elements of a vector of tolerances apply to corresponding components of the residual vector. AbsTol defaults to 1e-6.
FJacobian \ BCJacobian - Analytical partial derivatives of ODEFUN \ BCFUN
Computation of the Jacobian matrix at each mesh point can be a very expensive process. By passing an analytic derivative of the ODE and BC functions the user can greatly reduce computational time. For example when solving y′ = f(x, y), setting FJacobian to `@FJAC` where `∂f/∂y = FJAC(x, y)` evaluates the Jacobian of f with respect to y.
Stats - Display computational cost statistics [on — off]
Vectorized - Vectorized ODE function [on – off]
As will be discussed in section 6, bvp4c is able to accept a vectorised function which can markedly increase the efficiency of calculating local Jacobians over using finite differences with the odenumjac subroutine. Hence in the following programs, we will define

```
options = bvpset('Stats','on','RelTol',1e-5,'abstol',1e-4);
solinit = bvpinit(linspace(0,L,2), @guess);
```

And call the bvp4c routine with:

```
sol = bvp4c(@ode,@bc,solinit,options);
```

The above essentially ends the user input in solving the BVP system and the rest is left to bvp4c. Within the framework there are several notable steps which should be expounded.

3. Derivation of the guess

In this chapter, four guess functions are derived for the assistance of the MATLAB BVP solvers with the help of MATLAB symbolic toolbox.

3.1 1st Guess

If the constant guess is used as the initial values i.e., for the pump "Ip0" and for the Stokes "IsL" and `L = 10000;`

```
solinit = bvpinit(linspace(0,L,2),@guess);
options = bvpset('Stats','on','RelTol',1e-5);
function v = guess(x)
global Ip0  IsL
v=[Ip0 ; IsL];
```

It prompts as, "Unable to solve the collocation equations -- a singular Jacobian encountered". However, if the computation length is decreased as, `L = 1000`, the solver *is able* to solve coupled equations with these poor guesses v=[Ip0 ; IsL]. Therefore, with these guess values the convergence length (the maximum length which the solver is able to converge) is 1000 meter. The evolution of the guess values (estimate) with the real solution is shown in Fig. 1

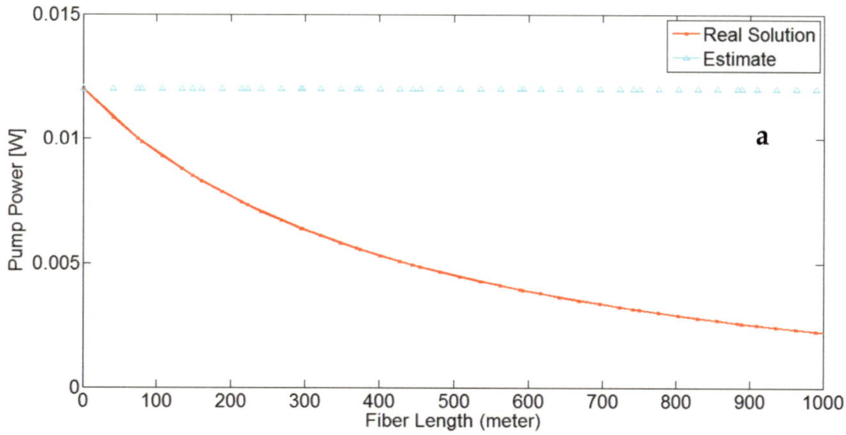

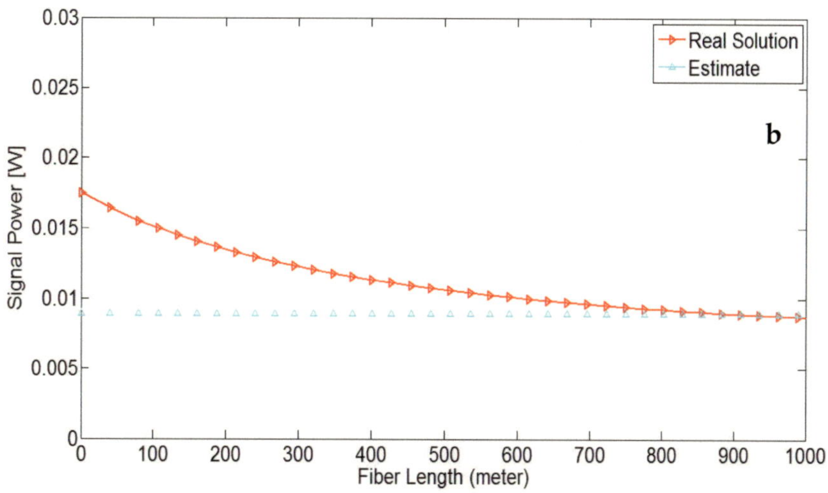

Fig. 1. Evolution of the guess values and real solution according to 1st guess

3.2 2nd Guess

If we guess that I_p and I_s is linearly changing as,

```
Ip ~ Ip0+A*z ;
Is ~ Is0+B*z ;
```

Exploiting with the MATLAB Symbolic Toolbox using the following script,

```
syms Is Ip Is0 Ip0 IsL gb L alpha A B z

 Ip = Ip0+A*z ;
 Is = Is0+B*z ;

 eqn1 = collect(diff(Ip,'z') + (gb)*Ip*Is+alpha*Ip);
 eqn2 = collect(diff(Is,'z') + (gb)*Ip*Is-alpha*Is);

 eqn3=collect(taylor(eqn1,1,0),z)
 eqn4=collect(taylor(eqn2,1,L),z)
```

The below output is produced;

```
eqn3 =  A + Ip0*alpha + (Ip0*Is0*gb)
eqn4 =  B - Is0*alpha - L*(B*alpha - (gb*(A*Is0 + B*Ip0))) +
        (Ip0*Is0*gb) + (A*B*L^2*gb)

Is0=IsL-B*L;
```

Here, there are two equations and two unknowns A and B. With the substitution of Is0, It can be solved simultaneously by the below script,

```
eqn=

solve(A + Ip0*alpha + (Ip0*(IsL-B*L)*gb),...
    B - (IsL-B*L)*alpha - L*(B*alpha - (gb*(A*(IsL-B*L) + B*Ip0)))+
    (Ip0*(IsL-B*L)*gb) + (A*B*L^2*gb),...
    'A','B')
eqn =

    A: [1x1 sym]
    B:  [1x1 sym]
```

Here A and B can be obtained as,

```
A=-(Ip0*alpha_s + Ip0^2*IsL*L*gb^2 + Ip0*IsL*gb -
    Ip0*IsL*L*alpha_s*gb)/(Ip0*IsL*L^2*gb^2);

B=(IsL*alpha_s + Ip0*IsL^2*L*gb^2 - Ip0*IsL*gb +
   Ip0*IsL*L*alpha_s*gb)/(Ip0*IsL*L^2*gb^2)

Ip ~ Ip0+A.*x ;
```

```
Is ~ (IsL-B.*L)+B.*x ;
```

The evolution of the 2nd guess values with the real solution is shown in Fig. 2

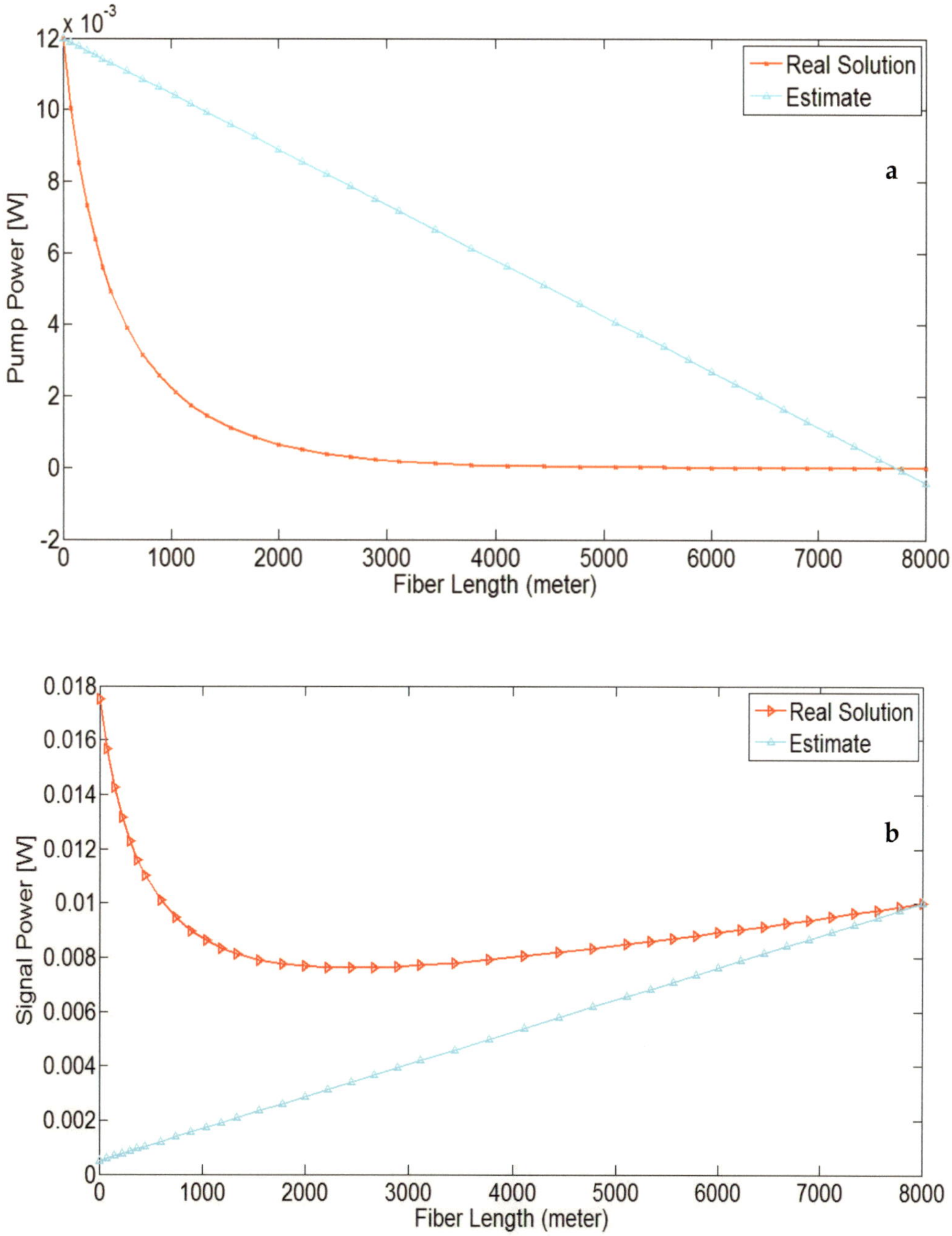

Fig. 2. Evolution of the guess values and real solution according to 2nd guess

3.3 3rd Guess

If it is guessed that I_p and I_s is exponentially changing as,

```
Ip ~ Ip0*exp(gamma1*z) ;
Is ~ Is0*exp(kappa1*z) ;
```

with using the following script,

```
syms Ip Is Is0 Ip0 gb z L IsL alpha gamma1 kappa1

Ip = Ip0*exp(gamma1*z) ;
Is = Is0*exp(kappa1*z) ;

eqn1 = collect(diff(Ip,'z') + (gb)*Ip*Is+alpha*Ip);
eqn2 = collect(diff(Is,'z') + (gb)*Ip*Is-alpha*Is);

eqn3=taylor(eqn1,1,0)
eqn4=taylor(eqn2,1,L)
```

The below output is produced;

```
eqn3 =Ip0*alpha + Ip0*gamma1 + (Ip0*Is0*gb)
eqn4 =Is0*kappa1*exp(L*kappa1) - Is0*alpha*exp(L*kappa1) +
       (Ip0*Is0*gb*exp(L*gamma1)*exp(L*kappa1))
```

`gamma1` and `kappa1` can be obtained as;

```
eqn5=solve(Ip0*alpha + Ip0*gamma1 + (Ip0*Is0*gb),'gamma1')
gamma1= -(alpha + Is0*gb)
```

using the same way;

```
kappa1 = (alpha - Ip0*gb*exp(L*gamma1));
```

Here, Is0 can be readily found by,

```
Is(z) = Is0*exp(kappa1*z) ;
For z=L
IsL= Is0*exp(kappa1*L);
Is0= IsL/exp(kappa1*L);
```

Therefore,

```
Ip ~ Ip0*exp(gamma1*z) ;
Is ~ IsL/exp(kappa1*L)*exp(kappa1*z) ;
```

The evolution of the 3rd guess values with the real solution is shown in Fig. 3

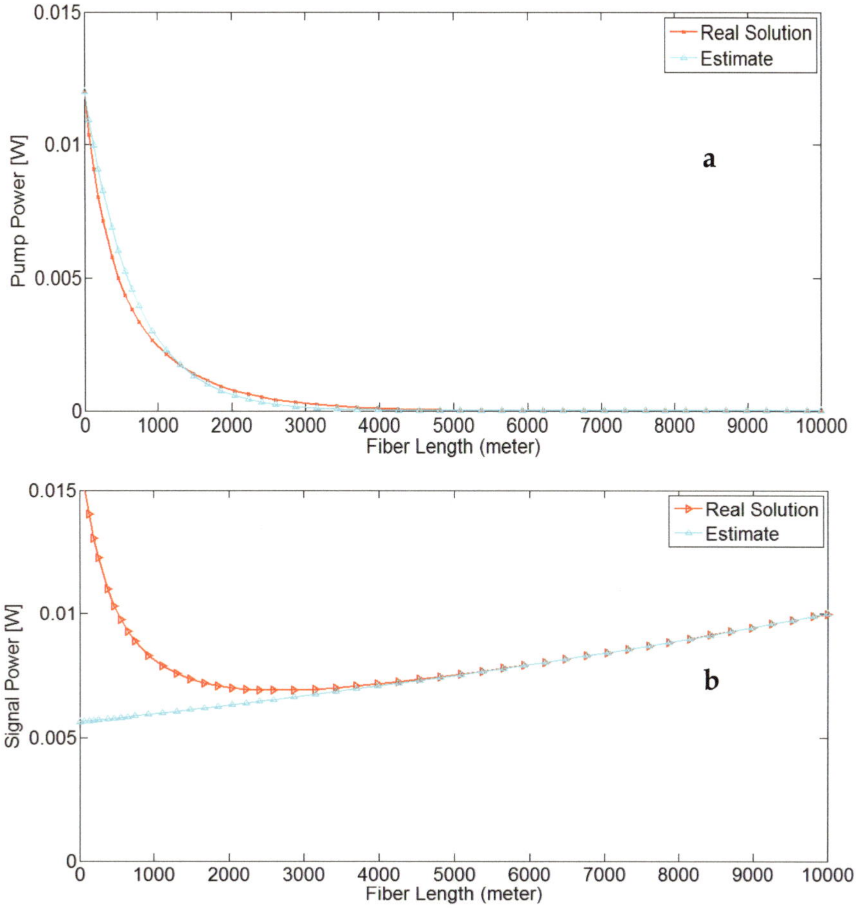

Fig. 3. Evolution of the guess values and real solution according to 3rd guess

3.4 4th Guess

Highly intuitive guess function may be derived the using the solution of lossless system, i.e., with eliminating the α coefficient in the Eq (3) and Eq. (4),

$$\frac{dIp}{dz} = -g_B I_P I_S \tag{5}$$

$$\frac{dIs}{dz} = -g_B I_P I_S \tag{6}$$

With neglecting the attenuation coefficient, the solution of the Eq.(5) and Eq.(6) is found as (Kobyakov *et al.*, 2006),

$$A(\zeta) = c_0[1 - (1 - c_0)\exp(-c_0 k\zeta)]^{-1} P_P(0) \tag{7}$$

$$B(\zeta) = c_0(1 - c_0)[\exp(c_0 k\zeta) - 1 + c_0]^{-1} P_P(0) \tag{8}$$

where,

$$c_0 \approx \frac{1}{k}\left\{\Lambda + \ln\left[\Lambda(1-\frac{\Lambda}{k})\right]\right\},\ k = \frac{g_B}{A_{eff}}P_P(0)L,\ \zeta = \frac{z}{L} \tag{9}$$

where,

$$\Lambda = -\ln(\frac{P_{SL}}{P_{p0}}k) = -\ln[\frac{g_B}{A_{eff}}P_{SL}L],\ \frac{P_{SL}}{P_{p0}}k \ll 1 \tag{10}$$

Exploiting the solution of Eq.(7) and Eq. (8), general expression of $P_p(z)$ and $P_S(z)$ can be derived as,

$$P_P(z) = A(z)\cdot[1 - a\cdot(A\cdot x + B\cdot x^2)] \tag{11}$$

$$P_S(z) = B(z)\cdot[1 - a\cdot(C\cdot x + D\cdot x^2)] \tag{12}$$

If a→0, then $P_P(z) = A(z)$ and $P_S(z) = B(z)$

```
syms z k A B C D a AA BB c0 x

AA=c0/(1-(1-c0)*exp(-c0*k*z));
BB=c0*(1-c0)/(exp(c0*k*z)-1+c0);
w=(AA*(1-a*(A*x+B*x^2)));

u=(BB*(1-a*(C*x+D*x^2)));
eqn1 = collect(diff(w,1,'z') + (k*u*w)+a*w)
eqn2 = collect(diff(u,1,'z') + (k*u*w)-a*u)
The output produces,

eqn1 =
 …+ ((c0^2*k*(A*a + C*a)*(c0 - 1))/(((c0 - 1)/exp(c0*k*z) + 1)*(c0 +
exp(c0*k*z) - 1)) - (A*a^2*c0)/((c0 - 1)/exp(c0*k*z) + 1) -
(2*B*a*c0)/((c0 - 1)/exp(c0*k*z) + 1) - (A*a*c0^2*k*(c0 -
1))/(exp(c0*k*z)*((c0 - 1)/exp(c0*k*z) + 1)^2))*x …
+ (a*c0)/((c0 - 1)/exp(c0*k*z) + 1) - (A*a*c0)/((c0 - 1)/exp(c0*k*z)
+ 1) + (c0^2*k*(c0 - 1))/(exp(c0*k*z)*((c0 - 1)/exp(c0*k*z) + 1)^2)
- (c0^2*k*(c0 - 1))/(((c0 - 1)/exp(c0*k*z) + 1)*(c0 + exp(c0*k*z) -
1))

 eqn2 =
 … + ((2*D*a*c0*(c0 - 1))/(c0 + exp(c0*k*z) - 1) - (C*a^2*c0*(c0 -
1))/(c0 + exp(c0*k*z) - 1) + (c0^2*k*(A*a + C*a)*(c0 - 1))/(((c0 -
1)/exp(c0*k*z) + 1)*(c0 + exp(c0*k*z) - 1)) -
(C*a*c0^2*k*exp(c0*k*z)*(c0 - 1))/(c0 + exp(c0*k*z) - 1)^2)*x …
+ (a*c0*(c0 - 1))/(c0 + exp(c0*k*z) - 1) + (C*a*c0*(c0 - 1))/(c0 +
exp(c0*k*z) - 1) - (c0^2*k*(c0 - 1))/(((c0 - 1)/exp(c0*k*z) + 1)*(c0
+ exp(c0*k*z) - 1)) + (c0^2*k*exp(c0*k*z)*(c0 - 1))/(c0 +
exp(c0*k*z) - 1)^2
```

We are interested in the behavior as $z \to 0$ and so, the higher the power of x, the less effect it has in these expansions. Our goal is to satisfy the equations as well as possible, so we want to choose coefficients that make as many successive terms zero as possible, starting with the lowest power. To eliminate the constant terms, we see from the expansions that we must take

```
A= 1; C=-1;
B= -(a - a/exp(c0*k*z) + (a*c0)/exp(c0*k*z) - (c0*k)/exp(c0*k*z) +
    (c0^2*k)/exp(c0*k*z))/((2*c0)/exp(c0*k*z) - 2/exp(c0*k*z) + 2)
D=  (a - a/exp(c0*k*z) + (a*c0)/exp(c0*k*z) - (c0*k)/exp(c0*k*z) +
    (c0^2*k)/exp(c0*k*z))/((2*c0)/exp(c0*k*z) - 2/exp(c0*k*z) + 2)
```

The evolution of the 4rd guess values with the real solution is shown in Fig. 4

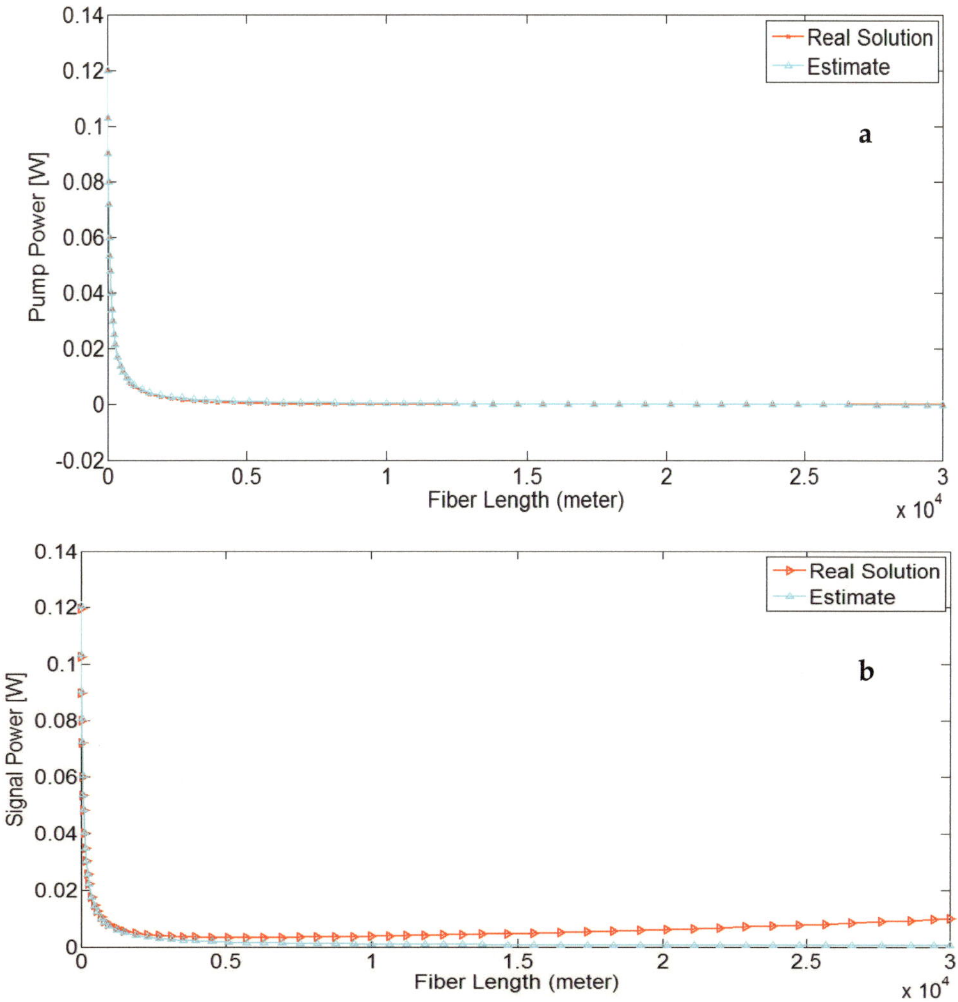

Fig. 4. Evolution of the guess values and real solution according to 4th guess

Guess	Length(mt) /mesh	Convergence length/mesh	Computation Time (with bvp4c) at 8000 meter
1st Guess - values (Ip0,IsL)	8000/ 40	8000/40	~1.18 sec
2nd Guess - functions (linear)	8000/ 40	9000/453	~1.13 sec
3rd Guess -functions (exponential)	8000/ 40	15000/56	~1.13 sec
4th Guess functions (modified exponential)	8000/ 35	30000/61	~1.0 sec

Table 1. Guess values/functions versus convergence length/mesh and run time.

As can be seen from Table 1 and Fig.4 the best estimation is the 4th guess. Because its' convergence length (30000) is more than the others (15000, 9000, 8000, respectively). The performance of the 2nd guess is approximately same as the first one. Because it hardly converge the solution using 453 points at 9000 meter. However, its performance is same as the first one with 40 points at 8000 meter.

4. Continuation

The method of continuation exploits the fact that generally the solution of one BVP is a good guess for the solution of another with slightly different parameters. If you have difficulty in finding a guess for the solution that is good enough to achieve convergence for the interval of interest, it is frequently the case that the problem is easier to solve on a shorter interval. The idea is then to solve a sequence of BVPs with the solution on one interval being used as a guess for the problem posed on a longer interval. Of course, this technique cannot be used to extend the interval *ad infinitum*; no matter how good the guess is, eventually the solver will not be able to distinguish the different kinds of solutions (Shampine *et al.*, 2003).
For the range of interested lengths bigger than the convergence lengths, the continuation process can be applied. Some types of snippets of continuation are illustrated below,

```
=================#1#=========================
options = bvpset('FJacobian',@sampleJac,...
                 'BCJacobian',@sampleBCJac,...
                 'Vectorized','on');

sol = bvpinit([-1 -0.5 0 0.5 1],[1 0]);

c = 0.1;
for i=2:4
    c = c/10;
    sol = bvp4c(@sampleODE,@sampleBC,sol,options);
end

=================#2#========================

infinity = 3;
maxinfinity = 6;

solinit = bvpinit(linspace(0,infinity,5),[0 0 1]);
sol = bvp4c(@fsode,@fsbc,solinit);
```

```
eta = sol.x;
f = sol.y;

for Bnew = infinity+1:maxinfinity

  solinit = bvpinit(sol,[0 Bnew]); % Extend solution to Bnew.
  sol = bvp4c(@fsode,@fsbc,solinit);
  eta = sol.x;
  f = sol.y;
```

=================#3#=====================

```
L=30000;
for i = 1:1000:L
D = 5*i/1000; d = 1/D;
if i == 1
solinit = bvpinit(linspace(1,i,10),@guess);
else
solinit = bvpinit(sol,[d,D]);
end

sol = bvp4c(@odes,@bcs,solinit);
end
```

==================#4#======================

```
function Boundary_value_increment
global a b

a= XL;     %[a
b= XR;     %   b]
sol = bvpinit(linspace(0,L,2),[Boundary values for each pump and
signal power]);

options = bvpset('Stats','on','RelTol',1e-5);

for k=1:Desired_Power
b=b+k;
sol = bvp4c(@bvpode,@bvpbc,sol,options);
end
```

If the interested length is bigger than the convergence length then continuation can be applied with the **bvpxtend** function. In the recent version of MATLAB, bvpinit function is simplified to a new function **bvpxtend**. Besides offering new possibilities, this function permits extension of length of interval to only one end point at a time (Kierzenka & Shampine, 2008). Briefly,

`solinit = bvpxtend(sol,xnew,ynew)` uses solution sol computed on [a,b] to form a solution guess for the interval extended to xnew. The extension point xnew must be outside the interval [a,b], but on either side. The vector ynew provides an initial guess for the solution at xnew.

For example, if it is assumed that the convergence and interested lengths are 15 and 30 km, respectively, the continuation can be applied via the below codes (Gokhan & Yilmaz, 2011a),

=================#5#=====================

```
L= 15000;
Interested=30000;
solinit = bvpinit(linspace(0,L,2),[Guess expression running with 15 km]);
sol = bvp4c(@bvpode,@bvpbc,solinit,options);
.
for Bnew=L:2000:Interested
    solinit=bvpxtend(sol,Bnew);
    sol = bvp4c(@bvpode,@bvpbc,solinit,options);
end
```

In the above codes, 2000 is the step size which is the modest increment range. In case of bigger step size, the solver may fail but the computation time reduces. On the other hand, if this increment is kept little, it takes more time to reach the end of the computation. Therefore, selecting the step size is important factor for the efficiency of the computation for continuation. One advantage of using bvpxtend function is the reduced computation time. Because, bvp solvers try to use mesh points as few as possible, the step size is incremented automatically depending on the previous mesh points. In bvpxtend, after obtaining convergence for the mesh, the codes adapt the mesh so as to obtain an accurate numerical solution with a modest number of mesh points. Here it must be emphasized that, for BVPs the most difficult part is providing an initial approximation to the solution.

5. Effect of the step size on the run time

Using the snippets 5 and the 1st Guess of Table 1, the performance of the continuation over step size is illustrated in Table 2.

Convergence Length (km)	Computation Length (km)	Linspace (0,L,**N**) Optimal *N*	Step Size (mt.)	Computation Time at Convergence Length (with bvp4c)	Total Computation time	Mesh number (between) (with bvp4c)
40	50	10	50	~3.2 sec	~110.0 sec	482-541
40	50	10	100	~3.2 sec	~60.0 sec	482-541
40	50	10	200	~3.2 sec	~32.8 sec	482-553
40	50	10	300	~3.2 sec	~25.3 sec	482-560
40	50	10	400	~3.2 sec	~23.6 sec	482-663
40	50	10	500	~3.2 sec	~44.5 sec	482-1984
40	50	10	600	Computation fails.		

Table 2. The performance of continuation method versus step size

If the step size is increased over the 600 meter, the computation fails with the below warning message;

```
Warning: Unable to meet the tolerance without using more than 5000 mesh points.
```

```
The last mesh of 4106 points and the solution are available in the
output  argument.

The maximum residual is 0.00018931, while requested accuracy is 1e-
005.
```

As can be seen on Table 2, for some step size over the modest increment, computation blows up (i.e. 600 m). When the step size is between 50 and 400, the number of used mesh is slightly different from each other. However, when it is 500 m, abruptly increase in the number of used mesh is a sign of lack of confidence.

In Fig.5, it can be seen that the distance between some mesh points, especially near the boundaries are denser than the others. This is because the solver tries to control the residual of the interpolating polynomial: $r(x) = S'(x) - f(x,S(x))$. The behavior of this residual depends on the behavior of some high derivatives of the solution (that the solver does not have access to). In the solver, the residual is estimated at each mesh subinterval, and additional mesh points are introduced if the estimate is bigger than the tolerance.

The mesh selection algorithm is 'localized', which means that if the residual is just above the tolerance, the interval will be divided into two (and likely on each of those subintervals, the residual will be much smaller than the tolerance). Also, the algorithm for removing mesh points is quite conservative, so there could be regions where the residual will be quite a bit smaller that the tolerance (i.e., the mesh could be quite a bit denser than necessary)(Kierzenka & Shampine, 2001).

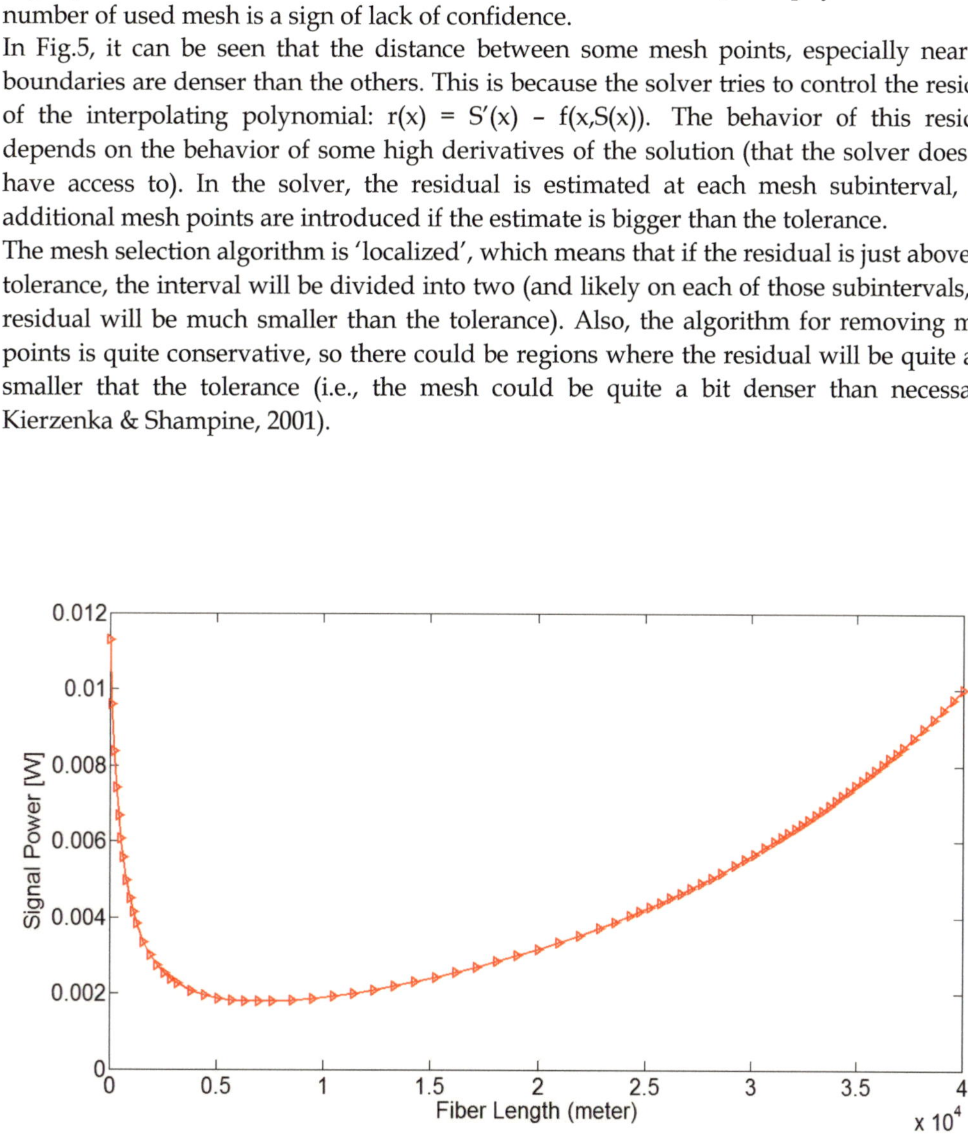

Fig. 5. Evolution of mesh density along the computation

5.1 Effect of the constructing an initial guess with bvpinit function on the run time

As can be seen from Table 3, when constructing an initial guess using `bvpinit(linspace(0,L,N)`, starting with a mesh of 5-10 points could often result in a more efficient run. It must be pointed out that with adaptive collocation solvers, using that many points (N=50,100) with a poor guess could often be counterproductive. In the case of N=100, the solver still achieved the sufficient accuracy as it is between 2 and 10.

Linspace (0,L,N) Optimal *N*	Computation Time (with bvp4c)	Mesh number (with bvp4c)	Maximum Residual
2-4	Singular Jacobian encountered		
5	~3.20 sec	498	9.791e-006
6	~2.85 sec	475	9.967e-006
7	~3.10 sec	483	9.983e-006
8	~2.75 sec	487	9.913e-006
9	~2.87 sec	464	9.848e-006
10	~2.68 sec	469	9.817e-006
50	~2.81 sec	478	9.938e-006
100	~3.10 sec	485	9.959e-006

Table 3. Performance of equally spaced N points for the mesh of a guess

6. Speeding up the run time of BVP solvers

The first technique which is used to reduce run time is vectorizing the evaluation of the differential equations. Vectorization is a valuable tool for speeding up MATLAB programs and this greatly reduces the run time (Shampine *et al.*, 2003). By vectorization, the function $f(x,y)$ is coded so that when given a vector $x=[x_1,x_2,...]$ and a corresponding array of column vectors $y=[y_1,y_2,...]$, it returns an array of column vectors $[f(x_1,y_1),f(x_2,y_2),...])$. By default, bvp4c and bvp4c approximate a Jacobian using finite differences. The evaluation of the ODEs is vectorized by changing the vectors to arrays and changing the multiplication to an array multiplication. It can be coded by changing scalar quantities like y(1) into arrays like y(1,:) and changing from scalar operations to array operations by replacing * and ^ with .* and .^, respectively. When vectorizing the ODEs, the solver must be informed about the presence of vectorization by means of the option `'Vectorized','on'`.

```
options = bvpset('Stats','on','RelTol',1e-3,'Vectorized','on');
```

The second technique is that of supplying analytical partial derivatives or to supply a function for evaluating the `Jacobian` matrix. This is because, in general, BVPs are solved much faster with analytical partial derivatives. However, this is not an easy task since it is too much trouble and inconvenient, although MATLAB Symbolic Toolbox can be exploited when obtaining analytical Jacobians. The third technique is to supply analytical partial derivatives for the boundary conditions. However, it has less effect on the computation time compared with supplying analytical Jacobians and vectorization. The solver permits the user to supply as much information as possible. It must be emphasized that supplying more information for the solvers results in a shorter computation run time (Gokhan & Yilmaz, 2011b).

The set of equations (3) and (4) is vectorized by changing the vectors to arrays and changing the multiplication to an array multiplication as seen below,

```
function dydx = bvpodevectorized(x,y)
global alpha_s gb K

dydx =   [ -gb *y(1,:).*y(2,:)-alpha_s*y(1,:)
           -gb *y(1,:).*y(2,:)+alpha_s*y(2,:) ];
```

Using vectorized ODEs with N=8, the performance of the vectorization is illustrated in Table 4.

Length (mt)	Computation Time with scalar evaluation (with bvp4c)	Computation Time with vectorization (with bvp4c)
5000	~1.83 sec	~1.79 sec
10000	~2.26 sec	~2.15 sec
20000	~2.60 sec	~2.45 sec
30000	~2.70 sec	~2.58 sec
40000	~3.00 sec	~2.85 sec

Table 4. Comparison of the computation time with scalar evaluation and with vectorization

The code bvp4c permits you to supply analytical partial derivatives for either the ODEs or the boundary conditions or both. It is far more important to provide partial derivatives for the ODEs than the boundary conditions. The solver is informed that a function is written for evaluating $\partial f/\partial y$ by providing its handle as the value of the FJacobian option. Similarly, the solver can be informed of a function for evaluating analytical partial derivatives of the boundary conditions with the option BCJacobian (Shampine *et al.*, 2003). FJacobian and BCJacobian can be introduced as with the below codes,

```
%options = bvpset(options,'FJacobian',@odeJac);
%options = bvpset(options,'BCJacobian',@bcJac);
```

The MATLAB Symbolic Toolbox has a function jacobian that can be very helpful when working out partial derivatives for complicated functions. Its use is illustrated with a script for the partial derivatives of the ODEs of this example.

```
syms res y1 y2 y1 y2 alpha_s gb

res = [ -gb*y1*y2 - alpha_s*y1
        -gb*y1*y2 + alpha_s*y2];
dFdy = jacobian(res,[y1; y2])

dFdy =
```

```
[ - alpha_s - gb*y2,          -gb*y1]
[          -gb*y2, alpha_s - gb*y1]
```

The performance of the insertion of analytical partial derivatives and vectorization, and both are compared in Table 5. As can be seen from Table 5, with vectorization and analytical partial derivatives, the computation time is reduced approximately 15 %. The calculations are simulated using the MATLAB 7.9 (R2009b) on an Intel Core i5 2.53 GHz laptop computer.

Length (mt)	Computation Time with scalar evaluation (with bvp4c)	Computation Time with only vectorization (with bvp4c)	Computation Time with only analytical partial derivatives (with bvp4c)	Computation Time with both vectorization & analytical partial derivatives (with bvp4c)
5000	~1.83 sec	~1.79 sec	~1.69 sec	~1.59 sec
10000	~2.26 sec	~2.15 sec	~2.05 sec	~1.80 sec
20000	~2.60 sec	~2.45 sec	~2.26sec	~1.96sec
30000	~2.70 sec	~2.58 sec	~2.40 sec	~2.04 sec
40000	~3.00 sec	~2.85 sec	~2.60 sec	~2.18 sec

Table 5. Comparison of the computation time of bvp4c with vectorization, with analytical partial derivatives and with both

In Table 6, the performance of the bvp5c is illustrated. In terms of scalar evaluation, the performance of bvp5c solver is better than bvpc4 and it is evident as the length is increased. This improvement is about 47 % at 40 km. As in the case of bvp4c, the performance can be increased with vectorization and analytical partial derivatives or with both. Compared with the scalar evaluation, only with vectorization and only with analytical partial derivatives this improvement is 8% and 13 %, respectively. If both is used this improvement is about 24 %.

Length (mt)	Computation Time with scalar evaluation (with bvp5c)	Computation Time with only vectorization (with bvp5c)	Computation Time with only analytical partial derivatives (with bvp5c)	Computation Time with both vectorization & analytical partial derivatives (with bvp5c)
5000	~1.32 sec	~1.32 sec	~1.30 sec	~1.23 sec
10000	~1.38 sec	~1.38 sec	~1.35 sec	~1.27 sec
20000	~1.44 sec	~1.42 sec	~1.38sec	~1.30sec
30000	~1.55 sec	~1.50 sec	~1.43 sec	~1.34 sec
40000	~1.60 sec	~1.52 sec	~1.47 sec	~1.36 sec

Table 6. Comparison of the computation time of bvp5c with vectorization, with analytical partial derivatives and with both

If the comparison among two solvers has made, it could be expressed that bvp5c "looks" exactly like bvp4c. However, bvp5c controls scaled residual and true error but bvp4c controls residual in a different norm. And, bvp5c is more efficient at stringent tolerances.

Also, bvp5c solves singular BVPs, but not multipoint BVPs. Moreover, bvp5c handles unknown parameters in a different way. And also, bvp5c was added to MATLAB at R2007b (Shampine, 2008)

7. Conclusion

Within the chapter, in order to analyze the effect of guess functions on the computation time, four guess functions are derived. For better understanding, while exploiting physical origin, guess functions are derived with the help of MATLAB Symbolic toolbox. Continuation method with functional snippets is presented to cope with poor guesses. Effect of the step size and bvpinit function on the computation time is analyzed. Speeding up the run time with vectorization and analytical partial derivatives are discussed and the comparison between bvp4c and bvp5c has been made.

As a conclusion, it is illustrated that, intuitive guess values/functions improves the convergence length, leads the computation with fewer mesh points and consequently lessens the computation time. On the other hand, regarding with the continuation, adjusting the step size is important for the reduction of run time. It is illustrated that, over the modest step size, the solver fails and below the optimum step size, the computation time is increased. Moreover, it is showed that when constructing an initial guess using bvpinit(linspace(0,L,N), starting with a mesh of 5-10 points could often result in a more efficient run. Another outcome of the chapter is the illustration of the efficiency of the vectorization and analytical partial derivatives. It is showed specifically with an example and with bvp4c that, with the application of vectorization and analytical partial derivatives, the computation time is reduced approximately 15 %. The performance of the bvp4c and bvp5c is also compared. In terms of scalar evaluation, the performance of bvp5c solver is better than bvpc4 and it is evident as the computation length is increased. Compared with the scalar evaluation, for the bvp5c, only with vectorization and only with analytical partial derivatives this improvement is 8% and 13 % respectively. If both is used this improvement is about 24 %.

8. Acknowledgments

The author gratefully acknowledges the financial support from the head of scientific research projects commission of Gazikent University.

9. References

Kierzenka J. & Shampine Lawrence F. (2001), *A BVP Solver Based on Residual Control and the MATLAB PSE*, ACM TOMS, vol. 27, No. 3, pp. 299-316.

Hale N.P., (2006), *A Sixth-Order Extension to the MATLAB bvp4c Software of J. Kierzenka and L. Shampine*, Msc Thesis. Accessed 06.04.2011, Available from: < http://people.maths.ox.ac.uk/hale/files/hale_mastersthesis.pdf >

MATLAB Documentation, *Continuation*, Accessed 06 April 2011, Available from: < http://www.mathworks.com/help/techdoc/math/f1-713877.html>

Shampine, L.F., Gladwell, I. & Thompson, S. (2003), *Solving ODEs with MATLAB*, 1st ed., Cambridge University Press, ISBN, 978-0-521-82404-4, New York

Agrawal G. P. (2001), *Nonlinear Fiber Optics*, 3rd ed. Academic, Chap. 9.

Kobyakov A., Darmanyan S., Sauer M. & Chowdhury D (2006), *High-gain Brillouin amplification: an analytical Approach*, Opt.Lett. 31 1960

Kierzenka, J. & Shampine, L.F. (2008), *BVP solver that controls residual and error*, Journal of Numerical Analysis, Industrial and Applied Mathematics (JNAIAM), Vol. 3 Nos 1/2, pp. 27-41, available at: www.jnaiam.org/downloads.php?did=44 (Accessed 06 April 2011).

Gokhan F. S., & Yilmaz G, (2011a), *Solution of Raman fiber amplifier equations using MATLAB BVP solvers*, COMPEL: The International Journal for Computation and Mathematics in Electrical and Electronic Engineering, Vol. 30 Iss: 2, pp.398 - 411

Gokhan F. S., & Yilmaz G, (2011b), *Novel Guess Functions for Efficient Analysis of Raman Fiber Amplifiers*, COMPEL: The International Journal for Computation and Mathematics in Electrical and Electronic Engineering, *accepted in 2010*

Shampine L.F, (2008). *Control of Residual and Error*, In: CAIMS-Canadian Mathematical Society, Accessed 06 April 2011,
Available from: < http://faculty.smu.edu/shampine/Montreal.pdf>

2

Revisiting the Ceschino Interpolation Method

Alain Hébert
École Polytechnique de Montréal
Canada

1. Introduction

The Ceschino polynomial expansion method is a generalization of the Taylor polynomial expansion method where higher derivatives of a function are predicted in addition to the value of the function itself. This technique was first introduced by (Ceschino, 1956), but was largely forgotten afterward. An unsuccessfull atempt was tried in 1975 to apply the Ceschino coupling relations to the solution of an elliptic space–dependent differential equation, but the resulting spatial discretization was found to be less accurate than competing finite-element approaches, as presented by (Pageau, 1975). No further published work was reported after the Pageau thesis.

Here, we propose to apply the Ceschino coupling relations to the basic interpolation problem, as an alternative to existing univariate interpolation schemes, such as the cubic spline approach. The interpolation problem consists to evaluate a functional $\mathcal{I}\{f(x);\xi\}$ of a continuous function (or dependent variable) $f(x)$ at a specific point ξ in the case where function $f(x)$ is only known at tabulated abscissa (or independent variables) $\{x_{m+1/2}\,;\ m = 0, M\}$. We also introduce the concept of interpolation factors (a. k. a., *terp factors*) that are useful for interpolating large databases with respect to a small number of independent variables, as presented by (MacFarlane, 1984). The Ceschino polynomial expansion method is the core component of the multiparameter reactor database system used in the reactor physics code DRAGON for performing cross section interpolation (Hébert, 2009). We will show that Ceschino polynomial expansion theory is an attractive choice for computing such interpolation factors and propose sample Matlab scripts for performing this task.

2. Ceschino polynomial expansion theory

The polynomial expansion theory is first applied over the one-dimensional domain depicted in Fig. 1. A continuous function $f(x)$ is defined over this domain and is known at specific abscissa points $x_{m+1/2}$. A $(J+1)$–th order Taylor series expansion of $f(x)$ around $x = x_{m-1/2}$ is written

$$f_{m+1/2} = \sum_{j=0}^{J} (\Delta x_m)^j \, M^{(j)}_{m-1/2} + \mathcal{O}(\Delta x_m)^{J+1} \tag{1}$$

where the mesh width is equal to

$$\Delta x_m = x_{m+1/2} - x_{m-1/2} \tag{2}$$

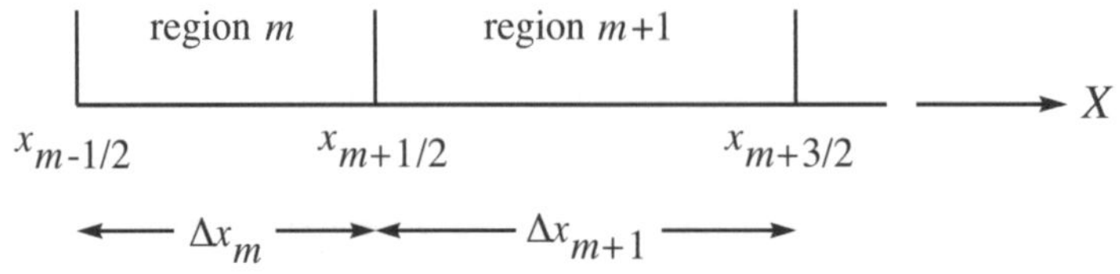

Fig. 1. Definition of the 1D domain.

and where

$$f_{m+1/2} \equiv f(x_{m+1/2}) \equiv M^{(0)}_{m+1/2} \text{ and } M^{(j)}_{m-1/2} \equiv \frac{1}{j!}\frac{d^j f}{dx^j}\bigg|_{x_{m-1/2}} . \tag{3}$$

A Ceschino expansion is nothing but the Taylor's expansion for the derivatives $f^{(k)}(x)$ of function $f(x)$. It is written

$$M^{(k)}_{m+1/2} = \sum_{j=k}^{J} (\Delta x_m)^{j-k} \binom{j}{k} M^{(j)}_{m-1/2} + \mathcal{O}(\Delta x_m)^{J-k+1} \tag{4}$$

where the binomial coefficients are defined as

$$\binom{j}{k} \equiv \frac{j!}{(j-k)!\,k!} . \tag{5}$$

Our interpolation strategy is based on two– and three–point coupling relations obtained directly from the Ceschino polynomial expansion (4). Two points relations are used at the extremities of the domain and three-point relations are used inside. Cubic Hermite polynomials will also be introduced to perform the interpolation operation.

2.1 Two–points Ceschino coupling relations

Our relations are coupling the first N derivatives of $f(x)$, with $N = 1$ leading to a cubic interpolation strategy. We set $J = 2N$ in Eq. (4), leading to a truncation error of order $2N+1$ if $k = 0$. We next perform a linear combination of the first N components $M^{(k)}_{m+1/2}$, introducing coefficients θ_k. The linear combination permits to maintain the order of the truncation error to $2N+1$. We write

$$\sum_{k=0}^{N} \theta_k\, M^{(k)}_{m+1/2} = \sum_{k=0}^{N}\sum_{j=k}^{2N} \theta_k\, (\Delta x_m)^{j-k} \binom{j}{k} M^{(j)}_{m-1/2} + \mathcal{O}(\Delta x_m)^{2N+1} . \tag{6}$$

After permutation of the two summations with the corresponding indices j and k in the right-hand-side, we get

$$\sum_{k=0}^{N} \theta_k\, M^{(k)}_{m+1/2} = \sum_{k=0}^{N}\sum_{j=0}^{k} \theta_j\, (\Delta x_m)^{k-j} \binom{k}{j} M^{(k)}_{m-1/2}$$
$$+ \sum_{k=N+1}^{2N}\sum_{j=0}^{N} \theta_j\, (\Delta x_m)^{k-j} \binom{k}{j} M^{(k)}_{m-1/2} + \mathcal{O}(\Delta x_m)^{2N+1} . \tag{7}$$

We choose coefficients θ_j in such a way that

$$\sum_{j=0}^{N} \theta_j \, (\Delta x_m)^{k-j} \binom{k}{j} = 0 \; ; \;\; k = N+1, 2N \tag{8}$$

and we define coefficients $\bar{\theta}_k$ as

$$\bar{\theta}_k = -\sum_{j=0}^{k} \theta_j \, (\Delta x_m)^{k-j} \binom{k}{j} \; ; \;\; k = 0, N \; . \tag{9}$$

We have obtained our $(2N+1)$–th order two–points Ceschino coupling relations as

$$\sum_{k=0}^{N} \left[\bar{\theta}_k \, M^{(k)}_{m-1/2} + \theta_k \, M^{(k)}_{m+1/2} \right] = 0 \; . \tag{10}$$

where the $\mathcal{O}(\Delta x_m)^{2N+1}$ error term is not given.
We need to determine a set of $2(N+1)$ coefficients θ_k and $\bar{\theta}_k$. Equations (8) and (9) permit to determine $2N+1$ of them, leaving θ_0 to be fixed. However, all values of θ_0 leads to valid solutions, making this choice arbitrary. We have chosen $\theta_0 = 1/(\Delta x_m)^2$ in order to simplify the resulting mathematical formalism.
In the specific case of cubic Ceschino interpolation, we set $N = 1$, so that Eqs. (8) and (9) reduce to

$$\begin{aligned} 2\Delta x_m \, \theta_1 &= -(\Delta x_m)^2 \, \theta_0 \\ \bar{\theta}_0 &= -\theta_0 \\ \text{and } \bar{\theta}_1 &= -\Delta x_m \, \theta_0 - \theta_1 \end{aligned} \tag{11}$$

so that our coefficients are

$$\begin{aligned} \bar{\theta}_0 &= -\frac{1}{(\Delta x_m)^2} \, , \quad \theta_0 = \frac{1}{(\Delta x_m)^2} \\ \bar{\theta}_1 &= -\frac{1}{2\Delta x_m} \;\; \text{and} \;\; \theta_1 = -\frac{1}{2\Delta x_m} \; . \end{aligned} \tag{12}$$

2.2 Three–points Ceschino coupling relations

The three–points Ceschino coupling relations span two consecutive regions along the X axis, as depicted in Fig. 1. We set $J = 3N$ in Eq. (4), leading to a truncation error of order $3N+1$ if $k = 0$. The Ceschino expansion are written

$$\begin{aligned} M^{(k)}_{m-1/2} &= \sum_{j=k}^{3N} (-\Delta x_m)^{j-k} \binom{j}{k} \, M^{(j)}_{m+1/2} + \mathcal{O}(\Delta x_m)^{3N-k+1} \\ M^{(k)}_{m+3/2} &= \sum_{j=k}^{3N} (\Delta x_{m+1})^{j-k} \binom{j}{k} \, M^{(j)}_{m+1/2} + \mathcal{O}(\Delta x_{m+1})^{3N-k+1} \end{aligned} \tag{13}$$

where the mesh widths are equal to

$$\Delta x_m = x_{m+1/2} - x_{m-1/2} \quad \text{and} \quad \Delta x_{m+1} = x_{m+3/2} - x_{m+1/2} \; . \tag{14}$$

We next perform a linear combination of the first N components $M^{(k)}_{m-1/2}$ and $M^{(k)}_{m+3/2}$, introducing coefficients $\breve{\beta}_k$ and β_k. The linear combination permits to maintain the order of the truncation error to $3N+1$. We write

$$\sum_{k=0}^{N} \breve{\beta}_k\, M^{(k)}_{m-1/2} + \beta_k\, M^{(k)}_{m+3/2} = \sum_{k=0}^{N}\sum_{j=k}^{3N} \left[\breve{\beta}_k\,(-\Delta x_m)^{j-k} + \beta_k\,(\Delta x_{m+1})^{j-k}\right] \binom{j}{k} M^{(j)}_{m+1/2} \tag{15}$$

where the truncation error is a linear combination of $\mathcal{O}(\Delta x_m)^{3N+1}$ and $\mathcal{O}(\Delta x_{m+1})^{3N+1}$. After permutation of the two summations with the corresponding indices j and k in the right-hand-side, we get

$$\begin{aligned}\sum_{k=0}^{N} \breve{\beta}_k\, M^{(k)}_{m-1/2} + \beta_k\, M^{(k)}_{m+3/2} &= \sum_{k=0}^{N}\sum_{j=0}^{k} \left[\breve{\beta}_j\,(-\Delta x_m)^{k-j} + \beta_j\,(\Delta x_{m+1})^{k-j}\right] \binom{k}{j} M^{(k)}_{m+1/2} \\ &+ \sum_{k=N+1}^{3N}\sum_{j=0}^{N} \left[\breve{\beta}_j\,(-\Delta x_m)^{k-j} + \beta_j\,(\Delta x_{m+1})^{k-j}\right] \binom{k}{j} M^{(k)}_{m+1/2}\ .\end{aligned} \tag{16}$$

We choose coefficients $\breve{\beta}_j$ and β_j in such a way that

$$\sum_{j=0}^{N} \left[\breve{\beta}_j\,(-\Delta x_m)^{k-j} + \beta_j\,(\Delta x_{m+1})^{k-j}\right] \binom{k}{j} = 0\,;\ \ k = N+1, 3N \tag{17}$$

and we define coefficients $\bar{\beta}_k$ as

$$\bar{\beta}_k = -\sum_{j=0}^{k} \left[\breve{\beta}_j\,(-\Delta x_m)^{k-j} + \beta_j\,(\Delta x_{m+1})^{k-j}\right] \binom{k}{j}\,;\ \ k = 0, N\ . \tag{18}$$

We have obtained our $(3N+1)$–th order three–points Ceschino coupling relations as

$$\sum_{k=0}^{N} \left[\breve{\beta}_k\, M^{(k)}_{m-1/2} + \bar{\beta}_k\, M^{(k)}_{m+1/2} + \beta_k\, M^{(k)}_{m+3/2}\right] = 0\ . \tag{19}$$

We need to determine a set of $3(N+1)$ coefficients $\breve{\beta}_k$, $\bar{\beta}_k$ and β_k. Equations (18) and (19) permit to determine $3N+1$ of them, leaving $\breve{\beta}_0$ and β_0 to be fixed. A first set of coefficients can be obtained by setting $\breve{\beta}_0 = -1/(\Delta x_m)^2$ and $\beta_0 = 1/(\Delta x_{m+1})^2$. A second independent set can be obtained by setting $\breve{\beta}'_0 = 1/(\Delta x_m)^3$ and $\beta'_0 = 1/(\Delta x_{m+1})^3$. Any other consistent set is a linear combination of these two.
In the specific case of cubic Ceschino interpolation, we set $N = 1$, so that Eqs. (17) and (18) reduce to

$$\begin{aligned} -2\Delta x_m\,\breve{\beta}_1 + 2\Delta x_{m+1}\,\beta_1 &= -(\Delta x_m)^2\,\breve{\beta}_0 - (\Delta x_{m+1})^2\,\beta_0 \\ 3(\Delta x_m)^2\,\breve{\beta}_1 + 3(\Delta x_{m+1})^2\,\beta_1 &= (\Delta x_m)^3\,\breve{\beta}_0 - (\Delta x_{m+1})^3\,\beta_0 \\ \bar{\beta}_0 &= -(\breve{\beta}_0 + \beta_0) \\ \text{and}\quad \bar{\beta}_1 &= \Delta x_m\,\breve{\beta}_0 - \Delta x_{m+1}\,\beta_0 - (\breve{\beta}_1 + \beta_1) \end{aligned} \tag{20}$$

so that our two independent sets of coefficients are

$$\begin{aligned}\breve{\beta}_0 &= -\frac{1}{(\Delta x_m)^2}, \ \bar{\beta}_0 = \frac{1}{(\Delta x_m)^2} - \frac{1}{(\Delta x_{m+1})^2}, \ \beta_0 = \frac{1}{(\Delta x_{m+1})^2}, \\ \breve{\beta}_1 &= -\frac{1}{3\Delta x_m}, \ \bar{\beta}_1 = -\frac{2}{3}\left[\frac{1}{\Delta x_m} + \frac{1}{\Delta x_{m+1}}\right], \ \beta_1 = -\frac{1}{3\Delta x_{m+1}}\end{aligned} \tag{21}$$

and

$$\begin{aligned}\breve{\beta}_0 &= \frac{1}{(\Delta x_m)^3}, \ \bar{\beta}_0 = -\frac{1}{(\Delta x_m)^3} - \frac{1}{(\Delta x_{m+1})^3}, \ \beta_0 = \frac{1}{(\Delta x_{m+1})^3}, \\ \breve{\beta}_1 &= \frac{1}{2(\Delta x_m)^2}, \ \bar{\beta}_1 = \frac{1}{2}\left[\frac{1}{(\Delta x_m)^2} - \frac{1}{(\Delta x_{m+1})^2}\right], \ \beta_1 = -\frac{1}{2(\Delta x_{m+1})^2}.\end{aligned} \tag{22}$$

2.3 Interpolation with cubic Hermite polynomials

Knowledge of $M^{(0)}_{m+1/2}$ and the capability to easily obtain $M^{(1)}_{m+1/2}$ on each tabulated point $x_{m+1/2}$ makes possible the interpolation of function $f(x)$ at each values of the independent variable x with a cubic Hermite polynomial in x. Such polynomial guarantee that the interpolated value and first derivative of the dependent variable remains continuous in x over the complete domain. As pointed out by (Rozon et al., 1981), this continuity property of the first derivative is often required in numerical applications such as those based on perturbation theory.

The first operation consists to solve a tridiagonal linear matrix system for obtaining the unknown vector $\boldsymbol{M}^{(1)} = \text{col}\{M^{(1)}_{m+1/2};\ m = 0, M\}$ over a M–region domain, considering the known values $M^{(0)}_{m+1/2}$ of $f(x)$ at tabulation points $x_{m+1/2}$. The linear matrix system is made with the first independent set of coefficients from Eq. (21) for linking the unknowns inside the domain. We have selected the first set in order to obtain a symmetric $\mathbb{C}$ matrix with minimum powers of Δx_m as coefficients. The first and last line coefficients are obtained from Eq. (12). Using coefficients from Eq. (12) with those from Eq. (22) leads to a singular $\mathbb{C}$ matrix. This last observation gives an additional clue for selecting three-point coefficients from Eq. (21).

The linear system is written

$$\mathbb{C}\ \boldsymbol{M}^{(1)} = \boldsymbol{S}^{(0)} \tag{23}$$

where the symmetric tridiagonal matrix is written

$$\mathbb{C} = \begin{bmatrix} \frac{1}{\Delta x_1} & \frac{1}{\Delta x_1} & 0 & \dots & 0 \\ \frac{1}{\Delta x_1} & 2\left(\frac{1}{\Delta x_1} + \frac{1}{\Delta x_2}\right) & \frac{1}{\Delta x_2} & \dots & 0 \\ 0 & \frac{1}{\Delta x_2} & 2\left(\frac{1}{\Delta x_2} + \frac{1}{\Delta x_3}\right) & \dots & 0 \\ \vdots & \vdots & \vdots & \ddots & \vdots \\ 0 & 0 & 0 & \dots & \frac{1}{\Delta x_M} \end{bmatrix} \tag{24}$$

and where the source term is written

$$\mathbf{s}^{(0)} = \begin{bmatrix} \frac{2}{(\Delta x_1)^2}\left(M^{(0)}_{3/2} - M^{(0)}_{1/2}\right) \\ \frac{3}{(\Delta x_1)^2}\left(M^{(0)}_{3/2} - M^{(0)}_{1/2}\right) + \frac{3}{(\Delta x_2)^2}\left(M^{(0)}_{5/2} - M^{(0)}_{3/2}\right) \\ \frac{3}{(\Delta x_2)^2}\left(M^{(0)}_{5/2} - M^{(0)}_{3/2}\right) + \frac{3}{(\Delta x_3)^2}\left(M^{(0)}_{7/2} - M^{(0)}_{5/2}\right) \\ \vdots \\ \frac{2}{(\Delta x_M)^2}\left(M^{(0)}_{M+1/2} - M^{(0)}_{M-1/2}\right) \end{bmatrix} . \tag{25}$$

The solution of the linear system in Eq. (23) can be performed without pivoting, as matrix $\mathbb{C}$ is diagonally dominant.
We next introduce the cubic Hermite polynomials defined over a reference region $-1/2 \leq u \leq 1/2$. They are

$$\begin{aligned} H_1(u) &= 3\left(\frac{1}{2} - u\right)^2 - 2\left(\frac{1}{2} - u\right)^3 \\ H_2(u) &= \left(\frac{1}{2} - u\right)^2 - \left(\frac{1}{2} - u\right)^3 \\ H_3(u) &= 3\left(\frac{1}{2} + u\right)^2 - 2\left(\frac{1}{2} + u\right)^3 \\ H_4(u) &= \left(\frac{1}{2} + u\right)^2 + \left(\frac{1}{2} + u\right)^3 \end{aligned} \tag{26}$$

so that a function $f(u)$ defined over this domain can be expressed as

$$f(u) \simeq f(-1/2)\, H_1(u) + f'(-1/2)\, H_2(u) + f(1/2)\, H_3(u) + f'(1/2)\, H_4(u) \tag{27}$$

where $-1/2 \leq u \leq 1/2$.
The above relation can be generalized to the interpolation of function $f(x)$ at ξ over region m. We first perform the change of variable

$$u = \frac{1}{\Delta x_m}\left[\xi - \frac{1}{2}\left(x_{m-1/2} + x_{m+1/2}\right)\right] \tag{28}$$

so that

$$\begin{aligned} \mathcal{I}\{f(x);\xi\} = {} & M^{(0)}_{m-1/2}\, H_1(u) + \Delta x_m\, M^{(1)}_{m-1/2}\, H_2(u) + M^{(0)}_{m+1/2}\, H_3(u) \\ & + \Delta x_m\, M^{(1)}_{m+1/2}\, H_4(u) \end{aligned} \tag{29}$$

where $x_{m-1/2} \leq \xi \leq x_{m+1/2}$.

2.4 Introduction of interpolation factors

Interpolation factors are useful to interpolate a large number of dependent variables at a unique value ξ of the independent variable. The interpolation factors are function only of the tabulated abscissas $\{x_{m+1/2}\,;\ m = 0, M\}$ and on the interpolation abscissa x. Using interpolation factors $\{t_{m+1/2}(\xi)\,;\ m = 0, M\}$, an interpolated dependent variable $\mathcal{I}\{f(x);\xi\}$ of $f(\xi)$ is obtained from

$$\mathcal{I}\{f(x);\xi\} = \sum_{m=0}^{M} t_{m+1/2}(\xi)\, f(x_{m+1/2}) \tag{30}$$

where

$$\sum_{m=0}^{M} t_{m+1/2}(\xi) = 1 \ . \tag{31}$$

Interpolation factors can be obtained if the interpolation operation is *distributive*, that is, if it can be distributed to the sum of two functions $f(x)$ and $g(h)$ according to

$$\begin{aligned}\mathcal{I}\{f(x)+g(x);\xi\} &= \sum_{m=0}^{M} t_{m+1/2}(\xi)\,[f(x_{m+1/2})+g(x_{m+1/2})] \\ &= \mathcal{I}\{f(x);\xi\} + \mathcal{I}\{g(x);\xi\} \ .\end{aligned} \tag{32}$$

The simplest form of interpolation factors are those corresponding to linear Lagrange interpolation. In this case, the interpolated value of $f(x)$, with $x_{m-1/2} \le \xi \le x_{m+1/2}$, is given by Eq. (30) with

$$t_\alpha(\xi) = \begin{cases} \frac{1}{2} - u, & \text{if } \alpha = m - 1/2\,; \\ \frac{1}{2} + u, & \text{if } \alpha = m + 1/2\,; \\ 0, & \text{otherwise.} \end{cases} \tag{33}$$

Similar interpolation factors exist for cubic Ceschino interpolation and can be obtained with the following procedure. The source term defined in Eq. (25) can be written in matrix form as

$$\mathbf{S}^{(0)} = \mathbb{S}\,\boldsymbol{M}^{(0)} \tag{34}$$

where

$$\mathbb{S} = \begin{bmatrix} -\frac{2}{(\Delta x_1)^2} & \frac{2}{(\Delta x_1)^2} & 0 & \cdots & 0 \\ -\frac{3}{(\Delta x_1)^2} & \frac{3}{(\Delta x_1)^2} - \frac{3}{(\Delta x_2)^2} & \frac{3}{(\Delta x_2)^2} & \cdots & 0 \\ 0 & -\frac{3}{(\Delta x_2)^2} & \frac{3}{(\Delta x_2)^2} - \frac{3}{(\Delta x_3)^2} & \cdots & 0 \\ \vdots & \vdots & \vdots & \ddots & \vdots \\ 0 & 0 & 0 & \cdots & \frac{2}{(\Delta x_M)^2} \end{bmatrix} . \tag{35}$$

The interpolated value of $f(\xi)$, with $x_{m-1/2} \le \xi \le x_{m+1/2}$, is therefore given by the relation

$$\mathcal{I}\{f(x);\xi\} = \left[\boldsymbol{H}_1(\xi)^\top + \boldsymbol{H}_2(\xi)^\top\,\mathbb{C}^{-1}\,\mathbb{S}\right] \boldsymbol{M}^{(0)} \tag{36}$$

where $\boldsymbol{H}_1(\xi) = \{H_{1,m+1/2}(\xi)\,;\ m = 0, M\}$ with

$$H_{1,\alpha}(\xi) = \begin{cases} 3\left(\frac{1}{2} - u\right)^2 - 2\left(\frac{1}{2} - u\right)^3, & \text{if } \alpha = m - 1/2\ ; \\ 3\left(\frac{1}{2} + u\right)^2 - 2\left(\frac{1}{2} + u\right)^3, & \text{if } \alpha = m + 1/2\ ; \\ 0, & \text{otherwise} \end{cases} \tag{37}$$

and $\boldsymbol{H}_2(\xi) = \{H_{2,m+1/2}(\xi)\,;\ m = 0, M\}$ with

$$H_{2,\alpha}(\xi) = \begin{cases} \left(\frac{1}{2} - u\right)^2 - \left(\frac{1}{2} - u\right)^3, & \text{if } \alpha = m - 1/2\ ; \\ \left(\frac{1}{2} + u\right)^2 + \left(\frac{1}{2} + u\right)^3, & \text{if } \alpha = m + 1/2\ ; \\ 0, & \text{otherwise.} \end{cases} \tag{38}$$

The vector $\boldsymbol{T}(\xi) = \{t_{m+1/2}(\xi)\,;\ m = 0, M\}$ of interpolation factors is obtained after transposition of Eq. (36), leading to

$$\mathcal{I}\{f(x);\xi\} = \boldsymbol{M}^{(0)\top}\left[\boldsymbol{H}_1(\xi) + \mathbb{S}^\top\,\mathbb{C}^{-1}\,\boldsymbol{H}_2(\xi)\right] \tag{39}$$

so that

$$\boldsymbol{T}(\xi) = \boldsymbol{H}_1(\xi) + \mathbb{S}^\top\,\mathbb{C}^{-1}\,\boldsymbol{H}_2(\xi)\ . \tag{40}$$

3. Matlab scripts and numerical examples

Two Matlab scripts are proposed in Appendices A and B as prototypes of the cubic Ceschino interpolation method. The first script, `alterp()` is used to obtain the terp factors corresponding to an interpolation (if `lderiv=false`) or to a derivation (if `lderiv=true`). The second script, `alteri()` is used to obtain the terp factors corresponding to the definite integration of $f(x)$. The following Matlab session is an example of interpolation similar to the `spline` Matlab tutorial.

```
x=0:10;  y=sin(x);
xx=0:.25:10;
yy=zeros(1,size(xx,2));
for i=1:size(xx,2)
   yy(i)=y*alterp(x,xx(i),false);
end
plot(x,y,'o',xx,yy)
```

Execution of the above script leads to Fig. 2. Similarly, the first derivative of $f(x) = sin(x)$ can be computed by setting `lderiv` $=$ `true`, as described in the following Matlab session.

```
yy=zeros(1,size(xx,2));
for i=1:size(xx,2)
   yy(i)=y*alterp(x,xx(i),true);
end
plot(x,cos(x),'o',xx,yy)
```

Execution of the above script leads to Fig. 3. We observe that the order of the numerical derivation approximation is less than the order of the interpolation, as expected. The higher derivation errors are observed at extremities of the domain, where two-point Ceschino coupling relation are used.

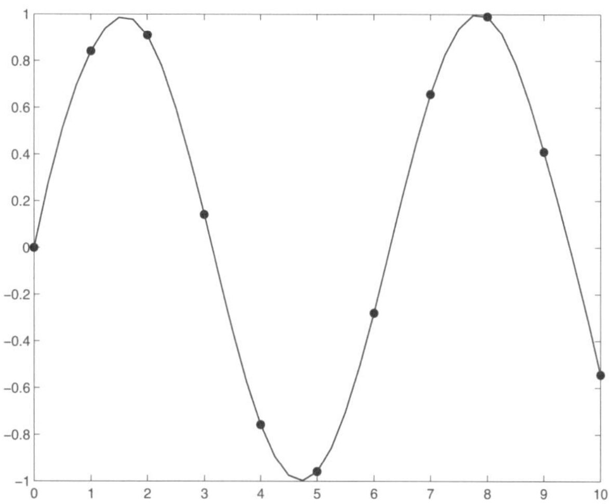

Fig. 2. Interpolation example.

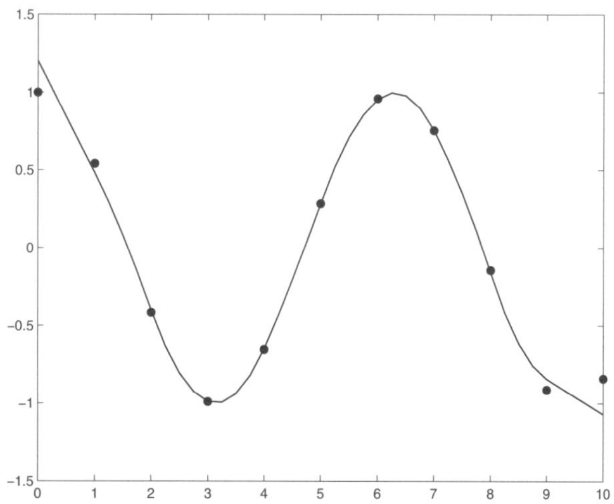

Fig. 3. Derivation example.

4. Conclusion

We have presented a straightforward numerical technique based on Ceschino polynomial expansion. Three applications of this approach permit to perform interpolation, derivation and definite integration of tabulated data. Equation (36) is efficient to interpolate few dependent variables over a large number of points ξ. Equation (39) introduces the concept of *interpolation factors* and is efficient to interpolate a large number of dependent variables over a few number of points ξ. Matlab scripts are provided as basic implementation of the Ceschino interpolating method.

The Ceschino interpolation technique is an alternative to the cubic spline approach based on different mathematical bases. In fact, the interpolating function obtained by this method is a piecewise polynomial function of degree 3 which is only a $\mathcal{C}^1$ function compared to the cubic spline which is a $\mathcal{C}^2$ function. It would be important to obtain error estimates to compare both approaches. However, the Ceschino interpolation technique is currently implemented in legacy applications and its behavior is already found acceptable.

Appendix A

The first Matlab script is used to compute interpolation/derivation factors (a. k. a., terp factors) using Eq. (40). The user must provide the tabulated abscissa defined as $\{x_{m+1/2}\,;\, m = 0, M\}$ and one interpolation point ξ. A logical variable, `lderiv`, select interpolation or derivation mode. The script returns a column vector containing the corresponding terp factors $\{t_{m+1/2}(\xi)\,;\, m = 0, M\}$.

```
function terp=alterp(x,val,lderiv)
% determination of the terp interpolation/derivation factors using
% the order 4 Ceschino method with cubic Hermite polynomials.
% function terp=alterp(x,val,lderiv)
% input parameters:
% x       abscissas (row vector)
% val     abscissa of the interpolated point.
% lderiv  set to true to compute the first derivative with respect to x.
%         set to false to interpolate.
% output parameters:
% terp    interpolation factors (column vector)
% (c) 2007 Alain Hebert, Ecole Polytechnique de Montreal
   n=size(x,2) ;
   if n <= 1
      error('invalid number of points')
   end
   terp=zeros(n,1) ;
   if n == 2
      if lderiv
         terp(1)=-1.0/(x(2)-x(1)) ;
         terp(2)=1.0/(x(2)-x(1)) ;
      else
         terp(1)=(x(2)-val)/(x(2)-x(1)) ;
         terp(2)=1.0-terp(1) ;
      end
   else
      wk=zeros(3,n) ;
%----
%  interval identification.
%----
      temp1=find(val>=x(1:end-1)) ;
      temp2=find(val<=x(2:end)) ;
      if (size(temp1,2) == 0) | (size(temp2,2) == 0)
         error('unable to interpolate')
      end
      i0=temp1(end) ;
      dx=x(i0+1)-x(i0) ;
      u=(val-0.5*(x(i0)+x(i0+1)))/dx ;
```

```
      if lderiv
         h1=(-6.0*(0.5-u)+6.0*(0.5-u)^2)/dx ;
         h2=(-2.0*(0.5-u)+3.0*(0.5-u)^2)/dx ;
         h3=(6.0*(0.5+u)-6.0*(0.5+u)^2)/dx ;
         h4=(-2.0*(0.5+u)+3.0*(0.5+u)^2)/dx ;
         test=0.0 ;
      else
         h1=3.0*(0.5-u)^2-2.0*(0.5-u)^3 ;
         h2=(0.5-u)^2-(0.5-u)^3 ;
         h3=3.0*(0.5+u)^2-2.0*(0.5+u)^3 ;
         h4=-(0.5+u)^2+(0.5+u)^3 ;
         test=1.0 ;
      end
      terp(i0)=h1 ;
      terp(i0+1)=h3 ;
      wk(3,i0)=h2*dx ;
      wk(3,i0+1)=h4*dx ;
%----
%  compute the coefficient matrix.
%----
      hp=1.0/(x(2)-x(1)) ;
      wk(1,1)=hp ;
      wk(2,1)=hp ;
      for i=2:n-1
         hm=hp ;
         hp=1.0/(x(i+1)-x(i)) ;
         wk(1,i)=2.0*(hm+hp) ;
         wk(2,i)=hp ;
      end
      wk(1,n)=hp ;
      wk(2,n)=hp ;
%----
%  forward elimination.
%----
      pmx=wk(1,1) ;
      wk(3,1)=wk(3,1)/pmx ;
      for i=2:n
         gar=wk(2,i-1) ;
         wk(2,i-1)=wk(2,i-1)/pmx ;
         pmx=wk(1,i)-gar*wk(2,i-1) ;
         wk(3,i)=(wk(3,i)-gar*wk(3,i-1))/pmx ;
      end
%----
%  back substitution.
%----
      for i=n-1:-1:1
         wk(3,i)=wk(3,i)-wk(2,i)*wk(3,i+1) ;
      end
%----
%  compute the interpolation factors.
%----
      gar=zeros(1,n+2) ;
      gar(2:n+1)=wk(3,:) ;
      wk=zeros(3,n) ;
      hp2=1.0/(x(2)-x(1)) ;
```

```
      wk(2,1)=-2.0*hp2*hp2 ;
      wk(1,2)=2.0*hp2*hp2 ;
      for i=2:n-1
         hp1=hp2 ;
         hp2=1.0/(x(i+1)-x(i)) ;
         wk(3,i-1)=-3.0*hp1*hp1 ;
         wk(2,i)=3.0*hp1*hp1-3.0*hp2*hp2 ;
         wk(1,i+1)=3.0*hp2*hp2 ;
      end
      wk(3,n-1)=-2.0*hp2*hp2 ;
      wk(2,n)=2.0*hp2*hp2 ;
      for j=1:n
         terp(j)=terp(j)+gar(j:j+2)*wk(:,j) ;
         test=test-terp(j) ;
      end
      if abs(test) > 1.0e-5
         error('wrong terp factors')
      end
      terp(find(abs(terp) <= 1.0e-7))=0.0 ;
   end
```

Appendix B

The second Matlab script is used to compute integration factors permitting to evaluate a definite integral. The user must provide the tabulated abscissa $\{x_{m+1/2}\,;\ m = 0, M\}$ and the integration limits. The script returns a column vector containing the corresponding terp factors.

```
function terp=alteri(x,val0,val1)
% determination of the terp integration factors using the order 4
% Ceschino method with cubic Hermite polynomials.
% function terp=alteri(x,val0,val1)
% input parameters:
% x       abscissas (row vector)
% val0    left integration limit.
% val1    right integration limit.
% output parameters:
% terp    integration factors (column vector)
% (c) 2007 Alain Hebert, Ecole Polytechnique de Montreal
   n=size(x,2) ;
   if n <= 1
      error('invalid number of points')
   elseif val1 <= val0
      error('invalid limits')
   elseif (val0 < x(1)) | (val1 > x(n))
      error('unable to integrate')
   end
   terp=zeros(n,1) ;
   if n == 2
      terp(1)=(x(2)-0.5*(val0+val1))*(val1-val0)/(x(2)-x(1)) ;
      terp(2)=(0.5*(val0+val1)-x(1))*(val1-val0)/(x(2)-x(1)) ;
   else
      wk=zeros(3,n) ;
%----
```

```
%  interval identification.
%----
      for i0=1:n-1
         if (val0 < x(i0+1)) & (val1 > x(i0))
            a=max(val0,x(i0)) ;
            b=min(val1,x(i0+1)) ;
            cc=0.5*(b-a) ;
            dx=x(i0+1)-x(i0) ;
            u1=(a-0.5*(x(i0)+x(i0+1)))/dx ;
            u2=(b-0.5*(x(i0)+x(i0+1)))/dx ;
            uu(1)=0.5*(-(u2-u1)/sqrt(3.0)+u1+u2) ;
            uu(2)=0.5*((u2-u1)/sqrt(3.0)+u1+u2) ;
            for js=1:2
               h1=(3.0*(0.5-uu(js))^2-2.0*(0.5-uu(js))^3)*cc ;
               h2=((0.5-uu(js))^2-(0.5-uu(js))^3)*cc ;
               h3=(3.0*(0.5+uu(js))^2-2.0*(0.5+uu(js))^3)*cc ;
               h4=(-(0.5+uu(js))^2+(0.5+uu(js))^3)*cc ;
               terp(i0)=terp(i0)+h1 ;
               terp(i0+1)=terp(i0+1)+h3 ;
               wk(3,i0)=wk(3,i0)+h2*dx ;
               wk(3,i0+1)=wk(3,i0+1)+h4*dx ;
            end
         end
      end
%----
%  compute the coefficient matrix.
%----
      hp=1.0/(x(2)-x(1)) ;
      wk(1,1)=hp ;
      wk(2,1)=hp ;
      for i=2:n-1
         hm=hp ;
         hp=1.0/(x(i+1)-x(i)) ;
         wk(1,i)=2.0*(hm+hp) ;
         wk(2,i)=hp ;
      end
      wk(1,n)=hp ;
      wk(2,n)=hp ;
%----
%  forward elimination.
%----
      pmx=wk(1,1) ;
      wk(3,1)=wk(3,1)/pmx ;
      for i=2:n
         gar=wk(2,i-1) ;
         wk(2,i-1)=wk(2,i-1)/pmx ;
         pmx=wk(1,i)-gar*wk(2,i-1) ;
         wk(3,i)=(wk(3,i)-gar*wk(3,i-1))/pmx ;
      end
%----
%  back substitution.
%----
      for i=n-1:-1:1
         wk(3,i)=wk(3,i)-wk(2,i)*wk(3,i+1) ;
      end
```

```
%----
% compute the integration factors.
%----
      test=1.0 ;
      gar=zeros(1,n+2) ;
      gar(2:n+1)=wk(3,:) ;
      wk=zeros(3,n) ;
      hp2=1.0/(x(2)-x(1)) ;
      wk(2,1)=-2.0*hp2*hp2 ;
      wk(1,2)=2.0*hp2*hp2 ;
      for i=2:n-1
         hp1=hp2 ;
         hp2=1.0/(x(i+1)-x(i)) ;
         wk(3,i-1)=-3.0*hp1*hp1 ;
         wk(2,i)=3.0*hp1*hp1-3.0*hp2*hp2 ;
         wk(1,i+1)=3.0*hp2*hp2 ;
      end
      wk(3,n-1)=-2.0*hp2*hp2 ;
      wk(2,n)=2.0*hp2*hp2 ;
      for j=1:n
         terp(j)=terp(j)+gar(j:j+2)*wk(:,j) ;
         test=test-terp(j)/(val1-val0) ;
      end
      if abs(test) > 1.0e-5
         error('wrong terp factors')
      end
      terp(find(abs(terp) <= 1.0e-7))=0.0 ;
   end
```

5. References

Ceschino, F. (1956). *L'intégration approchée des équations différentielles*, Compte Rendu de l'Académie des Sciences, Paris, 243, pp. 1478 – 1479.

Hébert, A. (2009). *Applied Reactor Physics*, Presses Internationales Polytechnique, ISBN 978-2-553-01436-9, 424 p., Montréal.

MacFarlane, R. E. (1984). *TRANSX-CTR: A code for Interfacing MATXS Cross-Section Libraries to Nuclear Transport Codes for Fusion Systems Analysis*, LA-9863-MS, Los Alamos Scientific Laboratory, New Mexico.

Pageau, R. (1975). *Application des méthodes TCNR et des séries de Fourier aux Problèmes statique bi-dimensionnels en physique des réacteurs*, Master Thesis, École Polytechnique de Montréal.

Rozon, D.; Hébert, A.; McNabb, D. (1981). *The Application of Generalized Perturbation Theory and Mathematical Programming to Equilibrium Refueling Studies of a CANDU Reactor*, Nucl. Sci. Eng., 78, pp. 211 – 226.

3

Matrix Based Operatorial Approach to Differential and Integral Problems

Damian Trif
Babes-Bolyai University of Cluj-Napoca
Romania

1. Introduction

Many problems of the real life lead us to linear differential equations of the form

$$\sum_{k=0}^{m} P_k(x)\frac{d^k y}{dx^k} = f(x), \quad x \in [a,b] \tag{1}$$

with the general conditions

$$\sum_{j=1}^{m} \alpha_{ij}^{(1)} y^{(j-1)}(x_{ij}^{(1)}) + \cdots + \sum_{j=1}^{m} \alpha_{ij}^{(m)} y^{(j-1)}(x_{ij}^{(m)}) = \beta_i, \quad i = 1,...,m \tag{2}$$

where $x_{ij}^{(k)} \in [a,b]$, $\forall i,j,k = 1,...,m$. These multipoint conditions include (for $m = 2$, for example)
- initial value conditions, $y(a) = \beta_1, y'(a) = \beta_2$,
- boundary value conditions $\alpha_{11}y(a) + \alpha_{12}y'(a) = \beta_1, \alpha_{21}y(b) + \alpha_{22}y'(b) = \beta_2$,
- periodic conditions $y(a) - y(b) = 0, y'(a) - y'(b) = 0$.

Eigenvalue problems for linear differential operators

$$\sum_{k=1}^{m} P_k(x)\frac{d^k y}{dx^k} + (P_0(x) - \lambda w(x))\, y = 0, \quad x \in [a,b]$$

$$\sum_{j=1}^{m} \alpha_{ij}^{(1)} y^{(j-1)}(x_{ij}^{(1)}) + \cdots + \sum_{j=1}^{m} \alpha_{ij}^{(m)} y^{(j-1)}(x_{ij}^{(m)}) = 0, \quad i = 1,...,m$$

are also included in this general form. Moreover, nonlinear problems where the r.h.s. $f(x)$ is replaced by $f(x, y(x), y'(x), ..., y^{(m-1)}(x))$ can be solved using Newton's method in the functional space $C^m[a,b]$ by solving a sequence of linear problems (1)+(2).
MATLAB uses different methods to solve initial condition problems (`ode` family) or boundary value problems (`bvp4c` or `bvp5c`) based on Runge-Kutta, Adams-Bashforth-Moulton, BDF algorithms, etc.
One of the most effective methods for solving (1)+(2) is to shift the problem to the interval $[-1,1]$ and then to use the *Chebyshev spectral methods*, i.e. to approximate the solution y by a finite sum of the Chebyshev series

$$y(x) = \frac{1}{2}c_0T_0(x) + c_1T_1(x) + c_2T_2(x).... \tag{3}$$

Here $T_k(x) = \cos(k \cos^{-1}(x)), k = 0, 1, ...$ are the Chebyshev polynomials of the first kind and the coefficients c_k, $k = 0, 1, ...$are unknown. A spectral method is characterized by a specific way to determine these coefficients. The Chebyshev spectral methods could be implemented as
- Galerkin and tau methods, where we work in the spectral space of the coefficients $\mathbf{c} = c_0, c_1, c_2, ...$ of y or as
- spectral collocation (or pseudospectral) methods, where we work in the physical space of the values of y at a specific grid $\mathbf{x} = x_1, x_2, ... \in [-1, 1]$.

The well known MATLAB packages which use spectral methods, *MATLAB Differentiation Matrix Suite* (*DMS*) (Weideman & Reddy, 2000) and *Chebfun* (Trefethen et al., 2011), are based on the pseudospectral methods. Usually, these methods are implemented in an operatorial form: a differentiation matrix D (or linear operator) is generated so that $Y' = DY$ where the vector Y' contains the values of the derivative y' at the specific grid while Y contains the values of y at the same grid. The equation (1) becomes

$$\left(\sum_{k=0}^{m} diag(P_k(\mathbf{x}))D^k \right) Y = f(\mathbf{x}) \text{ i.e. } AY = F$$

and the conditions (2) are enclosed in the matrix A and in the vector F. The numerical solution of the differential problem is now $Y = A^{-1}F$. We note that MATLAB capabilities of working with matrices make it an ideal tool for matrix based operatorial approach.

There is a price to pay for using pseudospectral methods: the differentiation matrix D is full (while for finite differences or finite element methods it is sparse) and, more importantly, D is very sensitive to rounding errors. We give here a comparison between *DMS*, *Chebfun* and our proposed package *Chebpack* (based on the tau spectral method) for an eigenvalue problem suggested by Solomonoff and Turkel. Let us consider the evolution problem

$$u_t = -xu_x, \; u(x, 0) = f(x), \; x \in [-1, 1],$$

with the exact solution $u(x,t) = f(xe^{-t})$. Here $x = \pm 1$ are outflow boundaries so that no boundary conditions are required. Using a Chebyshev spectral method to discretize the spatial part of the equation, the stability of time integration depends on the eigenvalues of that spatial part

$$-xu_x = \lambda u, \; x \in [-1, 1]. \tag{4}$$

The exact (polynomial) eigenvectors are the monomials x^n and the corresponding eigenvalues are $\lambda_n = -n, n = 0, 1, ...$

The commands for the *DMS* package

```
[x,D]=chebdif(64,1);L=eig(-diag(x)*D);
```

for *Chebfun*

```
N=chebop(@(x,u) -x.*diff(u),[-1,1]);L=eigs(N(66),64,'LR');
```

and for *Chebpack*

```
X=mult(64,[-1,1]);D=deriv(64,[-1,1]);L=eig(full(-X*D));
```

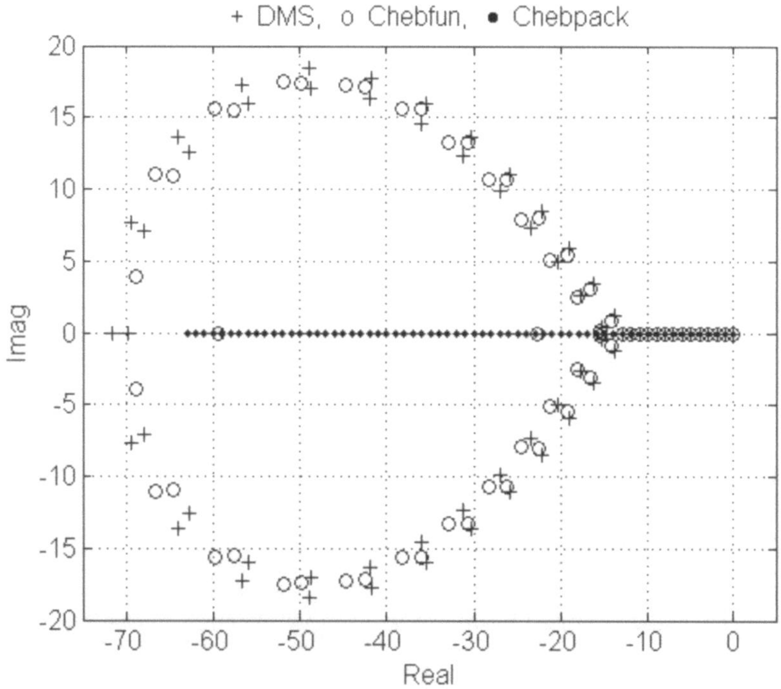

Fig. 1. Eigenvalues for the problem (4)

give the 64 approximated eigenvalues successively in the vector L and they are represented in Fig. 1. We see that *DMS* and *Chebfun* calculate accurately only a small number of eigenvalues, while *Chebpack* gives exactly all 64 eigenvalues.

The proposed package *Chebpack*, which is described in this chapter, is based on the representation (3) of the unknown functions and uses the *tau method* for linear operators (such as differentiation, integration, product with the independent variable,...) and the pseudospectral method for nonlinear operators – nonlinear part of the equations.

The tau method was invented by Lanczos (1938, 1956) and later developed in an operatorial approach by Ortiz and Samara (Ortiz & Samara, 1981). In the past years considerable work has been done both in the theoretical analysis and numerical applications.

Chebpack is freely accessible at `https://sites.google.com/site/dvtrif/` and at (Trif, 2011). All the running times in this chapter are the elapsed times for a 1.73GHz laptop and for MATLAB 2010b under Windows XP.

2. Chebpack, basic module

The package contains, at the basic module – level0, the tools which will be used in the next modules. Let us start with the Chebyshev series expansion of a given function y (Boyd, 2000):

THEOREM 1. *If y is Lipschitz continuous on [-1, 1], it has a unique representation as an absolutely and uniformly convergent series*

$$y(x) = \frac{c_0}{2}T_0(x) + c_1T_1(x) + c_2T_2(x) + ...,$$

and the coefficients are given by the formula

$$c_k = \frac{2}{\pi}\int_{-1}^{1}\frac{y(x)T_k(x)}{\sqrt{1-x^2}}dx,\ k = 0,1,2,....$$

Let y_{N-1} be the truncation of the above Chebyshev series

$$y_{N-1}(x) = \frac{c_0}{2}T_0(x) + c_1T_1(x) + c_2T_2(x) + \cdots + c_{N-1}T_{N-1}(x) \tag{5}$$

and $dom = [-1,1]$ be the working interval. Any interval $[a,b]$ can be shifted and scaled to $[-1,1]$ by using the shifted Chebyshev polynomials

$$T_k^*(x) = T_k(\alpha x + \beta),\ \alpha = \frac{2}{b-a},\ \beta = -\frac{b+a}{b-a},\ x \in [a,b].$$

First of all, we need a set of N collocation points $x_1,...,x_N \in dom$ in order to find a good transformation between the above spectral approximation (5) of y and its physical representation $y(x_1), y(x_2),..., y(x_N)$. Let

$$p_{N-1}(x) = \frac{a_0}{2}T_0(x) + a_1T_1(x) + ... + a_{N-1}T_{N-1}(x) \tag{6}$$

be the unique polynomial obtained by interpolating $y(x)$ through the points $x_1,...,x_N$, see (Trefethen, 2000) for more details on the coefficients a_k versus c_k. The next theorem of (Boyd, 2000) estimates the error:

THEOREM 2. *Let y have at least N derivatives on dom. Then*

$$y(x) - p_{N-1}(x) = \frac{1}{N!}y^{(N)}(\xi)\prod_{k=1}^{N}(x - x_k)$$

for some ξ on the interval spanned by x and the interpolation points. The point ξ depends on the function y, upon N, upon x and upon the location of the interpolation points.

Consequently, the optimal interpolation points are the roots of the Chebyshev polynomial $T_N(x)$, (**Chebyshev points of the first kind**)

$$x_k = -\cos\frac{(2k-1)\pi}{2N},\ k = 1,...,N. \tag{7}$$

For these points **x**, the polynomials $\{p_{N-1}\}$ are generally nearly as good approximations to y as the polynomials $\{y_{N-1}\}$ and if y is *analytic* on *dom*, then both $\|y - y_{N-1}\|$ and $\|y - p_{N-1}\|$ decrease geometrically as $N \to \infty$. This is the *spectral convergence property*, i.e. the convergence of $\|y - y_{N-1}\|$ and $\|y - p_{N-1}\|$ towards zero is faster than any power of $\frac{1}{N}$ as $N \to \infty$.

Numerical integration and Lagrangian interpolation are very closely related. The standard formulas for a continuous function f on $[-1,1]$ are of the type

$$\int_{-1}^{1} f(x)dx \approx \sum_{k=1}^{N} w_k f(x_k), \tag{8}$$

where w_k are the quadrature weights

$$w_k = \int_{-1}^{1}\prod_{j=1,j\neq k}^{N}\frac{x - x_j}{x_k - x_j}dx,\ k = 1,2,...,N.$$

The *Gauss quadrature formulas* are based on the optimal Legendre points $x_k,\ k = 1, ..., N$ and these formulas are exact for polynomials f up to degree $2N - 1$. The idea of *Clenshaw-Curtis quadrature* is to use Chebyshev points $\mathbf{x}$ instead of the above optimal nodes. By using the Chebyshev points of the first kind (7) one obtains the "classical" Clenshaw-Curtis formula while by using the zeros of the first derivative of a Chebyshev polynomial plus the endpoints ± 1, i.e. the Chebyshev extrema

$$x_k = -\cos\frac{(k-1)\pi}{N-1}, k = 1, ..., N \tag{9}$$

in $[-1, 1]$ (the so called **Chebyshev points of the second kind**) one obtains the "practical" Clenshaw-Curtis formula. Both formulas have all the good properties of the Gaussian quadrature, see (Trefethen, 2008) for more details.

Consequently, we may use Chebyshev points of the first kind or of the second kind both for quadrature formulas and for physical representation of a function y on $[-1, 1]$. Any interval $[a, b]$ may be scaled to $[-1, 1]$ and we obtain the corresponding formulas. Moreover, by using the mapping $x = \cos\theta$ and $T_k(x) = \cos k\theta$ we see that the following two series

$$y(x) = \frac{c_0}{2}T_0(x) + c_1T_1(x) + c_2T_2(x) + ...$$

$$y(\cos\theta) = \frac{c_0}{2} + c_1\cos\theta + c_2\cos 2\theta + ...$$

are equivalent. A Chebyshev series is in fact a Fourier cosine series so that the FFT and iFFT may be used to transform the spectral representation of y into the physical one and conversely, the physical representation into the spectral representation. The quadrature weights $\mathbf{w}$ could also be calculated by a fast algorithm given in (Waldvogel, 2006).

The first code of level0, inspired from `chebpts.m` of *chebfun* (Trefethen et al., 2011) is

```
[x,w] = pd(N,dom,kind)
```

(`pd` means "**p**hysical **d**omain"). It calculates the grid $\mathbf{x} = [x_1, ..., x_N]^T$ (column vector) and the quadrature weights $\mathbf{w} = [w_1, ..., w_N]$ (row vector) for the quadrature formula

$$\int_a^b f(x)dx \approx \sum_{j=1}^{N} w_j f(x_j) \equiv \mathbf{w}\cdot f(\mathbf{x}).$$

The input parameters are N – the dimension of the vectors $\mathbf{x}$ and $\mathbf{w}$, *dom* – the computational domain $[a, b]$ and *kind* which can be 1 or 2 in order to calculate $\mathbf{x}$ as the Chebyshev points of the first or of the second kind.

Some short tests show the performances of this code. Let us approximate

$$\int_0^1 x\sin\frac{1}{x}dx = \frac{cos(1) + sin(1) + Si(1)}{2} - \frac{\pi}{4} \approx 0.37853001712416130988...$$

for $N = 10, 10^2, ..., 10^6$. Here we use Chebyshev points of the first kind and hence we have no problems with the singularity at the origin. We have instead problems with the highly oscillatory behavior of the integrand near the origin. The code is `Chebpack\examples\ex_level0\quad_ex1.m` and the result for $N = 10^6$ is

```
Elapsed time = 0.938258074699438 seconds
err = 1.9568e-11.
```

A more efficient code is

```
[int,gridpts] = quadcheb(myfun,n,dom,kind,tol,gridpts,I)
```

in the folder `Chebpack\examples\ex_level0` which uses `pd` into a recursive procedure. Precisely, starting from the initial interval $dom = [a,b]$, `pd` is used with n points in $[a,b]$ and on two subintervals $[a,c]$ and $[c,b]$ where $c = (a+b)/2$. If the results differe by more than a tolerance ε, the interval $[a,b]$ is divided to that subintervals . Now `quadcheb` is called again for each subinterval and at each step we sum the results. For $N = 128$ we obtain

```
Elapsed time = 0.013672 seconds.
err = 4.907093620332148e-010
```

Of course, this non-optimized quadrature calculation is only a collateral facility in *Chebpack* and it does not work better than the basic quadrature command `quadgk` from MATLAB, which is designated for highly oscillatory integrals.
The next codes of level0

`v = t2x(c,kind)` and `c = x2t(v,kind)`

are inspired by `chebpolyval.m` and `chebpoly.m` from *chebfun* (Trefethen et al., 2011). These codes perform the correspondence between the spectral representation $\mathbf{c}$ of a function f and its physical representation $\mathbf{v} = f(\mathbf{x})$ on Chebyshev points of the first or second kind. It is important to remark that linear operators are better represented in the spectral space, while the nonlinear operators are easily handled in the physical space.
In `t2x` and `x2t`, $\mathbf{c}$ and $\mathbf{v}$ are matrices of the same dimension, each column represents the coefficients or the values for some other function, the number of rows is the above dimension N, while *kind* specifies the type of Chebyshev points used in $\mathbf{v}$. For example, the code

```
n=16;dom=[0,1];kind=2;x=pd(n,dom,kind);
vs=sin(x);vc=cos(x);ve=exp(x);c=x2t([vs,vc,ve],kind);
```

gives in the columns of $\mathbf{c}$ the coefficients of the Chebyshev series (6) of $\sin(x)$, $\cos(x)$ and $\exp(x)$ calculated by using the values of these functions on Chebyshev points of the second kind on $[0,1]$. We remark here that, taking into account the term $c_0T_0/2$, the coefficient c_0 is doubled.
Another code from level0, inspired from `bary.m` of *chebfun* (Trefethen et al., 2011) and useful for graphical representation of the functions is

```
fxn = barycheb(xn,fk,xk,kind)
```

It interpolates the values $\mathbf{fk}$ of a function f at the Chebyshev nodes $\mathbf{xk}$ of the first or second kind in *dom* by calculating the values $\mathbf{fxn}$ at the new (arbitrary) nodes $\mathbf{xn}$ in *dom*. The barycentric weights are calculated depending on kind.
Precisely, cf. (Berrut & Trefethen, 2004), the barycentric formula is

$$f(x) = \frac{\sum_{k=1}^{N} \frac{w_k}{x-x_k} f_k}{\sum_{k=1}^{N} \frac{w_k}{x-x_k}}, \quad w_k = \frac{1}{\prod\limits_{j \neq k} (x_k - x_j)}, \; k = 1, ..., N.$$

For Chebyshev points one can give explicit formula for barycentric weights $\mathbf{w}$. For the Chebyshev points of the first kind we have

$$x_k = -\cos\frac{(2k-1)\pi}{2N}, \; w_k = (-1)^k \sin\frac{(2k-1)\,\pi}{2N}, \; k = 1, ..., N$$

and for the Chebyshev points of the second kind we have

$$x_k = -\cos\frac{(k-1)\pi}{N-1},\ w_k = (-1)^k\delta_k,\ \delta_k = \begin{cases} \frac{1}{2}, & k=1,N \\ 1, & \text{otherwise} \end{cases},\ k = 1, ..., N.$$

We remark that for a general interval $dom = [a, b]$ and if the sign changes for all x_k and w_k the weights must be multiplicated by $\pm 2^{N-1}(b-a)^{1-N}$. This factor cancels out in the barycentric formula so that it is no need to include it.

Let us calculate now the differentiation matrix D such that if $\mathbf{f}$ is the column of the Chebyshev coefficients of a function f, then $D\mathbf{f}$ is the column of the Chebyshev coefficients of the derivative function $\frac{df}{dx}$. On $[-1, 1]$ the derivatives of T_i satisfy

$$T_0 = T_1',\ T_1 = \frac{T_2'}{4}, ..., T_i = \frac{T_{i+1}'}{2(i+1)} - \frac{T_{i-1}'}{2(i-1)},\quad i \geq 2$$

from where

$$\frac{T_0'}{2} = 0,\ T_i' = 2i\left(T_{i-1} + T_{i-3} + ... + T_1\right),\quad i \text{ even}$$
$$T_i' = 2i\left(T_{i-1} + T_{i-3} + ... + 0.5T_0\right),\quad i \text{ odd}.$$

Consequently, D is a sparse upper triangular matrix with

$$D_{ii} = 0,\ D_{ij} = 0 \text{ for } (j-i) \text{ even and } D_{ij} = 2j \text{ otherwise.}$$

Of course, the differentiation could be iterated, i.e. the coefficients of $f^{(p)}$ are $D^p\mathbf{f}$. The corresponding code from level0 is

```
D=deriv(n,dom)
```

where n is the dimension of the matrix D. For $dom = [a, b]$ the above matrix D is multiplied by $2/(b-a)$.

Similarly, the code

```
[J,J0]=prim(n,dom)
```

calculates the sparse integration matrix J such that the coefficients of $\int^x f(t)dt$ are $J\mathbf{f}$. *Here the first coefficient of the result* $J\mathbf{f}$ *may be changed in order to obtain the coefficients for a specific primitive of* f. For example, the coefficients of the primitive which vanishes at $a = dom(1)$ are obtained by using $J_0\mathbf{f}$.

The basic formulas for $dom = [-1, 1]$ are

$$\int \frac{T_0}{2}dx = \frac{T_1}{2},\ \int T_1 dx = \frac{T_0/2}{2} + \frac{T_2}{4},\ \int T_k dx = \frac{1}{2}\left(\frac{T_{k+1}}{k+1} - \frac{T_{k-1}}{k-1}\right),\ k \geq 2$$

from where

$$J_{k,k} = 0,\ J_{0,1} = \frac{1}{2},\ J_{k,k-1} = \frac{1}{2k} = -J_{k,k+1},\ k = 1, 2, ...$$

For a general $dom = [a, b]$ the above matrix J is multiplied by $(b-a)/2$.

As an important example, let us calculate the coeficients of a specific primitive $F(x)$ of the function $f(x)$. We must then solve the initial-value problem

$$\frac{dF}{dx} = f(x),\ y(-1) = \alpha,\ x \in [-1,1].$$

If $\mathbf{c}$ are the Chebyshev coefficients of F and $\mathbf{f}$ are the coefficients of f, the equation is discretized in spectral space as $D\mathbf{c} = \mathbf{f}$. In order to implement the initial condition, we remark that

$$y(-1) = c_0\frac{T_0}{2} + c_1T_1(-1) + c_2T_2(-1) + ... + c_{N-1}T_{N-1}(-1) = \alpha$$

can be written as $T\mathbf{c} = \alpha$ where

$$T = \left[\frac{T_0}{2}, T_1(-1), T_2(-1), ..., T_{N-1}(-1)\right].$$

This means that we can replace the last row of D by T and the last entry of $\mathbf{f}$ by α, thus obtaining a new matrix $\widetilde{D}$ and a new vector $\widetilde{f}$. Finally, $\mathbf{c} = \widetilde{D}^{-1}\widetilde{f}$ are the coefficients of the specific primitive.
The following code from level0

```
T=cpv(n,xc,dom)
```

(chebyshev **p**olynomial **v**alues) implements such conditions. Here $\mathbf{x}_c$ is an arbitrary vector in $dom = [a,b]$ and `cpv` calculates the values of the Chebyshev polynomials T_k, $k = 0,1,..,n-1$ at the column of nodes ξ

$$T = [T_0/2, T_1(\xi), T_2(\xi), ..., T_{N-1}(\xi)],\ \xi = \frac{2\mathbf{x}_c}{b-a} - \frac{b+a}{b-a},\ 1 \le \xi \le 1.$$

The code is based on the recurrence formulas of Chebyshev polynomials on $[-1,1]$

$$T_0(x) = 1,\ T_1(x) = x,\ T_k(x) = 2xT_{k-1}(x) - T_{k-2}(x),\ k \ge 2.$$

The test code `Chebpack\examples\ex_level0\quad_ex3` performs these calculations for the special case $y' = \cos x$, $y(0) = 0$, with the solution $y = \sin(x)$. The coefficients $\mathbf{c}$ are obtained by using the differentiation matrix, $\mathbf{cc}$ are the coefficients of the exact solution, $\mathbf{ccc}$ are obtained by using the integration matrix J and $\mathbf{cccc}$ are obtained by using the integration matrix J_0.
We also remark that if `T=cpv(n,x,dom)`,

$$f(x) = 0.5c_0T_0^*(x) + c_1T_1^*(x) + ... + c_{N-1}T_{N-1}^*(x) \tag{10}$$

and $\mathbf{c} = (c_0, ..., c_{N-1})^T$, we have $f(\mathbf{x}) = T\mathbf{c}$, for $\mathbf{x} \in [a,b]$. The code `cpv` could be used to transform between the spectral representation $\mathbf{f}$ of the function f and the physical representation $\mathbf{v} = f(\mathbf{x})$ of values at the Chebyshev grid $\mathbf{x}$,

$$\mathbf{v} = T\mathbf{f},\ \mathbf{f} = T^{-1}\mathbf{v}.$$

These transforms are performed by FFT in the codes `x2t` and `t2x`, but for a small dimension N we may use this direct matrix multiplication.

As another example, let us calculate the values at the grid points $\mathbf{x}$ of the specific primitive which vanishes at $a = dom(1)$

$$F(x_i) = \int_a^{x_i} f(t)dt, \ i = 1, ..., n$$

Starting with the values $\mathbf{f} = f(\mathbf{x})$ we have the Chebyshev coefficients $T^{-1}\mathbf{f}$, then $J_0T^{-1}\mathbf{f}$ are the Chebyshev coefficients of the specific primitive on $[a, b]$ and finally,

$$F(\mathbf{x}) = TJ_0T^{-1}\mathbf{f}. \tag{11}$$

Another code from level0

```
X=mult(n,dom)
```

calculates the sparse multiplication matrix X such that if $\mathbf{f}$ is the column vector of the Chebyshev coefficients of a function $f(x)$, then $X\mathbf{f}$ is the column vector of the coefficients of the function $xf(x)$. The code is based on the formulas

$$xT_0 = T_1, \ xT_1(x) = \frac{T_0}{2} + \frac{T_2}{2}, ..., \ xT_k(x) = \frac{T_{k-1}(x)}{2} + \frac{T_{k+1}(x)}{2}, \ k \geq 2$$

for $x \in [-1, 1]$. Consequently,

$$X_{k,k} = 0, \ X_{k,k-1} = X_{k,k+1} = \frac{1}{2}, \ k = 2, 3, ..., N-1,$$
$$X_{1,1} = 0, \ X_{1,2} = 1, \ X_{N,N-1} = \frac{1}{2}.$$

Then, in general, the coefficients of $x^p f(x)$ are given by $X^p\mathbf{f}$ and the coefficients of $a(x)f(x)$ are given by $a(X)\mathbf{f}$ for analytical functions $a(x)$, where $a(X)$ is the matricial version of the function a. Moreover, if $\dfrac{f(x)}{x^p}$ has no singularity at the origin, then its coefficients are $X^{-p}\mathbf{f}$.
Of course, X is a tri-diagonal matrix, X^2 is a penta-diagonal matrix and so on but, generally, the matrix version `funm(full(X))` of the scalar function $a(x)$ or $X^{-p} = [inv(X)]^p$ are not sparse matrices. For a general interval $dom = [a, b]$, X is replaced by $\frac{b-a}{2}X + \frac{b+a}{2}I_N$ where I_N is the sparse unit matrix `speye(N)`.
Another method to calculate $a(X)$ is to pass from the values $a(\mathbf{x})$ at the Chebyshev grid $\mathbf{x}$ to the Chebyshev coefficients $\mathbf{a}$ using `x2t` and to approximate

$$a(x) \approx .\frac{a_0}{2} + \sum_{k=1}^{m-1} a_k T_k(x). \tag{12}$$

Here m must be chosen sufficiently large, but $m \leq N$ so that the known function $a(x)$ is correctly represented by $a_0, a_1, ..., a_{m-1}$.
In order to calculate the coefficients of the product

$$a(x)f(x) = \left(\frac{a_0}{2} + \sum_{k=1}^{m-1} a_k T_k(x)\right)\left(\frac{f_0}{2} + \sum_{j=1}^{n-1} f_j T_j(x)\right)$$

we may use the formula

$$T_j(x)T_k(x) = \frac{T_{j+k}(x) + T_{|j-k|}(x)}{2}, \forall j,k.$$

The needed coefficients are given by $A\mathbf{f}$ where the matrix $A \approx a(X)$ is given by the code

```
A=fact(a,m)
```

from level0.
The test code `Chebpack\examples\ex_level0\fact_ex1.m` calculates `cosh(X)` using `fact` and `funm` from Matlab. We remark that X is a sparse matrix, so that `funm` must be applied to `full(X)`.

3. Chebpack, linear module

At the first level – level1, the package contains subroutines to solve
- initial and boundary value problems for high order linear differential equations
- initial value problems for first order linear differential systems
- linear integral equations
- eigenvalues and eigenfunctions for differential problems.

The main method used is the so called tau-method, see (Mason & Handscomb, 2003) or (Canuto et al., 1988) for more theoretical details and the implementation. It is based on
- discretization using the differentiation matrix D
- discretization using the integration matrix J
- splitting the interval $dom = [d_1, d_2, ..., d_p]$.

3.1 Discretization using the differentiation matrix D

The corresponding code is `Chebpack\level1\ibvp_ode.m`

```
[x,solnum]=ibvp_ode(n,dom,kind)
```

where *n, dom, kind* have the same significance as above, **x** is the Chebyshev grid and **solnum** is the numerical solution in the physical space calculated at the grid **x**.
The structure of `ivp_ode` is

```
function [x,solnum]=ibvp_ode(n,dom,kind)
x=pd(n,dom,kind);X=mult(n,dom);D=deriv(n,dom);
myDE;myBC;sol=A\b;solnum = t2x(sol,kind);myOUT;
end
```

where `myDE`, `myBC` and `myOUT` must be written by the user and describe the differential equation, the boundary conditions and the output of the program.
For example, for the problem

$$y''' - xy = (x^3 - 2x^2 - 5x - 3)e^x, \; x \in [0,1]$$
$$y(0) = 0, \; y'(0) = 1, \; y(1) = 0$$

we have

```
function myDE
A=D^3-X;b=x2t((x.^3-2*x.^2-5*x-3).*exp(x),kind);end
function myBC
T=cpv(n,dom,dom);A(n-2,:)=T(1,:);b(n-2)=0;
```

```
A(n-1,:)=T(1,:)*D;b(n-1)=1;A(n,:)=T(2,:);b(n)=0;end
```

The program is called by

```
[x,solnum]=ibvp_ode_test(32,[0 1],2);
```

Other examples are coded in `Chebpack\examples\ex_level1\ibvp_ode_ex*.m`
The general form for initial/boundary value problems for high order linear differential equations is (1) and its discrete form is

$$A\mathbf{c} \equiv \left(\sum_{k=0}^{m} P_k(X)D^k\right)\mathbf{c} = \mathbf{b}$$

where the unknown y is represented in the spectral space by its Chebyshev coefficients $\mathbf{c}$, while $\mathbf{b}$ are the Chebyshev coefficients of the r.h.s. $f(x)$.
We remark that the coefficients $P_k(X)$ of the equation can be defined in `myDE`
- directly, for example $P_k(x) = -x$ gives $P_k(X) = -X$
- using $funm$, for example $P_k(x) = \sin x$ gives $P_k(X) = funm(full(X), @sin)$, i.e. using the Taylor series of $\sin X$
- using $fact$, for example $P_k(x) = \cos x$ gives $P_k(X) = fact(x2t(cos(x), kind), m)$, i.e. using the Chebyshev series of $\cos X$
- if $P_k(x)$ is a constant, say P_k, then $P_k(X) = P_k \cdot speye(N)$.

The boundary conditions of the general type (2) are implemented using `cpv`. For example, for $y(x_{1c}) - y'(x_{2c}) + 2y''(x_{3c}) = y_c$ we calculate `T=cpv(N,[x1c,x2c,x3c],dom)`. One of the last rows of A is replaced by `T(1,:)-T(2,:)*D+2*T(3,:)*D^2` and the corresponding entry of the vector $\mathbf{b}$ is replaced by y_c.

3.2 Discretization using the integration matrix J

The corresponding code is `Chebpack\level1\ibvp_ode_int.m`

```
[x,solnum]=ibvp_ode_int(n,dom,kind)
```

We remark that the discretization using the differentiation matrix D does not work well for large N. For example, this type of discretization for the problem

$$\varepsilon y'' + xy\prime = -\varepsilon\pi^2 cos(\pi x) - \pi\, x\, sin(\pi x),\ x \in [-1,1], \varepsilon = 10^{-5}, \qquad (13)$$
$$y(-1) = -2,\ y(1) = 0$$

with $N = 2048$ and an error about 5.46×10^{-11} leads us to a sparse system $A\mathbf{c} = \mathbf{b}$ but with a sparsity factor about 25% that increases the computational time to 6.4 sec, see the example `ibvp_ode_ex.m` in the folder `Chebpack\examples\ex_level1`. A better idea is to integrate two times the above equation using the much more sparse integration matrix J. This integration make the coefficients c_0 and c_1 arbitrary and we may fix their values by using the boundary conditions, this time at the first two rows of A and $\mathbf{b}$.
Precisely, the first and the second integration of the equation (13) gives

$$\varepsilon y' + xy - \int^x y = \int^x \left[-\varepsilon\pi^2 cos(\pi x) - \pi\, x\, sin(\pi x)\right]$$
$$\varepsilon y + \int^x xy - \int^x\int^x y = \int^x\int^x \left[-\varepsilon\pi^2 cos(\pi x) - \pi\, x\, sin(\pi x)\right].$$

The discrete form is $(\varepsilon I_N + JX - J^2)\,\mathbf{c} = J^2\mathbf{f}$ where $\mathbf{c}$ are the Chebyshev coefficients of the solution y and $\mathbf{f}$ are the Chebyshev coefficients of the r.h.s. The new code

`ibvp_ode_int_ex.m` in the same folder as above gives the same accuracy for the same $N = 2048$, but needing only 0.12 sec. The new matrix A has now a sparsity factor of about 0.2439% for the dimension 2048.
This higher sparsity qualifies the integration method to be used for splitting the interval $dom = [a, b]$ into $dom = [a, d_1] \cup [d_1, d_2] \cup ... \cup [d_{m-1}, b]$ as well as for differential systems, where the dimension N of matrices is multiplied by the number of subintervals or by the number of differential equations in the system.
We give the formulas for first order equations and a general formula. For the first order we have in `myDE`

$$P_1(x)y' + P_0(x)y = F \implies P_1(x)y - \int P_1'(x)y + \int P_0(x)y = \int F,$$

$$A\mathbf{c} \equiv \left[P_1(X) + J\left[P_0(X) - P_1'(X)\right]\right]\mathbf{c} = J\mathbf{f} \equiv \mathbf{b}.$$

Generally, if we denote the differentiation operator on functions P by dP, the identity operator by I and the formal k power of the operator $I - Jd$ by $[\ ]^{(k)}$, we obtain, after m integrations, $A\mathbf{c} = \mathbf{b}$ where

$$A = \sum_{k=0}^{m} J^{m-k}\left[I - Jd\right]^{(k)} P_k(X),\ \mathbf{b} = J^m\mathbf{f}. \tag{14}$$

For example, for $m = 3$ we have

$$\iiint P_0(x)y(x) \to J^3 P_0(X)\mathbf{c},\ \iiint P_1(x)y'(x) \to J^2\left[P_1(X) - JP_1'(X)\right]\mathbf{c},$$

$$\iiint P_2(x)y''(x) \to J\left[P_2(X) - 2JP_2'(X) + J^2P''(X)\right]\mathbf{c},$$

$$\iiint P_3(x)y'''(x) \to \left[P_3(X) - 3JP_3'(X) + 3J^2P_3''(X) - J^3P_3'''(X)\right]\mathbf{c}.$$

It is important to remark that the absolute value of the Chebyshev coefficients gives us some information about the necessary dimension N of the discretized problem in order to capture the correct behavior of the solution. For example, let us consider the problem `ibvp_ode_int_ex2.m` in the folder `Chebpack\examples\ex_level1`

$$\varepsilon y'' + (x^2 - w^2)y = 0,\ y(-1) = 1, y(1) = 2,\ x \in [-1, 1]$$

for $w = 0.5$, $\varepsilon = 1.e - 6$. The command
`[x,solnum]=ibvp_ode_int_ex2(1024,[-1 1],2);`
gives the results in Fig. 2. We see that up to a dimension about $N = 400$, the algorithm cannot resolve y accurately, due to its highly oscillatory behavior. After that, the Chebyshev series begins to converge rapidly. For $N = 1024$ the elapsed time is about 0.05 sec.

3.3 Discretization using the integration matrix J and splitting the interval

The corresponding code is `Chebpack\level1\ibvp_ode_split.m`

```
[x,solnum]=ibvp_ode_split(n,dom,kind)
```

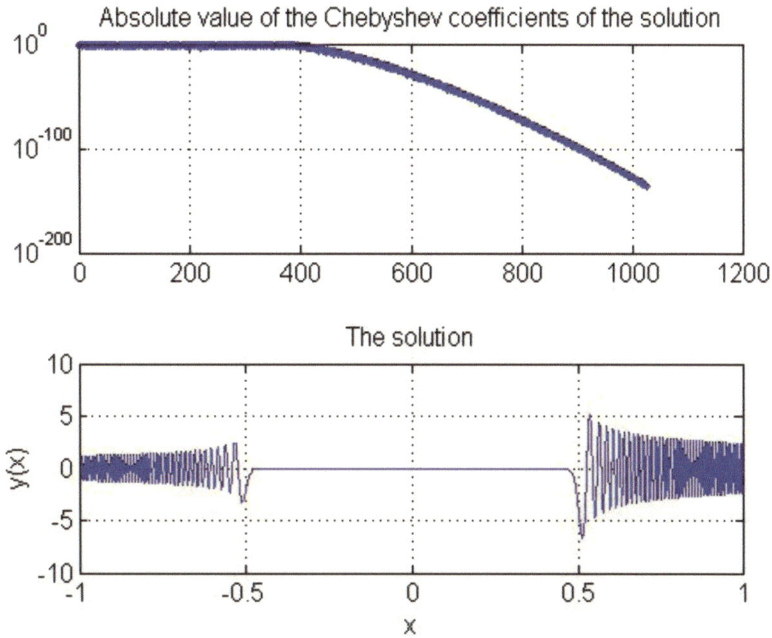

Fig. 2. The Chebyshev coefficients and the numerical solution for ex2

Sometimes, the solution of a differential problem has a different behavior in different subintervals. For example, for small ε the solution of the problem (13) has a shock near the origin and we need a very large N in order to capture its correct behavior. In these cases it is better to split the working interval $dom[a,b]$ into disjoint subintervals $[d_1,d_2] \cup [d_2,d_3] \cup \ldots \cup [d_{p-1},d_p] = [a,b]$ adapted to the behavior of the solution. The great advantage is to use a small N for each subinterval. The partial solutions on each subinterval are connected by some level of smoothness.

Precisely, let us consider for example a second order differential problem on $[a,b]$ and let us split the interval as $[a,b] = [d_1,d_2] \cup [d_2,d_3] \cup [d_3,d_4]$. This splitting is given by $dom = [d_1,d_2,d_3,d_4]$ on input. If we calculate the basic ingredients $\mathbf{xs}$, Xs, Ds, Js for the standard interval $[-1,1]$, then for each subinterval $[d_i,d_{i+1}]$, $i = 1,2,3$ the corresponding ingredients become

$$\mathbf{x} = len * \mathbf{xs} + med,\ X = len * Xs + med * I_N,\ D = \frac{Ds}{len},\ J = len * Js$$

where $len = \frac{d_{i+1}-d_i}{2}$, $med = \frac{d_{i+1}+d_i}{2}$.

Using the matrix J for the discretization we obtain on each subinterval $i = 1,2,3$ the discretized form $A^{(i)}c^{(i)} = b^{(i)}$ where the matrix $A^{(i)}$ and the vector $\mathbf{b}^{(i)}$ are given by (14) as above, while $\mathbf{c}^{(i)}$ are the Chebyshev coefficients of the solution $y^{(i)}$ on that subinterval i. Now, using the Kronecker product and the `reshape` command of Matlab, we build a large (but very sparse) system $A\mathbf{c} = \mathbf{b}$

$$\begin{pmatrix} A^{(1)} & O & O \\ O & A^{(2)} & O \\ O & O & A^{(3)} \end{pmatrix} \begin{pmatrix} \mathbf{c}^{(1)} \\ \mathbf{c}^{(2)} \\ \mathbf{c}^{(3)} \end{pmatrix} = \begin{pmatrix} \mathbf{b}^{(1)} \\ \mathbf{b}^{(2)} \\ \mathbf{b}^{(3)} \end{pmatrix}.$$

The boundary conditions are now the given boundary conditions say at d_1 and d_4 supplemented by smoothness conditions at d_2, d_3

$$y^{(1)}(d_2-0)=y^{(2)}(d_2+0),\ \frac{dy^{(1)}}{dx}(d_2-0)=\frac{dy^{(2)}}{dx}(d_2+0),\qquad (15)$$
$$y^{(2)}(d_3-0)=y^{(3)}(d_3+0),\ \frac{dy^{(2)}}{dx}(d_3-0)=\frac{dy^{(3)}}{dx}(d_3+0).$$

Of course, for a higher order equation (say m) we have coincidence conditions (15) until the derivatives of order $m-1$. The given boundary conditions are implemented in the first m rows of the first block-row of the matrix A and in the first entries of the first block of the vector $\mathbf{b}$, while the coincidence conditions are implemented in the first m rows of each of the following block-rows of A and in the first m entries of each following block of $\mathbf{b}$. The sparsity structure of A with 4 subintervals is given in Fig. 3. Here we have 16 blocks of size 64×64, the

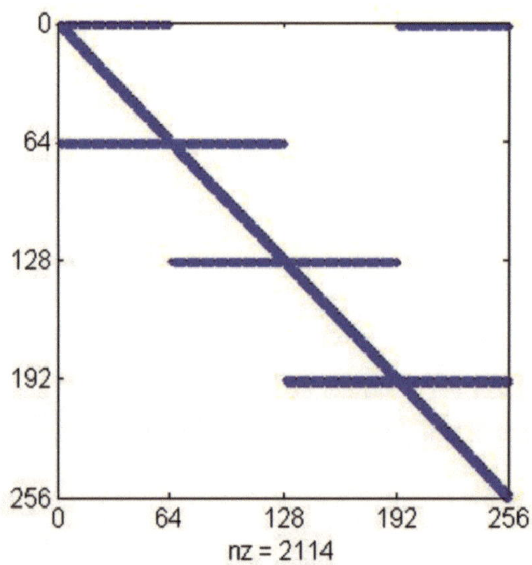

Fig. 3. The sparsity structure of the matrix A with boundary conditions implemented for 4 subintervals

4 diagonal segments come from the matrices $A^{(i)}$, $i=1,2,3,4$, the first horizontal segments come from the given boundary conditions while the next 3 pairs of horizontal segments come from connectivity conditions. Each block acts on the corresponding block coefficients $\mathbf{c}^{(i)}$, $i=1,2,3,4$.
Using this technique for the problem (13) for example, the command
```
[x,solnum]=ibvp_ode_split_ex(64,[-1 -0.05 0 0.05 1],2);
```
from the folder `Chebpack\examples\ex_level1` gives the numerical solution with an accuracy of about 6×10^{-15} with four subintervals with $N=64$ in only 0.014 sec. The new matrix A has now a sparsity factor of about 3.2257% and the dimension 256.

3.4 Linear first-order systems

Let us consider a first order linear differential system for $x \in [a,b]$

$$\begin{aligned} P_1(x)y_1' + P_{11}(x)y_1 + ... + P_{1m}(x)y_m &= f_1(x),\ y_1(a) = y_{1a}, \\ P_2(x)y_2' + P_{21}(x)y_1 + ... + P_{2m}(x)y_m &= f_2(x)\ ,\ y_2(a) = y_{2a}, \\ &\cdots\cdots \\ P_m(x)y_m' + P_{m1}(x)y_1 + ... + P_{mm}(x)y_m &= f_m(x),\ y_m(a) = y_{ma}. \end{aligned}$$

If we denote by $\mathbf{c} = (c^{(1)}, ..., c^{(m)})^T$ the Chebyshev coefficients of $y_1(x), ..., y_m(x)$ and by $\mathbf{f}^{(1)}, ..., \mathbf{f}^{(m)}$ the coefficients of $f_1, ..., f_m$ then the discretized version of the system is $\mathbf{Ac} = \mathbf{b}$ where

$$\mathbf{A} = \begin{pmatrix} P_1(X)D + P_{11}(X) & \cdots & P_{1m}(X) \\ \vdots & \ddots & \vdots \\ P_{m1}(X) & \cdots & P_m(X)D + P_{mm}(X) \end{pmatrix},\ \mathbf{b} = \begin{pmatrix} \mathbf{f}^{(1)} \\ \vdots \\ \mathbf{f}^{(m)} \end{pmatrix}.$$

The initial conditions are implemented like in (15): the last row of each block in the above matrix is replaced by T or zeros for the corresponding columns and the last entry of each block in the r.h.s. is replaced by y_{ka} such that $[O, ..., T, ..., O]\mathbf{c} = y_{ka}$ for each k. The corresponding code from level1 is

```
[x,solnum]=ibvp_sys(n,dom,kind,y0)
```

where **y0** is the column vector of the initial values $[y_{1a}, ..., y_{ma}]^T$. Of course, we may use the integration matrix J instead of D for discretization, obtaining again a system $\mathbf{Ac} = \mathbf{b}$ where

$$\mathbf{A} = \begin{pmatrix} P_1(X) - JP_1'(X) + JP_{11}(X) & \cdots & JP_{1m}(X) \\ \vdots & \ddots & \vdots \\ JP_{m1}(X) & \cdots & P_m(X) - JP_m'(X) + JP_{mm}(X) \end{pmatrix},\ \mathbf{b} = \begin{pmatrix} J\mathbf{f}^{(1)} \\ \vdots \\ J\mathbf{f}^{(m)} \end{pmatrix}$$

with the implementation of the initial conditions on the first row of each block, see `ibvp_sys_ex3_int.m`, or we may consider systems of higher order, see `ibvp_sys_ex2x2.m` from the folder `Chebpack\examples\ex_level1`.

3.5 Linear integral equations

Let us consider a Fredholm integral equation

$$y(x) = \int_a^b K(x,t)y(t)dt + f(x) \equiv A(y)(x) + f(x),\ x \in [a,b]. \tag{16}$$

The Fredholm integral operator $A(y)$ becomes after discretization with shifted Chebyshev polynomials

$$A(y)(x) = \int_a^b K(x,t) \sum_{k=0}^{N-1} c_k T_k^*(t)dt = \sum_{k=0}^{N-1} c_k \int_a^b K(x,t)T_k^*(t)dt =$$

$$\sum_{k=0}^{N-1} c_k \cdot I_k(x) = \sum_{k=0}^{N-1} c_k \sum_{j=0}^{N-1} k_{jk}T_j^*(x) = \sum_{j=0}^{N-1} \left[\sum_{k=0}^{N-1} k_{jk}c_k \right] T_j^*(x).$$

Consequently, if $\mathbf{c} = (c_0, ..., c_{N-1})^T$ are the coefficients of y, then $K\mathbf{c}$ are the coefficients of $A(y)$, given by the matrix $K = (k_{jk})_{j,k=0,...,N-1}$.
The matrix K can be calculated starting from the physical values

$$I_k(x_s) = \int_a^b K(x_s, t) T_k^*(t) dt = \sum_{i=0}^{N-1} w_i K(x_s, x_i) T_k^*(x_i), \;\; s, k = 0, ..., N-1.$$

In matrix form, this means

$$(I_k(x_s))_{k,s=0,...,N-1} = (K(x_s, x_i))_{s,i=0,...,N-1} \cdot diag((w_i)_{i=0,...,N-1}) \cdot T$$

where `T=cpv(n,x,dom)` and then we apply `x2t`, see also (Driscoll, 2010).
The Fredholm integral equation (16) becomes $(I_N - K)\mathbf{c} = \mathbf{f}$ where $\mathbf{f}$ are the Chebyshev coefficients of f and we obtain the solution by solving this linear system. The corresponding model code from the folder `Chebpack\level1` is

```
[x,solnum]=fred_eq(n,dom,kind)
```

Similarly, for a Volterra integral equation

$$y(x) = \int_a^x K(x, t) y(t) dt + f(x) \equiv A(y)(x) + f(x), \; x \in [a, b]$$

we obtain, using (11), for the Volterra integral operator

$$A(y)(x) = \int_a^x K(x, t) y(t) dt = \left[T J_0 T^{-1} .* K(x_i, x_j) \right] \mathbf{y},$$

where $\mathbf{y}$ are the values of $y(x)$ at the grid points $\mathbf{x}$. Consequently, the physical representation of the Volterra integral operator is the matrix $V_{phys} = T J_0 T^{-1} .* K(x_i, x_j)$, see again (Driscoll, 2010) while its spectral representation is $V_{spec} = T^{-1} V_{phys} T$. The Volterra integral equation becomes in physical representation $(I_N - K)\mathbf{y} = \mathbf{f}$ where $\mathbf{f}$ are now the values of f at the grid points $\mathbf{x}$.
The corresponding model code from *Chebpack* is

```
[x,solnum]=volt_eq(n,dom,kind)
```

from the folder `Chebpack\level1`. The folder `Chebpack\examples\ex_level1` contains some examples in the files `fred_eq_ex*` and `volt_eq_ex*`.
Of course, these codes work well only if the kernel $K(x, t)$ is sufficiently smooth such that it can be spectrally represented by an acceptable number of Chebyshev polynomials.

3.6 Eigenvalues/eigenfunctions for Sturm-Liouville problems

Let us consider now the second order spectral problem

$$P_2(x) y'' + P_1(x) y' + P_0(x) y = \lambda R(x) y$$

with homogeneous boundary value conditions as above. Using tau method, we get the following N – dimensional matrix eigenproblem

$$(P_2(X) D^2 + P_1(X) D + P_0(X))\mathbf{c} = \lambda R(X)\mathbf{c}$$

of the form $A\mathbf{c} = \lambda B\mathbf{c}$. The conditions give $T\mathbf{c} = 0$ and combining these equations we derive the generalized eigenproblem

$$\begin{pmatrix} T \\ A \end{pmatrix} c = \lambda \begin{pmatrix} \frac{1}{\lambda^*}T \\ B \end{pmatrix} c \text{ i.e. } \widetilde{A}\mathbf{c} = \lambda \widetilde{B}\mathbf{c}$$

where we retain only the first N rows of the matrices to obtain $\widetilde{A}$ and $\widetilde{B}$. Here λ^* is chosen by the user as a large and known value. We remark that for $\lambda \neq \lambda^*$ we get $Tc = 0$ as above but now the matrix $\widetilde{B}$ behaves well. Consequently, the eigenproblem has instead of two infinite eigenvalues two known λ^* eigenvalues that can be eliminated. The same procedure is applied for higher order problems.
The corresponding model code from the folder `Chebpack\level1` is

```
[lam,phi,x]=eig_ode2(n,dom,kind,numeigval)
```

The folder `Chebpack\examples\ex_level1` contains some other examples in the files `eig_ode2_ex*`, `eig_ode3_ex` and `eig_ode4_ex`. An older package *LiScEig* is also freely accessible at (Trif, 2005).

4. Chebpack, nonlinear module

At the second level – level2, we have subroutines to solve
- initial and boundary value problems for nonlinear differential equations
- nonlinear integral equations.

Here the codes of the first level are used at each step of the Newton method applied in the functional space. Another method could be the successive iteration method.

4.1 Successive iteration method

Let us consider, as an example, the nonlinear Emden boundary value problem

$$xy'' + 2y' = -xy^5,\ y'(0) = 0,\ y(1) = \frac{\sqrt{3}}{2},\ x \in [0,1].$$

If the starting spectral approximation of y is, for example, $Y_0 = 1$ then the discretization of the problem is $AY = F$. Here $A = XD^2 + 2D$ and $F = F(x, Y_0)$ are the coefficients of the r.h.s. modified by using the boundary value conditions. We apply successively

$$Y_{n+1} = A^{-1}F(x, Y_n),\ n = 0, 1, 2, ..., n_{\max}.$$

If Y_n converges, then it converges to a solution of the bvp.
The Matlab codes are `ibvp_ode_succapprox.m` from the folder `Chebpack\level2` or `ibvp_ode_ex1.m` from the folder `Chebpack\examples\ex_level2`.
Of course, the discretization could be performed using the integration matrix J instead of D.
Let us consider, for example, the Lotka-Volterra system

$$\begin{aligned} y_1' - Ay_1 &= -By_1y_2,\ y_2' + Cy_2 = By_1y_2,\ t \in [0, 100] \\ y_1(0) &= y_2(0) = 0.5,\ A = 0.1,\ B = 0.2,\ C = 0.05. \end{aligned}$$

We transform this system to integral form

$$y_1 - A\int y_1 dt = -B\int y_1 y_2 dt,\ y_2 + C\int y_2 dt = B\int y_1 y_2 dt$$

and the discretized form in spectral representation is

$$\begin{pmatrix} I_n - AJ & 0 \\ 0 & I_n + CJ \end{pmatrix} \begin{pmatrix} Y_1^{new} \\ Y_2^{new} \end{pmatrix} = \begin{pmatrix} -BJF \\ BJF \end{pmatrix}$$

where F is the column vector of the coefficients of $y_1^{old}(t)y_2^{old}(t)$ obtained by using `t2x.m` and `x2t.m`. In this discretized form we implement the initial conditions as usually and we must solve this system which has a sparsity factor of about 6% for $n = 32$ and about 3% for $n = 64$. For a long interval *dom* given as $dom = [d_0, d_1, ..., d_m]$, we apply the successive approximations method at each subinterval. The initial approximation for the following subinterval is given by the final values of the solution for the current subinterval. To test the numerical solution, we remark that the Lotka-Volterra system has as invariant $\Lambda = By_1 + By_2 - C\log y_1 - A\log y_2$. The code is used by the command

```
[x,solnum]=ibvp_sys_succapprox(32,[0:10:100],2,[0.5,0.5]);
```

and the result is given in Fig. 4, with the value of the invariant $\Lambda = 0.3039720770839$.

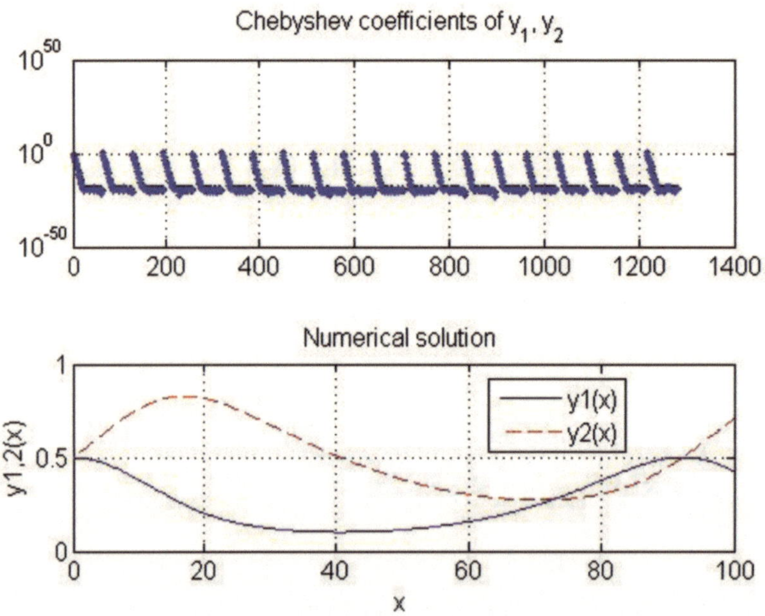

Fig. 4. The solution of the Lotka-Volterra problem

In the case of nonlinear integral equations, for example

$$y(x) = f(x) + \int_0^b K(x, t, y(t))dt,$$

we perform successive iterations (if this method works)

$$y^{new}(x) = f(x) + \int_0^b K(x, t, y^{old}(t))dt$$

starting with a suitable y^{old}. For each $x = x_s$ in the grid and at each iteration, the integral is evaluated as

$$\int_0^b K(x_s, t, y^{old}(t))dt \approx \sum_{k=1}^{n} w_k K(x_s, t_k, y^{old}(t_k)),$$

where $\{t_k, k = 1, ..., n\}$ is the Chebyshev grid on $[0, b]$ and $\{w_k, k = 1, ..., n\}$ are the corresponding weights. Consequently, we obtain

$$y^{new}(x_s) = \sum_{k=1}^{n} w_k K(x_s, t_k, y^{old}(t_k)),\ s = 1, ..., n.$$

Taking into account the nonlinearities, all the calculations are performed into the physical space. Next, $y^{old} \longleftarrow y^{new}$ until $\left\| y^{new} - y^{old} \right\| < \varepsilon$. The corresponding code is `ibvp_int_succapprox.m` from the folder `Chebpack\level2`.

4.2 Newton method

Let us consider again a nonlinear differential problem of the form

$$Ly(x) = f(x, y(x)),\ x \in [a, b]$$

where L is a linear differential operator, such as $Ly(x) = xy''(x) + 2y'(x)$ and f is the nonlinear part. We have also the boundary or initial conditions BC/IC. If we denote by

$$P(y)(x) = Ly(x) - f(x, y(x)),\ BC/IC$$

the problem is of the form $P(y)(x) = 0$ where P is the operator of the problem and y is the unknown.

The Newton method works as follows. Starting with an initial approximation $y_0(x)$ verifying the initial or boundary conditions, we must solve at each step n the linear problem

$$P'(y_n)(y_{n+1} - y_n)(x) = -P(y_n)(x),$$

for $y_{n+1} - y_n$, with the corresponding homogeneous IC/BC. Next, $y_{n+1} = y_n + (y_{n+1} - y_n)$ and we perform these iterations until $\|y_{n+1} - y_n\| < \varepsilon$. For our problem, the linear step is

$$\left[L - \frac{\partial f(x, y_n(x))}{\partial y}\right](y_{n+1} - y_n)(x) = -\left[Ly_n(x) - f(x, y_n(x))\right].$$

The corresponding code is `ibvp_ode_newton.m` from the folder `Chebpack \level2`. It starts with $y_0(x)$ verifying or not the IC/BC and solves at each step the above linear problem for y_{n+1} with the nonhomogeneous IC/BC.

A nonlinear system (of order 2 for example)

$$\begin{aligned} y_1' + a_{11}y_1 + a_{12}y_2 &= f_1(x, y_1, y_2),\ x \in [a, b] \\ y_2' + a_{21}y_1 + a_{22}y_2 &= f_2(x, y_1, y_2),\ y_1(a) = y_{1a}, y_2(a) = y_{2a} \end{aligned}$$

is in matrix form

$$Y'(x) + A(x)Y(x) = F(x, Y).$$

At the linear step it becomes

$$\left[Z' + \left[A(x) - JacF(x, Y_n)\right] Z = -\left[Y_n' + AY_n - F(x, Y_n)\right]\right.$$

where $Z = Y_{n+1} - Y_n$ is the correction, $Y_n \equiv Y(x_n)$ and

$$JacF(x, Y_n) = \begin{vmatrix} \frac{\partial f_1(x,y_{1n},y_{2n})}{\partial y_1} & \frac{\partial f_1(x,y_{1n},y_{2n})}{\partial y_2} \\ \frac{\partial f_2(x,y_{1n},y_{2n})}{\partial y_1} & \frac{\partial f_2(x,y_{1n},y_{2n})}{\partial y_2} \end{vmatrix}.$$

As above, $Y_{n+1} = Y_n + Z$ until $\|Z\| < \varepsilon$.
We remark that in the linear step we use the integration

$$Z + \int [A(x) - JacF(x, Y_n)]\, Z = -\int [Y_n' + AY_n - F(x, Y_n)]$$

which becomes in the discrete form

$$[I_n + J\,(A(X) - JacF(X, Y_n))]\, Z = -[Y_n + JA(x)]Y_n + JF(x, Y_n).$$

i.e $AZ = B$. In the l.h.s the matrix $J\,(A(X) - JacF(X, Y_n))$ is calculated using the code `fact.m`. This code uses the physical values of $A(x) - JacF(x, Y_n)$ and converts them into spectral coefficients. In the r.h.s the code also starts with the physical values and converts them into their spectral coefficients. The initial conditions are implemented now in the rows $1, n+1, ...$.
Of course, this code `ibvp_sys_newton.m` from the folder `Chebpack\level2` can be used in a long-term integration algorithm that starts with the initial values y_{a1}, y_{b1}, calculates the solution on $[a, b]$, extracts the final values y_{b1}, y_{b2} which become initial values for the same code on a new interval $[b, c]$ and so on.
A short comparison between the successive approximations method (SA) and the Newton method (N) for the example from `ibvp_sys_newton_ex1` shows that, for the same $n = 64$, $dom = [0, 1, 2 : 2 : 200]$ and $M = 8$,
- SA: 2910 iterations, 3.4 sec elapsed time, 12940 Chebyshev coefficients calculated
- N : 490 iterations, 6 sec elapsed time, 6475 Chebyshev coefficients calculated.
In the case of a nonlinear integral equation (of Fredholm or Volterra) type

$$P(y) \equiv y(x) - \int_a K(x, t, y(t))dt - f(x) = 0,$$

we start with an initial approximation y_0 (in physical space) and at each Newton step we obtain the linear equation for the correction z

$$z(x) - \int_a \frac{\partial K}{\partial y}(x, t, y_0(t))z(t)dt = -y_0(x) + \int_a K(x, t, y_0(t))dt + f(x).$$

We solve this equation in spectral form as in the previous section and the corrected value of y is $y_0 + z$. We repeat this step until convergence, i.e. until $\|z\| < \varepsilon$. There are many examples in the folder `Chebpack\examples\level2`.

5. Chebpack, experimental module

Finally, the package contains an experimental level – level3, in progress, for
- partial differential equations of evolution type
- fractional differential equations (i.e. differential equations of non-integer order).

5.1 Partial differential evolution equations

Let us consider, as a simple example, a problem from (Trefethen et al., 2011)

$$u_t = u_{xx},\ x \in [-4,2],\ t > 0$$
$$u(x,0) = u^{(0)}(x) \equiv \max(0, 1 - abs(x)),$$
$$u(-4,t) = 1,\ u(2,t) = 2.$$

First, we discretize in time by a backward finite difference on the grid $0 = t_0 < t_1 < ... < t_K$ starting with $u^{(0)}(x)$

$$\frac{u^{(k+1)}(x) - u^{(k)}(x)}{dt} = u_{xx}^{(k+1)}(x),$$

where $u^{(k)}(x) = u(x,t_k)$, $u_{xx}^{(k)}(x) = u_{xx}(x,t_k)$. We obtain the second order boundary value problems in x

$$\left(I - dt\frac{\partial^2}{\partial x^2}\right) u^{(k+1)}(x) = u^{(k)}(x),\ u^{(k+1)}(-4) = 1,\ u^{(k+1)}(2) = 2.$$

These problems, for each $k = 1,2,...,K$, are also discretized by the spectral Chebyshev method with some N, $dom = [-4,2]$, $kind$ as

$$\left(I_n - dtD^2\right) c^{(k+1)} = c^{(k)},\ u^{(k+1)}(-4) = 1,\ u^{(k+1)}(2) = 2.$$

Here $c^{(k)}$ are the Chebyshev spectral coefficients $\left(c_0^{(k)}, c_1^{(k)}, ..., c_{N-1}^{(k)}\right)$ of $u^{(k)}(x)$ corresponding to the grid $x_1, ..., x_N$ in dom. This way we may obtain the solution $u(x_j,t_k)$ on the computational grid $\left(x_j, t_k\right)_{j=1,...,N}^{k=1,...,K}$. The corresponding code is `pde_lin.m` from the folder `Chebpack\level3`.

Similarly, for nonlinear equations of the form $u_t = Lu + Nu$ where L is a linear operator and N a nonlinear one, for example for the Burgers equation

$$u_t = \nu u_{xx} - \left(\frac{u^2}{2}\right)_x,\ x \in [-1,1],\ t > 0,\ \nu = \frac{0.01}{\pi},$$
$$u(x,0) = \sin \pi x,\ u(0,t) = u(1,t) = 0,$$

we may take the backward Euler finite difference for the linear part while the forward Euler finite difference for the nonlinear part.

$$\frac{u^{(k+1)}(x) - u^{(k)}(x)}{dt} = Lu^{(k+1)}(x) + Nu^{(k)}(x),$$

We obtain

$$(I - dt\,L)\, u^{(k+1)}(x) = u^{(k)}(x) + dt\, Nu^{(k)}(x),\ u^{(k+1)}(0) = u^{(k+1)}(1) = 0$$

which is implemented in `pde_nonlin.m`.

Of course, we may take the approximating solution in the physical representation on the grid $x_1, ..., x_n$ and the semidiscrete problem becomes $u'(\mathbf{x},t) = \widetilde{D}u(\mathbf{x},t)$ where $\widetilde{D} = TD^2T^{-1}$ is the physical second order derivative. The boundary value condition imposes $u(x_1,t) = \alpha$,

$u(x_n, t) = \beta$ and therefore at these points we don't need to satisfy the equation. Consequently, if $\widehat{D} = \widetilde{D}(2 : n-1, 2 : n-1)$ is obtained by eliminating the first and last rows and columns from $\widetilde{D}$, the problem becomes

$$\widehat{u}'(t) = \widehat{D} * \widehat{u}(t) + \widetilde{D}(2 : n-1, [1, n]) * BC, \ \widehat{u}(0) = \widehat{u}^{(0)},$$

where $BC = (\alpha, \beta)^T$, i.e. $\widehat{u}'(t) = \widehat{D} * \widehat{u}(t) + b, \widehat{u}(0) = \widehat{u}^{(0)}$ with the solution

$$\widehat{u}(t) = expm(t\widehat{D}) \cdot \widehat{u}^{(0)} + \widehat{D}^{-1} \cdot \left(expm(t\widehat{D}) - I_{n-2}\right) \cdot b.$$

Here *expm(A)* is the matricial exponential function of A. The code `pde_lin_matr.m` uses this procedure.
The same thing may be performed in spectral space. The problem

$$u' = L \cdot u, \ u(0) = u_0, \ BC = T \cdot u$$

(where L is a linear differential operator with constant coefficients and T is given by `cpv` from `level0`) may be expanded as

$$\begin{pmatrix} \widehat{u}' \\ BC \end{pmatrix} = \begin{pmatrix} \widehat{L} & \widehat{\widehat{L}} \\ \widehat{T} & \widehat{\widehat{T}} \end{pmatrix} \cdot \begin{pmatrix} \widehat{u} \\ \widehat{\widehat{u}} \end{pmatrix}.$$

Therefore, successively,

$$\widehat{u}' = \widehat{L}\widehat{u} + \widehat{\widehat{L}}\widehat{\widehat{u}}, \ BC = \widehat{T}\widehat{u} + \widehat{\widehat{T}}\widehat{\widehat{u}}, \ \widehat{\widehat{u}} = \widehat{\widehat{T}}^{-1}\left(BC - \widehat{T}\widehat{u}\right), \tag{17}$$

$$\widehat{u}' = \left(\widehat{L} - \widehat{\widehat{L}}\widehat{\widehat{T}}^{-1}\widehat{T}\right)\widehat{u} + \widehat{\widehat{L}}\widehat{\widehat{T}}^{-1} BC, \ \widehat{u}' = \widetilde{L} \cdot \widehat{u} + \widetilde{\widetilde{L}} \cdot BC.$$

The exact solution of the last equation is given by

$$\widehat{u}(t) = e^{t\widetilde{L}} \cdot \widehat{u}_0 + \frac{e^{t\widetilde{L}} - I}{\widetilde{L}} \widetilde{\widetilde{L}} \cdot BC$$

and, using (17), $u = (\widehat{u}, \widehat{\widehat{u}})^T$.
This procedure is coded in `pde_lin_ex2.m` from the folder `Chebpack\examples\ex_level3`.
In the case of a nonlinear problem

$$u' = L \cdot u + Nu, \ u(0) = u_0, \ BC = T \cdot u$$

the same procedure leads to

$$\widehat{u}(t) = e^{t\widetilde{L}} \cdot \widehat{u}_0 + \frac{e^{t\widetilde{L}} - I}{\widetilde{L}} \left(\widetilde{\widetilde{L}} \cdot BC + \widehat{Nu}\right)$$

and to the same $\widehat{\widehat{u}}$ given by (17). This fixed point equation must now be solved using successive iterations method (for t sufficiently small) or using Newton method. It is coded in `pde_nonlin_ex4.m` in the folder `Chebpack\examples\ex_level3` for the Korteweg-de Vries problem

$$u_t + 6u\, u_x + u_{xxx} = 0,\ x \in [-20,20],\ t \in [0,4]$$
$$u(x,0) = 2sech(x)^2,\ u(-20,t) = u(20,t) = u_x(20,t) = 0.$$

This problem of the form $u_t = Lu + N(u)$ is numerically solved in spectral space $c'(t) = Lc(t) + N(c(t))$ by using the so called implicit exponential time differencing Euler method

$$c^{(k+1)} = e^{Ldt}c^{(k)} + \frac{e^{Ldt} - I}{L} N(c^{(k+1)}),$$

applied in a symmetric form

$$c = e^{Ldt/2}c^{(k)} + \frac{e^{Ldt/2} - I}{L} N(c),\ c^{(k+1)} = e^{Ldt/2}c + \frac{e^{Ldt/2} - I}{L} N(c).$$

Here, the first fixed point problem is solved using successive iterations starting with $c^{(k)}$, where $c^{(k)}$ are the Chebyshev coefficients of the numerical solution at the time level k.

5.2 Fractional differential equations

The fractional derivative $D^q f(x)$ with $0 < q < 1, 0 < x \le b$, in the Riemann-Liouville version, is defined by (Podlubny, 1999)

$$D^q f(x) = \frac{1}{\Gamma(1-q)} \frac{d}{dx} \int_0^x f(t)(x-t)^{-q} dt$$

while the Caputo fractional derivative is

$$D_*^q f(x) = \frac{1}{\Gamma(1-q)} \int_0^x f'(t)(x-t)^{-q} dt$$

and we have

$$D^q f(x) = \frac{f(0)x^{-q}}{\Gamma(1-q)} + D_*^q f(x).$$

Let us consider a function $f : [0,b] \to \mathbb{R}$, with the spectral representation

$$f(x) = \sum_{k=0}^{n-1} c_k T_k(\alpha x + \beta),\ \alpha = \frac{2}{b},\ \beta = -1$$

Using the spectral derivative matrix D, we have

$$f'(x) = \sum_{k=0}^{n-1} (Dc)_k\, T_k(\alpha x + \beta)$$

and using the linearity of the fractional derivative of order $q \in (0,1)$, we obtain

$$D_*^q f(x) = \frac{1}{\Gamma(1-q)} \int_0^x \frac{f'(t)dt}{(x-t)^q} = \frac{1}{\Gamma(1-q)} \sum_{k=0}^{n-1} (Dc)_k \int_0^x \frac{T_k(\alpha x + \beta)}{(x-t)^q} dt.$$

By calculating the physical values of the above integrals in the columns k of a matrix I, each row corresponding to a sample of x from the Chebyshev grid, the formula for the fractional derivative is

$$D_*^q f(x) = \frac{1}{\Gamma(1-q)} \cdot I \cdot D \cdot T^{-1} f(x)$$

where T is the matrix given by `cpv.m`. This means that the Caputo fractional differentiation matrix $\mathbf{D}$ in physical form is given by

$$\mathbf{D}_{phys} = \frac{1}{\Gamma(1-q)} \cdot I \cdot D \cdot T^{-1}$$

i.e. $\mathbf{D}_{phys}$ times the vector of physical values of f gives the vector of physical values of $D_*^q f$. For the spectral form,

$$\mathbf{D}_{spec} = \frac{1}{\Gamma(1-q)} \cdot T^{-1} \cdot I \cdot D,$$

i.e. $\mathbf{D}_{spec}$ times the vector $T^{-1}f(x)$ of the coefficients of f gives the vector of the coefficients of $D_*^q f$.

If $q > 1$ then let ex be $[q]$ and q will be replaced by $q - [q]$. In this case, the differentiation matrix will be

$$\mathbf{D}_{spec} = \frac{1}{\Gamma(1-q)} \cdot T^{-1} \cdot I \cdot D^{(ex+1)}.$$

In order to avoid the singularity of the fractional derivative $D^q f$ if $f(0) \neq 0$, **we suppose that** $\mathbf{f(0) = 0}$. The problem of computing the integrals

$$I_k(x) = \int_0^x \frac{T_k(\alpha x - 1)}{(x-t)^q} dt$$

for each x of the grid may be solved iteratively, see (Piessens & Branders, 1976). Indeed, we have, by direct calculation, using the recurrence formula for Chebyshev polynomials, as well as for the derivatives of the Chebyshev polynomials, for $k = 3, 4, ..$

$$I_k(x) \cdot \left(1 + \frac{1-q}{k}\right) = 2(\alpha x - 1) \cdot I_{k-1}(x) + \left(\frac{1-q}{k-2} - 1\right) \cdot I_{k-2}(x) - \frac{2(-1)^k}{k(k-2)} x^{1-q}$$

and

$$I_0(x) = \frac{x^{1-q}}{1-q}/2,\ I_1(x) = \frac{\alpha x^{2-q}}{(2-q)(1-q)} - \frac{x^{1-q}}{1-q},$$

$$I_2(x) = \frac{4\alpha^2 x^{3-q}}{(3-q)(2-q)(1-q)} - \frac{4\alpha x^{2-q}}{(2-q)(1-q)} + \frac{x^{1-q}}{1-q}.$$

This recurrence is as stable as the recurrence which calculates the Chebyshev polynomials. The calculation of the fractional derivative matrix $\mathbf{D}_{spec}$ is coded in `deriv_frac.m` from the folder `Chebpack\level3`. Next, if needed, $\mathbf{D}_{phys} = \frac{1}{\Gamma(1-q)} \cdot I \cdot D^{(ex+1)} \cdot T^{-1} = T \cdot \mathbf{D}_{spec} \cdot T^{-1}$.

Using an idea of Sugiura & Hasegawa (Sugiura & Hasegawa, 2009), let $J(s; f)$ be

$$J(s; f) = \int_0^s f'(t)(s-t)^{-q} dt$$

and, approximating $f(t)$ by a combination $p_n(t)$ of Chebyshev polynomials on $(0,1)$ we have the approximations $|J(s;f) - J(s;p_n)| \sim O(n\rho^{-n})$, for some $\rho > 1$.
Of course, this method is not suitable for the functions with a singularity in $[0,1]$ or singularities of lower-order derivatives, like $x^{0.1}$ for example. In this case, n must be excessively large.
For the initial value problems for fractional differential equations, let us consider the problem

$$D_*^q y(x) = x^2 + \frac{2}{\Gamma(3-q)} x^{2-q} - y(x),\ y(0) = 0,\ q = 0.5,\ \ x \in [0,1].$$

The physical discretization is

$$A\mathbf{y} = \mathbf{b},\ A = T \cdot DF \cdot T^{-1} + I_N,\ \mathbf{b} = x^2 + 2/\Gamma(3-q) \cdot x^{2-q}$$

where, in order to implement the initial condition, the first row of A is replaced by $[1, 0, ..., 0]$ and $\mathbf{b}(1)$ is replaced by 0. The solution is now $y(x) = A^{-1}B$. The example is coded in `deriv_frac_ex1.m` from the folder `Chebpack\examples\ex_level3`.
If we use the spectral representation, for example for the problem

$$D^q y(x) + y(x) = 1,\ y(0) = 0,\ y\prime(0) = 0,\ q = 1.8,\ \ x \in [0,5],$$

with the exact solution $yex = x^q E_{q,q+1}(-x^q)$, the spectral discretized form becomes

$$Ay \equiv (D^q + I_n)\, y = T^{-1} \cdot \mathbf{1} = B,$$
$$A(n-1,:) = T(1,:),\ B(n-1) = 0,\ A(n,:) = T(1,:) * D,\ B(n) = 0,$$

see `deriv_frac_ex2.m`
For nonhomogeneous initial conditions like $y(0) = c_0$, $y'(0) = c_1$, we perform a function change $y(x) = c_0 + c_1 x + z(x)$ where z verifies the same equation but with homogeneous initial conditins ($c_0 + c_1 x$ disappears by differentiation), see `deriv_frac_ex3.m`. Examples for discontinuous data, boundary value problems or eigenproblems are also given.

6. Conclusion

The new package *Chebpack* (Trif, 2011) is a large and powerful extension of *LiScEig* (Trif, 2005). It is based on the Chebyshev tau spectral method and it is applied to linear and nonlinear differential or integral problems, including eigenvalue problems. An experimental module contains applications to linear or nonlinear partial differential problems and to fractional differential problems. Each module is illustrated by many examples. A future version will handle also piecewise functions as well as functions with singularities.
The following comparisons with MATLAB codes *bvp4c, bvp5c* as well as with *DMS* or *Chebfun* prove the efficiency of *Chebpack*. The elapsed time was evaluated after three code executions. The first test problem (`test1.m` in the folder `Chebpack\tutorial`) is

$$-u'' - \frac{1}{6x}u' + \frac{1}{x^2}u = \frac{19}{6}x^{1/2},\ u(0) = u(1) = 0,\ x \in [0,1]$$

with the exact solution $u_{ex}(x) = x^{3/2} - x^{5/2}$. The elapsed time and the errors are presented in Table 1. Here *Chebpack* uses the differentiation matrix.
The second test problem (`test2.m` in the folder `Chebpack\tutorial`) is (13) with $\varepsilon = 10^{-4}$. The elapsed time and the errors are presented in Table 2. Here *Chebpack* uses the integration matrix.

	bvp4c RelTol=1.e-5	bvp5c RelTol=1.e-4	dms N=64	Chebfun N=98	Chebpack N=80
elapsed time (sec)	0.737	0.744	0.004	0.192	0.005
errors	3.2e-7	9.2e-8	2.3e-7	1.8e-7	4.6e-7

Table 1. Test 1

	bvp4c default	bvp5c default	dms N=1024	Chebfun N=[13,114,109,14]	Chebpack N=1024
elapsed time (sec)	0.131	0.244	3.471	1.053	0.041
errors	8.6e-5	6.6e-6	8.4e-13	1.0e-12	1.e-14

Table 2. Test 2

7. References

Berrut, J. P. & Trefethen, L. N. (2004). Barycentric Lagrange interpolation, *SIAM Review* Vol.46(No.3): 501–517.

Boyd, J. P. (2000). *Chebyshev and Fourier Spectral Methods*, Dover Publications, Inc.

Canuto, C., Hussaini, M. Y., Quarteroni, A. & Zang, T. A. (1988). *Spectral Methods in Fluid Dynamics*, Springer-Verlag, Berlin.

Driscoll, T. A. (2010). Automatic spectral collocation for integral, integro-differential, and integrally reformulated differential equations, *J. Comp. Phys.* Vol.229: 5980–5998.

Mason, J. & Handscomb, D. (2003). *Chebyshev Polynomials*, Chapman & Hall/CRC.

Ortiz, E. L. & Samara, H. (1981). An operational approach to the tau method for the numerical solution of non-linear differential equations, *Computing* Vol.27: 15–25.

Piessens, R. & Branders, M. (1976). Numerical solution of integral equations of mathematical physics, using Chebyshev polynomials, *J. Comp. Phys. (1976)* Vol.21: 178–196.

Podlubny, I. (1999). *Fractional Differential Equations*, Academic Press.

Sugiura, H. & Hasegawa, T. (2009). Quadrature rule for Abel's equations: Uniformly approximating fractional derivatives, *J. Comp. Appl. Math.* Vol.223: 459–468.

Trefethen, L. N. (2000). *Spectral Methods in MATLAB*, SIAM, Philadelphia.

Trefethen, L. N. (2008). Is Gauss quadrature better than Clenshaw–Curtis?, *SIAM Review* Vol.50(No.1): 67–87.

Trefethen, L. N. et al. (2011). *Chebfun Version 4.0*, The Chebfun Development Team. URL: *http://www.maths.ox.ac.uk/chebfun/*

Trif, D. (2005). LiScEig, MATLAB Central. URL: *http://www.mathworks.com/matlabcentral/fileexchange/8689-lisceig*

Trif, D. (2011). Chebpack, MATLAB Central. URL: *http://www.mathworks.com/matlabcentral/fileexchange/32227-chebpack*

Waldvogel, J. (2006). Fast construction of the Fejér and Clenshaw–Curtis quadrature rules, *BIT Numerical Mathematics* Vol.46: 195–202.

Weideman, J. A. C. & Reddy, S. C. (2000). A MATLAB differentiation matrix suite. URL: *http://www.mathworks.com/matlabcentral/fileexchange/29-dmsuite*

4

Comparison of Methodologies for Analysis of Longitudinal Data Using MATLAB

João Eduardo da Silva Pereira, Janete Pereira Amador
and Angela Pellegrin Ansuj
Federal University of Santa Maria
Brazil

1. Introduction

In several areas of scientific knowledge there is a need for studying the behavior of one or more variables using data generated by repeated measurements of the same unit of observations along time or spatial region. Due to this, many experiments are constructed in which various treatments are applied on the same plot at different times, or only one treatment is applied to an experimental unit and it is made a measurement of a characteristic or a set of features in more than one occasion [Khattree & Naik, 2000]. Castro and Riboldi [Castro & Riboldi, 2005] define data collected under these kinds of experimental setups as repeated measures. More specifically, he asserts that "repeated measures is understood as the data generated by repeatedly observing a number of investigation units under different conditions of evaluation, assuming that the units of investigation are a random sample of a population of interest". In order to analyze repeated measures data it is necessary to take a care about not independency between observations. This is so because it is expected a high degree of correlation between data collected on the same observation unit over time, and there is usually more variability in the measurements between the subjects than within a given subject. A very common type of repeated measures is longitudinal data, i.e., repeated measures where the observations within units of investigation were not or can not have been randomly assigned to different conditions of evaluation, usually time or position in space.

There are basically two paths to be taken in the analysis of longitudinal data; univariate analysis, which requires as a precondition a rigid structure of covariances, or multivariate analysis, which, despite being more flexible, is less efficient in detecting significant differences than the univariate methodology.

In Advances in Longitudinal Data Analysis [Fitzmaurice et al., 2009], Fitzmaurice comments that despite the advances made in statistical methodology in the last 30 years there has been a lag between recent developments and their widespread application to substantive problems, and adds that part of the problem why the advances have been somewhat slow to move into the mainstream is due to their limited implementation in widely available standard computer software.

In this context this work proposes to develop a single and easy computational implementation to solve a great number of practical problems of analysis of longitudinal

data, through the decomposition of the sum of squares error of the polynomial models of regression.
In light of the above, not independents the computational support MatLab looks likes an ideal tool for the implementation and dissemination of this kind of statistical analysis methods, and linear models, first because its matrix structure fits perfectly well for linear models which facilitates the construction of models for univariate and multivariate analysis, and second because being a large diffusion tool of, it allows for that the models to be implemented, modified and reused in several uses in different situations by several users who have access to a MatLab community on the internet. This avoids the need for the acquisition of expensive software with black box structure.

2. Review

As far as the analysis of experiments using longitudinal data is concerned the methods traditionally used are: univariate analyis or Univariate Profile Model whereby longitudinal data is considered as if it were observations done in subdivisions of the slots, usually requiring that the variance of the response be constant in the occasions of evaluation and that the covariance between responses in different occasions be equal; multivariate analysis or Multivariate Profile Model whereby it is admitted that these variances and covariances be distinct. Despite its apparent versatility, as far as the dimension of the matrix of variances and covariances, the multivariate model becomes less attractive, because its results are hard to interpret, and its estimates are not consistent. The univariate profile model gives consistent estimates and should be used every time when its presuppositions are met. Otherwise, the multivariate profile model is a viable alternative [Castro & Riboldi, 2005; Johnson & Wichern, 1998].
Using the univariate analysis in split-plot designs, regarding time as a sub-plot may cause problems because, as it is known, this design presupposes that the covariance matrix meets the condition of sphericity which does not always happen. What is found in the literature is that repeated measures in one same experimental unit along time are in general correlated, and that these correlations are greater for closer times [Malheiros, 1999].
Xavier [Xavier, 2000] asserts that a sufficient condition for the F test of the analysis of variance of the sub-plots for the time factor and the interaction time*treatments, be valid, is that the covariance matrix has a so called composite symmetry shape. The composite symmetry occurs when the variance and covariance matrix may be expressed as:

$$\Sigma = \begin{bmatrix} (\sigma^2+\sigma_1^2) & \sigma_1^2 & \sigma_1^2 & \sigma_1^2 \\ \sigma_1^2 & (\sigma^2+\sigma_1^2) & \sigma_1^2 & \sigma_1^2 \\ \sigma_1^2 & \sigma_1^2 & (\sigma^2+\sigma_1^2) & \sigma_1^2 \\ \sigma_1^2 & \sigma_1^2 & \sigma_1^2 & (\sigma^2+\sigma_1^2) \end{bmatrix} \quad (1)$$

where:

σ^2 : is the variance of the sub-plot (within-subjects);

σ_1^2 : is the variance of the plot (among-subjects).

The composite symmetry condition implies that the random variable be equally correlated and has equal variances considering the different occasions. A more general condition of the

$\sum$ is described by Huynh and Feldt [Huynh & Feldt, 1970]. This condition, called HUYNH-FELDT (H-F) or sphericity condition (circularity), specifies that the elements of the $\sum$ matrix be expressed for one $\lambda > 0$, as:

$$\Sigma = \begin{bmatrix} \sigma_1^2 & \frac{(\sigma_1^2+\sigma_2^2)}{2}-\lambda & \frac{(\sigma_1^2+\sigma_3^2)}{2}-\lambda & \frac{(\sigma_1^2+\sigma_4^2)}{2}-\lambda \\ \frac{(\sigma_1^2+\sigma_2^2)}{2}-\lambda & \sigma_2^2 & \frac{(\sigma_2^2+\sigma_3^2)}{2}-\lambda & \frac{(\sigma_2^2+\sigma_4^2)}{2}-\lambda \\ \frac{(\sigma_3^2+\sigma_1^2)}{2}-\lambda & \frac{(\sigma_3^2+\sigma_2^2)}{2}-\lambda & \sigma_3^2 & \frac{(\sigma_3^2+\sigma_4^2)}{2}-\lambda \\ \frac{(\sigma_4^2+\sigma_1^2)}{2}-\lambda & \frac{(\sigma_4^2+\sigma_2^2)}{2}-\lambda & \frac{(\sigma_4^2+\sigma_3^2)}{2}-\lambda & \sigma_4^2 \end{bmatrix} \quad (2)$$

where λ is the difference between the means of the variances and the means of the covariances.

The H-F condition is necessary and sufficient for the F test in the usual analysis of variance in split-plot in time to be valid. This condition is equivalent to specifying that the variances of the difference between pairs of errors are equal, and if the variances are all equal then the condition is equivalent to compound symmetry [Xavier, 2000].

To check the condition of circularity Mauchly [Mauchly, 1940] presents the test of sphericity. This test uses H-F condition for the covariance matrix of (t-1) normalized orthogonal contrasts for repeated measures not correlated with equal variances. Vonesh and Chinchilli [Vonesh & Chinchilli, 1997] state that the sphericity test is not very powerful for small samples and is not robust when there is violation of the normality assumption.

According to Box; Greenhouse & Geisser; and Huynh & Feldt [Box, 1954; Greenhouse & Geisser, 1959; Huynh & Feldt, 1976], although the matrix $\sum$ may not satisfy the condition of sphericity, the central F distribution may be used, in an approximate form, if a correction in the degrees of freedom associated with the causes of variation involving the time factor is made. The degrees of freedom correction in these sources of variation is done by multiplying the original degrees by a factor ε. When $\sum$ is uniform, the value of $\varepsilon = 1$.

According to Freitas [Freitas, 2007] the correction of the number of degrees of freedom should be made only in statistics that involve comparisons within subjects (time factor and interaction time*treatments). The statistics involving comparisons between subjects do not need corrections in the degrees of freedom because there is always an exact central F distribution.

When the pattern of the $\sum$ matrix is not satisfied, not even close, the multivariate techniques are used since this type of solution is applicable to any $\sum$ matrix. The only requirement of the multivariate procedure is that the $\sum$ matrix should be common to all treatments.

Due to the essentially multivariate nature of the response vectors, in studies involving longitudinal data, the multivariate analysis technique also known as multivariate profile analysis is a natural alternative to the problem at hand [Wald, 2000]. The multivariate profile analysis is well discussed in the literature by authors such as [Lima, 1996; Morrison, 1990; Singer, 1986].

The multivariate profile analysis is one of the statistics technique used to analyze observations derived from experiments that use longitudinal data. This technique bases itself both in the number of experimental units and the sample size [Castro, 1997].
Unlike the univariate profile analysis model, the multivariate profile analysis model does not require that the variance of the repeated measures or that the correlation between pairs of repeated measures remain constant along time. Nevertheless, both models require that the variances and the correlations be homogeneous in each moment in time [Vieira, 2006].
The routine techniques for analysis of variance impose the condition of independence of observations. However, this restriction generally does not apply to longitudinal data where the observations in the same individual are usually correlated. In such case, the adequate manner for treating the observations would be the multivariate form [Vonesh & Chinchilli, 1997].
Cole & Grizzle [Cole & Grizzle, 1966] use the multivariate analysis of variance according to the Smith et al. [Smith et al., 1962] formulation and comment on its versatility in the construction of specific hypothesis testing that may be obtained as particular cases of the general linear multivariate hypothesis test procedure. They assert that such hypothesis may be tested by three alternative criterions, all of which dependent on characteristic roots of matrix functions due to the hypothesis and of the matrix due to the error: criterion of the maximum characteristic root, criterion of the product of the roots (criterion of the verosimilarity ratio) and criterion of the sum of the roots. The authors illustrate the application of the multivariate analysis of variance and demonstrate that the information requested from these experiments may be formulated in terms of the following null hypotheses:

i. there are no principal effects of "measured conditions" (occasions);
ii. there are no effects of treatments;
iii. there is no interaction of treatment and occasions.

The multivariate analysis of variance is a powerful instrument to analyze longitudinal data but if the uniformity hypothesis of the variance and covariance matrix is not rejected the univariate analysis should be employed. Nonetheless, if the variance and covariance matrix of repeated measures has the serial correlation structure one should use an analysis method that takes into account the structure of this matrix in order that one might have an increment in the testing power. In this way the multivariate analysis of variance becomes the most convenient one if not the only appropriate one among the available procedures [Cole & Grizzle, 1966; Smith et al., 1962].
Lima [Lima, 1996] asserts that the multivariate profile analysis possesses as its main advantage the fact that is allows for the adoption of a very general model to represent the structure of covariances admitting that the variances of responses in each time and the covariances of responses between distinct times be different.
In studying longitudinal data investigation methods, Greenhouse & Geisser [Greenhouse & Geisser, 1959] observed that the ratios between the mean squares obtained in the analysis of variance for the mixed univariate model will only have exact distribution of probability F if the observations in time be normally distributed with equal variances and be mutually independent or equally correlated. Because these presuppositions are strict, the authors prefer considering the observations in time as a vector of samples of a normal multivariate distribution with an arbitrary variance and covariance matrix. Being so, the multivariate perspective presented by Morrison [Morrison, 1990] allows for the adoption of a general model to represent the covariance structure of the observations. In this case, the covariance

matrix is known as being non structured where all variances and covariances might be different and, as pointed out by Andreoni [Andreoni, 1989], it is only applicable when:
- there be no theoretical or empirical basis to establish any pattern for this matrix;
- there be no need to extrapolate the model beyond the occasions of the considered observations.

The quantity of parameters associated with the non structured matrix that need to be estimated is proportional to the number of conditions of evaluation. In situations where the number is large, when the number of experimental units is small in relation to the number of evaluation events or when there is the presence of many incomplete observations the efficiency of the estimators might be affected. In some cases it may be impossible to estimate the parameters of this covariance matrix [Wald, 2000].

Meredith & Stehman [Meredith & Stehman, 1991] state that the disadvantage of the multivariate analysis is the lack of power to estimate the parameters of the covariance matrix in case when t (number of measurement events or times) is large and n is small.

Stuker [Stuker, 1986] comments on the restriction of the multivariate analysis of covariance in which the number of experimental units minus the number of treatments should be greater than the number of observations taken in each experimental unit otherwise the required matrix due to error for these tests is singular.

Timm [Timm, 1980] claims that the restrictions to the application of the multivariate profile analysis occur due to the need for complete individual response profiles and to the low power of these hypothesis tests due to excessive parametering. On the other hand, except for these restrictions, the majority of the cases in longitudinal data studies, the analysis procedure of multivariate analysis of variance is the most convenient if not the only appropriate one among the available techniques.

3. Materials and methods

3.1 Data

In order to conduct the study it was created a data matrix with the following structure: $\underline{Y} = y_{ijk}$, where y_{ijk} is the observation j belonged the period i of the treatment k. To simulate growth curves composed of two treatments, seven observations over time and five repetitions, each observation of Y matrix was defined as $y_{ijk} = f_i + \varepsilon_{ijr}$ with a fixed part f_i, with i = 1,2, and where $f_1 = 46 + 88X - 57X^2$ and $f_2 = 42 + 88X + 53X^2$ and a variable portion ε_{ijk} randomly generated with normal distribution with zero mean and variance proportional to $E(f_i)$ in which the variation coefficient remains constant in 0,05, under these conditions is imposed on the model f_1 a linear growth higher than compared to the f_2 model and both with the same regression model.

3.1.1 Data base structure

To analyze the longitudinal data, the data base was structured in the following way; the first column refers to the independent variable $X = [x_i]$ or to periods with $i = 1 \ldots p$, the second column the response variable $Y = [y_{ijk}]$, in which y_{ijk}, refers to the observation referring to the repetition j of the period i of treatment k, with $j = 1 \ldots r$., and the third column refers to the control variable $F = [f_k]$ or treatments, with $j = 1 \ldots t$.

$$\text{File.txt}=\begin{bmatrix} 1 & y_{111} & 1 \\ \cdot & y_{121} & \cdot \\ . & . & . \\ . & . & . \\ p & y_{prt} & t \end{bmatrix} \tag{3}$$

The following Matlab commands upload and dimension the file in addition to determining the index of the column of each variable.

```
M=load('-ascii', 'file.txt');
[n,c]=size(M);
a=input('column of the independent variable X  =');
b=input('column of the dependent variable Y  =');
aa=input('initial column of the control variable curve =');
nc=input('number of curves to be compared =');
npc=input('number of points per curve =');
```

3.2 Data analysis

Once the data base is correctly structured the first step is to adjust the best polynomial model that explains the variation of Y in function of the X periods. Towards this, the parameters of the polynomial of adjustment will be estimated by the matrix expression below.

$$\hat{Y} = BX \tag{4}$$

$$\beta = [bo \quad b_1 \quad .... \quad b_g] \tag{5}$$

in which g is a degree of the polynomial

$$X = [1 \quad x_i \quad x_i^2 . \quad . \quad . \quad x_i^g] \tag{6}$$

$$\hat{\beta} = (X'X)^{-1}(X'Y) \tag{7}$$

To determine what is the best degree of the polynomial for the data under analysis it was used a scatterplot. The following commands prepare the data for visualization.

```
x=M(:,a:(b-1));
Y=M(:,b:(aa-1));
Trat=M(:,aa);
M=[x Y Trat];
[tmp,idx]=sort(M(:,aa));
M=M(idx,:),
set(plot(x,Y,'o'))
```

From the scatterplot, choose the degree of polynomial to be adjusted.

```
g=input('choose the degree of polynomial Degree  =');
```

The following procedures were used to estimate $\hat{\beta}$

```
[n,r]=size(M);
X=ones(n,npc);
```

```
y1=ones(n,1);
for i=2:npc
X(:,i)=M(:,a).*y1;
y1=X(:,i);
end
X=X(:,1:(d+1));
BT=(inv((X'*X)))*(X'*(M(:,b:aa-1)));
```

To test the hypothesis: $H_0 : \beta = 0$ against $H_1 : \beta \neq 0$, the F test is employed.

$$F = \frac{QMr}{QM\varepsilon} \tag{8}$$

that have the Snedecor F distribution with (g-1) and (n-g) degrees of freedom.

$$QMr = \frac{1}{(g-1)}\beta(X'Y) - n\bar{Y}^2 \tag{9}$$

$$QM\varepsilon = \frac{1}{(n-g)}[(Y'Y) - \beta(X'Y)] = \frac{1}{(n-g)}(Y-\hat{Y})'(Y-\hat{Y}) \tag{10}$$

And to measure the degree of explanation of the variability of Y according to the polynomial model it is used the coefficient of determination.

$$R^2 = \frac{SQr}{SQT} \tag{11}$$

$$SQr = \beta(X'Y) - n\bar{Y}^2 \tag{12}$$

$$SQT = (Y'Y) - n\bar{Y}^2 \tag{13}$$

And to measure the degree of explanation of the Y variability in function of the polynomial model it is employed the determination coefficient.

$$R^2 = \frac{SQr}{SQT} \tag{14}$$

in which

$$SQr = \beta(X'Y) - n\bar{Y}^2 \tag{15}$$

and

$$SQT = (Y'Y) - n\bar{Y}^2 \tag{16}$$

After the adjustment of the polynomial model for the data set, the next step is to adjust the same model for each of the k treatments separately, so

$$\hat{Y}_k = (X'X)^{-1}(X'Y_k) \tag{17}$$

Where

$$\hat{b}_k = (X'X)^{-1}(X'Yk) \tag{18}$$

The test for comparing the curves is based on the decomposition of SQε in one part explained by the variation between the curves and the other by the variation within the curves.

$$SQ\varepsilon = \sum_{k=1}^{t} (\hat{Y} - \hat{Y}k)'(\hat{Y} - \hat{Y}k) + \sum_{k=1}^{t} (\hat{Y}k - Y_{.}k)'(\hat{Y}k - Yk) \tag{19}$$

in which $\sum_{K=1}^{t} (\hat{Y} - \hat{Y}k)'(\hat{Y} - \hat{Y}k)$ is the variation explained by the treatments, and $\sum_{K=1}^{t} (\hat{Y}k - Y_{.}k)'(\hat{Y}k - Yk)$ is the variation within each treatment.

$$\text{And the } F = \frac{\sum_{k=1}^{t} ((\hat{Y} - \hat{Y}k)'(\hat{Y} - Yk))(n-t)(p-1)}{\sum_{K=1}^{t} ((\hat{Y} - Yk)'(\hat{Y} - Yk))(p-1)(t-1)} \tag{20}$$

has a Snedecor F distribution with $(p-1)(t-1)$ and $(n-t)(p-1)$ degrees of freedom.

$$\text{And the reason } F = \frac{\sum_{k=1}^{t} ((\hat{Y} - \hat{Y}k)'(\hat{Y} - Yk))(n-t)(p-1)}{\sum_{K=1}^{t} ((\hat{Y} - Yk)'(\hat{Y} - Yk))(p-1)(t-1)} \tag{21}$$

Has a Snedecor F distribution with $(p-1)(t-1)$ and $(n-t)(p-1)$ degrees of freedom.

The following commands calculate the regression parameters for the individual curves.

```
[c,r]=size(M1);
Yobs(:,i)=M1(:,b)
X=ones(c,npc);
y1=ones(c,1);
for j=2:npc
X(:,j)=M1(:,a).*y1;
y1=X(:,j);
end
Y=M1(:,b);
X=X(:,1:(d+1));
B(:,i)=(inv((X'*X)))*(X'*Y);
Y1est(:,i)=X*BT;
end
```

The following commands print the graph with the curves estimated.

```
Yest=X*B;
y=[Y1est Yest];
x=X(:,b);
plot(x,y)
```

The following commands execute analysis of variance.

```
[n,c]=size(M)
 SQmodelo=sum(sum((Y1est-Yest).*(Y1est-Yest)))
SQerro=sum(sum((Yest-Yobs).*(Yest-Yobs)))
SQtotal=sum(sum((Y1est-Yobs).*(Y1est-Yobs)))
glmodelo=(npc-1)*(nc-1)
gltotal=(n-nc)
glerro=gltotal-glmode
R=(SQmodelo/SQtotal)
F=(SQmodelo/glmodelo)/(SQerro/glerro)
p=fpdf(F,glmodelo,glerro)
```

The following commands format the ANOVA Table printout.

```
Table=zeros(3,5);
Table(:,1)=[ RSS SSE TSS]';
Table(:,2)=[df1 df2 df3]';
Table(:,3)=[ RSS/df1 SSE/df2 Inf ]';
Table(:,4)=[ F Inf Inf ]';
Table(:,5)=[ p Inf Inf ]';
colheads = ['Source      ';'      SS ';'      df ';...
        '    MS   ';'      F ';'   Prob>F  '];
  atab = num2cell(Table);
for i=1:size(atab,1)
  for j=1:size(atab,2)
    if (isinf(atab{i,j}))
      atab{i,j} = [];
    end
  end
end
if (nargout > 1)
  anovatab = atab
end
```

The following commands prepare the file for the multivariate analysis.

```
M=[X Yobs];
nt=M(:,2);
    x=nt(1);
    n=1;
    idx=1;
    for i=2:length(nt)
       if nt(i)==x(idx)
          n(idx)=n(idx)+1;
       else
```

```
        idx=idx+1;
        x(idx)=nt(i);
        n(idx)=1;
    end
 n=cumsum(n);
      B=ones(d+1,nc);
      for i=1:length(n)
        idx=find(M(:,aa)==M(n(i),aa));
M2=M(idx,:);
      end
```

For the multivariate analysis it was employed a new structure of the data file.

File2.txt= $[x_{jk} \quad y_{1jk} \quad . \quad . \quad . \quad y_{pjk}]$

File2.txt=[X Y]

In which, the first column has the values for the j repetitions for each of the k treatments, each one of the following i columns contains the values of Y for the j repetitions of the k treatments. As seen in the structure below.

$$\text{File2.txt} = \begin{bmatrix} x_{11} & y_{111} & \cdot & \cdot & \cdot & \cdot & \cdot & y_{711} \\ x_{21} & y_{121} & \cdot & \cdot & \cdot & \cdot & \cdot & y_{721} \\ x_{31} & y_{131} & \cdot & \cdot & \cdot & \cdot & \cdot & y_{731} \\ x_{41} & y_{141} & \cdot & \cdot & \cdot & \cdot & \cdot & y_{741} \\ x_{51} & y_{151} & \cdot & \cdot & \cdot & \cdot & \cdot & y_{751} \\ x_{12} & y_{112} & \cdot & \cdot & \cdot & \cdot & \cdot & y_{712} \\ x_{22} & y_{122} & \cdot & \cdot & \cdot & \cdot & \cdot & y_{722} \\ x_{32} & y_{132} & \cdot & \cdot & \cdot & \cdot & \cdot & y_{732} \\ x_{42} & y_{142} & \cdot & \cdot & \cdot & \cdot & \cdot & y_{742} \\ x_{52} & y_{152} & \cdot & \cdot & \cdot & \cdot & \cdot & y_{752} \end{bmatrix} \tag{22}$$

The following commands change the structure of the file.

```
           M=Mtemp;
     [n,c]=size(M);
    nt=M(:,1);
    z=nt(1);
    n=1;
    idx=1;
    for i=2:length(nt);
      if nt(i)==z(idx)
        n(idx)=n(idx)+1;
      else
        idx=idx+1;
        z(idx)=nt(i);
        n(idx)=1;
      end
```

```
end
 n=cumsum(n);
 for i=1:npc
     idx=find(M(:,a)==M(n(i),a));
     M1=M(idx,:);
     trat=M1(:,aa);
     M1=M1(:,b);
     Ymult(:,i)=M1;
 end
 Y=[trat Ymult];
```

For the multivariate data analysis the employed procedure was proposed by Johnson and Wishern [Johnson and Wishern, 1998] in which the standardized variable employed for the comparison of the curves is

$$\Lambda = \frac{|W|}{|W_p|} \tag{23}$$

in which $W = (X'\beta - X'\beta T)' * (X'\beta - X'\beta T)$ (24)

$$\beta = \begin{bmatrix} b_{10} & b_{20} \\ b_{11} & b_{21} \\ b_{12} & b_{22} \end{bmatrix} = \left[b_{dk} \right] \tag{25}$$

where $\left[b_{dk} \right]$ is the polynomial coefficient of d order of the k treatment.

$$\beta = (X'S^{-1}X)^{-1}(X'S^{-1}\bar{Y}) \tag{26}$$

$$S = \frac{1}{(rt)}(Y - \bar{Y})'(Y - \bar{Y}) \tag{27}$$

$$W_p = (Y - X'\beta T)' * (Y - X'\beta T) \tag{28}$$

$$\beta T = (X'S_p^{-1}X)^{-1}(X'S_p^{-1}\bar{Y}) \tag{29}$$

$$S_p = \frac{1}{(n-t)} \sum_{K=1}^{t} (n_k - 1)S_k^2 \tag{30}$$

Where $S_k^2 = matrix.of.\text{cov}\,ariance.of.the.treatment.k$

In order to test if there is a difference between curves the standardized variable is employed

$$\chi^2 = -\left(N - \frac{1}{2}(p - d - t) \right) \ln \Lambda \tag{31}$$

has a chi square distribution with (p-q-1) degrees of freedom.
The following commands run the multivariate analysis.

```
    x=x';
    [n,c]=size(Y);
    M=Y
    temp=M(:,b:c);
Y1obs=temp';
V=cov(temp);
S=inv(V);
temp=(sum(temp))./n;
Y=temp;
[n,c]=size(V);
    X=ones(n,c);
    y1=ones(n,1);
    for i=2:c
      X(:,i)=x.*y1;
      y1=X(:,i);
    end
    d=input('choose the polynomial degree =');
    X=X(:,1:(d+1));
    BT=(inv(X'*S*X))*(X'*S*Y');
    Y1est=X*BT;
    plot(x,Y1est)
    [n,c]=size(Y1obs);
    temp=ones(n,c);
    for i=1:c
      temp(:,i)=Y1est;
    end
    Y1est=temp;
    Temp=Y1obs-Y1est;
    W=Temp*Temp';
```

The following commands run the analysis of individual curves.

```
    nt=M(:,a);
    z=nt(a);
  n=1;
    idx=1;
    for i=2:length(nt)
      if nt(i)==z(idx)
        n(idx)=n(idx)+1;
      else
        idx=idx+1;
        z(idx)=nt(i);
        n(idx)=1;
      end
    end
   k=n;
   n=cumsum(n);
```

```
B=zeros(d+1,length(n));
v=zeros(length(W));
sp=zeros(length(S));
for i=1:length(n)
      idx=find(M(:,a)==M(n(i),a));
      M1=M(idx,:);
      [r,c]=size(M1);
      temp=M1(:,b:c);
      Yobs=temp';
      V=cov(temp);
      V=(k(i)-1)*V;
      temp=(sum(temp))./r;
      Y(i,:)=temp;
      temp=(V+v)/(n(i)-2);
      v=temp;
      S=inv(v);
      B=(inv(X'*S*X))*(X'*S*Y');
end
Temp=zeros(npc);
 for i=1:length(n)
      idx=find(M(:,1)==M(n(i),1));
      M1=M(idx,:);
      [r,c]=size(M1);
      temp=M1(:,b:c);
      Yobs=temp';
      temp=zeros(npc,r);
      Yest=X*B(:,z(i));
      for j=1:5
          temp(:,j)=Yest;
       end
       temp=((Yobs-temp)*(Yobs-temp)');
       Temp=temp+Temp;
       Wp=Temp;
 end
       Wilks=((det(Wp))/(det(W)))
      Qsquare=-(N-0.5*(npc-nc-2+d))*log(Wilks)
      df=(npc-nc-1)*d
      chi2pdf(Qsquare,df)
```

4. Results

The following parameters must be furnished when running the program:
independent variable column X =1
dependent variable column Y =2
initial column of the control variable curve =3
number of curves to be compared =2
number of points per curve =7

The following graph is generated in order to choose the degree of the polynomial to be adjusted.

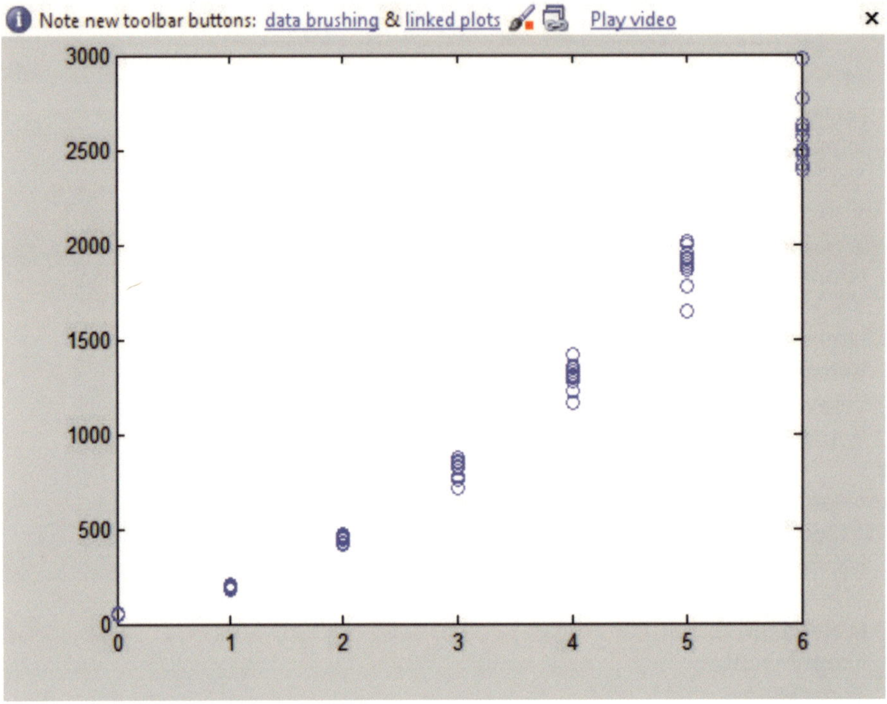

Fig. 1. Scatterplot of the data.

A second degree polynomial was chosen to model the data according to the scatterplot above.
The estimated coefficients for the second order polynomial were:

$$\hat{Y}_T = 48.464 + 81965X + 56.806X^2]$$

with (P<0000,1)

$$R^2 = 0.3405$$

The analysis of variance of the complete polynomial model is presented in table 1.

Causes of variation	DF	SS	SQ	F	P
Polynomial	2	5.2799E+007	2.6384E+007	3.8235E+003	1.2054E-072
Error	68	4.6924E+005	6.9006E+003		
Total	69	5.3238E+007			

Table 1. ANOVA for polynomial model

The output of the program has the following format
anovatab1 =

[5.2769e+007]	[2]	[2.6384e+007]	[3.8235e+003]	[1.2054e-072]
[4.6924e+005]	[68]	[6.9006e+003]	[]	[]
[5.3238e+007]	[69]	[]	[]	[]

After the choice of the polynomial model and its test of significance, the same model was applied on each one of the treatments separately, the results are as follows:

$$\hat{Y}_1 = 50.31 + 89.10X + 57.10X^2$$

$$\hat{Y}_2 = 46.90 + 76.82X + 56.55X^2$$

$$R^2 = 0.3405$$

The analysis of variance for decomposition of error was employed to test the difference between the curves and is presented in table 2.

Causes of variation	DF	SS	SQ	F	P
Polynomial	6	1.5976E+005	2.6626E+004	5.4202	2.52652E-004
Error	63	3.0948E+005	4.912E+003		
Total	69	4.6924E+005			

Table 2. Analysis of variance to compare the curves.

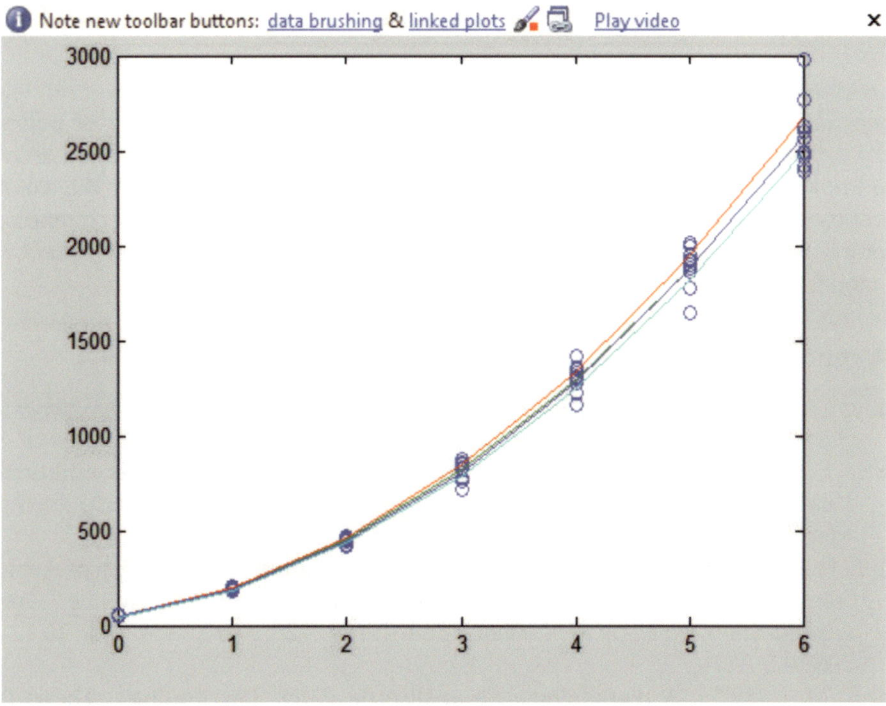

Fig. 2. Central line resulting from the estimated polynomial for the entire data set and the external lines, one for each treatment.

The output of the program has the following format:

```
B =  50.3069  46.9023
     89.0928  76.8230
     57.0744  56.5484
```

After the choice of the polynomial model and its test of significance, the same model was applied on each one of the treatments separately, the results are as follows:

```
anovatab =
   [1.5976e+005]  [ 6]  [2.6626e+004]  [5.4202]  [2.5262e-004]
   [3.0948e+005]  [63]  [4.9124e+003]       []            []
   [4.6924e+005]  [69]            []        []            []
```

The graph below presents a central line resulting from the estimated polynomial for the whole data set and the external lines are one for each treatment.

For the multivariate test it was calculated the standardized variable

$$\chi^2 = -\left(N - \frac{1}{2}(p - d - t)\right)\ln\Lambda = 192.0591 \text{ with } (P<0,001).$$

The program outputs were as follows.

```
Wilks =   0.0581
Chi square =  192.0591
df =    8
ans =  1.4552e-037
```

5. Conclusion

Given its matrix structure, Matlab presented itself as an efficient tool for linear models. The programs and the methodology presented were efficient to the comparing of polynomial growth curves. The modular sequence in which the programs were developed allows the user to implement new routines as well as new methodology proposals for the solution of the proposed problem. The solutions presented for the problem of comparison of polynomial growth curves may be used in part or in conjunction for the solution of other linear models problems.

6. References

Andrade, D. F. & Singer, J. M. (1986). Análise de dados longitudinais. *Proceedings of VII Simpósio Nacional de Probabilidade e Estatística*, pp. 19-26, Campinas, SP, Brazil, 1986.

Andreoni, S. (1989). Modelos de efeitos aleatórios para a análise de dados longitudinais não balanceados em relação ao tempo. Dissertation (MS. in Statistics) Institute of Mathematics, São Paulo University, São Paulo, Brazil, 1989.

Box, G. E. P. (1954). Some Theorems on Quadratic Forms Applied in the Study of Analysis of Variance Problems, I. Effect of Inequality of Variance in the One-Way Classification. *Annals of Mathematical Statistics*, Vol.25, No. 2, 1954, DOI: 10.1214, pp. 290-302.

Castro, S. M. J. (1997). A metodologia de análise de dados longitudinais. Thesis (BS. in Statistics), Federal University of Rio Grande do Sul, Porto Alegre, Brazil.

Castro, S. M. J. & Riboldi, J. (2005). A construção do modelo em dados longitudinais: escolha dos efeitos fixos e aleatórios, modelagem das estruturas de covariância. *Proceedings of the Annual Meeting of the Brazilian Region of the International Biometrics Society, and of the Simpósio de Estatística Aplicada a Experimentação Agronômica*, pp. 157-158, Londrina, Paraná, Brazil, 2005.

Cole, J. W. L. & Grizzle, J. E. (1966). Applications of Multivariate Analysis of Variance to Repeated Measurements Experiments. *Biometrics*, Vol. 22, 1966, ISSN 0006341x, pp. 810 - 828.

Fitzmaurice, G. et al. Ed(s).). (2009). *Longitudinal Data Analysis*. Chapman & Hall/CRC Taylor & Francis Group, ISBN 978-1-58488-658-7, Boca Raton, Florida.

Freitas, G. E. (2007). Análise de dados longitudinais em experimentos com cana-de-açúcar. Dissertation (MS. in Agronomics), Escola Superior de Agricultura "Luis de Queiroz", São Paulo University, Piracicaba, Brazil, 2007.

Greenhouse, S. W. & Geisser, S. (1959). On methods in the analysis of profile data. *Psychometrika*, Vol.24, No. 2, June 1959, DOI: 10.1007, pp.95-112.

Huynh, H. & Feldt, L.S. (1970) Condition under which mean square ratios in repeated measurements designs have exact F-distributions. *J. Am. Stat. Assoc.*, Vol.72, 1970, ISSN 0162-1459, pp.320-340.

Huynh, H. & Feldt, L. S. (1976). Estimation of the box correction for degrees of freedom from sample data in randomized block and split-plot designs. *J. Educational and Behavioral Statistics*, Vol.1, No.1, March 1976, DOI: 10.3102/10769986001001069, pp.69-82.

Johnson, R. A. & Wichern, D. W. (1998). *Applied multivariate statistical analysis*, 4 ed. Prentice Hall, ISBN 0-13-834194-x, Upper Saddle River, New Jersey.

Khattree, R. & Naik, D. N. (2000). Multivariate data reduction and discrimination with SAS software. SAS Institute Inc., ISBN 1-58025-696-1, Cary, North Carolina, USA.

Lima, C. G. (1996). Análise de dados longitudinais provenientes de experimento em blocos casualizados. Dissertation (PhD in Agronomics), Escola Superior de Agricultura "Luiz de Queiroz", São Paulo University, Piracicaba, Brazil, 1996.

Malheiros, E.B. (1999). Precisão da análise de dados longitudinais, com diferentes estruturas para a matriz de variâncias e covariância, quando se utiliza o esquema em parcelas subdivididas. *Revista de Matemática e Estatística UNESP*, Vol.17, 1999, ISSN 0102-0811, pp.263-273.

Mauchly, J. W. (1940). Significance test for sphericity of a normal n-variate distribution. *An. Math. Stat.*, Vol.11, No. 2, June 1940,ISSN 00034851, pp.204-209.

Meredith, M.P.; Stehman, S.V. (1991). Repeated measures experiments in forestry: focus on analysis of response curves. *Canadian Journal of Forest Research*, Vol.21, 1991, ISSN 0045-5067, pp.957-965.

Smith, H. R. et al. (1962). Multivariate Analysis of Variance. (MANOVA). *Biometrics*, Vol.2, 1962, ISSN 0006-341X, pp. 61 - 67.

Morrison, D. F. (1990). *Multivariate Statistical Methods*. 3 ed, McGraw-Hill, ISBN 0-07-043187-6, Singapore.

Stuker, H. (1986). Análise multivariada para dados onde a característica observada é subdividida em K classes. Dissertation (MS in Agronomics), Escola Superior de Agricultura "Luiz de Queiroz", São Paulo University, Piracicaba, 1986.

Timm, N.H. (1980). Multivariate analysis of variance of repeated measurements. In: *Handbook of Statistics Analysis of Variance*, Vol. 1, P. R. Krishnaiah (Ed), pp.41-87, North-Holland, ISBN:0444853359, New York.

Vieira, F. T. P. A. (2006). Uma Abordagem Multivariada em Experimento Silvipastoril com Leucaena leucocephala (Lam.) de Wit. no Agreste de Pernambuco. Dissertation (MS. in Biometrics), Rural Federal University of Pernambuco, Pernambuco, Brazil, 2006.

Vonesh, F. E. & Chinchilli, V.M. (1997). *Linear and nonlinear models for the analysis of repeated measurements.* Marcel Dekker, ISBN 0-8247-8248-8, New York.

Wald, V. B. (2000). A metodologia de modelos mistos não lineares aplicados à análise de dados longitudinais em plantas forrageiras. Dissertation (MS in Zootechnique), Federal University of Rio Grande do Sul, Brazil, 2000.

Xavier, L. H. (2000). Modelos univariado e multivariado para análise de medidas repetidas e verificação da acurácia do modelo univariado por meio de simulação. Dissertation (MS in Statistics and Agronomics experimentation), Escola Superior de Agricultura "Luiz de Queiroz", São Paulo University, Piracicaba, Brazil, 2000.

5

Educational Simulator for Particle Swarm Optimization and Economic Dispatch Applications

Woo Nam Lee and Jong Bae Park
Konkuk University
Korea

1. Introduction

Optimization problems are widely encountered in various fields in science and technology. Sometimes such problems can be very complex due to the actual and practical nature of the objective function or the model constraints. Most of power system optimization problems have complex and nonlinear characteristics with heavy equality and inequality constraints. Recently, as an alternative to the conventional mathematical approaches, the heuristic optimization techniques such as genetic algorithms (GAs), Tabu search, simulated annealing, and particle swarm optimization (PSO) are considered as realistic and powerful solution schemes to obtain the global or quasi-global optimums (K. Y. Lee et al., 2002).

In 1995, Eberhart and Kennedy suggested a PSO based on the analogy of swarm of bird and school of fish (J. Kennedy et al., 1995). The PSO mimics the behavior of individuals in a swarm to maximize the survival of the species. In PSO, each individual makes his decision using his own experience together with other individuals' experiences (H. Yoshida et al., 2000). The algorithm, which is based on a metaphor of social interaction, searches a space by adjusting the trajectories of moving points in a multidimensional space. The individual particles are drawn stochastically toward the present velocity of each individual, their own previous best performance, and the best previous performance of their neighbours (M. Clerc et al., 2002).

The practical economic dispatch (ED) problems with valve-point and multi-fuel effects are represented as a non-smooth optimization problem with equality and inequality constraints, and this makes the problem of finding the global optimum difficult. Over the past few decades, in order to solve this problem, many salient methods have been proposed such as a hierarchical numerical method (C. E. Lin et al., 1984), dynamic programming (A. J. Wood et al., 1984), evolutionary programming (Y. M. Park et al., 1998; H. T. Yang et al., 1996; N. Sinba et al., 2003), Tabu search (W. M. Lin et al., 2002), neural network approaches (J. H. Park et al., 1993; K. Y. Lee et al., 1998), differential evolution (L. S. Coelho et al., 2006), particle swarm optimization (J. B. Park et al., 2005; T. A. A. Victoire et al., 2004; T. A. A. Victoire et al., 2005), and genetic algorithm (D. C. Walters et al., 1993).

This chapter would introduce an educational simulator for the PSO algorithm. The purpose of this simulator is to provide the undergraduate students with a simple and useable tool for gaining an intuitive feel for PSO algorithm, mathematical optimization problems, and power system optimization problems. To aid the understanding of PSO, the simulator has been developed under the user-friendly graphic user interface (GUI) environment using MATLAB. In this simulator, instructors and students can set parameters related to the performance of PSO and can observe the impact of the parameters to the solution quality. This simulator also displays the movements of each particle and convergence process of a group. In addition, the simulator can consider other mathematical or power system optimization problems with simple additional MATLAB coding.

2. Overview of particle swarm optimization

Kennedy and Eberhart (J. Kennedy et al., 1995) developed a PSO algorithm based on the behavior of individuals of a swarm. Its roots are in zoologist's modeling of the movement of individuals (e.g., fishes, birds, or insects) within a group. It has been noticed that members within a group seem to share information among them, a fact that leads to increased efficiency of the group (J. Kennedy et al., 2001). The PSO algorithm searches in parallel using a group of individuals similar to other AI-based heuristic optimization techniques.
In a physical n-dimensional search space, the position and velocity of individual i are represented as the vectors $X_i = (x_{i1}, \cdots, x_{in})$ and $V_i = (v_{i1}, \cdots v_{in})$ in the PSO algorithm. Let $Pbest_i = \left(x_{i1}^{Pbest}, \cdots, x_{in}^{Pbest}\right)$ and $Gbest = \left(x_1^{Gbest}, \cdots, x_n^{Gbest}\right)$ be the best position of individual i and its neighbors' best position so far, respectively. The modified velocity and position of each individual can be calculated using the current velocity and the distance from $Pbest_i$ to $Gbest$ as follows:

$$\begin{aligned} V_i^{k+1} = \omega V_i^k + c_1 rand_1 \times (Pbest_i^k - X_i^k) \\ + c_2 rand_2 \times (Gbest^k - X_i^k) \end{aligned} \tag{1}$$

$$X_i^{k+1} = X_i^k + V_i^{k+1} \tag{2}$$

where,
V_i^k velocity of individual i at iteration k,
ω weight parameter,
c_1, c_2 acceleration coefficients,
$rand_1, rand_2$ random numbers between 0 and 1,
X_i^k position of individual i at iteration k,
$Pbest_i^k$ best position of individual i until iteration k,
$Gbest^k$ best position of the group until iteration k.
The constants c_1 and c_2 represent the weighting of the stochastic acceleration terms that pull each particle toward the Pbest and Gbest positions. Suitable selection of inertia weight provides a balance between global and local explorations, thus requiring less iteration on average to find a sufficiently optimal solution. In general, the inertia weight ω has a linearly

decreasing dynamic parameter framework descending from ω_{max} to ω_{min} as follows (K. Y. Lee et al., 2002; H. Yoshida et al., 2000; J. B. Park et al., 2005).

$$\omega = \omega_{max} - \frac{\omega_{max} - \omega_{min}}{Iter_{max}} \times Iter \tag{3}$$

Were, $Iter_{max}$ is maximum iteration number and $Iter$ is current iteration number.

3. Structure of educational PSO simulator

3.1 Purpose and motivation of simulator

As a result of the rapid advances in computer hardware and software, computer-based power system educational tools have grown from very simple implementations, providing the user with little more than a stream of numerical output, to very detailed representations of the power system with an extensive GUI. Overbye, et al. had developed a user-friendly simulation program, PowerWorld Simulator, for teaching power system operation and control (T. J. Overbye et al., 2003). They applied visualization to power system information to draw user's attention and effectively display the simulation results. Through these works, they expected that animation, contouring, data aggregation and virtual environments would be quite useful techniques that are able to provide efficient learning experience to users. Also they presented experimental results associated with human factors aspects of using this visualization (D. A. Wiegmann et al., 2005; D. A. Wiegmann et al., 2006; N. Sinba et al., 2003).

Therefore, like other previous simulators, the motivation for the development of this simulator is to provide the students with a simple and useable tool for gaining an intuitive feel for the PSO algorithm, mathematical and power system optimization problems.

3.2 Functions of simulator

The basic objectives of this simulator were to make it easy to use and to provide effective visualization capability suitable for presentations as well as individual studies. This educational simulator was developed by MATLAB 2009b. MATLAB is a scientific computing language developed by The Mathworks, Inc. that is run in an interpreter mode on a wide variety of operating systems. It is extremely powerful, simple to use, and can be found in most research and engineering environments.

The structure and data flow of the developed PSO simulator is shown in Fig. 1. The simulator consists of 3-parts, that is, i) user setting of optimization function as well as parameters, ii) output result, and iii) visualized output variations, as shown in Figs. 2, 3, and 4, respectively. Since the main interaction between user and the simulator is performed through the GUI, it presents novice users with the information they need, and provides easy access for advanced users to additional detailed information. Thus, the GUI is instrumental in allowing users to gain an intuitive feel of the PSO algorithm, rather than just learning how to use this simulator.

In this simulator, parameters (i.e., maximum number of the iteration, maximum and minimum number of inertia weight, acceleration factors c_1 and c_2, and number of particles) that have the influence of PSO performance can be directly inputted by users. In addition,

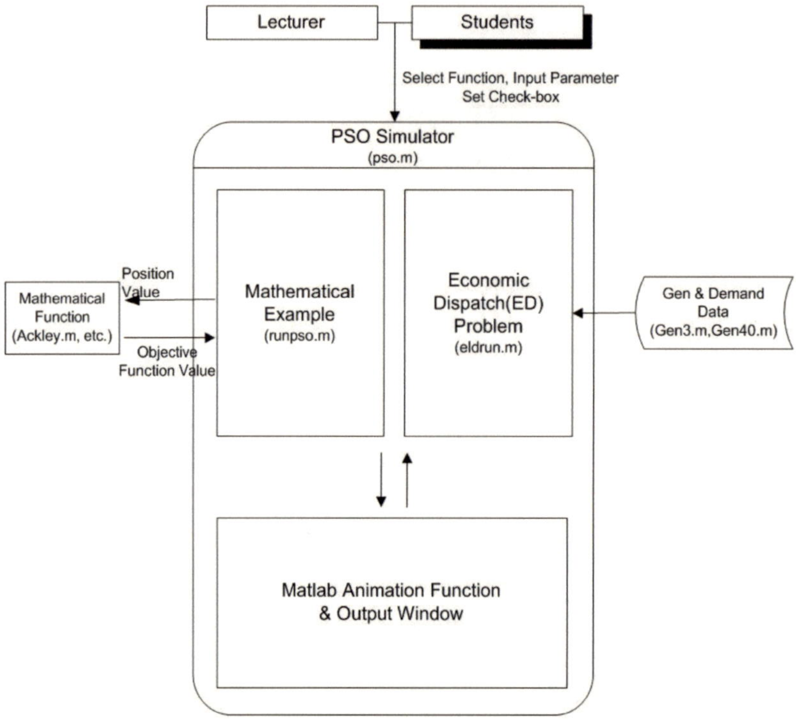

Fig. 1. Structure of the developed PSO simulator

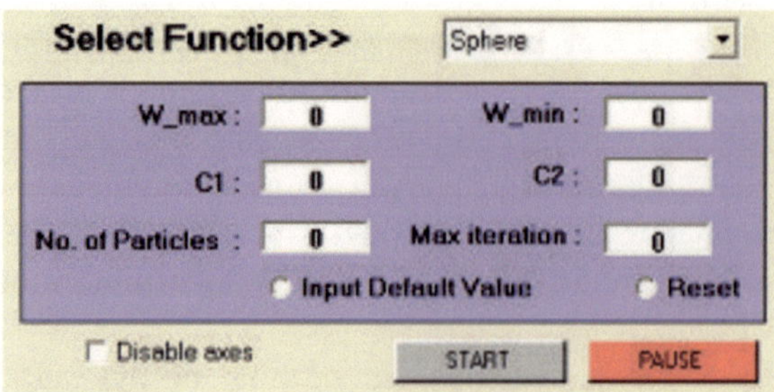

Fig. 2. A window for user setting

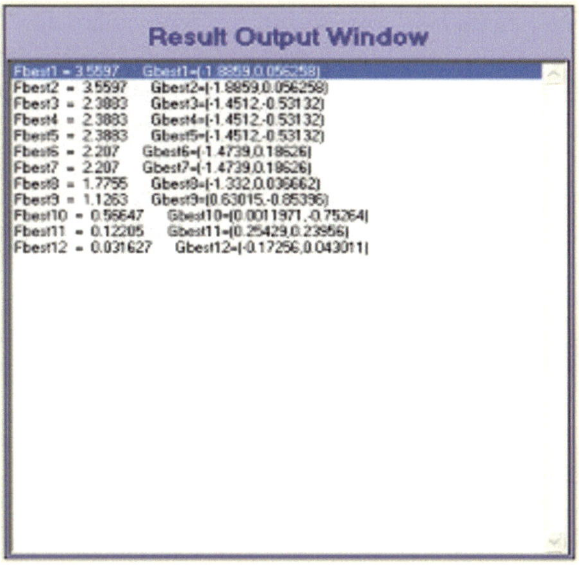

Fig. 3. Output result window

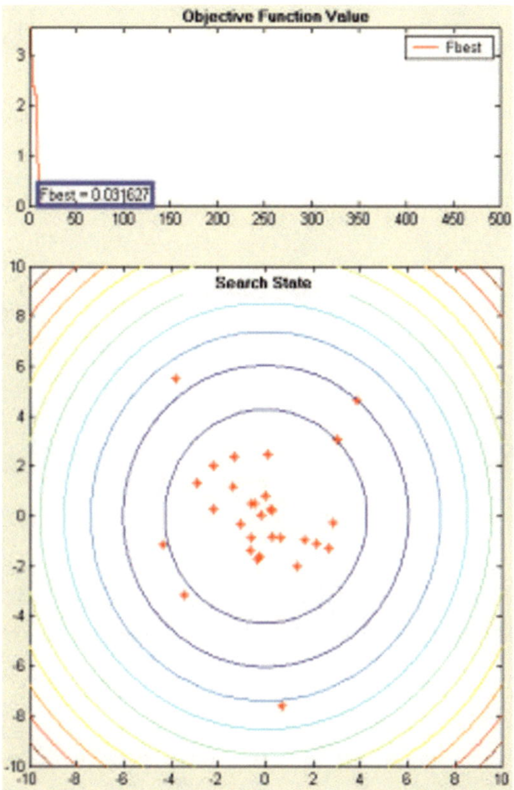

Fig. 4. Viewing parts of output variation

"Input Default Value" check-box was added for users who don't know the proper parameter values of the PSO. If the users push the "START" button finally, then the users can observe the evolution process of the particles on contours of the objective function (in case of a mathematical example) or the output histogram of each generator through MATLAB animation functions and check the changes of the values of the objective function and control variables at each iteration. The "Disable axes" check-box is used when the users want to show only the values of the final result fast. When the check-box is checked, only the final results (i.e., the value of the objective function and control variables) are expressed in the "Result Output Window". At any point in time in the simulation, the user can pause or restart the simulation by pushing the "PAUSE" button. As shown in Figs. 5 and 6, user can observe movements of each particle as well as the trend of the value of the objective function.

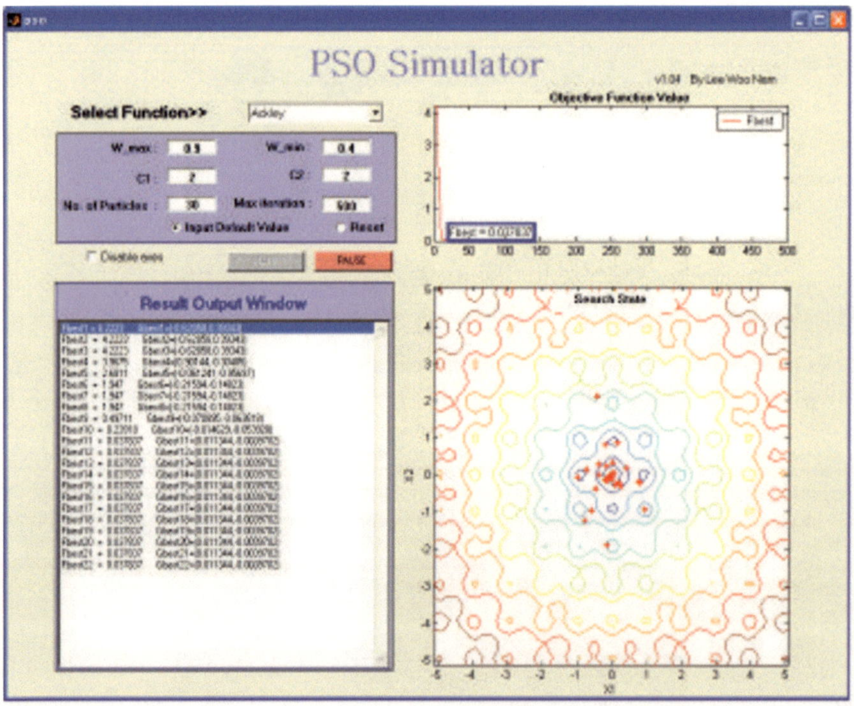

Fig. 5. Simulation for a mathematical example

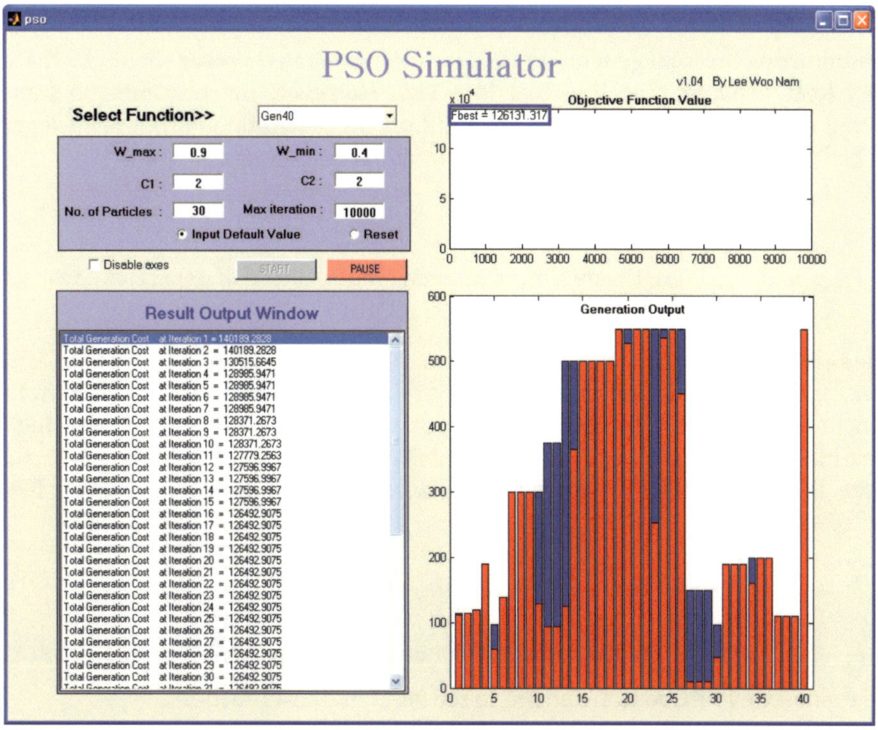

Fig. 6. Simulation for an economic dispatch problem.

4. Economic dispatch(ED) problem

4.1 Basic ED problem formulation

The ED problem is one of the basic optimization problems for the students who meet the power system engineering. The objective is to find the optimal combination of power generations that minimizes the total generation cost while satisfying an equality constraint and a set of inequality constraints. The most simplified cost function can be represented in a quadratic form as following (A. J. Wood et al., 1984):

$$C = \sum_{j \in J} F_j(P_j) \tag{4}$$

$$F_j(P_j) = a_j + b_j P_j + c_j P_j^2 \tag{5}$$

where,

C total generation cost;

F_j cost function of generator j;

a_j, b_j, c_j cost coefficients of generator j;

P_j electrical output of generator j;

J set for all generators.

While minimizing the total generation cost, the total generated power should be the same as the total load demand plus the total line loss. However, the transmission loss is not considered in this paper for simplicity. In addition, the generation output of each generator should be laid between minimum and maximum limits as follows:

$$P_{j\min} \le P_j \le P_{j\max} \tag{6}$$

where $P_{j\min}$ and $P_{j\max}$ are the minimum and maximum output of generator j, respectively.

4.2 Valve-point effects

The generating units with multi-valve steam turbines exhibit a greater variation in the fuel-cost functions. Since the valve point results in ripples, a cost function contains high order nonlinearities (H. T. Yang et al., 1996; N. Sinba et al., 2003; D. C. Walters et al. 1993). Therefore, the cost function (5) should be replaced by the following to consider the valve-point effects:

$$F_j(P_j) = a_j + b_j P_j + c_j P_j^2 + \left| e_j \times \sin(f_j \times (P_{j\min} - P_j)) \right| \tag{7}$$

where e_j and f_j are the cost coefficients of generator j reflecting valve-point effects. Here, the sinusoidal functions are added to the quadratic cost functions.

5. Case studies

This simulator can choose and run five different mathematical examples and two different ED problems: (i) The Sphere function, (ii) The Rosenbrock (or banana-valley) function, (iii) Ackley's function, (iv) The generalized Rastrigin function, (v) The generalized Griewank function, (vi) 3-unit system with valve-point effects, and (vii) 40-unit system with valve-point effects. In the case of each mathematical example (functions (i)-(v)), two input variables (i.e., 2-dimensional space) have been set in order to show the movement of particles on contour. For the case study, 30 independent trials are conducted to observe the variation during the evolutionary processes and compare the solution quality and convergence characteristics.

To successfully implement the PSO, some parameters must be assigned in advance. The population size NP is set to 30. Since the performance of PSO depends on its parameters such as inertia weight ω and two acceleration coefficients (i.e., c_1 and c_2), it is very important to determine the suitable values of parameters. The inertia weight is varied from 0.9 (i.e., ω_{max}) to 0.4 (i.e., ω_{min}), as these values are accepted as typical for solving wide varieties of problems. Two acceleration coefficients are determined through the experiments for each problem so as to find the optimal combination.

5.1 Mathematical examples

For development of user's understanding of the PSO algorithm, five non-linear mathematical examples are used here. In each case, the maximum number of iterations (i.e., $iter_{max}$) was set to 500. The acceleration coefficients (i.e., c_1 and c_2) was equally set to 2.0

from the experimental results for each case using the typical PSO algorithm. And all of the global minimum value of each function is known as 0. The global minimum value was successfully verified by the simulator.

5.1.1 The sphere function

The function and the initial position range of input variables (i.e., x_i) are as follows:

$$f_0(x) = \sum_{i=1}^{n} x_i^2 \tag{8}$$

$$-5.12 \le x_i \le 5.12$$

Initial and final stages of the optimization process for the Sphere function are shown in Fig. 7.

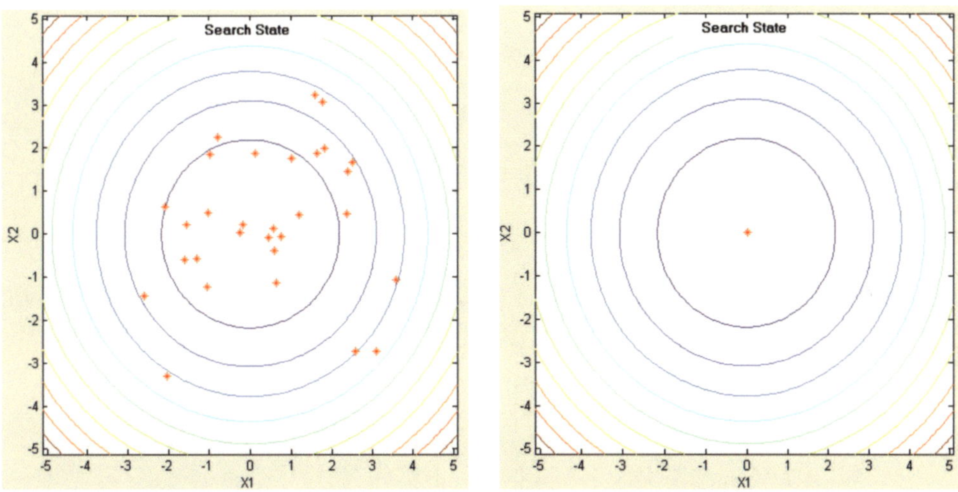

(a) Initial stage (b) Final stage

Fig. 7. Optimization process for the sphere function.

5.1.2 The rosenbrock (or banana-valley) function

The function and the initial position range of input variables (i.e., x_i) are as follows:

$$f_1(x) = \sum_{i=1}^{n/2} (100(x_{2i} - x_{2i-1}^2)^2 + (1 - x_{2i-1})^2) \tag{9}$$

$$-2.048 \le x_i \le 2.048$$

Initial and final stages of the optimization process for the Rosenbrock function are shown in Fig. 8.

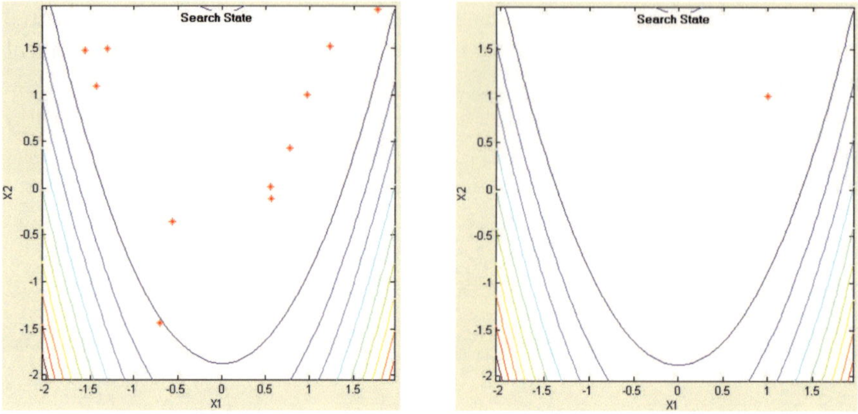

(a) Initial stage b) Final stage

Fig. 8. Optimization process for the Rosenbrock function.

5.1.3 The ackley's function

The function and the initial position range of input variables (i.e., x_i) is as follows:

$$f_2(x) = -20\exp\left(-0.2\sqrt{\frac{1}{n}\sum_{i=1}^{n} x_i^2}\right) - \exp\left(\frac{1}{n}\sum_{i=1}^{n}\cos(2\pi x_i)\right) + 20 + e \tag{10}$$

$$-30 \le x_i \le 30$$

Initial and final stages of the optimization process for the Ackley's function are shown in Fig. 9.

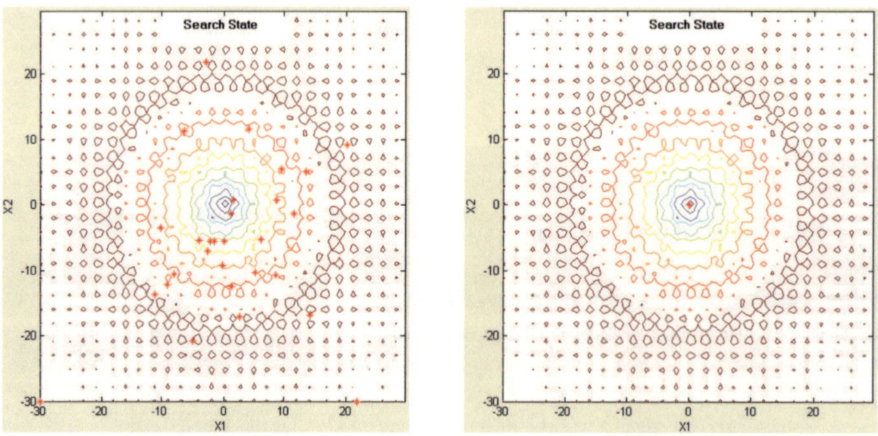

(a) Initial stage (b) Final stage

Fig. 9. Optimization process for Ackley's function.

5.1.4 The generalized rastrigin function

The function and the initial position range of input variables (i.e., x_i) is as follows:

$$f_3(x) = \sum_{i=1}^{n} (x_i^2 - 10\cos(2\pi x_i) + 10) \tag{11}$$

$$-5.12 \le x_i \le 5.12$$

Initial and final stages of the optimization process for the generalized Rastrigin function are shown in Fig. 10.

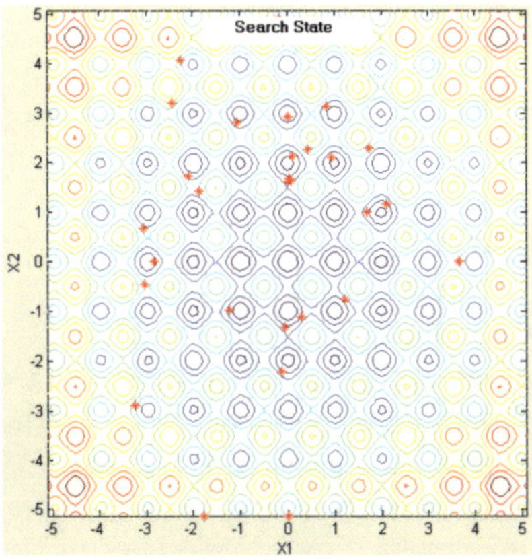

(a) Initial stage

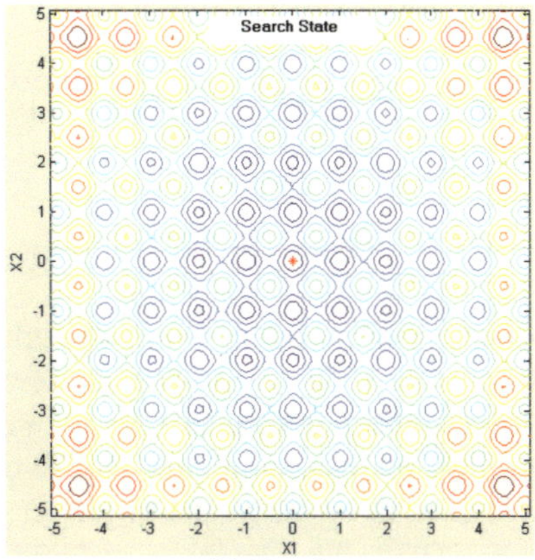

(b) Final stage

Fig. 10. Optimization process for Rastrigin function.

5.1.5 The generalized griewank function

The function and the initial position range of input variables (i.e., x_i) is as follows:

$$f_4(x) = \frac{1}{4000}\sum_{i=1}^{n} x_i^2 - \prod_{i=1}^{n} \cos\left(\frac{x_i}{\sqrt{i}}\right) + 1 \tag{12}$$

$$-200 \le x_i \le 200$$

Initial and final stages of the optimization process for the generalized Griewank function are shown in Fig. 11.

Table 1 shows the average values of objective functions and two input variables for each function achieved by the PSO simulator.

Function Name	Objective Function Value	x_1	x_2
Sphere	0	0	0
Rosenbrock	0	1	1
Ackley	-8.8818e-16	-2.9595e-16	1.6273e-16
Rastrigin	0	9.7733e-10	-7.9493e-10
Griewank	0	100	100

Table 1. Results for Each Test Function

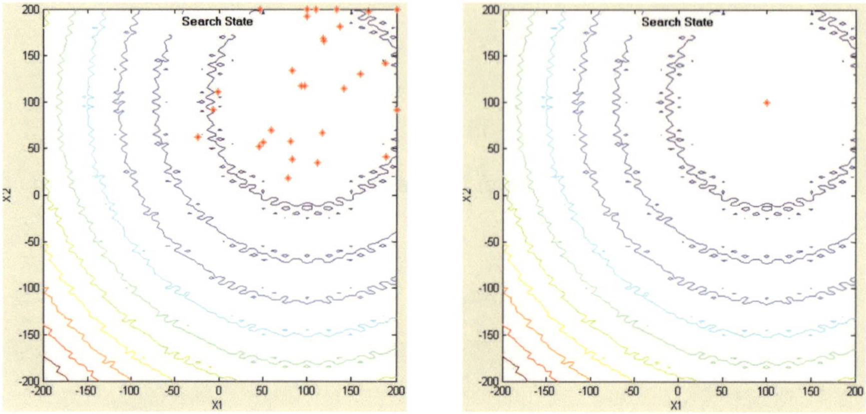

(a) Initial stage (b) Final stage

Fig. 11. Optimization process for Griewank function.

5.2 Economic dispatch(ED) problems with valve-point effects

This simulator also offers examples to solve ED problem for two different power systems: a 3-unit system with valve-point effects, and a 40-unit system with valve-point effects. The total demands of the 3-unit and the 40-unit systems are set to 850MW and 10,500MW, respectively. All the system data and related constraints of the test systems are given in (N. Sinba et al., 2003). Because these systems have more than 3 input variables, the simulator shows a histogram for the generation output instead of the contour and particles. Since the global minimum for the total generation cost is unknown in the case of the 40-unit system, the maximum number of iterations (i.e., $iter_{\max}$) is set to 10,000 in order to sufficiently search for the minimum value.

Table 2 shows the minimum, mean, maximum, and standard deviation for the 3-unit system obtained from the simulator. The generation outputs and the corresponding costs of the best solution for 3-unit system are described in Table 3.

Case	Minimum Cost ($)	Average Cost ($)	Maximum Cost ($)	Standard Deviation
3-Unit System	8234.0717	8234.0717	8234.0717	0

* Global value of the 3-unit system was known as 8234.0717.T

Table 2. Convergence Results for 3-Unit System

Unit	Generation	Cost
1	300.2669	3087.5099
2	400.0000	3767.1246
3	149.7331	1379.4372
TP/TC	850.0000	8234.0717

*TP: total power [MW], TC: total generation cost [$]

Table 3. Generation Output of Each Generator and The Corresponding Cost in 3-Unit System

In order to find the optimal combination of parameters (i.e., ω_{max}, ω_{min}, c_1, and c_2 B), six cases are considered as given in Table 4. The parameters are determined through the experiments for 40-unit system using the simulator. In Table 4, the effects of parameters are illustrated

Cases	ω_{max}	ω_{min}	c1,c2	Minimum Cost ($)	Average Cost ($)	Maximum Cost ($)	Standard Deviation
1	1.0	0.5	1	121755.49	122221.90	122624.07	156.97
2	0.9	0.4	1	121761.40	122343.32	123087.16	303.62
3	0.8	0.3	1	121949.15	122842.59	124363.11	602.06
4	1.0	0.5	2	121865.23	122285.12	122658.29	175.19
5	0.9	0.4	2	121768.69	122140.32	122608.27	187.74
6	0.8	0.3	2	121757.09	122158.00	122615.71	212.36

Table 4. Influence of Acceleration Coefficients for 40-Unit System

The result screens for 3-unit and 40-unit system are shown in Figs. 12 and 13, respectively. Each histogram expresses the result of generation output for each generator.

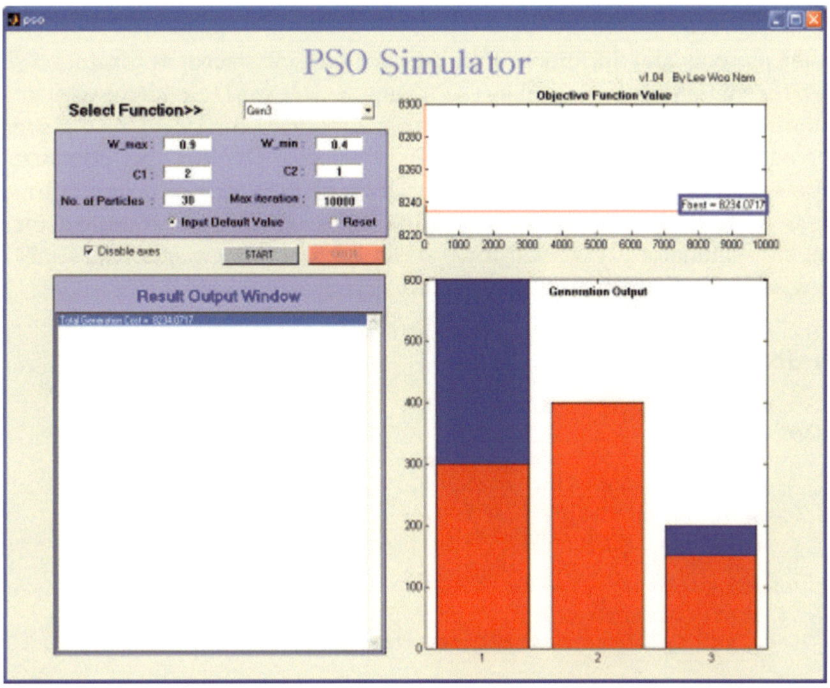

Fig. 12. Result screen for the 3-units system.

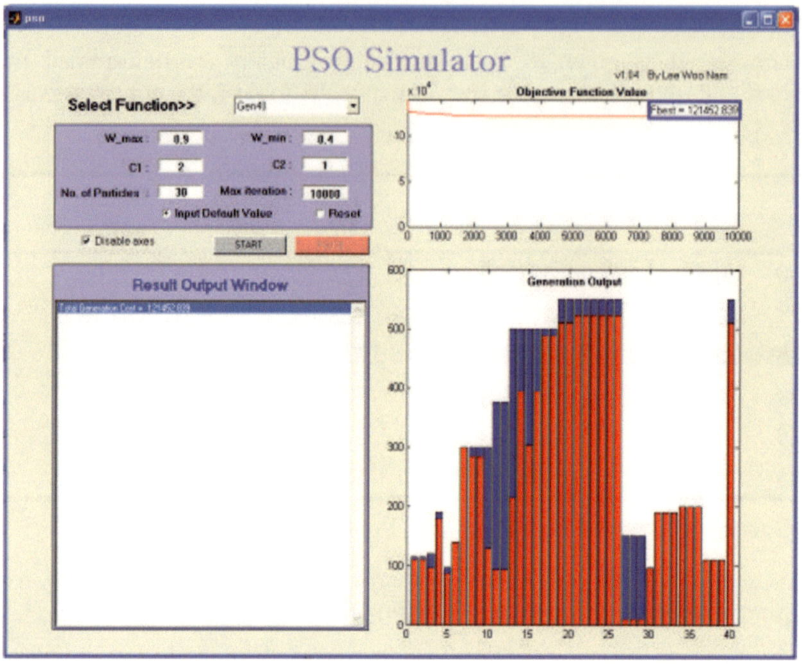

Fig. 13. Result screen for the 40-units system.

6. Conclusion

This chapter presents an educational simulator for particle swarm optimization (PSO) and application for solving mathematical test functions as well as ED problems with non-smooth cost functions. Using this simulator, instructors and students can select the test functions for simulation and set the parameters that have an influence on the PSO performance. Through visualization process of each particle and variation of the value of objective function, the simulator is particularly effective in providing users with an intuitive feel for the PSO algorithm. This simulator is expected to be an useful tool for students who study electrical engineering and optimization techniques.

7. Appendix 1: pso.m

```
function varargout = pso(varargin)
gui_Singleton = 1;
gui_State = struct('gui_Name',       mfilename, ...
    'gui_Singleton',  gui_Singleton, ...
    'gui_OpeningFcn', @pso_OpeningFcn, ...
    'gui_OutputFcn',  @pso_OutputFcn, ...
    'gui_LayoutFcn',  [] , ...
    'gui_Callback',   []);
if nargin & isstr(varargin{1})
    gui_State.gui_Callback = str2func(varargin{1});
end
if nargout
    [varargout{1:nargout}] = gui_mainfcn(gui_State, varargin{:});
else
```

```
    gui_mainfcn(gui_State, varargin{:});
end
function pso_OpeningFcn(hObject, eventdata, handles, varargin)
handles.output = hObject;
guidata(hObject, handles);
function varargout = pso_OutputFcn(hObject, eventdata, handles)
varargout{1} = handles.output;
function select_func_CreateFcn(hObject, eventdata, handles)
if ispc
    set(hObject,'BackgroundColor','white');
else
    set(hObject,'BackgroundColor',get(0,'defaultUicontrolBackgroundColor'));
end
function select_func_Callback(hObject, eventdata, handles)
function default_value_Callback(hObject, eventdata, handles)
set(handles.default_value, 'Value', 1);
set(handles.reset, 'Value', 0);
set(handles.wmax, 'String', 0.9);
set(handles.wmin, 'String', 0.4);
set(handles.X_max, 'String', 5.12);
set(handles.X_min, 'String', -5.12);
set(handles.c1, 'String', 2);
set(handles.c2, 'String', 2);
set(handles.N, 'String', 30);
set(handles.itmax, 'String', 500);
function reset_Callback(hObject, eventdata, handles)
set(handles.default_value, 'Value', 0);
set(handles.reset, 'Value', 1);
set(handles.wmax, 'String', 0);
set(handles.wmin, 'String', 0);
set(handles.X_max, 'String', 0);
set(handles.X_min, 'String', 0);
set(handles.c1, 'String', 0);
set(handles.c2, 'String', 0);
set(handles.N, 'String', 0);
set(handles.itmax, 'String', 0);
function wmax_CreateFcn(hObject, eventdata, handles)
if ispc
    set(hObject,'BackgroundColor','white');
else
set(hObject,'BackgroundColor',get(0,'defaultUicontrolBackgroundColor'));
end
function wmax_Callback(hObject, eventdata, handles)
wmax = str2double(get(hObject,'String'));
if isnan(wmax)
    set(hObject, 'String', 0);
    errordlg('Input must be a number','Error');
end
pso_para = getappdata(gcbf, 'metricdata');
pso_para.wmax = wmax;
setappdata(gcbf, 'metricdata', pso_para);
function wmin_CreateFcn(hObject, eventdata, handles)
if ispc
    set(hObject,'BackgroundColor','white');
else
set(hObject,'BackgroundColor',get(0,'defaultUicontrolBackgroundColor'));
end
```

```
function wmin_Callback(hObject, eventdata, handles)
wmin = str2double(get(hObject,'String'));
if isnan(wmin)
    set(hObject, 'String', 0);
    errordlg('Input must be a number','Error');
end
pso_para = getappdata(gcbf, 'metricdata');
pso_para.wmin = wmin;
setappdata(gcbf, 'metricdata', pso_para);
function c1_CreateFcn(hObject, eventdata, handles)
if ispc
    set(hObject,'BackgroundColor','white');
else
set(hObject,'BackgroundColor',get(0,'defaultUicontrolBackgroundColor'));
end
function c1_Callback(hObject, eventdata, handles)
c1 = str2double(get(hObject,'String'));
if isnan(c1)
    set(hObject, 'String', 0);
    errordlg('Input must be a number','Error');
end
pso_para = getappdata(gcbf, 'metricdata');
pso_para.c1 = c1;
setappdata(gcbf, 'metricdata', pso_para);
function c2_CreateFcn(hObject, eventdata, handles)
if ispc
    set(hObject,'BackgroundColor','white');
else
set(hObject,'BackgroundColor',get(0,'defaultUicontrolBackgroundColor'));
end
function c2_Callback(hObject, eventdata, handles)
c2 = str2double(get(hObject,'String'));
if isnan(c2)
    set(hObject, 'String', 0);
    errordlg('Input must be a number','Error');
end
pso_para = getappdata(gcbf, 'metricdata');
pso_para.c2 = c2;
setappdata(gcbf, 'metricdata', pso_para);
function N_CreateFcn(hObject, eventdata, handles)
if ispc
    set(hObject,'BackgroundColor','white');
else
set(hObject,'BackgroundColor',get(0,'defaultUicontrolBackgroundColor'));
end
function N_Callback(hObject, eventdata, handles)
N = str2double(get(hObject,'String'));
if isnan(N)
    set(hObject, 'String', 0);
    errordlg('Input must be a number','Error');
end
pso_para = getappdata(gcbf, 'metricdata');
pso_para.N = N;
setappdata(gcbf, 'metricdata', pso_para);
function itmax_CreateFcn(hObject, eventdata, handles)
if ispc
    set(hObject,'BackgroundColor','white');
```

```
else
set(hObject,'BackgroundColor',get(0,'defaultUicontrolBackgroundColor'));
end
function itmax_Callback(hObject, eventdata, handles)
itmax = str2double(get(hObject,'String'));
if isnan(itmax)
    set(hObject, 'String', 0);
    errordlg('Input must be a number','Error');
end
function start_Callback(hObject, eventdata, handles)
if get(handles.select_func,'value')>=7
    eldrun
else
    runpso
end
function Result_window_CreateFcn(hObject, eventdata, handles)
if ispc
    set(hObject,'BackgroundColor','white');
else
set(hObject,'BackgroundColor',get(0,'defaultUicontrolBackgroundColor'));
end
function Result_window_Callback(hObject, eventdata, handles)
function pause_Callback(hObject, eventdata, handles)
if isequal(get(handles.pause,'String'),'PAUSE')
    set(handles.start,'Enable','on');
    set(handles.pause,'String','RESUME');
    uiwait;
else
    set(handles.start,'Enable','off');
    set(handles.pause,'String','PAUSE');
    uiresume;
end
function disable_Callback(hObject, eventdata, handles)
function close_Callback(hObject, eventdata, handles)
delete(get(0,'CurrentFigure'));
function X_max_Callback(hObject, eventdata, handles)
X_max = str2double(get(hObject,'String'));
if isnan(X_max)
    set(hObject, 'String', 0);
    errordlg('Input must be a number','Error');
end
pso_para = getappdata(gcbf, 'metricdata');
pso_para.X_max = X_max;
setappdata(gcbf, 'metricdata', pso_para);
function X_max_CreateFcn(hObject, eventdata, handles)
if ispc
    set(hObject,'BackgroundColor','white');
else
set(hObject,'BackgroundColor',get(0,'defaultUicontrolBackgroundColor'));
end
function X_min_Callback(hObject, eventdata, handles)
X_min = str2double(get(hObject,'String'));
if isnan(X_min)
    set(hObject, 'String', 0);
    errordlg('Input must be a number','Error');
end
pso_para = getappdata(gcbf, 'metricdata');
```

```
pso_para.X_min = X_min;
setappdata(gcbf, 'metricdata', pso_para);
function X_min_CreateFcn(hObject, eventdata, handles)
if ispc
    set(hObject,'BackgroundColor','white');
else
set(hObject,'BackgroundColor',get(0,'defaultUicontrolBackgroundColor'));
end
```

8. Appendix 2: runpso.m

```
cla;
set(handles.start,'Enable','off');
set(handles.pause,'String','PAUSE','Enable','on');
set(handles.text14,'String','Search State ');
functnames = get(handles.select_func,'String');
functname = functnames{get(handles.select_func,'Value')};
wmax = str2double(get(handles.wmax, 'String'));
wmin = str2double(get(handles.wmin, 'String'));
X_max = str2double(get(handles.X_max, 'String'));
X_min = str2double(get(handles.X_min, 'String'));
c1 = str2double(get(handles.c1, 'String'));
c2 = str2double(get(handles.c2, 'String'));
N = str2double(get(handles.N, 'String'));
itmax = str2double(get(handles.itmax, 'String'));
pso_para = getappdata(gcbf, 'metricdata');
pso_para.wmax = wmax;
pso_para.wmin = wmin;
pso_para.X_max = X_max;
pso_para.X_min = X_min;
pso_para.c1 = c1;
pso_para.c2 = c2;
pso_para.N = N;
pso_para.itmax = itmax;
setappdata(gcbf, 'metricdata', pso_para);
D=2; % Dimension
% Weight Parameter
for iter=1:pso_para.itmax
    W(iter)= pso_para.wmax-((pso_para.wmax-
pso_para.wmin)/pso_para.itmax)*iter;
end
%Initialization of positions of agents
% agents are initialized between -5.12,+5.12 randomly
a= X_min;  %min
b= X_max;   %max
x=a+(b-a)*rand(pso_para.N,D,1);
%Initialization of velocities of agents
%Between -5.12 , +5.12, (which can also be started from zero)
m=X_min;
n=X_max;
V=m+(n-m)*rand(pso_para.N,D,1);
%Function to be minimized.
```

```
F = feval(functname,x(:,:,1));
% Saving address and value; C:Value of E, I: The Number of Particle
[C,I]=min(abs(F(:,1,1))); B(1,1,1)=C;
XX(1,1,1)=I;
gbest(1,:,1)=x(I,:,1);
%Matrix composed of gbest vector
for p=1:pso_para.N
    for r=1:D
        G(p,r,1)=gbest(1,r,1);
    end
end
Fbest(1,1,1) = feval(functname,G(1,:,1));
pbest=x;
% Calculating Velocity
V(:,:,2) = W(1) * V(:,:,1) + pso_para.c1*rand*(pbest(:,:,1)-
x(:,:,1)) + pso_para.c2*rand*(G(:,:,1)-x(:,:,1));
x(:,:,2)=x(:,:,1) + V(:,:,2);
for i=1:pso_para.N
    for j=1:D
        if x(i,j,2)<a
            x(i,j,2)=a;
        else
            if x(i,j,2)>b
                x(i,j,2)=b;
            else
            end
        end
    end
end
Fb(1,1,1) = feval(functname,gbest(1,:,1));
if get(handles.disable,'Value')==0
    %%%%%%%%%%%%%%%%%%%%%% Contour Plot %%%%%%%%%%%%%%%%%%%%%%
    axes(handles.axes2);
    axis([a b a b])
    con_m=a:0.1:b;
    con_n=con_m;
    [con_m,con_n]=meshgrid(con_m,con_n);
    for q=1:length(con_m(1,:))
        for z=1:length(con_n(1,:))
            r(q,z)= feval(functname,[con_m(q,z),con_n(q,z)]);
        end
    end
    r_save=r;
    [c,h]=contour(con_m,con_n,r_save,10);
    xlabel('X1')
    ylabel('X2')
    title('Search State')
    %%%%%%%%%%%%%%%%%%%%%%%%%%%%%%%%%%%%%%%%%%%%
end

for j=2:pso_para.itmax
```

```
    % Calculation of new positions
    F(:,1,j) = feval(functname,x(:,:,j));
    [C,I]=min(abs(F(:,1,j)));
    B(1,1,j)=C;
    for i=1:D
        gbest(1,i,j)=x(I,i,j);
    end
    Fb(1,1,j) = feval(functname,gbest(1,:,j));
    [C,I]=min(Fb(1,1,:));
    if Fb(1,1,j)<=C
        for k=1:D
            gbest(1,k,j)=gbest(1,k,j);
        end
    else
        for m=1:D
            gbest(1,m,j)=gbest(1,m,I);
        end
    end
    %Matrix composed of gbest vector
    for p=1:pso_para.N
        for r=1:D
            G(p,r,j)=gbest(1,r,j);
        end
    end
    Fbest(1,1,j) = feval(functname,G(1,:,j));
    for i=1:pso_para.N;
        [C,I]=min(F(i,1,:));
        if  F(i,1,j)<=C
            pbest(i,:,j)=x(i,:,j);
        else
            pbest(i,:,j)=x(i,:,I);
        end
    end
    V(:,:,j+1)= W(j)*V(:,:,j) + pso_para.c1*rand*(pbest(:,:,j)-
x(:,:,j)) + pso_para.c2*rand*(G(:,:,j)-x(:,:,j));
    x(:,:,j+1)=x(:,:,j)+V(:,:,j+1);
    for k=1:pso_para.N
        for m=1:D
            if x(k,m,j+1)<a
                x(k,m,j+1)=a;
            else
                if x(k,m,j+1)>b
                    x(k,m,j+1)=b;
                else
                end
            end
        end
    end
    if get(handles.disable,'Value')==0
        set(gcf,'Doublebuffer','on');
```

```
        %%%%%%%%% Display to the ListBox%%%%%%%%%
        ResultStr(1) = [{['Fbest','1',' ','=',' ',
num2str(Fbest(1,1,1)),'
','Gbest','1','=','(',num2str(gbest(1,1,1)),',',num2str(gbest(1,2,1)
),')']}];
        ResultStr(j) = [{['Fbest',num2str(j),'  ','=','  ',
num2str(Fbest(1,1,end)),'
','Gbest',num2str(j),'=','(',num2str(gbest(1,1,end)),',',num2str(gbe
st(1,2,end)),')']}];
        set(handles.Result_window, 'String', ResultStr);
        %%%%%%%%% end of Display %%%%%%%%%%%%%%%%%

        %%%%%%%%%%%%%%%%  AXE-1  %%%%%%%%%%%%%%%%%
        axes(handles.axes1);
        cla;
        set(gca,'xlim',[0 pso_para.itmax],'ylim',[0 Fbest(1,1,1)]),
        plot(Fbest(:),'r-')
        if j<=pso_para.itmax/2
            text(j,Fbest(1,1,end),['Fbest = ',
num2str(Fbest(1,1,end))],'HorizontalAlignment','Left','VerticalAlign
ment','bottom','EdgeColor','blue','LineWidth',3);
        else
            text(j,Fbest(1,1,end),['Fbest = ',
num2str(Fbest(1,1,end))],'HorizontalAlignment','Right','VerticalAlig
nment','bottom','EdgeColor','blue','LineWidth',3);
        end
        legend('Fbest');
        hold on
        %%%%%%%%%%%%%%%%%%%%%%%%%%%%%%%%%%%%%%%%%%

        %%%%%%%%%%%%%%%%%  AXE-2  %%%%%%%%%%%%%%%%
        axes(handles.axes2);
        axis([a b a b])
        [c,h]=contour(con_m,con_n,r_save,10);
        hold on
        plot(pbest(:,1,j),pbest(:,2,j),'r*')
        xlabel('X1')
        ylabel('X2')
        drawnow
        hold off
        %%%%%%%%%%%%%%%%%%%%%%%%%%%%%%%%%%%%%%%%%%
    end
end
if get(handles.disable,'Value')==1
    ResultStr = [{['Fbest  ','=','  ', num2str(Fbest(1,1,end)),'
','Gbest','=','(',num2str(gbest(1,1,end)),',',num2str(gbest(1,2,end)
),')']}];
    set(handles.Result_window, 'String', ResultStr);
end
set(handles.start,'Enable','on');
set(handles.pause,'String','PAUSE','Enable','off');
```

9. Appendix 3: eldrun.m

```
cla;
set(handles.start,'Enable','off');
set(handles.pause,'String','PAUSE','Enable','on');
set(handles.text14,'String','Generation Output');
functnames = get(handles.select_func,'String');
functname = functnames{get(handles.select_func,'Value')};
wmax = str2double(get(handles.wmax, 'String'));
wmin = str2double(get(handles.wmin, 'String'));
c1 = str2double(get(handles.c1, 'String'));
c2 = str2double(get(handles.c2, 'String'));
N = str2double(get(handles.N, 'String'));
itmax = str2double(get(handles.itmax, 'String'));
pso_para = getappdata(gcbf, 'metricdata');
pso_para.wmax = wmax;
pso_para.wmin = wmin;
pso_para.c1 = c1;
pso_para.c2 = c2;
pso_para.N = N;
pso_para.itmax = itmax;
setappdata(gcbf, 'metricdata', pso_para);

[Gen,Demand]=feval(functname);

%Initialization of PSO parameters
D=size(Gen,1); % Dimension (Number of Generator)
CR = 0.5;
for iter=1:pso_para.itmax
    W(iter)= pso_para.wmax-((pso_para.wmax-
pso_para.wmin)/pso_para.itmax)*iter;
end
%Initialization of positions of agents
%agents are initialized between P_min,P_max randomly
for i=1:D
    P_min(i) = Gen(i,6);     % P_min
    P_max(i) = Gen(i,7);     % P_max
end
% Constraints handling
for i=1:pso_para.N
    yes=1;
    while yes==1
        p=randperm(D);

        for n=1:D-1
            g = p(n);
            x(i,g) = P_min(g) +  (P_max(g)-P_min(g)) * rand;
            A(n) = x(i,g);
        end
        SUM=0;
        for f=1:D-1
```

```
            SUM = SUM + A(f);
        end
        A(D) = Demand - SUM;
        g=p(D);
        if A(D) < P_min(g)
            A(D) = P_min(g);
            ok=0;
        else
            if A(D) > P_max(g)
                A(D) = P_max(g);
                ok=0;
            else
                ok=1;
                yes=0;
            end
        end

        L=1;
        while ok==0
            A(L) = Demand -(sum(A(:))-A(L));
            if A(L) < P_min(p(L))
                A(L) = P_min(p(L));
                ok=0;
                L = L+1;
                if L==D+1
                    ok=1;
                    yes=1;
                else
                end
            else
                if A(L) > P_max(p(L))
                    A(L) = P_max(p(L));
                    ok=0;
                    L= L+1;
                    if L==D+1
                        ok=1;
                        yes =1;
                    else
                    end
                else
                    ok=1;
                    yes=0;
                end
            end
        end
    end
    for k=1:D
        x(i,p(k))=A(k);
    end
end
%Initialization of velocities of agents
```

```
%Between V_min , V_max, (which can also be started from zero)
for i=1:pso_para.N
    for j=1:D
        m(j) = Gen(j,6) - x(i,j);  %V_min
        n(j) = Gen(j,7) - x(i,j);  %V_max
        V(i,j) = m(j) + (n(j)-m(j)) * rand;
    end
end
% End of Initialization
% Function to be minimized.
for i=1:pso_para.N;
    for j=1:D;
        Cost(i,j) = Gen(j,1) + Gen(j,2)*x(i,j) + Gen(j,3)*x(i,j).^2
+ abs(Gen(j,4)*sin(Gen(j,5)*(Gen(j,6)-x(i,j))));
    end
    F(i,1) = sum(Cost(i,:)); % Total Cost
end
pbest=x;
[C,I]=min(abs(F(:,1)));
B(1,1)=C;
XX(1,1)=I;
gbest(1,:)=x(I,:);
Gen_sum(1,1) = sum(gbest(1,:));
%Matrix composed of gbest vector
for j=1:D;
    Cost_Best(1,j) =
Gen(j,1)+Gen(j,2)*gbest(1,j)+Gen(j,3)*gbest(1,j).^2
+abs(Gen(j,4)*sin(Gen(j,5)*(Gen(j,6)-gbest(1,j))));
end
Fbest(1,1) = sum(Cost_Best(1,:)); % Total Cost
% Constraints handling
for i=1:pso_para.N
    yes=1;
    while yes==1
        p=randperm(D);
        for n=1:D-1
            g = p(n);
            V(i,g) = W(1) * V(i,g) + c1*rand*(pbest(i,g)-x(i,g)) +
c2*rand*(gbest(1,g)-x(i,g));
            x(i,g)=x(i,g) + V(i,g);
            if rand<=CR
                x_adj(i,g) = x(i,g);
            else
                x_adj(i,g) = pbest(i,g);
            end
            A(n) = x_adj(i,g);
            if A(n) < P_min(g)
                A(n) = P_min(g);
            else
                if A(n) > P_max(g)
                    A(n) = P_max(g);
```

```
            else
            end
        end
    end
    SUM=0;
    for u=1:D-1
        SUM = SUM + A(u);
    end
    A(D) = Demand - SUM;

    g=p(D);
    if A(D) < P_min(g)
        A(D) = P_min(g);
        ok=0;
    else
        if A(D) > P_max(g)
            A(D) = P_max(g);
            ok=0;
        else
            ok=1;
        end
        yes=0;
    end

    L=1;
    while ok==0
        A(L) = Demand -(sum(A(:))-A(L));
        if A(L) < P_min(p(L))
            A(L) = P_min(p(L));
            ok=0;
            L = L+1;
            if L==D+1
                ok=1;
                yes=1;
            else
            end
        else
            if A(L) > P_max(p(L))
                A(L) = P_max(p(L));
                ok=0;
                L= L+1;
                if L==D+1
                    ok=1;
                    yes =1;
                else
                end
            else
                ok=1;
            end

            yes=0;
```

```
            end
        end
    end
    for k=1:D
        x_adj(i,p(k))=A(k);
    end
end

for j=2:pso_para.itmax
    % Calculation of new positions
    for i=1:pso_para.N
        for k=1:D
            Cost(i,k) =
Gen(k,1)+Gen(k,2)*x_adj(i,k)+Gen(k,3)*x_adj(i,k).^2
+abs(Gen(k,4)*sin(Gen(k,5)*(Gen(k,6)-x_adj(i,k))));
        end
        F(i,j) = sum(Cost(i,:)); % Total Cost
    end

    for i=1:pso_para.N
        [C,I]=min(F(i,:));
        if  F(i,j)<=C
            pbest(i,:)=x_adj(i,:);
        else
        end
    end
    for i=1:pso_para.N
        for k=1:D
            Cost_pbest(i,k) =
Gen(k,1)+Gen(k,2)*pbest(i,k)+Gen(k,3)*pbest(i,k).^2
+abs(Gen(k,4)*sin(Gen(k,5)*(Gen(k,6)-pbest(i,k))));
        end
        F_pbest(i,1) = sum(Cost_pbest(i,:)); % Total Cost
    end
    [C,I]=min(F_pbest(:,1));
    for k=1:D
        gbest(1,k)=pbest(I,k);
    end
    Gen_sum(j,1) = sum(gbest(1,:));
    Fbest(j,1) = C;
% Constraints handling
    for i=1:pso_para.N
        yes=1;
        while yes==1
            p=randperm(D);
            for n=1:D-1
                g = p(n);
                V(i,g) = W(j) * V(i,g) + c1*rand*(pbest(i,g)-x(i,g))
+ c2*rand*(gbest(1,g)-x(i,g));
                x(i,g) = x(i,g) + V(i,g);
                if rand<=CR
```

```
            x_adj(i,g) = x(i,g);
        else
            x_adj(i,g) = pbest(i,g);
        end
        A(n) = x_adj(i,g);
        if A(n) < P_min(g)
            A(n) = P_min(g);
        else
            if A(n) > P_max(g)
                A(n) = P_max(g);
            else
            end
        end
    end
    SUM=0;
    for f=1:D-1
        SUM = SUM + A(f);
    end
    A(D) = Demand - SUM;

    g=p(D);
    if A(D) < P_min(g)
        A(D) = P_min(g);
        ok=0;
    else
        if A(D) > P_max(g)
            A(D) = P_max(g);
            ok=0;
        else
            ok=1;
            yes=0;
        end

    end
    L=1;
    while ok==0
        A(L) = Demand -(sum(A(:))-A(L));
        if A(L) < P_min(p(L))
            A(L) = P_min(p(L));
            ok=0;
            L = L+1;
            if L==D+1
                ok=1;
                yes=1;
            else
            end
        else
            if A(L) > P_max(p(L))
                A(L) = P_max(p(L));
                ok=0;
                L= L+1;
```

```
                        if L==D+1
                            ok=1;
                            yes=1;
                        else
                        end
                    else
                        ok=1;
                        yes=0;
                    end
                end
            end
        end
        for k=1:D
            x_adj(i,p(k))=A(k);
        end
    end

    if get(handles.disable,'Value')==0
        set(gcf,'Doublebuffer','on');
        %%%%%%%%% Display to the ListBox%%%%%%%%%
        ResultStr(1) = [{['Total Generation Cost    at Iteration
','1',' ','=',' ', num2str(Fbest(1,1))]}];
        ResultStr(j) = [{['Total Generation Cost    at Iteration
',num2str(j),'  ','=','  ', num2str(Fbest(end,1))]}];
        set(handles.Result_window, 'String', ResultStr);
        %%%%%%%%% end of Display %%%%%%%%%%%%%%%%

        %%%%%%%%%%%%%%%%  AXE-1  %%%%%%%%%%%%%%%%%
        axes(handles.axes1);
        cla;
        set(gca,'xlim',[0 pso_para.itmax],'ylim',[0 Fbest(1,1)]),
        plot(Fbest(:),'r-')
        if j<=pso_para.itmax/2
            text(j,Fbest(end,1),['Fbest = ',
num2str(Fbest(end,1))],'HorizontalAlignment','Left','VerticalAlignme
nt','bottom','EdgeColor','blue','LineWidth',3);
        else
            text(j,Fbest(end,1),['Fbest = ',
num2str(Fbest(end,1))],'HorizontalAlignment','Right','VerticalAlignm
ent','bottom','EdgeColor','blue','LineWidth',3);
        end
        legend('Fbest');
        hold on
        %%%%%%%%%%%%%%%%%%%%%%%%%%%%%%%%%%%%%%%%%%%

        %%%%%%%%%%%%%%%%%  AXE-2  %%%%%%%%%%%%%%%%
        axes(handles.axes2);
        axis([0 D+1 0 max(Gen(:,7))+50])
        bar(Gen(:,7),'r')
        hold on
        bar(gbest,'w')
```

```
        drawnow
        %%%%%%%%%%%%%%%%%%%%%%%%%%%%%%%%%%%%%%%%%%%
    else
    end
end
if get(handles.disable,'Value')==1
    cla;
    ResultStr = [{['Total Generation Cost ','=','  ',
num2str(Fbest(end,1))]}];

    set(handles.Result_window, 'String', ResultStr);
end
%%%%%%%%%%%%%%%%%%  AXE-2  %%%%%%%%%%%%%%%%%
axes(handles.axes2);
axis([0 D+1 0 max(Gen(:,7))+50])
bar(Gen(:,7),'r')
hold on
bar(gbest(end,:),'w')
drawnow
%%%%%%%%%%%%%%%%%%%%%%%%%%%%%%%%%%%%%%%%%%%
set(handles.start,'Enable','on');
set(handles.pause,'String','PAUSE','Enable','off');
```

10. References

A. J. Wood and B. F. Wollenbergy (1984). Power Genration, Operation, and Control, *New York: Wiley*.

C. E. Lin and G. L. Viviani (1984). Hierarchical economic dispatch for piecewise quadratic cost functions, *IEEE Trans. Power App. System*, vol. PAS-103, no. 6, pp. 1170-1175.

D. A. Wiegmann, G. R. Essenberg, T. J. Overbye, and Y. Sun (2005). Human Factor Aspects of Power System Flow Animation, *IEEE Trans. Power Syst.*, vol. 20, no. 3, pp. 1233-1240.

D. A. Wiegmann, T. J. Overbye, S. M. Hoppe, G. R. Essenberg, and Y. Sun (2006). Human Factors Aspects of Three-Dimensional Visualization of Power System Information, *IEEE Power Eng. Soci. Genral Meeting*, pp. 7.

D. C. Walters and G. B. Sheble (1993). Genetic algorithm solution of economic dispatch with the valve point loading, *IEEE Trans. Power Syst.*, vol. 8, pp. 1325-1332.

H. T. Yang, P. C. Yang, and C. L. Huang (1996). Evolutionary programming based economic dispatch for units with nonsmooth fuel cost functions, *IEEE Trans. Power Syst.*, vol. 11, no. 1, pp. 112-118.

H. Yoshida, K. Kawata, Y. Fukuyama, S. Takayama, and Y. Nakanishi (2000). A particle swarm optimization for reactive power and voltage control considering voltage security assessment, *IEEE Trans. Power System*, vol. 15, pp. 1232-1239.

J. B. Park, K. S. Lee, J. R. Shin, and K. Y. Lee (2005). A particle swarm optimization for economic dispatch with nonsmooth cost functions, *IEEE Trans. Power Syst.*, vol. 20, no. 1, pp. 34-42.

J. H. Park, Y. S. Kim, I. K. Eom, and K. Y. Lee (1993). Economic load dispatch for piecewise quadratic cost function using Hopfield neural network, *IEEE Trans. Power Syst.*, vol. 8, pp. 1030-1038.

J. Kennedy and R. Eberhart (1995). Particle swarm optimization, *Proc. IEE Int. Conf. Neural Networks (ICNN'95)*, vol. IV, Perth, Australia, pp.1942-1948.

J. Kennedy and R. C. Eberhart (2001). Swarm Intelligence. *San Francisco, CA: Morgan Kaufmann.*

K. Y. Lee, A. Sode-Yome, and J. H. Park (1998). Adaptive Hopfield neural network for economic load dispatch, *IEEE Trans. Power Syst.*, vol. 13, pp. 519-526.

K. Y. Lee and M. A. El-Sharkawi, Eds. (2002). Modern Heuristic Optimization Techniques with Applications to Power Systems: *IEEE Power Engineering Society (02TP160).*

L. S. Coelho and V. C. Mariani (2006). Combining of chaotic differential evolution and quadratic programming for economic dispatch optimization with valve-point effect, *IEEE Trans. Power Syst.*, vol. 21, No. 2.

M. Clerc and J. Kennedy (2002). The particle swarm-expolsion, stability, and convergence in a multidimensional complex space, *IEEE Trans. Evol. Comput.*, vol. 6, no. 1, pp. 58-73.

N. Sinha, R. Chakrabarti, and P. K. Chattopadhyay (2003). Evolutionary programming techniques for economic load dispatch, *IEEE Trans. on Evolutionary Computations*, Vol. 7, No. 1, pp. 83-94.

T. A. A. Victoire and A. E. Jeyakumar (2004). Hybrid PSO-SQP for economic dispatch with valve-point effect, *Electric Power Syst. Research*, vol. 71, pp. 51-59.

T. A. A. Victoire and A. E. Jeyakumar (2005). Reserve constrained dynamic dispatch of units with valve-point effects, *IEEE Trans. Power Syst.*, vol. 20, No. 3, pp. 1273-1282.

T. J. Overbye, D. A. Wiegmann, A. M. Rich, and Y. Sun (2003). Human Factor Aspects of Power System Voltage Contour Visualizations, *IEEE Trans. Power Syst.*, vol. 18, no. 1, pp. 76-82.

W. M. Lin, F. S. Cheng, and M. T. Tasy (2002). An improved Tabu search for economic dispatch with multiple minima, *IEEE Trans. Power Syst.*, vol. 17, pp. 108-112.

Y. M. Park, J. R. Won, and J. B. Park (1998). A new approach to economic load dispatch based on improved evolutionary programming, *Eng. Intell. Syst. Elect. Eng. Commun.*, vol. 6, no. 2, pp. 103-110.

6

Decomposition Approach for Inverse Matrix Calculation

Krasimira Stoilova and Todor Stoilov
Institute of Information and Communication Technologies
Academy of Sciences
Bulgaria

1. Introduction

Frequently, numerical algorithms are based on sequentially solution of linear set of equation *Ax=b*, applying small influences of few components of matrix *A*, which changes to a new one A^*. Thus, new equation set is defined, with new matrix A^*, which has to be solved for the current numerical iteration. Instead of solving the new equation set, it is beneficial to evaluate a new inverse matrix A^{*-1}, having the evaluations for the previous inverse matrix A^{-1}. Many control algorithms, on-line decision making and optimization problems reside on the prompt evaluation of the inverse matrix A^{-1}, stated as a quadratic nonsingular, e.g. $A.A^{-1}=A^{-1}.A=I$, where *I* is identity matrix. Currently, for the evaluation of the inverse matrix A^{-1} three general types of *A* factorization are applied: LU factorization, QR – decomposition and SVD-decomposition to singular values of *A*.

LU – factorization. It results after the application of Gauss elimination to linear set of equations *Ax=b* to obtain a good computational form of *A* (Fausett, 1999). The factorization of *A* is obtained by multiplication of two triangular matrices, upper *U* and lower *L* triangular, related to the initial one by *LU=A* , or

$$\begin{vmatrix} l_{11} & 0 & 0 \\ l_{21} & l_{22} & 0 \\ l_{31} & l_{32} & l_{33} \end{vmatrix} . \begin{vmatrix} u_{11} & u_{12} & u_{13} \\ 0 & u_{22} & u_{23} \\ 0 & 0 & u_{33} \end{vmatrix} = \begin{vmatrix} a_{11} & a_{12} & a_{13} \\ a_{21} & a_{22} & a_{23} \\ a_{31} & a_{32} & a_{33} \end{vmatrix} .$$

The LU factorization can be applied for the solution of linear set of equations to evaluate the inverse matrix of *A*: A^{-1}. The evaluation of A^{-1} is performed on two steps, for given LU factorization of *A*, *A=LU (L,U* - given):

First: the matrix equation *LY=I* is solved. The first column of matrix *Y* is found from the linear equation system $LY(:,1) = |1 \quad 0 \quad ... \quad 0|^T$. The next columns of *Y* are calculated by solving this linear equation set with the next columns of matrix *I*. The solution of this set of equations is found by sequential substitution from top to down, because the matrix *L* is a lower triangular and there is no need to find the inverse L^{-1}.

Second: Using the solution matrix Y^* a new linear matrix equation system is solved $U.X=Y^*$. Because *U* is upper triangular, each column of *X* is calculated with the corresponding

column of Y^* by substitutions from bottom to top. Thus, no inverse matrix U^{-1} is calculated, which speeds up the calculations.
The solution $X=A^{-1}$ is the inverse matrix of the initial one A. Thus, the inverse matrix A^{-1} is found by LU factorization of A and twice solution of triangular linear matrix equation systems, applying substitution technique.
QR decomposition The QR decomposition of matrix A is defined by the equality $A=Q.R$, where R is upper triangular matrix and Q is orthogonal one, $Q^{-1}=Q^T$. Both matrices Q and R are real ones. As the inverse A^{-1} is needed, $A^{-1}=R^{-1}.Q^{-1}$. Following the orthogonal features of Q, it is necessary to evaluate only R^{-1}, which can be done from the linear matrix system $R.Y=I$. Because R is upper triangular matrix, the columns of the inverse matrix $Y=R^{-1}$ can be evaluated with corresponding columns of the identity matrix I by merely substitutions from bottom to down. Hence, the inverse matrix A^{-1} is found by QR factorization of A, sequential evaluation of R^{-1} by substitutions in linear upper triangular matrix system and finally by multiplication of R^{-1} and Q^T.
SVD – decomposition to singular values This decomposition is very powerful, because it allows to be solved system equations when A is singular, and the inverse A^{-1} does not exist in explicit way (Flannery, 1997). The SVD decomposition, applied to a rectangular MxN matrix A, represents the last like factorization of three matrices:

$$A=U.W.V^T,$$

where U is MxN orthogonal matrix, W is NxN diagonal matrix with nonnegative components (singular values) and V^T is a transpose NxN orthogonal matrix V or

$$U^TU=V^TV=I_{NxN}.$$

The SVD decomposition can always be performed, nevertheless of the singularity of the initial matrix A. If A is a square NxN matrix, hence all the matrices U, V and W are square with the same dimensions. Their inverse ones are easy to find because U and V are orthogonal and their inverses are equal to the transpose ones. W is a diagonal matrix and the corresponding inverse is also diagonal with components $1/w_j$, $j=1,N$. Hence, if matrix A is decomposed by SVD factorization, $A=U.W.V^T$, then the inverse one is $A^{-1}=V.[diag1/w_j].U^T$. The problem of the evaluation of the inverse A^{-1} appears if a singular value w_j exists, which tends to zero value. Hence, if matrix A is a singular one, the SVD decomposition easily estimates this case.
Hence, the peculiarities of LU, QR and SVD factorizations determine the computational efficiency of the evaluations for finding the inverse matrix A^{-1}. Particularly, the simplest method, from evaluation point of view, is LU factorization followed by QR decomposition and SVD factorization. All these methods do not use peculiarities, if matrix A^* slightly differs from the initial matrix A. The inverse of A^* has to be evaluated starting with its factorization and sequentially solution of linear matrix equation systems. Hence, it is worth to find methods for evaluation of the inverse of A^*, which differs from A in few components and A^{-1} is available. The new matrix A^* can contain several modified components a_{ij}. Hence, the utilization of components from the inverse A^{-1} for the evaluation of the new inverse matrix A^{*-1} can speed up considerably the numerical calculations in different control algorithms and decreases the evaluation efforts. Relations for utilization of components of A^{-1} for evaluation

of a corresponding inverse of a modified matrix $A^{*\,-1}$ are derived in (Strassen, 1969). The components of the inverse matrix can be evaluated analytically.
Finding the inverse matrix is related with a lot of calculations. Instead of direct finding an inverse matrix, it is worth to find analytical relations where lower dimensions inverse matrices components are available. Here analytical relations for inverse matrix calculation are derived and the corresponding MATLAB codes are illustrated.

2. Analytical relations among the components of inverse matrix

Initial optimization problem is given in the form

$$\min_x \left\{ \frac{1}{2} \begin{vmatrix} x_1^T & x_2^T \end{vmatrix} \begin{vmatrix} Q_1 & 0 \\ 0 & Q_2 \end{vmatrix} \begin{vmatrix} x_1 \\ x_2 \end{vmatrix} + \begin{vmatrix} R_1^T & R_2^T \end{vmatrix} \begin{vmatrix} x_1 \\ x_2 \end{vmatrix} \right\} \tag{1}$$

$$\begin{aligned} a_1 x_1 + a_2 x_2 &= d \\ b_1 x_1 \qquad &= C_1 \\ b_2 x_2 &= C_2 \end{aligned}$$

where the matrices dimensions are: $x_1 |_{n_1 x1}$; $Q_1 |_{n_1 x n_1}$; $R_1 |_{n_1 x1}$; $a_1 |_{m_0 x n_1}$; $d |_{m_0 x1}$

$$x_2 |_{n_2 x1} \;; Q_2 |_{n_2 x n_2} \;; R_2 |_{n_2 x1} \;; a_2 |_{m_0 x n_2} \;;\; b_1 |_{m_1 x n_1} \;;\; C_1 |_{m_1 x1} \;;\; b_2 |_{m_2 x n_2} \;;\; C_2 |_{m_2 x1} \;;$$

$$Q = \begin{vmatrix} Q_1 & 0 \\ 0 & Q_2 \end{vmatrix} ; R = \begin{vmatrix} R_1 \\ R_2 \end{vmatrix}$$

Peculiarity of problem (1) is that the connected condition $a_1 x_1 + a_2 x_2 = d$ distributes a common resource d while the subsystems work with own resources C_1 and C_2. For simplicity of the writing it can be put

$$A_1 |_{(m_0+m_1+m_2) x n_1} = \begin{vmatrix} a_1 \\ b_1 \\ 0 \end{vmatrix} \begin{matrix} m_0 x n_1 \\ m_1 x n_1 \\ m_2 x n_1 \end{matrix} ; A_2 |_{(m_0+m_1+m_2) x n_2} = \begin{vmatrix} a_2 \\ 0 \\ b_2 \end{vmatrix} \begin{matrix} m_0 x n_2 \\ m_1 x n_2 \\ m_2 x n_2 \end{matrix} ;$$

$$D = \begin{vmatrix} d \\ C_1 \\ C_2 \end{vmatrix}_{(m_0+m_1+m_2) x1} ; A = \begin{vmatrix} A_1 & A_2 \end{vmatrix} |_{(m_0+m_1+m_2) x (n_1 x n_2)} . \tag{2}$$

2.1 Decomposition of the initial problem by goal coordination

The initial problem (1) can be solved by two manners using hierarchical approach according to the hierarchical multilevel systems (Mesarovich et al, 1973; Stoilov & Stoilova, 1999): by goal coordination and by predictive one. Taking into account the substitutions

$$Q = \begin{vmatrix} Q_1 & 0 \\ 0 & Q_2 \end{vmatrix} ; R = \begin{vmatrix} R_1 \\ R_2 \end{vmatrix} ; A = \begin{vmatrix} A_1 & A_2 \end{vmatrix} ; x = \begin{vmatrix} x_1 \\ x_2 \end{vmatrix} , \tag{3}$$

the solution of (1) can be found in analytical form (Stoilova, 2010) :

$$x^{opt} = -Q^{-1}\left[R - A^T(AQ^{-1}A^T)^{-1}(AQ^{-1}R + D)\right] \tag{4}$$

or

$$x_1^{opt} = -Q_1^{-1}R_1 + Q_1^{-1}A_1^T\left(A_1Q_1^{-1}A_1^T + A_2Q_2^{-1}A_2^T\right)^{-1}\left(A_1Q_1^{-1}R_1 + A_2Q_2^{-1}R_2 + D\right) \tag{5}$$

$$x_2^{opt} = -Q_2^{-1}R_2 + Q_2^{-1}A_2^T\left(A_1Q_1^{-1}A_1^T + A_2Q_2^{-1}A_2^T\right)^{-1}\left(A_1Q_1^{-1}R_1 + A_2Q_2^{-1}R_2 + D\right).$$

It is necessary to be known the matrices A_1, A_2, Q_1, Q_2, R_1, R_2 for evaluating the solutions (5)
Determination of $AQ^{-1}A^T$
Applying (3) it is obtained

$$AQ^{-1}A^T = \begin{vmatrix} A_1 & A_2 \end{vmatrix} \begin{vmatrix} Q_1^{-1} & 0 \\ 0 & Q_2^{-1} \end{vmatrix} \begin{vmatrix} A_1^T \\ A_2^T \end{vmatrix} = A_1Q_1^{-1}A_1^T + A_2Q_2^{-1}A_2^T . \tag{6}$$

Using (2) it follows

$$A_1Q_1^{-1}A_1^T = \begin{vmatrix} a_1Q_1^{-1}a_1^T{}_{m_0xm_0} & a_1Q_1^{-1}b_1^T{}_{m_0xm_1} & 0_{m_0xm_2} \\ b_1Q_1^{-1}a_1^T{}_{m_1xm_0} & b_1Q_1^{-1}b_1^T{}_{m_1xm_1} & 0_{m_1xm_2} \\ 0_{m_2xm_0} & 0_{m_2xm_1} & 0_{m_2xm_2} \end{vmatrix}, \tag{7}$$

$$A_2Q_2^{-1}A_2^T = \begin{vmatrix} a_2Q_2^{-1}a_2^T{}_{m_0xm_0} & 0_{m_0xm_1} & a_2Q_2^{-1}b_2^T{}_{m_0xm_2} \\ 0_{m_1xm_0} & 0_{m_1xm_1} & 0_{m_1xm_2} \\ b_2Q_2^{-1}a_2^T{}_{m_2xm_0} & 0_{m_2xm_1} & b_2Q_2^{-1}b_2^T{}_{m_2xm_2} \end{vmatrix}. \tag{8}$$

After substitution of (7) and (8) in (6) $AQ^{-1}A^T$ and $(AQ^{-1}A^T)^{-1}$ can be determined

$$AQ^{-1}A^T = A_1Q_1^{-1}A_1^T + A_2Q_2^{-1}A_2^T = \begin{vmatrix} a_1Q_1^{-1}a_1^T + a_2Q_2^{-1}a_2^T{}_{m_0xm_0} & a_1Q_1^{-1}b_1^T{}_{m_0xm_1} & a_2Q_2^{-1}b_2^T{}_{m_0xm_2} \\ b_1Q_1^{-1}a_1^T{}_{m_1xm_0} & b_1Q_1^{-1}b_1^T{}_{m_1xm_1} & 0_{m_1xm_2} \\ b_2Q_2^{-1}a_2^T{}_{m_2xm_0} & 0_{m_2xm_1} & b_2Q_2^{-1}b_2^T{}_{m_2xm_2} \end{vmatrix} \tag{9}$$

$$(AQ^{-1}A^T)^{-1} = (A_1Q_1^{-1}A_1^T + A_2Q_2^{-1}A_2^T)^{-1} =$$
$$= \begin{vmatrix} a_1Q_1^{-1}a_1^T + a_2Q_2^{-1}a_2^T{}_{m_0xm_0} & a_1Q_1^{-1}b_1^T{}_{m_0xm_1} & a_2Q_2^{-1}b_2^T{}_{m_0xm_2} \\ b_1Q_1^{-1}a_1^T{}_{m_1xm_0} & b_1Q_1^{-1}b_1^T{}_{m_1xm_1} & 0_{m_1xm_2} \\ b_2Q_2^{-1}a_2^T{}_{m_2xm_0} & 0_{m_2xm_1} & b_2Q_2^{-1}b_2^T{}_{m_2xm_2} \end{vmatrix}^{-1}. \tag{10}$$

The manner of definition of matrix $AQ^{-1}A^T$ shows that it is a symmetric one.

Determination of $AQ^{-1}R+D$

Using (2) and (3) it follows

$$AQ^{-1}R+D=\begin{vmatrix} a_1Q_1^{-1}R_1+a_2Q_2^{-1}R_2+d \\ b_1Q_1^{-1}R_1+C_1 \\ b_2Q_2^{-1}R_2+C_2 \end{vmatrix} \tag{11}$$

Determination of $(AQ^{-1}A^T)^{-1}(AQ^{-1}R+D)$

Using (10) and (11), it is obtained

$$(AQ^{-1}A^T)^{-1}(AQ^{-1}R+D)=\begin{vmatrix} a_1Q_1^{-1}a_1^T+a_2Q_2^{-1}a_{2\,m_0xm_0}^T & a_1Q_1^{-1}b_{1\,m_0xm_1}^T & a_2Q_2^{-1}b_{2\,m_0xm_2}^T \\ b_1Q_1^{-1}a_{1\,m_1xm_0}^T & b_1Q_1^{-1}b_{1\,m_1xm_1}^T & 0_{m_1xm_2} \\ b_2Q_2^{-1}a_{2\,m_2xm_0}^T & 0_{m_2xm_1} & b_2Q_2^{-1}b_{2\,m_2xm_2}^T \end{vmatrix}^{-1} \begin{vmatrix} a_1Q_1^{-1}R_1+a_2Q_2^{-1}R_2+d \\ b_1Q_1^{-1}R_1+C_1 \\ b_2Q_2^{-1}R_2+C_2 \end{vmatrix}$$

$$(AQ^{-1}A^T)^{-1}(AQ^{-1}R+D)=\begin{vmatrix} \alpha_{11m_0xm_0} & \alpha_{12m_0xm_1} & \alpha_{13m_0xm_2} \\ \alpha_{21m_1xm_0} & \alpha_{22m_1xm_1} & \alpha_{23m_1xm_2} \\ \alpha_{31m_2xm_0} & \alpha_{32m_2xm_1} & \alpha_{33m_2xm_2} \end{vmatrix} \begin{vmatrix} a_1Q_1^{-1}R_1+a_2Q_2^{-1}R_2+d \\ b_1Q_1^{-1}R_1+C_1 \\ b_2Q_2^{-1}R_2+C_2 \end{vmatrix}$$

where

$$(AQ^{-1}A^T)^{-1}=\alpha=\begin{vmatrix} \alpha_{11} & \alpha_{12} & \alpha_{13} \\ \alpha_{21} & \alpha_{22} & \alpha_{23} \\ \alpha_{31} & \alpha_{32} & \alpha_{33} \end{vmatrix}_{(m_0+m_1+m_2)x(m_0+m_1+m_2)} \tag{12}$$

Taking into account the structure of matrix $(AQ^{-1}A^T)^{-1}$, then $\alpha_{23}=0$, $\alpha_{32}=0$. The manner of definition of the inverce matrix α shows that it is a symmetric one. Consequently, the term $(AQ^{-1}A^T)^{-1}(AQ^{-1}R+D)$ is

$$(AQ^{-1}A^T)^{-1}(AQ^{-1}R+D)=\begin{vmatrix} \alpha_{11}(a_1Q_1^{-1}R_1+a_2Q_2^{-1}R_2+d)+\alpha_{12}(b_1Q_1^{-1}R_1+C)_1+\alpha_{13}(b_2Q_2^{-1}R_2+C_2) \\ \alpha_{21}(a_1Q_1^{-1}R_1+a_2Q_2^{-1}R_2+d)+\alpha_{22}(b_1Q_1^{-1}R_1+C_1)+\underbrace{\alpha_{23}(b_2Q_2^{-1}R_2+C_2)}_{0} \\ \alpha_{31}(a_1Q_1^{-1}R_1+a_2Q_2^{-1}R_2+d)+\underbrace{\alpha_{32}(b_1Q_1^{-1}R_1+C_1)}_{0}+\alpha_{33}(b_2Q_2^{-1}R_2+C_2) \end{vmatrix} \begin{matrix} m_0x1 \\ m_1x1 \\ m_2x1 \end{matrix} \tag{13}$$

Determination of $A^T(AQ^{-1}A^T)^{-1}(AQ^{-1}R+D)$

After a substitution of (2) in (13) it follows

$$\begin{vmatrix} a^T_{1\,n_1xm_0} & b^T_{1\,m_1xm_0} & 0_{n_1xm_2} \\ a^T_{2\,n_2xm_0} & 0_{n_2xm_1} & b^T_{2\,n_2xm_2} \end{vmatrix} (AQ^{-1}A^T)^{-1}(AQ^{-1}R+D) =$$

$$= \begin{vmatrix} \begin{vmatrix} a_1^T & b_1^T \end{vmatrix} \begin{vmatrix} \underbrace{\alpha_{11}}_{m_0xm_0} \\ \underbrace{\alpha_{21}}_{m_1xm_0} \end{vmatrix} \underbrace{(a_1Q_1^{-1}R_1 + a_2Q_2^{-1}R_2 + d)}_{m_0x1} + \begin{vmatrix} a_1^T & b_1^T \end{vmatrix} \begin{vmatrix} \underbrace{\alpha_{12}}_{m_0xm_1} \\ \underbrace{\alpha_{22}}_{m_1xm_1} \end{vmatrix} \underbrace{(b_1Q_1^{-1}R_1 + C_1)}_{m_1x1} + \begin{vmatrix} a_1^T & b_1^T \end{vmatrix} \begin{vmatrix} \underbrace{\alpha_{13}}_{m_0xm_2} \\ \underbrace{0}_{m_1xm_2} \end{vmatrix} \underbrace{(b_2Q_2^{-1}R_2 + C_2)}_{m_2x1} \\ \begin{vmatrix} a_2^T & b_2^T \end{vmatrix} \begin{vmatrix} \underbrace{\alpha_{11}}_{m_0xm_0} \\ \underbrace{\alpha_{31}}_{m_2xm_0} \end{vmatrix} \underbrace{(a_1Q_1^{-1}R_1 + a_2Q_2^{-1}R_2 + d)}_{m_0x1} + \begin{vmatrix} a_2^T & b_2^T \end{vmatrix} \begin{vmatrix} \underbrace{\alpha_{12}}_{m_0xm_1} \\ \underbrace{0}_{m_1xm_2} \end{vmatrix} \underbrace{(b_1Q_1^{-1}R_1 + C_1)}_{m_1x1} + \begin{vmatrix} a_2^T & b_2^T \end{vmatrix} \begin{vmatrix} \underbrace{\alpha_{13}}_{m_0xm_2} \\ \underbrace{\alpha_{33}}_{m_2xm_2} \end{vmatrix} \underbrace{(b_2Q_2^{-1}R_2 + C_2)}_{m_2x1} \end{vmatrix}$$

Consequently, the term $A^T(AQ^{-1}A^T)^{-1}(AQ^{-1}R+D)$ becomes

$$A^T(AQ^{-1}A^T)^{-1}(AQ^{-1}R+D) = \begin{bmatrix} \begin{bmatrix} \begin{vmatrix} a_1^T & b_1^T \end{vmatrix} \begin{vmatrix} \alpha_{11} & \alpha_{12} & \alpha_{13} \\ \alpha_{21} & \alpha_{22} & 0 \end{vmatrix} \begin{vmatrix} a_1Q_1^{-1}R_1 + a_2Q_2^{-1}R_2 + d \\ b_1Q_1^{-1}R_1 + C_1 \\ b_2Q_2^{-1}R_2 + C_2 \end{vmatrix} \end{bmatrix} \\ \begin{bmatrix} \begin{vmatrix} a_2^T & b_2^T \end{vmatrix} \begin{vmatrix} \alpha_{11} & \alpha_{12} & \alpha_{13} \\ \alpha_{31} & 0 & \alpha_{33} \end{vmatrix} \begin{vmatrix} a_1Q_1^{-1}R_1 + a_2Q_2^{-1}R_2 + d \\ b_1Q_1^{-1}R_1 + C_1 \\ b_2Q_2^{-1}R_2 + C_2 \end{vmatrix} \end{bmatrix} \end{bmatrix} \quad (14)$$

After putting (3) and (14) in (5) the analytical solutions of the initial problem (1) are

$$x_1^{opt} = -Q_1^{-1}R_1 + Q_1^{-1} \begin{bmatrix} \begin{vmatrix} a_1^T & b_1^T \end{vmatrix} \begin{vmatrix} \alpha_{11} & \alpha_{12} & \alpha_{13} \\ \alpha_{21} & \alpha_{22} & 0 \end{vmatrix} \begin{vmatrix} a_1Q_1^{-1}R_1 + a_2Q_2^{-1}R_2 + d \\ b_1Q_1^{-1}R_1 + C_1 \\ b_2Q_2^{-1}R_2 + C_2 \end{vmatrix} \end{bmatrix} \quad (15)$$

$$x_2^{opt} = -Q_2^{-1}R_2 + Q_2^{-1} \begin{bmatrix} \begin{vmatrix} a_2^T & b_2^T \end{vmatrix} \begin{vmatrix} \alpha_{11} & \alpha_{12} & \alpha_{13} \\ \alpha_{31} & 0 & \alpha_{33} \end{vmatrix} \begin{vmatrix} a_1Q_1^{-1}R_1 + a_2Q_2^{-1}R_2 + d \\ b_1Q_1^{-1}R_1 + C_1 \\ b_2Q_2^{-1}R_2 + C_2 \end{vmatrix} \end{bmatrix}$$

Analytical relations (15) are a result of applying a goal coordination for solving the initial problem (1). They are useful only if the components α_{ij} of the inverse matrix (12) are known. However, if α_{ij} are not known (the usual case) relations (15) can not be applied.

2.2 Decomposition of the initial problem by predictive coordination

According to the hierarchical approach, the subsystems work independently. The idea of the predictive coordination is that the coordinator influences to each subsystem by independent impacts instead of common impact in goal coordination. For the initial problem (1) decomposition by goal coordination can not be fully accomplished because of the connected relation $a_1x_1 + a_2x_2 = d$. Applying predictive coordination, the connected restriction can be decomposed to:

$$a_1x_1 = y_1 \,;\, a_2x_2 = y_2 \tag{16}$$

observing the condition for resource limitation

$$y_1 + y_2 = d \tag{17}$$

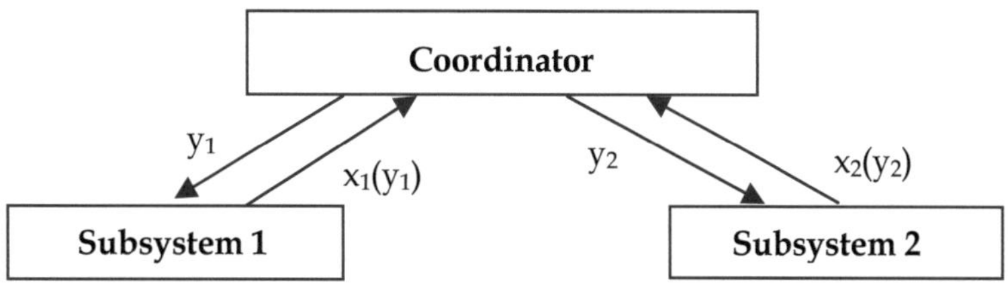

Fig. 1. Hierarchical approach for solving (1)

Applying (16), the initial optimization problem (1) is decomposed to two optimization subproblems with lower dimensions than the initial one:

$$\min\left\{\frac{1}{2}x_1^TQ_1x_1 + R_1^Tx_1\right\} \quad \min\left\{\frac{1}{2}x_2^TQ_2x_2 + R_2^Tx_2\right\} \tag{18}$$

$$\underbrace{a_1}_{m_0xn_1}\ x_1 = \underbrace{y_1}_{m_0x1} \quad \underbrace{a_2}_{m_0xn_2}\ x_2 = \underbrace{y_2}_{m_0x1}$$

$$\underbrace{b_1}_{m_1xn_1}\ x_1 = \underbrace{C_1}_{m_1x1} \;;\; \underbrace{b_2}_{m_2xn_2}\ x_2 = \underbrace{C_2}_{m_2x1}$$

where

$$A_1\,|_{(m_0+m_1+m_2)xn_1} = \begin{vmatrix} a_1 \\ b_1 \\ 0 \end{vmatrix}\begin{matrix} m_0xn_1 \\ m_1xn_1 \\ m_2xn_1 \end{matrix} \;;\; A_2\,|_{(m_0+m_1+m_2)xn_2} = \begin{vmatrix} a_2 \\ 0 \\ b_2 \end{vmatrix}\begin{matrix} m_0xn_2 \\ m_1xn_2 \\ m_2xn_2 \end{matrix} \;;\; \overset{=}{y}_1 = \begin{vmatrix} d_1 \\ C_1 \\ 0 \end{vmatrix}\begin{matrix} m_0x1 \\ m_1x1 \\ m_2x1 \end{matrix} \;;\; \overset{=}{y}_2 = \begin{vmatrix} d_2 \\ 0 \\ C_2 \end{vmatrix}\begin{matrix} m_0x1 \\ m_1x1 \\ m_2x1 \end{matrix}$$

and it can be realized

$$\overset{=}{y}_1 + \overset{=}{y}_2 = D \text{ or } y_1 + y_2 = d\ .$$

The analytical solution of the first subproblem (18), according to (4), is

$$x_1^{opt} = -Q_1^{-1}\left[R_1 - A_1^T(A_1Q_1^{-1}A_1^T)^{-1}(A_1Q_1^{-1}R_1 + D)\right].$$

The analysis of matrix A_1 shows that it has zero rows. Respectively, the square matrix

$$A_1 Q_1^{-1} A_1^T = \begin{vmatrix} a_1 \\ b_1 \\ 0 \end{vmatrix}_{(m+l_1+l_2)xn_1} Q_1 \,|_{n_1 x n_1} \begin{vmatrix} a_1^T & b_1^T & 0 \end{vmatrix}_{n_1 x(m+l_1+l_2)} = \begin{vmatrix} a_1 Q_1^{-1} a_1^T & a_1 Q_1^{-1} b_1^T & 0 \\ b_1 Q_1^{-1} a_1^T & b_1 Q_1^{-1} b_1^T & 0 \\ 0 & 0 & 0 \end{vmatrix}$$

has zero rows and columns, which means that the inverse matrix $(AQ^{-1}A^T)^{-1}$ does not exist. However, in the solution of problem (1) takes part a sum of the matrices $(A_i Q_i^{-1} A_i^T)^{-1}$, so that the sum matrix $(AQ^{-1}A^T)^{-1}$ has a full rank. This matrix has a high dimension and for it can not be used the specific structure $A_i Q_i^{-1} A_i^T$. To use the less rank of matrices $A_i Q_i^{-1} A_i^T$, the definition of subproblems (18) has to be done by rejecting the zero rows in matrices A_1 and A_2.

Respectively, the subproblems are obtained of the initial problem (1) by additional modification of the admissible areas, determined by the matrices A_1 and A_2 instead of direct decomposition. In that manner the modified subproblems will present only the corresponding meaning components as follows:

$$A_1 = \begin{vmatrix} a_1 \\ b_1 \\ 0 \end{vmatrix} \Rightarrow \bar{A}_1 = \begin{vmatrix} a_1 \\ b_1 \end{vmatrix};\ A_2 = \begin{vmatrix} a_2 \\ 0 \\ b_2 \end{vmatrix} \Rightarrow \bar{A}_2 = \begin{vmatrix} a_2 \\ b_2 \end{vmatrix};\ \bar{\bar{y}}_1 = \begin{vmatrix} y_1 \\ C_1 \\ 0 \end{vmatrix} \Rightarrow \bar{y}_1 = \begin{vmatrix} y_1 \\ C_1 \end{vmatrix};\ \bar{\bar{y}}_2 = \begin{vmatrix} y_2 \\ 0 \\ C_2 \end{vmatrix} \Rightarrow \bar{y}_2 = \begin{vmatrix} y_2 \\ C_2 \end{vmatrix}.$$

The modified subproblems (19) have lower dimension in comparison with (18), obtained by direct decomposition

$$\min\left\{\frac{1}{2}x_1^T Q_1 x_1 + R_1^T x_1\right\};\min\left\{\frac{1}{2}x_2^T Q_2 x_2 + R_2^T x_2\right\} \tag{19}$$

$$\bar{A}_1 x_1 = \bar{y}_1\ ;\ \bar{A}_2 x_2 = \bar{y}_2$$

$$\bar{A}_1 = \begin{vmatrix} a_1 \\ b_1 \end{vmatrix}_{(m_0+m_1)xn_1};\ \bar{A}_2 = \begin{vmatrix} a_2 \\ b_2 \end{vmatrix}_{(m_0+m_2)xn_2}$$

$$\bar{y}_1 = \begin{vmatrix} y_1 \\ C_1 \end{vmatrix}_{(m_0+m_1)x1};\ \bar{y}_2 = \begin{vmatrix} y_2 \\ C_2 \end{vmatrix}_{(m_0+m_2)x1}.$$

The solutions of (18), obtained in analytical forms using (4), are

$$x_i^{opt} = -Q_i^{-1}\left[R_i - \bar{A}_i^T(\bar{A}_i Q_i^{-1}\bar{A}_i^T)^{-1}(\bar{A}_i Q_i^{-1} R_i + \bar{y}_i)\right] \quad i = 1,2.$$

After substitution of matrices $\bar{A}_i$ with the corresponding matrix components, it follows

$$x_1(y_1) = -Q_1^{-1}\left[R_1 - \begin{vmatrix} a_1^T & b_1^T \end{vmatrix} \begin{vmatrix} a_1 Q_1^{-1} a_1^T & a_1 Q_1^{-1} b_1^T \\ b_1 Q_1^{-1} b_1^T & b_1 Q_1^{-1} a_1^T \end{vmatrix}^{-1} \begin{vmatrix} a_1 Q_1^{-1} R_1 + y_1 \\ b_1 Q_1^{-1} R_1 + C_1 \end{vmatrix}\right].$$

It is put

$$\begin{vmatrix} \underbrace{a_1Q_1^{-1}a_1^T}_{m_0xm_0} & \underbrace{a_1Q_1^{-1}b_1^T}_{m_0xm_1} \\ \underbrace{b_1Q_1^{-1}a_1^T}_{m_1xm_0} & \underbrace{b_1Q_1^{-1}b_1^T}_{m_1xm_1} \end{vmatrix}^{-1} = \beta = \begin{vmatrix} \underbrace{\beta_{11}}_{m_0xm_0} & \underbrace{\beta_{12}}_{m_0xm_1} \\ \underbrace{\beta_{21}}_{m_1xm_0} & \underbrace{\beta_{22}}_{m_1xm_1} \end{vmatrix} . \qquad (20)$$

where the matrix β is a symmetric one by definition. Consequently, $x_1(y_1)$ can be developed to:

$$x_1(y_1) = -Q_1^{-1}R_1 + Q_1^{-1}\left[\begin{vmatrix} a_1^T & b_1^T \end{vmatrix} \begin{vmatrix} \beta_{11} & \beta_{12} \\ \beta_{21} & \beta_{22} \end{vmatrix} \begin{vmatrix} a_1Q_1^{-1}R_1 + y_1 \\ b_1Q_1^{-1}R_1 + C_1 \end{vmatrix} \right] . \qquad (21)$$

Analogically, $x_2(y_2)$ is

$$x_2(y_2) = -Q_2^{-1}R_2 + Q_2^{-1}\left[\begin{vmatrix} a_2^T & b_2^T \end{vmatrix} \begin{vmatrix} \gamma_{11} & \gamma_{12} \\ \gamma_{21} & \gamma_{22} \end{vmatrix} \begin{vmatrix} a_2Q_2^{-1}R_2 + y_2 \\ a_2Q_2^{-1}R_2 + C_2 \end{vmatrix} \right] . \qquad (22)$$

where matrix γ is a symmetric one by definition, $\gamma_{12} = \gamma_{21}^T$

$$\gamma = \begin{vmatrix} \underbrace{\gamma_{11}}_{m_0xm_0} & \underbrace{\gamma_{12}}_{m_0xm_2} \\ \underbrace{\gamma_{21}}_{m_2xm_0} & \underbrace{\gamma_{22}}_{m_2xm_2} \end{vmatrix} = \begin{vmatrix} \underbrace{a_2Q_2^{-1}a_2^T}_{m_0xm_0} & \underbrace{a_2Q_2^{-1}b_2^T}_{m_0xm_2} \\ \underbrace{b_2Q_1^{-1}a_2^T}_{m_2xm_0} & \underbrace{b_2Q_2^{-1}b_2^T}_{m_2xm_2} \end{vmatrix}^{-1} .$$

If the optimal resources y_1^{opt}, y_2^{opt} are known, after their substitution in (21)-(22), the solution of the initial problem (1) can be obtained

$$x_1^{opt} = x_1(y_1^{opt}), \qquad x_2^{opt} = x_2(y_2^{opt}) .$$

The determination of the optimal resources y_1^{opt}, y_2^{opt} is done by solution of the coordination problem.

2.2.1 Determination of the coordination problem

After substitution of relations $x_1(y_1)$ and $x_2(y_2)$ in the initial problem (1) and taking into account the resource constraint (17), the coordination problem becomes

$$\min_{y \in S_y} w(y) = \min\left\{ \frac{1}{2}x_1^T(y_1)Q_1x_1(y_1) + R_1^Tx_1(y_1) + \frac{1}{2}x_2^T(y_2)Q_2x_2(y_2) + R_2^Tx_2(y_2) \right\}$$

$$S_y \equiv y_1 + y_2 = d \ ,$$

or

$$\min\{w(y) = w_1(y_1) + w_2(y_2)\} \tag{23}$$

$$y_1 + y_2 = d$$

where

$$w_i(y_i) = \frac{1}{2} x_i^T (y_i) Q_i x_i(y_i) + R_i^T x_i(y_i), \quad i = 1,2\,.$$

As $x_i(y_i)$ is inexplicit function, it can be approximated in Mac-Laurin series at point y_i=0

$$x_1(y_1)_{n_1 x1} = x_{10 n_1 x1} + X_{1 n_1 x m_0} y_{1 m_0 x1} \quad (24)$$

where

$$x_{i0}^1 = -Q_1^{-1} R_1 + Q_1^{-1} \begin{vmatrix} a_1^T & b_1^T \end{vmatrix} \begin{vmatrix} \beta_{11} & \beta_{12} \\ \beta_{21} & \beta_{22} \end{vmatrix} \begin{vmatrix} a_1 Q_1^{-1} R_1 \\ b_1 Q_1^{-1} R_1 + C_1 \end{vmatrix} \tag{25}$$

$$X_{1 n_1 x m_0} = Q_1^{-1}{}_{n_1 x n_1} \begin{vmatrix} \underbrace{a_1^T}_{n_1 x m_0} & \underbrace{b_1^T}_{n_1 x m_1} \end{vmatrix} \begin{vmatrix} \beta_{11 m_0 x m_0} \\ \beta_{21 m_1 x m_0} \end{vmatrix} \tag{26}$$

where x_{10} is solution of subproblem (19) having zero resource, y_1=0 .
Analogically, for the second subproblem is valid:

$$x_2(y_2)_{n_2 x1} = x_{20 n_2 x1} + X_{2 n_2 x m_0} y_{2 m_0 x1} \tag{27}$$

where

$$x_{20} = -Q_2^{-1} R_2 + Q_2^{-1} \begin{vmatrix} a_2^T & b_2^T \end{vmatrix} \begin{vmatrix} \gamma_{11} & \gamma_{12} \\ \gamma_{21} & \gamma_{22} \end{vmatrix} \begin{vmatrix} a_2 Q_2^{-1} R_2 \\ b_2 Q_2^{-1} R_2 + C_2 \end{vmatrix} \tag{28}$$

$$X_{2 n_2 x m_0} = Q_2^{-1}{}_{n_2 x n_2} \begin{vmatrix} \underbrace{a_2^T}_{n_2 x m_0} & \underbrace{b_2^T}_{n_2 x m_2} \end{vmatrix} \begin{vmatrix} \gamma_{11 m_0 x m_0} \\ \gamma_{21 m_2 x m_0} \end{vmatrix} \tag{29}$$

After substitution of (24) in $w_1(y_1)$ of (23), it follows:

$$w_1(y_1) = \frac{1}{2}(x_{10}^T + y_1^T X_1^T) Q_1 (x_{10} + X_1 y_1) + R_1^T (x_{10} + X_1 y_1) =$$

$$= \frac{1}{2} x_{10}^T Q_1 x_{10} + \frac{1}{2} x_{10}^T Q_1 X_1 y_1 + \frac{1}{2} y_1^T X_1^T Q_1 x_{10} + \frac{1}{2} y_1^T X_1^T Q_1 X_1 y_1 + R_1^T x_{10} + R_1^T X_1 y_1$$

The components $x_{10}^T Q_1 X_1 y_1$ and $y_1^T X_1^T Q_1 x_{10}$ are equal, as they are transposed of corresponding equal relations. Consequently, the coordination problem becomes

$$w_1(y_1) \equiv \frac{1}{2} y_1^T X_1^T Q_1 X_1 y_1 + y_1^T X_1^T Q_1 x_{10} + y_1^T X_1^T R_1 \tag{30}$$

or

$$w_1(y_1) \equiv \frac{1}{2} y_1^T q_1 y_1 + y_1^T r_1$$

where

$$q_1 = X_1^T Q_1 X_1 \,;\, r_1 = X_1^T Q_1 x_{10} + X_1^T R_1$$

Analogically, for the second subproblem, it follows:

$$w_2(y_2) \equiv \frac{1}{2} y_2^T X_2^T Q_2 X_2 y_2 + y_2^T X_2^T Q_2 x_{20} + y_2^T X_2^T R_2 \tag{31}$$

or

$$w_2(y_2) \equiv \frac{1}{2} y_2^T q_2 y_2 + y_2^T r_2$$

where

$$q_2 = X_2^T Q_2 X_2 \,;\, r_2 = X_2^T Q_2 x_{20} + X_2^T R_2 \,.$$

Functions $w_i(y_i)$ has to be presented in terms of the initial problem (1) by the following transformations.

Development of q_1

Relation q_1 is presented like

$$q_1 = X_1^T Q_1 X_1 = \begin{vmatrix} \beta_{11}^T & \beta_{21}^T \end{vmatrix} \begin{vmatrix} a_1 \\ b_1 \end{vmatrix} Q_1^{-1} \underbrace{Q_1 Q_1^{-1}}_{I} \begin{vmatrix} a_1^T & b_1^T \end{vmatrix} \begin{vmatrix} \beta_{11} \\ \beta_{21} \end{vmatrix} = \begin{vmatrix} \beta_{11}^T & \beta_{21}^T \end{vmatrix} \begin{vmatrix} a_1 \\ b_1 \end{vmatrix} Q_1^{-1} \begin{vmatrix} a_1^T & b_1^T \end{vmatrix} \begin{vmatrix} \beta_{11} \\ \beta_{21} \end{vmatrix}$$

or

$$q_1 = \begin{vmatrix} \beta_{11}^T & \beta_{21}^T \end{vmatrix} \begin{vmatrix} a_1 Q_1^{-1} a_1^T & a_1 Q_1^{-1} b_1^T \\ b_1 Q_1^{-1} a_1^T & b_1 Q_1^{-1} b_1^T \end{vmatrix} \begin{vmatrix} \beta_{11} \\ \beta_{21} \end{vmatrix} = \begin{vmatrix} \beta_{11}^T & \beta_{21}^T \end{vmatrix} \begin{vmatrix} a_1 Q_1^{-1} a_1^T \beta_{11} + a_1 Q_1^{-1} b_1^T \beta_{21} \\ b_1 Q_1^{-1} a_1^T \beta_{11} + b_1 Q_1^{-1} b_1^T \beta_{21} \end{vmatrix} . \tag{32}$$

According to the manner of definition of matrix β from (20) the following matrix equality is performed

$$\begin{vmatrix} \underbrace{a_1 Q_1^{-1} a_1^T}_{m_0 x m_0} & \underbrace{a_1 Q_1^{-1} b_1^T}_{m_0 x m_1} \\ \underbrace{b_1 Q_1^{-1} a_1^T}_{m_1 x m_0} & \underbrace{b_1 Q_1^{-1} b_1^T}_{m_1 x m_1} \end{vmatrix} \begin{vmatrix} \underbrace{\beta_{11}}_{m_0 x m_0} & \underbrace{\beta_{12}}_{m_0 x m_1} \\ \underbrace{\beta_{21}}_{m_1 x m_0} & \underbrace{\beta_{22}}_{m_1 x m_1} \end{vmatrix}^{-1} = \begin{vmatrix} \underbrace{I}_{m_0 x m_0} & \underbrace{0}_{m_0 x m_1} \\ \underbrace{0}_{m_1 x m_0} & \underbrace{I}_{m_1 x m_1} \end{vmatrix} \tag{33}$$

i.e. an unit matrix is obtained. Consequently, the following equations are performed

$$a_1Q_1^{-1}a_1^T\beta_{11} + a_1Q_1^{-1}b_1^T\beta_{21} = I_{m_0xm_0} \tag{34}$$

$$b_1Q_1^{-1}a_1^T\beta_{11} + b_1Q_1^{-1}b_1^T\beta_{21} = 0_{m_1xm_0} .$$

After substitution of (34) in (32) it is obtained

$$q_1 = \begin{vmatrix} \underbrace{\beta_{11}^T}_{m_0xm_0} & \underbrace{\beta_{21}^T}_{m_0xm_1} \end{vmatrix} \begin{vmatrix} \underbrace{I}_{m_0xm_0} \\ \underbrace{0}_{m_1xm_0} \end{vmatrix} = \underbrace{\beta_{11}}_{m_0xm_0}$$

as β_{11} is a symmetric and square or

$$q_1 = \beta_{11} . \tag{35}$$

Analogically,

$$q_2 = \gamma_{11} \tag{36}$$

Development of r_i.
In a similar way the relations of r_i are developed to the expressions

$$r_1 = X_1^T(Q_1x_{10} + R_1) = \begin{vmatrix} \beta_{11}^T & \beta_{21}^T \end{vmatrix} \begin{vmatrix} a_1Q_1^{-1}R_1 \\ b_1Q_1^{-1}R_1 + C_1 \end{vmatrix} \tag{37}$$

$$r_2 = X_2^T(Q_2x_{20} + R_2) = \begin{vmatrix} \gamma_{11}^T & \gamma_{21}^T \end{vmatrix} \begin{vmatrix} a_2Q_2^{-1}R_2 \\ b_2Q_2^{-1}R_2 + C_2 \end{vmatrix} .$$

The coordination problem becomes

$$\min\left\{ w_1(y_1) + w_2(y_2) = \frac{1}{2}y_1^Tq_1y_1 + r_1^Ty_1 + \frac{1}{2}y_2^Tq_2y_2 + r_2^Ty_2 \right\} \tag{38}$$

$$y_1 + y_2 = d \quad \Rightarrow \quad \begin{vmatrix} I_{m_0xm_0} & I_{m_0xm_0} \end{vmatrix}_{m_0x2m_0} ; y = \begin{vmatrix} y_1 \\ y_2 \end{vmatrix} ; \; q = \begin{vmatrix} q_1 & 0 \\ 0 & q_2 \end{vmatrix} \; r = \begin{vmatrix} r_1 \\ r_2 \end{vmatrix} ;$$

The coordination problem (38) is a linear-quadratic one and its solution can be found in an analytical form according to (4) or

$$y^{opt} = -q^{-1}\left[r - A_I^T(A_Iq^{-1}A_I^T)^{-1}(A_Iq^{-1}r + d) \right] . \tag{39}$$

Relation (39) is developed additionally to the form

$$y_1^{opt} = -q_1^{-1}r_1 + q_1^{-1}(q_1^{-1} + q_2^{-1})^{-1}(q_1^{-1}r_1 + q_2^{-1}r_2 + d) \tag{40}$$

$$y_2^{opt} = -q_2^{-1}r_2 + q_2^{-1}(q_1^{-1} + q_2^{-1})^{-1}(q_1^{-1}r_1 + q_2^{-1}r_2 + d) .$$

2.2.2 Presenting the resources y_i^{opt} in terms of the initial problem

It is necessary the values of y_i^{opt} to be presented by the matrices and vectors of the initial problem a_i, b_i, Q_i, R_i, C_i, β, γ, $i=1,2$. According to (35) and (36), it is performed

$$q_1 = \beta_{11} \qquad \Rightarrow \quad q_1^{-1} = \beta_{11}^{-1} \tag{41}$$

$$q_2 = \gamma_{11} \qquad \Rightarrow \quad q_2^{-1} = \gamma_{11}^{-1}.$$

After additional transformations it follows

$$y_1^{opt} = \beta_{11}^{-1} \begin{vmatrix} \beta_{11}^T & \beta_{21}^T \end{vmatrix} \begin{vmatrix} a_1 Q_1^{-1} R_1 \\ b_1 Q_1^{-1} R_1 + C_1 \end{vmatrix} + \beta_{11}^{-1} (\beta_{11}^{-1} + \gamma_{11}^{-1})^{-1} \left[\beta_{11}^{-1} \begin{vmatrix} \beta_{11}^T & \beta_{21}^T \end{vmatrix} \begin{vmatrix} a_1 Q_1^{-1} R_1 \\ b_1 Q_1^{-1} R_1 + C_1 \end{vmatrix} + \gamma_{11}^{-1} \begin{vmatrix} \gamma_{11}^T & \gamma_{21}^T \end{vmatrix} \begin{vmatrix} a_2 Q_2^{-1} R_2 \\ b_2 Q_2^{-1} R_2 + C_2 \end{vmatrix} + d \right] \tag{42}$$

$$y_2^{opt} = \gamma_{11}^{-1} \begin{vmatrix} \gamma_{11}^T & \gamma_{21}^T \end{vmatrix} \begin{vmatrix} a_2 Q_2^{-1} R_2 \\ b_2 Q_2^{-1} R_2 + C_2 \end{vmatrix} + \gamma_{11}^{-1} (\gamma_{11}^{-1} + \beta_{11}^{-1})^{-1} \left[\beta_{11}^{-1} \begin{vmatrix} \beta_{11}^T & \beta_{21}^T \end{vmatrix} \begin{vmatrix} a_1 Q_1^{-1} R_1 \\ b_1 Q_1^{-1} R_1 + C_1 \end{vmatrix} + \gamma_{11}^{-1} \begin{vmatrix} \gamma_{11}^T & \gamma_{21}^T \end{vmatrix} \begin{vmatrix} a_2 Q_2^{-1} R_2 \\ b_2 Q_2^{-1} R_2 + C_2 \end{vmatrix} + d \right].$$

After substitution of optimal resources y_i^{opt}, i=1,2 from (42) in the expressions of $x_1(y_1)$ from (21) and $x_2(y_2)$ from (22) the analytical relations $x_1(y_1^{opt})$ and $x_2(y_2^{opt})$, which are solutions of the initial problem (1) are obtained. To get the explicit analytical form of relations $x_i(y_i^{opt})$, (42) is substituted in (21) and (22) and after transformations follows

$$x_1(y_1^{opt}) = -Q_1^{-1} R_1 + Q_1^{-1} \begin{vmatrix} a_1^T & b_1^T \end{vmatrix} \begin{vmatrix} (\beta_{11}^{-1} + \gamma_{11}^{-1})^{-1} & (\beta_{11}^{-1} + \gamma_{11}^{-1})^{-1} \beta_{11}^{-1} \beta_{21}^T & (\beta_{11}^{-1} + \gamma_{11}^{-1})^{-1} \gamma_{11}^{-1} \gamma_{21}^T \\ \beta_{21} \beta_{11}^{-1} (\beta_{11}^{-1} + \gamma_{11}^{-1})^{-1} & \begin{matrix} \beta_{21} \beta_{11}^{-1} (\beta_{11}^{-1} + \gamma_{11}^{-1})^{-1} \beta_{11}^{-1} \beta_{21}^T + \\ + \beta_{22} - \beta_{21} \beta_{11}^{-1} \beta_{21}^T \end{matrix} & \beta_{21} \beta_{11}^{-1} (\beta_{11}^{-1} + \gamma_{11}^{-1})^{-1} \gamma_{11}^{-1} \gamma_{21}^T \end{vmatrix} \tag{43}$$

$$* \begin{vmatrix} a_1 Q_1^{-1} R_1 + a_2 Q_2^{-1} R_2 + d \\ b_1 Q_1^{-1} R_1 + C_1 \\ b_2 Q_2^{-1} R_2 + C_2 \end{vmatrix}$$

$$x_2(y_2^{opt}) = -Q_2^{-1} R_2 + Q_2^{-1} \begin{vmatrix} a_2^T & b_2^T \end{vmatrix} \begin{vmatrix} (\beta_{11}^{-1} + \gamma_{11}^{-1})^{-1} & (\beta_{11}^{-1} + \gamma_{11}^{-1})^{-1} \beta_{11}^{-1} \beta_{21}^T & (\beta_{11}^{-1} + \gamma_{11}^{-1})^{-1} \gamma_{11}^{-1} \gamma_{21}^T \\ \gamma_{21} \gamma_{11}^{-1} (\beta_{11}^{-1} + \gamma_{11}^{-1})^{-1} & \gamma_{21} \gamma_{11}^{-1} (\beta_{11}^{-1} + \gamma_{11}^{-1})^{-1} \beta_{11}^{-1} \beta_{21}^T & \begin{matrix} \gamma_{21} \gamma_{11}^{-1} (\beta_{11}^{-1} + \gamma_{11}^{-1})^{-1} \gamma_{11}^{-1} \gamma_{21}^T + \\ + \gamma_{22} - \gamma_{21} \gamma_{11}^{-1} \gamma_{21}^T \end{matrix} \end{vmatrix} * \tag{44}$$

$$\begin{vmatrix} a_1 Q_1^{-1} R_1 + a_2 Q_2^{-1} R_2 + d \\ b_1 Q_1^{-1} R_1 + C_1 \\ b_2 Q_2^{-1} R_2 + C_2 \end{vmatrix}.$$

The obtained results in (43) and (44) $x_i(y_i^{opt})$, $i=1,2$ are after applying the predictive coordination for solving the initial problem (1). The solutions x_i^{opt}, $i=1,2$ from (15) are obtained by applying goal coordination to the same initial problem. As the solutions $x_i(y_i^{opt})$, $i=1,2$ and x_i^{opt}, $i=1,2$ are equal, after equalization of (15) with (43) and (44) relations among the components of the inverse matrix α and the components of the inverse β and γ are obtained. According to (15) and (43), it follows:

$$\alpha_{11} = (\beta_{11}^{-1} + \gamma_{11}^{-1})^{-1};\ \alpha_{12} = (\beta_{11}^{-1} + \gamma_{11}^{-1})^{-1}\beta_{11}^{-1}\beta_{21}^{T};\ \alpha_{13} = (\beta_{11}^{-1} + \gamma_{11}^{-1})^{-1}\gamma_{11}^{-1}\gamma_{21}^{T}$$
$$\alpha_{21} = \beta_{21}\beta_{11}^{-1}(\beta_{11}^{-1} + \gamma_{11}^{-1})^{-1};\ \alpha_{22} = \beta_{21}\beta_{11}^{-1}(\beta_{11}^{-1} + \gamma_{11}^{-1})^{-1}\beta_{11}^{-1}\beta_{21}^{T} + \beta_{22} - \beta_{21}\beta_{11}^{-1}\beta_{21}^{T};$$
$$\alpha_{23} = \beta_{21}\beta_{11}^{-1}(\beta_{11}^{-1} + \gamma_{11}^{-1})^{-1}\gamma_{11}^{-1}\gamma_{21}^{T} \quad (45)$$
$$\alpha_{31} = \gamma_{21}\gamma_{11}^{-1}(\beta_{11}^{-1} + \gamma_{11}^{-1})^{-1};\ \alpha_{32} = \gamma_{21}\gamma_{11}^{-1}(\beta_{11}^{-1} + \gamma_{11}^{-1})^{-1}\beta_{11}^{-1}\beta_{21}^{T};$$
$$\alpha_{33} = \gamma_{21}\gamma_{11}^{-1}(\beta_{11}^{-1} + \gamma_{11}^{-1})^{-1}\gamma_{11}^{-1}\gamma_{21}^{T} + \gamma_{22} - \gamma_{21}\gamma_{11}^{-1}\gamma_{21}^{T}.$$

Consequently, after applying the both coordination strategies towards the same initial problem (1) analytical relations (15) and respectively (43) and (44) are obtained. This allows to be received analytical relations among the components of the inverse matrices α, β and γ, which were not able to be determined directly because by definition:

$$\alpha = \begin{vmatrix} a_1Q_1^{-1}a_1^T + a_2Q_2^{-1}a_2^T & a_1Q_1^{-1}b_1^T & a_2Q_2^{-1}b_2^T \\ b_1Q_1^{-1}a_1^T & b_1Q_1^{-1}b_1^T & 0 \\ b_2Q_2^{-1}a_2^T & 0 & b_2Q_2^{-1}b_2^T \end{vmatrix}^{-1};$$

$$\beta = \begin{vmatrix} a_1Q_1^{-1}a_1^T & a_1Q_1^{-1}b_1^T \\ b_1Q_1^{-1}a_1^T & b_1Q_1^{-1}b_1^T \end{vmatrix}^{-1} \quad \gamma = \begin{vmatrix} a_2Q_2^{-1}a_2^T & a_2Q_2^{-1}b_2^T \\ b_2Q_2^{-1}a_2^T & b_2Q_2^{-1}b_2^T \end{vmatrix}^{-1}.$$

Consequently, using (45) the components of the inverse matrix α can be determined when β and γ are given. This allows the matrix α to be determined by fewer calculations in comparison with its direct inverse transformation because the inverse matrices β and γ have less dimensions. Relations (45) can be applied for calculation of the components α_{ij} of the inverse matrix α (with large dimension) by finding the inverse matrices β and γ (with fewer dimensions). The computational efficiency for evaluating the inverse matrix with high dimension using relations (45) is preferable in comparison with its direct calculation (Stoilova & Stoilov, 2007).

3. Predictive coordination for block-diagonal problem of quadratic programming with three and more subsystems

Analytical relations for predictive coordination strategy for the case when the subsystems in the bi-level hierarchy are more than two are developed. The case of bi-level hierarchical system with three subsystems is considered, figure 2

The initial optimization problem, solved by the hierarchical system is stated as

$$\min \frac{1}{2} \begin{vmatrix} x_1^T & x_2^T & x_3^T \end{vmatrix} \begin{vmatrix} Q_1 & 0 & 0 \\ 0 & Q_2 & 0 \\ 0 & 0 & Q_3 \end{vmatrix} \begin{vmatrix} x_1 \\ x_2 \\ x_3 \end{vmatrix} + \begin{vmatrix} R_1^T & R_2^T & R_3^T \end{vmatrix} \begin{vmatrix} x_1 \\ x_2 \\ x_3 \end{vmatrix} \quad (46)$$

$$a_1 x_{1 m_0 x n_1} + a_2 x_{2 m_0 x n_2} + a_3 x_{3 m_0 x n_3} = d \quad (47)$$

$$\begin{aligned} b_1 x_{1 m_1 x n_1} \quad\quad\quad\quad\quad\quad &= C_1 \\ b_2 x_{2 m_2 x n_2} \quad\quad\quad &= C_2 \\ b_3 x_{3 m_3 x n_3} &= C_3 \end{aligned}$$

where the dimensions of the vectors and matrices are appropriately defined

$$x_{1 n_1 x1}; x_{2 n_2 x1}; x_{3 n_3 x1}; R_{1 n_1 x1}; R_{2 n_2 x1}; R_{3 n_3 x1};$$

$$a_{1 m_0 x n_1}; a_{2 m_0 x n_2}; a_{3 m_0 x n_3}; d_{\ m_0 x1};$$

$$b_{1 m_1 x n_1}; b_{2 m_2 x n_2}; b_{3 m_3 x n_3}; C_{1 m_1 x1}; C_{2 m_2 x1}; C_{3 m_3 x1};$$

$$C = \begin{vmatrix} d \\ C_1 \\ C_2 \\ C_3 \end{vmatrix}_{(m_0+m_1+m_2+m_3)x(n_1+n_2+n_3)}; \; Q = \begin{vmatrix} Q_1 & 0 & 0 \\ 0 & Q_2 & 0 \\ 0 & 0 & Q_3 \end{vmatrix}; \; R = \begin{vmatrix} R_1 \\ R_2 \\ R_3 \end{vmatrix};$$

$$A = \begin{vmatrix} a_1 & a_2 & a_3 \\ b_1 & 0 & 0 \\ 0 & b_2 & 0 \\ 0 & 0 & b_3 \end{vmatrix}_{(m_0+m_1+m_2+m_3)x(n_1+n_2+n_3)}.$$

The peculiarity of problem (46), which formalizes the management of hierarchical system with three subsystems, concerns the existence of local resources C_1, C_2, C_3, which are used by each subsystem. According to the coupling constraint (47) additional resources d are allocated among the subsystems. Problem (46) can be presented in a general form, using the substitutions

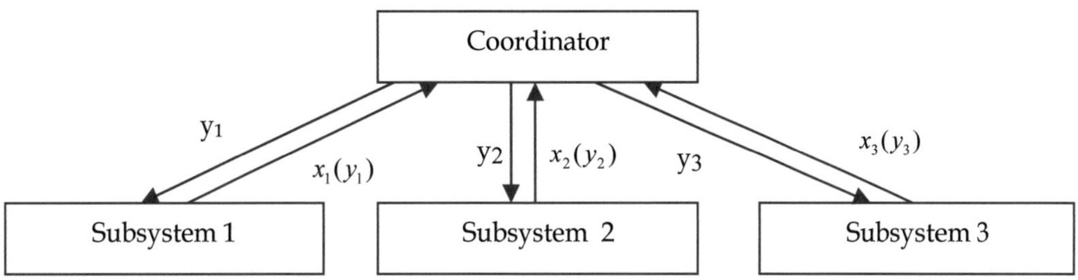

Fig. 2. Hierarchical approach with three subsystems for solving initial problem

$$\underset{(m_0+m_1+m_2+m_3)xn_1}{A_1} = \begin{vmatrix} a_1 \\ b_1 \\ 0 \\ 0 \end{vmatrix} \begin{matrix} m_0 x n_1 \\ m_1 x n_1 \\ m_2 x n_1 \\ m_3 x n_1 \end{matrix}; \quad \underset{(m_0+m_1+m_2+m_3)xn_3}{A_3} = \begin{vmatrix} a_3 \\ 0 \\ 0 \\ b_3 \end{vmatrix} \begin{matrix} m_0 x n_3 \\ m_1 x n_3 \\ m_2 x n_3 \\ m_3 x n_3 \end{matrix}; \; D = \begin{vmatrix} d \\ C_1 \\ C_2 \\ C_3 \end{vmatrix}_{(m_0+m_1+m_2+m_3)x1} \quad (48)$$

$$A = \left| A_1 \quad A_2 \quad A_3 \right|_{(m_0+m_1+m_2+m_3)x(n_1+n_2+n_3)}.$$

Analogically to the previous case with two subsystems, analytical relations for determining the inverse matrix components by matrices with fewer dimensions are obtained

$$\alpha_{11} = (\beta_{11}^{-1}+\gamma_{11}^{-1}+\delta_{11}^{-1})^{-1}; \ \alpha_{12} = (\beta_{11}^{-1}+\gamma_{11}^{-1}+\delta_{11}^{-1})^{-1}\beta_{11}^{-1}\beta_{21}^{T} \tag{49}$$

$$\alpha_{13} = (\beta_{11}^{-1}+\gamma_{11}^{-1}+\delta_{11}^{-1})^{-1}\gamma_{11}^{-1}\gamma_{21}^{T}; \ \alpha_{14} = (\beta_{11}^{-1}+\gamma_{11}^{-1}+\delta_{11}^{-1})^{-1}\delta_{11}^{-1}\delta_{21}^{T}$$

$$\alpha_{21} = \beta_{21}\beta_{11}^{-1}(\beta_{11}^{-1}+\gamma_{11}^{-1}+\delta_{11}^{-1})^{-1}; \ \alpha_{22} = \beta_{21}\beta_{11}^{-1}(\beta_{11}^{-1}+\gamma_{11}^{-1}+\delta_{11}^{-1})^{-1}\beta_{11}^{-1}\beta_{21}^{T}+\beta_{22}-\beta_{21}\beta_{11}^{-1}\beta_{21}^{T}$$

$$\alpha_{23} = \beta_{21}\beta_{11}^{-1}(\beta_{11}^{-1}+\gamma_{11}^{-1}+\delta_{11}^{-1})^{-1}\gamma_{11}^{-1}\gamma_{21}^{T}; \ \alpha_{24} = \beta_{21}\beta_{11}^{-1}(\beta_{11}^{-1}+\gamma_{11}^{-1}+\delta_{11}^{-1})^{-1}\delta_{11}^{-1}\delta_{21}^{T}$$

$$\alpha_{31} = \gamma_{21}\gamma_{11}^{-1}(\beta_{11}^{-1}+\gamma_{11}^{-1}+\delta_{11}^{-1})^{-1}; \ \alpha_{32} = \gamma_{21}\gamma_{11}^{-1}(\beta_{11}^{-1}+\gamma_{11}^{-1}+\delta_{11}^{-1})^{-1}\beta_{11}^{-1}\beta_{21}^{T}$$

$$\alpha_{33} = \gamma_{21}\gamma_{11}^{-1}(\beta_{11}^{-1}+\gamma_{11}^{-1}+\delta_{11}^{-1})^{-1}\gamma_{11}^{-1}\gamma_{21}^{T}+\gamma_{22}-\gamma_{21}\gamma_{11}^{-1}\gamma_{21}^{T}; \ \alpha_{34} = \gamma_{21}\gamma_{11}^{-1}(\beta_{11}^{-1}+\gamma_{11}^{-1}+\delta_{11}^{-1})^{-1}\delta_{11}^{-1}\delta_{21}^{T}$$

$$\alpha_{41} = \delta_{21}\delta_{11}^{-1}(\beta_{11}^{-1}+\gamma_{11}^{-1}+\delta_{11}^{-1})^{-1}; \ \alpha_{42} = \delta_{21}\delta_{11}^{-1}(\beta_{11}^{-1}+\gamma_{11}^{-1}+\delta_{11}^{-1})^{-1}\beta_{11}^{-1}\beta_{21}^{T}$$

$$\alpha_{43} = \delta_{21}\delta_{11}^{-1}(\beta_{11}^{-1}+\gamma_{11}^{-1}+\delta_{11}^{-1})^{-1}\gamma_{11}^{-1}\gamma_{21}^{T}; \ \alpha_{44} = \delta_{21}\delta_{11}^{-1}(\beta_{11}^{-1}+\gamma_{11}^{-1}+\delta_{11}^{-1})^{-1}\delta_{11}^{-1}\delta_{21}^{T}+\delta_{22}-\delta_{21}\delta_{11}^{-1}\delta_{21}^{T}.$$

The initial problem can be solved by four or more subsystems. The relations between the components of the matrix $\alpha = (\alpha_{ij})$ and the matrices with lower sizes $\beta, \gamma, \ldots \omega$ are given below

$$\left| \begin{array}{ccccc}
\alpha_{11} = & \alpha_{12} = & \alpha_{13} = & & \alpha_{1j} = \\
(\beta_{11}^{-1}+\cdots+\omega_{11}^{-1})^{-1} & (\beta_{11}^{-1}+\cdots+\omega_{11}^{-1})^{-1}\beta_{11}^{-1}\beta_{21}^{T} & (\beta_{11}^{-1}+\cdots+\omega_{11}^{-1})^{-1}\gamma_{11}^{-1}\gamma_{21}^{T} & \cdots & \begin{array}{c}(\beta_{11}^{-1}+\cdots+\omega_{11}^{-1})^{-1} * \\ *\omega_{11}^{-1}\omega_{21}^{T}\end{array} \\
\alpha_{21} = & \alpha_{22} = & \alpha_{23} = & & \alpha_{2j} = \\
\beta_{21}\beta_{11}^{-1}(\beta_{11}^{-1}+\cdots+\omega_{11}^{-1})^{-1} & \begin{array}{c}\beta_{21}\beta_{11}^{-1}(\beta_{11}^{-1}+\cdots+\omega_{11}^{-1})^{-1} * \\ *\beta_{11}^{-1}\beta_{21}^{T}+\beta_{22}-\beta_{21}\beta_{11}^{-1}\beta_{21}^{T}\end{array} & \begin{array}{c}\beta_{21}\beta_{11}^{-1}(\beta_{11}^{-1}+\cdots+\omega_{11}^{-1})^{-1} * \\ *\gamma_{11}^{-1}\gamma_{21}^{T}\end{array} & \cdots & \begin{array}{c}\beta_{21}\beta_{11}^{-1}(\beta_{11}^{-1}+\cdots+\omega_{11}^{-1})^{-1} * \\ *\omega_{11}^{-1}\omega_{21}^{T}\end{array} \\
\alpha_{31} = & \alpha_{32} = & \alpha_{33} = & & \alpha_{3j} = \\
\gamma_{21}\gamma_{11}^{-1}(\beta_{11}^{-1}+\cdots+\omega_{11}^{-1})^{-1} & \begin{array}{c}\gamma_{21}\gamma_{11}^{-1}(\beta_{11}^{-1}+\cdots+\omega_{11}^{-1})^{-1} * \\ *\beta_{11}^{-1}\beta_{21}^{T}\end{array} & \begin{array}{c}\gamma_{21}\gamma_{11}^{-1}(\beta_{11}^{-1}+\cdots+\omega_{11}^{-1})^{-1} * \\ *\gamma_{11}^{-1}\gamma_{21}^{T}+\gamma_{22}-\gamma_{21}\gamma_{11}^{-1}\gamma_{21}^{T}\end{array} & \cdots & \begin{array}{c}\gamma_{21}\gamma_{11}^{-1}(\beta_{11}^{-1}+\cdots+\omega_{11}^{-1})^{-1} * \\ *\omega_{11}^{-1}\omega_{21}^{T}\end{array} \\
\vdots & & & & \\
\alpha_{i1} = & \alpha_{i2} = & \alpha_{i3} = & & \alpha_{ij} = \\
\omega_{21}\omega_{11}^{-1}(\beta_{11}^{-1}+\cdots+\omega_{11}^{-1})^{-1} & \begin{array}{c}\omega_{21}\omega_{11}^{-1}(\beta_{11}^{-1}+\cdots+\omega_{11}^{-1})^{-1} * \\ *\beta_{11}^{-1}\beta_{21}^{T}\end{array} & \begin{array}{c}\omega_{21}\omega_{11}^{-1}(\beta_{11}^{-1}+\cdots+\omega_{11}^{-1})^{-1} * \\ *\gamma_{11}^{-1}\gamma_{21}^{T}\end{array} & \cdots & \begin{array}{c}\omega_{21}\omega_{11}^{-1}(\beta_{11}^{-1}+\cdots+\omega_{11}^{-1})^{-1} * \\ \omega_{11}^{-1}\omega_{21}^{T}+\omega_{22}-\omega_{21}\omega_{11}^{-1}\omega_{21}^{T}\end{array}
\end{array} \right| \tag{50}$$

4. Assessment of the calculation efficiency of the analytical results for determination of inverse matrix components

For simplicity of working the notations for right matrices with lower dimensions are introduced. In the case of 2 subsystems, the matrices *c* and *d* are the corresponding right matrices of the inverse matrices β and γ. By definition having in mind (46) c and d are symmetric ones

$$c = \begin{vmatrix} \underbrace{c_{11}}_{m_0 x m_0} & \underbrace{c_{12}}_{m_0 x m_1} \\ \underbrace{c_{21}}_{m_1 x m_0} & \underbrace{c_{22}}_{m_1 x m_1} \end{vmatrix} = \begin{vmatrix} \underbrace{a_1 Q_1^{-1} a_1^T}_{m_0 x m_0} & \underbrace{a_1 Q_1^{-1} b_1^T}_{m_0 x m_1} \\ \underbrace{b_1 Q_1^{-1} a_1^T}_{m_1 x m_0} & \underbrace{b_1 Q_1^{-1} b_1^T}_{m_1 x m_1} \end{vmatrix} ; \ \beta = \begin{vmatrix} \beta_{11} & \beta_{12} \\ \beta_{21} & \beta_{22} \end{vmatrix} = c^{-1}$$

$$d = \begin{vmatrix} \underbrace{d_{11}}_{m_0 x m_0} & \underbrace{d_{12}}_{m_0 x m_2} \\ \underbrace{d_{21}}_{m_2 x m_0} & \underbrace{d_{22}}_{m_2 x m_2} \end{vmatrix} = \begin{vmatrix} \underbrace{a_2 Q_2^{-1} a_2^T}_{m_0 x m_0} & \underbrace{a_2 Q_2^{-1} b_2^T}_{m_0 x m_2} \\ \underbrace{b_2 Q_1^{-1} a_2^T}_{m_2 x m_0} & \underbrace{b_2 Q_2^{-1} b_2^T}_{m_2 x m_2} \end{vmatrix} \quad \gamma = \begin{vmatrix} \gamma_{11} & \gamma_{12} \\ \gamma_{21} & \gamma_{22} \end{vmatrix} = d^{-1}.$$

Analogically, for 3 subsystems the right matrix is e and the corresponding inverse matrix is δ ($e - \delta$); for 4 subsystems - ($f - \varphi$).

An *example* for computational efficiency of the proposed relations (45) /2 subsystems is given below with a symmetric matrix AL with dimension from 17×17 to 26×26 which varies according to variation of dimension m_1 from 2 to 11, while m_0 is 4 and m_2 is 11. Matrix AL is in the form

	m_0=4	m_1=2÷11	m_2=11
	$c_{11}+d_{11}$	c_{12}	d_{12}
AL =	c_{21}	c_{22}	0
	d_{21}	0	d_{22}

The MATLAB's codes are given below:

```
%example of inversion of AL  (dimension 26x26) when m1=11

c11=[1 2 3 1;  2 3 2 2;  3 2 4 2;   1 2 2 1];

c12=[ -2  1  0  -1  2  4   0  -1  -3  2  2;    -5  0  2  1  4  6  -5
7  1  9  1;   0  7  2  1  3  -8  9  1  0  2  3;   4  2 -1  0  2  -1
2  1  3  1  1];

c21=c12';

c22=[ 1    2    1   -3    1    0    1    5    2    8    2;
   2    3   -4    1    0    2    9    8    5    1   -3;
   1   -4    1   -1    1    5   -6    2   1     3    1;
  -3    1   -1    4    3    2    1    0   -1   -2    2;
        1    0    1    3    2    1    1    5   -3    3   -1;
   0    2    5    2    1    4    2    1    0    1    1;
   1    9   -6    1    1    2    6    3    1    0    2;
   5    8    2    0    5    1    3    5   -2    7    0;
        2    5    1   -1   -3    0    1   -2    3    1    1;
```

```
    8   1   3  -2   3  1   0    7   1   4   2;
    2  -3  1    2  -1  1   2   0    1   2  4];

c=[c11 c12; c21 c22];
d11=[3  0  0 -2;     0 -6  2  0;    0  2 -2 -1;     -2  0 -1  2];

d12=[1  0  2  1  3  -4  2  0  1  -3  1 ;
    3 -1  0  2 -2  -1  0  1  1   0  2 ;
    3  0  1  0  5   3  7  1  2  -2  0;
    2  2  0  1  3   2  1  0  1  -1  1];

d21=d12';

d22=[ 1   3  7  2  2  1  1  0  -2  -1  1;
           3   2  1  1  1 -1 -2 -3   0   1  0 ;
           7   1  5  2  4  2  3 -1  -3  -2  1 ;
           2   1  2  1  2  3  0  1  -2  -4  2;
           2   1  4  2  1 -1  3  7  -1   2  0;
           1  -1  2  3 -1  0  2  1   4   1  2;
           1  -2  3  0  3  2  2  1  -3  -1  1;
           0  -3 -1  1  7  1  1  0   1   2  1;
          -2   0 -3 -2 -1  4 -3  1  -2   0  2;
          -1   1 -2 -4  2  1 -1  2   0   1  1;
           1   0  1  2  0  2  1  1   2   1  5];

d=[d11 d12; d21 d22];

%definition of AL

mm=size(c12);
m0=mm(1);              %m0=4
m1=mm(2);              %m1=11
mm=size(d12);
m2=mm(2);              %m2=11
m10=zeros(m1,m2);
m20=m10';

al=[c11+d11   c12   d12;  c21   c22   m10;   d21   m20   d22];

flops(0);
alpha1=inv(al);          %direct inversion  of AL
fl_al=flops              %flops for direct matrix inversion

%matrix inversion by hierarchical approach
flops(0);

beta=inv(c);
gama=inv(d);
invbeta11=inv(beta(1:m0,1:m0));
invgama11=inv(gama(1:m0,1:m0));
invbeta11beta21T=invbeta11*beta(m0+1:m0+m1,1:m0)';
invgama11gama21T=invgama11*gama(m0+1:m0+m2,1:m0)';
```

```
ff=flops
flops(0);
alpha11=inv(invbeta11+invgama11);
alpha12=alpha11*invbeta11beta21T;
alpha13=alpha11*invgama11*gama(m0+1:m0+m2,1:m0)';

alpha21=alpha12';
alpha22=invbeta11beta21T'*alpha12+beta(m0+1:m0+m1,m0+1:m0+m1)-
beta(m0+1:m0+m1,1:m0)*invbeta11beta21T;
alpha23=invbeta11beta21T'*alpha13;

alpha31=alpha13';
alpha32=alpha23';
alpha33=invgama11gama21T'*alpha13+gama(m0+1:m0+m2,m0+1:m0+m2)-
gama(m0+1:m0+m2,1:m0)*invgama11gama21T;

alpha=[alpha11 alpha12 alpha13; alpha21 alpha22 alpha23; alpha31
alpha32 alpha33];

fl_nic=flops
fl_full=ff+fl_nic                    %flops using noniterative coordination


al2=inv(alpha);            %verification
```

This code has been used for two types of calculations:

1. Direct calculation of α - inversion of matrix *AL* by built-in MATLAB function *INV*. The amount of calculations is presented as a dashed red line in Figure 3.
2. Evaluation of α applying relations (45). The amount of calculation is presented as a solid blue line in Figure 3.

The comparison of the both manners of calculations shows that the analytical relations are preferable when the matrix dimension increases. From experimental considerations it is preferable to hold the relation $3m_0 < m_1 + m_2$, which gives boundaries for the decomposition of the initial matrix *AL*. For the initial case of $m_0=4$ $m_1=2$ $m_2=11$ these values are near to equality of the above relation and that is why the decomposition approach does not lead to satisfactory result.

Second example A 29×29 symmetric block-diagonal matrix denoted by *AL* is considered. It has to be inversed to the matrix α by two manners: direct MATLAB's inversion and using relations (45) and (50). This matrix will be calculated by hierarchical approach and decomposition with 2, 3, and 4 subsystems.

Case 1. The right matrix *AL* can be inversed to α by the above analytical relations applying 4 subsystems where *AL* is presented by the matrices *c, d, e* and *f* in the manner:

	m_0	m_1	m_2	m_3	m_4
	$c_{11}+d_{11}+e_{11}+f_{11}$	c_{12}	d_{12}	e_{12}	f_{12}
	c_{21}	c_{22}	0	0	0
$AL =$	d_{21}	0	d_{22}	0	0
	e_{21}	0	0	e_{22}	0
	f_{21}	0	0	0	f_{22}

$$
AL=\left|\begin{array}{ccc|cccccc|cccccc|ccccccc|ccccccc}
\multicolumn{3}{c|}{m_0=3} & \multicolumn{6}{c|}{m_1=6} & \multicolumn{6}{c|}{m_2=6} & \multicolumn{7}{c|}{m_3=7} & \multicolumn{7}{c}{m_4=7} \\
5&1&-3&-1&2&4&-1&2&1&-4&1&0&1&-3&2&0&2&1&1&-2&0&-3&1&0&3&6&-1&1&4\\
1&4&5&-3&1&0&5&4&-1&-2&-1&0&-2&1&4&2&4&0&-5&7&1&-4&3&2&1&-1&4&-1&-2\\
-3&5&-4&3&2&1&0&3&2&-2&1&0&1&-1&-2&1&-2&1&3&1&0&1&4&1&3&2&4&1&-2\\
-1&-3&3&3&-4&1&0&2&1&0&0&0&0&0&0&0&0&0&0&0&0&0&0&0&0&0&0&0&0\\
2&1&2&-4&1&-1&1&5&-1&0&0&0&0&0&0&0&0&0&0&0&0&0&0&0&0&0&0&0&0\\
4&0&1&1&-1&7&3&2&3&0&0&0&0&0&0&0&0&0&0&0&0&0&0&0&0&0&0&0&0\\
-1&5&0&0&1&3&9&1&2&0&0&0&0&0&0&0&0&0&0&0&0&0&0&0&0&0&0&0&0\\
2&4&3&2&5&2&1&8&-1&0&0&0&0&0&0&0&0&0&0&0&0&0&0&0&0&0&0&0&0\\
1&-1&2&1&-1&3&2&-1&2&0&0&0&0&0&0&0&0&0&0&0&0&0&0&0&0&0&0&0&0\\
-4&-2&-2&0&0&0&0&0&0&1&-1&-2&-1&-1&1&0&0&0&0&0&0&0&0&0&0&0&0&0&0\\
1&-1&1&0&0&0&0&0&0&-1&-2&3&0&1&2&0&0&0&0&0&0&0&0&0&0&0&0&0&0\\
0&0&0&0&0&0&0&0&0&-2&3&-1&1&-2&4&0&0&0&0&0&0&0&0&0&0&0&0&0&0\\
1&-2&1&0&0&0&0&0&0&-1&0&1&-2&-4&2&0&0&0&0&0&0&0&0&0&0&0&0&0&0\\
-3&1&1&0&0&0&0&0&0&-1&1&-2&-4&1&3&0&0&0&0&0&0&0&0&0&0&0&0&0&0\\
2&4&-2&0&0&0&0&0&0&1&2&4&2&3&2&0&0&0&0&0&0&0&0&0&0&0&0&0&0\\
0&2&1&0&0&0&0&0&0&0&0&0&0&0&0&2&1&5&1&1&-2&1&0&0&0&0&0&0&0\\
2&4&-2&0&0&0&0&0&0&0&0&0&0&0&0&1&3&2&4&1&3&2&0&0&0&0&0&0&0\\
1&0&1&0&0&0&0&0&0&0&0&0&0&0&0&5&2&3&2&1&-1&1&0&0&0&0&0&0&0\\
1&-5&3&0&0&0&0&0&0&0&0&0&0&0&0&1&4&2&5&-1&3&-2&0&0&0&0&0&0&0\\
-2&7&1&0&0&0&0&0&0&0&0&0&0&0&0&1&1&1&-1&6&1&-1&0&0&0&0&0&0&0\\
0&1&0&0&0&0&0&0&0&0&0&0&0&0&0&-2&3&-1&3&1&2&1&0&0&0&0&0&0&0\\
-3&-4&1&0&0&0&0&0&0&0&0&0&0&0&0&1&2&1&-2&-1&1&3&0&0&0&0&0&0&0\\
1&3&4&0&0&0&0&0&0&0&0&0&0&0&0&0&0&0&0&0&0&0&1&-1&3&1&2&1&4\\
0&2&1&0&0&0&0&0&0&0&0&0&0&0&0&0&0&0&0&0&0&0&-1&2&1&3&-2&1&0\\
3&1&3&0&0&0&0&0&0&0&0&0&0&0&0&0&0&0&0&0&0&0&3&1&1&-2&-1&-2&1\\
6&-1&2&0&0&0&0&0&0&0&0&0&0&0&0&0&0&0&0&0&0&0&1&3&-2&1&-3&1&-2\\
-1&4&4&0&0&0&0&0&0&0&0&0&0&0&0&0&0&0&0&0&0&0&2&-2&-1&-3&2&1&-1\\
1&-1&1&0&0&0&0&0&0&0&0&0&0&0&0&0&0&0&0&0&0&0&1&1&-2&1&1&3&1\\
4&-2&-2&0&0&0&0&0&0&0&0&0&0&0&0&0&0&0&0&0&0&0&4&0&1&-2&-1&1&1
\end{array}\right|
$$

$$
c=\left|\begin{array}{ccc|cccccc}
\multicolumn{3}{c|}{m_0=3} & \multicolumn{6}{c}{m_1=6} \\
2&-1&2&-1&2&4&-1&2&1\\
-1&1&2&-3&1&0&5&4&-1\\
2&2&3&3&2&1&0&3&2\\
\hline
-1&-3&3&3&-4&1&0&2&1\\
2&1&2&-4&1&-1&1&5&-1\\
4&0&1&1&-1&7&3&2&3\\
-1&5&0&0&1&3&9&1&2\\
2&4&3&2&5&2&1&8&-1\\
1&-1&2&1&-1&3&2&-1&2
\end{array}\right|
\qquad
d=\left|\begin{array}{ccc|cccccc}
\multicolumn{3}{c|}{m_0=3} & \multicolumn{6}{c}{m_2=6} \\
-1&-1&-1&-4&1&0&1&-3&2\\
-1&2&0&-2&-1&0&-2&1&4\\
-1&0&-2&-2&1&0&1&-1&-2\\
\hline
-4&-2&-2&1&-1&-2&-1&-1&1\\
1&-1&1&-1&-2&3&0&1&2\\
0&0&0&-2&3&-1&1&-2&4\\
1&-2&1&-1&0&1&-2&-4&2\\
-3&1&1&-1&1&-2&-4&1&3\\
2&4&-2&1&2&4&2&3&2
\end{array}\right| \quad (51)
$$

$$e=\left|\begin{array}{ccc|ccccccc} \multicolumn{3}{c|}{m_0=3} & \multicolumn{7}{c}{m_3=7} \\ 3 & 0 & -2 & 0 & 2 & 1 & 1 & -2 & 0 & -3 \\ 0 & -4 & 2 & 2 & 4 & 0 & -5 & 7 & 1 & -4 \\ -2 & 2 & 1 & 1 & -2 & 1 & 3 & 1 & 0 & 1 \\ \hline 0 & 2 & 1 & 2 & 1 & 5 & 1 & 1 & -2 & 1 \\ 2 & 4 & -2 & 1 & 3 & 2 & 4 & 1 & 3 & 2 \\ 1 & 0 & 1 & 5 & 2 & 3 & 2 & 1 & -1 & 1 \\ 1 & -5 & 3 & 1 & 4 & 2 & 5 & -1 & 3 & -2 \\ -2 & 7 & 1 & 1 & 1 & 1 & -1 & 6 & 1 & -1 \\ 0 & 1 & 0 & -2 & 3 & -1 & 3 & 1 & 2 & 1 \\ -3 & -4 & 1 & 1 & 2 & 1 & -2 & -1 & 1 & 3 \end{array}\right| \qquad f=\left|\begin{array}{ccc|ccccccc} \multicolumn{3}{c|}{m_0=3} & \multicolumn{7}{c}{m_4=7} \\ 1 & 3 & -2 & 1 & 0 & 3 & 6 & -1 & 1 & 4 \\ 3 & 5 & 1 & 3 & 2 & 1 & -1 & 4 & -1 & -2 \\ -2 & 1 & -4 & 4 & 1 & 3 & 2 & 4 & 1 & -2 \\ \hline 1 & 3 & 4 & 1 & -1 & 3 & 1 & 2 & 1 & 4 \\ 0 & 2 & 1 & -1 & 2 & 1 & 3 & -2 & 1 & 0 \\ 3 & 1 & 3 & 3 & 1 & 1 & -2 & -1 & -2 & 1 \\ 6 & -1 & 2 & 1 & 3 & -2 & 1 & -3 & 1 & -2 \\ -1 & 4 & 4 & 2 & -2 & -1 & -3 & 2 & 1 & -1 \\ 1 & -1 & 1 & 1 & 1 & -2 & 1 & 1 & 3 & 1 \\ 4 & -2 & -2 & 4 & 0 & 1 & -2 & -1 & 1 & 1 \end{array}\right|$$

Here is assessed the efficiency of usage of relations (50) for finding the inverse matrix α when the matrices with fewer dimensions *c, d, e* and *f* are given. The assessment is done by measurement of "flops" in MATLAB environment. A part of the MATLAB's codes which performs relations (50) for inverse matrix calculations and assess the computational performance are given below

```
al=[c11+d11+e11    c12    d12    e12 ;    c21    c22    m10    m30;    d21
m20    d22    m40;    e21    m50    m60    e22];
flops(0);
alpha1=inv(al);
fl_al=flops
flops(0);
beta=inv(c);
gama=inv(d);
delta=inv(e);
invbeta11=inv(beta(1:m0,1:m0));
invgama11=inv(gama(1:m0,1:m0));
invdelta11=inv(delta(1:m0,1:m0));
invbeta11beta21T=invbeta11*beta(m0+1:m0+m1,1:m0)';
invgama11gama21T=invgama11*gama(m0+1:m0+m2,1:m0)';
invdelta11delta21T=invdelta11*delta(m0+1:m0+m3,1:m0)';
ff=flops
flops(0);
alpha11=inv(invbeta11+invgama11+invdelta11);
alpha12=alpha11*invbeta11beta21T;
alpha13=alpha11*invgama11*gama(m0+1:m0+m2,1:m0)';
alpha14=alpha11*invdelta11delta21T;
alpha21=alpha12';
alpha22=invbeta11beta21T'*alpha12+beta(m0+1:m0+m1,m0+1:m0+m1)-
beta(m0+1:m0+m1,1:m0)*invbeta11beta21T;
alpha23=invbeta11beta21T'*alpha13;
alpha24=alpha21*invdelta11delta21T;
alpha31=gama(m0+1:m0+m2,1:m0)*invgama11*alpha11;
alpha32=alpha31*invbeta11beta21T;
alpha33=invgama11gama21T'*alpha13+gama(m0+1:m0+m2,m0+1:m0+m2)-
gama(m0+1:m0+m2,1:m0)*invgama11gama21T;
alpha34=alpha31*invdelta11delta21T;
```

```
alpha41=delta(m0+1:m0+m3,1:m0)*invdelta11*alpha11;
alpha42=alpha41*invbeta11beta21T;
alpha43=alpha41*invgama11gama21T;
alpha44=alpha41*invdelta11delta21T+delta(m0+1:m0+m3,m0+1:m0+m3)-
delta(m0+1:m0+m3,1:m0)*invdelta11delta21T;
alpha=[alpha11   alpha12   alpha13   alpha14;
alpha21    alpha22   alpha23   alpha24;
alpha31    alpha32   alpha33   alpha34;
alpha41    alpha42   alpha43   alpha44];
fl_nic=flops;
fl_full=ff+fl_nic
al2=inv(alpha);%verification
```

For direct inversion of AL the flops are 50220 and for using (50) - 16329, figure 4.

Case 2. The same matrix AL is given however α is determined by a different manner - by 3 subsystems:

$$AL = \left|\begin{array}{c:c:c:c} c_{11}+d_{11}+e_{11} & c_{12} & d_{12} & e_{12} \\ \hdashline c_{21} & c_{22} & 0 & 0 \\ \hdashline d_{21} & 0 & d_{22} & 0 \\ \hdashline e_{21} & 0 & 0 & e_{22} \end{array}\right|$$

where c and d are the same as in (51) , however the right matrix e is different. It utilizes the previous matrices e and f:

$$e = \left|\begin{array}{ccc:cccccccccccccc} \multicolumn{3}{c:}{m_0=3} & \multicolumn{14}{c}{m_3=14} \\ 4 & 3 & -4 & 0 & 2 & 1 & 1 & -2 & 0 & -3 & 1 & 0 & 3 & 6 & -1 & 1 & 4 \\ 3 & 1 & 3 & 2 & 4 & 0 & -5 & 7 & 1 & -4 & 3 & 2 & 1 & -1 & 4 & -1 & -2 \\ -4 & 3 & -5 & 1 & -2 & 1 & 3 & 1 & 0 & 1 & 4 & 1 & 3 & 2 & 4 & 1 & -2 \\ \hdashline 0 & 2 & 1 & 2 & 1 & 5 & 1 & 1 & -2 & 1 & 0 & 0 & 0 & 0 & 0 & 0 & 0 \\ 2 & 4 & -2 & 1 & 3 & 2 & 4 & 1 & 3 & 2 & 0 & 0 & 0 & 0 & 0 & 0 & 0 \\ 1 & 0 & 1 & 5 & 2 & 3 & 2 & 1 & -1 & 1 & 0 & 0 & 0 & 0 & 0 & 0 & 0 \\ 1 & -5 & 3 & 1 & 4 & 2 & 5 & -1 & 3 & -2 & 0 & 0 & 0 & 0 & 0 & 0 & 0 \\ -2 & 7 & 1 & 1 & 1 & 1 & -1 & 6 & 1 & -1 & 0 & 0 & 0 & 0 & 0 & 0 & 0 \\ 0 & 1 & 0 & -2 & 3 & -1 & 3 & 1 & 2 & 1 & 0 & 0 & 0 & 0 & 0 & 0 & 0 \\ -3 & -4 & 1 & 1 & 2 & 1 & -2 & -1 & 1 & 3 & 0 & 0 & 0 & 0 & 0 & 0 & 0 \\ 1 & 3 & 4 & 0 & 0 & 0 & 0 & 0 & 0 & 0 & 1 & -1 & 3 & 1 & 2 & 1 & 4 \\ 0 & 2 & 1 & 0 & 0 & 0 & 0 & 0 & 0 & 0 & -1 & 2 & 1 & 3 & -2 & 1 & 0 \\ 3 & 1 & 3 & 0 & 0 & 0 & 0 & 0 & 0 & 0 & 3 & 1 & 1 & -2 & -1 & -2 & 1 \\ 6 & -1 & 2 & 0 & 0 & 0 & 0 & 0 & 0 & 0 & 1 & 3 & -2 & 1 & -3 & 1 & -2 \\ -1 & 4 & 4 & 0 & 0 & 0 & 0 & 0 & 0 & 0 & 2 & -2 & -1 & -3 & 2 & 1 & -1 \\ 1 & -1 & 1 & 0 & 0 & 0 & 0 & 0 & 0 & 0 & 1 & 1 & -2 & 1 & 1 & 3 & 1 \\ 4 & -2 & -2 & 0 & 0 & 0 & 0 & 0 & 0 & 0 & 4 & 0 & 1 & -2 & -1 & 1 & 1 \end{array}\right|$$

The calculations in flops for direct inversing of AL are 50220 and using (49) - 23082, figure 4

Case 3. The inverse matrix α is determined by 2 subsystems and AL is in the form

$$AL \quad \left|\begin{array}{c:c:c} c_{11}+d_{11} & c_{12} & d_{12} \\ \hdashline c_{21} & c_{22} & 0 \\ \hdashline d_{21} & 0 & d_{22} \end{array}\right|$$

where c is the same as in (51) but the right matrix d covers d, e and f from *Case* 1 or d and e from *Case* 2.
The calculations for direct inversing AL are 50232 flops and for using (45) are 37271, figure 4
The results of the experiments of the second example show that if the number of the subsystems increases, the computational efficiency increases because the matrices' dimensions decrease. This is in harmony with the multilevel hierarchical idea for decomposition of the initial problem leading to better efficiency of the system's functionality.

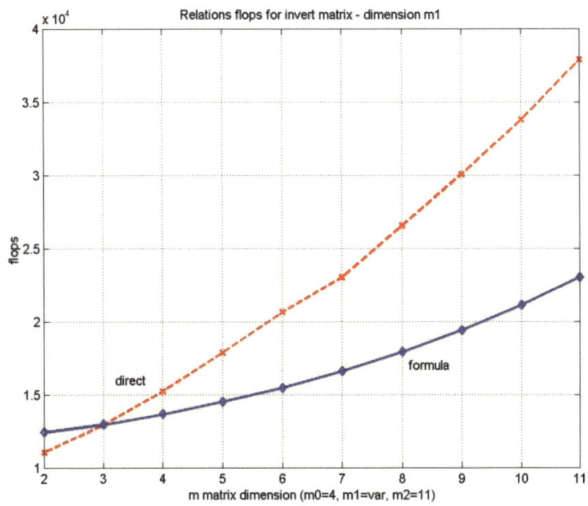

Fig. 3. Relation flops- m_1 matrix dimension

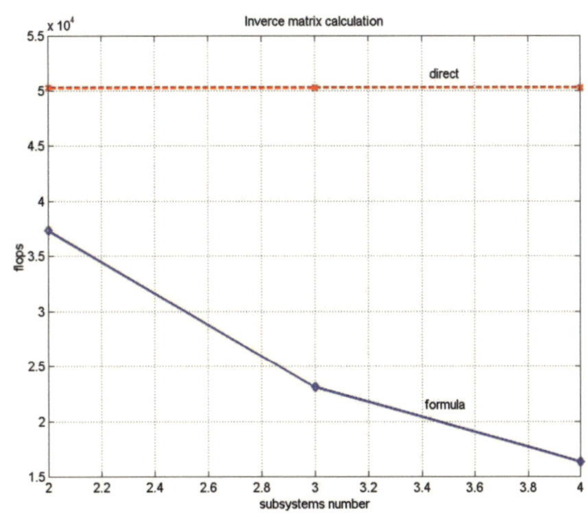

Fig. 4. Relation flops-subsystems number

5. Conclusion

The inverse matrix evaluations are decomposed to a set of operations, which does not consist of calculations of inverse high order matrix. Such decomposition benefits the inverse calculations when the initial large scale matrix is composed of low order matrices, which inverses are calculated with less computational efforts. The decomposition approach benefits the case when an initial matrix is known with its inverse, but few modifications of its components change it and new inverse has to be calculated. The decomposition approach for the inverse calculations is assessed and increase of the computational efficiency is illustrated. The MATLAB implementation of the presented sequence of calculations (49)−(50) is easy to perform because it results in consequent matrix sum and multiplications, and low order inverse matrix evaluations.

6. References

Fausett, L.(1999). *Applied numerical analysis*. Prentice Hall, NY, 596 p.

Flannery, B.(1997) *Numerical recipes in C. The art of Scientific Computing*. Cambridge University press, William Press, Second edition, 965p.

Mesarovich, M., D. Mako I. Takahara (1973) *Theory of Hierarchical Multilevel Systems*, Moscow, Mir (in Russian)

Stoilov T., K. Stoilova (1999). *Noniterative coordination in multilevel systems*. Kluwer Academic Publisher, ISBN 0-7923-5879-1, Dordrecht /Boston/London.

Stoilova, K. (2010). *Noniterative predictive coordination*. Professor M. Drinov Academic Publisher, ISBN 978-954-322-268-1, Sofia (in Bulgarian)

Stoilova K., T. Stoilov (2007) Computational efficiency of inverse matrix evaluations. Proceedings of International Conference Computer Systems and Technologies "CompSysTech 2007", ISBN 978-954-9641-50-9, Russe, Bulgaria, pp.IIIA.2-1 - IIIA.2-6.

Strassen V., (1969). Numerische Mathematik, vol.13, pp.354-356.

Part 2

Database Development

7

A Cluster-Based Method for Evaluation of Truck's Weighing Control Stations

Abbas Mahmoudabadi[1] and Arezoo Abolghasem[2]
[1]*PhD Candidate, Technical and Engineering Faculty, Payam-e-Noor University & General Director of Traffic Safety Department, Road Maintenance and Transportation Organization, Tehran*
[2]*Transportation Engineer, Road Maintenance and Transportation Organization, Tehran Iran*

1. Introduction

Effective and safe road network is essential to economic growth and social welfare (Islamic Republic of Iran Majlis, 2005). More than 550 million tons of goods are transported by road network in Islamic Republic of Iran, which is a large amount of total cargo transportation's rate (RMTO, 2009). Overloading of vehicles increases safety risk and pavement damages (Planning and Management Organization, 1996), so to improve road safety and restrain pavement damages, legislation based on maximum allowable axle and total load is applied for heavy vehicles, which are passing on the roads (Mohammadi, 1999). Law enforcement control is done by weighing control equipments, which have been installed near the arterial roads, and to evaluate law enforcement, clustering method can be used as an effective technique.

Clustering method is used to classify data and decision making in transportation studies. Some researchers (Ahmed and Kanhere, 2007) used clustering method for public transport modeling in order to improve situation and possibility of changing decision in public transportation. They showed that using a step forward algorithm for clustering the nodes in finding routes problems while using clustering method, improves effectiveness of algorithm.

Clustering has been used to classify accident types (Depaire et al. 2008). They used a model based on clustering data, which divide accident data to 7 homogenous groups and finally analyzed injuries in each group .Comparing results based on divided groups and total data analysis showed that classifying data could be used for safety issues researchers with more accuracy.

(Fielding et. al 1985) used clustering method for analyzing transit systems equipments, considering vehicle's size, average speed, urban transportation situation, and bus specified routes, and have classified transit situation to 12 categories. Difference of characteristics for all categories was identified using variance analysis, detached group and tree decision-making method. Grouping data were made by seven main transit efficiency factors and finally some suggestion for each group was supposed to productivity evaluation.

In this paper after a brief review on methods of controlling cargo transportation and existing regulation in rural roads network, an evaluation method of trucks weighing control is presented using clustering analysis method. For evaluation and comparing results, available data on trucks weighing control, which have been collected by local authorities in all over the country, have been analyzed based on clustering and finally weighing stations have been categorized in different groups.

2. Goods transportation controlling on road network

Overloading vehicles are important from two sides of decreasing transportation safety and fateful damages on roads surface and infrastructures. Overloaded vehicles in addition to damage road surface, because of Pre-designing of braking system particularly at slides and curves, endanger other vehicles. Increasing goods' transportation will lead to economical growth from one side of the view, and the other side will increase maintenance costs and safety risks. Studies show that the most important factor of roads destruction is heavy vehicle's axle load. Based on researches the damage on roads surface is related to the vehicle axle load by a non-linear acceleration rate mostly in a polynomial equation of forth degree. Because of limited budget in roads maintenance activities, it is essential to apply over loaded vehicles limitation rules effectively. In spite of heavy maintenance costs, do not repairing road surfaces leads to destroy vehicles and decreasing traffic speed, so pavement management is very important issue because of overloading vehicles passage .
At the present, the method of trucks weighing control in Iran is using weighing control equipments including static, dynamic, and portable scales at weighing stations (and Weigh in Motion System in 6 points). Maximum permitted axle load for different types of heavy vehicles, which has been identified by laws, is under the control of weighing stations.

3. Proposed method

According to importance of controlling overloaded vehicles, performance evaluation of weighing control is inevitable. Identifying effective parameters on weighing control, data standardizing and ranking weighing stations have done in this paper in the sequence process using a well-known method of statistical process of clustering.

3.1 Clustering method

Clustering method is a statistical method that divides observation data according to their similarity to homogenous and detached groups (Sharma, 1996). In this method, similarity criterion is firstly identified. The number of groups would be analyzed and recognized. Observation data in each group are similar to each other based on similarity criterion and each group is different from the other groups. It is possible to consider more than one variable simultaneously as similarity criterion in clustering method. However, there are some different methods of identifying similarity criterions, but the common method for defining similarity is known as equation number 1 while the similarity of itk and jtk observed data of k_{th} variable is defined by P2ij.

$$P^2_{ij} = \sum_{k=1}^{p} (x_{ik} \ x_{jk})^2 \tag{1}$$

Clustering is a hierarchically process means that the nearest observations are merged continuously to make larger groups. This process will be continued until number of groups is reached to the proposed number of desired clusters. Merging observations is done by different methods such as Centroid, Farthest- Neighbour, Nearest- Neighbour, Average

Linkage, and Ward method usually chosen by analysts based on acceptable frequency. Based on experience, experts' view and comparing results of clustering Ward method is used to merge data in this research.

3.2 Data normalization

Because of existing the effective parameters in decision-making techniques, if there are different dimensions, for variables normalization or standardizing methods are used to assimilate (Sharma, 1996). If data can be fitted by a normal distribution function, normalization method is used. In addition, there are different methods of output and input data normalization, which the most regular methods convert data to, numbers between 0 to 1 and -1 to 1. Equations (2) and (3) converts data to zero to 1 numbers and are used for data more than zero.

$$X_{new} = \frac{X_{old}}{X_{\max}} \tag{2}$$

$$X_{new} = \frac{X_{old} - X_{\min}}{X_{\max} - X_{\min}} \tag{3}$$

If it is necessary to convert data in the range of -1 to 1, equation (4) is used:

$$\left\{\begin{array}{ll} X_{new} = \dfrac{X_{old}}{X_{\max}} & \forall X_{old} \geq 0 \\ X_{new} = \dfrac{X_{old}}{X_{\min}} & \forall X_{old} \leq 0 \end{array}\right\} \tag{4}$$

In order to standardize data assuming distribution function is normal, equation (5) is used which X_{old} is preliminary amount of factor and X_{new} is standardized form:

$$X_{new} = \frac{X_{old} - \overline{X}}{\sqrt{\sum_{i=1}^{n} \frac{(X_i - \overline{X})^2}{n-1}}} \tag{5}$$

3.3 Data gathering

To evaluate truck's weighing control performance, number of registered overloaded vehicles, amount of detected overload, the type of scale, average heavy vehicle's daily traffic, and number of overloaded vehicles with more than 5 tons overload are collected from all over the country in 6 mount period to use defined below parameters:

- Number of registered overloaded vehicles of six months period
- Detected amount of overloading of six months period
- Proportion of registered overloaded vehicles of six months period to the same period in last year
- Proportion of detected amount of overloading of six months period to the same period in last year
- Average heavy vehicles daily traffic of six months period

- The fraction of number of overloaded vehicles with more than 5 ton overload to total registered overloaded vehicles of six months period

Tables 1 and 2 show maximum, minimum, average, and standard deviation of collected data before and after standardizing data respectively. As it is observed, to homogenize data, standardization is used because of having a normal distribution function.

Row	Parameter's Name	Experimental Data			
		Max	Min	Average	Standard Deviation
1	Number of registered overloaded vehicles	1754	2	193	255
2	Detected amount of overloading(ton)	4014	2	519	655
3	Proportion of detected overloaded vehicles of six months period to the same period in last year	615	-96	88	143
4	Amount of detected overloading proportion of six months period to the same period in last year	718	-94	89	162
5	Average daily heavy vehicles traffic	41059	103	3887	6493
6	Number of more than 5 ton overloaded vehicles to number of total overload proportion	0.35	0	0.07	0.09

Table 1. Parameters, experimental data

Row	Parameter's Name	Standardized Data			
		Max	Min	Average	Standard Deviation
1	Number of detected overloaded vehicles	6.12	-0.75	0	1
2	Detected amount of overloading(ton)	5.37	-0.79	0	1
3	Proportion of detected overloaded vehicles of six months period to the same period in last year	3.69	-1.29	0	1
4	Amount of detected overloading proportion of six months period to the same period in last year	3.89	-1.13	0	1
5	Average daily heavy vehicles traffic	5.72	-0.58	0	1
6	Number of more than 5 ton overloaded vehicles to number of total overload proportion	3.16	-0.87	0	1

Table 2. Parameters, standardized data

3.4 Setting number of clusters

The number of clusters is specified in two ways. In the first method, analysts specify number of clusters when the number of clusters needs to be applied to other decision-making process, for example using clustering method to fuzzy modeling. Second method of specifying number of clusters, is minimizing Within-Group Sum of Squares (Sharma, 1996) while the sum of total deviation is calculated and number of clusters is identified in such a way that inter clusters sum of squares, which is named missed sum of squares, would be minimized. Also proportional sum of deviation squares as Between-Group Sum of Squares is used as a criterion to specifying number of clusters.

Since the number of clusters in this research work is not too important, second method which is more scientific has been used and the number of clusters is specified in such a way that minimizes Within-Group, deviation. Table 3 shows total deviation, Within-Group and Between-Group deviation and proportion of Within-Group to total deviation which is decision making parameter.

According to table (3), if it is proposed that 85 percent of deviation is reserved, number of clusters would be 16, and if it is proposed to reserve 90 percent of deviation, number of clusters would be 22. As it is shown at table (3) rest of deviations after 22 would change slowly means increasing the number of clusters doesn't have significant rule in decision process.

Figure (1) shows changes in total deviation, Within-Group and Between-Group deviation based on the number of clusters. As it has been shown in this figure, difference between Total deviation and Between-Group deviation would be decreased after 16, since 16 covers 85 percent of deviations, so in this research 16 number of clusters has been considered to evaluate weighing stations performance in controlling goods transported by heavy vehicles.

Row	Number of Clusters	Deviation From Average Sum of Square Errors			
		Total	Within Groups	Between Groups	Proportion of Between Groups to Total
1	4	750	352	398	53
2	6	750	236	514	69
3	8	750	183	567	76
4	10	750	156	594	79
5	12	750	145	605	81
6	14	750	122	628	84
7	16	750	113	637	85
8	18	750	102	648	86
9	20	750	81	669	89
10	22	750	77	673	90
11	24	750	68	682	91
12	26	750	63	687	92
13	28	750	61	689	92
14	30	750	55	695	93

Table 3. Deviation from average sum of square errors

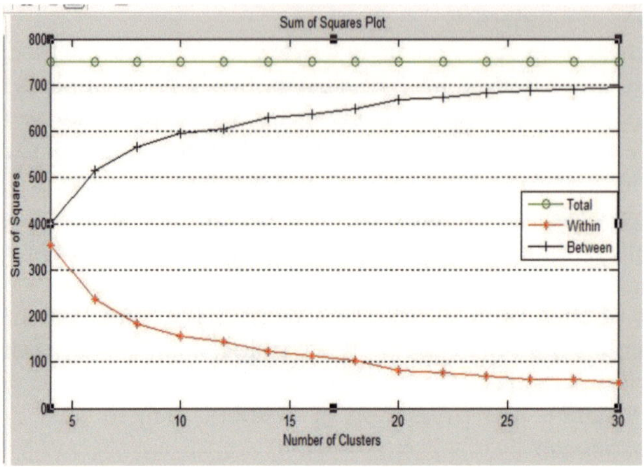

Fig. 1. Plot of square errors (Within, Between and Total)

4. How to use MATLAB software

There is a command in MATLAB software, which has ability to cluster observations based on many parameters. As shown in tables 1 and 2, there are six parameters for clustering. Clusterdata is a well-known command in order to cluster data. There is a matrix 126×6 contains data used in this research work. If matrix named as X figure 2 shows the format of data.

Code	X(:,1)	X(:,2)	X(:,3)	X(:,4)	X(:,5)	X(:,6)
5707	0.011113	-0.0353	-0.64109	-0.81193	-0.46864	-0.86858
5704	0.819076	0.992241	-0.65484	-0.90436	-0.36345	-0.86858
...	...	...	...	...	...	...
5108	0.611202	1.519068	-0.08919	-0.82648	0.333153	0.958812
5106	-0.68703	-0.72033	0.783371	1.209399	0.448663	-0.86858

Fig. 2. Matrix contains data with six parameters

When command "clusterdata" is typed, results, are generated and are shown in a matrix contain two columns. The first column corresponds the row of observation and the second corresponds assigned cluster. For example if the first row of result matrix contains, 1 and 15, it means that station coded as 5707 in the first row of matrix X, belong to the 14th cluster.
The other command in MATLAB is kmeans, which is used to calculate the distance between observation and centre of the cluster. There is a output variable of SUMD in kmeans command to set distances and within group sum of square errors will be calculated by sum of the square distances of variable SUMD. Between sum of square errors will be calculated by total sum of square errors minus within sum of square errors while total sum of square errors is calculated as below (Sharma, 1996):

$$\text{Total sum of square errors} = (126-1) \times 6 = 750$$

When 126 is the number of observations and 6 is the number of standardized parameters.

5. Results

Considering the number of clusters by 16 and Ward Method to merging data, using clustering method of well-known software of MATLAB version R2008a, weighing station grades considering six identified variables are presented as table 4.

Class	Station's code	Number of stations
1	1126, 3603	2
2	3607, 3601	2
3	4507, 4102, 8708, 2109	4
4	1106	1
5	1125, 1104, 5408, 8701	4
6	5409, 8705, 8706, 3202, 2110, 9101	6
7	5108, 5107, 5109, 9703, 9702	5
8	1190, 1112, 3609, 3606, 3602, 7504	6
9	1108, 3608, 3604	3
10	9748, 4502, 8709, 3203, 3303, 7702, 2107	7
11	5102, 1122, 7503, 5401, 5406, 1403, 4110, 2104, 5703, 5704	11
12	5106, 1116, 4508, 4553, 4506, 4106, 41014, 4108, 4106, 4104, 6108, 6107, 2116, 2106, 9104, 9105	14
13	2105, 6401, 5402, 5403, 5404, 9701, 9506, 9502, 2111, 2105	10
14	5104, 1103, 1114, 7502, 4503, 4501, 4504, 1405, 4117, 6110, 6105, 8702, 7701, 2108, 2101, 5701, 5702, 5707	19
15	6402, 6404, 6403, 5407, 6106, 6102, 6101, 8704, 3201, 3301, 7706, 9505, 9501, 2103, 2102, 9103, 9102	17
16	3610, 7505, 6405, 4114, 4111, 4122, 4109, 4105, 4112, 4101, 6108, 6103, 7704, 9503, 5706	15

Table 4. Results (Clusters contain the number of stations)

6. Conclusion and future research

In this research, number of detected overloaded vehicles, amount of overload, scale's type, average heavy vehicle's daily traffic, and number of overloaded vehicles with more than 5 ton overload are collected from all over the country in a six month period and using standardization method are homogenized. By using minimum deviation method of Average within-Groups, number of clusters is calculated and considering Ward method for merging data, and using clustering method, the performance of weighing stations have been classified in 16 groups. Results show that this method is appropriate to use evaluation of weighing control performance in weighing stations.

Future studies, recommended using ranking method by similarity factors for traffic laws enforcement control, and any other important factors such as vehicles speed, overtaking, and left diversion control. Ranking enforcement stations and at a wider view ranking provinces could provide a comprehensive and precise image for mangers about enforcement stations performance.

7. References

Ahmed, S.; Kanhere, S.S, (Oct 2007), "Cluster-based Forwarding in Delay Tolerant Public Transport, Networks", 32nd IEEE Conference, Pages 625-634.

Bolghari, M., (2010, 1389 local calender), "Driving laws and regulations", Second version, Department of transportation, Tehran municipality, 2010.

Depaire, B., Wets, G., Vanhoof, K., (July 2008), "Traffic accident segmentation by means of latent class clustering", Accident Analysis and Preventation, Vol, 40, Issue 4, Pages 1257-1266.

Fielding, G.J., Brenner, M.E., Faust, K., (May 1985), "Typology for Bus Transit", Transportation Research, Part A, Vol 40, Issue 4, Pages 1257-1266.

Islamic Republic of Iran Majlis, (2005, 1384 local calender) "Forth five-year developing plan of Islamic republic of Iran", available on www.majlis.ir

Mohammadi Asa, A., (1999, 1378 local calender), "Laws and regulations in road transport", Road maintenance and transportation organization.

Planning and management organization, (1996, 1375 local calender) "Road pavement and asphalt manual", Vol. 234.

Road Maintenance and Transportation Organization, (2009, 1388 local calender) "Annual survey of road transport in Iran", available on www.rmto.ir

Subhash Sharma, (1996), "Applied Multivariable Techniques", University of South Carolina, USA.

The Impact of the Data Archiving File Format on Scientific Computing and Performance of Image Processing Algorithms in MATLAB Using Large HDF5 and XML Multimodal and Hyperspectral Data Sets

Kelly Bennett[1] and James Robertson[2]
[1]*U.S. Army Research Laboratory, Sensors and Electron Devices Directorate, Adelphi, MD*
[2]*Clearhaven Technologies LLC, Severna Park, MD*
U.S.A

1. Introduction

Scientists require the ability to effortlessly share and process data collected and stored on a variety of computer platforms in specialized data storage formats. Experiments often generate large amounts of raw and corrected data and metadata, which describes and characterizes the raw data. Scientific teams and groups develop many formats and tools for internal use for specialized users with particular references and backgrounds. Researchers need a solution for querying, accessing, and analyzing large data sets of heterogeneous data, and demand high interoperability between data and various applications (Shasharina et al., 2007; Shishedjiev et al., 2010).

Debate continues regarding which data format provides the greatest transparency and produces the most reliable data exchange. Currently, Extensible Markup Language (XML) and Hierarchical Data Format 5 (HDF5) formats are two solutions for sharing data. XML is a simple, platform-independent, flexible markup meta-language that provides a format for storing structured data, and is a primary format for data exchange across the Internet (McGrath, 2003). XML data files use Document Type Definitions (DTDs) and XML Schemas to define the data structures and definitions, including data formatting, attributes, and descriptive information about the data. A number of applications exist that use XML-based storage implementations for applications, including radiation and spectral measurements, simulation data of magnetic fields in human tissues, and describing and accessing fusion and plasma physics simulations (Shasharina et al., 2007; Shishedjiev et al., 2010).

HDF5 is a data model, library, and file format for storing and managing data. HDF5 is portable and extensible, allowing applications to evolve in their use of HDF5 (HDF Group). HDF5 files provide the capability for self-documenting storage of scientific data in that the HDF5 data model provides structures that allow the file format to contain data about the file structure and descriptive information about the data contained in the file (Barkstrom, 2001). Similar to XML, numerous applications using the HDF5 storage format exist, such as fusion and plasma physics, astronomy, medicine and bio-imaging (Shasharina et al., 2007; Dougherty et al., 2009).

In this chapter, we will use hyperspectral images stored in XML and HDF5 format to compare the relative performance of the file format using computationally intensive signal and image processing algorithms running in MATLAB on Windows® 64-bit and Linux 64-bit workstations. Hyperspectral imaging refers to the multidimensional character of the spectral data set, where the acquisition of images takes place over many contiguous spectral bands throughout the visible and infrared (IR) regions (Goetz et al., 1985). Sensor fusion and advanced image processing techniques are now possible using the information from these different bands that allow applications in aerospace, defense, medicine, and other fields of study.

To assist researchers in exchanging the data needed to develop, test, and optimize the techniques, selecting the best file format for computing environments (such as MATLAB) requires additional analysis. Such analysis includes analyzing the relative performance of the file format, including scalability, with respect to various computational tools, computer architectures, and operating systems (Bennett & Robertson, 2010). In this chapter we provide insights into the challenges researchers face with a growing set of data, along with expectations for performance guidelines on workstations for processing large HDF5 and XML hyperspectral image data. Additionally, in this chapter, we provide specific results comparing data load, process, and memory usage for the differing data formats, along with detailed discussions and implications for researchers.

2. Analysis of HDF5 and XML Formats

The goals of this analysis are to:

1. Determine strengths and weaknesses of using HDF5 and XML formats for typical processing techniques associated with large hyperspectral images;
2. Compare and analyze processing times on Windows and Linux 64-bit workstations for HDF5 and XML hyperspectral images; and
3. Identify areas that require additional research to help improve efficiencies associated with processing large HDF5 and XML files, such as hyperspectral images.

3. Methodology for Analysis of HDF5 and XML Formats

To address the analysis goals a set of 100 files containing multimodal hyperspectral images, ranging in size from 57 MB to 191 MB, stored in HDF5 format provided the input for the creation of HDF5 and XML dataset files as part of a preprocessing step for further analysis. The created HDF5 and XML dataset files provided the input to a series of analysis techniques typically associated with image and signal processing. Two different workstations running 64-bit Windows and Linux operating systems are used. The workstations are equipped with MATLAB (scientific programming language). Table 1 displays the descriptions of each of the workstations.

The hyperspectral images were originally stored in HDF5 format and included several different types of metadata in the form of HDF5 Groups and Datasets. Metadata in a typical HDF5 file includes ground truth, frequency bandwidths, raw image data, TIFF (Tagged

---

® Registered trademark of Microsoft Corporation.

Image File Format)-formatted images, collection information, and other ancillary information, allowing researchers to understand the images and their collection parameters.

Descriptor	Windows 64-bit	Linux 64-bit
Operating System	Windows 7 home premium	Red Hat Enterprise Linux 5
CPU	Intel i7 920 @2.67 GHz	2 processor, quad core Xeon 2.0 GHz
Memory	6 GB	16 GB
MATLAB version	7.11.0 (R2010b)	7.11.0 (R2010b)

Table 1. Research Equipment Descriptions.

Each original HDF5 file went through a number of preprocessing steps to remove the metadata in preparation for analysis. For analysis purposes, we needed to remove the metadata from the original HDF5 files and create new HDF5 and XML formatted files consisting of only raw sensor data prior to performing image processing. These steps included loading the original HDF5 file structures, searching through the HDF5 groups to find the raw image data, saving the new HDF5 file, creating and populating an XML document node, and saving the XML file. Figure 1 shows the overall steps in processing the original HDF5 file, along with some critical MATLAB code associated with each of those steps.

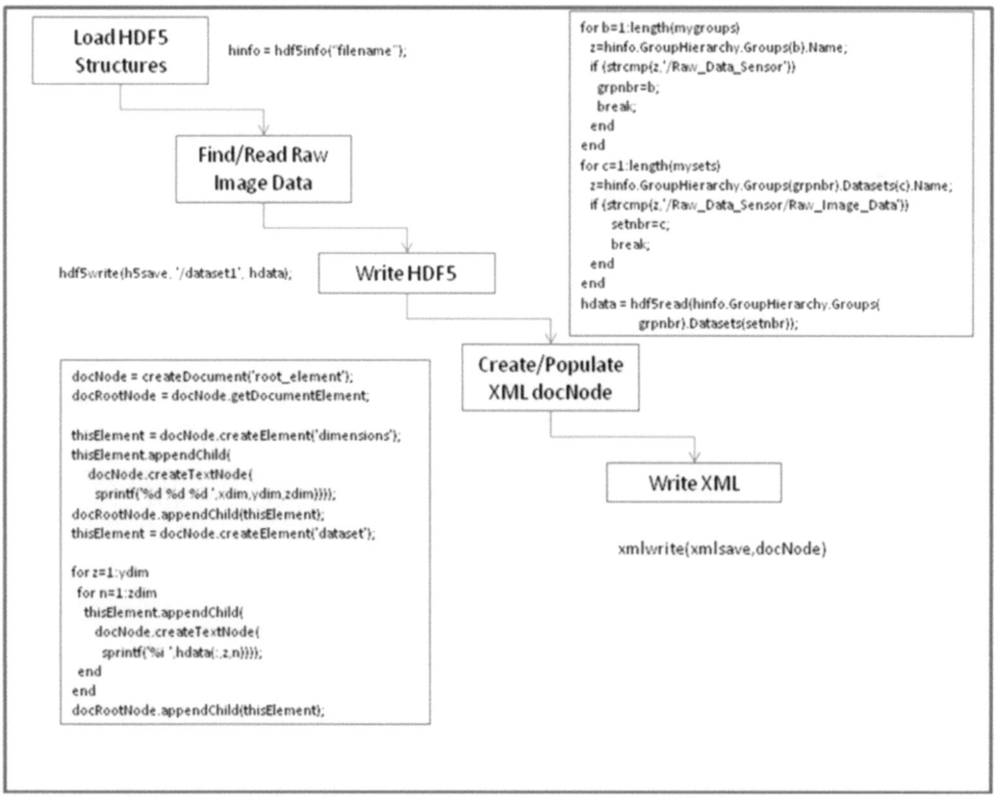

Fig. 1. Original HDF5 File Preprocessing Overview for the creation of HDF5 and XML Dataset Files.

After creating the HDF5 and XML files for the raw sensor data, each file was loaded into MATLAB, converted to an array as needed, and run through a number of image processing steps. XML stores the array data as a large ASCII character string, which requires converting the character array into a numeric array before beginning any processing. Unfortunately, the arrays were too large to use MATLAB's str2num() function, so a novel custom method was developed to read each character and convert it into numbers before writing the numbers into a MATLAB array.

Technique	Description	Example MATLAB Call
Image Adjustment	Maps the values in intensity to new values such that 1% of data saturates at low and high intensities of the original image.	im2= imadjust(im);
Histogram	Calculates a histogram where the variable bin specifies the number of bins used in the histogram.	[COUNTS,X] = imhist(im2,bin);
Descriptive Statistics	Computes the mean and standard deviations of the image values.	imagemean=mean2(im2); imagestd=std2(im2);
Median Noise Filter	Performs a median filtering of the image using a 3-by-3 neighborhood.	J=medfilt2(im2);
Weiner Noise Filter	Performs a filtering of the image using pixel-wise adaptive Wiener filtering, using neighborhoods of size fx-by-fy to estimate the local image mean and standard deviation	K = wiener2(im2,[fx fy]);
Sobel Edge Detection	Sobel method finds edges using the Sobel approximation to the derivative. It returns edges at those points where the gradient is maximum	BW1 = edge(im2,'sobel');
Canny Edge Detection	The Canny method finds edges by looking for local maxima of the gradient. The derivative of a Gaussian filter provides the approach for calculating the gradient.	BW2 = edge(im2,'canny');

FFT 2D Threshold Feature Detection	FFT approach to template matching and feature detection.	z= im2(minx:maxx,miny:maxy);
		
		C = real(ifft2(fft2(im2) .* fft2(rot90(z,2),dims(1),dims(2))));
		t=max(C(:)) - .05*max(C(:));

Table 2. Image Processing Technique Descriptions.

Once stored as numeric arrays, the processing for the XML and the HDF5 files were the same and these processing steps include image adjustment, histogram calculation, and descriptive statistics, filtering to remove noise, edge detection and 2-D FFT threshold feature detection. Each of these image-processing techniques includes possible techniques users may invoke when processing hyperspectral images. Table 2 provides a brief description of each of these techniques and an example call within MATLAB. In Table 2, "im" represents the original image and 'im2' represents a processed image of 'im'. Each row in Table 2 shows various processing operations performed on 'im' or 'im2'. Figure 2 shows the flow of the image processing techniques.

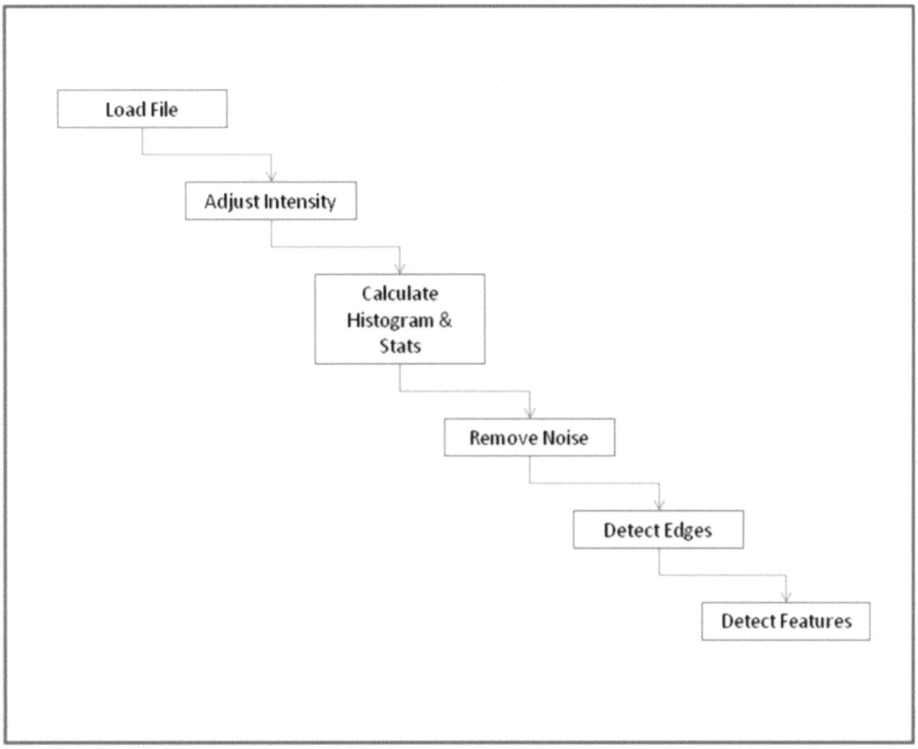

Fig. 2. Image Processing Overview.

Some of the metrics used for assessing the performance of each file format are calculation of load times, process times, and memory usage statistics for each file format and machine. These metrics reveal the computational performance of processing large archived data files in MATLAB using typical image processing algorithms. MATLAB's tic and toc methods were convenient to measure elapsed times associated with each processing step. Hyperspectral images consist of multiple segments representing different spectral bands or narrow frequency bands, with data collected for each image segment and averaged for reporting purposes. For example, an image with 62 segments would generate data for each of the 62 segments and the mean of those values, with the results described in the Results section of this paper. A typical sequence of elapsed time measurement would occur as shown in Figure 3. In the Figure 3 example, all files ("i") and segments ("j") perform the timing process for the image adjustment algorithm.

```
% Adjust the image for better display
tic;
im2= imadjust(im);
adjustIM(i,j)=toc;
```

Fig. 3. Elapsed Time Measurement Example Code.

After loading each created dataset file, both in HDF5 and XML, measuring the memory will determine the average memory usage. For the Windows environment, MATLAB's memory functions perform the process of determining the physical memory available at that point in time. For the Linux environment, system calls to the Linux memory functions determine the physical memory available after loading the file. MATLAB does not provide a Linux memory function at this time. Figure 4 shows a typical Windows memory call.

```
% Measure Windows Memory
[USERVIEW, SYSTEMVIEW] = memory;
pmem(i,j)=SYSTEMVIEW.PhysicalMemory.Available;
```

Fig. 4. Windows Memory Measurement Example Code.

Test	Description	Performance Factors
LU	Perform LU of a full matrix	Floating-point, regular memory access
FFT	Perform FFT of a full vector	Floating-point, irregular memory access
ODE	Solve van der Pol equation with ODE45	Data structures and MATLAB function files
Sparse	Solve a symmetric sparse linear system	Mixed integer and floating-point
2-D	Plot Bernstein polynomial graph	2-D line drawing graphics
3-D	Display animated L-shape membrane logo	3-D animated OpenGL graphics

Table 3. MATLAB's Benchmark Descriptions.

Prior to running the algorithms, each computer system performed baseline benchmarks. MATLAB has a convenient built-in benchmark named "bench" that executes six different MATLAB tasks and compares the execution speed with the speed of several other computers. Table 3 shows the six different tasks.

The LU test performs a matrix factorization, which expresses a matrix as the product of two triangular matrices. One of the matrices is a permutation of a lower triangular matrix and the other an upper triangular matrix. The fast Fourier transform (FFT) test performs the discrete Fourier transform computed using an FFT algorithm. The ordinary differential equation (ODE) test solves equations using the ODE45 solver. The Sparse test converts a matrix to sparse form by removing any zero elements. Finally, the 2-D and 3-D measure 2-D and 3-D graphics performance, including software or hardware support for OpenGL (Open Graphics Library).

The benchmark results in a speed comparison between the current machine and industry-available machines.

4. Data analysis

Data analysis included calculating descriptive statistics on each test to include mean, standard deviation, variance, minimum and maximum values, and t-test analysis; to determine relationships and differences in performance measurements comparing XML and HDF5 formats for both computer systems. The t-test is one of the most commonly used statistics to determine whether two datasets are significantly different from one another (Gay & Airasian, 2003). The t-test determines if the observed variation between the two datasets is sufficiently larger than a difference expected purely by chance. For this research, the significance level (α) was set at 0.05. This value is commonly accepted and is the default value for many statistical packages that include the t-test (Gay & Airasian, 2003; SAS Institute, 2003; MathWorks, 2011).

For each processing, memory, or loading algorithm, the descriptive statistics for each hyperspectral image create relevant data for a final analysis. The information obtained from averaging across each segment of the multiple segmented images creates the analytical data products used in the results.

In addition to the descriptive statistics for each process, graphical plots illustrate the load times, process times, and memory usage as a function of file size for each data type and test environment. These plots provide an ability to identify differences between the XML and HDF5 data types and possible processing bottlenecks and limitations.

5. Results and Implications

Scientists and researchers need a reliable format for exchanging large datasets for use in computational environments (such as MATLAB). MATLAB has many advantages over conventional languages (such as FORTRAN, and C++) for scientific data analysis, such as ease of use, platform independence, device-independent plotting, graphical user interface, and the MATLAB compiler (Chapman, 2008). Previous results have shown HDF5 format provided faster load and process times than XML formats, and loads large amounts of data without running into memory issues (Bennett & Robertson, 2010). This research supports these findings.

This section provides results and discussion of this current research. After the baseline benchmarks provide results for each machine, the analysis will show example images and descriptive statistics for each image-processing algorithm, along with tables, plots, and discussion comparing HDF5 and XML formats for each task.

Table 4 shows the average of 10 MATLAB bench time results for each of the machines for the LU, FFT, ODE, Sparse, 2D, and 3D tests. For most tests, the Windows 64-bit machine performed better (as indicated by smaller execution times) than the Linux 64-bit machine. One exception to this was the 2D graphics, where the Linux 64-bit machine was slightly faster than the Windows machine. Based on these results, the Windows 64-bit machine should perform slightly faster for the subsequent image processing tasks.

Machine	LU	FFT	ODE	Sparse	2D	3D
Windows 64-bit	0.0389	0.0511	0.1353	0.1789	0.4409	0.7531
Linux 64-bit	0.0872	0.1221	0.2267	0.3137	0.3301	0.8154

Table 4. MATLAB's Bench Results.

Figure 5 shows a typical image used in this analysis. This image represents one specific frequency range (spectral band) for a 460 x 256 image after adjusting of the intensity for display.

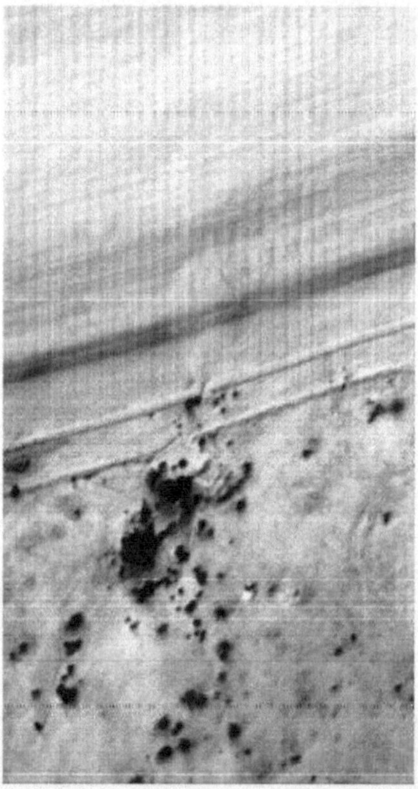

Fig. 5. Example 460 x 256 Image.

A quad chart (Figure 6) displays processed images showing some of the techniques. The first image in Figure 6 is an image in the upper-left corner representing the image adjusted for intensity. The image in the upper-right corner represents the image after the Weiner noise filter is applied. Next, the image in the lower-left corner represents the image after the Canny edge detection is applied. Lastly, the image in the lower-right corner represents the FFT threshold results.

Recall from Figure 1, preparing the images for processing requires several steps. The first step was to load the HDF5 structures, followed by finding and loading the HDF5 raw image data, saving the HDF5 raw image data, populating the XML docNode, and saving the XML raw image data.

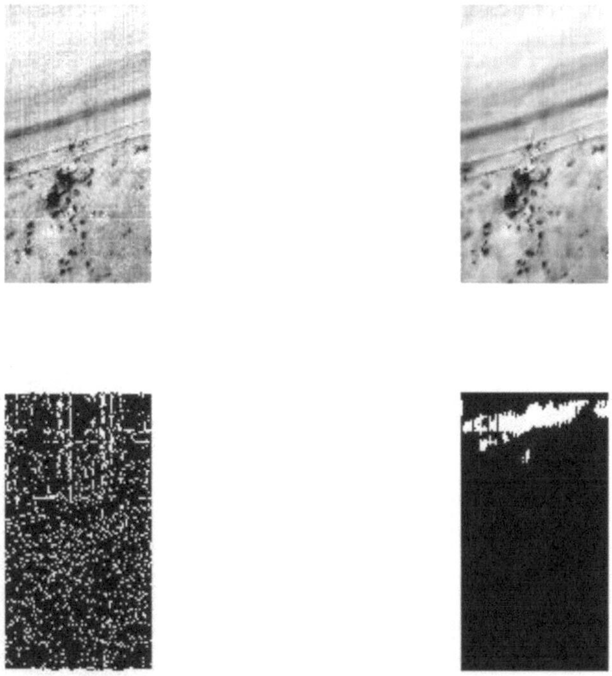

Fig. 6. Quad Image Example 460 by 256 Image.

A total of 100 original HDF5 files, ranging from 57 to 191 MB in size, provide the input for the creation of the HDF5 and XML dataset files. Table 5 displays the original HDF5 file size statistics for this research. The original HDF5 files contained ground truth, collection information, processed data, and spectral content, in addition to the raw image data. The computed image processing statistics use only the raw image data extracted from the HDF5 files and saved to HDF5 and XML formats.

Descriptor	Value (MB)
Mean	116.7304
Minimum	56.9807
Maximum	191.7729
Standard Deviation	28.5472
Variance	814.9406

Table 5. Original HDF5 File Size Descriptions.

The average times associated with each of these steps are shown in Table 6 for the Windows 64-bit and Table 7 for Linux 64-bit machine. The column labeled **"Total (s)"** represents the sum of each of the processing steps for the respective machines. For the current configuration of the Windows 64-bit machine, the mean preparation time per file was just over 9 s, with preparation times ranging between almost 7 and approximately 16.5 s. For the current configuration of the Linux 64-bit machine, the mean preparation time per file was almost 11 s, with times ranging between almost 9 and approximately 19.5 s.

Statistic	Load (s)	Read (s)	HDF5 Save (s)	docNode (s)	XML Save (s)	Total (s)
Mean	0.3313	0.3665	0.0996	7.129	1.1577	9.0841
Minimum	0.0261	0.0097	0.0168	6.0196	0.9191	6.9913
Maximum	1.1602	0.7236	0.5047	12.2276	1.9504	16.567
Standard Deviation	0.2269	0.1384	0.1275	1.8607	0.301	
Variance	0.0515	0.0192	0.0163	3.4623	0.0906	

Table 6. Windows 64-bit HDF5 Data Average Preparation Times.

Statistic	Load (s)	Read (s)	HDF5 Save (s)	docNode (s)	XML Save (s)	Total (s)
Mean	0.043	0.0226	0.0653	9.5711	1.0478	10.75
Minimum	0.0076	0.0107	0.044	8.146	0.7723	8.9806
Maximum	0.3131	0.1311	0.1404	16.775	2.1607	19.52
Standard Deviation	0.0382	0.0171	0.0245	2.6023	0.3637	
Variance	0.0015	0.0003	0.0006	6.7721	0.1322	

Table 7. Linux 64-bit HDF5 Data Average Preparation Times.

Table 8 shows the average free physical memory for each system during the preprocessing steps. Free physical memory can vary throughout a run based on system processing during the run and the amount of memory allocated to MATLAB for processing the run. For all runs during this research, the MATLAB Java heap memory was set to its maximum possible value to avoid any potential out-of-memory issues. In MATLAB version 2010b, selecting File, then Preferences, then General, and then Java Heap Memory, and then using the scroll bar to set its maximum setting changes the memory. The maximum setting for the Windows 64-bit machine was 1533 MB, while the maximum setting for the Linux 64-bit machine was 4011 MB. One trade-off with the Java heap memory being larger in Linux is that less physical memory is available for the run. However, increasing the Java heap memory does allow for larger possible Java objects, which is useful when dealing with large image arrays.

Statistic	Windows 64-bit (GB)	Linux 64-bit (GB)
Mean	2.7223	0.2374
Minimum	2.5234	0.0791
Maximum	2.9228	1.8715
Standard Deviation	0.0738	0.3696
Variance	0.0054	0.1366

Table 8. Free Physical Memory during HDF5 Preparation Steps.

After the preparation steps are complete, saving the raw image data to HDF5 and XML files is the next step. The new raw image files in HDF5 and XML contain only the image dimension information and the raw image pixel values. Table 9 provides the file statistics of the raw image data in both HDF5 and XML format. In all cases, the XML files are larger compared to the HDF5 files. In most cases, the resulting XML file is between 2.5 and 3 three times as large as the similar HDF5 file. This finding is consistent with other published results (Bennett & Robertson, 2010).

Statistic	HDF5 Raw Image Size (MB)	XML Raw Image Size (MB)
Mean	17.8374	49.3223
Minimum	13.9301	41.0791
Maximum	30.1252	86.0207
Standard Deviation	6.6819	13.7911
Variance	44.6480	190.1954

Table 9. HDF5 and XML Raw Image File Size Statistics.

After saving the raw image data to HDF5 and XML files, each file was loaded and processed according to the steps shown previously in Figure 2. These steps include loading the file, adjusting the image, calculating image statistics, removing noise, detecting edges, and detecting features. Algorithms include two different noise removal algorithms (Median and Weiner Filtering) and two different edge detection algorithms (Sobel and Canny). All of these algorithms, unmodified for this research effort, are available within the MATLAB Image Processing toolbox.

Table 10 shows the statistical results of the execution times for each of these image-processing algorithms for HDF5 and XML formats for the Windows 64-bit. Table 11 shows the results for the Linux 64-bit machine.

	HDF5					XML				
Process	Mean	Min	Max	Std	Var	Mean	Min	Max	Std	Var
Load (s)	0.0258	0.0013	0.0530	0.0072	0.0001	0.7309	0.6117	1.3135	0.2059	0.0424
Adjust (s)	0.0162	0.0058	0.0778	0.0235	0.0006	0.0419	0.0055	0.2366	0.0828	0.0069
Histogram (s)	0.0128	0.0013	0.0730	0.0262	0.0007	0.0225	0.0022	0.1256	0.0447	0.0020
Mean2 (s)	0.0005	0.0001	0.0026	0.0008	0.0000	0.0007	0.0001	0.0037	0.0013	0.0000
STD2 (s)	0.0124	0.0009	0.0735	0.0261	0.0007	0.0089	0.0005	0.0489	0.0179	0.0003
Median (s)	0.0057	0.0021	0.0273	0.0081	0.0001	0.0822	0.0097	0.4280	0.1545	0.0239
Weiner (s)	0.1111	0.0098	0.6541	0.2309	0.0533	0.1307	0.0088	0.7117	0.2597	0.0674
Sobel (s)	0.0663	0.0069	0.3890	0.1347	0.0181	0.0661	0.0051	0.3542	0.1288	0.0166
Canny (s)	0.7276	0.0673	4.1964	1.4975	2.2425	0.5622	0.0532	2.9744	1.0781	1.1622
FFT Feature (s)	0.1222	0.0124	0.6884	0.2398	0.0575	0.1461	0.0122	0.7627	0.2759	0.0761
Total (s)	1.1006	0.1079	6.2351			1.7922	0.7090	6.9594		

Table 10. Windows 64-bit HDF5 and XML Image Processing Execution Times.

On both the Windows and Linux machines, the total execution times for the HDF5 files were significantly less than the total execution times for the XML files. Comparing the results for the mean execution time for the Windows machine, HDF5 demonstrates excellent performance (~1.1 s) compared to XML (~1.8 s). The execution times for the windows machine ranged between ~0.1 and ~6.2 s for the HDF5 files, compared to ~0.7 - ~6.9 s for the XML files. Similarly, comparing the results for the mean execution time for the Linux machine, HDF5 demonstrates excellent performance (~1.5 s) compared to XML (~3.1 s). The execution times for the Linux machine ranged between ~0.15 and ~9.2 s for the HDF5 files, compared to ~1.3 - ~12.3 s for the XML files.

The total execution time difference for both the Windows and Linux machines is primarily due to the "load" process. Loading XML files requires far more execution time due to the larger file sizes of the created XML data files (~3 times larger file size when storing the raw data in XML format).

Additional loading difficulties with XML files include:

1. Slowness of the serialization process of converting Unicode XML into binary memory storage (McGrath, 2003).
2. MATLAB loading algorithm ('xmlread' method) uses the Document Object Model (DOM) to load XML files. DOM is memory and resource intensive, and can consume as much as 10 times the computer memory as the size of the actual XML data file (Wang et al., 2007).
3. In general, and of particular concern for users performing 32-bit processing, processing speeds associated with XML loading can be greatly diminished as virtual memory becomes insufficient compared with the size of the XML file as the computer starts to run out of memory.

	HDF5					XML				
Process	Mean	Min	Max	Std	Var	Mean	Min	Max	Std	Var
Load (s)	0.0199	0.0021	0.0509	0.0095	0.0001	1.3520	1.2015	2.0415	0.2444	0.0597
Adjust (s)	0.0250	0.0087	0.1276	0.0371	0.0014	0.0757	0.0095	0.4293	0.1503	0.0226
Histogram (s)	0.0160	0.0017	0.0914	0.0326	0.0011	0.0290	0.0028	0.1697	0.0598	0.0036
Mean2 (s)	0.0007	0.0003	0.0036	0.0010	0.0000	0.0020	0.0004	0.0106	0.0036	0.0000
STD2 (s)	0.0216	0.0019	0.1309	0.0447	0.002	0.0136	0.0012	0.0806	0.0285	0.0008
Median (s)	0.0631	0.0074	0.3595	0.1265	0.0160	0.1135	0.0127	0.6524	0.2291	0.0525
Weiner (s)	0.1564	0.0179	0.8985	0.3137	0.0984	0.1615	0.0140	0.9496	0.3351	0.1123
Sobel (s)	0.0699	0.0090	0.4486	0.1385	0.0192	0.1221	0.0095	0.7272	0.2573	0.0662
Canny (s)	0.8779	0.0746	5.1806	1.8290	3.3453	0.9195	0.0667	5.4927	1.9447	3.7817
FFT Feature (s)	0.2810	0.0229	1.8790	0.5845	0.3416	0.2960	0.0235	1.7437	0.6157	0.3791
Total (s)	**1.5315**	**0.1465**	**9.1706**			**3.0850**	**1.3417**	**12.2973**		

Table 11. Linux 64-bit HDF5 and XML Image Processing Execution Times.

Some other results worth mentioning confirm the expected relative calculation times between differing noise filters and edge detection methods. As expected, the Weiner Filter (using adaptive techniques) took more time than the Median Filter. In addition, the more complex Canny edge detection algorithm took more time than the Sobel edge detection algorithm.

The load times were larger for the XML files compared to the HDF5 files. This difference is most likely due to the larger XML file size. Figure 7 visually displays the load times for the XML and HDF5 files for the Linux 64-bit machine. Figure 8 shows a similar result for the Windows 64-bit machine.

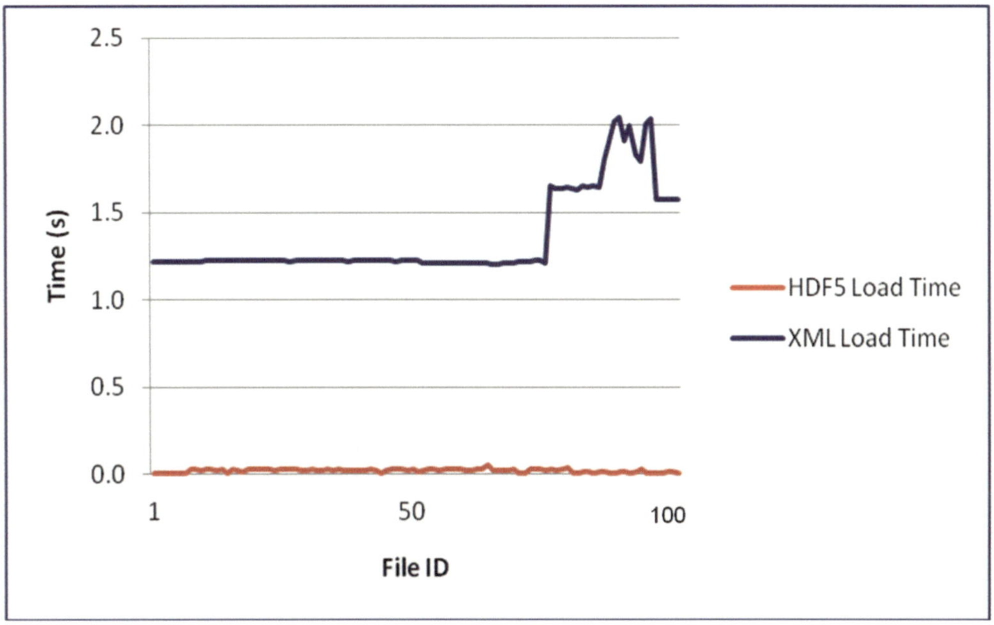

Fig. 7. Linux 64-bit XML and HDF5 Load Times.

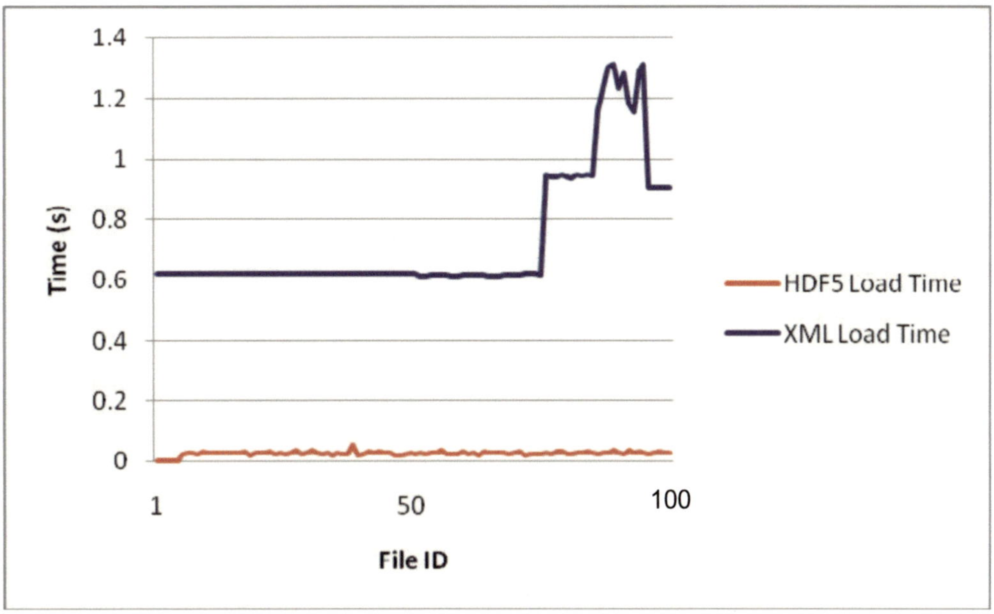

Fig. 8. Windows 64-bit XML and HDF5 Load Times.

Corresponding increases in XML file size contribute to the large jumps observed in the XML load times around file ID 75 and 90 (Figures 7 and 8). Similar arguments made earlier in the chapter (slowness of serialization of converting Unicode to binary storage and resource intensive DOM loading methods) offer explanation of the larger loading process times compared to the more efficient loading of HDF5 binary files.

HDF5 load times do not significantly vary depending on file size. Efficient methods of loading HDF5 binary data files, combined with excellent memory usage and use of computing resources, into the MATLAB workspace, demonstrate the superior benefit of archiving data in HDF5 versus XML. HDF5 provides seamless integration of data into MATLAB without performance degradation (especially for large data sets) and is the 'de facto' standard for MATLAB data files containing workspaces over 2 GB in size (Mather & Rogers, 2007).

The load times (Figures 7 and 8) for both HDF5 and XML show similar behavior on both the Windows and Linux machines. The cross platform behavior demonstrates the file size dependency for XML loading performance, and the lack of file size dependency for HDF5 loading performance. As expected from the benchmark testing results, the XML loading performance on the Windows machine is slightly faster than the Linux.

An additional processing step is required to prepare the large raw data for processing. In XML files, the raw image data is stored as ASCII characters with whitespace separators. As the image gets larger, converting from the ASCII character data to a MATLAB array can take considerable time. MATLAB has a num2str() function that works very nice for small arrays, but this function would not work for these large character arrays. A novel process allows the reading of each character, one at a time, parse on spaces, and then load into the array, resulting in a tremendous savings (as much as two orders of magnitude) in processing time. C or other software development languages may provide other more efficient methods to reduce this processing restriction. However, preparing the XML data for processing is a very important process step. Additional new research and software tools may simplify and expedite the process.

T-test analysis on the total image processing times confirmed that there was a significant difference between the HDF5 and XML file processing times not attributable to random chance. Specifically, HDF5 files took less processing time than XML files on the Windows 64-bit machine ($t\ (198) = 2.27$, $\rho = .0014$) and the Linux 64-bit machine ($t\ (198) = 3.25$, $\rho = .0244$). The t (198), or t-value, represents the difference of the mean values for total processing times for HDF5 and XML, respectively, divided by the standard error of the two means. The 198 represents the degrees of freedom, or sample size minus 2 for an unpaired t-test, which is appropriate for the independent groups in this analysis. The important value (ρ) represents the probability of the difference (t-value) being due to chance is .0014 for the Windows 64-bit machine, and .0244 for the Linux 64-bit machine. Setting the significance level to .05 indicates that in both cases, the difference in processing times between HDF5 and XML is not by chance. These results suggest a significant difference between the total process times for HDF5 and XML files for both machines. Further t-test analysis on the individual components contributing to the total process time indicated significant differences in execution times for load, adjust, and mean calculations for the Linux 64-bit machine and load, adjust, and median noise filter for the Windows 64-bit machine. It seems reasonable the load times would be different between the XML and HDF5 formats. To provide insight into the differences between the XML and HDF5 formats for the image adjust, median noise filter, and image mean calculations, requires additional research and analysis, since these routines should provide similar results because the data format should not impact the results for these processes.

Table 12 displays the t-test results for each of the components, resulting in significant differences between the XML and HDF5 files. The t-test results for each of the other components shows no significant difference between XML and HDF files.

Test	Windows 64-bit	Linux 64-bit
Load	t (198) = 34.39, ρ < .0001	t (198) = 54.73, ρ < .0001
Image Adjust	t (198) = 2.99, ρ = .0031	t (198) = 3.29, ρ = .0012
Image Mean	t (198) = 1.55, ρ = .122 (Not significant)	t (198) = 3.35, ρ = .0009
Median Filter	t (198) = 4.97, ρ < .0001	t (198) = 1.93, ρ = .050 (Not significant)

Table 12. T-test Process Time Components Results.

Figures 9 and 10 graphically depict these findings by displaying the total processing time for the HDF5 and XML files for the Linux 64-bit and Windows 64-bit test systems. In both cases, the XML process times were significantly greater than the HDF5 process times.

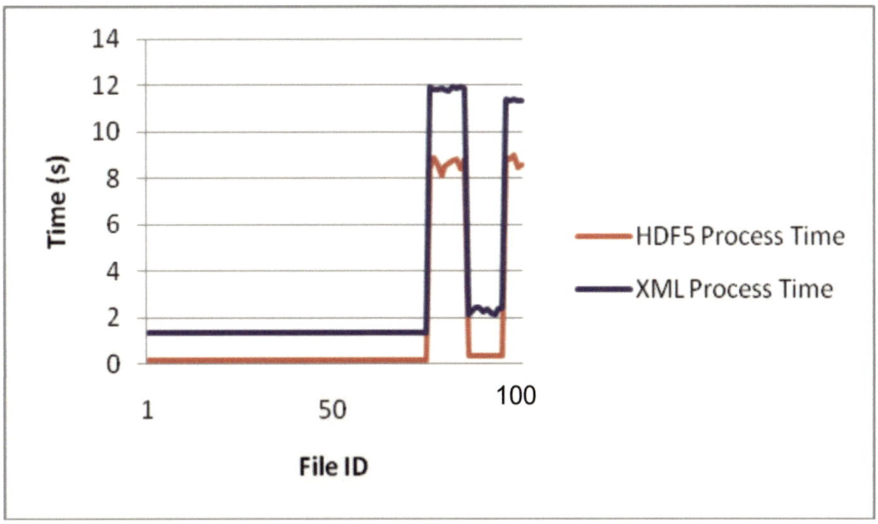

Fig. 9. Linux 64-bit Image Processing Times- HDF5 and XML.

For each file format and test machine, the amount of calculated free physical memory usage during the image processing stage shows definite differences between the file formats. Table 13 shows the descriptive statistics of these data. Similar to the preprocessing step, setting the maximum Java heap memory to maximum for each run results in no out-of-memory errors. For both machines, the XML files required more physical memory than the HDF5 files, as indicated by less free physical memory in Table 13. This result is consistent with XML loading requiring relatively large amounts of memory compared to the XML file size (Wang et al., 2007).

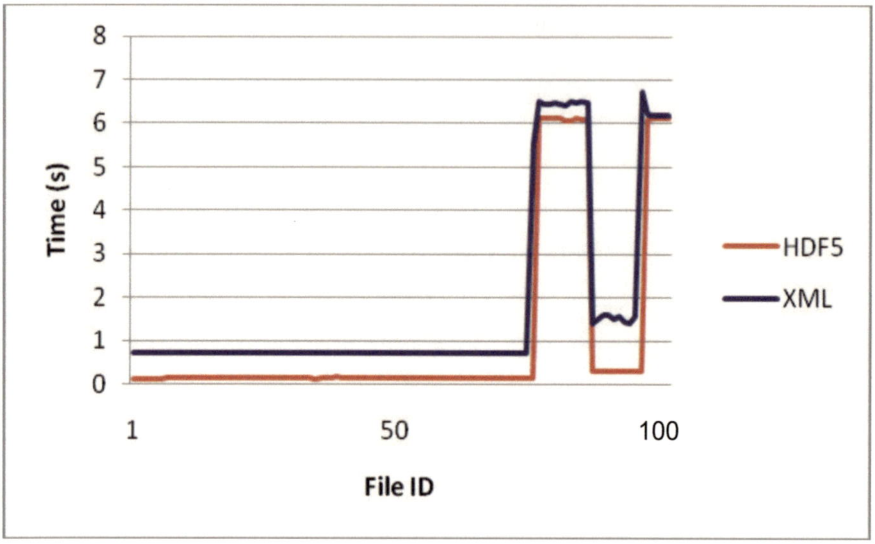

Fig. 10. Windows 64-bit Image Processing Times- HDF5 and XML.

Statistic	Windows 64-bit (GB)		Linux 64-bit (GB)	
	HDF5	XML	HDF5	XML
Mean	3.6608	3.2726	13.6388	11.0808
Minimum	3.5995	3.0064	11.9786	11.0215
Maximum	3.6874	3.7858	14.4033	11.1872
Standard Deviation	0.0194	0.4446	0.6277	0.0924
Variance	0.0004	0.1976	0.394	0.0085

Table 13. Free Physical Memory during Image Processing Steps.

6. Ethics of data sharing

There is a large, complex set of concerns when openly sharing data – especially electronic data over the Internet. From a scientific viewpoint of discovery, open sharing of scientific data allows many researchers and scientists the ability to form a common understanding of data, which is essential for furthering science. However, there are many ethical concerns in the process of sharing data, particularly over the Web. For example, a given medical study group collects sensitive, personal medical information as part of a medical case study using public government funds. All of the data is stored (archived) on a government computer system. Many years later, another researcher wants to use the data for another study, which could help save the lives of many people. Should the second researcher be able to use the archived data for a purpose other than the intent of the original study? Many arguments come into discussion in this situation. The right to use data paid for with publically collected funds seems reasonable; however, what about the right of human participants to privacy? What happens if a data release into the public domain harms any of the participants? Such harm may take the form of job loss or denial of life insurance, etc. The ethics of sharing data is complex and the ethical dilemma of sharing data is an area of study requiring much thought and discussion.

Many of the ethical concerns stem from a balance of beneficial results from sharing data versus ethical concerns researchers have in such sharing. Ethical data sharing and management involves reconciliation of diverse conflicting values (Sieber, 2005). Among these concerns are the sharing of data for the benefit of society and science, while protecting the interest of human participants in data collections (Mauthner & Perry, 2010). For many years, researchers took the position of protecting the interests of the human participants in such data; however, with the advent of sharing data across the Web, the interest of human participants is certainly less sure and threatens the overall fabric of the trust-based relationship that exists between researcher and participant. A definite loss of data control can exist when sharing data across the Web, possibility resulting in the loss of privacy and protection of human participants (Mauthner & Perry, 2010).

Another ethical concern is the rights of those who collect data and receive no recognition by those who download the data through public Web interfaces for use in their research. The process of collecting high quality data requires much time, effort, and expense; moreover, many of the individuals who collect data (data producers) are in a positional or career situation where they are vulnerable to receiving little recognition for their data collection efforts by indiscriminate availability of data over the Web. Such individuals are not nearly as protected as data users, such as algorithm designers, who can protect their interests through intellectual property rights (Mauthner & Perry, 2010).

Along with recognition of the data as a contribution deserving recognition, intellectual property rights assigning ownership and rightful claims to the data are another ethical concern. Reductions or even elimination of researcher's data rights occurs when funding agencies require a researcher to share data, especially over the Web, allowing anyone to access the information. Certain government agencies are always balancing the public's right to information collected with public funds, and the right to protect both the researcher's intellectual property and the test participant's privacy rights.

Archiving and disseminating data over the Web creates a "data as commodity" mindset, where the ethical concerns of both the researcher and human participant become lost in the impersonal downloading of archived data (Mauthner & Perry, 2010). When sharing data, regardless of the methods, confidentially of human participants is important at all times. Data providers must take great care in judging the sensitivity of the data and may find it necessary to restrict access based on ethical, legal, or security justifications, even in the case of publicly funded data collections. Further safeguards in data dissemination include restricting others (end users) of disseminating data as a third party; thus, requiring an end user to go to the original source to acquire the data (MIT Libraries, 2011).

The ethics of data sharing is clearly more complex today than before the advent of the Internet. However, many general guiding principles apply to all data sharing situations. As a core group of guiding principles, every data collector and provider has a duty to:

1. Protect the confidentially of human participants in data collections (UK Data Archive, 2011).
2. Avoid providing sensitive information of human test participants, which may endanger data test participants (UK Data Archive, 2011).
3. Consult with the test participants on making data publically available and be sensitive to their wishes (UK Data Archive, 2011).
4. Inform the test participants on the use of the data, and the methods, procedures, and intentions of archiving and disseminating the data, prior to using them as test participants (UK Data Archive, 2011).

5. Make data available to the public, which doesn't violate ethical, legal, or security principles (UK Data Archive, 2011).

7. Conclusions

This research processed 100 large hyperspectral images in both HDF5 and XML formats on Windows 64-bit and Linux 64-bit machines. A number of image processing steps available within MATLAB, including intensity adjustment, histogram calculation, statistical analysis, noise removal, edge detection and feature extraction, provided the algorithms to fulfill the goals of the research:

1. Determine strengths and weaknesses of using HDF5 and XML formats for typical processing techniques associated with large hyperspectral images.
2. Compare and analyze processing times on Windows and Linux 64-bit machines for HDF5 and XML hyperspectral images.
3. Identify areas that require additional research to help improve efficiencies associated with processing large HDF5 and XML hyperspectral images.

The research identified a number of strengths and weaknesses. First, the overall image processing results show reduced processing times for images stored in HDF5 compared to XML format. The main contribution to this difference is the large load time and the preprocessing step required to convert an ASCII XML character string to a numeric array in MATLAB. The relative size of the files is the main factor in the difference in load speed with the XML files being almost three times as large as the HDF5 files. A larger file will always take more time to load using any application.

The preprocessing required to convert an ASCII XML character string to a numeric array was very time-consuming and a potential huge process bottleneck. The processing of large XML files requires additional tools and approaches with an easier out-of-the-box solution, making XML processing more practical. In addition to the processing time differences, HDF5 requires less physical memory and, hence, allows larger objects to be loaded without out-of-memory errors. HDF5 data files are much smaller (~3 times) than the corresponding XML versions of same data files. Binary files in general are far more efficient in storing numerical data than XML files using Unicode. As discussed earlier, XML loading of data can consume as much as 10 times the amount of computer memory as the size of the actual XML file (Wang et al., 2007), and conversion of Unicode to binary storage is memory intensive requiring much more physical memory and resources than the loading of HDF5 files of similar data (McGrath, 2003). MATLAB can process very large arrays, but it will run out of memory quickly when processing very large XML files. On another test machine that was running MATLAB with only 760 MB Java heap memory, several of the larger XML datasets would not load. HDF5 files on any machine even when experimenting with HDF5 files as large as 800MB did not experience any problems. Clearly, for machines with less memory available and smaller processing capability, HDF5 files are preferred. Defining upper limit processing for both HDF5 and XML files requires additional research and analysis. The upper limit appears to have relationships to processing speed, physical memory, and other constraints. Exploring these limits as a function of different environmental parameters requires recommended future research.

The archiving and processing of large image data requires the use of HDF5, until additional tools and processes are in place that allow for the quick and efficient processing of XML files using computational tools such as MATLAB.

There are many important ethical considerations when sharing data, especially over the Web. Additional considerations to protect the privacy and interests of human participants in data collections require additional guidance when sharing data in a completely public forum where the researcher (and organization) has no control over how the data is used. There will always exist a balance between sharing data for scientific discovery and advancement, and ethical concerns and requirements.

8. References

Barkstrom, B., "Ada 95 Bindings for the NCSA Hierarchical Data Format", proceedings of the 2001 annual ACM SIGAda International Conference on ADA (2001).

Bennett, K., Robertson, J., "The Impact of the Data Archiving Format on the Sharing of Scientific Data for Use in Popular Computational Environments", Proc. SPIE 7687, Orlando Florida (April 2010).

Chapman, S.J., "MATLAB Programming for Engineers; 4th edition; Thomson publishing, Ontario, Canada, 2008.

Dougherty, M., Folk, M., Zadok, E., Bernstein, H., Bernstein, F., Eliceiri, K., Benger, W., Best, C., "Unifying Biological Image Formats with HDF5", communications of the ACM (CACM), 52(10): p. 42-47 (2009).

Gay, L.R. Airasian, P. Educational Research. Prentice Hall, Columbus, Ohio, 2003.

Goetz, A.F.H., Vane, G., Solomon, E., Rock, B.N., "Imaging Spectrometry for Earth Remote Sensing", *Science*, Vol. 228, p. 1147-1153 (1985).

Mather, J., Rogers, A., "HDF5 in MATLAB", Presentation at the HDF5 and HDF-EOS Workshop X, Raytheon System Corporation, Upper Marlboro, MD (November 2007).

MATLAB User's Guide, "Statistical Toolbox, Ttest2", http://www.mathworks.com/help/toolbox/stats/ (April, 2011).

Mauthner, M., Perry, O., "Ethical Issues in Digital Data Archiving and Sharing", eResearch Ethics, http://eresearch-ethics.org (October 2010).

McGrath, R., "XML and Scientific File Formats," Report generated by National Center for Supercomputing Applications, University of Illinois, Urbana-Champaign, in support of work under a Cooperative Agreement with NASA under NASA grant NAG 5-2040 and NAG NCCS-599 (August 2003).

MIT Libraries, "Data Management and Publishing: Ethical and Legal Issues", http://libraries.mit.edu (November 2011).

SAS/STAT User's Guide, "T-Test Procedure", http://support.sas.com/documentation (April, 2011).

Shasharina, S., Li, C., Nanbor, W., Pundaleeka, R., Wade-Stein, D., "Distributed Technologies for Remote Access of HDF Data", proceedings of the 16th IEEE International Workshop on Enabling Technologies: Infrastructure for Collaborative Enterprises (2007).

Shishedjiev, B., Goranova M., Georgieva, J., "XML-based Language for Specific Scientific Data Description",proceedings of the 2010 Fifth International Conference on Internet and Web Applications and Services (2010).

Sieber, J., "Ethics of Sharing Scientific and Technological Data: A Heuristic for Coping with Complexity & Uncertainty", Data Science Journal, Vol 4, p. 165 (December 2005).

UK Data Archive, "Create and Manage Data - Consent and Ethics: Ethical/Legal/Overview", http://www.data-archive.ac.uk (2011).
Wang, F., Li, J., Homayounfar, "A Space Efficient XLM DOM Parser", Data and Knowledge Engineering,Volume 60, Issue 1, p. 185-207 (2007).

9

Energy Management in Buildings Using MATLAB

Shahram Javadi
Islamic AZAD University, Central Tehran Branch
Iran

1. Introduction

MATLAB is an applicable software in various aspects of engineering such as Electrical engineering and its different sub majors. There are a lot of examples and demos on these majors, although there is a few text or example on MATLAB application in energy management. In this text, I have provided a general application of energy management in buildings using MATLAB software.
Considering limit source of fuel energy, we need to use energy and resources carefully and it is an economical and ecological challenge as well as being one which is important for survival and which can only be mastered by highly qualified engineers. A significant percentage of the energy used nationally is consumed in buildings, which means there are considerable potential for savings and a corresponding need for responsible behavior.The building sector worldwide uses up to 40% of primary energy requirements and also a considerable amount of overall water requirements.
Building Energy Management Systems (BEMS), aims to improve environment within the building and may control temperature, carbon dioxide levels. BEMS is not sufficient enough due to human interference. Human is a dynamic part of the building; therefore he/she should be taken into account in the control strategy. Latest trends in designing Intelligent Building Energy management Systems (IBEMS) integrate a Man Machine Interface that could store the human's preferences and adapt the control strategy accordingly.
BEMS have been developed after the Energy crisis in the late 70's combined with the fast development of computers science. The aims of these systems are to monitor and control the environmental parameters of the buildings and at the same time to minimize the energy consumption and cost. Since then, BEMS have become commercial tools and are implemented in a wide range of applications, especially in large office buildings; thus useful experience is available regarding their benefits and drawbacks.
Systems linked to a BMS typically represent 40% of a building's energy usage; if lighting is included, this number approaches 70%.
Some Benefits of BMS are:

- Building tenant/occupants
- Good control of internal comfort conditions
- Possibility of individual room control
- Increased staff productivity

- Effective monitoring and targeting of energy consumption
- Improved plant reliability and life
- Effective response to HVAC-related complaints
- Save time and money during the maintenance

BEMS is used to create a central computer controlled method which has three basic functions: controlling, monitoring and optimizing. It comprises:

- Power systems
- Illumination system
- Electric power control system
- Heating, Ventilation and Air-conditioning HVAC System
- Security and observation system
- Magnetic card and access system
- Fire alarm system
- Lifts, elevators etc.
- Plumbing system
- Burglar alarms
- Other engineering systems
- Trace Heating

BEMS uses a control strategy with the following objectives:

i. To obtain a flexible system for operator to maintain thermal, visual, security, illumination and air quality in a building.
ii. To reduce the energy consumption for all loads in a building.
iii. To provide a monitoring/controlling system in a building.

The above objectives are achieved by the use of a fuzzy controller at each zone level of the building, supervised by a suitable cost function. The detailed description of the control strategy has been described in next parts.

2. Fuzzy systems

Fuzzy logic originally is identified and set forth by Lotfi A. Zadeh is a form of multi-valued logic derived from fuzzy set theory to deal with reasoning that is fluid or approximate rather than fixed and exact. In contrast with "crisp logic", where binary sets have two-valued logic, fuzzy logic variables may have a truth value that ranges in degree between 0 and 1. Put more simply, fuzzy logic is a superset of conventional (boolean) logic that has been extended to handle the concept of partial truth, where the truth value may range between completely true and completely false. Furthermore, when linguistic variables are used, these degrees may be managed by specific functions. As the complexity of a system increases, it becomes more difficult and eventually impossible to make a precise statement about its behavior, eventually arriving at a point of complexity where the fuzzy logic method born in humans is the only way to get at the problem.

Fuzzy logic is used in system control and analysis design, because it shortens the time for engineering development and sometimes, in the case of highly complex systems, is the only way to solve the problem.

A fuzzy controller consists of the following major components depicted in figure 1:

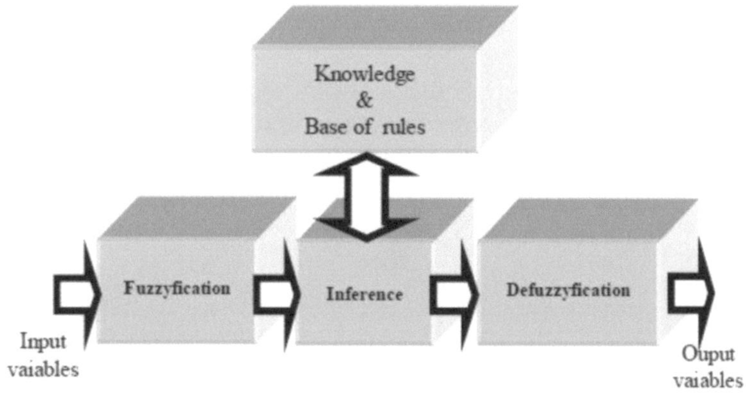

Fig. 1. Fuzzy system diagram

3. Considered systems for energy management

3.1 Illumination system

Lighting or illumination is the deliberate application of light to achieve some aesthetic or practical effect. Lighting includes use of both artificial light sources such as lamps and natural illumination of interiors from daylight. Daylighting (through windows, skylights, etc.) is often used as the main source of light during daytime in buildings given its high quality and low cost. Artificial lighting represents a major component of energy consumption, accounting for a significant part of all energy consumed worldwide. Artificial lighting is most commonly provided today by electric lights, but gas lighting, candles, or oil lamps were used in the past, and still are used in certain situations. Proper lighting can enhance task performance or aesthetics, while there can be energy wastage and adverse health effects of poorly designed lighting. Indoor lighting is a form of fixture or furnishing, and a key part of interior design. Lighting can also be an intrinsic component of landscaping

Providing daylight in a building does not by itself lead to energy efficiency. Even a well day building may have a high level of lighting energy use if the lighting controls are inappropriate. However, improved control in building management and automation system through research and development will definitely help to improve energy savings in buildings. This part presents the development of an automated fuzzy lighting/dimming control system. The schematic diagram of the system is shown in Fig. 1. Fuzzy logic is an innovative technology that allows the description of desired system behavior using everyday spoken language Fuzzy logic can be derived into three stages which are: Fuzzification, Fuzzy Inference and Defuzzification. In a typical application, all three stages must be employed.

3.1.1. Indoor natural lighting

What we have to do is solve an equation of the type

$$E = \frac{\Phi_{rec}}{A}$$

Where E is the illumination level required at the work surface and A is the total area of the plane where the work is done. The factor Φ_{rec} is the flux of light received on the working surface.

The average indoor illuminance E_{in} (lx) is calculated (DHW Li and JC Lam, 2000, *"Measurements of solar radiation and illuminance on vertical surfaces and daylighting implications"*) using the equation:

$$E_{in} = \frac{A_w \tau E_v}{A_{in}(1-\rho)} \tag{1}$$

where

A_w (m2) the window surface

τ (-) the light transmittance of the window glazing

E_v (lx) the vertical illuminance on the window

A_{in} (m2) the total area of all indoor surfaces

ρ (-) the area weighted mean reflectance of all indoor surfaces.

The vertical illuminance on the window Ev (lx) is given by the following equation

$$E_v = k_G G_v \tag{2}$$

with

k_G (lm.W-1) the luminous efficacy of global solar radiation

G_v (W.m-2) the global solar radiation on the window surface

The luminous efficacy of global solar radiation (M. Perraudeau, 1994, *"Estimation of illuminances from solar radiation data"*) can be calculated by the following relation

$$k_G = \frac{D_h}{G_h} k_D + \left(1 - \frac{D_h}{G_h}\right) k_s \tag{3}$$

with

D_h (W.m-2) the diffuse horizontal solar radiation

G_h (W.m-2) the global horizontal solar radiation

k_D (lm.W-1) the luminous efficacy of diffuse solar radiation

k_S (lm.W-1) the luminous efficacy of beam solar radiation.

The luminous efficacy of diffuse solar radiation is calculated (P. Littlefair, 1993, S. Ashton and H. Porter, "*Luminous efficacy algorithms*",) using the equation:

$$k_D = 144 - 29C \tag{4}$$

$$1 - C = 0.55NI - 1.22NI^2 + 1.68NI^3 \tag{5}$$

$$NI = \frac{1 - \dfrac{D_h}{G_h}}{1 - 0.12037 \sin^{-0.82}(\theta_z)} \tag{6}$$

with θ_z (deg) the solar zenith angle.

Finally, the luminous efficacy of the beam solar radiation can be calculated (S. Aydinli and J. Krochmann, 1983, *"Data on daylight and solar radiation: Guide on Daylight"*) using the relation

$$k_S = 17.72 + 4.4585\ \theta z - 8.7563 \times 10\text{-}2\ (\theta z)2 + 7.3948 \times 10\text{-}4\ (\theta z)3 - 2.167 \times 10\text{-}6\ (\theta z)4 - 8.4132 \times 10\text{-}10\ (\theta z)5 \quad (7)$$

3.1.2 Artificial lighting

The Equation below is used to calculate the average artificial light intensity inside the buildings:

$$E_{AL} = \frac{u^*_{AL} \cdot N \cdot (P \cdot V \cdot n)}{2\pi \cdot (H-h)^2} \quad (8)$$

Where:

u^*_{AL} : The actuating signal of the artificial light controller, ranging from 0-1. This signal is driven by the artificial lighting fuzzy controller. The same signal is also fed into the building model (Archimed.bui) to drive the actuator for the artificial lights. If $u^*_{AL} = 0$ means that all lights are off. If $u^*_{AL} = 1$ means that all lights are on at full power.

3.1.3 Fuzzy controller for lighting

All lighting control systems are based on one of the following strategies:

- Occupancy sensing, in which lights are turned on and off or dimmed according to occupancy;
- Scheduling, in which lights are turned off according to a schedule;
- Tuning, in which power to electric lights is reduced to meet current user needs;
- Daylight harvesting (daylighting control), in which electric lights are dimmed or turned off in response to the presence of daylight;
- Demand response, in which power to electric lights is reduced in response to utility curtailment signals or to reduce peak power charges at a facility;
- Adaptive compensation, in which light levels are lowered at night to take advantage of the fact that people need and prefer less light at night than they do during the day.

Daylight is a dynamic source of lighting and the variations in daylight can be quite large depending on season, location or latitude, and cloudiness. Different skylight levels can be found under the same sunlight conditions, and, even when the sky pattern remains the same, the range of solar illuminances may increase as a result of a momentary turbidity filter or scattering of particles over the sun. In consequence, any prediction system has to be flexible to allow for the multivariate changes that characterize the combination of sunlight and skylight.

The proposed daylighting fuzzy control uses two sensing devices (an occupancy/motion sensor and a photosensor), continuously electronic dimming ballasts for every luminaries aiming the control of the electric lighting output, and a fuzzy controller.

A proposed algorithm is assigned to control the illumination:

if *illuminance is between 500 and 550 lux and motion sensor is ON* **then** *all lamps is full powered*

else *use the fuzzy controller for lighting control*

The input linguistic variables of the fuzzy controller are the level of the illuminance measured by the photosensor (A) while the output variable is the level of the DC control signal sent to electronic ballasts in the control zone (μ_1). The fuzzy membership functions of Input/Output variables are shown in figures 2 and 3:

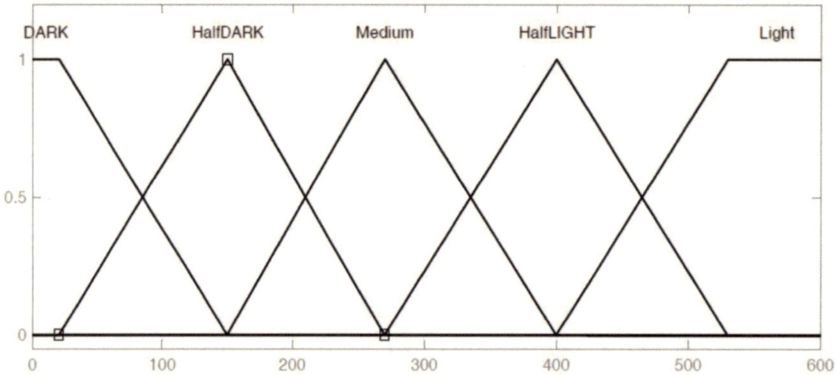

Fig. 2. Membership Function of Input A

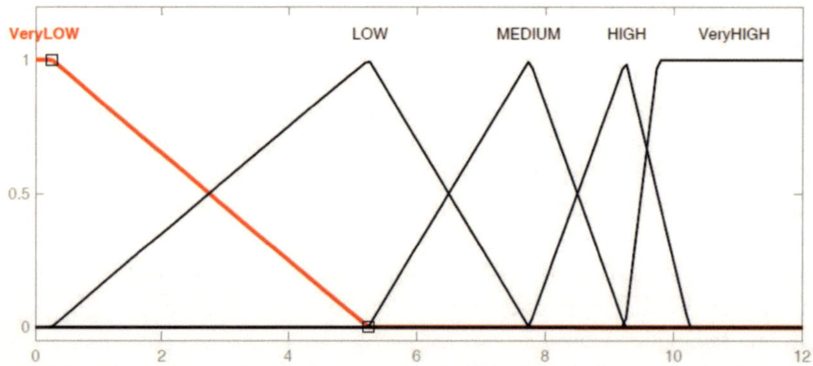

Fig. 3. Membership Function of Output (DC Voltage Level)

A rule-based fuzzy controller is evaluated for this system as follow:

1. If A is DARK then DC-Output-Level is VERY-HIGH
2. If A is HALF-DARK then DC-Output-Level is HIGH
3. If A is MEDIUM then DC-Output-Level is MEDIUM
4. If A is HALF-LIGHT then DC-Output-Level is LOW
5. If A is LIGHT then DC-Output-Level is VERY-LOW

Control surface of this system is shown in figure 4. As it is seen, the controller is very smooth action and it causes the ballast has a long life with a low harmonic feed into the grid.

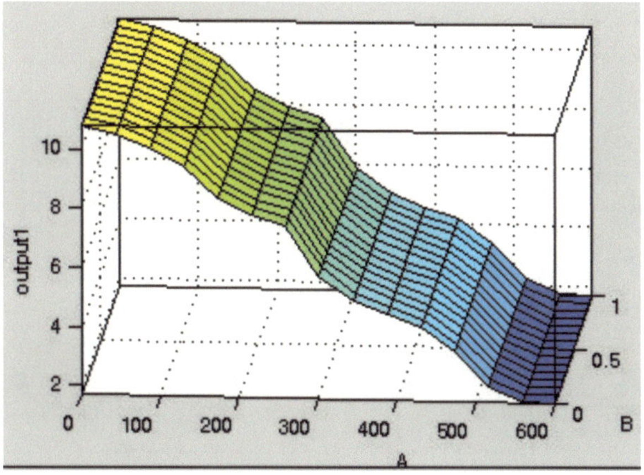

Fig. 4. Control Surface of Controller

3.2 HVAC system

In this part the role of fuzzy modeling in heating, ventilating and air conditioning (HVAC) and control models is presented. HVAC design professionals are required to evaluate numerous design alternatives and properly justify their final conceptual selection through modeling. This trend, coupled with the knowledge of experienced designers, increasing complexity of the systems, unwillingness to commit additional funds to the design phase itself, can only be satisfied by approaching the conceptual design process in more scientific, comprehensive and rational manner as against the current empirical and often adhoc approach. Fuzzy logic offers a promising solution to this conceptual design through fuzzy modeling. Numerous fuzzy logic studies are available in the non- mechanical engineering field and allied areas such as diagnostics, energy consumption analysis, maintenance, operation and its control. Relatively little exists in using fuzzy logic based systems for mechanical engineering and very little for HVAC conceptual design and control. Temperature and relative humidity are essential factors in meeting physiological requirements.

To identify the FLC's variables, various (control or explicit) parameters may be considered depending on the HVAC system, sensors and actuators such as:

- Room Temperature as a thermal comfort index
- Relative Humidity
- Difference between supply and room temperatures
- Indoor Air Quality (CO2 concentration)
- Outdoor Temperature
- HVAC system actuators (valve positions, operating modes, fan speeds, etc.)

As man is more sensitive to temperature than to humidity, most of the comforts air-conditioning systems are designed to provide relatively accurate temperature control and relative humidity.

Two parameters T (Temperature) and H (Humidity) are controlled by Fuzzy controller system in order to regulate the room temperature and humidity to their desired values, T_{ref} and H_{ref} (Zheng Xiaoqing, 2002 , "*Self-Tuning Fuzzy Controller for Air-Conditioning Systems*"). The block diagram of the air-conditioning control system is a simple closed loop system as shown in figure 5.

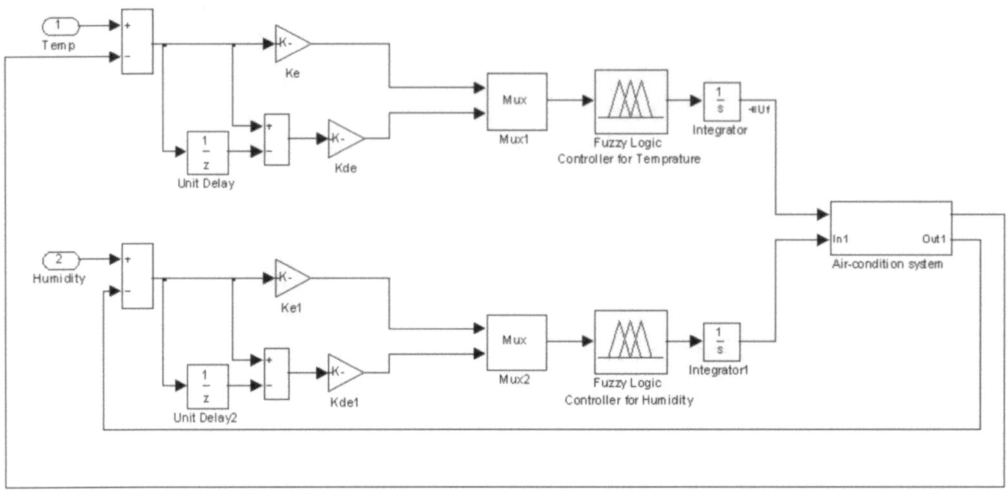

Fig. 5. Block diagram of the air-conditioning control system

As it is seen, two independent fuzzy controllers are assigned to control Temperature and Humidity parameters. Error signal and its derivation are fed to each fuzzy controller. The output of fuzzy controllers is assigned as inputs of air conditioner system. The output of system is feedback to controller to make a closed-loop controller.

The control strategy used can be expressed by the following linguistic rules:

If **room temperature** *is higher than the set point, then increase the* **supply air fan speed**.

If **room humidity** *is higher than the set point, then increase the* **chilled water valve opening.**

Seven linguistic variables are chosen for each of Temperature and Humidity error and also their derivations as follow:

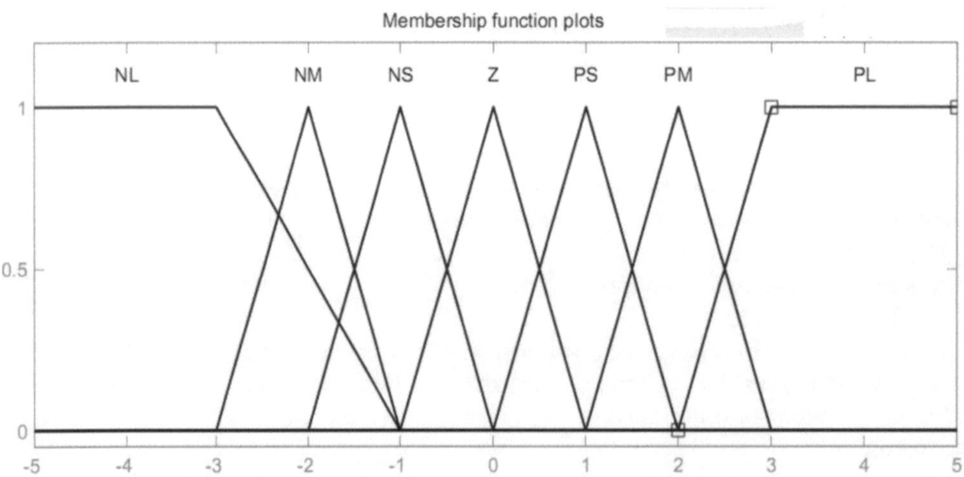

Fig. 6. Membership functions of inputs

Also seven linguistic variables are chosen for **supply air fan speed** and **chilled water valve opening** as its outputs. It is show in figure 7.

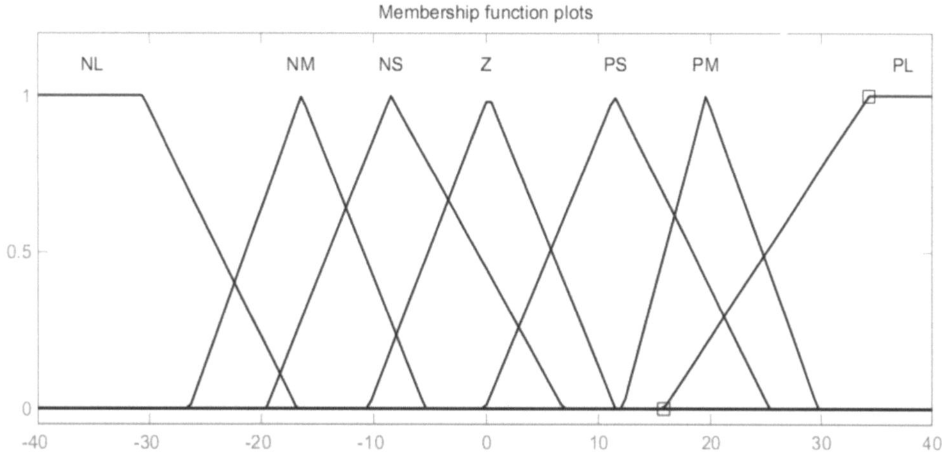

Fig. 7. Membership functions of outputs

Rule base of this controller is defined as table 1:

	NL	NM	NS	Z	PS	PM	PL
NL	PL	PL	PM	PM	PS	PS	NS
NM	PL	PL	PM	PS	PS	NS	NS
NS	PM	PS	PS	PS	NS	NS	NM
Z	PM	PM	PS	Z	NS	NM	NM
PS	PM	PS	PS	NS	NS	NM	NM
PM	PS	PS	NS	NS	NM	NL	NL
PL	PS	NS	NS	NM	NM	NL	NL

Table 1. Rules of Fuzzy HVAC

For example:

If the **room temperature error** *is NL and its* **rate of change** *is NL, then* **supply air fan speed** *is PL*

or

If the **room humidity error** *is NL and its* **rate of change** *is NL, then* **chilled water valve opening** *is PL*

In this case we have 49 rules to have smooth control surface for HVAC control.

3.3 Elevator system

With the advancement of intelligent computerized buildings in recent years, there have been strong demands for intelligent elevator control with more sophistication and diverse functions. The design criteria of an intelligent elevator control system would include optimizing the movement of a group of elevators with respect to time, energy, load, etc. In this paper, a new elevator group supervisory control system based on the ordinal structure fuzzy logic algorithm is proposed. The system determines the optimum car to answer a hall call using the knowledge and experiential rules of experts. Software has been developed to simulate the traffic flow of three elevator cars in a 15-floor building. The software simulates the movements of the cars as found in practical elevator systems. It can be verified through simulation that the new system can bring about considerable improvements in the average waiting time, riding time, etc. in comparison with conventional methods.

In a conventional elevator system, the task of controlling a large number of elevators is numerically evaluated by calculating a specified fixed-evaluation function. It has been realized that knowledge and experiential rules of experts can be incorporated in the elevator system to improve performance. However, such expert knowledge is fragmentary and fuzzy which are difficult to organize. Furthermore, the choice of "good" rules and evaluation functions are too complicated in many cases. It is difficult to adequately incorporate such knowledge into products using conventional software and hardware technology.

In order to overcome such problems as described above, a new elevator control system using fuzzy logic algorithm is proposed based on the ordinal structure theory. This system determines the optimum car within a group of elevators to answer a hall call using the knowledge and experiential rules of experts. Instead of using the simple up and down hall call buttons, destination oriented keypads at each floor is used. This system requires the passengers to enter their desired floors on the keypad before they enter the car. The system then assigns the passenger the respective optimal car to take through information displayed on dot matrix displays near the keypad. This new elevator supervisory control system has several objectives which can meet users' satisfaction. It can improve not only the average waiting time, but also the riding time, load, energy and so on. This paper discusses the design and operations of the proposed fuzzy logic elevator control system.

In order to achieve good traffic performance, the elevator fuzzy control system uses six kinds of parameters as the control inputs and one parameter for the output. These parameters represent the criteria or objectives to be optimized in this elevator system which are as follows:

- Waiting Time: Total time an elevator needed to travel from its current position to the new hall call.
- Riding Time: Total time a passenger spent in the elevator until he reached as his destination.
- Loading: Number of passengers in an elevator.
- Travelling Distance: Distance between elevator position and new hall call in terms of number of floors.
- Hall call Area Weight: The area weight of the elevator which goes to the floor where a new hall call is generated.
- Destination Area Weight: The area weight of the elevator which goes to the floor where the destination of the new hall call is generated.
- Priority: Output of the fuzzy controller, where the elevator with highest value will be assigned.

As can be observed, it is difficult to configure six kinds of parameters at a time using the conventional fuzzy reasoning method. Thus, the ordinal structure model of fuzzy reasoning is used. With this model, all the fuzzy inference rules are described in one dimensional space for each input and output. The membership function of the inputs and output variables are shown in Figures 9 and 10.

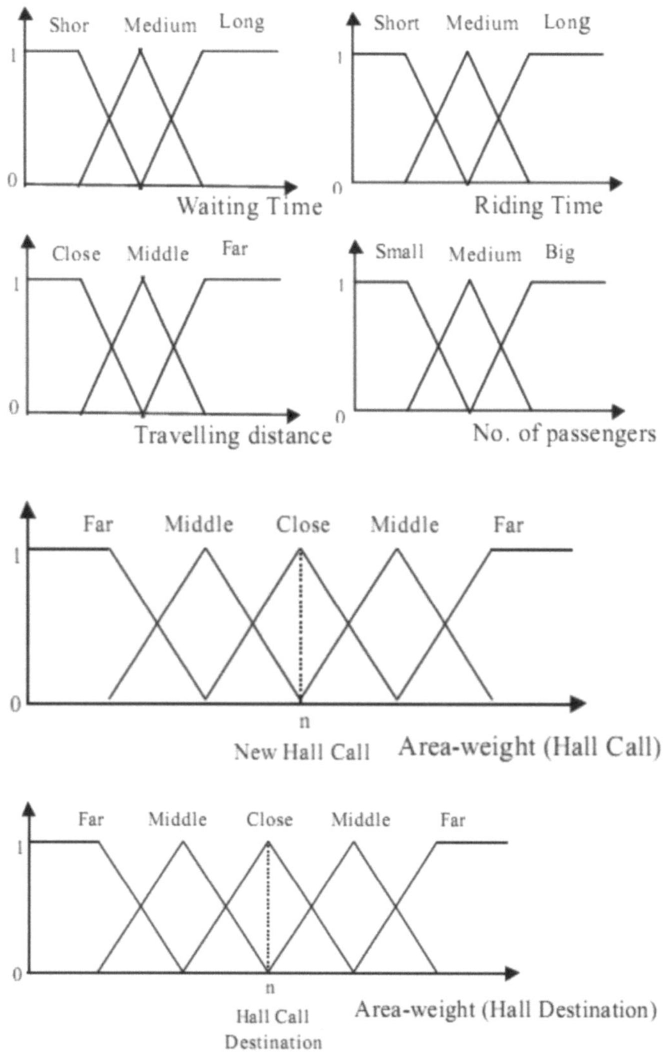

Fig. 8. Membership functions of the elevator system inputs.

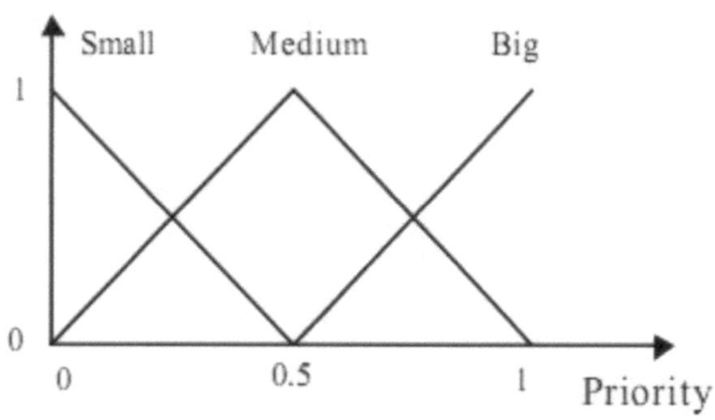

Fig. 9. The membership function of the output of the elevator system.

The proposed fuzzy inference rules are shown in Table 2:

Rule No.	Inference Rules
R1	If waiting time is *Short* then priority is *Big.*
R2	If waiting time is *Medium* then priority is *Medium*
R3	If waiting time is *Long* then priority is *Small.*
R4	If riding time is *Short* then priority is *Big.*
R5	If riding time is *Medium* then priority is *Medium.*
R6	If loading is *Long* then priority is *Small*
R7	If loading is *Small* then priority is *Big*
R8	If loading is *M*edium then priority is *Medium*
R9	If loading is *Big* then priority is *Small*
R10	If travelling distance is *Close* then priority is *Big*
R11	If travelling distance is *Middle* then priority is *Medium*
R12	If travelling distance is *Far* then priority is *Small.*
R13	If hall call area weight is *Close* then priority is *Big.*
R14	If hall call area weight is *Middle* then priority is *Medium*
R15	If hall call area weight is *Far* then priority is *Small.*
R16	If destination area weight is *Close* then priority is *Big.*
R17	If destination area weight is *Middle* then priority is *Medium.*
R18	If destination area weight is *Far* then priority is *Small.*

Table 2. A total of 18 fuzzy inference rules

4. Conclusion

In this chapter one of the applications of MATLAB is introduced in order to apply energy management in buildings. Three major systems were considered and a fuzzy controller was developed for each of them. It can be open a new vision to the students to learn MATLAB more applicable and more efficient.

5. References

A. Guillemin and N. Morel, 2001, *"An innovative lighting controller integrated in a self-adaptive building control system"*, Energy and Buildings, vol. 33, no. 5, pp. 477–87.

DHW Li and JC Lam, 2000, *"Measurements of solar radiation and illuminance on vertical surfaces and daylighting implications"*, Renewable Energy, vol. 20, pp. 389-404

M. Perraudeau, 1994, *"Estimation of illuminances from solar radiation data"*, Joule 2 DAYLIGHT II Program: Availability of Daylight - Design of a European Daylighting Atlas, CSTB Nantes.

P. Littlefair, 1993, S. Ashton and H. Porter, *"Luminous efficacy algorithms"*, Joule 1 Program - Dynamic characteristics of daylight data and daylighting design in Buildings, Final Report, CEC Brussels.

S. Aydinli and J. Krochmann, 1983, *"Data on daylight and solar radiation: Guide on Daylight"*, Draft for CIE TC 4.2.

Zheng Xiaoqing, 2002 , *"Self-Tuning Fuzzy Controller for Air-Conditioning Systems"*, M.Sc. Thesis

Part 3

Control Applications

10

Synchronous Generator Advanced Control Strategies Simulation

Damir Sumina, Neven Bulić, Marija Mirošević and Mato Mišković
University of Zagreb/Faculty of Electrical Engineering and Computing,
University of Rijeka, Faculty of Engineering,
University of Dubrovnik/Department of Electrical Engineering and Computing
Croatia

1. Introduction

During the last two decades, a number of research studies on the design of the excitation controller of synchronous generator have been successfully carried out in order to improve the damping characteristics of a power system over a wide range of operating points and to enhance the dynamic stability of power systems (Kundur, 1994; Noroozi et.al., 2008; Shahgholian, 2010). When load is changing, the operation point of a power system is varied; especially when there is a large disturbance, such as a three-phase short circuit fault condition, there are considerable changes in the operating conditions of the power system. Therefore, it is impossible to obtain optimal operating conditions through a fixed excitation controller. In (Ghandra et.al., 2008; Hsu & Liu, 1987), self-tuning controllers are introduced for improving the damping characteristics of a power system over a wide range of operating conditions. Fuzzy logic controllers (FLCs) constitute knowledge-based systems that include fuzzy rules and fuzzy membership functions to incorporate human knowledge into their knowledge base. Applications in the excitation controller design using the fuzzy set theory have been proposed in (Karnavas & Papadopoulos, 2002; Hiyama et. al., 2006; Hassan et. al., 2001). Most knowledge-based systems rely upon algorithms that are inappropriate to implement and require extensive computational time. Artificial neural networks (ANNs) and their combination with fuzzy logic for excitation control have also been proposed, (Karnavas & Pantos, 2008; Salem et. al., 2000a, Salem et. al., 2000b). A simple structure with only one neuron for voltage control is studied in (Malik et. al., 2002; Salem et. al., 2003). The synergetic control theory (Jiang, 2009) and other nonlinear control techniques, (Akbari & Amooshahi, 2009; Cao et.al., 2004), are also used in the excitation control.
One of the disadvantages of artificial intelligence methods and nonlinear control techniques is the complexity of algorithms required for implementation in a digital control system. For testing of these methods is much more convenient and easier to use software package Matlab Simulink. So, this chapter presents and compares two methods for the excitation control of a synchronous generator which are simulated in Matlab Simulink and compared with conventional control structure. The first method is based on the neural network (NN) which uses the back-propagation (BP) algorithm to update weights on-line. In addition to

the function of voltage control the proposed NN has the function of stabilizing generator oscillations. The second method proposes a fuzzy logic controller (FLC) for voltage control and the stabilization of generator oscillations. The proposed control algorithms with neural networks and a fuzzy controller are tested on a simulation model of synchronous generator weakly connected through transmissions lines to an AC network. The simulations are carried out by step changes in voltage reference.

2. Simulation models

Simulation models of synchronous generator and different control structures are made in Matlab Simulink. The generator is connected over transformer and transmission lines to the AC network (Fig. 1).

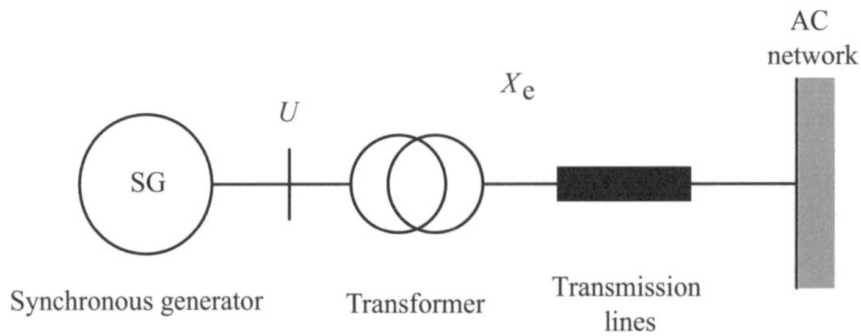

Fig. 1. Synchronous generator connected to AC network

2.1 Simulation model of a synchronous generator

Mathematical model of synchronous generator is represented in *dq* axis form. Based on that it is necessary to perform transformation from *abc* coordinate system to *dq* coordinate system. Assumption is that voltages are symmetrical in all phases and there is only one harmonic of magnetic flux in air gap. Equations are represented in per-unit system and time is absolute.

The synchronous generator under consideration is assumed to have three armature windings, one field winding, and damper windings. One damper winding is located along the direct axis (D) and another is located along the quadrature axis (Q). Accordingly, the basis for the mathematical model of the synchronous generator is a system of voltage equations of the generator in the rotating *dq* coordinate system, where *u, i, r, x* and Ψ denote voltage, current, resistance, reactance and flux, respectively (Kundur, 1994):

$$-u_d = r \cdot i_d + \frac{1}{\omega_s} \cdot \frac{d\Psi_d}{dt} + \omega \cdot \Psi_q \tag{1}$$

$$-u_q = r \cdot i_q + \frac{1}{\omega_s} \cdot \frac{d\Psi_q}{dt} - \omega \cdot \Psi_d \tag{2}$$

$$u_f = r_f \cdot i_f + \frac{1}{\omega_s} \cdot \frac{d\Psi_f}{dt} \tag{3}$$

$$0 = r_D \cdot i_D + \frac{1}{\omega_s} \cdot \frac{d\Psi_D}{dt} \tag{4}$$

$$0 = r_Q \cdot i_Q + \frac{1}{\omega_s} \cdot \frac{d\Psi_Q}{dt} \tag{5}$$

The equations defining the relations between fluxes and currents are:

$$\Psi_d = x_d \cdot i_d + x_{ad} \cdot i_f + x_{dD} \cdot i_D \tag{6}$$

$$\Psi_q = x_q \cdot i_q + x_{qQ} \cdot i_Q \tag{7}$$

$$\Psi_f = x_{ad} \cdot i_d + x_f \cdot i_f + x_{fD} \cdot i_D \tag{8}$$

$$\Psi_D = x_{dD} \cdot i_d + x_{fD} \cdot i_f + x_D \cdot i_D \tag{9}$$

$$\Psi_Q = x_{qQ} \cdot i_q + x_Q \cdot i_Q \tag{10}$$

The motion equations are defined as follows:

$$\frac{d\delta}{dt} = (\omega - 1) \cdot \omega_s \tag{11}$$

$$\frac{d\omega}{dt} = \frac{1}{2H} \cdot (T_m - T_e) \tag{12}$$

where δ is angular position of the rotor, ω is angular velocity of the rotor, ω_s is synchronous speed, H is inertia constant, T_m is mechanical torque, and T_e is electromagnetic torque.
The electromagnetic torque of the generator T_e is determined by equation:

$$T_e = \Psi_q \cdot i_d - \Psi_d \cdot i_q \tag{13}$$

Connection between the synchronous generator and AC network is determined by the following equations:

$$u_d = i_d \cdot r_e + \frac{x_e}{\omega_s} \cdot \frac{di_d}{dt} + \omega \cdot x_e \cdot i_q + u_{sd} \tag{14}$$

$$u_q = i_q \cdot r_e + \frac{x_e}{\omega_s} \cdot \frac{di_q}{dt} - \omega \cdot x_e \cdot i_d + u_{sq} \tag{15}$$

$$u_{sd} = U_m \cdot (-\sin\delta) \tag{16}$$

$$u_{sq} = U_m \cdot \cos\delta \tag{17}$$

transformer and transmission line resistance, x_e is transformer and transmission line reactance, and U_m is AC network voltage. Synchronous generator nominal data and simulation model parameters are given in Table 1.

Terminal voltage	400 V
Phase current	120 A
Power	83 kVA
Frequency	50 Hz
Speed	600 r/min
Power factor	0,8
Excitation voltage	100 V
Excitation current	11.8 A
d-axis synchronous reactance X_d	0.8 p.u.
q-axis synchronous reactance X_q	0.51 p.u.
Inertia constant H	1.3
d-axis transient open-circuit time constant $T_{do'}$	0.55 s
d-axis transient reactance X_d'	0.35 p.u.
d-axis subtransient reactance X_d''	0.15 p.u.
q-axis subtransient reactance X_q''	0.15 p.u.
Short-circuit time constant T_d''	0.054 s
Short-circuit time constant T_q''	0.054 s
Transformer and transmission line resistance r_e	0.05 p.u.
Transformer and transmission line reactance x_e	0.35 p.u.

Table 1. Synchronous generator nominal data and simulation model parameters

2.2 Conventional control structure

Conventional control structure (CCS) for the voltage control of a synchronous generator is shown in Fig. 3. The structure contains a proportional excitation current controller and, subordinate to it, a voltage controller. Simulation model of conventional control structure is shown in Fig. 4.

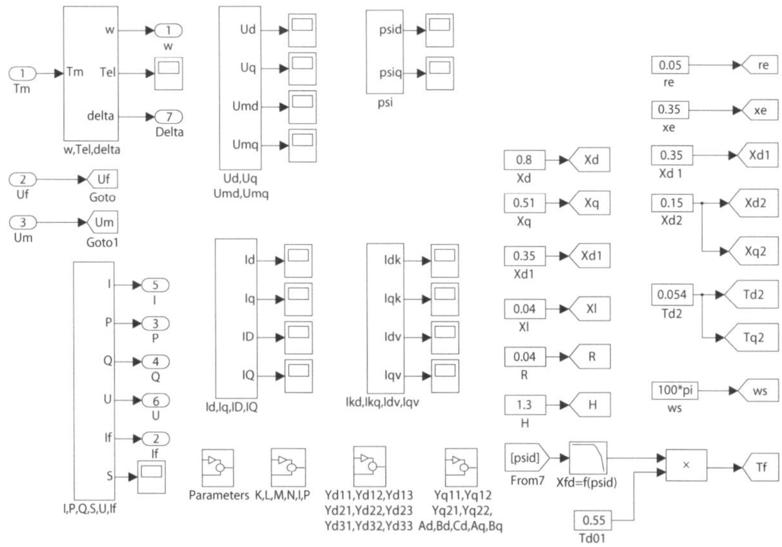

Fig. 2. Simulation model of synchronous generator

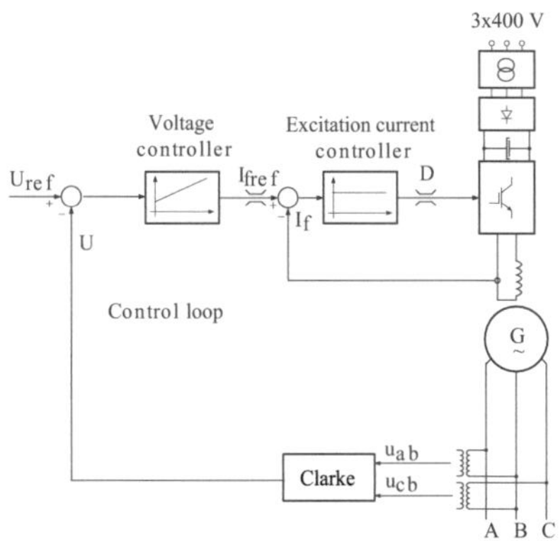

Fig. 3. Conventional control structure

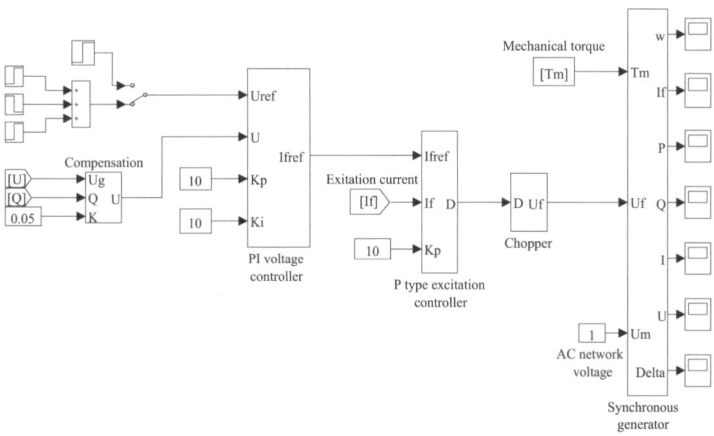

Fig. 4. Simulation model of conventional control structure

For supplying the generator excitation current, an AC/DC converter is simulated. The AC/DC converter includes a three-phase bridge rectifier, a DC link with a detection of DC voltage, a braking resistor, and a DC chopper (Fig. 5).

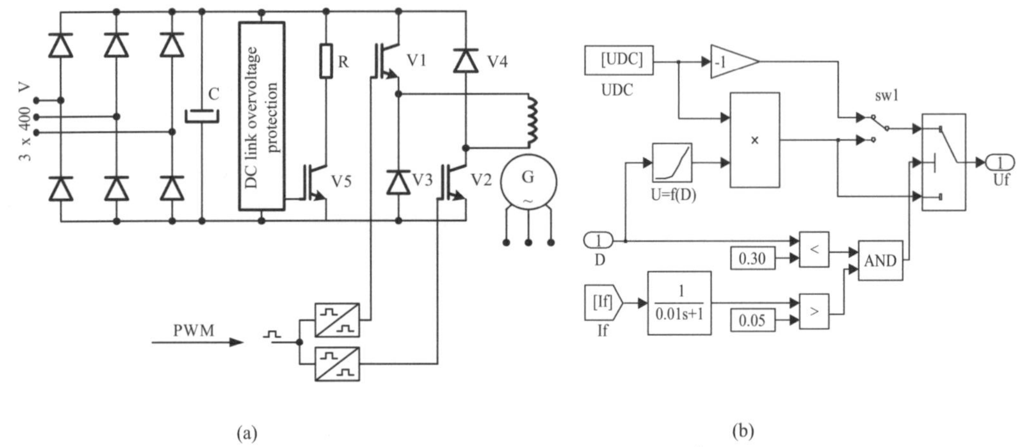

Fig. 5. AC/DC converter for supplying generator excitation current (a) and simulation model (b)

2.3 Neural network based control

The structure of the proposed NN is shown in Fig. 6. The NN has three inputs, six neurons in the hidden layer and one neuron in the output layer. The inputs in this NN are the voltage reference U_{ref}, the terminal voltage U and the previous output from the NN y(t-1). Bringing the previous output to the NN input is a characteristic of dynamic neural networks. The function tansig is used as an activation function for the neurons in the hidden layer and for the neuron in the output layer.

The graphical representation of the tansig function and its derivation is shown in Fig. 7. The numerical representation of the tansig function and its derivation are given as follows (Haykin, 1994):

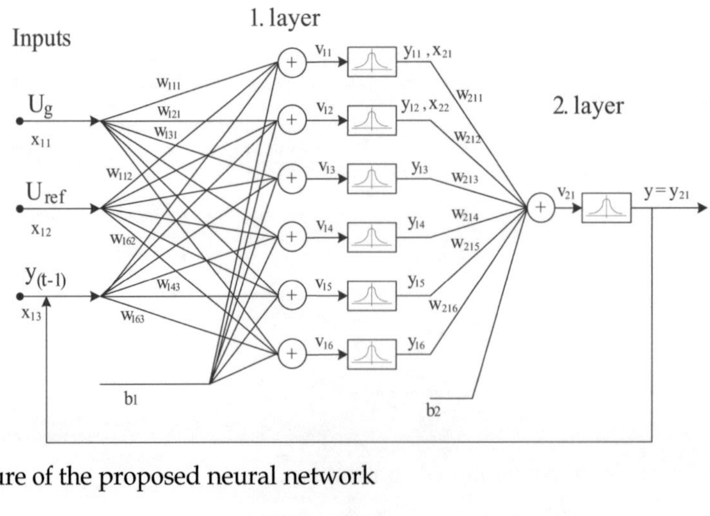

Fig. 6. Structure of the proposed neural network

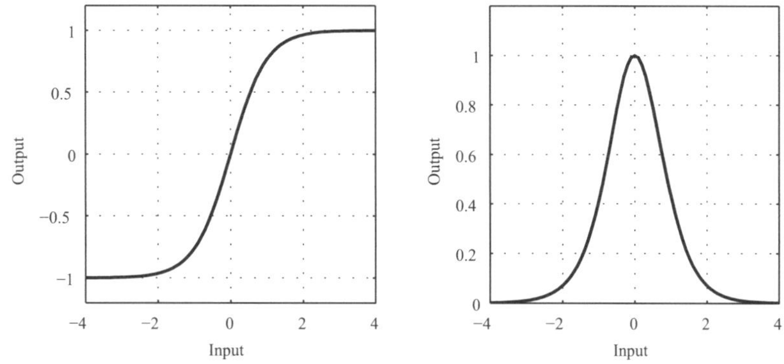

Fig. 7. Tansig activation function and its derivation

$$\psi(v) = \frac{1}{1+e^{-cv}} - 1 \tag{18}$$

$$\psi'(v) = c\frac{4e^{-2cv}}{(1+e^{-2cv})^2} = c\cdot(1-\psi^2) \tag{19}$$

The NN uses a simple procedure to update weights on-line and there is no need for any off-line training. Also, there is no need for an identifier and/or a reference model. The NN is trained directly in an on-line mode from the inputs and outputs of the generator and there is no need to determine the states of the system. The NN uses a sampled value of the machine quantities to compute the error using a modified error function. This error is back-propagated through the NN to update its weights using the algorithm shown in Fig. 8. When the weights are adjusted, the output of the neural network is calculated.

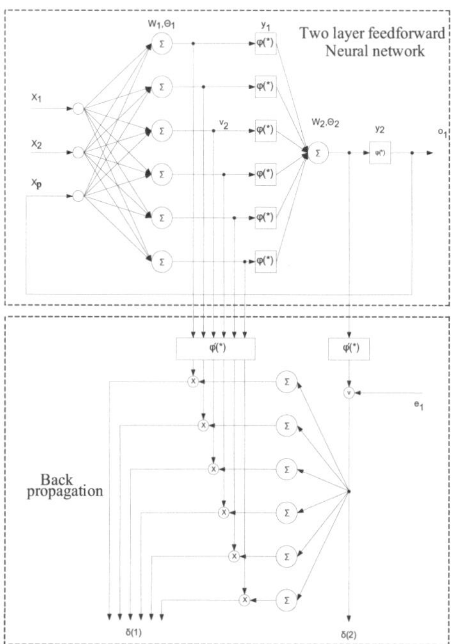

Fig. 8. Back-propagation algorithm

Training of the NN with the BP algorithm is described in (Haykin, 1994). Inputs and outputs of one neuron in the NN can be determined as follows:

$$y_{ki} = \psi\left(\sum_{k} w_{kij} \cdot x_{kj} + b_1\right) \tag{20}$$

The BP algorithm is an iterative gradient algorithm designed to minimize the mean square error between the actual output and the NN desired output. This is a recursive algorithm starting at the output neuron and working back to the hidden layer adjusting the weights according to the following equations:

$$w_{kij}(t+1) = w_{kij}(t) + \Delta w_{kij}(t) \tag{21}$$

$$\Delta w_{ji}(n) = \eta \cdot \delta_j(n) \cdot y_i(n) \tag{22}$$

$$\delta_j(n) = e_j(n) \cdot \phi_j'(v_j(n)) \tag{23}$$

The error function commonly used in the BP algorithm can be expressed as:

$$\Im = \frac{1}{2}\left(t_{ki} - y_{ki}\right)^2 \tag{24}$$

If the neuron is in the output layer, the error function is:

$$\frac{\partial \Im}{\partial y_{ki}} = t_{ki} - y_{ki} \tag{25}$$

If the neuron is in the hidden layer, the error function is recursively calculated as (Haykin, 1994):

$$\frac{\partial \Im}{\partial y_{ki}} = \sum_{p=1}^{n(k+1)} \frac{\partial \Im}{\partial y_{k+1,p}} \cdot \psi'_{k+1,p} \cdot w_{k+1,1,i} \tag{26}$$

If the NN is used for the excitation control of a synchronous generator, it is required that we not only change the weights based only on the error between the output and the desired output but also based on the change of the error as follows:

$$\frac{\partial \Im}{\partial y_{ki}} = \left(t_{ki} - y_{ki}\right) - \frac{dy_{ki}}{dt} \tag{27}$$

In this way, the modified error function speeds up the BP algorithm and gives faster convergence. Further, the algorithm becomes appropriate for the on-line learning implementation. The error function for the NN used for voltage control is expressed as:

$$\frac{\partial \Im}{\partial y_{ki}} = K(U_{ref} - U) - k_1 \frac{dU}{dt} \tag{28}$$

In order to perform the power system stabilization, the active power deviation ΔP and the derivation of active power dP/dt are to be imported in the modified error function. The complete modified error function for the excitation control of a synchronous generator is given as follows:

$$\frac{\partial \Im}{\partial y_{ki}} = \left[K(U_{ref} - U) - k_1 \frac{dU}{dt} \right] - \left[k_3 (\Delta P) + k_2 \frac{dP}{dt} \right] \tag{29}$$

The modified error function is divided into two parts. The first part is used for voltage control and the second part for power system stabilization. Parameters K, k_1, k_2 and k_3 are given in Table 2. Simulation model of NN control structure is shown in Fig. 9.

K	2.5
k_1	0.3
k_2	0.6
k_3	0.25

Table 2. Parameters of neural network

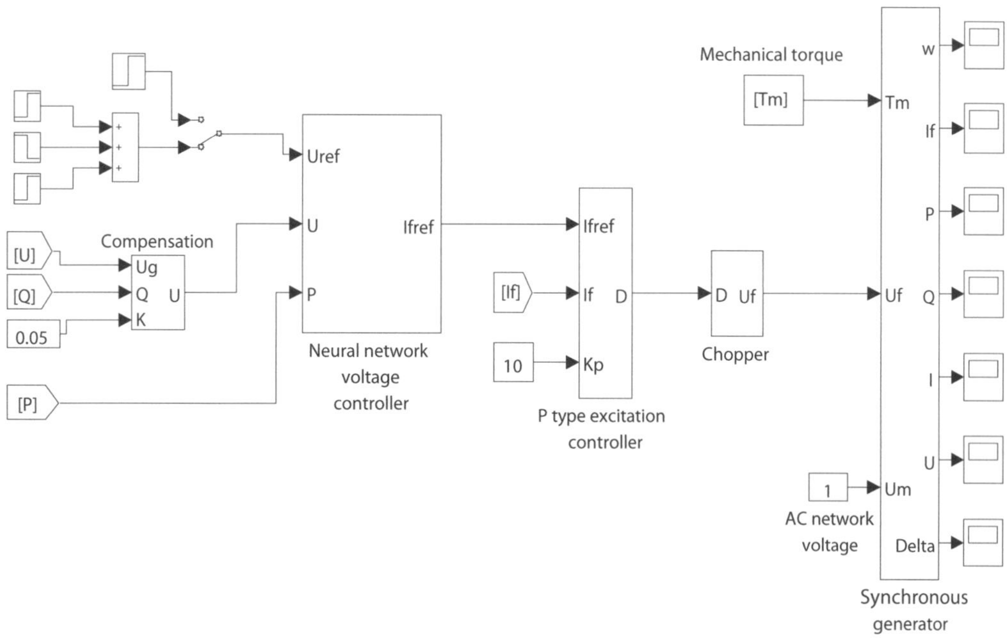

Fig. 9. Simulation model of neural network control structure

Neural network based controller is realized as S-function in Matlab and is called in every simulation step.

2.4 Fuzzy logic controller

The detailed structure of the proposed fuzzy logic controller (FLC) is shown in Fig. 10. The FLC has two control loops. The first one is the voltage control loop with the function of voltage control and the second one is the damping control loop with the function of a power system stabilizer. A fuzzy polar control scheme is applied to these two control loops.

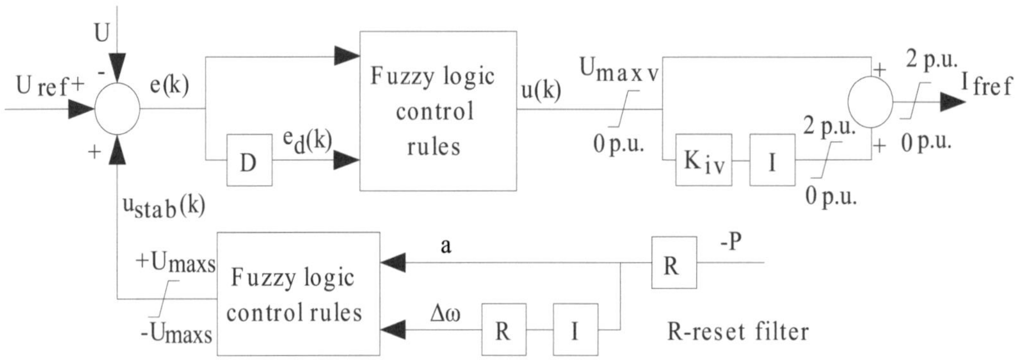

Fig. 10. Structure of the fuzzy logic stabilizing controller

The PD information of the voltage error signal *e* (k) is utilized to get the voltage state and to determine the reference I_{fref} for the proportional excitation current controller. To eliminate the voltage error, an integral part of the controller with parameter K_{iv} must be added to the output of the controller. The damping control signal u_{stab} is derived from the generator active power P. The signal *a* is a measure of generator acceleration and the signal Δω is a measure of generator speed deviation. The signals *a* and Δω are derived from the generator active power through filters and the integrator. The damping control signal u_{stab} is added to the input of the voltage control loop.
The fuzzy logic control scheme is applied to the voltage and stabilization control loop (Hiyama et. al., 1996). The generator operating point in the phase plane is given by *p*(k) for the corresponding control loop (Fig. 11a):

$$p(k) = (X(k), A_s \cdot Y(k)) \tag{30}$$

where *X*(k) is *e*(k) and *Y*(k) is e_d(k) for the voltage control loop, and *X*(k) is Δω(k) and *Y*(k) is *a*(k) for the stabilization control loop. Parameter A_s is the adjustable scaling factor for *Y*(k). Polar information, representing the generator operating point, is determined by the radius *D*(k) and the phase angle Θ(k):

$$D(k) = \sqrt{X(k)^2 + (A_s \cdot Y(k))^2} \tag{31}$$

$$\Theta(k) = arctg(\frac{A_s \cdot Y(k)}{X(k)}) \tag{32}$$

The phase plane is divided into sectors A and B defined by using two angle membership functions *N*(Θ(k)) and *P*(Θ(k)) (Fig. 11b).
The principles of the fuzzy control scheme and the selection of the membership functions are described in (Hiyama et. al., 1996). By using the membership functions *N*(Θ(k)) and *P*(Θ(k)) the output control signals *u*(k) and u_{stab}(k) for each control loop are given as follows:

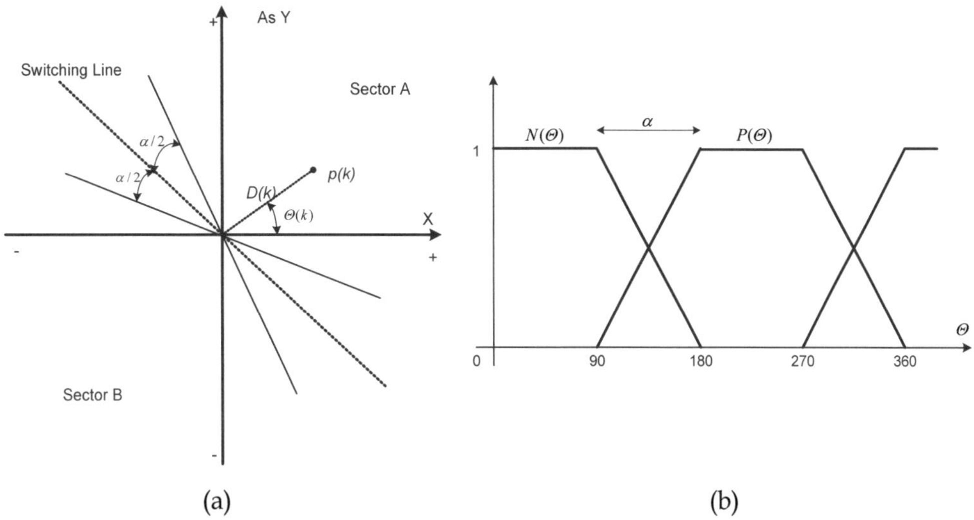

Fig. 11. Phase plane (a) and angle membership functions (b)

$$u(k)=\frac{N(\Theta(k))-P(\Theta(k))}{N(\Theta(k))+P(\Theta(k))}\cdot G(k)\cdot U_{\max v} \tag{33}$$

$$u_{\text{stab}}(k)=\frac{N(\Theta(k))-P(\Theta(k))}{N(\Theta(k))+P(\Theta(k))}\cdot G(k)\cdot U_{\max s} \tag{34}$$

The radius membership function G (k) is given by:

$$G(k) = D(k) / D_r \text{ for } D(k) \leq D_r$$

$$G(k) = 1 \text{ for } D(k) > D_r (35)$$

Simulation models of the voltage control loop, stabilization control loop and fuzzy logic control structure are presented on the Figs. 12, 13, and 14, respectively. Parameters A_s, D_r and α for the voltage control loop and the damping control loop are given in Tables 3 and 4.

A_S	0.1
D_r	1
K_{iv}	10
U_{maxv}	2 p.u.
α	90°

Table 3. FLC parameters for voltage control loop

A_S	0.01
D_r	0.01
U_{maxs}	0.1 p.u.
α	90°

Table 4. FLC parameters for damping control loop

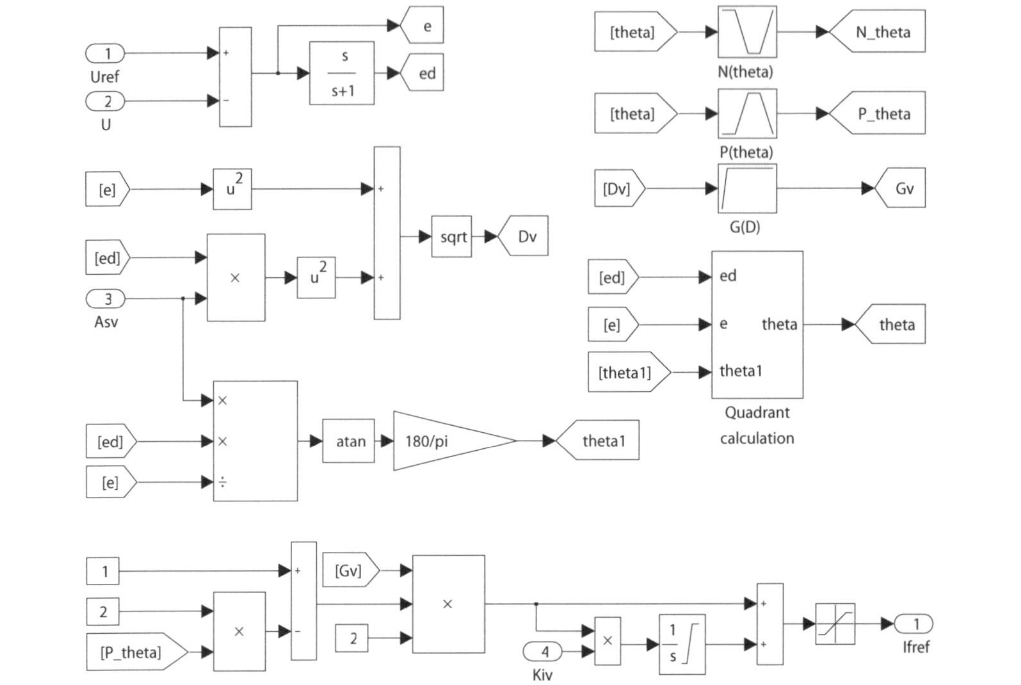

Fig. 12. Simulation model of voltage control loop

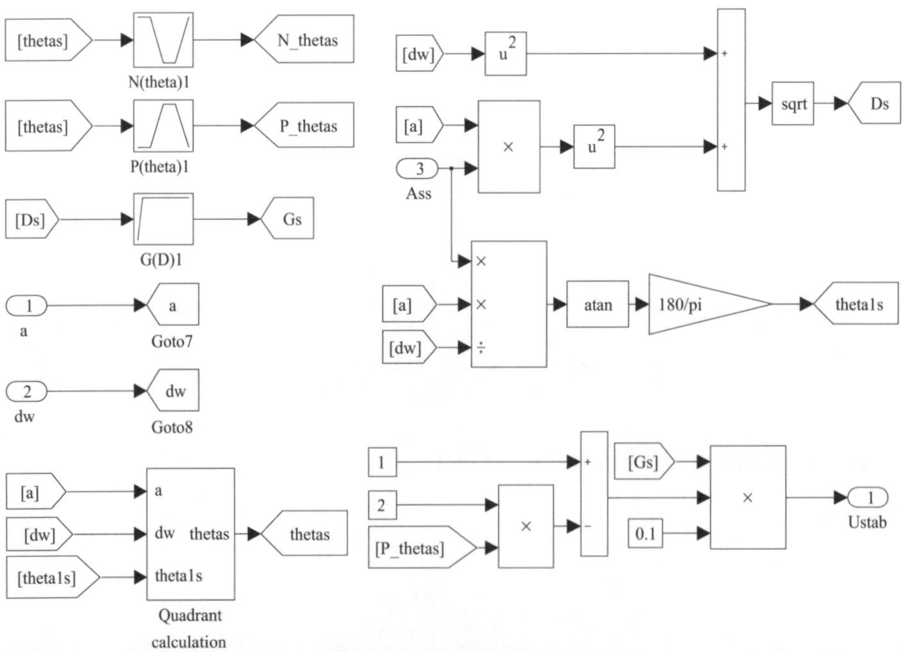

Fig. 13. Simulation model of stabilization control loop

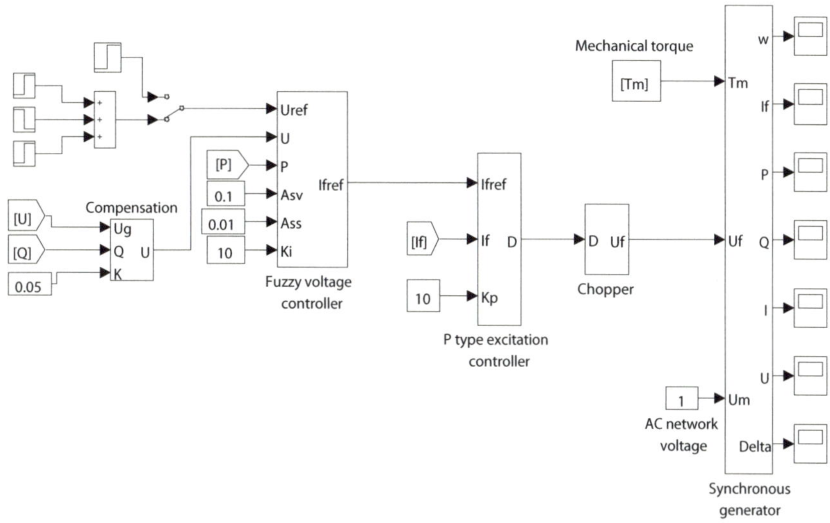

Fig. 14. Simulation model of fuzzy logic control structure

3. Simulation results

In order to verify the performance of the proposed control structures several simulations were carried out. In these experiments, voltage reference is changed in 0.1 s from 1 p.u. to 0.9 p.u. or 1.1 p.u. and in 1 s back to 1 p.u. at a constant generator active power.

For the quality analysis of the active power oscillations two numerical criteria are used: the integral of absolute error (IAE) and the integral of absolute error derivative (IAED). If the response is better, the amount of criteria is smaller.

Fig. 15 presents active power responses for step changes in voltage reference from 1 p.u. to 0.9 p.u. and back to 1 p.u. at an active power of 0.5 p.u. The numerical criteria of the responses in Fig. 15 are given in Table 5.

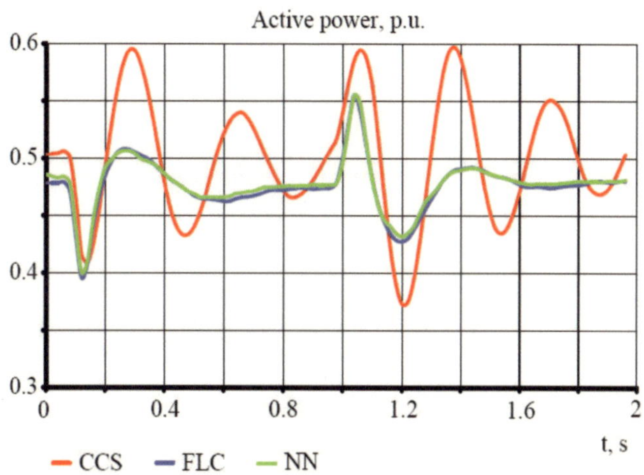

Fig. 15. Active power responses for step changes in voltage reference 1 p.u.-0.9 p.u.-1 p.u. at an active power of 0.5 p.u.

	IAE	IAED
CCS	0.389	0.279
FLC	0.255	0.097
NN	0.235	0.090

Table 5. Numerical criteria for step changes in voltage reference 1 p.u.-0.9 p.u.-1 p.u. at an active power of 0.5 p.u.

Fig. 16 shows active power responses for step changes in voltage reference from 1 p.u. to 1.1 p.u. and back to 1 p.u. at an active power of 0.5 p.u. The numerical criteria of the responses in Fig. 16 are given in Table 6.

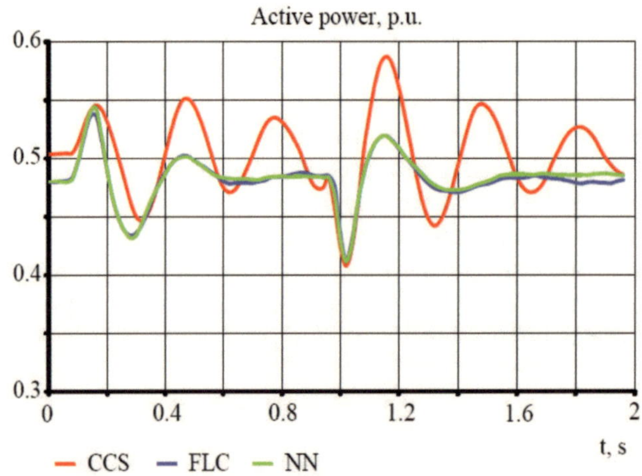

Fig. 16. Active power responses for step changes in voltage reference 1 p.u.-1.1 p.u.-1 p.u. at an active power of 0.5 p.u.

	IAE	IAED
CCS	0.264	0.196
FLC	0.202	0.092
NN	0.192	0.091

Table 6. Numerical criteria for step changes in voltage reference 1 p.u.-1.1 p.u.-1 p.u. at an active power of 0.5 p.u.

Fig. 17 presents active power responses for step changes in voltage reference from 1 p.u. to 0.9 p.u. and back to 1 p.u. at an active power of 0.8 p.u. The numerical criteria of the responses in Fig. 17 are given in Table 7.

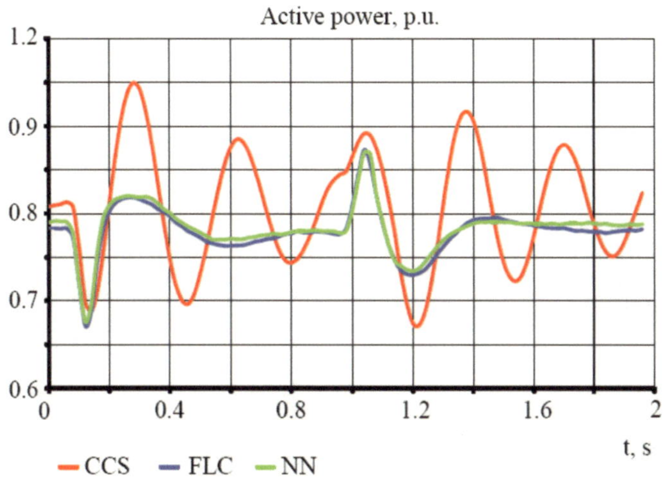

Fig. 17. Active power responses for step changes in voltage reference 1 p.u.-0.9 p.u.-1 p.u. at an active power of 0.8 p.u.

	IAE	IAED
CCS	0.52	0.373
FLC	0.248	0.114
NN	0.219	0.106

Table 7. Numerical criteria for step changes in voltage reference 1 p.u.-0.9 p.u.-1 p.u. at an active power of 0.8 p.u.

Fig. 18 shows active power responses for step changes in voltage reference from 1 p.u. to 1.1 p.u. and back to 1 p.u. at an active power of 0.8 p.u. The numerical criteria of the responses in Fig. 18 are given in Table 8.

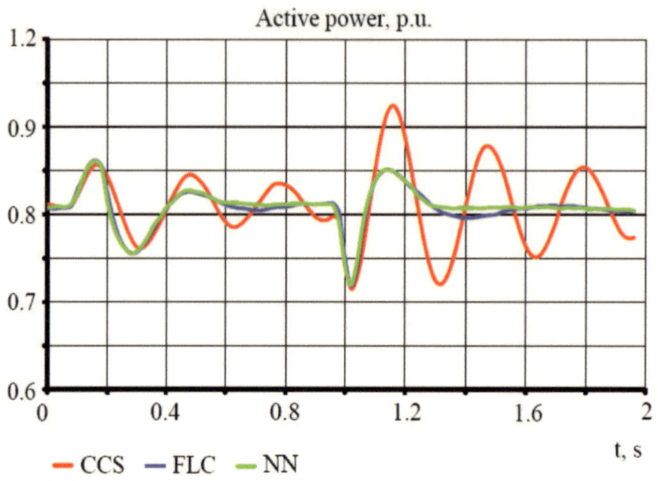

Fig. 18. Active power responses for step changes in voltage reference 1 p.u.-1.1 p.u.-1 p.u. at an active power of 0.8 p.u.

	IAE	IAED
CCS	0.312	0.234
FLC	0.130	0.097
NN	0.119	0.090

Table 8. Numerical criteria for step changes in voltage reference 1 p.u.-1.1 p.u.-1 p.u. at an active power of 0.8 p.u.

Based on the numerical criteria it can be concluded that the neural network-based controller with stabilization effect in the criteria function has two to three percent better damping of oscillations than the fuzzy logic controller.

4. Conclusion

Three different structures for the excitation control of a synchronous generator were simulated in Matlab Simulink: the first structure is a conventional control structure which includes a PI voltage controller, while the second structure includes a fuzzy logic controller, and the third structure includes a neural network-based voltage controller. Performances of the proposed algorithms were tested for step changes in voltage reference in the excitation system of a synchronous generator, which was connected to an AC network through a transformer and a transmission line.

For the performance analysis of the proposed control structures two numerical criteria were used: the integral of absolute error and the integral of absolute error derivative. In the comparison with the PI voltage controller neural network-based controller and the fuzzy logic controller show a significant damping of oscillations. It is important to emphasize that

the stabilizer was not used in the conventional control structure, which would definitely reduce the difference between the conventional and the proposed control structures.
The simulation results show justification for the use of the advanced control structure based on neural networks and fuzzy logic in the excitation control system of a synchronous generator. Also, using the software package Matlab Simulink allows users to easily test the proposed algorithms.

5. References

Akbari, S., & Karim Amooshahi, M. (2009). Power System Stabilizer Design Using Evolutionary Algorithms, *International Review of Electrical Engineering*, 4, 5, (October 2009), pp. 925-931.

Cao, Y., Jiang, L., Cheng, S., Chen, D., Malik, O.P., & Hope, G.S. (1994). A nonlinear variable structure stabilizer for power system stability, *IEEE Transactions on Energy Conversion*, 9, 3, (1994), pp. 489-495.

Ghandra, A., Malik, & O. P., Hope, G.S. (1988). A self-tuning controller for the control of multi-machine power systems, *IEEE Trans. On Power Syst.*, 3, 3, (August 1988), pp. 1065-1071.

Hassan, M.A., Malik, O.P., & Hope, G.S. (1991). A Fuzzy Logic Based Stabilizer for a Synchronous Machine, *IEEE Trans. Energy Conversion*, 6, 3, (1991), pp. 407-413.

Haykin, S. (1994). *Neural Networks: A Comprehensive Foundation*, IEEE Press

Hiyama T., Oniki S., & Nagashima H. (1996). Evaluation of advanced fuzzy logic PSS on analog network simulator and actual installation on hydro generators, *IEEE Trans. on Energy Conversion*, 11, 1, (1996), pp. 125-131.

Hsu, Y.Y., & Liou, K.L. (1987). Design of self-tuning PID power system stabilizers for synchronous generators, *IEEE Trans. on Energy Conversion*, 2, 3, (1987), pp. 343-348.

Jiang, Z. (2009). Design of a nonlinear power system stabilizer using synergetic control theory, *Electric Power Systems Research*, 79, 6, (2009), pp. 855-862.

Karnavas, Y.L., & Pantos, S. (2008). Performance evaluation of neural networks for µC based excitation control of a synchronous generator, *Proceedings of 18th International Conference on Electrical Machines ICEM 2008*, Portugal, September 2008.

Karnavas, Y.L., & Papadopoulos, D. P. (2002). AGC for autonomous power system using combined intelligent techniques, *Electric Power Systems Research*, 62, 3, (July 2002), pp. 225-239.

Kundur, P. (1994). *Power System Stability and Control*, McGraw-Hill

Malik, O.P., Salem, M.M., Zaki, A.M., Mahgoub, O.A., & Abu El-Zahab, E. (2002). Experimental studies with simple neuro-controller based excitation controller, *IEE Proceedings Generation, Transmission and Distribution*, 149, 1, (2002), pp. 108-113.

Noroozi, N., Khaki, B., & Seifi, A. (2008). Chaotic Oscillations Damping in Power System by Finite Time Control, *International Review of Electrical Engineering*, 3, 6, (December 2008), pp. 1032-1038.

Salem, M.M., Malik, O.P., Zaki, A.M., Mahgoub, O.A., & Abu El-Zahab, E. (2003). Simple neuro-controller with modified error function for a synchronous generator, *Electrical Power and Energy Systems*, 25, (2003), pp. 759-771.

Salem, M.M., Zaki, A.M., Mahgoub, O.A., Abu El-Zahab, E., & Malik, O.P. (2000a). Studies on Multi-Machine Power System With a Neural Network Based Excitation Controller, *Proceedings of Power Engineering Society Summer Meeting*, 2000.

Salem, M.M., Zaki, A.M., Mahgoub, O.A., Abu El-Zahab, E., & Malik, O.P. (2000b). Experimental Veification of Generating Unit Excitation Neuro-Controller, *Proceedings of* IEEE Power Engineering Society Winter Meeting, 2000.

Shahgholian, G. (2010). Development of State Space Model and Control of the STATCOM for Improvement of Damping in a Single-Machine Infinite-Bus, *International Review of Electrical Engineering*, 5, 1, (February 2010), pp. 1367-1375.

11

Design of PSO-Based Optimal/Tunable PID Fuzzy Logic Controller Using FPGA

Zeyad Assi Obaid[1], Saad Abd Almageed Salman[1], Hazem I. Ali[2], Nasri Sulaiman[3], M. H. Marhaban[3] and M. N. Hamidon[3]

[1]*College of Engineering University of Diyala*
[2]*Control Engineering Department University of Technology*
[3]*Faculty of EngineeringUniversity Putra Malaysia*
[1,2]*Iraq*
[3]*Malaysia*

1. Introduction

Fuzzy Logic controllers have been successfully applied in a large number of control applications, with the most commonly used controller being the PID controller. Fuzzy logic controllers provide an alternative to PID controllers, as they are a good tool for the control of systems that are difficult to model. The control action in fuzzy logic controllers can be expressed with simple "if-then" rules (Poorani et al., 2005). Fuzzy controllers are more sufficient than classical controllers as they can cover a much wider range of operating conditions than classical Controllers. In addition, fuzzy controllers operate with noise and disturbances of a different nature. The common method for designing a fuzzy controller is to realize it as a computer program. Higher density programmable logic devices, such as the FPGA, can be used to integrate large amounts of logic in a single IC. The FPGA provides greater flexibility than ASIC, and can be used with tighter time-to-market schedules. The term programmable highlights the customization of the IC by the user. Many researchers have discussed the design of the hardware implementation of fuzzy logic controllers. A number was specialized for control applications, and aimed to get better control responses. These researches have concern using new techniques in fuzzy control, in order to get higher processing speed versus low utilization of chip resource (Jain et al., 2009 and Islam et al., 2007)

The hardware implementation of fuzzy logic controllers has many requirements, such as high-speed performance, low complexity and high flexibility (Leonid, 1997). With this type of application, and to provide these requirements, it is necessary to avoid various limitations and challenges. In deriving a practical PIDFC structure, it is desirable to reduce the number of inputs. In addition, it is difficult to formulate the fuzzy rules with the variable sum of error ($\sum e$), as its steady-state value is unknown for most control problems (Mann et al., 1999), (Hassan et al., 2007), (Obaid et al., 2009). Hence, it is necessary to design the FPGA-based PIDFC with fewer inputs and rules to get higher processing speed versus low utilization of chip resources. In addition, the design of digital fuzzy controllers has limitations concerning the structure. These include the restriction or limitation of the shapes of fuzzy sets implemented in the fuzzifier block, such as those in the controllers proposed in (Hassan et al., 2007) and (Seng et al., 1999). It is desirable to simplify the structure of the PIDFC controller to offer higher flexibility versus low-chip resources. The majority of PID fuzzy controller applications belong to the direct action (DA) type; here the fuzzy inference is used to compute the PID controller actions, not to tune the PID parameters (Mann et al., 1999). Therefore, it is necessary to design a tuning method inside the digital fuzzy chip, especially with the DA type, in order to scale the universe of discourse for the inputs/outputs variable in the PIDFC, and to obtain the best tuning case in the operational range. Changing the scaling gains at the input and output of PIDFC has a significant impact on the performance of the resulting fuzzy control system, as well as the controller's stability and performance (Leonid et al., 2000). Therefore, it is necessary to use an optimization method to calculate the optimal values of these gains. In recent years, several researchers have designed fuzzy controllers with different ranges of accuracy. Most of these controllers have 6-8 bits of accuracy (Poorani et al., 2005), (Tipsuwanpornet al., 2004), (Hassan et al., 2007), (Solano et al., 1997), (Gabrielli et al., 2009). This accuracy has a trade off with the speed of the process and it may affect the process behavior inside the digital fuzzy chip (Jantzen, 1998), (Ibrahim, 2004). Furthermore, increasing the accuracy will also increase the hardware complexity versus low-speed performance and vice versa. However, none have evaluated the same controller with different ranges of accuracy. Hence, it is necessary to find the best accuracy inside the digital chip that offers low hardware complexity versus high-speed performance. The aim of this chapter is to design a PIDFC that can efficiently replace other fuzzy controllers realized as a computer program, that have the ability to serve a wide range of systems with real-time operations. To achieve this aim, the following points are addressed:

Ref No.	Controller type	Optimization and tuning method	System Type
(Li and Hu , 1996)	PID with FIS	Tuned by FIS	Process control
(Tipsuwanpornet al., 2004)	Gain scheduling PID FC	Gain scheduling Tuning method	Level and temperature
(Poorani et al., 2005)	Specific FC 6-inputs, 1-output	No method	Speed control of electric vehicle
(Alvarez et al., 2006)	Optimal FC 2-inputs, 1-output	No method	Multi phase converter
(Gonzalez-Vazquez et al, 2006)	PD FC	No method	No system
(Khatr and Rattan, 2006)	Multi-layered PDFC	No method	Autonomous mobile robot
(Hassan et al., 2007)	PID FC	No method	Linear system
(Jain et al., 2009)	Optimal PID controller	Bacterial Foraging Optimization method	Inverted pendulum

Table 1. Summary of the Related FPGA-Based Controller in the Literature

1. To design a PIDFC with improved fuzzy algorithm that offers low implementation size versus high processing speed.
2. To aid the PIDFC with a tuning gains block inside the FPGA chip that makes the design able to accept PSO-based optimal scaling gains.
3. To design two versions of the proposed PIDFC. The first one is an 8-bits PIDFC, while the second one is a 6-bits PIDFC.
4. To test the proposed design with different plants models with a unity feedback control system.

Many researchers have discussed different approaches to the present fuzzy algorithms that offer high-processing speed and small chip size. Many of the fuzzy controllers implemented in the literature using FPGA, have many limitations and challenges with the structure, such as those in the shape of fuzzy sets implemented in the Fuzzifier block. This thesis will deal with some of these limitations. Table I lists the related FPGA-based controllers in the literature, highlighting the tuning and optimization methods used as well as the type of application and the type of controller.

2. PID fuzzy logic controller

A PID fuzzy controller is a controller that takes error, summation of error and rate of change of error (rate for short) as inputs. Fuzzy controller with three inputs is difficult and not easy to implement, because it needs a large number of rules and memory (Leonid, 1997). In the proposed design, if each input is described with eight linguistic values, then 8x8x8=512 rules will be needed. The PIDFC can be constructed as a parallel structure of a PDFC and a PIFC, and the output of the PIDFC is formed by algebraically adding the outputs of the two fuzzy control blocks (Leonid, 1997). In deriving a practical PIDFC structure, the following remarks are made (Hassan et al., 2007) (Mann et al., 1999), (Leonid, 1997), (Obaid et al., 2009): *Remark 1:* For any PIDFC, the error (e) is considered as the necessary input for deriving any PID structure. *Remark 2:* It is difficult to formulate control rules with the input variable sum-of-error $\sum e$, as its steady-state value is unknown for most control problems. To overcome the problem stated in remark 2, a PDFC may be employed to serve as a PIFC in incremental form, where a PD fuzzy logic controller, with summation at its output, is used instead of the PIFC (Hassan et al., 2007), (Obaid et al., 1999).

3. Particle swarm optimization

PSO is an evolutionary computation technique-based developed by Eberhart and Kennedy in 1995 (Wang et al., 2006). It was inspired by the social behavior of birds flocking or fish schooling, more specifically, the collective behaviors of simple individuals interacting with their environment and each other (Wang et al., 2006). PSO has been successfully applied in many areas: function optimization, artificial neural network training, fuzzy system control, and other areas where evolutionary computation can be applied. Similar to evolutionary computation (EC), PSO is a population-based optimization tool (Wang et al., 2006), (Allaoua et al., 2009). The system is initialized with a population of random solutions and searches for optima by updating generations. All of the particles have fitness values that are evaluated by the fitness function to be optimized, and have velocities that direct the flying of the particles (Wang et al., 2006). In a PSO system, particles change their positions by flying around in a multidimensional search space until computational limitations are exceeded.

The concept of the modification of a searching point by PSO is shown in Fig. 1 (Allaoua et al., 2009).

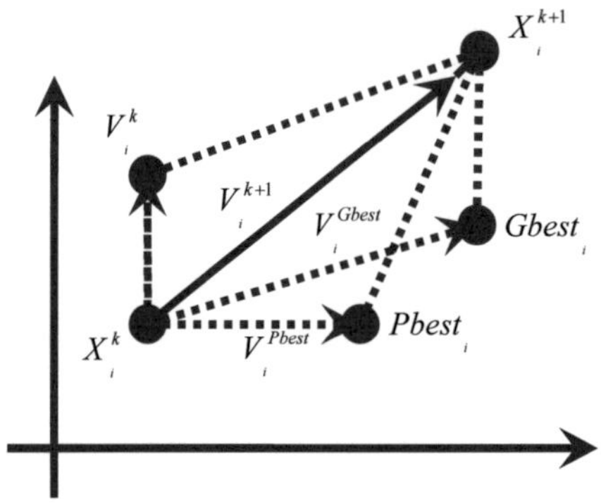

Fig. 1. Concept of the Modification of a Searching Point by PSO (Allaoua et al., 2009).

In the PSO algorithm, instead of using evolutionary operators such as mutation and crossover, to manipulate algorithms, for a d-variable optimization problem, a flock of particles are put into the d-dimensional search space with randomly chosen velocities and positions knowing their best values so far (Pbest) and the position in the d-dimensional space. The velocity of each particle, adjusted according to its own flying experience and the other particle's flying experience. For example, the *i*-th particle is represented as *xi* = (*xi,* 1, xi, 2… *xi,* d) in the d-dimensional space. The best previous position of the *i*-th particle is recorded and represented as (Allaoua et al., 2009):

$$\text{Pbest}i = (\text{Pbest}i, 1, \text{Pbest}i, 2 \ldots \text{Pbest } i, d) \tag{1}$$

The index of best particle among all of the particles in the group is gbest*d*. The velocity for particle *i* is represented as *vi* = (*vi,*1 ,*vi,*2 ,…, *vi,*d). The modified velocity and position of each particle can be calculated using the current velocity and the distance from Pbest*i,* d to gbestd as shown in the following formulas (Allaoua et al., 2009):

$$V_{i,m}^{(t+1)} = W.V_{i,m}^{(t)} + c_1 * rand() * (Pbest_{i,m} - X_{i,m}^{(t)}) + c_2 * rand() * (gbest_m - X_{i,m}^{(t)}) \tag{2}$$

$$X_{i,m}^{(t+1)} = X_{i,m}^{(t)} + V_{i,m}^{(t+1)} \; ; \quad i= 1, 2\ldots n; \quad m=1, 2\ldots d \tag{3}$$

Where:
N: Number of particles in the group,
D: dimension,
t: Pointer of iterations (generations),
$V_{i,m}^{(t)}$: Velocity of particle I at iteration t, $V_d^{\min} \le V_{i,m}^{(t)} \le V_d^{\max}$
W: Inertia weight factor,
*c*1, *c*2: Acceleration constant,
rand ( ): Random number between 0 and 1
$X_{i,m}^{(t)}$: Current position of particle *i* at iterations,
Pbesti: Best previous position of i-th particle,
Gbest: Best particle among all the particles in the population.

4. The proposed PSO algorithm

The main aim of the PSO algorithm is to tune the controller parameters [Kp, Kd, Ki, Ko], by minimizing the cost function for minimum values in order to get the optimal gains value for these parameters. The target cost function is the integral square error (ISE), this is simple function and can easy represented in the fuzzy algorithm. The cost function (equation 4) is calculated by swapping the searching results in the local position with the minimum value of the function until reaching the best global search. In this case, the proposed PSO algorithm is 6-dimension in the population size for PIDFC (also can do it by 4-dimenssion), 3-dimension in the case of the PIFC and PDFC. This dimension belongs to the controller parameters, which represent the particle (X) inside the population space. These particles are explained in equations (5, 6 and 7) with *ith* iteration path. Note that during the search process the resulting gains were constrained by the interval [Xmin Xmax] to search with these limits in order to cover the range of the operational range (universe of discourse). Fig. 2 shows the flow chart of the proposed PSO algorithm.

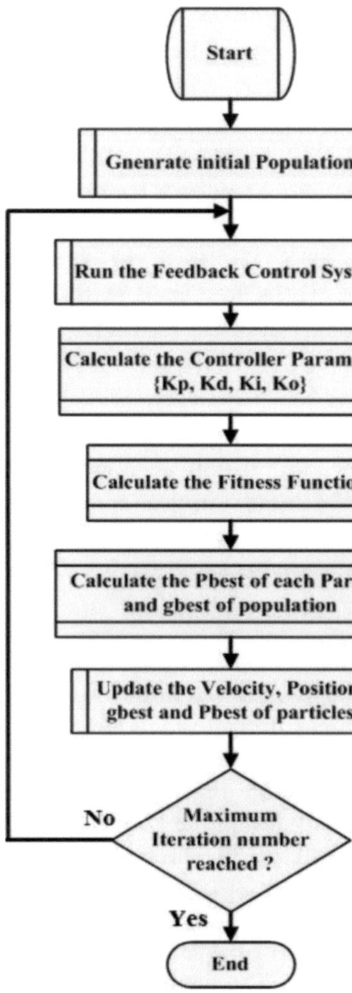

Fig. 2. Flowchart of the Proposed PSO Algorithm

$$ISE = \sum_{t=0}^{Maxiteration} (e(t))^2 \tag{4}$$

$$\begin{aligned} X(PIDFC) &= [x(1)\ \ x(2)\ \ x(3)\ \ x(4)\ x(5)\ \ x(6)] = \\ &[Kp\ \ Kd\ Ko + Kp\ \ Ki\ \ Ko] \quad , \text{Dimension} = 6 \end{aligned} \tag{5}$$

$$X(PIFC) = [x(1)\ \ x(2)\ \ x(3)] = [Kp\ \ Ki\ \ Ko] \qquad , \text{Dimension} = 3 \tag{6}$$

$$X(PDFC) = [x(1)\ \ x(2)\ \ x(3)] = [Kp\ \ Kd\ \ Ko] \qquad , \text{Dimension} = 3 \tag{7}$$

5. Block diagram of the PIDFC

The proposed controller accepts two signals, the first one is the plant output (y_p) and the second one is the desired output (y_d), both of them are digital signals, and deliver the control action signal as a digital output. It also accepts four 8-bit digital signals that represent the optimal gain parameters needed by the controller (K_p , K_d , K_i , and K_o). These parameters are used to aid the tuning block with optimal values of the scaling gains online with the digital FPGA chip. Other two (one-bit) signals have been used to select the type of the controller (PDFC, PIFC, or PIDFC) online with the chip. Fig. 3 shows the general block diagram of the controller chip in a unity feedback control system. In recent years, many of the digital fuzzy applications have different ranges of the accuracy. Most of them have 6-8 bits of accuracy (Poorani et al., 2005), (Tipsuwanpornet al., 2004), (Hassan et al., 2007), (Solano et al., 1997), (Gabrielli et al., 2009), (Obaid et al., 2009), (Obaid et al., 1999). This accuracy may affect the process behavior inside the digital fuzzy chip; also it has a trade off with the speed of the process (Leonid , 1997), (Jantzen, 1998), (Ibrahim, 2004). Therefore, it is necessary to find which range has better accuracy inside the digital chip. Two versions of the proposed PIDFC were designed, the first one is an 8-bit which uses 8 bits for each input/output variables. The second version is a 6-bit which uses 6 bits for each input/output variable. To make the discussion clear and general for the proposed controller in the following sections, symbol (q) will be used to represent the range of accuracy, (q=8) in the proposed 8-bits design, and (q=6) in the 6-bits version of the proposed design.

6. Structure of the PIDFC design

Generally, to represent PIDFC, it is required to design a fuzzy inference system with three inputs that represent the proportional, derivative, and integral components, and each one of them can have up to eight fuzzy sets. Therefore, the maximum number of the required fuzzy rules is 8^3=512 rules. To avoid this huge number of rules, the proposed controller was designed using two parallel PDFC to design the PIDFC as discussed earlier (Hassan et al., 2007), (Obaid et al., 2009), (Obaid et al., 1999). The second PDFC was converted to a PIFC by accumulating its output. Fig. 4 shows the structure of proposed PIDFC, where FIS refers to the fuzzy inference system with its three blocks, Fuzzifier, inference engine and defuzzifier. Both controllers, PDFC and PIFC, receive the same error signal. The structure of the single PDFC is discussed in the next sections. The main block in the PDFC is the fuzzy inference block which has two inputs ($e(n)$ and $\Delta e(n)$), one output (U(n)) fuzzy system of Mamdani type that uses singleton membership functions for the output variable. Initially, the two input signals are multiplied by a gain coefficient (K_p and K_d or K_p and K_i) before entering the fuzzy inference block. Similarly, the output of the fuzzy inference block is multiplied by a gain coefficient (K_o) (Hassan et al., 2007), (Obaid et al., 2009), (Obaid et al., 1999). At the same time, the output of the fuzzy inference block in the second PDFC is multiplied by a gain coefficient and then accumulated to give the output of the PIFC. Subsequently, both outputs of the PDFC and PIFC are added together to give the PIDFC output (u_{PID}). The final design works as a PDFC, PIFC, or PIDFC, depending on the two selection lines sw_1 and sw_0, which provide a more flexible design to cover a wide range of systems. The PIDFC is designed using two blocks of PDFC, and the main block in the proposed design is the PDFC block. The main components inside the PDFC block are: *Tuning-gain* block, *Fuzzifier* block, *inference engine* block, and *Defuzzifier* block.

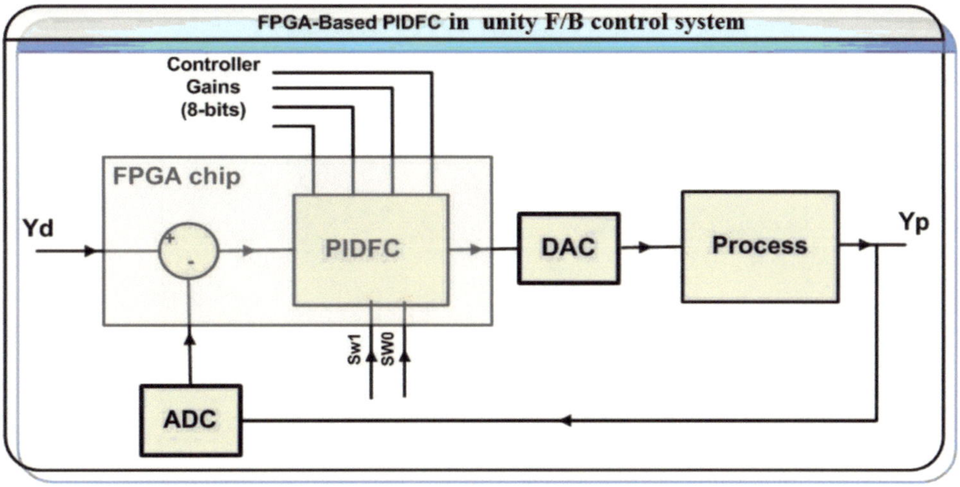

Fig. 3. Block Diagram of the PIDFC in a Unity Feedback Control System.

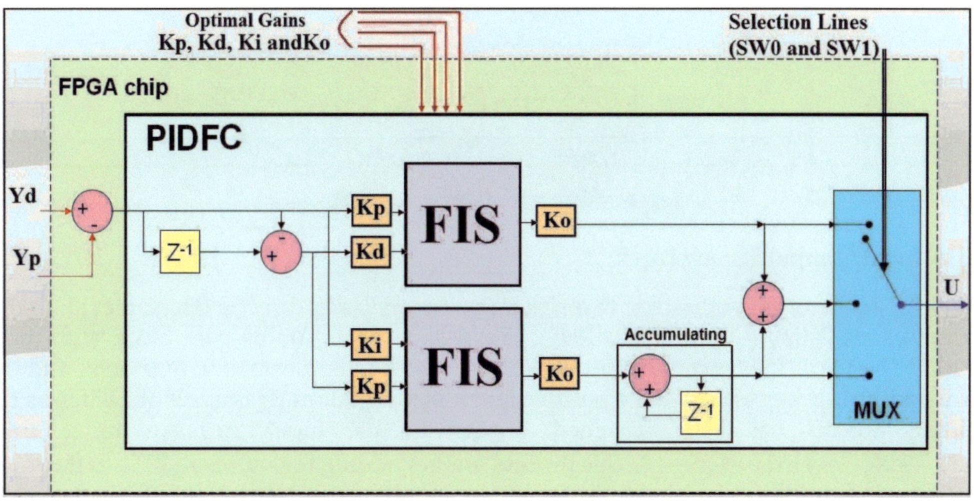

Fig. 4. Main structure of the Proposed Controller

Tuning-Gain Block

The tuning-gain block is used at each of the two inputs and also at the output of each PDFC block. This block receives and multiplies two inputs: the variable to be scaled (input or output) and its related gains, this implies the proposed tuning method via scaling the universe of discourse. An eight-bit latch was used at each Tuning-gain block to store the gain coefficient value received from one of the gain ports, depending on selection line values. The "*" operator was used in the VHDL files of the design to express a multiplication process just like a conventional language. This process has been designed at the *behavioral* level of abstraction in VHDL code, i.e. during the design synthesis process, if the library "*IEEE.std_logic_signed*" was included in the VHDL files (Hassan et al., 2007), (Obaid et al., 2009), (Obaid et al., 1999). Fig. 5 shows the Tuning-gain block with more details.

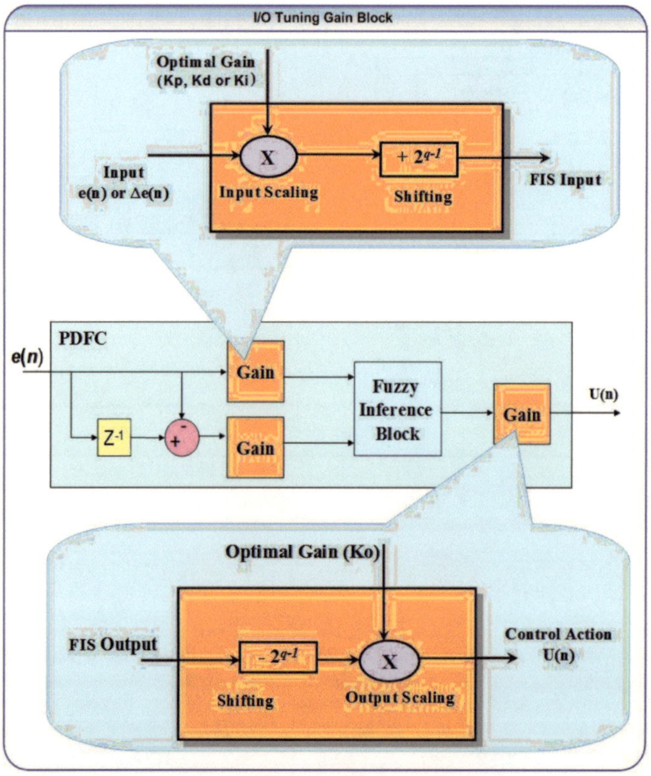

Fig. 5. Input/Output Tuning Block

Every "*" operator is synthesized to a *signed number multiplier* directly (Hassan et al., 2007), (Obaid et al., 2009), (Obaid et al., 1999). Fig. 6 shows the Tuning-gain block with more details. The fuzzy inference block in each PDFC can handle positive values only, and the error and its rate signals can have positive and negative values (Hassan et al., 2007), as the shifting process has been designed to convert the input variables range from $[-2^{q-1} \rightarrow 2^{q-1}-1]$ to $[0 \rightarrow 2^{q}-1]$. This process implies adding the number (2^{q-1}) to the input variable. This addition has been designed by inverting the last bit (MSB) of the input variable (Hassan et al., 2007), (Obaid et al., 2009), (Obaid et al., 1999). The shift process at the output has been designed using subtraction, instead of addition, to convert the range of the output variable from $[0 \rightarrow 2^q - 1]$ to $[-2^{q-1} \rightarrow 2^{q-1} - 1]$. This specification will increase the flexibility of the proposed design.

Fuzzifier Block

The overlapping degree (V) in the proposed design is two, which means that at each time instance there are two active, (have nonzero membership values), fuzzy sets for each input variable at maximum. The proposed fuzzification process has been designed using two fuzzifier blocks, one for each input variable. The fuzzifier block implies the fuzzification process by taking the input and producing four output values. These values represent the sequence numbers of the two active fuzzy sets (e1, e2 and de1, de2) and the membership degrees of the variable for each one of them (μe1, μe2 and μde1, μde2). The memory base was designed using ROM. The use of ROM is better than RAM when the programmability is directly achieved by the implementation techniques (as in the case of FPGA) (Barriga et al., 2006). The fuzzifier block was designed using memory based membership functions (MBMSF) (Solano et al., 1997), (Barriga et al., 2006). This method reduces the restrictions of the fuzzy set shapes, even it needs a smaller memory size than other method such as the arithmetic method. The memory model has been implemented with maximum possible membership values in the proposed design, where the maximum coded in p values is $(2^p - 1)$, where p=4 bits in the 6-bits version of the PIDFC, and p=6 bits in the 8-bits version of the PIDFC. This dictates that the summation of membership values of two consecutive fuzzy set is always equal to $(2^p - 1)$. Each word in the MBMSF is divided into two parts. The first part represents the sequence number of the active fuzzy set (3-bits, in both versions). Assigning 3 bits for the sequence number of the fuzzy sets, gives the controller flexibility to accept for each input variable for up-to 8 fuzzy sets. The second part of the memory word is p bits data word which represents the membership value of the input in the active fuzzy set. The total memory length for each input is equal to (2^q).

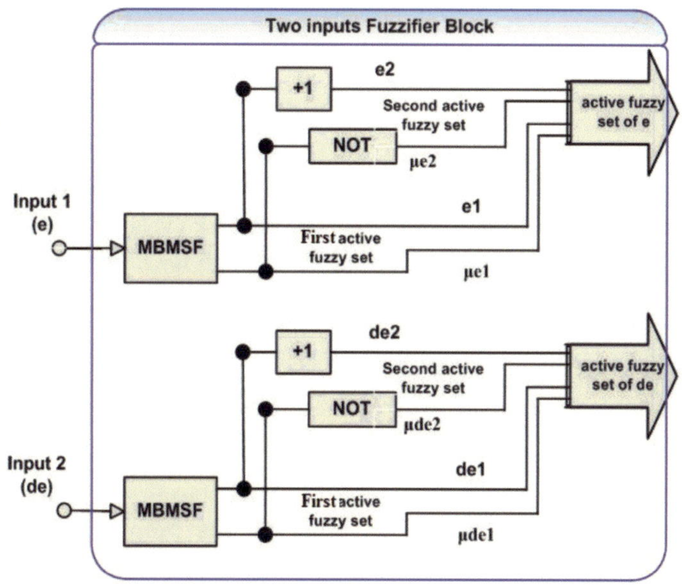

Fig. 6. Two Inputs Fuzzifier Block.

Inference Engine Block

The inference engine consists of three blocks: rule selector, rule memory, and minimum circuit as shown in Fig. 7. Different mechanisms have been used to minimize both the calculation time and the area of the fuzzy inference system; among the most interesting methods is the active rules selector concept (Hassan et al., 2007), (Solano et al., 1997), (Obaid et al., 2009), (Barriga et al., 2006), (Huang and Lai, 2005), (Obaid et al., 1999). This block uses the information from fuzzifier, which belongs to the active fuzzy sets to launch only active rules. This reduces the number of processed rules. Furthermore, by using an active rule selector, the number of rules to be processed will be reduced according to this equation (Hassan et al., 2007):

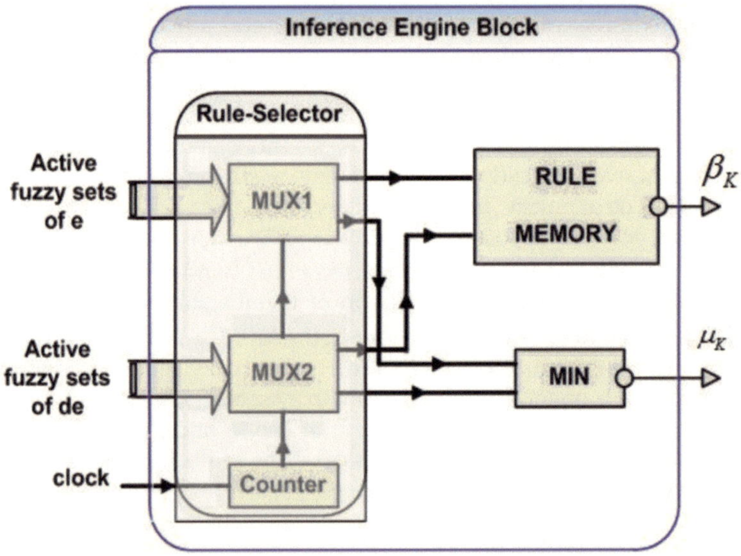

Fig. 7. Inference Engine Block

$$\text{Number of active rules} = V^m \tag{8}$$

Where m is the number of inputs, and V is the maximum number of overlapped fuzzy sets. In the proposed design, it is assumed that $m = 2$ and $V = 2$. Hence, the number of active rules at each time is: $V^m = 2^2 = 4$ rules. In each counter cycle, the membership degrees delivered from the two multiplexers are combined through the minimum circuit to calculate the applicability degree of the rule (μ_k), while the active fuzzy set sequence numbers are combined directly to address a rule memory location that contains the corresponding rule consequent (β_k). The rule memory is a ($2^{2\times3} \times q$) bits ROM, and each word in it represents the position of the output singleton membership functions of one rule.

Defuzzifier Block

The defuzzification process in the defuzzifier block has been designed using the *Centroid* method. The four main components that represent the proposed defuzzifier are: two accumulators, one multiplier, and one divider. The defuzzifier block accepts the information from the inference engine (four (μ_k), and four (β_k) each time), and produces an output (crisp set) to the output -tuning gain block, as shown in Fig. 8.

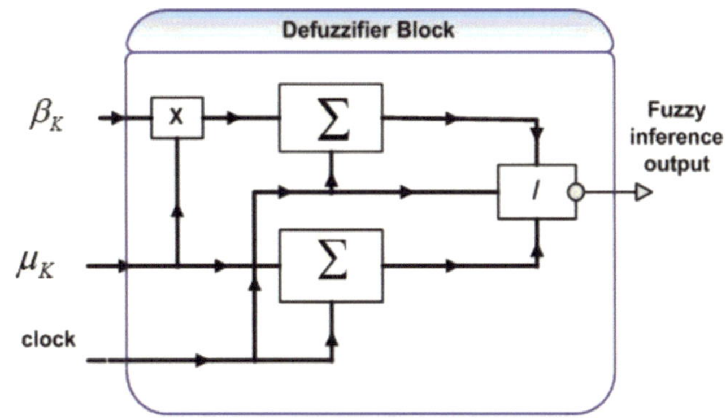

Fig. 8. Defuzzifier Block.

		e							
		NB	NM	NS	NZ	PZ	PS	PM	PB
de	NB	-1	-1	-1	-0.7	-0.7	-0.4	-0.1	0.1
	NM	-1	-1	-0.7	-0.7	-0.4	-0.1	0.1	0.1
	NS	-1	-0.7	-0.7	-0.4	-0.1	0.1	0.1	0.4
	NZ	-0.7	-0.7	-0.4	-0.1	0.1	0.1	0.4	0.7
	PZ	-0.7	-0.4	-0.1	-0.1	0.1	0.4	0.7	0.7
	PS	-0.4	-0.1	-0.1	0.1	0.4	0.7	0.7	1
	PM	-0.1	-0.1	0.1	0.4	0.7	0.7	1	1
	PB	-0.1	0.1	0.4	0.7	0.7	1	1	1

Table 2. Fuzzy Rules.

The defuzzifier block was designed with two stages to reduce the memory size of the target device. Both accumulators are reset every four clock cycles to receive the next four active rules of the next input. Note that μ_k and β_k are delivered from the inference engine in series during four consecutive clock cycles, instead of being produced in parallel in one clock cycle. This will reduce the used area of the FPGA device, at the expense of increasing time interval between input latching and output producing (Hassan et al., 2007). However, during the design, whenever a trade off between area and speed is found, it is directed to optimize (reduce) area at the expense of speed reduction, since the maximum time delay caused by controller is still much less than the minimum sampling time in many control systems. Even less than other controllers proposed in the literature (Poorani et al., 2005), (Tipsuwanpornet al., 2004), (Hassan et al., 2007), (Obaid et al., 2009), (Alvarez et al., 2006), (Lund et al., 2006), (Obaid et al., 1999). Here, the multiplication process was designed at the *behavioral* level (the method used in the tuning-gain block). The only difference is that another library called *"IEEE.std_logic_unsigned"* must be used instead of the library *"IEEE.std_logic_signed"*, to ensure that the produced multiplier after the synthesis process is an unsigned number multiplier (because the proposed fuzzy inference block can only handle positive numbers only) (Hassan et al., 2007), (Obaid et al., 2009). The group involves eight triangular membership functions for each input variable, eight singleton membership functions for output variable, and the rule table of 64 rules has been used in the proposed

PIDFC, as shown in Fig. 9 and Table II. The use of a singleton membership function is to increase the computation speed versus low complexity (Leonid , 1997). And also for the majority of applications, using singleton fuzzy sets is more sufficient (Ying, 2000).

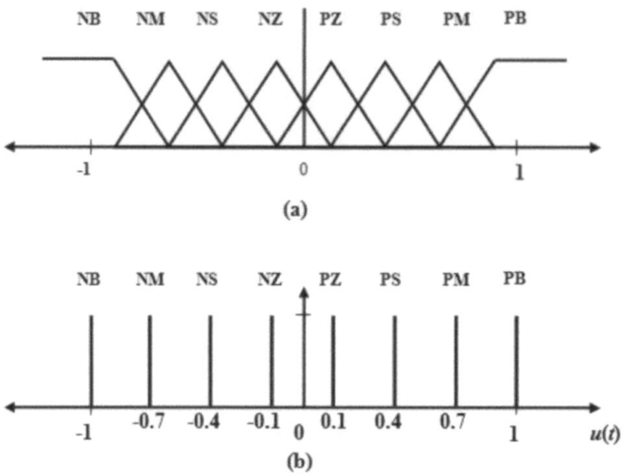

Fig. 9. (a) Inputs Membership Functions, (b) Output Membership Functions.

7. FPGA design considerations

The proposed device for the hardware implementation is the Virtex FPGAs family from Xilinx Company. Vertex FPGAs family is a useful device to the proposed design, it has internal RAM block. Virtex FPGAs consist of several large block memories. These complement the Look Up Table (LUT). This performance is very useful because the fuzzy system always needs large memory to store fuzzy sets information and rules table (Xilinx Company, 2009). The final design of the PIDFC has (3*q + 36) pins, four 8-bit input ports, two q-bits input ports and one q-bit output ports as well as 4 control signal pins, Table (III) lists the port names, sizes, and types.

Port name	Port size (bit)	Port type
Desired output	q	Input data
Plant output	q	Input data
Control action	q	Output data
K_p	8	Input data
K_d	8	Input data
K_i	8	Input data
K_o	8	Input data
sw1	1	Control signal
sw0	1	Control signal
Reset	1	Control signal
Clock	1	Control signal

Table 3. Port Names, Sizes, and Types Which Used In the Proposed Controller.

Note that the Reset signal does not change the contents of ROM or gain coefficients latches. However, the contents of ROM, as stated before can not be altered during the operation of the controller. The clock speed has a maximum frequency of 40 MH. This is necessary to cover a wide range of systems with a high sampling time.

8. Simulation environments

The Altera Quartus II 9.0 program was used to get the compilation and timing test results as well as the synthesized design. The ModelSim simulation program was also used for the purpose of simulation for all tests with the proposed design. The same design was designed in Matlab environments in order to make comparisons. The ModelSim stores the simulation data in text files, these files are used in Matlab and convert it to decimal vectors, which are used to plot the analog responses. Fig. 10 shows the Coding and Simulation environments used with the proposed design.

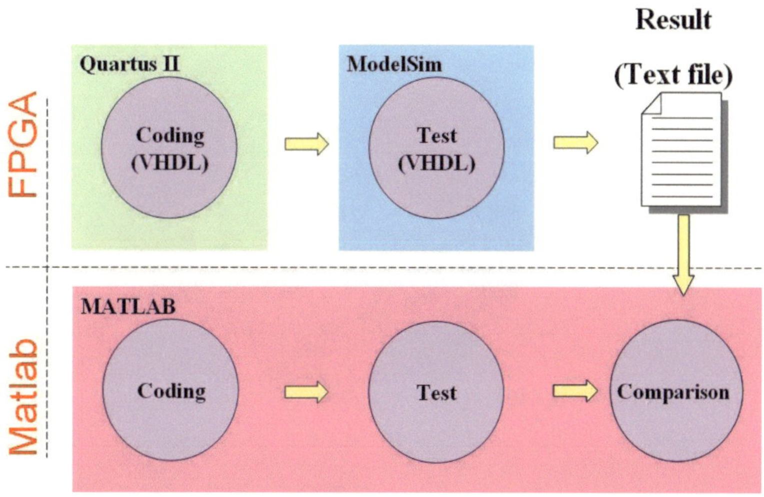

Fig. 10. Coding and Simulation Environments.

9. Timing analysis

The overall structure of the proposed PIDFC needs 16 clock cycles to complete one process. The input tuning-gain block needs one clock cycle. The fuzzification process needs one clock cycle. The inference engine needs four clock cycles to generate the four active rules consequent, $\beta_1, \beta_2, \beta_3, \beta_4$ and their corresponding applicability degrees $\mu_1, \mu_2, \mu_3, \mu_4$. Another four clock cycles are needed to calculate the terms $\sum_{k=1}^{4} \mu_k$ and $\sum_{k=1}^{4} \mu_k \times \beta_k$. Three of these four clocks are parallel to the four clocks of the inference engine, because the accumulation process starts after delivering the first rule consequent β_1 and its applicability degree μ_1. Subsequently, the division process starts and it takes eight clock cycles, which are split into two four-clock stages. The last clock cycle is needed to perform the output tuning-gain block.

10. Control surfaces test (comparison case study)

This test is performed to make sure that the fuzzy inference system used inside the FPGA-based controller (FBC) is working properly. This test involves generating the control surface using fuzzy sets and the rule shown in Fig. 9 and Table 2. This test has been used to make a comparison between both types of FBC with MSBC in order to evaluate the accuracy of the digital design implemented on FPGA with respect to the Matlab design. The control surfaces generated by MSBPD, 6FBC, MSBC and 8FBC are shown in Fig. 11 and Fig. 12. This surface reveals the effect of rounding and approximation processes (inside the FPGA design) on the result and also shows the accuracy of each version of the controller with respect to the Matlab-Based design. Generally, these statistics show that the surfaces generated by the fuzzy inference system of 8FBC are smoother than the surfaces generated by the fuzzy inference system of 6FBC with respect to MSBC, since the 8FBC has better accuracy and is adequate for this design.

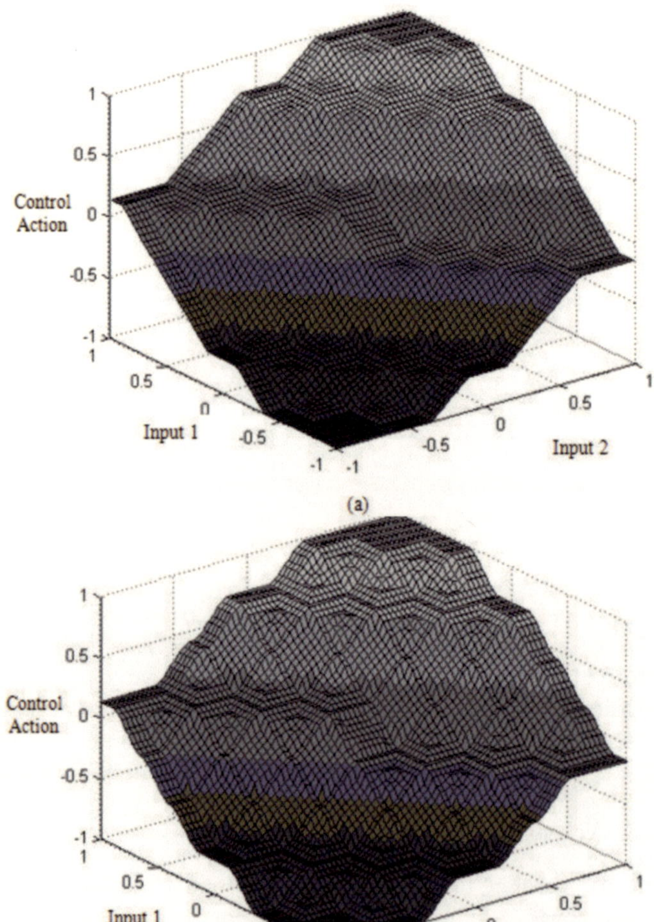

Fig. 11. (a) Control surface of MSBC (b) Control surface of 6FBC

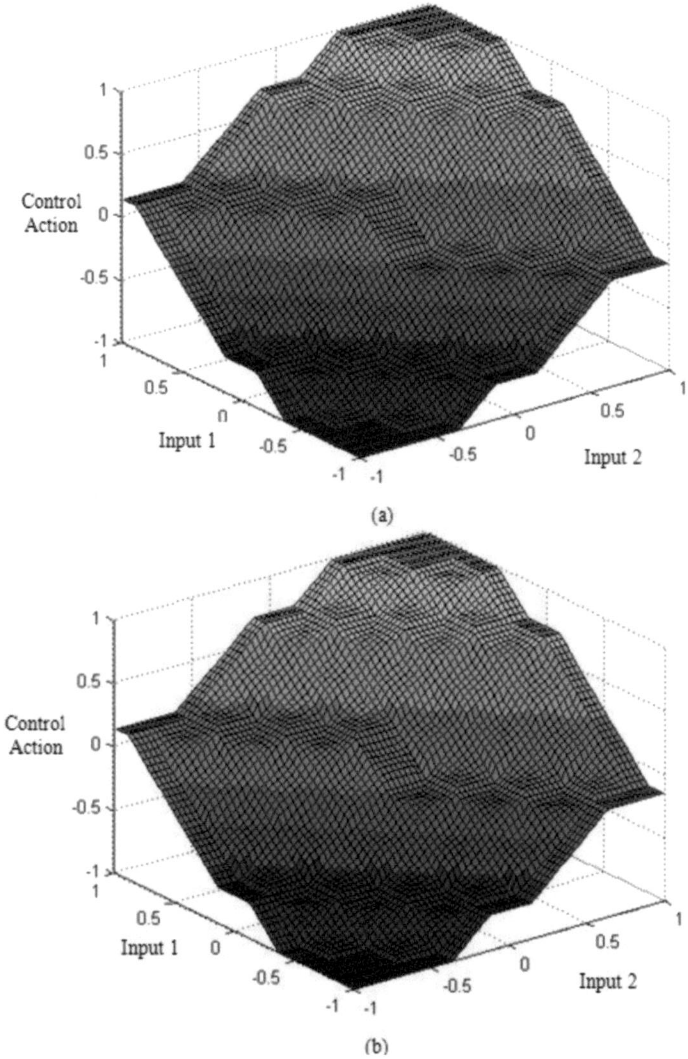

Fig. 12. (a) Control surface of MSBC (b) Control surface of 8FBC

11. The proposed controller with unity feedback control system

As mentioned before, the simplest and most usual way to implement a fuzzy controller is to realize it as a computer program on general purpose computers. Therefore, a comparison has been made between the simulation results of the two FPGA-based controller versions. The 6 bits **F**PGA-**B**ased **C**ontroller (6FBC) and the 8 bits **F**PGA-**B**ased **C**ontroller (8FBC), and the simulation results of the **S**oftware **B**ase **C**ontroller designed using **M**atlab (MSBC). These comparisons are necessary to show that how FPGA-based design is close to Matlab-based design. The first level of this comparison was made using ModelSim as the test bench simulation before generating the results in a Text File. Subsequently, as explained before, these files were taken to the Matlab environment to do the comparison. The controllers

(6FBC, 8FBC, and MSBC) have been used in unity feedback control systems, and subjected to 0.5 step input. Mathematical models of five different plants have been used for this test. These consist of four case studies with linear systems and one case study with a nonlinear system. Each one of these plants has been designed in MATLAB software (for simulation in MATLAB), and also in non-synthesizable VHDL code (for simulation in ModelSim). Since each controller could serve as PDFC, PIFC, or PIDFC, a test was made for each one of these types. PSO was used to obtain the optimal values of the controller parameters that represent the tuning gains. Where the information of the proposed PSO algorithm is listed as follows: Population size: 100, W= [0.4 to 0.9], C1, C2=2, Iteration reached with every case is=1000 iteration path, and the particle searching range depends on the trial and is different in every case. All X-axes represent the time.

11.1 First order plant (first case study)

Many industrial processes such as level process can be represented by a first order model (Hu et al., 1999). Equation (9) shows the mathematical plant model (in s-plane). A discrete transfer function of this model has been obtained using the ZOH method, and the selected sampling period (T) is 0.1. Equation (10) shows the discrete transfer functions, (in z-plane). The searching range of the particle for this case ranges from [Xmin Xmax], and by using trial to reach the operational range with the universe of discourse. The optimal values of Kp, Kd, Ki, and Ko used in this test were selected using PSO; and listed in Table 4.

$$CS_1(s) = \frac{1}{s+1} \tag{9}$$

$$CS_1(z) = \frac{0.09516}{z-0.9048}, \ \mathrm{T} = 0.1 \tag{10}$$

Range of Particle X	Controller type	Gain type	Value
$0.0001 \le X \le 5$	PIDFC	K_p	4.5111
		K_d	0.8751
		K_i	4.6875
		K_o	0.5625
$0.0001 \le X \le 3.5$	PIFC	K_p	0.6875
		K_i	2.4375
		K_o	1.0212
$0.0001 \le X \le 15$	PDFC	K_p	13.7501
		K_d	0.6251
		K_o	0.5011

Table 4. Optimal Gains Values Used With Cs1.

Fig. 13 shows the test bench simulation results using ModelSim. This test is generated using non-synthesizable VHDL code, and the controller gives action at 0.3 μs. The 6FBC has the same procedure except the real data which has different values. ModelSim stores the results as digital data in a text file; this file is manipulated in Matlab environments to change the data to decimal before using it as a comparison. The closed loop responses with 0.5 step input are shown in Fig. 14. In Fig. 14-a, it seems that the response has a large study state error. This is because the controller is PDFC, this controller affects the transient response (rise time, overshoot), but has no effect on the steady state error (at most). When the PIFC is applied on the first order system, the error disappears, and the system is first order, since there is no overshoot in this system (Fig. 14-b). When the PIDFC is applied for this system, as shown in Fig. 14-c, the response has a fast rising time with zero overshoot and error. However, although the 6FBC can sometimes give a response close to the MSBC response, at most, the 8FBC has smoother responses to MSBC than the 6FBC. The response performance of the proposed controllers is listed in Table 5.

Controller type	Error	Over shoot	Rising time	Settling time
PDFC	0.025	0.0	0.89	0.1
PIFC	0.0	0.0	0.3	0.4
PIDFC	0.0	0.0	0.15	0.198

Table 5. Responses Performance of the Proposed 8fbc with Cs1.

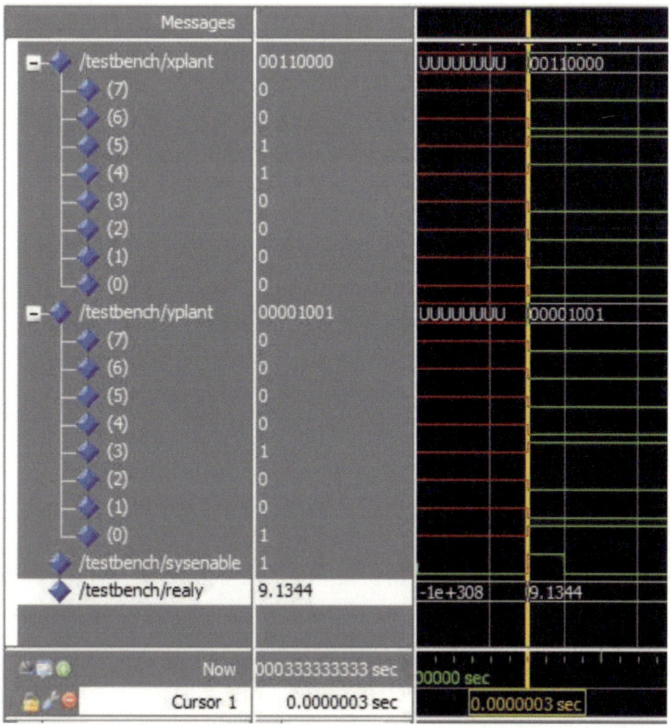

Fig. 13. Test Bench Results using ModelSim of the Proposed Controller (8FBC) with CS1 in unity Feedback Control system.

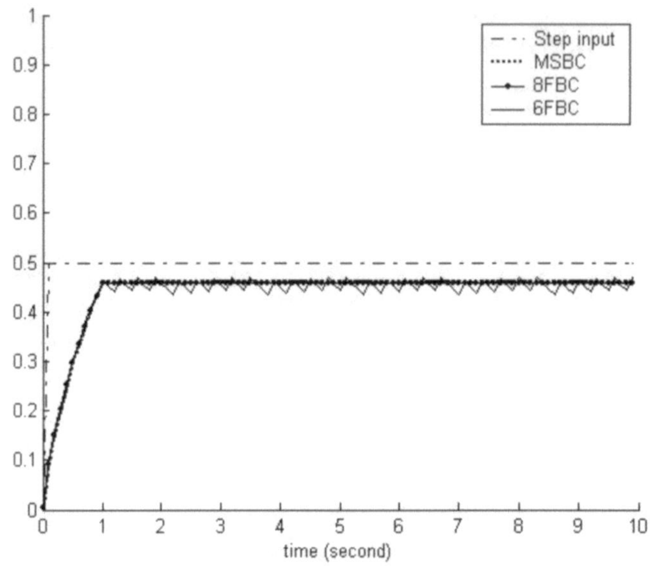
Step input
MSBC
8FBC
6FBC
0
0.1
0.2
0.3
0.4
0.5
0.6
0.7
0.8
0.9
1
0
1
2
3
4
5
6
7
8
9
10
time (second)

(a)

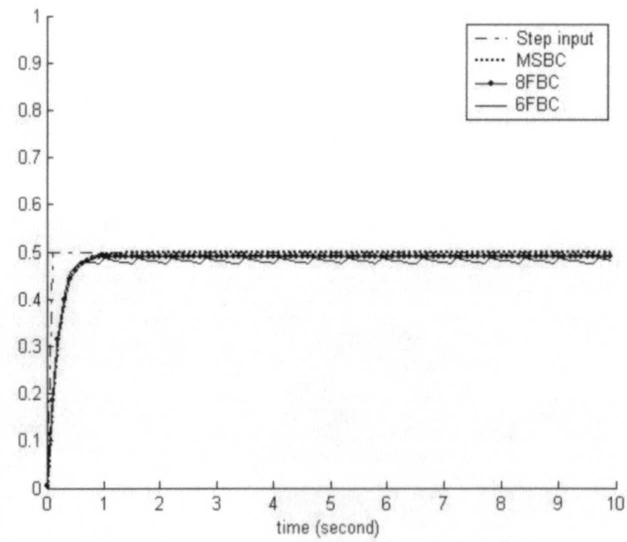
Step input
MSBC
8FBC
6FBC
0
0.1
0.2
0.3
0.4
0.5
0.6
0.7
0.8
0.9
1
0
1
2
3
4
5
6
7
8
9
10
time (second)

(b)

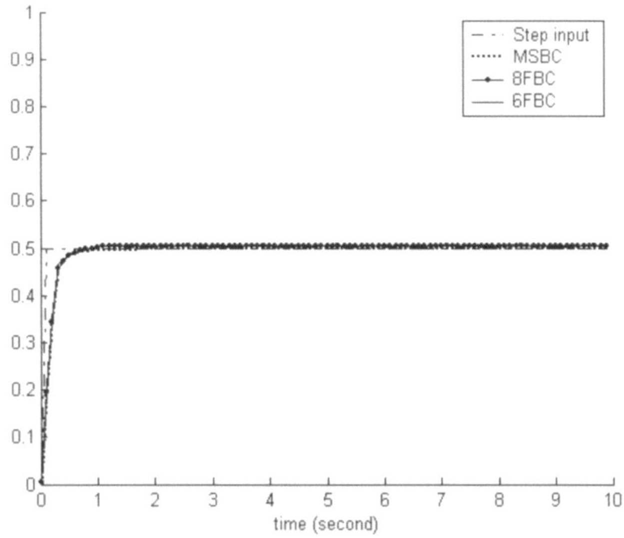

(c)

Fig. 14. First Order Linear Plant Controlled by (a) PDFC, (b) PIFC and (c) PIDFC.

11.2 Delayed first order plant (second case study)

The time delay occurs when a sensor or an actuator is used with a physical separation (Hu et al., 1999). Equation (11) shows the mathematical plant model (in *s-plane*). The discrete transfer functions of this model were obtained using the ZOH method, and the selected sampling period (T) is 0.1. Equation (12) shows the discrete transfer functions, (in *z-plane*). The searching range of the particle for this case is [Xmin Xmax], and by using trial to reach the operational range with the universe of discourse. The optimal values of K_p, K_d, K_i, *and* K_o used in this test were selected using PSO; and listed in Table 6.

Range of Particle X	Controller type	Gain type	Value
$0.0001 \le X \le 1.9$	PIDFC	K_p	1.4372
		K_d	1.687
		K_i	0.5625
		K_o	0.437
$0.0001 \le X \le 1.9$	PIFC	K_p	0.501
		K_i	1.5
		K_o	0.51
$0.0001 \le X \le 6$	PDFC	K_p	5
		K_d	0.125
		K_o	0.375

Table 6. Optimal Gains Values Used With CS2.

$$CS_2(z) = z^{-2} \times CS_1(z) \tag{11}$$

$$CS_2(z) = z^{-2} \times \left(\frac{0.09516}{z - 0.9048} \right) \quad , \mathrm{T} = 0.1 \tag{12}$$

Fig. 15 shows the test bench simulation results using ModelSim. This test is generated in the same procedure as explained before. The controller gives action at 0.3 μs (Fig. 15), the delay with the systems affects the beginning of the real data (the response). The closed loop responses with 0.5 step input are shown in Fig. 16. In Fig. 16-a, again the response has a large study state error with the PDFC. When the PIFC is applied on the first order system (see Fig. 16-b), the error disappears with 8FBC. The 6FBC has a large steady state error, as the responses of the systems that use 8FBC are closer to the MSBC responses. When the PIDFC is applied for this system, as shown in Fig. 16-c, the response is close to the responses when using the PIFC. In all this, 8FBC has smoother responses to the MSBC than the 6FBC. The responses performance of the 8FBC are listed in Table 7.

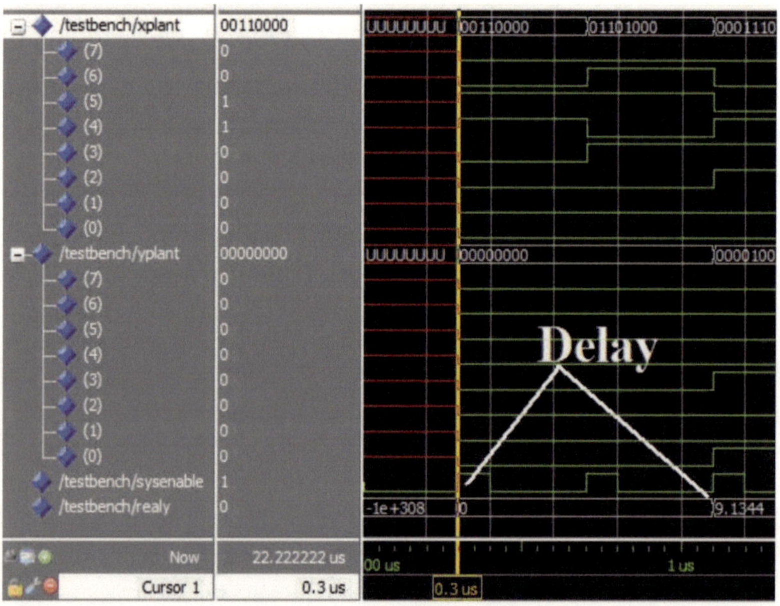

Fig. 15. Timing Diagram using ModelSim of the Controller (8FBC) with CS2 in unity Feedback Control system.

Controller type	Error	Over shoot	Rising time	Settling time
PDFC	0.11	0.01	1.12	1.2
PIFC	0.01	0.0	0.8	0.9
PIDFC	0.02	0.0	0.48	0.49

Table 7. Responses Performance of the Proposed 8fbc with CS2.

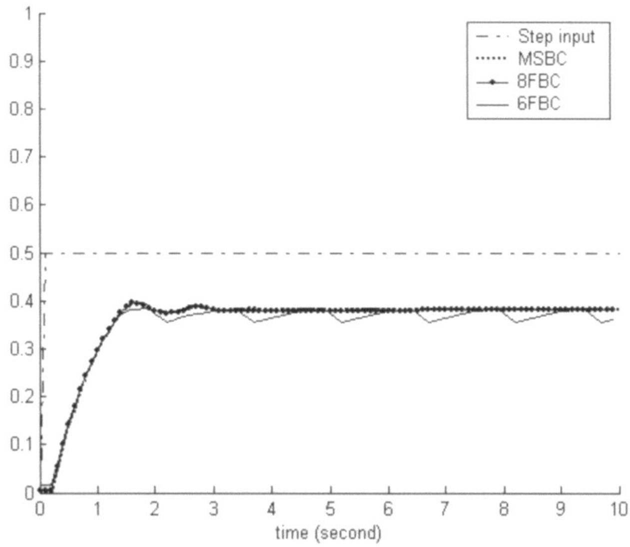
Step input
MSBC
8FBC
6FBC
time (second)

(a)

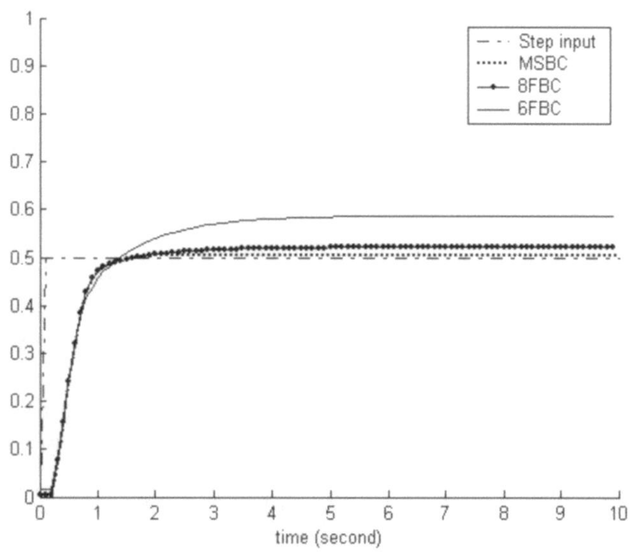
Step input
MSBC
8FBC
6FBC
time (second)

(b)

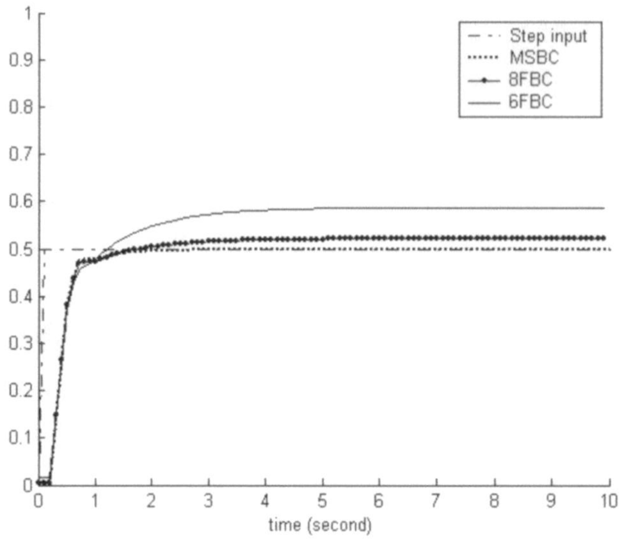

(c)

Fig. 16. Delayed first order linear plant controlled by(a) PDFC, (b) PIFC and (c) PIDFC.

11.3 Second order plant (third case study)

The position control of an AC motor process or temperature control can be represented by a second order model (Hu et al., 1999). Equation (13) shows the mathematical plant model (in *s-plane*). Discrete transfer functions of this model were obtained using the ZOH method, and the selected sampling period (T) is 0.2. Equation (14) shows the discrete transfer functions, (in *z-plane*). The searching range of the particle for this case is ranging as [Xmin Xmax], and by using trial to reach the operational range with the universe of discourse. The optimal values of K_p, K_d, K_i, *and* K_o used in this test were selected using PSO; and listed in Table 8.

$$CS_3(s)=\frac{1}{s^2+4s+3} \tag{13}$$

$$CS_3(z)=\frac{0.01544\ z+0.01183}{z^2-1.368\ z+0.4493}\ ,\ T=0.2 \tag{14}$$

Fig. 17 shows the test bench simulation results using ModelSim for 8FBC; this test is generated using the same procedure as explained. The controller gives action at 0.3 μs (Fig. 17). This means the same action with CS1 and CS2, which represent the linear models. The closed loop responses with 0.5 step input are shown in Fig. 17. CS3 is a second order plant, and has a steady state error with non-controlled response. In Fig. 18-a, when PDFC is applied the overshoot is limited by the action of this controller, but the response still has a steady state error. When the PIFC is applied to this system (see Fig. 18-b), the error is disappears with 8FBC, and the system still has overshoot. The 6FBC has a rough and non-smooth response as can be seen in the control action figures where sharp spikes appear along the steady state part, while the responses of the systems that use 8FBC are closer to the MSBC responses. When the PIDFC is applied for this system, as shown in Fig. 18-c, the

8FBC response is close to the responses using MSBC, with zero error and little overshoot. The Responses Performance of the proposed 8FBC with CS3 is listed in Table 9.

Range of Particle X	Controller type	Gain type	Value
$0.0001 \le X \le 8.5$	PIDFC	K_p	5.0191
		K_d	7.101
		K_i	1.6875
		K_o	0.937
$0.0001 \le X \le 2$	PIFC	K_p	1.02
		K_i	1.812
		K_o	1.75
$0.0001 \le X \le 15$	PDFC	K_p	14.625
		K_d	6.021
		K_o	1.062

Table 8. Optimal Gains Values Used With CS3.

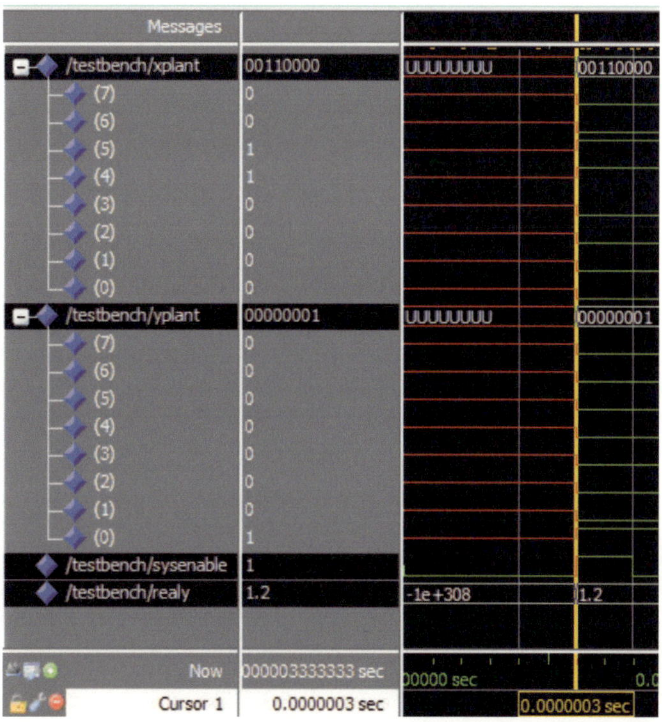

Fig. 17. Timing Diagram using ModelSim of the Controller (8FBC) with CS3 in unity Feedback Control system.

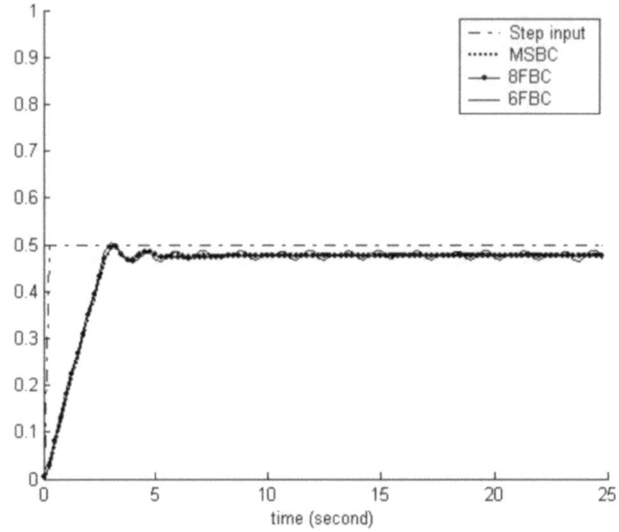
Step input
MSBC
8FBC
6FBC
0
0.1
0.2
0.3
0.4
0.5
0.6
0.7
0.8
0.9
1
0
5
10
15
20
25
time (second)

(a)

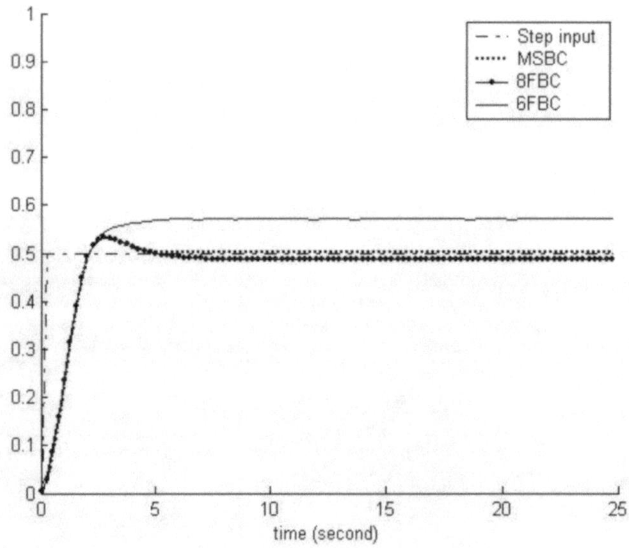
Step input
MSBC
8FBC
6FBC
0
0.1
0.2
0.3
0.4
0.5
0.6
0.7
0.8
0.9
1
0
5
10
15
20
25
time (second)

(b)

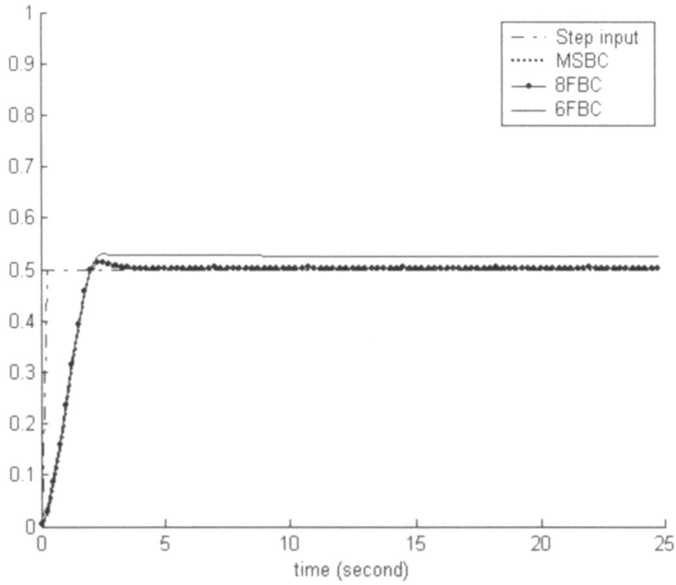

(c)

Fig. 18. Second order linear plant controlled by(a) PDFC, (b) PIFC and (c) PIDFC.

Controller type	Error	Over shoot	Rising time	Settling time
PDFC	0.02	0.02	2.1	2.3
PIFC	0.005	0.03	1.89	2
PIDFC	0.0	0.005	1.6	1.8

Table 9. Responses Performance of the Proposed 8fbc with CS3.

11.4 Delayed second order plant (fourth case study)

The time delay occurs when a sensor or an actuator are used with a physical separation (Hu et al., 1999). Equation (15) shows the mathematical plant model (in *s-plane*). Discrete transfer function of this model was obtained using the ZOH method, and the selected sampling period (T) is 0.2. Equation (16) shows the discrete transfer functions, (in *z-plane*). The searching range of the particle for this case is ranging as [Xmin Xmax], and by using trial to reach the operational range with the universe of discourse. The optimal values of K_p, K_d, K_i, *and* K_o used in this test were selected using PSO; and listed in Table 10.

$$CS_4(z) = z^{-2} \times CS_3 \tag{15}$$

$$CS_4(z) = z^{-2} \times \left(\frac{0.01544\ \ z+ 0.01183}{z^2 - 1.368\ \ z+ 0.4493} \right) ;\ \mathrm{T} = 0.2 \tag{16}$$

Range of Particle X	Controller type	Gain type	Value
$0.0001 \leq X \leq 8.5$	PIDFC	K_p	2.11
		K_d	1.687
		K_i	0.5012
		K_o	0.375
$0.0001 \leq X \leq 2$	PIFC	K_p	0.253
		K_i	1.185
		K_o	1.251
$0.0001 \leq X \leq 15$	PDFC	K_p	7.18
		K_d	8.754
		K_o	0.503

Table 10. Optimal Gains Values Used with CS4.

Fig. 19 shows the test bench simulation results using ModelSim for 8FBC. This test is generated using the same procedure as explained before. The delay with the system only affects the value of the real data (response). The controller gives action at 0.3 μs. The closed loop responses with 0.5 step input are shown in Fig. 20. CS4 is the same model as CS3 but with delay. In Fig. 20-a, when the PDFC is applied, the overshoot is limited by the action of this controller, but the response has a large steady state error. In this case the 8FBC is very close to the MSBC while the 6FBC has a non-smooth response. When the PIFC is applied to

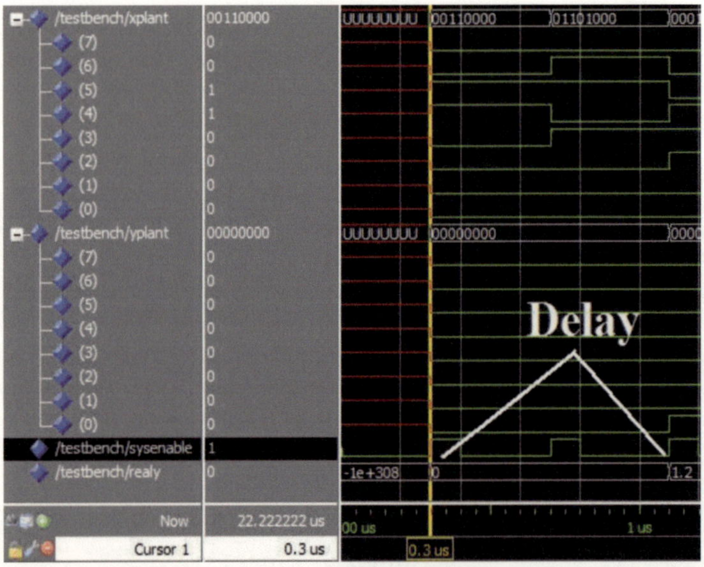

Fig. 19. Timing Diagram using ModelSim of the Controller (8FBC) with CS4 in unity Feedback Control system.

this system (see Fig. 20-b), the error disappears with the 8FBC with little overshoot. The 6FBC has a large steady state error while the responses of the systems that use 8FBC arc closer to the MSBC responses. When the PIDFC is applied for this system, as shown in Fig. 20-c, the 8FBC response has better overshoot to the responses using MSBC, and is very close to the MSBC in the steady state response. The 6FBC has a long rising time with steady state error. The Responses Performance of the proposed 8FBC with CS4 is listed in Table 11.

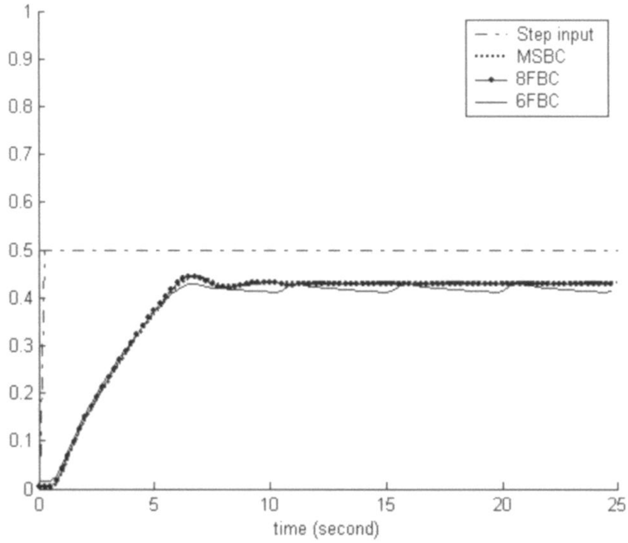

(a)

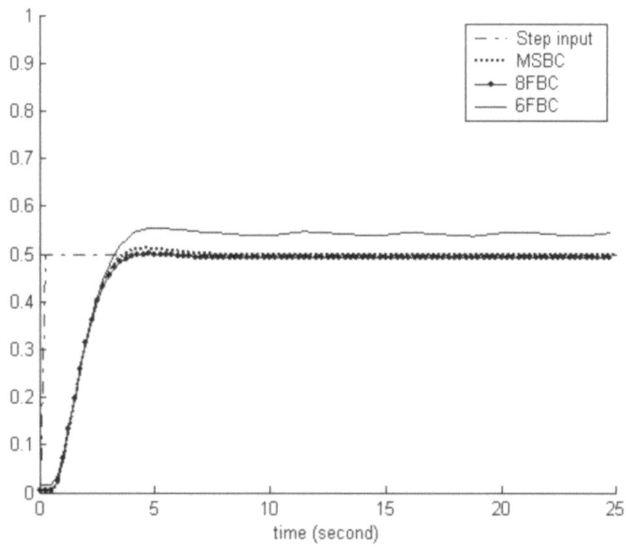

(b)

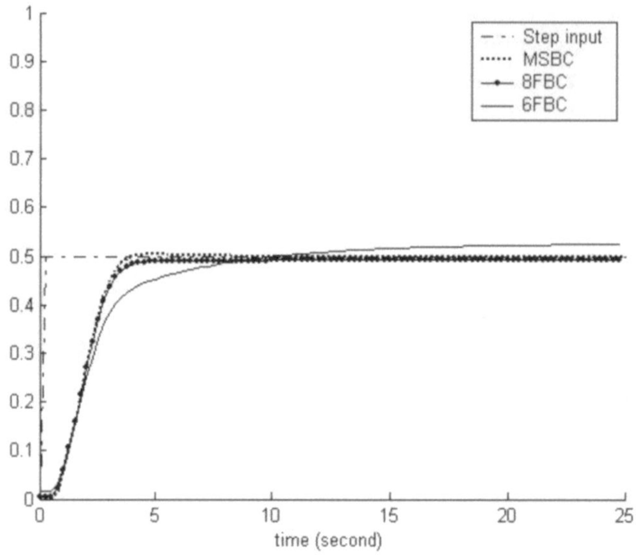

(c)

Fig. 20. Delayed second order linear plant controlled by (a) PDFC, (b) PIFC and (c) PIDFC.

Controller type	Error	Over shoot	Rising time	Settling time
PDFC	0.07	0.02	4.9	5.3
PIFC	0.0	0.0	2.3	2.4
PIDFC	0.0	0.0	2.4	2.5

Table 11. Responses Performance of the Proposed 8FBC with CS4.

11.5 Non-linear plant model (fifth case study)

A mathematical model of nonlinear plant (inverted pendulum) has been used to test the PIDFC with unity feedback control system; this model is characterized by Equation (17) and Equation (18) (Passino and Yurkovich, 1998).

$$CS_5 = \ddot{y} = \frac{9.8\sin(y) + \cos(y)\left[\dfrac{-\bar{u} - 0.25\dot{y}^2\sin(y)}{1.5}\right]}{0.5\left[\dfrac{4}{3} - \dfrac{1}{3}\cos^2(y)\right]} \tag{17}$$

$$\dot{\bar{u}} = -100\bar{u} + 100u \tag{18}$$

The first order filter on u to produce $\bar{u}$ represents an actuator. Assuming the initial conditions $y(0) = 0.1$ radians (= 5.73 deg.), $\dot{y}(0) = 0$, and the initial condition for the actuator state is zero. For simulation of the fourth-order, the Runge-Kutta method was used with an integration step size of 0.01 (Passino and Yurkovich, 1998), (Obaid et al., 1999). Again, this plant has been designed using MATLAB software (for simulation in MATLAB), and in

VHDL code (for simulation in ModelSim). A special package was designed in VHDL code to represent the trigonometric functions and fourth-order Runge-Kutta method, which are not available in Quartus II (or in ISE) standard libraries (Obaid et al., 1999). The searching range of the particle for this case is [Xmin Xmax], and by using trial to reach the proposed algorithm, the values of K_p, K_d, K_i, *and* K_o used in this test were selected using PSO. These values are listed in Table XII.

Range of Particle X	Controller type	Gain type	Value
$0.0001 \le X \le 11.5$	PIDFC	K_p	1.1012
		K_d	10.1103
		K_i	1.5013
		K_o	5.0032

Table 12. Optimal Gains Values Used With CS5.

Fig. 21 shows the test bench simulation results using ModelSim for 8FBC and the controller gives an output at 0.7 μs after the input latching (Fig. 21). The 6FBC has the same procedure in ModelSim and produces an output at 0.62 μs. The Responses Performance of the proposed controller with CS5 is listed in Table 13. Where the bound of the settling time of the pendulum to reach its initial position with the force applied to the cart is -0.02 and +0.02 with both versions. The first time of the pendulum reach s the initial position is listed as the rising time. When using a nonlinear system for testing, both versions (6FBC and 8FBC) provide generally good responses although there is some oscillation. One must not be deceived by the steady state error that appears in Fig. 22, as it represents less than 1% of the output range in the case of 6FBC and less than 0.5% of the output range, in the case of 8FBC. The absolute mean difference between the nonlinear plant response, using MSBC, and the

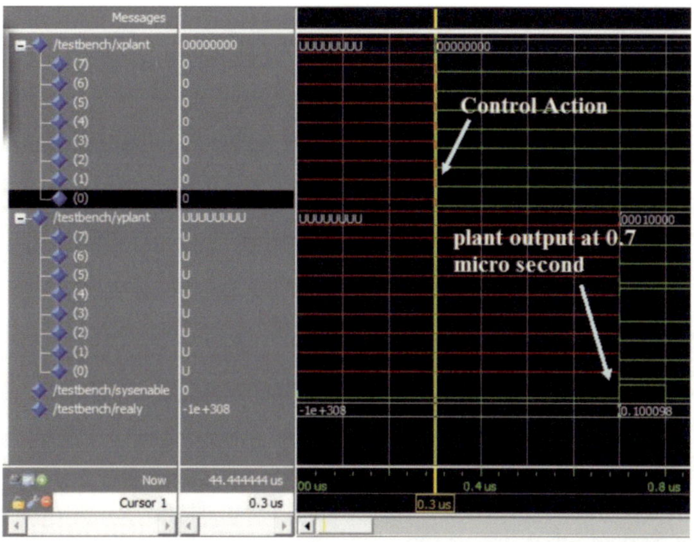

Fig. 21. Timing Diagram using ModelSim of the Controller (8FBC) with CS5 in unity Feedback Control system.

nonlinear plant response, using 6FBC is less than 0.017. The absolute mean difference between the nonlinear plant response, using MSBC, and the nonlinear plant response, using 8FBC is less than 0.006 as shown in Fig. 22. The experimental result is carried out by using the nonlinear inverted pendulum (the last case study CS5). The experimental data recorded to the inverted pendulum has been used in this test in unity feedback control system. This data has been recorded by Sultan (Sultan, 2006) to analyze, design & develop a control loop for the given inverted pendulum (with servomechanism). The pendulum reaches the initial position zero at 0.058 second with overshoot equal to 0.025 and undershoot equal to 0.02. Fig. 23 shows the experimental data simulation of the inverted pendulum with the PIDFC in 8-bit version. The controller (8FBC) provides a good control performance with respect to the simulation results of the same case as shown in Table 13.

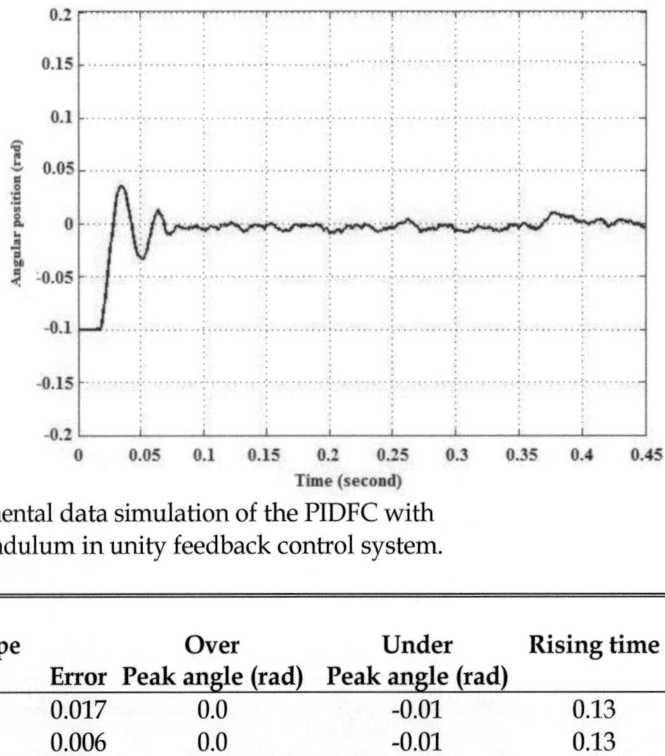

Fig. 23. Experimental data simulation of the PIDFC with the inverted pendulum in unity feedback control system.

Controller type	Error	Over Peak angle (rad)	Under Peak angle (rad)	Rising time	Settling time
6FBC	0.017	0.0	-0.01	0.13	0.1
8FBC	0.006	0.0	-0.01	0.13	0.1
6MSBC	0.0	0.018	-0.041	0.13	0.1
8MSBC	0.0	0.018	-0.041	0.13	0.1
Experimental case	0.0	0.025	0.024	0.029	0.058

Table 13. Responses Performance of the Proposed 8fbc with CS5.

12. Results comparison and discussion

The proposed design has been coded in Matlab environments as explained before. The aim of this test is to find to what extent the 6FBC and 8FBC responses are close to the MSBC responses with respect to the accuracy. In contrast to the 6FBC, the responses of the systems that use 8FBC are smooth (as MSBC responses). When the 6FBC or 8FBC is used as PIFC or

PIDFC, the system responses will settle at a value close to the response settling value of systems that use MSBC. The reason being the rounding error in the PI component, the proposed PIDFC consists of a PDFC and PIFC, the PIFC is a PDFC with a summation block at its output. This error could be positive or negative. Sometimes, during the summation process, the rounding error cancels itself. Commonly, in CS1 and CS2, it is clear that the responses have a steady state error with PDFC, because these systems do not have an overshoot, only a steady state error (no need to use PDFC), and this test is used to evaluate the multi structure in the proposed PIDFC. The absolute mean of differences between the MSBC and 6FBC was less than 0.07 with the linear systems and less than 0.017 with the nonlinear system, while the absolute mean of differences between MSBC and 8FBC was less than 0.017 with the linear systems and less than 0.006 with the nonlinear system. The proposed controller has good responses performance with respect to the classical controller proposed in the literature, and also better responses as compared it with other type of fuzzy PID controller.

CS1, CS2 and CS3 have been used in the work proposed in (Hu et al., 1999). In this work, Genetic algorithm (GA) based optimal fuzzy PID controller was used with new methodology (Matlab-based). Table 14 lists the comparison of the responses performance of this work with respect to the proposed PIDFC (8FBC) with CS1, CS2 and CS3. This comparison consists of rising time (Tr), settling time (Ts) and overshoot (OV). The proposed PSO-PIDFC with the linear cases CS1 and

CS2 have no overshoot and a short rising and settling time with respect to other types of controller designed in the literature with the same models. For the CS3, there is a 0.005 overshoot and short rising and settling time with respect to other types of controller designed in the literature with the same model. The proposed PSO-PIDFC with the nonlinear cases (CS5) have zero overshoot and 0.13, 0.1 rising and settling time respectively, while other types of controller with the same nonlinear model have an overshoot and longer rising and settling time. In CS5, a mathematical model of nonlinear plant (inverted pendulum) was used to test the controller with a unity feedback control system. This case has been used in (Jain et al., 2009), (Masmoudi et al., 1999) and (Jain et al., 1999) (Matlab-based) with different types of controllers. In (Jain et al., 2009), Bacterial Foraging (BF) algorithm was used for tuning the parameters of the PID controller for optimal performance, while (Jain et al., 1999) used a comparison between Evolutionary Algorithms namely Gas (Genetic Algorithms), and Swarm Intelligence i.e. PSO and BG. In (Jain et al., 1999) as there was no need to know the value of rising time as they used a reference input equal to zero. It is not considered by this author either. Therefore, a comparison is made with the proposed 8FB (PIDFC) with those presented in (Jain et al., 2009), (Masmoudi et al., 1999) and (Jain et al., 1999). This comparison is listed in Table 15. In the case of (Jain et al., 1999), PSO had the best responses with respect to the other methods proposed by this author, hence, we will compare with PSO and ISE only. Other comparison has been made to the proposed design with respect to FPGA chip resources. This comparison involves the utilization of the chip resources in the proposed FPGA-based PIDFC with respect to the other FPGA-based controllers proposed in the literature. It also involves a comparison with respect to the time required per one action with the maximum frequency. This comparison was made after compiling the design using the ISE program provided by Xilinx Company, because this tool provides a clear Report for the chip resources, even it was used by the authors in the literature. This comparison is listed in Table 16.

Case	Performance	Proposed FPGA-based PIDFC with PSO	GA - Fuzzy PID In (Hu et al., 1999)	GA -Optimal PID In (Hu et al., 1999)
CS1	Tr (s)	0.19	0.16	0.2
	Ts(s)	0.23	0.2	0.36
	OV	0.0	0.0	0.0039
CS2	Tr (s)	0.48	0.16	0.38
	Ts(s)	0.49	0.46	0.74
	OV	0.0	0.0051	0.0162
CS3	Tr (s)	1.6	0.74	0.88
	Ts(s)	1.8	2.34	1.34
	OV	0.005	0.0622	0.0107

Table 14. Performance Comparison of the PIDFC with the Work Proposed by Hu et al. In (Hu et al., 1999)

Performance	The proposed Controller In Experimental Case with CS5	The Proposed FPGA-based PIDFC With PSO	Optimal PID In (Jain et al., 2009) With BG	Fuzzy logic controller in (Masmoudi et al., 1999)	Optimal PD-PI In (Jain et al., 1999) With PSO
Ts (s)	0.058	0.1	0.4	0.21	2.4
Tr(s)	0.029	0.13	0.2	0.22	---
Peak angle (rad)	0.025	0.0	0.178	0.75	0.00127

Table 15. Performance Comparison of the PIDFC (8FBC) With Those Proposed In (Jain et al., 2009), (Masmoudi et al., 1999) and (Jain et al., 1999) By Using CS5.

References	Number of CLBs	Number of IOBs	Frequency	Time per action
PIDFC	494	68	40 MHz	0.3 μs
(Poorani et al., 2005)	757	39	8 KHz	41.1 ms
(Tipsuwanpornet al., 2004)	---	---	40.55 MHz	2.1 μs
(Hassan et al., 2007)	1394	61	40.245 MHz	0.421 μs
(Alvarez et al., 2006)	3492	51	100 MHz	1.4 μs
(Lund et al., 2006)	63	---	20 MHz	1 μs

Table 16. FPGA Chip Resources Comparison between the PIDFC and Other Type of Controllers Proposed In the Literature.

13. Conclusion

From the design and simulation results of the PIDFC, it can be concluded that: Higher execution speed versus small chip size is achieved by designing PIDFC with a simplified fuzzy algorithm as a parallel structure of PDFC and PIFC and also by designing PIFC by accumulating the output of the PDFC. These methods significantly reduce the number of rules needed. It also enables the controller to work as a PIFC, PDFC or PIDFC depending on two external signals to provide high-flexibilities with different applications. The controller needs 16 clock cycles to generate an output with a maximum clock frequency of 40 MHz. Therefore, the proposed controller will be able to control a wide range of systems with a high sampling rate. Higher flexibility versus good control performance is achieved by designing tuning-gains block at each input/output stage. This block involves a tuning by scaling the universe of discourse for the input/output variables (renormalization). This block makes the controller chip accept the PSO-based optimal scaling gains, and also enables the digital controller chip able to accept unsigned inputs. The PSO algorithm has better simulation results than other intelligent optimization methods proposed in the literature such as genetic algorithm. This block is very important and is useful for providing a best tuning case for the universe of discourse.
In addition, it makes the design applicable for different systems without requiring reprogramming the controller chip. Higher execution speed and small chip size versus acceptable accuracy is achieved by designing each one of the scaling gains as two parts: integer and fraction, and perform all mathematical operations using integer number algorithms, which are smaller in the implementation size than floating number algorithms, and even faster. Sufficient design accuracy can be achieved with 8FBC in Particular. 8FBC is superior to 6FBC since it presents higher accuracy versus moderately low target device utilizations. 8FBC was able to produce a control action in 0.3 μs after input latching (the computational time of the controller is 0.3 μs). The 8FBC produced responses approximately similar or better than the MSBC compared with the 6FBC or with the results in the literature. The absolute mean of differences between the responses of the 6FBC and the MSBC, was less than 4% of the output range, for the linear plants, and less than 0.5% of the output range for the nonlinear plant, while the absolute mean of differences between the responses of 8FBC and the MSBC, was less than 1% of the output range, for the linear plants, and less than 0.3% of the output range for the nonlinear plant. Both versions showed some error at the steady state part of the response when serving as PIFLC or PIDFLC because of the accumulation of the rounding error at the summation block. This error depends on the rounding error; therefore it becomes larger when using the 6FBC than when using 8FBC. As a result, the proposed controller could be used to control many industrial applications with high sampling time. Its small size versus high speed makes it a good choice for other applications, such as robots. It is hoped that some future work could settle down the feasibility of the suggestions: Increasing the number of the first part of the fuzzy set in the MBMSF inside the fuzzifier block more than (3-bits) could make the design accept more than 8 fuzzy sets at each input. Increasing the number of bits of the entire design may be useful in decreasing the error in the PIFC component (in some cases) of the controller at the expense of increasing design area and processing time.

14. Acknowledgment

The authors would firstly like to thank God, and all friends who gave us any help related to this work. Other Appreciation goes to the Assist chancellor amend to Diyala University-Iraq

(Prof. Dr Amer Mohammed Ibrahim) and the Dean of Collage of Engineering-Diyala University- Iraq (Assist. Prof. Dr. Adel Khaleel Mahmoud). Further appreciation goes to My Colleagues Mr. Waleed Fawwaz and Mrs. Areej Sadiq for their wide help and support. Finally, a heartfelt thank to our families and home countries.

15. References

Poorani, S., Priya, T.V.S.U., Kumar, K.U., and Renganarayanan, S., (2005) "*FPGA Based Fuzzy Logic Controller for Electric Vehicle*," Journal of the Institution of Engineers, Singapore, Vol. 45 Issue 5.

Jain, T., Patel, V., Nigam and M.J., "*Implementation of PID Controlled SIMO Process on FPGA Using Bacterial Foraging for Optimal Performance*," International Journal of Computer and Electrical Engineering, Vol. 1, No. 2, p: 1793-8198, June.

Tipsuwanporn, V., Intajag, S. and Krongratana, V., (2004) "*Fuzzy Logic PID Controller Based on FPGA for Process Control*," Proceedings of IEEE International Symposium on Industrial Electronics, Vol. 2, May 4-7, page(s):1495-1500.

Karasakal, O., Yesl, E., Guzelkaya, M. and Eksin, I., (2005) "*Implementation of a New Self-Tuning Fuzzy PID Controller on PLC*," Turk J Elec Engin, Vol.13, NO.2.

Hassan, M.Y., and Sharif, W.F., (2007) "*Design of FPGA based PID-like Fuzzy Controller for Industrial Applications*," IAENG International Journal of Computer Science, Vol. 34 Issue 2, November.

Kim, D., (2000) "*An Implementation of Fuzzy Logic Controller on the Reconfigurable FPGA System*," IEEE Transactions on Industrial Electronics, Vol. 47, No. 3, p: 703- 715, June.

Solano, S.S., Barriga, A., Jimenez, C.J and Huertas, J.L., (1997) "*Design and Application of Digital Fuzzy Controllers*", Proceedings of Sixth IEEE International Conference on Fuzzy Systems (FUZZ-IEEE'97), Vol. 2, July 1-5, page(s):869-874.

Islam, S., Amin, N., Bhuyan, M.S, Zaman, M., Madon, B. and Othman, M., (2007) "*FPGA Realization of Fuzzy Temperature Controller for Industrial Application*", WSEAS Transactions on Systems and Control, Volume 2, Issue 10, p: 484- 490, October.

Mann, G.K.I., Hu, B.G. and Gosine, R.G., (1999) "*Analysis of Direct Action Fuzzy PID Controller Structures*", IEEE Transactions on Systems, Man, and Cybernetics—Part B: Cybernetics, Vol. 29, No. 3, p: 371 - 388, June.

Seng, T.L., Khalid, M. and Yusuf, R., (1999) "*Tuning of a Neuro-Fuzzy Controller by Genetic Algorithm*", IEEE Transactions on Systems, Man, and Cybernetics—Part B: Cybernetics, Vol. 29, No. 2, P: 226- 236, April.

Leonid, R., Ghanayem, O. and Bourmistrov, A., (2000) "*PID plus fuzzy controller structures as a design base for industrial applications*", Engineering Applications of Artificial Intelligence, Elsevier Science Ltd, 13, p: 419-430.

Leonid, R. (1997). *Fuzzy Controllers*, first edition, Newnes.

Gabrielli, Gandolfi, E. and Masetti, M., (2009) "*Design of a Very High Speed Fuzzy Processor by VHDL Language*", Physics Department University of Bologna, URL:http://www.bo.infn.it/dacel/papers/96_03_parigi_EDTC.pdf. Accessed on 4 October 2009.

Jantzen, J., (1998) "*Design of Fuzzy Controllers*". Technical University of Denmark, and Department of Automation, reports no 98-H 869 (soc), 19 Aug.

Ibrahim, A.M., (2004) "*Fuzzy Logic for Embedded Systems Applications*", USA, Elsevier Science.

Obaid, Z.A., Sulaiman, N. and Hamidon, M.N., (2009) *"Developed Method of FPGA-based Fuzzy Logic Controller Design with the Aid of Conventional PID Algorithm"*, Australian Journal of Basics and Applied Science, Vol. 3(3), P: 2724-2740.

Ying, H., (2000) *"Fuzzy Control and Modeling, Analytical Foundations and Applications"*, Institute of Electrical and Electronic Engineers Inc., USA.

Wang, J., Zhang, Y. and Wang, W., (2006) *"Optimal design of PI/PD controller for non-minimum phase system"*, Transactions of the Institute of Measurement and Control, Vol. 28 No. 1, p: 27-35.

Allaoua, B., Gasbaoui, B. and Mebarki, B., (2009) "Setting Up PID DC Motor Speed Control Alteration Parameters Using Particle Swarm Optimization Strategy", Leonardo Electronic Journal of Practices and Technologies, Issue 14, p: 19-32, January-June 2009.

Barriga, A., Sanchez-Solano, S., Brox, P., Cabrera, A., and Baturone, I., (2006) *"Modeling and implementation of Fuzzy Systems Based on VHDL"*, International Journal of Approximate Reasoning, Elsevier Inc, Vol. 41, p: 164–178.

Huang, S.H. and Lai, J.Y., (2005) *"A High Speed Fuzzy Inference Processor with Dynamic Analysis and Scheduling Capabilities"*, IEICE Transaction Information & System., Vol. E88-D, No.10 October.

Alvarez, J., Lago, A. and Nogueiras, A., (2006) *"FPGA Implementation of a Fuzzy Controller for Automobile DC-DC Converters"* Proceeding of IEEE International Conference on Field Programmable Technology, December, page(s): 237-240.

Lund, T., Aguirre, M. and Torralba, A., (2004) "Fuzzy Logic Control via an FPGA: A Design using techniques from Digital Signal Processing", Proceedings of IEEE International Symposium on Industrial Electronics, vol. 1, May 4-7, page(s): 555- 559.

Sultan, KH., *"Inverted Pendulum, Analysis, Design and Implementation"* IIEE Visionaries Document Version 1.0, Institute of Industrial Electronics Engineering, Karachi, Pakistan. [Available online at] Matlab Central File Exchange http://www.Mathworks.com.

Xilinx Company. 2009. Virtex 2.5 V Field Programmable Gate Arrays, Data Sheet DS003, URL www.xilinx.com. Accessed on 2009.

Hu, B.G., Mann, G.K. and Gosine, R.G, (1999) *"New Methodology for Analytical and Optimal Design of Fuzzy PID Controllers"*, IEEE Transactions on Fuzzy Systems, Vol. 7, No. 5, pp. 521-539, October.

Passino, K.M., and Yurkovich, S., (1998) *"Fuzzy Control*, Addison-Weslwey Longman Inc., USA.

Masmoudi, N., Hachicha, M. and Kamoun, L., (1999) *"Hardware Design of Programmable Fuzzy Controller on FPGA"*, Proceedings of IEEE International Fuzzy Systems Conference Proceedings, August 22-25, page(s):1675-1679.

Jain, T. and Nigam, M.J., (2008) *"Optimization of PD-PI Controller Using Swarm Intelligence"*, Journal of Theoretical and Applied Information Technology, Page: 1013-1018, 2008.

Obaid, Z.A., Sulaiman, N., Marhaban, M.H. and Hamidon, M.N. (2010), "Implementation of Multistructure PID-like Fuzzy Logic Controller using Field Programmable Gate Array" IEICE Electronics Express, Vol. 7 No. 3, P: 132-137, 10 February.

Li J. and Hu B.S., (1996) "The Architecture of Fuzzy PID Gain Conditioner and its FPGA Prototype Implementation", Proceedings of the Second International Conference on ASIC, October 21-24, page(s):61-65.

Khatr, A. P., and Rattan, K.S., (2006) "Implementation of a Multi-Layered Fuzzy Controller on an FPGA", Annual meeting of the North America, by IEEE Fuzzy Information Processing Society, Page(s): 420- 425.

J.L. Gonzalez-vazquez, O. Castillo and L.T. Aguilar-bustos, "A Generic Approach to Fuzzy Logic Controller Synthesis on FPGA", Proceedings of IEEE international conference on fuzzy systems, 2006, page(s): 2317 - 2322.

Gonzalez-Vazquez, J.L., Castillo, O. and Aguilar-bustos, L.T., (2006) "A Generic Approach to Fuzzy Logic Controller Synthesis on FPGA", Proceedings of IEEE international conference on fuzzy systems, page(s): 2317 - 2322.

12

Cascaded NPC/H-Bridge Inverter with Simplified Control Strategy and Superior Harmonic Suppression

Tom Wanjekeche, Dan V. Nicolae and Adisa A. Jimoh
Tshwane University of Technology
South Africa

1. Introduction

In recent decades the electric power systems has suffered significant power quality problems caused by the proliferation of non linear loads, such as arc furnace lighting loads adjustable ac drives etc., which causes a large amount of characteristic harmonics, low power factor and significantly deteriorates the power quality of the distribution system (Benslimane, 2007; Franquelo et. al., 2008; Gupta et al., 2008). The increasing restrictive regulations on power quality have significantly stimulated the development of power quality mitigation equipments. For high power grid connected systems, the classical two level or three level converters topology are insufficient due to the rating limitations imposed by the power semiconductors (Holmes & McGrath, 2001; Koura et al., 2007). Hence considerable attention has been focused on multilevel inverter topologies. This important multilevel technology has found widespread application in medium and high voltage electric drives, renewable energy - grid interface, power conditioning, and power quality application (Lai & Peng, 1996; Peng et al., 1996; Rodriguez et al., 2002; Sinha & Lipo, 1996; Tolbert et al., 1999).

Multilevel converters offer several advantages compared to their conventional counterparts (Manjrekar & Lipo, 1988, 1998, 200; Corzine & Familiant, 2002; Lund et. al., 1999; Sneineh et. al., 2006; Park et. al., 2003; Zhang et al., 2002; Ding et. al., 2004; Duarte et al., 1997; Rojas &. Ohnishi, 1997). By synthesizing the AC output terminal voltage from several voltage levels, staircase waveforms can be produced, which in their turn approach the sinusoidal waveform with low harmonic distortion, thus reducing filters requirements. However the several sources on the DC side of the converter make multilevel technology difficult to control by the need to balance the several DC voltages. For the class of multilevel inverter called diode clamped, if a higher output voltage is required one of the viable methods is to increase the number of inverter voltage levels. For Neutral Point Clamped (NPC) inverter voltage can only be increased up to five level beyond which DC voltage balancing becomes impossible. For single Phase H Bridge inverter, an increase in the number levels leads to increase in the number of separate DC sources, thus the proposed hybrid model is developed by combining the NPC and H- bridge topologies (Wu et al., 1999).

A lot of research has been done on single phase H- Bridge inverter where each inverter level generate three different voltage outputs, $+V_{dc}$, 0, and $-V_{dc}$ by connecting the dc source to the ac output using different combinations of the four switches of the Bridge (Peng et al., 1996). There has also been more emphasis on modeling and control of a five level NPC/H-bridge inverter without cascading the bridge (Cheng & Wu, 2007). This fails to address the principle of realizing a general cascaded n- level NPC/H-Bridge. It is on this need of realizing a higher voltage output with simplified control algorithm that this book chapter proposes a simplified control strategy for a cascaded NPC/H-bridge inverter with reduced harmonic content. Because of the modularity of the model only two cascaded cells which gives a 9 level cascaded NPC/H-bridge inverter is considered. The new control strategy is achieved by decomposing the nine level output into four separate and independent three-level NPC PWM output. By combining the three- level NPC PWM back to back using DC sources and properly phase shifting the modulating wave and carrier a simplified control strategy is achieved with reduced number of components. The control strategy is applied on cascaded NPC/H-bridge inverter that combines features from NPC inverter and cascaded H-Bridge inverter. For higher voltage applications, this structure can be easily extended to an n- level by cascaded NPC/H-Bridge PWM inverters.
The article starts by developing a control algorithm based on novel phase shifted PWM technique on the proposed inverter model. This is done on a two cell of the cascaded model to realize nine level voltage output. A theoretical harmonic analysis of the model with the proposed control algorithm is carried out based on double Fourier principle. Spectral characteristics of the output waveforms for all operating conditions are studied for a five-level and nine- level voltage output. Theoretical results are verified using MATLAB simulation.The results shows that the spectrum can be made to only consist of the multiples of fourth order for a five level and with proper phase shift combination, a multiple of eighth order is achieved for nine level voltage output. The results are compared with those of a conventional multicarrier PWM approach; it is shown that with the proposed phase shifted PWM approach, the inverter exhibits reduced harmonic content are present. Finally the article compares the components count of the the model with the convetional cascaded H-bridge inverter, it is clealry shown that the proposed model requires a lesser number of separate dc sources as compared to conventional cascaded H-bridge inverter.

2. System topology and switching technique

2.1 Main system configuration

Fig 1 shows the circuit configuration of the proposed nine- level cascaded NPC/H-Bridge PWM inverter which consists of two legs for each cell connected to a common bus. Four active switches, four freewheeling diodes and two diodes clamped to neutral are adopted in each leg. The voltage stress of all the eight power switches is equal to half of DC bus voltage. The power switches in each leg are operated in high frequency using phase shifted PWM control technique to generate the three voltage levels on the ac terminal to neutral voltage point
The building block of the whole topology consists of two identical NPC cascaded cells. The inverter phase voltage V_{an} is the sum of the two cascaded cells, i.e.,

$$V_{an} = V_{01} + V_{02} \tag{1}$$

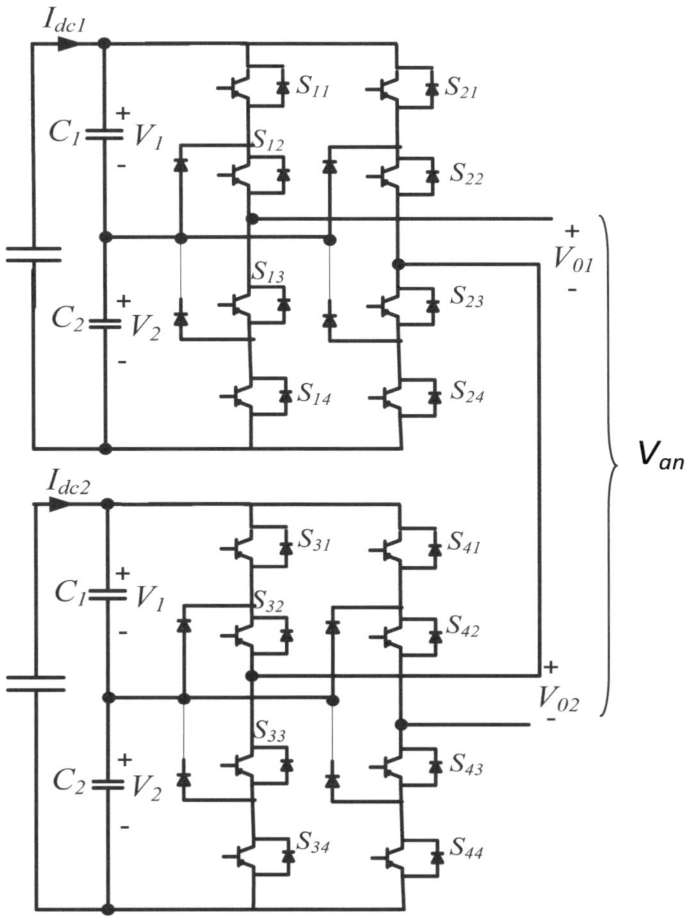

Fig. 1. Schematic diagram of the proposed cascaded NPC/H-bridge inverter model

Assuming that the two capacitor voltages on the DC bus voltage are equal, five different voltage levels +2Vdc, $+V_{dc}$, 0, $-V_{dc}$ and $-2V_{dc}$, are generated on the ac terminal V_{01} which consist of two legs. Same applies to V_{02} fig. 2 shows the switching model for a nine- level output [6]. This implies that by cascading two NPC/H-Bridge inverters (V_{01} and V_{02}) and properly phase shifting the modulating wave and carriers, a nine- level PWM output is achieved. The number of output voltage levels is given by

$$m = 4N + 1 \tag{2}$$

Where N is the number of series connected NPC/H-Bridges. The topology is made up of four three level legs and each leg has four active switches and four freewheeling diodes.

2.2 System operation

Most of the past research on modeling of cascaded multilevel inverter has concentrated on realizing a switching model of conventional H- bridge inverter without giving a guideline

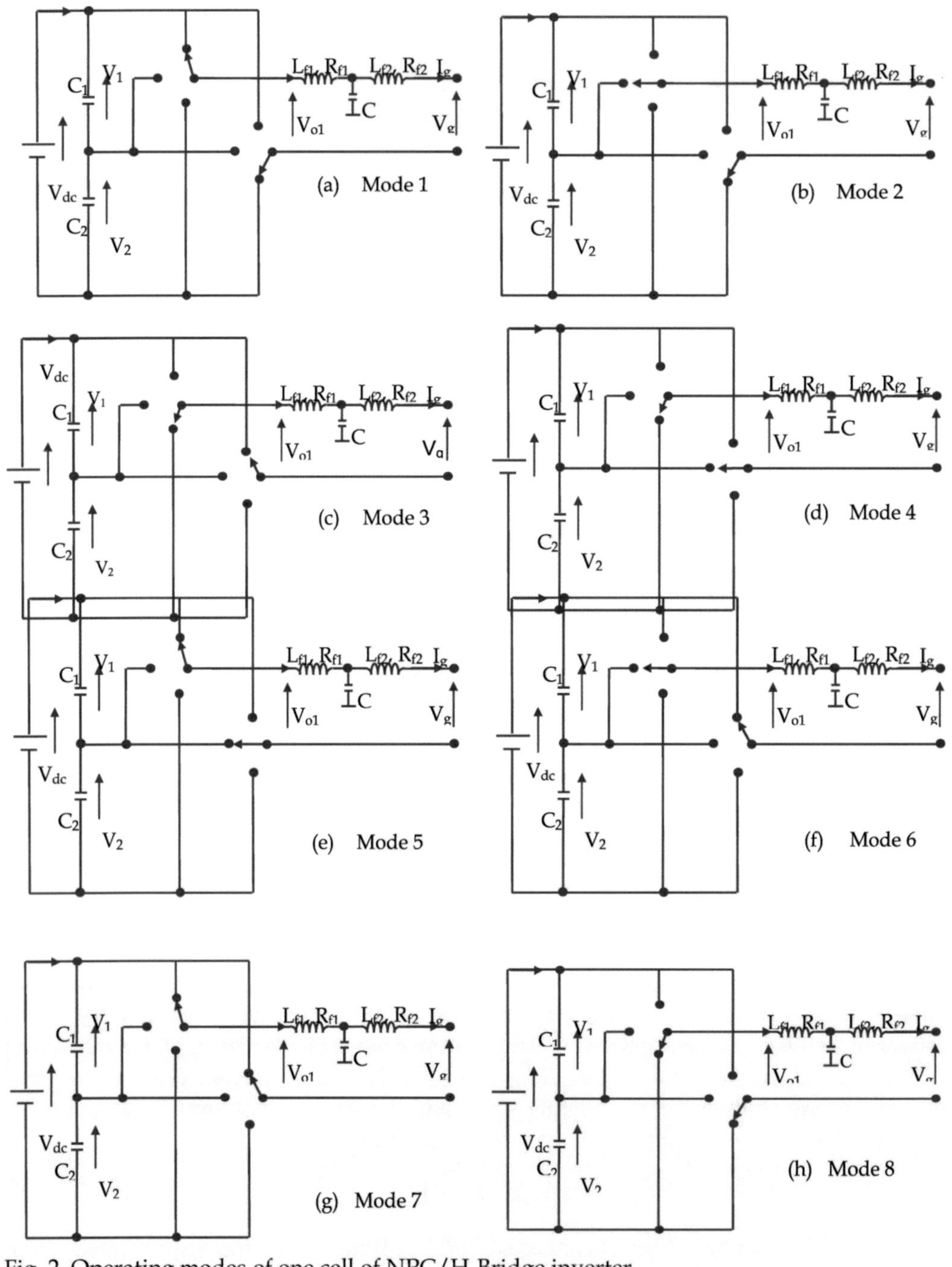

Fig. 2. Operating modes of one cell of NPC/H-Bridge inverter

on how one can get operating modes of cascaded NPC/H-bridge inverter and hence obtain a valid model for the topology. This section analyses eight valid operating modes of one cell of the proposed topology. The following assumptions are made in the modeling and analysis process:

- All components (power switches and capacitors) are ideal.
- The DC- link capacitors V_1, V_2, V_3 and V_4 have the same capacitance.
- PV cells supplies constant and equal voltages to the four DC link capacitors.
- The reference phase voltage is assumed to be a constant value during one switching period.

Figure 3 shows the operation modes for one NPC/H-bridge cell from the 9-level inverter.
In mode 1 the power switches S_{11} & S_{12} and S_{23} & S_{24} are turned on to supply voltage at the output of first NPC/H-bridge cell that is equal to $V_{01}= V_1+ V_2$. The capacitors C_1 and C_2 are discharged as they supply power to the utility as shown in figure 2 (a). The modes 2 to 8 are as shown in figures 2 (b) to 2 (h) respectively. In mode 2 the output voltage is $V_{01}= V_2$, in mode 3: $V_{01}= -(V_1+ V_2)$, in mode 4: $V_{01}= -V_2$, in mode 5: $V_{01}= V_1$, in mode 6: $V_{01}= -V_1$: in mode 7: $V_{01}= 0$ and in mode 8: $V_{01}= 0$.
Based on the analysis of the operation model, the state variable equation for the proposed inverter can be estimated. To prevent the top and bottom power switched in each inverter leg from conducting at the same time, the constraints of power switches can be expressed as:

$$S_{i1} + S_{i3} = 1;\ S_{i2} + S_{i4} = 1\} \tag{3}$$

Where i = 1, 2. Let's define the switch operator as: $T_1 = S_{11}$ & S_{12}; $T_2 = S_{13}$ & S_{13}; $T_3 = S_{21}$ & S_{22} $T_4 = S_{23}$ & S_{24}. The four valid expressions are given by:

$$T_1 = \begin{cases} 1\ if\ both\ S_{11}\ \&\ S_{12}\ are\ ON \\ 0\ Otherwise \end{cases} \tag{4}$$

$$T_2 = \begin{cases} 1\ if\ both\ S_{13}\ \&\ S_{14}\ are\ ON \\ 0\ Otherwise \end{cases} \tag{5}$$

$$T_3 = \begin{cases} 1\ if\ both\ S_{21}\ \&\ S_{22}\ are\ ON \\ 0\ Otherwise \end{cases} \tag{6}$$

$$T_4 = \begin{cases} 1\ if\ both\ S_{23}\ \&\ S_{24}\ are\ ON \\ 0\ Otherwise \end{cases} \tag{7}$$

From fig. 4 taking two legs for each cell to be *a* and *b*, the equivalent switching function are:

$$K_a = \begin{cases} 1\ if\ T_1 = 1 \\ 0\ if\ S_{12}\ \ 1 \\ -1 if\ T_2 = 1 \end{cases} \&\ K_b = \begin{cases} 1\ if\ T_3 = 1 \\ 0\ if\ S_{22}\ \ 1 \\ -1 if\ T_4 = 1 \end{cases} \tag{8}$$

Using equation (3 - 7), a switching state and corresponding voltage output V_{o1} can be generated as shown in table 1 which clearly indicates that there are 8 valid switching states; From table 1, the voltage V_{01} generate by the inverter can be expressed as:

$$V_{01} = V_a + V_b \tag{9}$$

For the control technique stated above; the voltage level for one leg of the cell is given as:

K_a	K_b	T_1	T_2	S_{12}	T_3	T_4	S_{21}	V_a	V_b	V_{01}	Mode
1	-1	1	0	1	0	1	0	V_1	$-V_2$	V_1+V_2	1
0	-1	0	0	1	0	1	0	0	$-V_2$	V_2	2
-1	0	0	1	0	0	0	1	0	V_2	$-V_2$	3
1	0	1	0	1	0	0	1	V_1	0	V_1	4
0	1	0	0	1	1	0	1	$-V_1$	0	$-V_1$	5
1	1	1	0	1	1	0	1	V_1	V_1	0	6
-1	-1	0	1	1	0	1	1	V_2	V_2	0	7
-1	-1	0	1	0	1	0	1	V_2	V_1	$-V_1-V_2$	8

Table 1. Switching States and Corresponding Voltage(s) for One Cell of NPC/H-bridge Inverter

$$V_a = K_a\left(\frac{K_a+1}{2}\right)V_1 - K_a\left(\frac{K_a-1}{2}\right)V_2 \tag{10}$$

Similarly for the second leg the expression is given by (11)

$$V_b = K_b\left(\frac{K_b+1}{2}\right)V_1 - K_b\left(\frac{K_b-1}{2}\right)V_2 \tag{11}$$

S_{11}	S_{12}	S_{21}	S_{22}	S_{31}	S_{32}	S_{41}	S_{42}	V_{01}	V_{02}	V_{an}
0	0	0	0	0	0	0	0	0	0	0
0	0	0	1	0	0	0	0	$-V_{dc}$	0	$-V_{dc}$
0	0	0	1	0	0	0	1	$-V_{dc}$	$-V_{dc}$	$-2V_{dc}$
0	0	0	1	0	0	1	1	$-V_{dc}$	$-2V_{dc}$	$-3V_{dc}$
0	0	0	1	0	1	0	0	$-V_{dc}$	V_{dc}	0
0	0	0	1	1	1	0	0	$-V_{dc}$	$2V_{dc}$	V_{dc}
0	0	1	1	0	0	0	0	$-2V_{dc}$	0	$-2V_{dc}$
0	0	1	1	0	0	0	0	$-2V_{dc}$	$-V_{dc}$	$-3V_{dc}$
0	0	1	1	0	0	1	0	$-2V_{dc}$	$-2V_{dc}$	$-4V_{dc}$
0	0	1	1	0	1	0	0	$-2V_{dc}$	V_{dc}	$-V_{dc}$
0	0	1	1	1	1	0	0	$-2V_{dc}$	$2V_{dc}$	0
0	1	0	0	0	0	0	0	V_{dc}	0	V_{dc}
0	1	0	0	0	0	0	1	V_{dc}	$-V_{dc}$	0
0	1	0	0	0	0	1	1	V_{dc}	$-2V_{dc}$	$-V_{dc}$
0	1	0	0	0	1	0	0	V_{dc}	V_{dc}	$2V_{dc}$
0	1	0	0	1	1	0	0	V_{dc}	$2V_{dc}$	$3V_{dc}$
1	1	0	0	0	0	0	0	$2V_{dc}$	0	$2V_{dc}$
1	1	0	0	0	0	0	1	$2V_{dc}$	$-V_{dc}$	V_{dc}
1	1	0	0	0	0	1	1	$2V_{dc}$	$-2V_{dc}$	0
1	1	0	0	0	1	0	0	$2V_{dc}$	V_{dc}	$3V_{dc}$
1	1	0	0	1	1	0	0	$2V_{dc}$	$2V_{dc}$	$4V_{dc}$
1	1	1	1	1	1	1	1	0	0	0

Table 2. Switching scheme for one phase leg of a nine level cascaded NPC/H- bridge inverter

From equation (9), the voltage output for one cell of the model can be deduced as;

$$V_{01} = \frac{K_a - K_b}{2}(V_1 + V_2) + \frac{K^2{}_a - K^2{}_b}{2}(V_1 - V_2) \tag{12}$$

For the compound nine level inverter let's assume that $V_1 = V_2 = V_3 = V_4 = \text{V}$, the switching states are as shown in Table 2.
For a nine level cascaded NPC/H-bridge inverter, there are 22 valid switching states though two of the switching states are short circuits and thus cannot compensate the DC capacitor as current do not pass through either of the four DC- link capacitors.

3. Mathematical analysis

Most of the past research on modeling of cascaded multilevel inverter has concentrated on realizing a switching model of conventional H- bridge inverter without giving a guideline on how one can get operating modes of cascaded NPC/H-bridge inverter and hence obtain a valid model for the topology. This section analyses eight valid operating modes of one cell of the proposed topology and proposes an equivalent circuit for the topology.
The following assumptions are made for deriving the mathematical model of the cascaded H-bridge inverters.

- The grid is assumed to be AC current source,
- The power losses of the whole system are categorized as series loss and parallel loss. The series loss and interfacing inductor loss are represented as equivalent series resistance (ESR). Parallel losses are represented as shunt connected resistances across the dc-link capacitors.

The differential equations describing the dynamics of the coupling inductor between the NPC/H-bridge inverter and the grid of the model shown in fig. 1 can be derived as:

$$\begin{cases} L_{f1}\dfrac{di_{fx}}{dt} = -V_{cx} - i_{fx}R_{f1x} + \delta_{1x}V_1 + \delta_{2x}V_2 \\ L_{f2}\dfrac{di_{sx}}{dt} = -V_{cx} - i_{sx}R_{f2x} - V_{sx} \end{cases} \tag{13}$$

According to Kirchhoff's law, the currents flowing into the dc link capacitors C_1 and C_2 can be expressed as:

$$\begin{cases} i_{C1} = C_1\dfrac{dV_1}{dt} = \delta_{1x}i_{fx}\dfrac{V_1}{R} + \dfrac{V_2}{R} \\ i_{C2} = C_2\dfrac{dV_2}{dt} = -\delta_{2x}i_{fx}\dfrac{V_1}{R} + \dfrac{V_2}{R} \\ i_{CX} = C_f\dfrac{dV_{fx}}{dt} = i_{fx} - i_{sx} \\ C_1\dfrac{dV_1}{dt} - C_2\dfrac{dV_2}{dt} = \delta_3 i_{fx} \end{cases} \tag{14}$$

The equations (13) and (14) can be rearranged as:

$$\begin{cases} \dfrac{di_{fx}}{dt} = \dfrac{R_{f1x}}{L_{f1}} - \dfrac{V_{cx}}{L_{f1}} + \dfrac{\delta_{1x}V_1}{L_{f1}} + \dfrac{\delta_{2x}V_2}{L_{f1}} \\ \dfrac{di_{sx}}{dt} = \dfrac{V_{cx}}{L_{f2}} - \dfrac{R_{f1}}{L_{f2}} - \dfrac{V_{sx}}{L_{f2}} \\ \dfrac{dV_1}{dt} = \dfrac{\delta_{1x}i_{fx}}{C_1} - \left(\dfrac{V_1}{RC_1} + \dfrac{V_2}{RC_1}\right) \\ \dfrac{dV_2}{dt} = \dfrac{\delta_{2x}i_{fx}}{C_2} - \left(\dfrac{V_1}{RC_2} + \dfrac{V_2}{RC_2}\right) \\ \dfrac{dV_f}{dt} = \dfrac{i_{fx}}{C_f} - \dfrac{i_{sx}}{C_f} \\ \delta_3 i_{fx} = C_1\dfrac{dV_1}{dt} - C_2\dfrac{dV_2}{dt} \end{cases} \tag{15}$$

Equation (16) can be written in the format of:

$$Z\dot{x} = Ax + B \tag{16}$$

Capacitor current, inverter current and utility line current and DC- Link capacitors are taken as state variables:

$$x = [i_{fx}\ i_{sx}\ V_c\ V_1\ V_2]^T \tag{17}$$

$$Z = \begin{bmatrix} L_{f1} & 0 & 0 & 0 & 0 \\ 0 & L_{f2} & 1 & 0 & 0 \\ 0 & 0 & C & 0 & 0 \\ 0 & 0 & 0 & C_1 & 0 \\ 0 & 0 & 0 & 0 & C_2 \end{bmatrix} \tag{18}$$

$$B = [0\ -V_s\ 0\ 0\ 0\ ]^T \tag{19}$$

Matrix A depends on each operating mode as such

- For $V_{01} = +V_2$

$$A_1 = \begin{bmatrix} -R_{f1} & 0 & -1 & 0 & 1 \\ 0 & -R_{f2} & 1 & 0 & 0 \\ 1 & -1 & 0 & 0 & 0 \\ 0 & 0 & 0 & R^{-1} & R^{-1} \\ -1 & 0 & 0 & R^{-1} & R^{-1} \end{bmatrix} \tag{20}$$

- For $V_{01} = -V_2$

$$A_5 = A_1{}^T \tag{21}$$

- For $V_{01} = +V_1$

$$A_2 = \begin{bmatrix} -R_{f1} & 0 & -1 & 1 & 0 \\ 0 & -R_{f2} & 1 & 0 & 0 \\ 1 & -1 & 0 & 0 & 0 \\ -1 & 0 & 0 & R^{-1} & R^{-1} \\ 0 & 0 & 0 & R^{-1} & R^{-1} \end{bmatrix} \tag{22}$$

- For $V_{01} = - V_1$

$$A_6 = A_2^T \tag{23}$$

- For $V_{01} = 0$

$$A_4 = \begin{bmatrix} -R_{f1} & 0 & -1 & -1 & -1 \\ 0 & -R_{f2} & 1 & 0 & 0 \\ 1 & -1 & 0 & 0 & 0 \\ -1 & 0 & 0 & 0 & 0 \\ -1 & 0 & 0 & 0 & 0 \end{bmatrix} \tag{24}$$

Considering the same assumption made earlier that the dc link capacitors have the same capacitance $C_1 = C_2 = C$ which implies $V_1 = V_2 = V_{dc}/2$, the state space equation (17) can be simplified to:

$$Z'\dot{x} = A'x + B' \tag{25}$$

With

$$x = [i_{fx}\ i_{sx}\ V_c\ V_{dc}/2]^T \tag{26}$$

$$Z' = \begin{bmatrix} L_{f1} & 0 & 0 & 0 \\ 0 & L_{f2} & 1 & 0 \\ 0 & 0 & C & 0 \\ 0 & 0 & 0 & C_T \end{bmatrix} \tag{27}$$

$$B = [0\ V_s\ 0\ 0\ 0\ ]^T \tag{28}$$

$$A' = \begin{bmatrix} -R_{f1} & 0 & -k & k \\ 0 & -R_{f2} & k & 0 \\ k & -1 & 0 & 0 \\ -k & 0 & 0 & 0 \end{bmatrix} \tag{29}$$

Where k depends on the operating mode and can take five different values: 1. 0.5 0, -05, -1.

For a three phase system, V_s is replaced $V_s(\cos\omega_o t)$, $V_s(\cos\omega_o - 2\pi/3)$ and $V_s(\cos\omega_o + 2\pi/3$. similarly the Z, A and B matrices are expanded accordingly to three phase. Where V_s is the grid voltage.

3.1 Harmonic analysis of a nine level cascaded NPC/H-bridge inverter

Having realized a nine- level output from the a cascaded 9- level model, it is important to theoretically investigate its harmonic structure and show how harmonic suppression is achieved. Based on the principle of double Fourier integral (Holmes & Thomas, 2003). the first modulation between triangular carrier v_{cr1}, and the positive sinusoidal waveform a naturally sampled PMW output $V_p(t)$ of equation (30). Where M is the modulation index, V_{dc} is the DC link voltage of the PWM inverter and J_n is the nth order Bessel function of the first kind. Using v_{cr2} which is the same carrier but displaced by minus unity, the naturally sampled PWM output V_n is as given in equation (31)

$$V_p(t) = \begin{cases} \dfrac{V_{dc1}}{2} + \dfrac{V_{dc1}M}{2}\cos\omega_s t + \dfrac{2V_{dc1}}{\pi}\sum\limits_{m=1}^{\infty}\dfrac{1}{m}J_0(m\dfrac{\pi}{2}M) \\ \sin m\dfrac{\pi}{2}\cos\omega_s t + \dfrac{2V_{dc1}}{\pi}\sum\limits_{m=1}^{\infty}\sum\limits_{\substack{n=-\infty \\ n\mp 0}}^{\infty}\dfrac{1}{m}J_n \\ (m\dfrac{\pi}{2}M)\sin(m+n)\dfrac{\pi}{2}\cos(n\omega_c t + n\omega_s t) \end{cases} \tag{30}$$

$$V_n(t) = \begin{cases} \dfrac{V_{dc1}}{2} - \dfrac{V_{dc1}M}{2}\cos\omega_s t - \dfrac{2V_{dc1}}{\pi}\sum\limits_{m=1}^{\infty}\dfrac{1}{m}J_0(m\dfrac{\pi}{2}M) \\ \sin m\dfrac{\pi}{2}\cos\omega_s t + \dfrac{2V_{dc1}}{\pi}\sum\limits_{m=1}^{\infty}\sum\limits_{\substack{n=-\infty \\ n\mp 0}}^{\infty}\dfrac{1}{m}J_n \\ (m\dfrac{\pi}{2}M)\sin(m+n)\dfrac{\pi}{2}\cos(n\omega_c t + n\omega_s t) \end{cases} \tag{31}$$

The output of leg 'a' is given by V_a (t) = V_p (t) $-V_n$ (t) which is:

$$V_a(t) = \begin{cases} V_{dc1}\cos(\omega_s t) + \dfrac{4V_{dc1}}{\pi}\sum\limits_{m=2,4,6}^{\infty}\sum\limits_{n=\pm1\pm3\pm5}^{\infty}\dfrac{1}{m}J_n \\ (m\dfrac{\pi}{2}M)\cos(m\omega_c t + n\omega_s t) \end{cases} \tag{32}$$

The output of leg 'b' is realized by replacing ω_s with $\omega_s + \pi$ and using v_{cr2} which is same as phase displacing v_{cr1} by minus unity which gives

$$V_b(t) = \begin{cases} -V_{dc1}\cos(\omega_s t) - \dfrac{4V_{dc1}}{\pi}\sum\limits_{m=2,4,6}^{\infty}\sum\limits_{n=\pm1\pm3\pm5}^{\infty}\dfrac{(-1)^{m+n}}{m}J_n \\ (m\dfrac{\pi}{2}M)\cos(m\omega_c t + n\omega_s t) \end{cases} \tag{33}$$

From equations (32) and (33), it can be clearly deduced that that odd carrier harmonics and even sideband harmonics around even carrier harmonic orders are completely eliminated. Five- level obtained by taking the differential output between the two legs and is given by (35). Similarly the output between the other two legs of the second cell of the hybrid model is achieved by replacing ω_s with $\omega_s+\pi$ and ω_c with ωc + $\pi/4$ which gives another five level inverter for equation given by equation (34)

$$V_{01}(t)=\begin{cases}2V_{dc1}\cos(\omega_s t)+\dfrac{8V_{dc1}}{\pi}\sum\limits_{m=4,8,12}^{\infty}\sum\limits_{n=\pm1\pm3\pm5}^{\infty}\dfrac{1}{m}J_n\\(m\dfrac{\pi}{2}M)\cos(m\omega_c t+n\omega_s t)\end{cases} \tag{34}$$

$$V_{02}(t)=\begin{cases}-2V_{dc1}\cos(\omega_s t)-\dfrac{8V_{dc1}}{\pi}\sum\limits_{m=4,8,12}^{\infty}\sum\limits_{n=\pm1\pm3\pm5}^{\infty}\dfrac{(-1)^{\frac{m}{4}+n}}{m}J_n\\(m\dfrac{\pi}{2}M)\cos(m\omega_c t+n\omega_s t)\end{cases} \tag{35}$$

Equations (34) and (35) clearly show that for five- level inverter, the proposed control strategy has achieved; Suppression of carrier harmonics to multiples of four; Elimination of even side harmonics around multiples of four carrier harmonics of Multiples of four carrier harmonics. Finally the output for a nine level is achieved differentiating the output voltage between the two cells of the five level cells and this is given by equation (36). It can be concluded that for a cascaded N-level inverter the carrier harmonic order is pushed up by factor of $4N$ where N is the number of cascaded hybrid inverters. The output voltages and spectral waveforms to confirm the validation of the control strategy using this approach of double Fourier transform will be discussed later.

$$V_{an}(t)=\begin{cases}4V_{dc1}\cos(\omega_s t)+\dfrac{8V_{dc1}}{\pi}\sum\limits_{m=8,16,24}^{\infty}\sum\limits_{n=\pm1\pm3\pm5}^{\infty}\dfrac{1}{m}J_n\\(m\dfrac{\pi}{2}M)\cos(m\omega_c t+n\omega_s t)\end{cases} \tag{36}$$

4. Proposed hybrid control method

The above section has illustrated in general the switching technque for one cell of the cascaded NPC/H-bridge model, because of the modularity of the model, two cells will be considered for modulatin and analysis in this section.For the two cells an improved strategy for realizing nine level output is proposed in this book chapter. The article uses the principle of decomposition where each leg is treated independently and gives a three level output (Naderi &. Rahmati, 2008).

Positive and negative legs are connected together back to back and they share the same voltage source V_{dc}. PD modulation is used for achieving three level output (Rodriguez et al., 2002). To achieve a five level PWM output two triangular carriers V_{cr1} and V_{cr2} in phase but vertically disposed and modulating wave phase shifted by π are used. The multilevel converter model is modulated using phase shifted PWM technique as illustrated in fig. 3

and 4 for the two NPC/H-Bridge cells. Finally a nine- level PWM output is achieved by using the same two carriers but phase shifted by π/4 and modulating wave phase shifted by π as shown in fig. 5. This is a simple control strategy that can be easily implemented in a digital signal processor. The switching states for one phase leg of a nine- level NPC/H-bridge inverter is shown in table 2, as can be seen there several redundant states which can be utilized in DC voltage balance, this is not within the scope of this paper.

The control strategy has two advantages as compared to multicarrier PWM approach (Holmes & McGrath, 2001). First for an N-level cascaded NPC/H-bridge PWM inverter, we can use a switching frequency of 4N times less to achieve the same spectrum as multicarrier approach. This has an advantage of reducing the switching losses, which is an important feature in high power application. Secondly the multicarrier PWM approach requires 8 carriers to achieve nine level output, but the proposed control strategy requires only one carrier phase shifted by (N-1)π/4 where N is the number of series connected NPC/H-Bridge inverter.

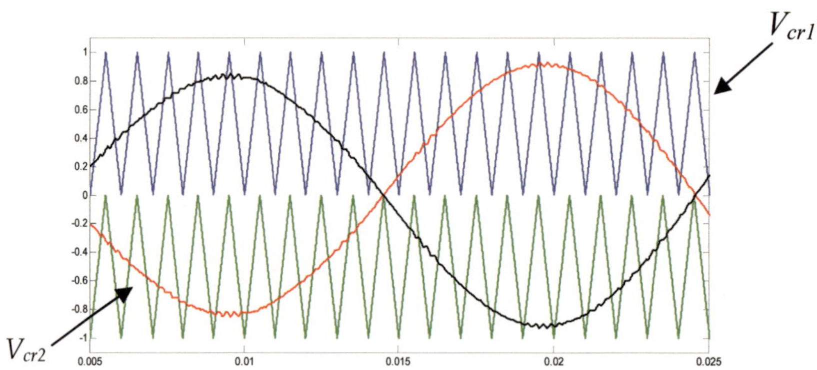

(a)

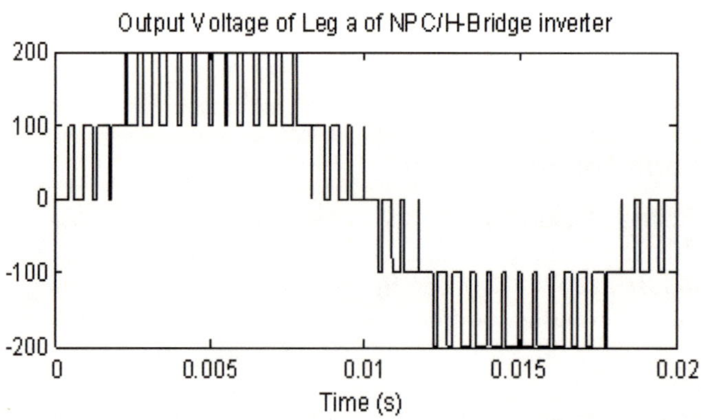

(b)

Fig. 3. (a) PWM scheme and (b) output voltage waveform for one cell of NPC/H-Bridge inverter

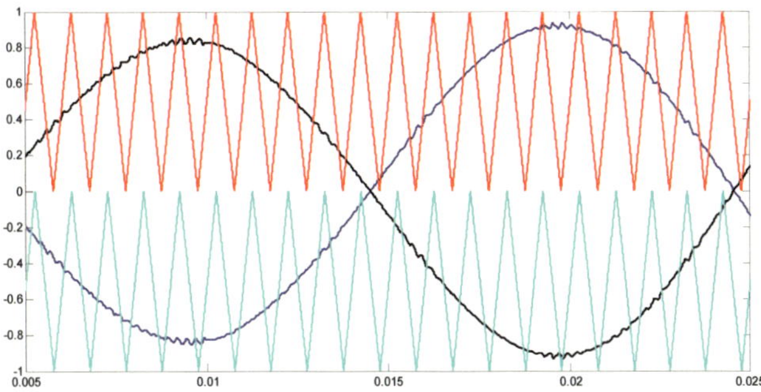

(a)

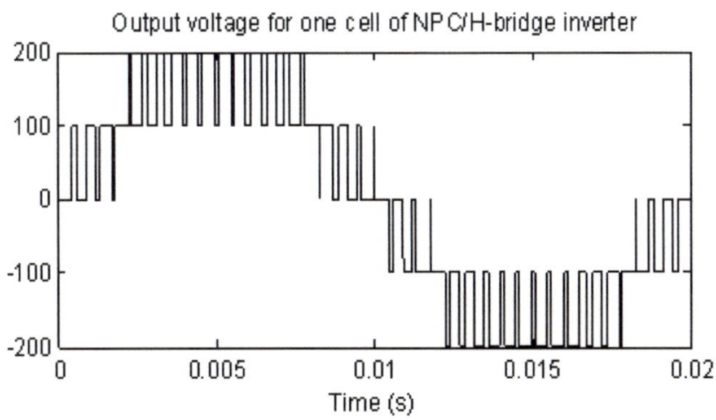

(b)

Fig. 4. (a) Phase shifted PWM scheme and (b) output voltage waveform for the second cell of cascaded NPC/H-Bridge inverter

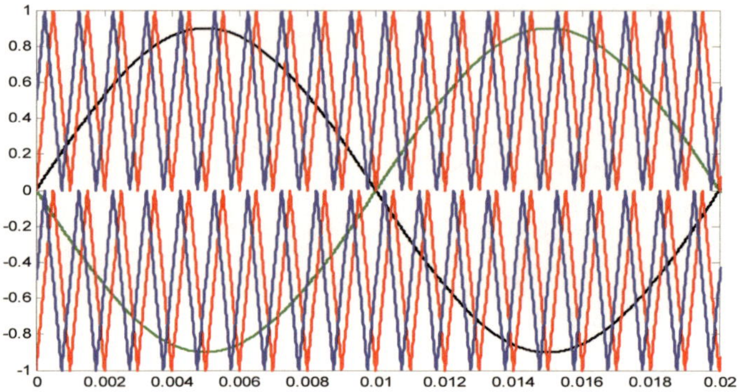

(a)

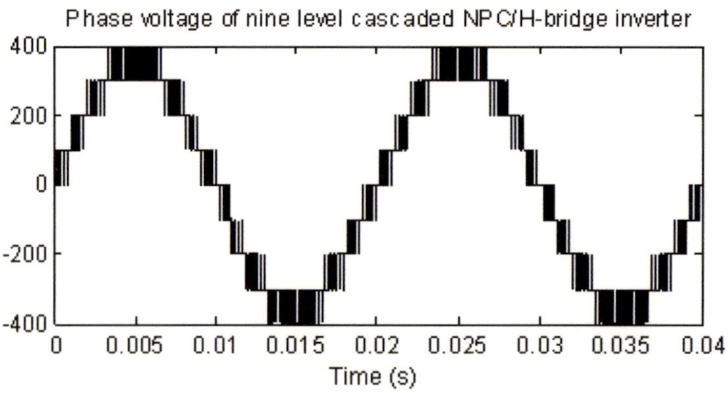

(b)

Fig. 5. (a) PWM scheme and (b) output voltage waveform for a nine level cascaded NPC/H-Bridge inverter

5. MATLAB simulation

Part of the Matlab simulation has already been carried out in section 4 to investigate the proposed phase shifted PWM control technique. In order verify that a nine- level output is achieved by cascading two NPC/H-Bridge PWM inverter and properly phase shifting the carrier and the modulating wave, a model as shown in fig. 6 was developed and simulated in MATLAB. The control strategy to minimize harmonics was designed and developed in MATLAB as shown in fig. 7 (wanjekeche et.al., 2009). It is assumed that the dc voltage input for each module is E = 1OOV. The inverter operates under the condition of f_m=50HZ, m_f=20 for a five level output and m_a=0.9. The device switching frequency is found from $f_{sw,dev}$= m_f/2 X f_m=500HZ

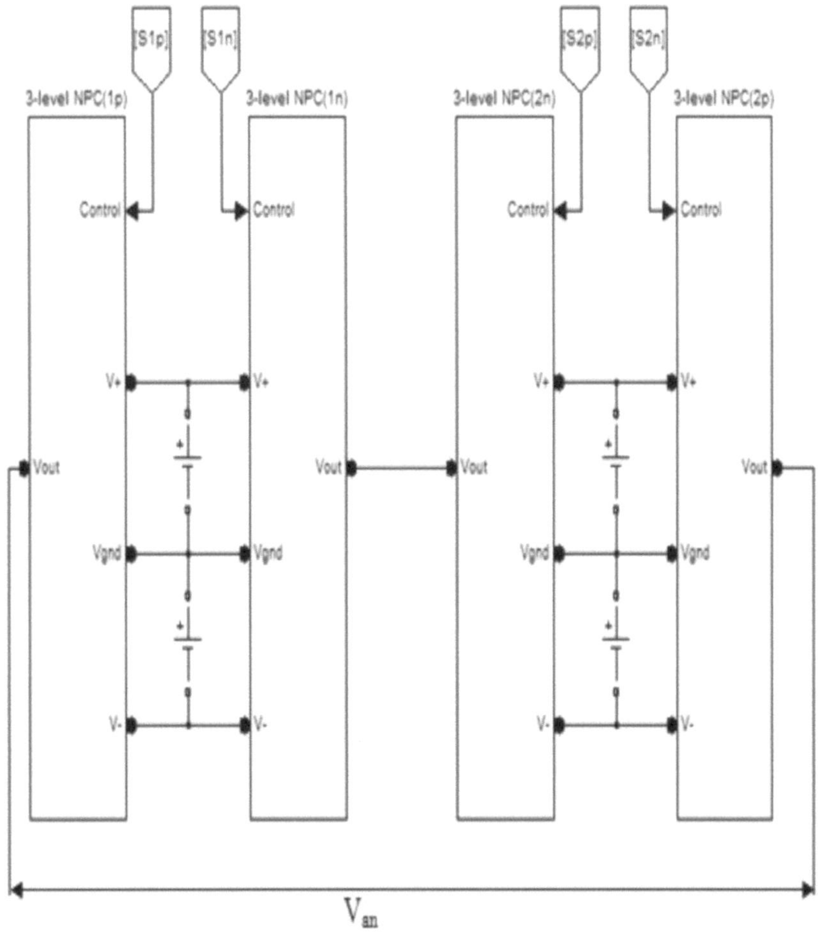

Fig. 6. Four legs of a nine-level cascaded NPC/H-bridge inverter

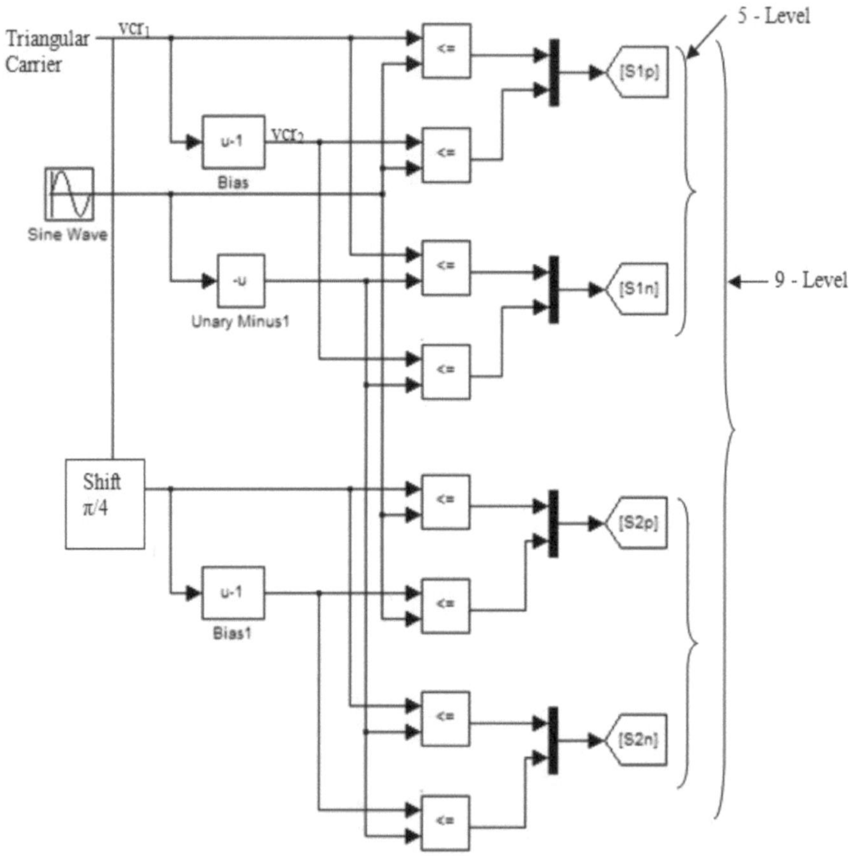

Fig. 7. Control strategy for a nine-level cascaded NPC/H-bridge inverter

5.1 Simulation results and discussion

Five- level inverter output are shown in figs.8, 9 and 10 for various switching frequency. Fig.8 shows the simulated waveform for the phase voltage V_{01} of the NPC/H-Bridge PWM inverter and its harmonic content. The waveform V_{01} is a five voltage levels, whose harmonics appear as sidebands centered around $2m_f$ and its multiples such as $4m_f$, $6m_f$. This simulation verifies analytical equation (34) which shows that the phase voltage does not contain harmonics lower than the 31st, but has odd order harmonics (i.e. $n=\pm1\pm3\pm5$) centered around $m=4, 8, 12$. Figs. 9 & 10 shows five- level NPC/H-Bridge inverter output for device inverter switching frequency of 1000HZ and 200HZ respectively.

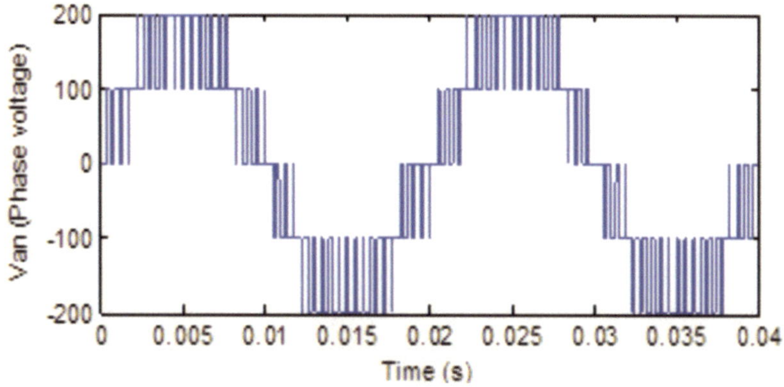

(a)

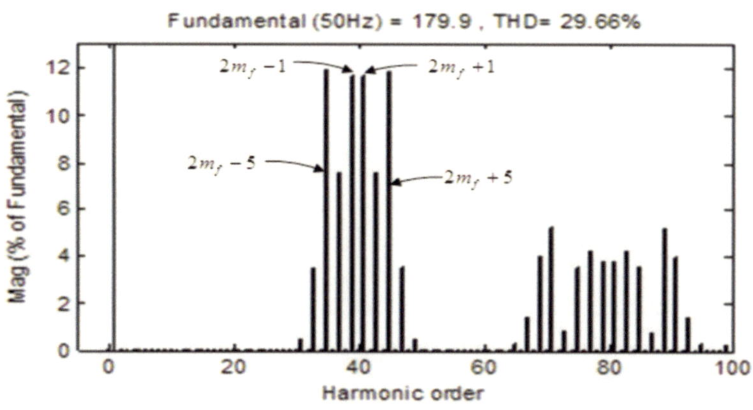

(b)

Fig. 8. (a) Waveform and (b) Spectrum for a five level NPC/H-Bridge inverter phase voltage (f_m=50HZ, $f_{sw,dev}$=500HZ, m_f=20, m_a=0.9)

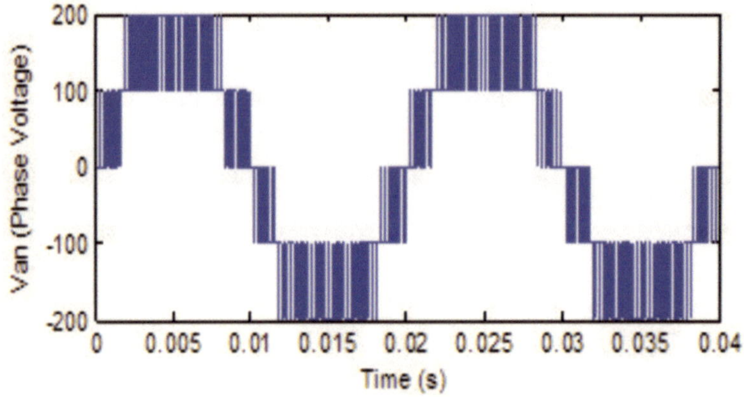

(a)

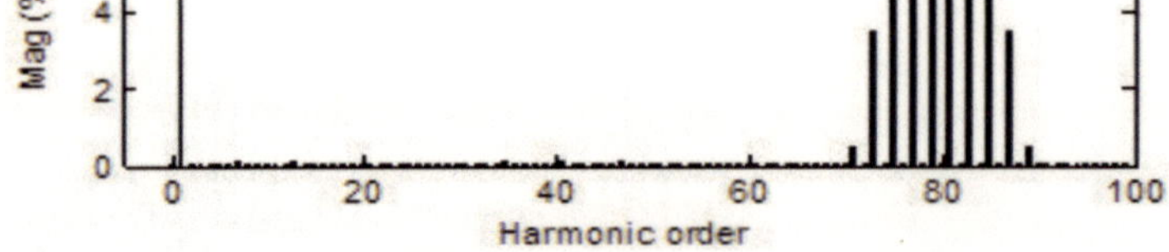

(b)

Fig. 9. (a) Waveform and (b) Spectrum for a five level NPC/H-Bridge inverter phase voltage (f_m=50HZ, $f_{sw,dev}$=1000HZ, m_f=40, m_a=0.9)

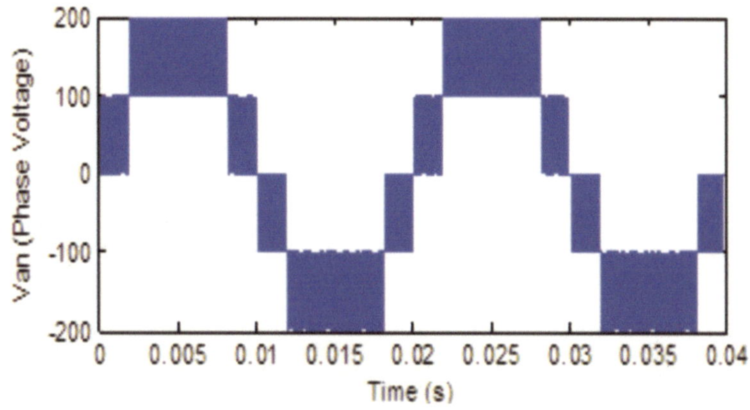

(a)

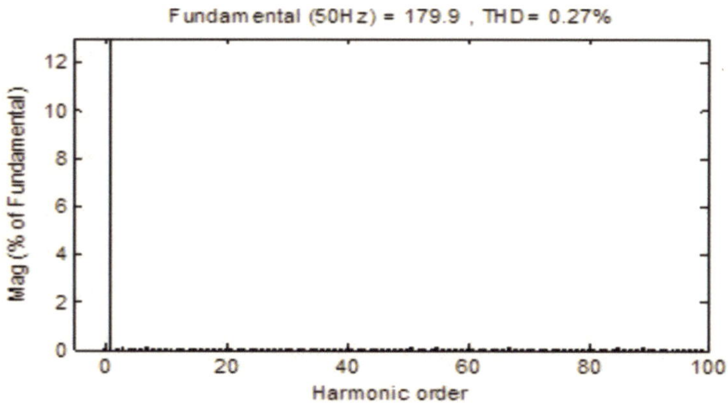

(b)

Fig. 10. (a) Waveform and (b) Spectrum for a five level NPC/H-Bridge inverter phase voltage (f_m=50HZ, $f_{sw,dev}$=2000HZ, m_f=80, m_a=0.9

Fig. 11 shows the waveform of the phase voltage of a nine level NPC/H-Bridge PWM inverter. It has sidebands around $4m_f$ and its multiples, this shows further suppression in harmonic content. This topology operates under the condition of f_m=50HZ, m_f=40 and m_a=0.9. The device switching frequency is found from $f_{sw,dev}$= m_f/4 X f_m=500HZ. This simulation verifies analytical equation (36) which shows that the phase voltage does not contain harmonics lower than the 67th, but has odd order harmonics (i.e. n=±1±3±5) centered around m=8, 16, 32. As can be seen from fig. 12, a switching frequency of 1KHZ which fits most of high power switching devices has a THD of 0.18% this makes the topology a perfect fit for most high power application such as utility interface power quality control and Medium Voltage drives.

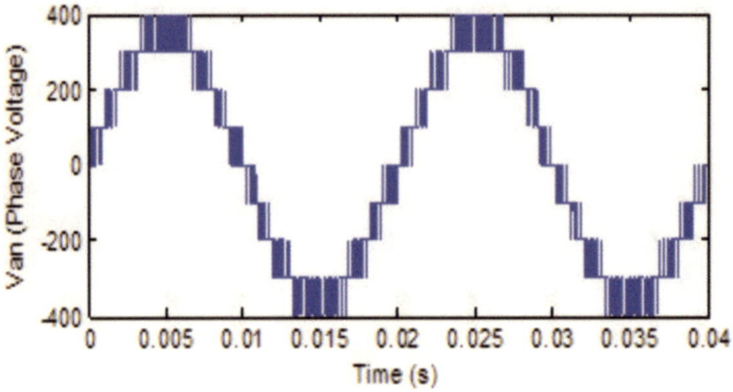

(a)

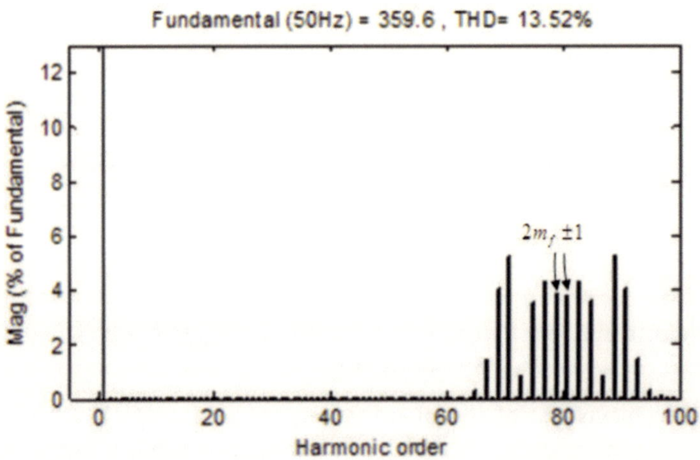

(b)

Fig. 11. (a) Waveform and (b) Spectrum for a nine- level cascaded NPC/H-Bridge inverter phase voltage (f_m=50HZ, $f_{sw,dev}$=500HZ, m_f=40, m_a=0.9)

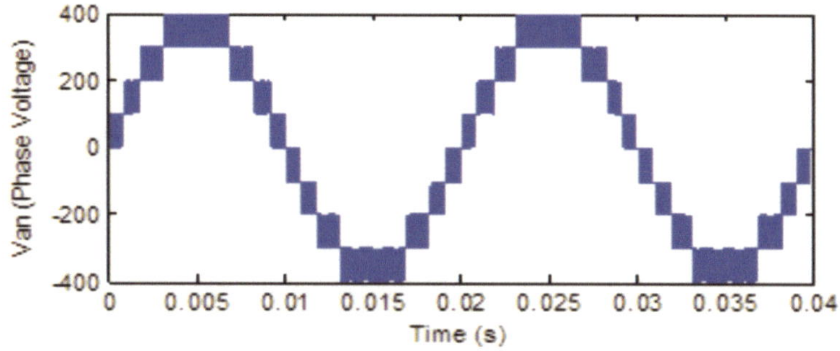

(a)

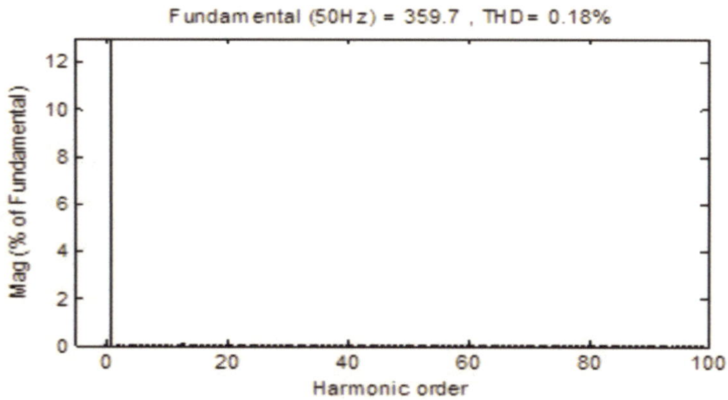

(b)

Fig. 12. (a) Waveform and (b) Spectrum for a nine- level cascaded NPC/H-Bridge inverter phase voltage (f_m=50HZ, $f_{sw,dev}$=1000HZ, m_f=80, m_a=0.9)

6. Comparison of the proposed control technique with conventional PWM multicarrier approach

As can be seen from fig. 1, to achieve the same voltage levels N for each phase, only *(N-1)/4* separate dc sources are needed for one phase leg converter of the cascaded NPC/H-bridge model, whereas *(N-1)/2* separate voltage voltages is need for cascaded H -bridge inverter. Thus for an n- cascaded NPC/H-bridge inverter, the number of separate DC sources S is given by:

$$S = \frac{N-1}{4} \tag{37}$$

Table 3 shows comparison on the number of components for various multilevel inverters, cascaded NPC/H-bridge inverter requires 16 switching devices just as the other topologies but used only two carriers for any level of voltage output. For comparison between the two cascaded inverters it is readily shown in table 4 that the NPC/H-bridge inverter has an advantage of realizing the same voltage level as cascaded H-bridge inverter with a half number of separate DC sources which is more expensive as compared to clamping diodes.

Topology / No. of Components	Diode clamped	Flying capacitor	Cascaded H- bridge	Cascaded NPC/H-bridge
Switching devices	16	16	16	16
Clamping diodes	56	0	0	8
Flying capacitors	0	56	0	0
Carriers	8	8	4	2
Separate cells	0	0	4	2
Separate dc sources	1	0	4	2

Table 3. Component comaprison for different multilevel inverters for nine level voltage output

Topology / No. of Components	Cascaded H- bridge	Cascaded NPC/H-bridge
Switching devices	2N-1	2N-1
Clamping diodes	0	N-1
Flying capacitors	0	0
Carriers	(N-1)/2	2
Separate cells	(N-1)/2	(N-1)/4
Separate dc sources	(N-1)/2	(N-1)/4

Table 4. Component comaprison for different multilevel inverters for nine level voltage output

6.1 Comparison of the MATLAB simulation results of the two PWM control methods

To clearly investigate the superiority of the model under the proposed PWM control technique, Matlab simulation results was carried out on a cascaded NPC/H-bridge nine level inverter model under the conditions of f_m=50HZ, fc =1000Hz and m_a=0.9.

With the proposed Phase - shifted PWM technique, there is further harmonic suppression as shown in fig. 13 (b), as compared to conventional PWM Phase shifted approach. This is clearly illustrated in fig. 13 (a) where Phase Disposition and Phase shifted PWM modulation strategy is adopted (Jinghua & Zhengxi, 2008). This is beacuse with conventional PWM multicarrier approach, optimum harmonic cancellation is achieved by phase shifting each carrier by $(i-1)\pi/N$ (Holmes & Thomas, 2003). where i is the ith converter, N is the number of series - connected single the multicarrier PWM approach requires 8 carriers to achieve nine level output, but the proposed control strategy requires only one carrier phase shifted by (N-1)п/4 as stated in section 4.1(Wanjekeche et al., 2009).

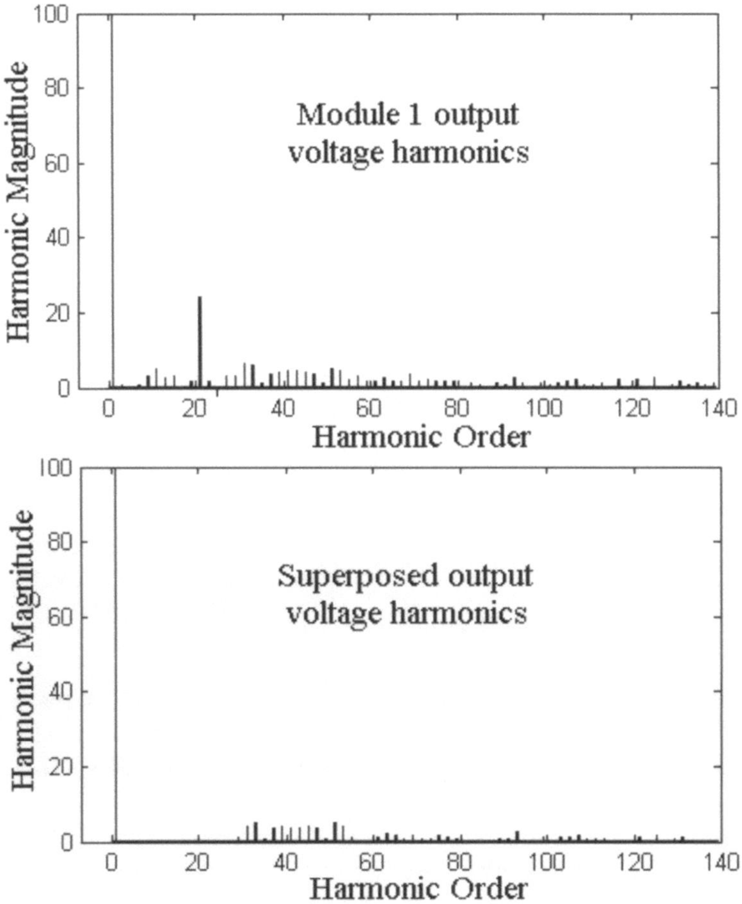
Module 1 output
voltage harmonics
Harmonic Magnitude
Harmonic Order
Superposed output
voltage harmonics
Harmonic Magnitude
Harmonic Order
0
20
40
60
80
100
120
140

(a)

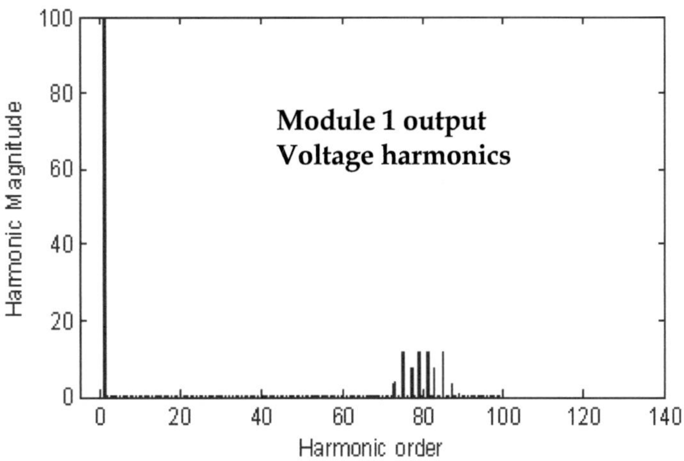
Module 1 output
Voltage harmonics
Harmonic Magnitude
Harmonic order
0
20
40
60
80
100
120
140

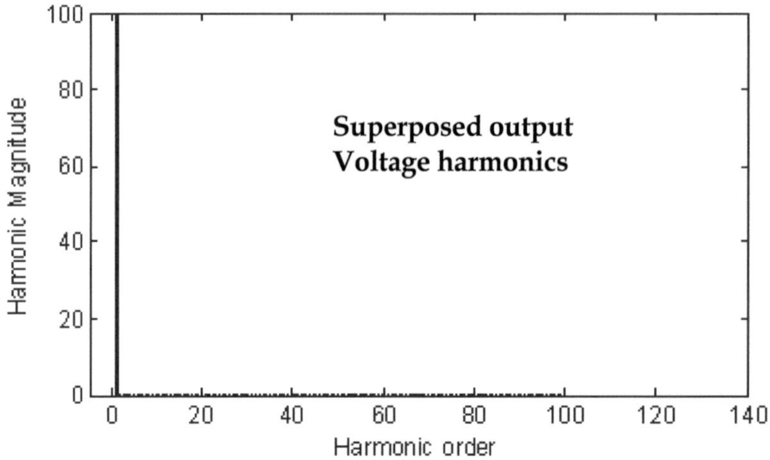

(b)

Fig. 13. Spectra voltage waveforms of NPC/H-bridge topology using (a) conventional multicarrier phase shifted PWM approach (b) proposed phase shifted PWM approach

7. Conclusion

In this chapter it has been demonstrates with proper modeling of the converter, the operating characteristic and the control technique to be applied on the model can be easily found. This can be used to develop standard model for cascaded NPC/H-bridge inverter which is currently not available.

The article has developed an improved topology that can be used to achieve a nine- level NPC/H-Bridge PWM inverter. It has been clearly shown that five level NPC/H-Bridge inverter that has been proposed by many researchers gives a higher THD which is not acceptable in most high and medium power application unless a filter is used. And since there is limited research on cascaded this important hybrid model, the chapter has developed a novel phase shifted PWM control technique that was tested on a two cell cascaded NPC/H-bridge model. In the proposed control technique it has been shown that by properly phase shifting both the modulating wave and the carrier, a nine- level voltage output can be achieved with a reduced harmonic content. With a THD of 0.18% without a filter, this makes the control strategy for a cascaded nine level NPC/H-bridge inverter a good option for medium and high power application such as utility interface and medium drives.

The simulation results obtained clearly verifies the analytical equations from double Fourier transform, showing that a nine- level output has multiples of eighth- order cross modulated harmonics. From the mathematical analysis it has been shown that cross modulated harmonics for a generalized m- level cascaded NPC/H-Bridge inverter is a multiple of $4N$ where N is the number of series connected NPC/H-Bridge inverter

And finally the superiority of the proposed phase shifted PWM control technique is validated by comparing its waveform spectra with that of the conventional phase shifted PWM technique and it was shown the inverter exhibits reduced harmonic content

8. References

Benslimane, T. (2007). Open Switch Faults Detection and Localization Algorithm for Three Phase Shunt Active Power Filter based on Two Level Voltage Source Inverter," *Electronics and Electrical Engineering Conference* 2(74), pp. 21- 24, ISSN 1392 -1215

Franquelo, L.G.; Rodriquez, J.; Leon, J.I.; Kouro, S.; Portillo, R. & Prats, M.A.M. (2008). The Age of Multilevel Converters Arrives, *IEEE Industrial Electronics Magazine*, pp. 28-39, ISSN 1932-4529

Gupta, R.; Ghosh, A. & Joshi, A. (2008). Switching Characteristics of Cascaded Multilevel Inverter Controlled Systems, *IEEE Transactions on Industrial Electronics*, vol.55, no.3, pp. 1047- 1058, ISSN: 0278-0046

Holmes, D.G. & McGrath, B.P. (2001). Opportunities for harmonic cancellation with carrier-based PWM for two - level and multilevel cascaded inverters, *IEEE Transaction on Industrial Applications*, vol. 37, no. 2, pp.547 - 582, ISSN 0093-9994, August 2002

Kouro, S.; Rebolledo J. & Rodriquez J. (2005). Reduced switching frequency modulation algorithm for high power multilevel inverters, *IEEE Transaction on Industrial Electronics*, vol.54, no.5, pp. 2894- 2901, ISBN 0-7803-9033-4, January 2006

Lai, J. S. & Peng, F. Z. (1995). Multilevel Converters - A New Breed of Power Converters," *IEEE Transactions on Industry Applications*, vol. 32, no. 3, pp. 509-517, ISBN 0-7803-3008-0 August 2002

Peng, F. Z.; Lai, J. S.; McKeever, J. W. & VanCoevering, J. (1996). A Multilevel Voltage-Source Inverter with Separate DC Sources for Static Var Generation, *IEEE Transactions on Industry Applications*, vol. 32, no. 5, pp. 1130-1138, Aug. 2002. ISBN: 0-7803-3008-0

Rodriguez, J.; Lai, J. S. & Peng, F. Z. (1995). Multilevel Inverters: Survey of Topologies, Controls, and Applications, *IEEE Transactions on Industry Applications*, vol. 49, no. 4, pp. 724-738, ISSN 0278-0046

Sinha, G. & Lipo, T. A. (1996). A Four Level Rectifier-Inverter System for Drive Applications, *IEEE-IAS Conference Record*, pp. 980-987, ISBN 0-7803-3544-9, August 2002

Tolbert, L. M.; Peng, F. Z. & Habetler, T. (1999). Multilevel Converters for Large Electric drives, *IEEE Trans. Ind. Application*, vol.35, pp. 36-44, ISSN 0093-9994, August 2002

Manjrekar, M.D. & Lipo, T.A. (1988). A hybrid multilevel inverter topology for drive applications, *IEEE APEC*, pp. 523-529, ISBN 0-7803-4340-9, August 2002

Manjrekar, M.D. & Lipo, T.A. (1998). A generalized structure of multilevel power converter, *Proc. IEEE PEDS*, 62-67, ISBN 0-7803-4879-6

Manjrekar, M.D. & Lipo, T.A. (2000). Hybrid multilevel power conversion system: A competitive solution for higher power application, IEEE *Transaction on Industry Application*, Vol. 36, no. 3, pp. 834-841, ISSN 0093-9994, August 2002

Corzine, K. & Familiant, Y. (2002). A new cascaded multilevel H- bridge drive, *IEEE Trans on Power Electronics*, Vol. 17, no.1, pp. 125-131, ISSN 0885-8993

Lund, R. et. al., (1999). Control strategies for hybrid seven level inverter, *EPE Conference Proceedings*

Sneineh, A.A.; Wang, M. W. & Tian, K. (2006). A new topology for capacitor clamp cascaded multilevel converters, *IEEE –IPEMC*, pp. 1-5, ISSN 1-4244-0448-7, February 2009

Park J. et. al., (2003). A new single phase 5 - level PWM inverter employing a deadbeat control scheme, *IEEE Transaction on Power Electronics*, vol.18, no.3, pp. 831-843, ISSN 0885-8993

Zhang, L.; Watkins, S.J. & Shepherd, W. (2002). Analysis and control of multilevel flying capacitor inverter, *IEEE CIEP*, pp. 66-71, ISBN 0-7803-7640-4, August 2003

Ding, K. et. al., (2004). A novel hybrid diode clamp cascade multilevel converter for high power application, *IEEE Transaction on Industry Application, 39th IAS Annual Meeting*, 820-827, ISBN 0-7803-8486-5

Duarte, J.L.; Jullicher, P.J.M.; Offringa L.J.J. & Groningen, W.D.H. (1997). Stability analysis of multilevel converters with imbricated cells, *EPE Conference Proceedings*, pp. 168-174.

Rojas, R. & Ohnishi, T. (1997). PWM control method with reduced of total capacitance required in a three- level inverter, *COBEP Conference Proceedings*, pp. 103-108

Wu, C.M.; Lau W.H. & Chung, H. (1999). A five-level neutral-point-clamped H-bridge PWM inverter with superior harmonics suppression: A theoretical analysis, *ISACS '99, proceedings of the 1999 IEEE international symposium,* vol. 5, pp.198-201

Cheng, Z. & Wu, B. (2007). A novel switching sequence design for five-Level NPC/H-Bridge inverters with improved output voltage spectrum and minimized device switching frequency, *IEEE Transactions on Power Electronics*, vol. 22 no.6, 2138 – 2145, ISSN 0885-8993

Naderi, R. & Rahmati, A. (2008). Phase shifted carrier PWM technique for general cascade inverters, *IEEE Transactions on power electronics*, vol. 23, no.3, pp.1256-1269, ISSN 0885-8993

Jinghua, Z. & Zhengxi, L. (2008). Research on hybrid modulation strategies based on general hybrid topology of multilevel inverter, *International symposium on power electronics and electric drives, automation and motion (SPEEDAM)*, pp. 784 – 788, ISBN 978-1-4244-1663-9

Holmes, D.G. & Thomas, A.L. (2003). *Pulse Width Modulation for Power Converters –principles and practices*, IEEE press series, A John Wiley & Sons inc. publication, ISBN: 978-0-471-20814-3, 445 Hoes Lane, Piscataway NJ 0885

Wanjekeche, T. Jimoh, A.A. & Nicolae, D.V. (2009). A Novel Multilevel 9- level inverter based on 3 – level NPC/H-Bridge topology for Photovoltaic application" *international review of electrical engineering,* Vol. 4, No.5, ISSN 1827- 6679

Wanjekeche, T. Nicolae, D.V. & Jimoh, A.A. (2009). A Cascaded NPC/H-bridge inverter with simplified control strategy and minimum component count, *IEEE – Africon*, pp. 1-6, ISBN 978-1-4244-3918-8

13

MATLAB: A Systems Tool for Design of Fuzzy LMI Controller in DC-DC Converters

Carlos Andrés Torres-Pinzón and Ramon Leyva
Department of Electronic, Electrical, and Automatic Control Engineering
Rovira i Virgili University
Tarragona, Spain

1. Introduction

DC-DC switching converters are devices usually used to adapt primary energy sources to the load requirements (Erickson & Macksimovic, 2001). These devices produce a regulated output voltage despite changes in the feed voltage or in the load current. There are three basic topologies of dc-dc converters, namely the buck, the boost and the buck-boost converter. The buck converter is used to reduce output voltage, while the boost converter increase the output voltage. In the buck-boost converter, the output voltage can be maintained either higher or lower than the source but in the opposite polarity. These basic converters consist of two reactive elements; namely, an inductor and a capacitor, besides a transistor and a diode to perform the commutation, the size of reactive elements are chosen to guarantee a low level of ripple and hence an averaged dynamical model behavior is a good approximation of the switched behavior.

In order to maintain a regulated output and to have a damped enough response some control loops are added to command the converter. The signal which drives the transistor used to be a squared, constant-period and high frequency signal.

The design of the control loops is commonly based on linearized dynamic models around equilibrium point of the converter (Erickson & Macksimovic, 2001). Nevertheless, commonly the averaged dynamical models of these plants are nonlinear and their linearization is non minimum phase. Therefore, using linear controllers can only ensures stability and dynamic performances around equilibrium point, and hence, instabilities or bad performances may appear when large signal perturbations occur. This fact has prompted several authors to apply nonlinear control methods to regulate switching converters.

Some of the first researches on nonlinear controller design for dc-dc converters can be found in the studies of (Sanders & Verghese, 1992) and (Kawasaki et al., 1995). These authors propose non-linear strategies based on Lyapunov functions, which allows the converter to ensure stability over a wide range of operating conditions. More recent studies are those of (Leyva et al., 2006) and (He & Luo, 2006) which derive robust non-linear controller for large-signal stability in dc-dc converters and present efficient implementations.

Furthermore, robust control approaches have been applied in dc-dc converters which take into account nonlinearities and uncertainties (Olalla et al., 2009; 2010).

Another promising nonlinear technique for controlling power converters is the model-based fuzzy control technique. The model-based fuzzy approaches begin by constructing the corresponding (T-S) Takagi–Sugeno fuzzy model representation of the nonlinear system (Tanaka & Wang, 2001). This T-S fuzzy representation is described by fuzzy rules IF-THEN which represent local linear input-output relations of the nonlinear plant. Once fuzzy rules are obtained with linear submodels, the control design is based on the technique known as Parallel Distributed Compensator (PDC), where each control rule is designed from the corresponding rule of the T-S fuzzy model (Korba et al., 2003). The stability analysis is carried out using Lyapunov functions on the closed-loop system. The Lyapunov functions are formulated into linear matrix inequalities (LMIs). This approach is fundamentally different from heuristics based fuzzy control (Tanaka & Wang, 2001) where the rules are based on heuristic knowledge. A model-based fuzzy control for dc-dc converters have been described in (Kuang et al., 2006), where the authors show a fuzzy law for the buck and ZVT buck converters. Other authors who applied this technique in dc-dc converters are (Lan & Tan, 2009)

Nowadays, thanks to the powerful computational tools and optimization techniques, many robust and fuzzy control designs based on LMIs can be readily solved. Matlab is a powerful tool in this process. The LMI Toolbox of Matlab is an efficient software tool based on interior point methods (Gahinet et al., 1995), which it can be used to numerically solve many LMI control problems that otherwise could not be solved since they have not an analytical solution. The main advantage of the LMI formulations is the ability to combine various design constraints and objectives in a numerically tractable manner.

This chapter presents a synthesis of LMI fuzzy controllers for dc-dc converters. The chapter describes in detail a compact control design methodology which takes into account constraints such as: control effort and the decay rate of state variables. The chapter is organized as follows: First, in section 2, we review the dynamics of a buck and a boost converter. In section 3, we introduce the T-S fuzzy representation of dc-dc converters, with their corresponding uncertainties. Aspects of the LMI fuzzy control design are explained in section 4. In section 5, we present two design examples to illustrate the advantages of the procedure. The first example shows the LMI controller of a buck converter, while in the second, we obtain an LMI Fuzzy controller for a boost converter working at different operating point. Both examples have been simulated with Matlab and the results are in perfect agreement with the design specification. Finally, we summarize the main ideas in section 6.

2. Modeling of DC-DC converters. A dynamical review

This section presents basic PWM converters and their state-space models which are used in the following sections. Specifically, the section describes the dynamic behavior of buck and boost converters.

2.1 Model of PWM buck converters

Fig.1 shows a dc-dc step-down (buck) converter, this power electronic stage reduces and regulates the output voltage from a primary voltage source.

The converter switch alternates periodically between two positions. Fig. 2 shows the circuits corresponding to on and off during intervals T_{on} and T_{off}, respectively. These positions are driven by the binary signal u whose values are $u = 1$ during T_{on} and $u = 0$ during T_{off}. The voltage reduction of this converter in steady state corresponds to the ratio T_{on}/T_s. We model the converter dynamics at each position by using the Kirchhoff laws. Its dynamic expressions

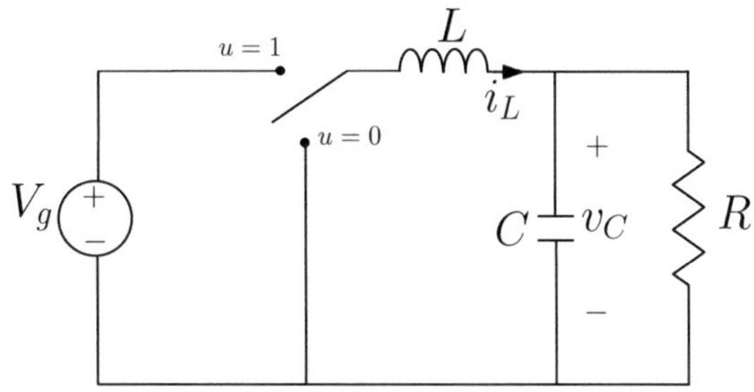

Fig. 1. Schematic circuit of a buck converter

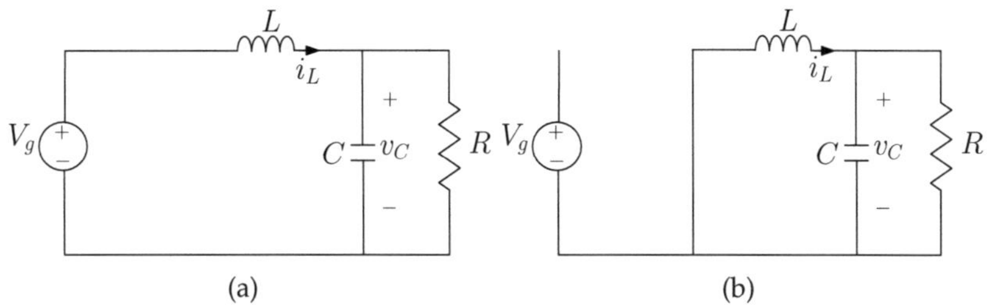

Fig. 2. Equivalent circuit during T_{on} (a) and T_{off} (b).

in state-space at each position correspond to

$$\begin{aligned} \dot{x}(t) &= A_{on}x(t) + B_{u_{on}} \;\; during\ T_{on} \\ \dot{x}(t) &= A_{off}x(t) + B_{u_{off}} \;\; during\ T_{off} \end{aligned} \tag{1}$$

being

$$A_{on} = A_{off} = \begin{bmatrix} 0 & -\frac{1}{L} \\ \frac{1}{C} & -\frac{1}{RC} \end{bmatrix} \; B_{u_{on}} = \begin{bmatrix} \frac{V_g}{L} \\ 0 \end{bmatrix} \; B_{u_{off}} = \begin{bmatrix} 0 \\ 0 \end{bmatrix} \tag{2}$$

and

$$x(t) = \left[i_L(t) \; v_C(t) \right]^T$$

where V_g is the feed voltage or primary source and v_C is the output voltage. R models the load, while L and C stand for inductance and capacitance values, respectively. The state vector $x(t)$ consists of the inductor current $i_L(t)$ and the capacitor voltage $v_C(t)$. A_{on} and $B_{u_{on}}$ are the transition matrix and input vector, respectively, during T_{on} and A_{off} and $B_{u_{off}}$ are the transition matrix and input vector during T_{off}.
The binary signal u turn on and off the switch which is controlled by means of a pulse width modulator (PWM), whose switching period T_s is equals to the sum of T_{on} and T_{off}. The PWM duty cycle is noted as d.
The expressions (1) and (2) can be written compactly in terms of the binary signal u as follows

$$\dot{x}(t) = A_{off}x(t) + B_{off} + \left(A_{on} - A_{off}\right) xu + \left(B_{on} - B_{off}\right) u \tag{3}$$

The converter operates in continuous conduction mode (CCM) when the inductor current i_L is ever greater than zero. We assume this operation mode then the switched model (3) can be approximated using state-space averaging method (Middlebrook & Cuk, 1976), replacing the binary signal u by its respective duty cycle d and the state variables by their averaged values during the switching period. The result of this averaging process can be written as

$$\dot{\overline{x}}(t) = A_{off}\overline{x}(t) + B_{off} + \left(A_{on} - A_{off}\right)\overline{x}d + \left(B_{on} - B_{off}\right)d \tag{4}$$

Thus, the averaged state vector $\overline{x}$ corresponds to $\overline{x} = \left(\overline{i}_L, \overline{v}_C\right)^T$; where $\overline{i}_L$ and $\overline{v}_C$ are the averaged values of inductor current and capacitor voltage during a switching period.
Usually the bilinear model (4) is linearized around equilibrium point by considering that the system variables consist of two components:

$$\begin{aligned} \overline{x}(t) &= X + \hat{x}(t) \\ d(t) &= D + \hat{d}(t) \end{aligned} \tag{5}$$

where X and D represent the equilibrium values and $\hat{x}$ and $\hat{d}$ are the perturbed values of the state and duty cycle. Therefore, equation (4) can be written as follows

$$\dot{\hat{x}} = \left[A_{off} + \left(A_{on} - A_{off}\right)D\right]\hat{x} + \left[\left(B_{on} - B_{off}\right) + \left(A_{on} - A_{off}\right)X\right]\hat{d} \tag{6}$$

The equilibrium state in the buck converter corresponds to

$$X = \begin{bmatrix} \frac{V_g D}{R} \\ V_g D \end{bmatrix} \tag{7}$$

Taking into account (2), we can model the buck converter as

$$\dot{\hat{x}}(t) = \begin{bmatrix} 0 & -\frac{1}{L} \\ \frac{1}{C} & -\frac{1}{RC} \end{bmatrix}\hat{x}(t) + \begin{bmatrix} \frac{V_g}{L} \\ 0 \end{bmatrix}\hat{d}(t) \tag{8}$$

The model can be augmented to ensure zero steady-state error of v_C by introducing a new state variable x_3 corresponding to

$$x_3(t) = \int \left(v_C(t) - V_{ref}\right)dt \tag{9}$$

where V_{ref} is the voltage reference.
Thus, the augmented model can be written as

$$\dot{\hat{x}}(t) = A\hat{x}(t) + B_u\hat{d}(t) \tag{10}$$

where

$$A = \begin{bmatrix} 0 & -\frac{1}{L} & 0 \\ \frac{1}{C} & -\frac{1}{RC} & 0 \\ 0 & 1 & 0 \end{bmatrix} \quad B_u = \begin{bmatrix} \frac{V_g}{L} \\ 0 \\ 0 \end{bmatrix} \tag{11}$$

In the next subsection, we develop the same procedure for the boost converter.

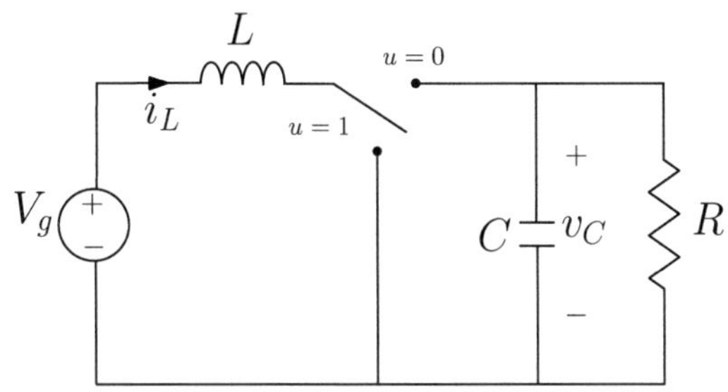

Fig. 3. Schematic circuit of a boost converter

2.2 Model of PWM boost converters

The Fig.3 shows the well-known boost converter (Erickson & Macksimovic, 2001), which is capable of regulating a dc output voltage when it is higher than the dc feed voltage.
The dynamic behavior of boost converter during T_{on} and T_{off} shown in the Fig. 4 can be written as

$$A_{on} = \begin{bmatrix} 0 & 0 \\ 0 & -\frac{1}{RC} \end{bmatrix} \; A_{off} = \begin{bmatrix} 0 & -\frac{1}{L} \\ \frac{1}{C} & -\frac{1}{RC} \end{bmatrix} \; B_{u_{on}} = B_{u_{off}} = \begin{bmatrix} \frac{V_g}{L} \\ 0 \end{bmatrix} \tag{12}$$

$$x(t) = \left[i_L(t) \; v_C(t) \right]^T$$

where $x(t)$ is the state-space vector composed of i_L, which represents the inductor current, and v_C, which represents the capacitor voltage. These variables are measurable and available for feedback purposes.

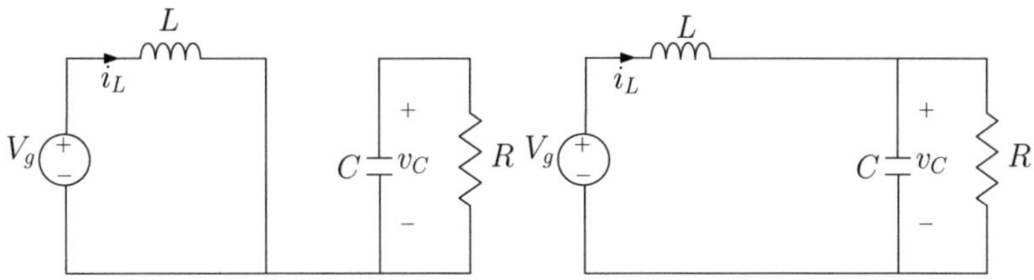

(a) (b)

Fig. 4. Equivalent circuit of boost converter for T_{on} (a) and T_{off} (b).

Therefore, according to (12), the equilibrium state in the boost converter corresponds to

$$X = \begin{bmatrix} \frac{V_g}{RD'^2} \\ \frac{V_g}{D'} \end{bmatrix} \tag{13}$$

where $D' = 1 - D$ is the complementary steady-state duty-cycle.
Since $A_{on} \neq A_{off}$, the average model of the boost converter is bilinear, which can be written as:

$$\dot{\hat{x}} = A\hat{x} + B_u(\hat{x})\hat{d} \tag{14}$$

being

$$A = \begin{bmatrix} 0 & -\frac{D'}{L} & 0 \\ \frac{D'}{C} & -\frac{1}{RC} & \\ 0 & 1 & 0 \end{bmatrix} \; B_u(\hat{x}) = \begin{bmatrix} \frac{V_g}{D'L} + \frac{\hat{v}_C(t)}{L} \\ -\frac{V_g}{(D'^2R)C} - \frac{\hat{i}_L(t)}{C} \\ 0 \end{bmatrix} \tag{15}$$

In next section, we describes the T-S fuzzy modeling method for the DC-DC converters.

3. Takagi-Sugeno fuzzy representation of DC-DC converters

There exist several approaches to fuzzy representation of dynamic systems, between them the most common are the Mamdani fuzzy representation (Driankov et al., 1993) and the T-S fuzzy representation (Tanaka & Wang, 2001). In the first representation, it is assumed that there is no model of the plant, while the second representation is always based on a dynamical model of the plant.
This T-S representation describes the dynamic system by means of an interpolation of linear submodels. The performance requirements of a linear model may be expressed by means of LMI.

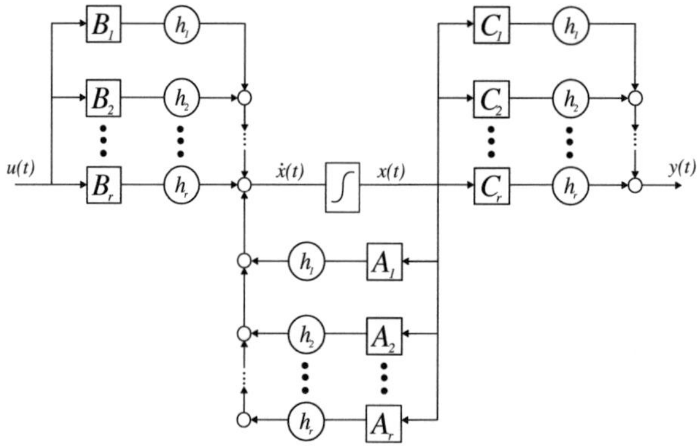

Fig. 5. Final structure of the Takagi-Sugeno fuzzy model

Figure 5 shows the model of the nonlinear plant as a group of linear models, which locally represent the relationship input-output system (Takagi & Sugeno, 1985), described of the form:

$$R_i : If \ \delta_1 \ is \ M_{i1} \ and \ldots and \ \delta_j \ is \ M_{ji} \ then$$
$$\dot{x}_i(t) = A_i x(t) + B_i u(t) \ i = 1, 2, \ldots r \tag{16}$$

Where r is the number of submodels, A_i is the system matrix of the i-th linear submodel, B_i is the input matrix, $x(t)$ is the global state-space vector, $u(t)$ is the input vector, M_{ji} are fuzzy sets, and δ_j is the scheduling vector (Korba et al., 2003).
Fuzzy sets M_{ji} have associated membership functions $\eta's$ which characterize the degree of membership (Takagi & Sugeno, 1985). The nonlinearities of the plant will determine the variables of the scheduling vector δ_i used in the antecedent, i.e., a correct election of scheduling variables will capture all the nonlinearities of the plant, in the case of the dc-dc converters the scheduling variables are function of the state variables $\delta(t) = \delta(x(t))$ (Korba et al., 2003; Tanaka & Wang, 2001). The entire fuzzy model of the plant corresponds to a fuzzy weighting of the locally valid linear submodel associated to each implications R_i (Korba et al., 2003), i.e.,

$$\dot{x}(t) = \frac{\sum_{i=1}^{r} w_i(\delta(t)) \left[A_i x(t) + B_i u(t)\right]}{\sum_{i=1}^{r} w_i(\delta(t))} \tag{17}$$

Weights $w_i(\delta(t))$ are zero or positive time-variant values and the sum of all the weights is positive.

$$\sum_{i=1}^{r} w_i(\delta(t)) > 0, \quad w_i(\delta(t)) \geq 0 \quad \forall \quad i = 1, 2, \ldots, r$$

We use the next normalized weight function $h_i(\delta(t))$ replacing $w_i(\delta(t))$,

$$h_i(\delta(t)) = \frac{w_i(\delta(t))}{\sum_{i=1}^{r} w_i(\delta(t))}$$

that fulfill with

$$0 \leq h_i(\delta(t)) \leq 1, \quad \sum_{i=1}^{r} h_i(\delta(t)) = 1 \tag{18}$$

Therefore the fuzzy model (17) can be rewritten as

$$\dot{x}(t) = \sum_{i=1}^{r} h_i(\delta(t)) \left[A_i x(t) + B_i u(t)\right] \tag{19}$$

The T-S fuzzy model of the buck converter is expressed by only one rule given that it is linear. The T-S fuzzy models of other topologies require several rules given that their dynamic behaviour is bilinear. The boost converter case is shown in the next subsection.

3.1 Takagi-Sugeno model of a boost converter

We propose the next boost converter fuzzy model consisting of the following four rules.

- $\mathbf{R}_1$:

$$\textbf{If } \hat{i}_L \; is \; i_{small} \; and \; \hat{v}_C \; is \; v_{small} \; \textbf{then}$$
$$\dot{\hat{x}}_1(t) = A_1\hat{x}(t) + B_1\hat{d}(t) \tag{20}$$

- $\mathbf{R}_2$:

$$\textbf{If } \hat{i}_L \; is \; i_{big} \; and \; \hat{v}_C \; is \; v_{small} \; \textbf{then}$$
$$\dot{\hat{x}}_2(t) = A_2\hat{x}(t) + B_2\hat{d}(t) \tag{21}$$

- $\mathbf{R}_3$:

$$\textbf{If } \hat{i}_L \; is \; i_{small} \; and \; \hat{v}_C \; is \; v_{big} \; \textbf{then}$$
$$\dot{\hat{x}}_3(t) = A_3\hat{x}(t) + B_3\hat{d}(t) \tag{22}$$

- $\mathbf{R}_4$:

$$\textbf{If } \hat{i}_L \; is \; i_{big} \; and \; \hat{v}_C \; is \; v_{big} \; \textbf{then}$$
$$\dot{\hat{x}}_4(t) = A_4\hat{x}(t) + B_4\hat{d}(t) \tag{23}$$

where

$$A_1 = A_2 = A_3 = A_4 = A = \begin{bmatrix} 0 & -\frac{D'}{L} & 0 \\ \frac{D'}{C} & -\frac{1}{RC} \\ 0 & 1 & 0 \end{bmatrix}$$

$$B_1 = \begin{bmatrix} \frac{V_g}{D'L} + \frac{v_{min}}{L} \\ -\frac{V_g}{(D'^2R)C} - \frac{i_{min}}{C} \\ 0 \end{bmatrix} \quad B_2 = \begin{bmatrix} \frac{V_g}{D'L} + \frac{v_{min}}{L} \\ -\frac{V_g}{(D'^2R)C} - \frac{i_{max}}{C} \\ 0 \end{bmatrix}$$
$$B_3 = \begin{bmatrix} \frac{V_g}{D'L} + \frac{v_{max}}{L} \\ -\frac{V_g}{(D'^2R)C} - \frac{i_{min}}{C} \\ 0 \end{bmatrix} \quad B_4 = \begin{bmatrix} \frac{V_g}{D'L} + \frac{v_{max}}{L} \\ -\frac{V_g}{(D'^2R)C} - \frac{i_{max}}{C} \\ 0 \end{bmatrix} \tag{24}$$

being the membership function of the fuzzy sets i_{small}, i_{big}, v_{small} and v_{big} the following ones,

$$\begin{aligned} \eta_{i_{small}}(\hat{i}_L) &= \frac{i_{max}-\hat{i}_L}{i_{max}-i_{min}} \quad \eta_{i_{big}}(\hat{i}_L) = 1 - \eta_{i_{small}}(\hat{i}_L) \\ \eta_{v_{small}}(\hat{v}_C) &= \frac{v_{max}-\hat{v}_C}{v_{max}-v_{min}} \quad \eta_{v_{big}}(\hat{v}_C) = 1 - \eta_{v_{small}}(\hat{v}_C) \end{aligned} \tag{25}$$

Note that (20) correspond to the dynamic behavior around (i_{min}, v_{min}) values, and (21)-(23) describe the local behavior around the other interval bounds. Thus, the normalized weight functions are

$$\begin{aligned} h_1(\hat{i}_L, \hat{v}_C) &= \eta_{i_{small}} \cdot \eta_{v_{small}} \quad h_3(\hat{i}_L, \hat{v}_C) = \eta_{i_{small}} \cdot \eta_{v_{big}} \\ h_2(\hat{i}_L, \hat{v}_C) &= \eta_{i_{big}} \cdot \eta_{v_{small}} \quad h_4(\hat{i}_L, \hat{v}_C) = \eta_{i_{big}} \cdot \eta_{v_{big}} \end{aligned} \tag{26}$$

therefore the entire fuzzy converter model corresponds to

$$\dot{\hat{x}}(t) = \sum_{i=1}^{r} h_i\left(\hat{i}_L, \hat{v}_C\right)\left(A_i\hat{x}(t) + B_i\hat{d}(t)\right) \tag{27}$$

since $\sum_{i=0}^{r} h_i = 1$ and $A_i = A$ then

$$\dot{\hat{x}}(t) = A\hat{x}(t) + \left(\sum_{i=1}^{r} h_i(\hat{i}_L, \hat{v}_C)B_i\right)\hat{d}(t) \tag{28}$$

and it is worth to remark that (28) corresponds with the bilinear model (14) inside the polytope region $[\hat{i}_{min}, \hat{i}_{max}] \times [\hat{v}_{min}, \hat{v}_{max}]$. This operating space is depicted in Fig. (6).

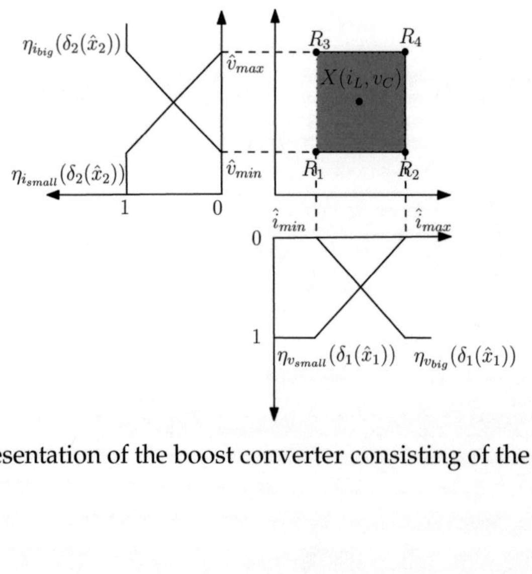

Fig. 6. *T-S* Fuzzy representation of the boost converter consisting of the 4 rules

The approach shown here can be easily adapted for the buck-boost converter, such as shown in (Torres-Pinzón & Leyva, 2009).
In next section, we explain a control strategy where the law consist of a normalized weight sum of linear feedback gains at each interval limit, which takes into account constraints such as: control effort and the decay rate of state variables.

4. LMI performance requeriments

This section presents the concept and basic procedure of the parallel distributed compensation (PDC) technique and the definitions and LMI constraints used in the synthesis of control. First, we introduce the basic concept of Lyapunov-based stability. Then, we discuss on stability concepts for fuzzy systems in form of LMI. These concepts will be applied in Section 5 to find a LMI fuzzy controller for the buck and boost converters. It can be observed that since the buck converter dynamics is linear, we obtain a linear control law for this converter that is a fuzzy controller with only one rule.

4.1 Quadratic stability conditions

Given the linear dynamic system

$$\dot{x}(t) = Ax(t) \tag{29}$$

the existence of a quadratic function of the form

$$V(x(t)) = x(t)^T \mathbf{P} x(t) \tag{30}$$

that satisfies $\dot{V}(x(t)) < 0$, is a necessary and sufficient condition to ensure that the system is asymptotically stable, i.e., all trajectories converge to zero. Where $\mathbf{P}$ is a symmetric positive definite matrix $\in \mathbb{R}^{n \times n}$. Since the expression $\dot{V}(x(t)) < 0$ has form quadratic, this condition is referred as quadratic stability, and it can be rewritten as follows

$$\dot{V}(x(t)) = x(t)^T \left(A^T \mathbf{P} + \mathbf{P} A\right) x(t) \tag{31}$$

Thus, the system is asymptotically stable if and only if there exist a symmetric matrix $\mathbf{P}$ such that

$$A^T \mathbf{P} + \mathbf{P} A < 0 \tag{32}$$

The main interest of the quadratic stability condition is that by means of a convex envelope and numerically simple test, it is possible to conclude about the overall stability of a dynamics system.
For an in-deep explanation on quadratic stability see (Boyd et al., 1994).
Based on the results (32), the following subsection present some basic results on the stability of fuzzy control systems.

4.2 Performance constraints

In this subsection, we review in detail the Parallel Distributed Compensation (PDC) technique (Tanaka & Wang, 2001). In such fuzzy technique, each control rule is associated with the corresponding rule of the fuzzy model, thus the controller rules are as follows,

$$R_i : \textbf{If} \;\; \delta_1 \;\; is \;\; M_{i1} \;\; and \ldots and \;\; \delta_j \;\; is \;\; M_{ji} \;\; \textbf{Then}$$

$$u(t) = -\mathbf{F}_i x(t) \;\; i = 1, \ldots, r \tag{33}$$

where $\mathbf{F}_i$ are lineal feedback gain vectors associate with each rule. And the overall fuzzy controller is represented as

$$u(t) = -\frac{\sum_{i=1}^{r} w_i \mathbf{F}_i x(t)}{\sum_{i=1}^{r} w_i} = -\sum_{i=1}^{r} h_i \mathbf{F}_i x(t) \tag{34}$$

Substituting the control law (34) in the fuzzy model (19), the closed loop system dynamics is given by

$$\dot{x}(t) = \sum_{i=1}^{r} \sum_{j=1}^{r} h_i h_j \left(A_i - B_i \mathbf{F}_j \right) x(t) \tag{35}$$

In order to select the suitable feedback gain vectors $\mathbf{F}_i$, we impose Lyapunov stability constraints and performance constraints on decay rate and control effort in form of LMIs. Therefore, the sufficient conditions for the stability of the open-loop fuzzy system (19) and closed-loop one (35) are obtained using quadratic stability condition of the equation (32). These conditions, derived from (Tanaka & Wang, 2001), it can be expressed by means of the next propositions.

Proposition 4.1. *The equilibrium of the continuous fuzzy system* (19) *with* $u(t) = 0$ *is asymptotically stable if there exists a common positive definite matrix* $\mathbf{P}$ *such that*

$$\begin{array}{c} A_i^T \mathbf{P} + \mathbf{P} A_i < 0, \ i=1,\ldots,r \\ \mathbf{P} > 0 \end{array} \tag{36}$$

that is, a common P has to exist for all subsystems

where A_i are system matrices of the linear submodels defined in the previous section.

Proposition 4.2. *The equilibrium of the continuous fuzzy control system described by* (35) *is asymptotically stable if there exists a common positive definite matrix* $\mathbf{P}$ *such that*

$$\begin{array}{c} \left(A_i - B_i \mathbf{F}_j \right)^T \mathbf{P} + \mathbf{P} \left(A_i - B_i \mathbf{F}_j \right) < 0, \ j > i \\ \mathbf{P} > 0 \end{array} \tag{37}$$

Note that the condition (37) is not linear because involves the multiplication of the variables $\mathbf{P}$ and $\mathbf{F}_j'$s. Thus, in order to rewrite (37) in a linear manner, we multiply the inequality (37) on the left and right by $\mathbf{P}^{-1}$, and we define a new variable $\mathbf{W} = \mathbf{P}^{-1}$, then proposition 4.2 can be rewritten as follows.

Proposition 4.3. *The continuous fuzzy system* (35) *is quadratically stable for some feedback gain* $\mathbf{F}_i$ *if there exists a common positive definite matrix* $\mathbf{W}$ *such that*

$$\begin{array}{lr} A_i \mathbf{W} + \mathbf{W} A_i^T - B_i \mathbf{Y}_i - \mathbf{Y}_i^T B_i^T < 0, & i = 1, \ldots r \\ A_i \mathbf{W} + \mathbf{W} A_i^T + A_j \mathbf{W} + \mathbf{W} A_j^T - B_i \mathbf{Y}_j - \mathbf{Y}_j^T B_i^T - B_j \mathbf{Y}_i - \mathbf{Y}_i^T B_j^T \leq 0, & i < j \leq r \end{array} \tag{38}$$

being $\mathbf{Y}_i = \mathbf{F}_i \mathbf{W}$ *so that for* $\mathbf{W} > 0$, *we have* $\mathbf{F}_i = \mathbf{Y}_i \mathbf{W}^{-1}$

Using these LMI conditions, we establish the first controller design constraint, next we describe the second design restriction.
As dc-dc converter control signal corresponds to the incremental duty cycle, then the control signal is bounded in the interval $[-D, 1-D]$. In order to satisfy with this limitation, we constrain the control signal by the next proposition.
The satisfaction of the next proposition will assure that control signal $d(t)$ is inside the interval $[-D, 1-D]$ from starting condition $x(0)$ to the equilibrium point.

Proposition 4.4. *Assume that initial condition x(0) is known. The constraint $\|d(t)\|_2 \leq \mu$ is enforced at all times $t \geq 0$ if the LMIs* (39) *hold*

$$\begin{bmatrix} 1 & x(0)^T \\ x(0) & \mathbf{W} \end{bmatrix} \geq 0, \qquad \begin{bmatrix} \mathbf{W} & \mathbf{Y}_i^T \\ \mathbf{Y}_i & \mu^2\mathbf{I} \end{bmatrix} \geq 0 \tag{39}$$

where $\mathbf{W} = \mathbf{P}^{-1}$ *and* $\mathbf{Y}_i = \mathbf{F}_i\mathbf{W}$.

Also, it will be desirable a suitable transient performances of the closed loop system. The entire fuzzy system transient performances depends on the localizations of the poles of its linear systems corresponding to each rule. In our case, this poles are expressed in terms of decay rate introduced via exponential stability, which it can be seen as a special case of pole-placement on the closed-loop system.
Consequently, we impose that this poles must be inside a predetermined region as the one pictured in Fig. 7. Therefore, the design process will add the next proposition, adapted from (Tanaka & Wang, 2001).

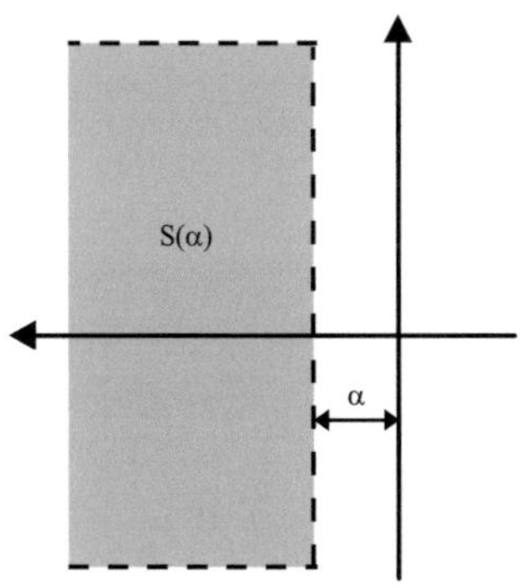

Fig. 7. $S(\alpha)$ region

Proposition 4.5. *The eigenvalues of $\left(A_i - B_iF_j\right)$ in each linear fuzzy system are inside the region* $\mathbf{S}(\alpha)$ *if there exist a common positive definite matrix* $\mathbf{W}$ *such that*

$$\begin{aligned} &A_i\mathbf{W} + \mathbf{W}A_i^T - B_i\mathbf{Y}_i - \mathbf{Y}_i^T B_i^T + 2\alpha\mathbf{W} < 0, \qquad i = 1, \ldots r \\ &A_i\mathbf{W} + \mathbf{W}A_i^T + A_j\mathbf{W} + \mathbf{W}A_j^T - B_i\mathbf{Y}_j - \mathbf{Y}_j^T B_i^T - B_j\mathbf{Y}_i - \mathbf{Y}_i^T B_j^T + 4\alpha\mathbf{W} \leq 0, \; i < j \leq r \end{aligned} \tag{40}$$

being $\mathbf{F}_i = \mathbf{Y}_i\mathbf{W}^{-1}$.

Between all the feasible set of feedback gains, the proposed algorithm finds the largest possible decay rate (α) of the state variables, satisfying the previous LMIs. Hence, the design procedure of the LMI Fuzzy control can be formulated by the following optimization algorithm.

$$\begin{array}{ll} max & \alpha \ subject \ to \\ \mathbf{W}, \mathbf{Y}_i & \\ i = 1, \ldots, r & (39), \ and \ (40) \end{array} \tag{41}$$

The solution of this optimization program with its corresponding LMIs will provide the set of feedback gains $F_{LMI-Fuzzy} = \{F_1, F_2, F_3, F_4\}$. The solution of this algorithm can be carried out by means of GEVP function in MATLAB LMI toolbox.

5. Design examples

This section shows two examples of LMI-based control applied to dc-dc converters. The first case presents the control design of a step-down converter working around equilibrium point. This example takes into account the same LMIs constraints of the algorithm (41). The second example proposes an LMI Fuzzy control for a step-up converter, allowing working at different operating point. Both examples are tested during a start-up and under load disturbances.

5.1 LMI control of a Buck converter

In this first example, we presents an LMI control approach applied to the problem of regulating the output voltage of the buck converter. The values of the converter parameter set are shown in Table 1. The nominal load of the converter is equal to 10 Ω, while supply voltage equal to 48 V. Consequently, the equilibrium point satisfying (7) is equal to $[i_L \ v_C] = [4.8 \ 24]^T$. The simulation prototype is designed to process less than 60 W corresponding to a load resistance $R = 10 \ \Omega$. The inductance and capacitance values and switching frequency have been selected to ensure low ripple level. In order to limit the control signal in the range $[-D, 1-D]$, μ is set to 1500, since simulations show no saturation of the duty-cycle.

V_g	$48V$
$v_C(V_{ref})$	$24V$
L	$200 \ \mu H$
C	$200 \ \mu F$
R	$10 \ \Omega$
D'	$0.5 \ \Omega$
T_s	$10 \ \mu$ s

Table 1. Buck converter parameters

Once the parameters values of the converter and controller have been defined, the next step is to obtain the feedback gain vector. Thus, solving the optimization algorithm (41) for the system (11), by means of the LMI toolbox of MATLAB (Gahinet et al., 1995), the state-feedback controller obtained for the buck converter is

$$\mathbf{F}_{Buck} = \begin{bmatrix} 0.0963 \ 0.1133 \ -319.8021 \end{bmatrix}$$

with a decay rate of $\alpha = 3254$, which assures a maximum constant time of $1/3254$, and consequently a maximum settling time of $4 * (1/3254)$. In order to verify the behavior of

the buck converter under the control law described above, numerical simulations have been carried out in MATLAB/Simulink, as shown in Fig.8.
Fig. 9 shows the transient simulation of the state variables and duty-cycle during start-up, in fact, represents a large signal perturbation around the equilibrium point of the state variables. It is remark that the settling time is smaller than 1.2 *ms*, and agrees with the decay rate obtained.

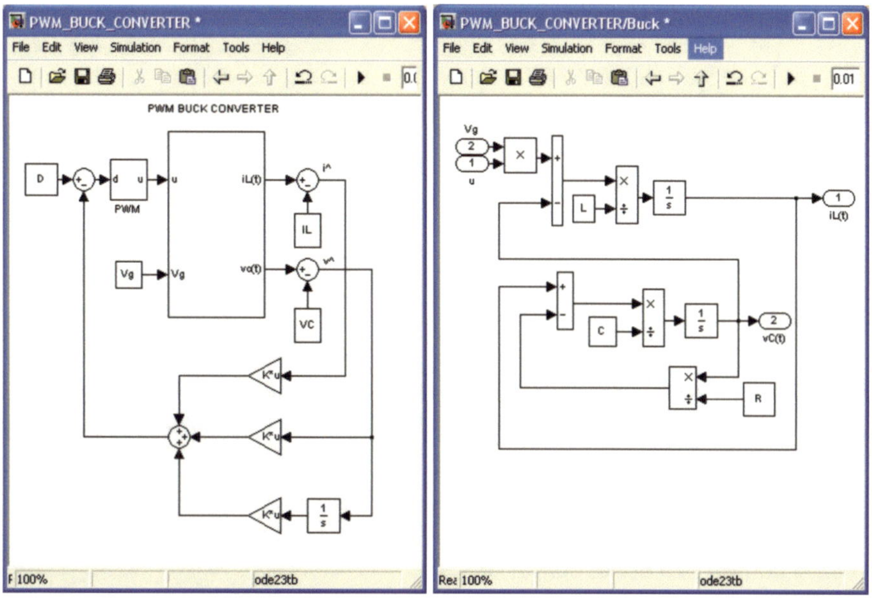

(a) (b)

Fig. 8. Simulink diagram of a buck converter with state-feedback regulation. (a) Implementation diagram in MATLAB/Simulink. (b) Simulink model of the buck converter.

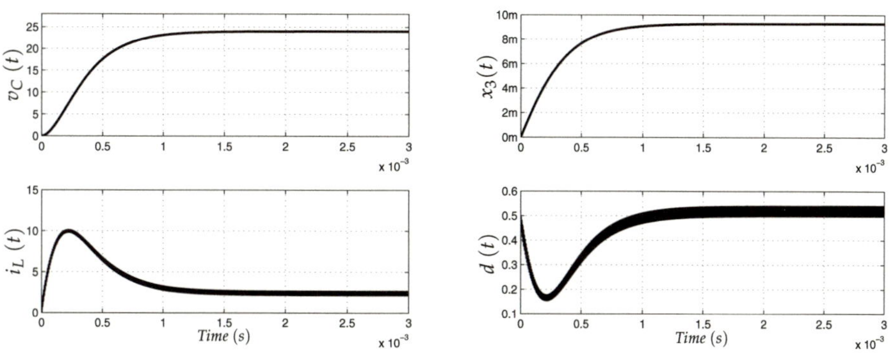

(a) (b)

Fig. 9. Simulated response of the dc-dc buck converter during start-up. (a) Inductor current $i_L(t)$ and capacitor voltage $v_C(t)$. (b) Steady-state error $x_3(t)$ and duty-cycle $d(t)$.

Fig. 10 illustrates the system responses for step changes in the load current from 2.4 A to 4.4 A at $2ms$ and then returns to 2.4 A at $8ms$. It can be observed that the controller regulates the output voltage v_C smoothly at 24 V after a short transient period. It can also be observed that the duty-cycle does not exceed the limits of interval $[-D, 1-D]$. In the next subsection, the

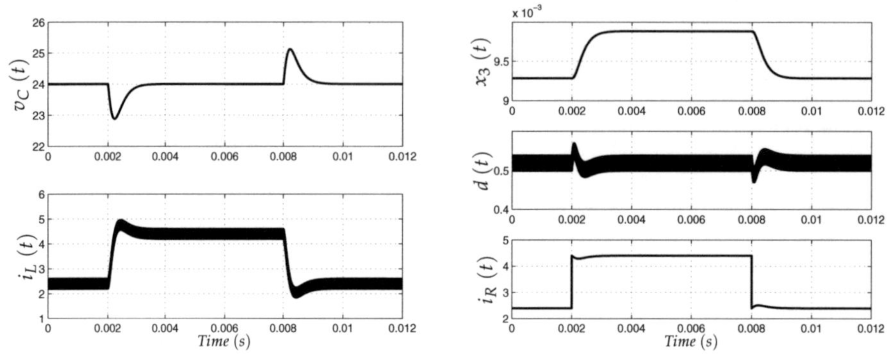

(a) (b)

Fig. 10. Simulated response of the buck converter under a load step transient of 2 A.
(a) Inductor current $i_L(t)$ and capacitor voltage $v_C(t)$. (b) Steady-state error $x_3(t)$, duty-cycle $d(t)$ and load current i_R.

LMI Fuzzy controller design for a boost converter is described.

5.2 LMI Fuzyy control of a boost converter

In this subsection, we present the results of the design of the LMI Fuzzy controller applied to fuzzy model of the boost converter shown in subsection 3.1, whose parameter set is shown in Table 2. Consequently, the equilibrium state is given by $[\,i_L \; v_C\,] = [4.8 \; 24]^T$.

The design of the control law consists of solving the optimization algorithm (41) for the

V_g	$12V$
$v_C(V_{ref})$	$24V$
L	$300\ \mu H$
C	$300\ \mu F$
R	$10\ \Omega$
D'	$0.5\ \Omega$
T_s	$20\ \mu$ s

Table 2. Boost converter parameters

four linear submodels of the fuzzy model. This submodels correspond to the vertices of the polytopic model of the boost converter in the region defined in Fig 6. Therefore, in order to ensure stability within the polytopic region during a start-up transition and disturbance, the polytopic region should be $[\hat{i}_{min} = 0, \hat{i}_{max} = 20] \times [\hat{v}_{min} = 0, \hat{v}_{max} = 10]$. To demonstrate the advantage of this Fuzzy approach, we will compare the LMI Fuzzy control with a LMI linear Control.

As in the previous subsection, the simulation prototype is designed to process less than 60 W, as well as the inductance and capacitance values and switching frequency are selected to ensure low ripple level. To maintain the control signal under the threshold limit value, μ is set to 350, for the two control designs. So, according to the optimization algorithm (41), the fuzzy state-feedback gains obtained via LMI Toolbox of Matlab are given follows:

$$\mathbf{F}_1 = \begin{bmatrix} 0.1737 \; 0.1019 \; -183.4507 \end{bmatrix}$$

$$\mathbf{F}_2 = \begin{bmatrix} 0.2737 \; 0.1871 \; -313.9974 \end{bmatrix}$$

$$\mathbf{F}_3 = \begin{bmatrix} 0.1814 \; 0.1157 \; -199.8689 \end{bmatrix}$$

$$\mathbf{F}_4 = \begin{bmatrix} 0.1877 \; 0.1149 \; -202.6875 \end{bmatrix}$$

The decay rate value obtained is 878, which assures a maximum settling time of $4 * (1/878)$. As mentioned above, to contrast the performance and robustness of the proposed control, we compare the LMI Fuzzy control law with a LMI linear law, which it presents the same optimization criteria (41). The resulting controller gain vector is

$$\mathbf{F}_{Boost} = \begin{bmatrix} 0.0895 \; 0.1018 \; -159.9759 \end{bmatrix}$$

with a decay rate of 1950, that assures a maximum settling time of $4 * (1/1950)$.
It can be observed that there exist differences between the decay rate obtained above. Next, we will show its properties during a start-up and in presence of load disturbances. Fig. 11 shows the simulation schematic of the boost converter with the LMI Fuzzy controller implemented in MATLAB/Simulink. Note that the MATLAB Function block is used to run the LMI Fuzzy

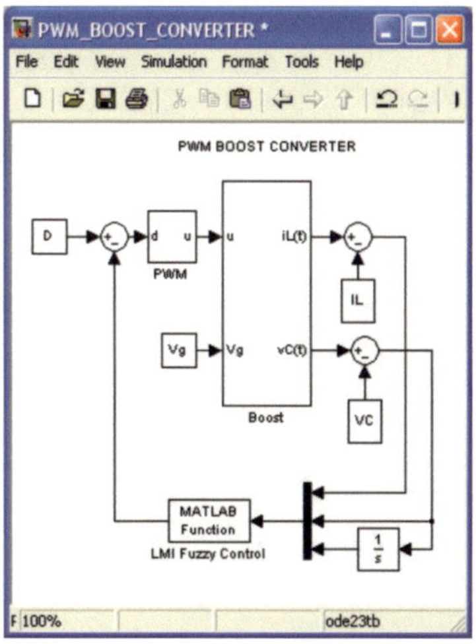

Fig. 11. Simulink implementation diagram of a boost converter with LMI Fuzzy regulation.

control on Simulink, which it is written by means of a code in the MATLAB Editor.
Fig. 12 illustrates the transient simulation of the boost converter during start-up. The waveforms depicted in the figure are the inductor current i_L, capacitor voltage v_C, steady-state error x_3 and duty-cycle $d(t)$. The response of the LMI linear contoller corresponds to dashed line, while the waveform of the LMI Fuzzy controller has been drawn with solid line. In Fig. 13, the converter reacts to large load disturbances. In this simulation the load current is initially 2.4 A. At $t = 2$ ms, the current changes to 6.4 A, and at $t = 8$ ms, it returns to its initial

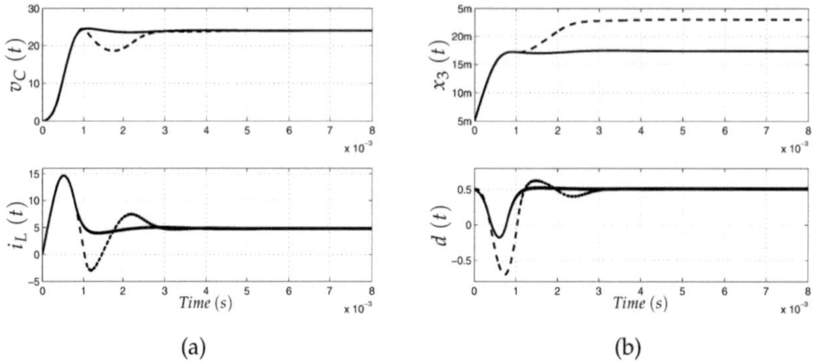

Fig. 12. Simulated responses of the dc-dc boost converter during start-up linearly controlled (dished) and fuzzy controlled (solid). (a) Inductor current $i_L(t)$ and capacitor voltage $v_C(t)$. (b) Steady-state error $x_3(t)$ and duty-cycle $d(t)$.

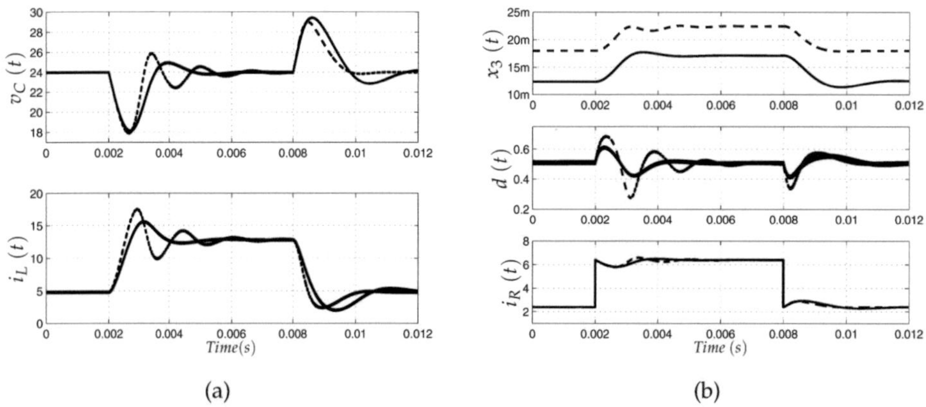

Fig. 13. Simulated responses of the boost converter under a load step transient of 4 A linearly controlled (dished) and fuzzy controlled (solid).
(a) Inductor current $i_L(t)$ and capacitor voltage $v_C(t)$. (b) Steady-state error $x_3(t)$, duty-cycle $d(t)$ and load current i_R.

value. It is worth noting that state variables and duty-cycle are better with the LMI Fuzzy controller (dashed line), since it maintains its stability properties under large disturbances, and despite that it is slower. The main advantage of this controller, is that it ensures robust stability in broad range of operation.

6. Conclusions

This chapter presents a LMI fuzzy controller design for dc-dc converters using MATLAB. The design methodology has been applied to a buck converter and to a boost converter where the control optimizes the decay rate of the state variables subject to a bound in the control effort. The methodology allows us to take into account the bilinear nature of the boost converter dynamics. We express the control objective and the bound as LMIs. The set of LMIs, which is solved by means of LMI Toolbox, provides the feedback gains.

The dynamical performances of LMI fuzzy controlled boost converter have been compared those of a linear-controlled boost considering the same design constraint. We have verified the closed-loop dynamic behavior using Simulink/MATLAB. The plots exhibit a perfect agreement with the design specifications. This design procedure ensures the stability of the converter in a wide region. On the contrary, a linear-controlled converter deteriorates its performances out of the operating point. The approach can be extended to more complex converters or other types of bilinear plants.

7. Acknowledgment

This work was partially supported by the Spanish Ministerio de Educación y Ciencia under grant DPI2010-16481

8. References

Boyd, S.; El Ghaoui, L.; Feron, E. & Balakrishnan, V. (1994). *Linear Matrix Inequalities in Systems and Control Theory*, ser. Studies in Applied and Numerical Mathematics, Philadelphia,PA:SIAM

Chilali, M. & Gahinet, P. (1996). H_∞ Design with Pole Placement Constraints: An LMI Approach, *IEEE Trans. on Autom. Control.*, Vol. 42, No.3, (358-367)

Driankov, D.; Hellendoorn, H. & Reinfrank, M. (1993). *An introduction to Fuzzy Control*, Springer-Verlag, Germanny

Erickson, R.W. & Macksimovic, D. (2001). *Fundamental of Power Electronics, Second ed.*, 920 pages, Kluwer Academic Publisher, ISBN 0-7923-7270-0, USA

Gahinet, P.; Nemirovski, A.; Laub, A.J.; & Chilali, M. (1995). LMI Control Toolbox for Use With Matlab, *The MathWorks, Inc*, Vol. 3, No.1, (75-85)

He, Y. & Luo, F.L. (2006). Sliding-mode control for dc-dc converters with constant switching frequency, *IEE Proc.-Control Theory Appl.*, Vol. 153, No.1, (37-45)

Kawasaki, N.; Nomura, H. & Masuhiro, M. (1995). A new control law of bilinear DC-DC converters developed by direct application of Lyapunov, *IEEE Trans. Power Electron.*, Vol. 10, No.1, (318-325)

Korba, P.; Babuska, R.; Verbruggen, H.B. & Frank, P.M. (2003). Fuzzy Gain Scheduling: Controller and Observer Design Based on Lyapunov Method and Convex Optimization, *IEEE Trans. on Fuzzy Syst.*, Vol. 11, No.3, (285-298)

Kuang-Yow, L.; Jeih-Jang, L. & Chien-Yu, H. (2006). LMI-Based Integral Fuzzy Control of DC-DC Converters, *IEEE Trans. on Fuzzy Syst.*, Vol. 14, No.1, (71-80)

Lan, H.K & Tan, S.C (2009). Stability analysis of fuzzy-model-based control systems: application on regulation of switching dc-dc converter, *IET Control Theory and Appl.*, Vol. 3, No.8, (1093-1106)

Leyva, R.;Cid-Pastor, A.; Alonso, C.; Queinnec, I.; Tarbouriech, S. & Martínez-Salamero, L. (2001). Passivity-based integral control of a boost converter for large-signal stability, *IEE Proc.-Control Theory Appl.*, Vol. 153, No.2, (March) (139-146)

Middlebrook, R. & Cuk, S. (1976). A general unified approach to modeling switching-converter power stages, *in IEEE Power Electron. Special. Conf.*, (June)(18-34), Cleveland

Olalla, C.;Leyva, R.; El Aroudi, A. & Queinnec, I. (2009). Robust LQR Control for PWM Converters: An LMI Approach, *IEEE Trans. Ind. Electron.*, Vol. 56, No.7, (July) (2548-2558)

Olalla, C.;Leyva, R.; El Aroudi, A.; Garcés, P. & Queinnec, I. (2009). Robust LQR Control for PWM Converters: An LMI Approach, *IET Power Electron.*, Vol. 3, No.1, (75-85)

Sanders, S.R. & Verghese G.C.(1992). Lyapunov-based control for switched power converters, *IEEE Trans. Power Electron.*, Vol. 7, No.3, (17-24)

Takagi, T. & Sugeno, M. (1985). Fuzzy Identification of Systems and Its Applications to Modeling and Control, *IEEE Trans. on Syst., Man, and Cyber.*, Vol. 15, No.1, (January) (116-132)

Tanaka, K. & Wang, H.O. (2001). *Fuzzy Control Systems Design an Analysis*, Jhon Wiley & Sons, INC, New York

Torres-Pinzón, C.A. & Leyva, R. (2009). Fuzzy Control in DC-DC Converters: an LMI Approach,*in Proc. of the IEEE Annual Conf. on Ind. Electron., IECON'09*, (November)(510-515),Porto

14

MATLAB as Interface for Intelligent Digital Control of Dynamic Systems

João Viana da Fonseca Neto and Gustavo Araújo de Andrade
Federal University of Maranhão
Department of Electrical Engineering
Control Process Laboratory
Brazil

1. Introduction

Digital control systems have shown to the developers the features and their applications in a wide variety of plants. Tools that help the developer to promote a design methodology that is efficient and at the same time reliable, has gained ground in the market and attributions of control engineers. Tasks such as data acquisition system, control design and system implementation can become arduous if there are prerequisites for sensitivity and complexity of the controller for these tasks take time and performance of the developer which will entail additional costs to the final product. These tools provide the designer with the scientist and the smooth progress of their work role has important and necessary in many areas will be subject to this study. The integration of technologies to speed and lower costs as it relates the design phases can be observed with a proper exploration of the work tool and how knowledge of plant and control techniques that meet in a less costly the goal of being achieved whatever the difficulties of the project. The choice of a tool properly can be a deciding factor in a world where time and efficiency of processes is become extremely important because the applications are growing in scale and more complex, Moudgalya (2007), Andrade (2010).
Intelligent Systems has considerable performance in accordance with plans and small large and its design encompasses more robustness to the system as well as ease of expansion. The mathematical simplicity that fuzzy systems can present and adaptability of neural networks are adopted more frequently in the academy and the industry.
An approach of intelligent systems requires a systematic and efficient operation because one works with a data stream that needs a consistency so that the iterations will be where made all the decisions may have minimal accounting. A tool that can assist in the design of this requirement is most welcome in engineering projects for control system parameter becomes constant with time,S. Sumathi (2010).
The *MATLAB* software designers can provide facilities for development and interface with different technologies for data acquisition through its communication protocols such as Serial Interface, OPC, Ethernet and others. This work is mainly focused on a methodology design of digital control systems using as development platform and implementing in software *MATLAB*.

2. Digital control and Data Acquisition Systems

The Data Acquisition System (DAS)is a key part to the project and implementation of digital controllers for the nature of digital systems is based on sampled analog system, ie played by the analog system a digital computer and its Since the interface Digital - Analog system performs the control actions . The Figure 1 shows a diagram of a system digital control and its special features such as the pool Analog - Digital and Digital - Analogue, responsible for interfacing with the analog environment.

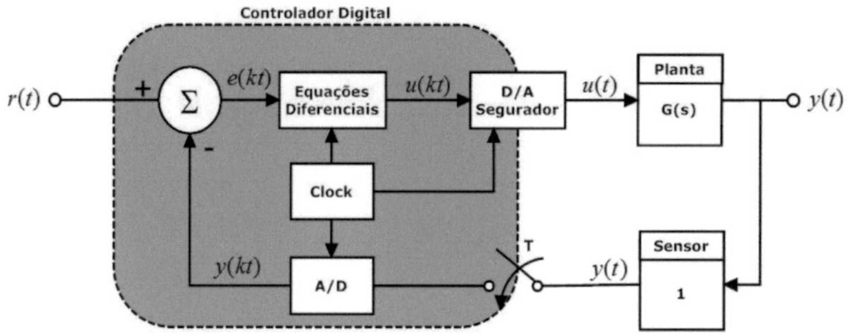

Fig. 1. Digital Control System Diagram

A digital control system is obtained from the reconstruction of analog signal contained in nature. This reconstruction is related mainly with the data acquisition system which is also involved modeling digital control system. Figure 2 illustrates the design of a system basic data acquisition of an industry.

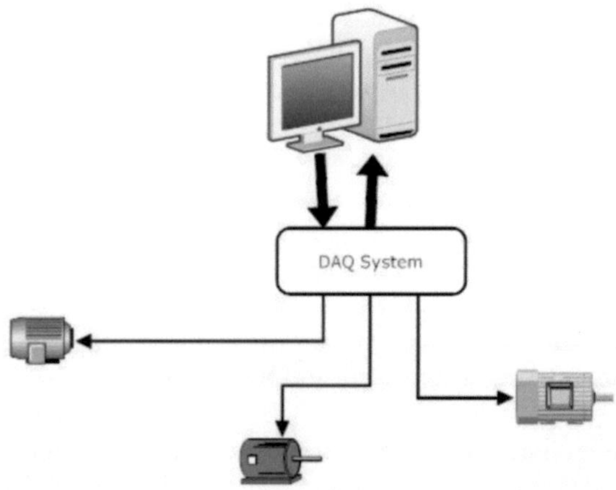

Fig. 2. DAQ System Diagram

The modern control concepts applied in the contemporary industry may be appropriated to the development of academic research activities. The introduction of a methodology parameters that specify and clarify the implementation of monitoring and control of dynamic systems.

In Figures 1 and 2 are shown at different levels, primary architectures to industrial control systems. In Figure 1 is exposed a system with minimal complexity, type SISO (Single Input - Single Output) that can occur in *n* times or a more complex system can be mapped as a black box system, where internal states of the process do not matter. In Figure 2 is noted, however, approach of discrete variables on the process that encompasses the entire plant worrying about sub stages.

In this work is explored a way to conceptualize these types of sound architecture in a way such that the system can be modeled and represented whatever its complexity, thus using a powerful tool when it comes to development concepts and analysis.

3. Discrete models of dynamic systems

To be held control of dynamic systems, it is necessary in this environment, the perception of some step that must be met for a procedure with minimum guarantees for the project. In the following sections will show important steps as ways to implement them by programming or graphical interface in *MATLAB*, Moudgalya (2007) and Charles L. Philips (1995).

3.1 Dynamic system identification tools

The identification of dynamic systems can be facilitated so as to make procedures the control design more efficient from the standpoint of technical feasibility and cost. processes of various types can be considered as chemical, mechanical or even behavior, used for macroeconomic modeling systems.

The use of tools that comply with the practicality of applying the concept and system design digital control is very suitable as mentioned before, so we introduce a way simple to obtain mathematical models of whatever the process, however in the case of linear or linearized process. To initiate an identification in the *MATLAB* we can proceed in two ways and the designer must choose whichever is most convenient to your time and level of knowledge that it is your process or your plan.

In *Command Window* use the following command to open the graphical user interface the *Identification Toolbox*:

```
>> ident
```

will produce the screens shown in Figure 3, where you can begin the process of identification.

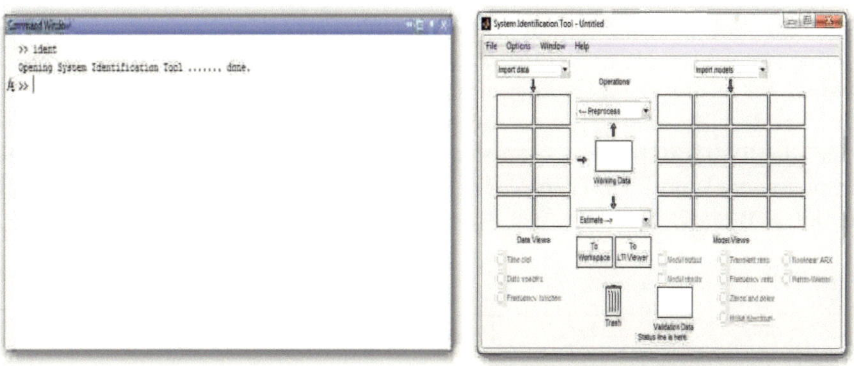

(a) Control to start *Ident* (b) *Ident* Main Screen

Fig. 3. Opening The Identification Tool Box - *MATLAB*

On these screens you can start importing the measurement data on the system or even with knowledge in the previous system

The main tool for modeling dynamic systems to digital control is the *MATLAB* Identification Tool Box of, a feature that helps the designer to seamlessly and generates discrete polynomial transfer functions and the user without the need of programming the algorithms used for system identification. The *IDENT* from *MATLAB Graphical User Interface* is shown in Figures 4 and 3 and in this figure that can be seen are located to the left set of data and the right answer, ie the model to be obtained.

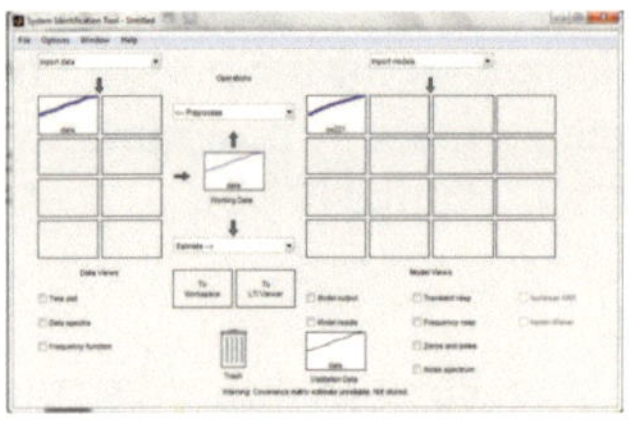

(a) Ident GUI

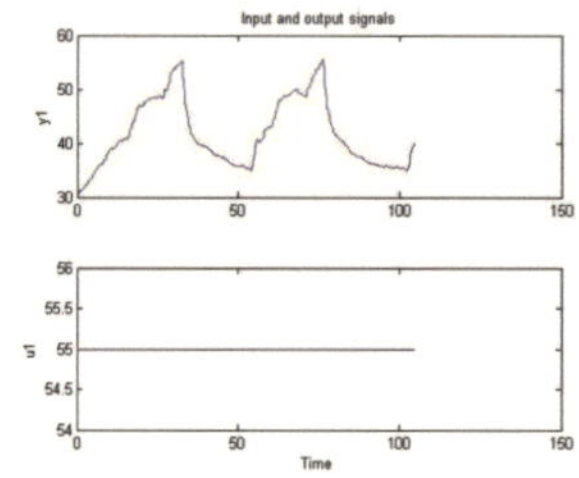

(b) Data - Time Response

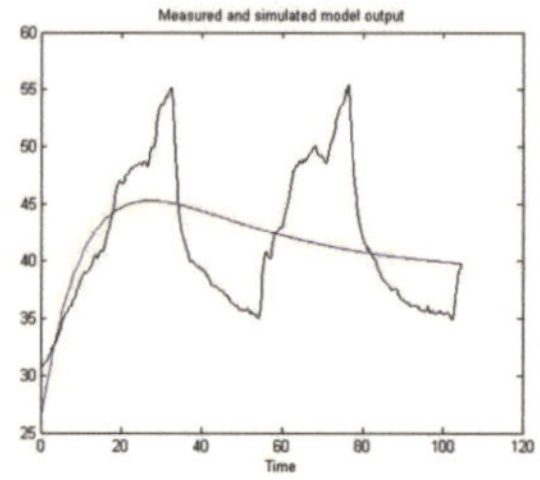

(c) Model- Time Response

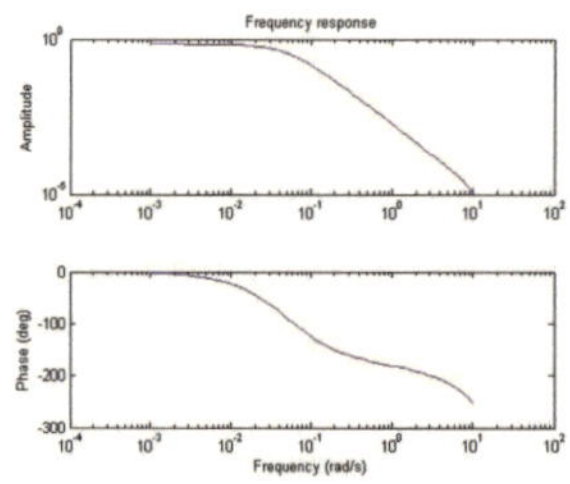

(d) Model -Frequency Response

Fig. 4. Results From The Identification Tool Box - MATLAB

Still in Figure 4 can observe that the user can define various aspects modeling systems such as filtering of data and type of modeling, as well as the analysis of response in time and frequency of the system model, Gene F. Franklin (1998).
Through this tool we can get two different ID type models in the output. The model based on parameters in the output shows a polynomial equation in discrete form
It should be added that among the numerous tools of identification, we will use polynomial will be the identification, because it gives us a response in discrete time, which makes this model implementable on digital computers. With the option to generate a polynomial model identification as described in Eq.1.

$$G(z) = \frac{Y(z)}{U(z)} = \frac{b_0 + b_1 z^{-1} + b_2 z^{-2} + \ldots b_n z^{-n}}{1 + a_1 z^{-1} + a_2 z^{-2} + \ldots a_n z^{-n}} \qquad (1)$$

3.2 The plant modeling

The estimation of parameters of the transfer function of the plant is performed with the *Toolbox* Identification Systems *MATLAB*. Using the observations of voltage and temperature measurements, table,we can get the parameters of a 2*nd* order transfer function.
In Figure 5 to represent the operation points thermal plant for a first evaluation of the algorithm, shows the temperature behavior from departure to variations in operating points.

The bands system operation are separated for purposes of calculation of the parameters of a model of second order. The band Operation of this plant is between 58^0 and $60^{\ 0}$ as observed in Figure 5.

3.2.1 Computational and hardware setups

It is understood by *Hardware* setups and computational specifications of the hardware and and design specifications that are the model order and delay. Description of procedure for conducting the experiment are presented in next sections.

3.2.2 OE model

Using *Identification Toolbox* to estimate the parameters of the discrete model **OE** (Output-Error) operated in the delay is given by

$$T(t) = \frac{B(q)}{F(q)}\omega(t) + e(t) \tag{2}$$

where

$$\begin{aligned} A(q) &= 1 - 1.52q^{-}1 + 0.5336q^{-2} \\ B(q) &= 0.7426q^{-1} - 0.7187q^{-2} \end{aligned}$$

Considering the transfer function of the deterministic signal from the ω input we have

$$\frac{T(t)}{\omega(t)} = \frac{B(q)}{F(q)} \tag{3}$$

3.2.3 The transfer function and polynomial form

The transfer function in Z plane is given by

$$\frac{W(z)}{V_a(z)} = \frac{B(z)}{F(z)} = \frac{0.7426z - 0.718}{z^2 - 1.52z + 0.5336} \tag{4}$$

The poles of the transfer function in Z, $pz_1 = 0.9697$ and $pz_1 = 0.5503$is the positive axis that divides the first and fourth quadrants. The zero is given by $z = 0.9678$ and is on top from one pole to the nearest two decimal places.
Applying the transformation *C2D* command of *Toolbox* Control gives the model transfer function continuously in the model time we have

$$\frac{T(s)}{V_a(s)} = \frac{B(s)}{F(s)} = \frac{0.9852s - 0.03224}{s^2 + 0.628s + 0.01837} \tag{5}$$

The poles of the transfer function at s,$pc_1 = -0.5973$and $pc_2 = -0.0308$. The zero at $zc = -0.0327$ nearly cancels the effect pole pc_2.
The *MATLAB scrip execution* has to read the temperature signals and actuator to estimate the parameters a mathematical model that represents the operating point system's thermal system.

```
Sys = OE(Data,[nb nf nk]
```

where
Data is the object containing the information input and output system;
nb is the order of the polynomial $B(q)$ from Equation 1;
nf is the order of the polynomial $F(q)$ from Equation 1;
nk is the input delay

We can also order the knowledge to perform analysis in continuous time by following the identification commands

```
M = idproc(type,value)
```

Thereby generating a frequency domain model type

$$G(s) = Kp\frac{1+T_z s}{(1+T_{p1}s)(1+T_{p2}s)(1+T_{p3}s)}e^{-T_d s} \tag{6}$$

Where the parameters of the function ***idproc*** are inherent in the system type, order and constant delay.
The graphs in Figure 5 are constructed in accordance with the instructions from design requirements . The first statement stores the vector *medt* values of temperature around the heat source (resistor) and the actuator speed ω. The third instruction is didactic and for implementation is not required to be codified.

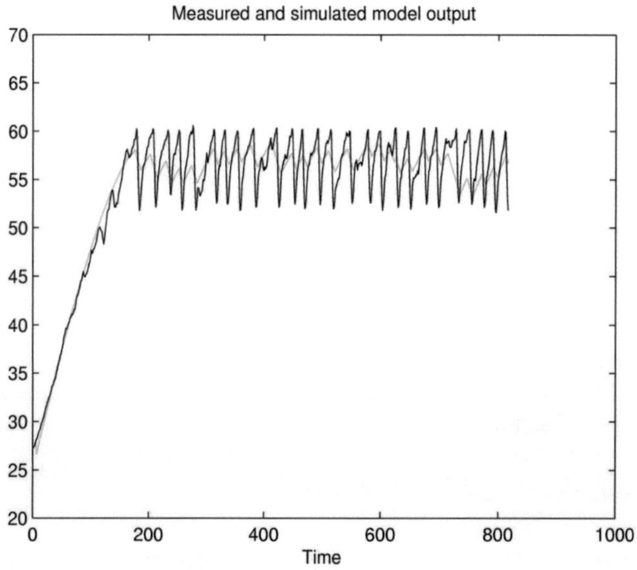

Fig. 5. Continuous Process Reaction Curve.

3.3 Model survey

The lifting of the method consists of parametric estimation conversion this model of transfer function in Z.

3.3.1 Model discrete time

The procedure for the identification of parameters of discrete time is encoded in the *script*, converting (describing) the discrete models in transfer function descriptions.
The Figure 5 shows the comparison of behavior temperature of the continuous model obtained by the process reaction curve

3.3.2 Transfer functions

The purpose of the transfer functions we generate the files contains models of the objects should be stored *OE* to conversion models.

3.3.3 Estimating parameters scripts

The establishment of a procedure for estimating parameters (connotation: scientific) or lifting of a model (connotation: engineering) presented in this section consists of three steps. The first step is the generation each measurement. The second step consists of estimating the parameters of functions transfer. The third step is the analysis of the model have the impulse response, Bode diagram and step.

3.4 A Platform to testing control systems

To validate our experiment we used a platform for experiments with micro digital circuits processed with the support of micro controllers that can be easily programmed using knowledge of language with C and a broad support to this type of application as in Ibrahim (2006),Lewis (2001) and Wilmshurst (2007).
Using the Microchip PIC micro controller family we can turn our platform to run on following code done in C programming language.

```
#device adc=10
#use delay(clock=4000000)
#fuses HS,NOWDT,PUT
#use rs232(baud=9600, xmit=PIN_C6,rcv=PIN_C7)
#include <mod_lcd.c>

main()
{
   long int value=0;
   float temp=0;
   int i=0;
   lcd_ini();
   setup_timer_2 (T2_DIV_BY_16, 61, 1);
   setup_ADC_ports (RA0_analog);
   setup_adc(ADC_CLOCK_INTERNAL );
   setup_ccp1(ccp_pwm);
   set_pwm1_duty ( 0 );
   setup_ccp2(ccp_pwm);
   set_pwm2_duty ( 0 );
   set_adc_channel(0);
   printf ("%%------------ DAQ - System ------------ \r\n");
   printf ("%%Temperature (žC) \r\n");
   while(true){
```

```
set_pwm1_duty(1023);
 delay_ms(100);
 value = read_adc();
    temp = ((5*(float) value)/(1024))*16.09;
    printf (" %f \r\n",temp);
    printf (lcd_write,"Temp = %f ",temp);
    lcd_write ('\f');

      if(temp>=60){
          set_pwm2_duty ( 1023 );
          }
      if(temp<=58){
      set_pwm2_duty ( 0 );
          }
delay_ms(500);

}
}
```

The code shown above is the implementation of a system that simulates the temperature, in the form of *Hardware* a thermal system with relative temperature variation in responses to time much smaller.
The dynamics of this system is well demonstrated in Figure 6

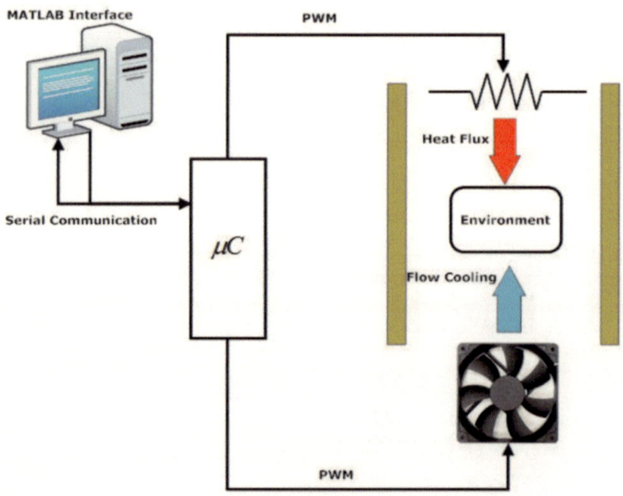

Fig. 6. A Diagram to System Hardware

Where the basis for the system of change of temperature in an open environment that is cooler acts as the system actuator. The control objective, as shown in the code is to keep a room temperature at a desired track with minimal accuracy in the output signal.

4. Implementing control systems on MATLAB

The *MATLAB* software provides support, form the implementation of acquisition system data to design a control system, which becomes possible with methods of identification and communication required in numerical methods implementation of a controller. This tool was incorporated for the purpose to help engineers and scientists in projects and systems design methods numeric, or for the resolution algorithms and systems simulation. In the following sections will be shown tools that are part of the suite of applications such as *MATLAB* concepts for implementation of digital control systems.

4.1 The serial interface

For the design of systems for data acquisition in *MATLAB*, an important tool are the protocols for data communications in environments that are common industries. The serial communication is known for its simplicity of connection and implementation in both hardware and software because there are a wide variety software and programming languages that provide libraries for development communication in serial protocol. In *MATLAB* the simplicity of applying this tool can be translated by code shown below

```
Serial_Obj = Serial('COM1');
fopen(Serial_Obj);
var_read = fscanf(Serial_Obj)
fprintf(var_read,'Data Receiveve');
fclose(Serial_Obj);
Delete(Serial_Obj);
```

With the above script you can communicate and receive data from an external device to your computer. With communication with the *external hardware* can open, using the following commands, send and receive data relevant to the control system

```
function send_data_tohard(data_ctrl,setpoint_ctrl)
fprintf(Serial_Obj,data_ctrl));
fprintf(Serial_Obj,setpoint_ctrl));
```

Therefore the system receives the data for the implementation of intelligent digital control system:

```
function receiv_data_fromhard(data_ctrl,data_error)
data_ctrl = fscanf(Serial_Obj,'data_ctrl');
data_error = fscanf(Serial_Obj,'data_error');
```

Always observing that the variable *Dataa_crtl* is used for timing and appropriateness of real-time system.

4.2 The user interface

The user interface development system shown in Figure 7 is used with supervisors and control environment of the platform.

Using the anointing of the environment development of ***GUIDE*** MATLAB can therefore obtain the convenience of the project environment be the same as the deployment environment

In the source code below is observed in connection with the generation via the serial port textbf GUID emph MATLAB.

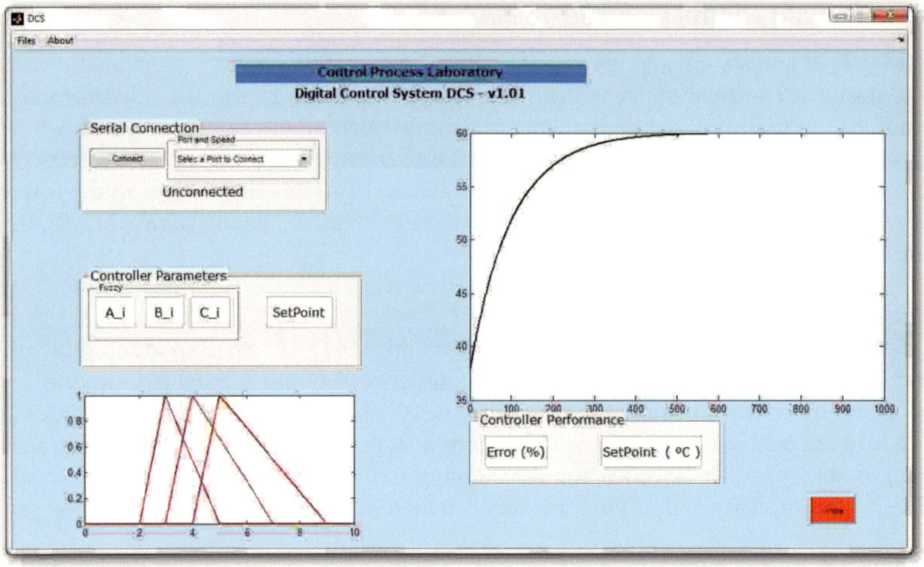

Fig. 7. Graphical Interface of the Platform System

```
function  Button_01_Callback(hObject, eventdata, handles, varargin)
Serial_Obj=serial('COM1','BaudRate',9600);
opcon2 =get(handles.menu_01,'Value');
opcon = get(handles.menu_01,'String');

switch opcon{opcon2}
    case 'COM1'
        Serial_Obj.Port='COM1';
    case 'COM2'
        Serial_Obj.Port='COM2';
    case 'COM3'
        Serial_Obj.Port='COM3';
    case 'COM4'
       Serial_Obj.Port='COM4';
    case 'COM5'
      Serial_Obj.Port='COM5';
    case 'COM6'
       Serial_Obj.Port='COM6';
    case 'COM7'
      Serial_Obj.Port='COM7';
    otherwise
        errordlg('Select a Valid Serial Port','Error')

end

fopen(Serial_Obj);
if Serial_Obj.Status ==open
```

```
set(handles.con_text,'String','Connected');
end
```

4.3 Real time control

Digital Control Systems has its roots in the interface with the analog world and thus the delay time this conversion to occur immediately. In real-time systems is a concern that the execution time of a given instruction does not exceed a predetermined threshold. Converging, the realtime systems are strictly necessary in digital control because it does necessary to guarantee instruction execution control U_c within the limit of sampling system T_s where a failure of this requirement may lead to instability as the plant design of discrete controllers is directly related T_s variable.

4.4 Implementing intelligent systems

The implementation of intelligent systems through *MATLAB* may well become a very profitable it facilitates the testing of new techniques that use features and tools already implemented in this software. Techniques computational intelligence can withdraw from the digital control system the important factor in the T_s, however the system still requires real time control. Each execution cycle lets you have the need to perform numerical derivatives and integrals and introducing a context of researching and mapping , which may require less computational effort. The diagram shown in Figure 8

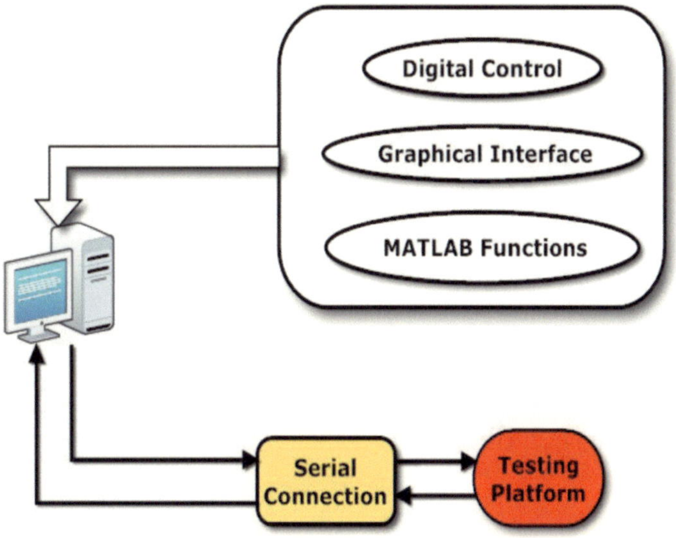

Fig. 8. Diagram of the General System

Itś possible conclude that with the development of both the hardware and software, these systems are likely to become the largest presence within the control and automation

4.4.1 A fuzzy method implementation

As described in Ross (2004),S. Sumathi (2010) and Andrade (2010) the commitment of systems based on fuzzy logic both in respect of the facility as implementation of policies that take into account not only the performance of closed loop of industrial process control as well as the experience acquired human with the process that can be transferred directly to the core of the *Fuzzy Logic Controller*(*FLC*) with its implementation process described in Figure 9

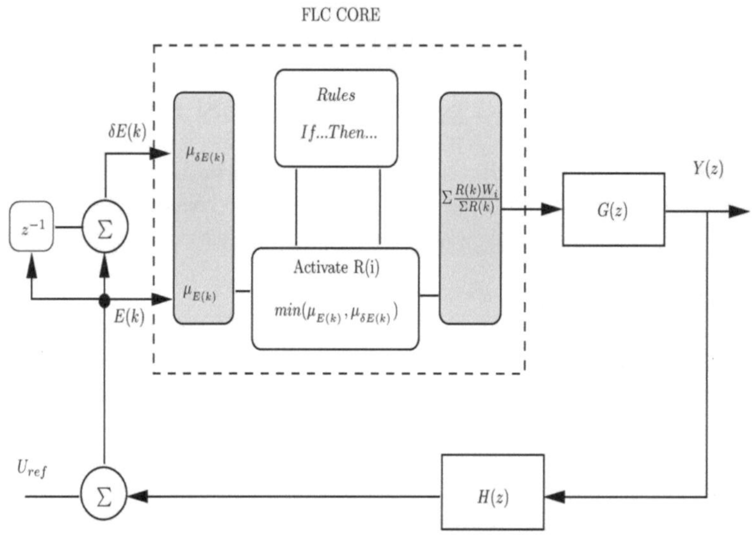

Fig. 9. Diagram of the General System

The consolidation of this type of system could provide designers with a feature not found on controllers classical, ie the aforementioned expertise. To use the Fuzzy controller is needed for the project prior knowledge on the implementation of systems based on fuzzy logic and can be found in Andrade (2010) and especially in Zadeh (1965). In *MATLAB* the design begins by checking the feasibility of the controller and can be done by graphical interface *Fuzzy Logic Toolbox* with a significant help from MathWorks (2010).
To open the *FLT (Fuzzy Logic Toolbox)* typed:

```
>>fuzzy
```

and the following screen will open
However the system to be implemented with *MATLAB* using the serial communication is necessary to implement the intelligent system in *script* and can be done as follows

```
error = data_ctrl;
NG(k) = trimf(error, [a_i b_i c_i]);
NS(k) = trimf(error, [a_i b_i c_i]);
ZR(k) = trimf(error, [a_i b_i c_i]);
PS(k) = trimf(error, [a_i b_i c_i]);
PB(k) = trimf(error, [a_i b_i c_i]);
chang_error = data_ctrl;
NL(k) = trimf(chang_error, [a_i b_i c_i]);
NS(k) = trimf(chang_error, [a_i b_i c_i]);
ZR(k) = trimf(chang_error, [a_i b_i c_i]);
PS(k) = trimf(chang_error, [a_i b_i c_i]);
PL(k) = trimf(chang_error, [a_i b_i c_i]);
```

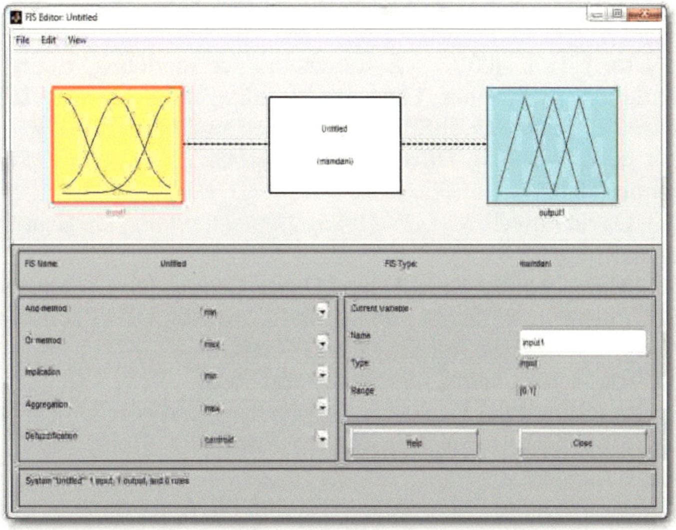

Fig. 10. The FLT Main Screen

Where N*egative* ***L****arge*, *N****egative*** ***S****mall*, ***Z****e****R****o*, ***P****ositive* ***S****mall* and ***P****ositive* ***L****arge* are linguistics vary based on experience. The system output can be given as shown in Figure 9 with a bank of rules based on Table 1 decision-making as an example

$Error \setminus changing_{E}rror$	**NL**	**NS**	**ZR**	**PS**	**PL**
NL	PL	PL	PL	PL	NL
NS	PS	PS	PS	PS	NS
ZR	PS	ZR	ZR	NS	ZR
PS	NS	NS	NS	NS	PS
PL	NL	NL	NL	NS	PS

Table 1. The knowledge from the Rules of Decision System

And the controller output and results in a weighted sum that depends exclusively on the method chosen.

5. Conclusion

With the aid of this important tool can facilitate the development of applications to interface with and control devices industries. A overview of these tools has been shown here to that may be developed to greater diversity of applications according to the need of the designer. As an environment of the computational complex, *MATLAB* can provide solutions for engineering, physics and mathematics with the use of its functions basic and therefore leaving the search more efficient and less costly. This platform is an important and necessary tool, it can lead a project, with integration between *Software* and *Hardware*, for a safe convergence of results, thus integrating computational resources for simulation design and implementation from a direct single platform.

6. References

Andrade, G.A. Neto, J. L. L. (2010). A framework for modeling, digital control design and simulations of dynamic, *Computer Modelling and Simulation (UKSim), 2010 12th International Conference on*, IEEE Computer Society Digital Library.

Charles L. Philips, H. T. N. (1995). *Digital Control Systems: Analisys and Design*, third edition edn, Prentice Hall.

Gene F. Franklin, J. David Powell, M. L. W. (1998). *Digital Control of Dynamic Systems*, 3rd edn, Prentice Hall.

Ibrahim, D. (2006). *Microcontroller Based Applied Digital Control*, John Wiley and Sons.

Lewis, C. S. (2001). *Programming Microcontrollers in C*, 2nd edn, LLH Publishing.

MathWorks, T. (2010). *Fuzzy Logic Tool Box : User's Guide.*

Moudgalya, K. (2007). *Digital Control*, John Wiley and Sons.

Ross, T. J. (2004). *Fuzzy Logic With Engineering Applications*, 2nd edn, John Wiley and Sons.

S. Sumathi, S. P. (2010). *Computational Intelligence Paradigms: Theory and Applications Using MATLAB*, CRC Press.

Wilmshurst, T. (2007). *Designing Embedded Systems with PIC Microcontrollers*, Newnes.

Zadeh, L. A. (1965). Fuzzy sets, *Information and Control Proceedings* .

15

A Fuzzy Finite Element Method Programmed in MATLAB for the Analysis of Uncertain Control Systems of Structures

Angel L. Morales[1], Jem A. Rongong[2] and Neil D. Sims[2]

[1]*Universidad de Castilla - La Mancha*
[2]*The University of Sheffield*
[1]*Spain*
[2]*United Kingdom*

1. Introduction

Vibration is an important aspect of many engineering systems. In most cases, such vibration is undesirable and requires attenuation or control, which explains the huge quantity of vibration control techniques that can be found in the literature. Nevertheless, sometimes all this knowledge is not enough to guarantee the success in this purpose. Model inaccuracies or parameter uncertainty are unavoidable in all relevant practical application and not only can they degrade the performance of an otherwise well-designed control system, but they may also lead to instability and even structural failure.

For these reasons, robustness is of crucial importance in control-system design. Although always being appreciated, it was not until late 1970s when a theory capable to explicitly handle the robustness issue in feedback design was developed: the H_∞ optimal control theory (Zames, 1981; Zames & Francis, 1983). This optimization approach is well developed and we can even find a full *Robust Control Toolbox* in MATLAB which, in collaboration with the *Control System Toolbox*, let us identify worst-case scenarios and generate optimal controllers so that the stability and good performance of the plant is ensured (Gu et al., 2005).

Obviously, the H_∞ optimal control theory shows some disadvantages, like the high level of mathematical understanding needed to apply them successfully and the fact that it sometimes leads to potentially very conservative results (Gu et al., 2005). Indeed, even when a solution via H_∞ techniques is eventually found, the process may have been too expensive in terms of designer's time and the sensitivity to the uncertainty sources is not analyzed. These motivations make us think that a straightforward possibilistic methodology for simulating and analyzing the uncertainty propagation in control system would be a very valuable, complementary and time saving tool.

This work focuses on how MATLAB can supply suitable tools in order to manage uncertainty propagation in finite element models of structures from the point of view of fuzzy arithmetic. More specifically, we will describe a methodology fully programmed in MATLAB in order to deal with uncertain control systems of vibrating structures and we will illustrate the application of this approach to a case study.

In order to develop this work we need to integrate two different problems: the calculation of the dynamic response of a vibrating structure via finite element models and the study of the

uncertainty propagation via fuzzy arithmetic. Both problems can be solved using MATLAB code obtaining very good results in terms of accuracy and computational cost.
The motivation behind this work is threefold: firstly, it is meant to show how MATLAB provides suitable functions and specialized toolboxes in order to study the static or dynamic response of a controlled structure via finite elements and control theory; secondly, it demonstrates the suitability of MATLAB to solve uncertainty propagation problems through fuzzy arithmetic minimizing the computational cost; and thirdly, it illustrates the application of a Fuzzy Finite Element procedure, which integrates these two tools, with a specific case study.
The chapter is organized in the following way: Section 1 has summarized the aims and concerns of the chapter; Section 2 deals with dynamic analysis of structures with active damping by means of the *OpenFEM Toolbox* and the *Control System Toolbox* of MATLAB; Section 3 discusses the different types of uncertainty and how they could be analyzed using fuzzy arithmetic programmed in MATLAB; Section 4 describes a Fuzzy Finite Element procedure in MATLAB in order to study the propagation of uncertain parameters in control systems of structures; Section 5 shows a case study in which the Fuzzy Finite Element procedure is tested; Section 6 deals with the main conclusions of this work; and finally the acknowledgements and references included through the text are included.

2. Dynamic analysis and control of structures

2.1 Finite Element analysis and the OpenFEM Toolbox

The study of the dynamic behaviour of a structure can be carried out by means of finite element analysis. Among all the different possibilities to solve finite elements problems, in this chapter we focus on the use of a specific toolbox of MATLAB: the *OpenFEM Toolbox* (Balmes et al., 2009).
It is an open-source toolbox for finite element analysis within the matrix computing environment MATLAB. The software is developed in collaboration between Macs and the SDTools Company and it is distributed under a GNU Lesser General Public License, that is, a free software license which also allows the user to make modifications in the code. Performing finite element analysis within a matrix computing environment is of considerable interest, in particular as regards the ease of new developments, integration of external software, portability, post-processing, etc. This relatively young software is already quite successful in the finite element community as it is proven by the about 300 downloads per month (OpenFEM, 2011).
Though the toolbox architecture includes graphical user interfaces for visualization, analysis and animation of results, the powerful of this toolbox does not lie in this fact but in the standard and advanced methods which are implemented. Moreover, the provided functions are open and can be easily extended to suit particular needs of the user (Balmes et al., 2009), as it is our case.
Let us consider a vibrating structure. The first step in order to carry out its finite element analysis consists in discretizing the structure. The mesh nodes, elements which join the nodes, material properties, element properties and any additional information such as boundary conditions, loads, etc., are stored in a *struct* class variable which defines the model of the multi degree of freedom vibrating structure which is governed by the next set of equations of motion

$$M\ddot{x} + C\dot{x} + Kx = f \tag{1}$$

where M, K and C are the mass, the stiffness and the damping matrices, respectively, x the vector of displacements of all the degrees of freedom of the structure and f a general vector of forces. Matrices M and K arise from the finite element analysis of the structure whereas C is usually obtained under the hypothesis of Rayleigh damping.

Both in the state space approach and in the transfer function approach, working with physical coordinates is not practical because of the usually high number of degrees of freedom. Thus, a change of variables into modal coordinates is suggested. In addition, in this way the problem can be restricted to the bandwidth of interest, neglecting the high frequency dynamics of the system. After the computation of modes via finite element analysis one obtains the natural frequencies of the modes and the matrix of the mode shapes Φ. After performing the change of variables $x = \Phi z$, where z is the vector of modal coordinates and Φ is normalized in such a way that the modal mass matrix is the identity matrix, the governing equations in modal coordinates read

$$\ddot{z} + 2\xi\Omega\dot{z} + \Omega^2 z = \Phi^{\mathrm{T}} f \tag{2}$$

where Ω and ξ define the diagonal matrices of natural frequencies and damping factors.

Finally, the software also provides several commands related to the definition of the actuators and sensors or, strictly speaking, the input force influence vector L_u and the sensor influence vector L_y, both of them required for the definition of either the transfer function or the state space matrices.

The finite element models which are obtained with this toolbox can be used to solve both static and dynamic problems, the results of which being ready to be plotted or post-processed under any other MATLAB toolbox. In this work, we blended these commands which those corresponding to the *Control System Toolbox*.

2.2 Active damping and the Control System Toolbox

The *Control System Toolbox* provides a collection of matrix-based functions, usually expressed as M-files, for the topic of control engineering. The control systems may be modelled as transfer functions, zero-pole-gain or even using the state space approach, which allows the designer to apply classic techniques as well as modern techniques. However, it is not our purpose to study thoroughly this topic, so we will concentrate on briefly reviewing, as an example, one of the most common active control techniques of structures (Preumont, 2002): active damping with collocated piezoelectric pairs via Positive Position Feedback, which, in the end, will be the case study discussed in Section 5.

The transfer function of the multi degree of freedom vibrating structure obtained via modal expansion reads

$$G(\omega) = \frac{X(\omega)}{F(\omega)} = \sum_{n=1}^{\infty} \frac{\Phi_n \Phi_n^{\mathrm{T}}}{\omega_n^2 + 2\mathrm{j}\omega\xi_n\omega_n - \omega^2} \tag{3}$$

where Φ_n, ω_n and ξ_n are the mode shape, the natural frequency and the damping ratio for the nth mode of vibration, respectively. The same model based upon the first N modes of vibration leads to the expression

$$\hat{G}(\omega) \approx \sum_{n=1}^{N} \frac{\Phi_n \Phi_n^{\mathrm{T}}}{\omega_n^2 + 2\mathrm{j}\omega\xi_n\omega_n - \omega^2} \tag{4}$$

where the residual term due to the contributions of the truncated nodes has been neglected.

Combining the equations for the surface-bonded actuator and sensor (Dosch et al., 1992; Sims et al., 2005) and Equation 4 which governs the structural dynamics, we obtain the frequency response function between the voltage V_a applied to the actuator and the voltage V_s at the output of the charge amplifier of the sensor

$$H(\omega) = \frac{V_s(\omega)}{V_a(\omega)} = k_a k_s \sum_{n=1}^{N} \frac{L_u^T \Phi_n \Phi_n^T L_y}{\omega_n^2 + 2j\omega\xi_n\omega_n - \omega^2} \tag{5}$$

where k_s and k_a are the sensor gain and the actuator gain, respectively.
As far as the Positive Position Feedback scheme is concerned, it is appropriate for a structure equipped with strain actuators and sensors (Preumont, 2002). The objective of a Positive Position Feedback controller is to use a second order filter to improve the roll-off of the control system, allowing high frequency gain stabilization. The implementation of this control system is given by the following equations

$$\begin{aligned} M\ddot{x} + C\dot{x} + Kx &= L_u u \\ y &= L_u^T x \\ \ddot{v} + \beta_f \dot{v} + \Omega_f^2 v &= y \\ u &= -Gv \end{aligned} \tag{6}$$

where u is the control force acting on the structure through the influence vector L_u, y is the difference of slope between the ends of the sensor, $G = \text{diag}(g_i)$ is the positive gain matrix, and v is the output of the second order filter defined by the matrices $\beta_f = \text{diag}(2\xi_f\omega_f)$ and $\Omega_f^2 = \text{diag}(\omega_f^2)$. Note that the fact that the same localization vector (L_u) rules the actuator and sensors is a consequence of collocation.
The transfer function of the controller (a second order low pass filter) can be written as follows

$$gD(w) = g\frac{\omega_f^2}{\omega_f^2 + 2j\omega\xi_f\omega_f - \omega^2} \tag{7}$$

This compensator has both advantages and drawbacks. On the one hand, the open-loop transfer function has a roll-off of -40dB/decade, larger in comparison to Direct Velocity Feedback (-20dB/decade), which may decrease the risk of destabilizing high frequency dynamics. On the other hand, there is a stability limit which is reached when the open-loop static gain is equal to 1, this fact being independent of the damping (Preumont, 2002).
Once the open loop transfer functions of the plant and the regulator are defined, they can be used in the *Control System Toolbox* as *transfer function* class variables. Then, the desired active damping can be obtained by selecting the proper gain g of the regulator. In order to do this, several techniques can be used such as Bode Diagram Design, Root Locus Design, Nichols Plot design, etc.
Finally, the *Control System Toolbox* also provides valuable functions in order to analyze the stability and performance in terms of stability margins, time responses or the position of the closed loop poles and zeros in the pole-zero map. They will be used in our Fuzzy Finite Element methodology as fuzzy outputs in order to analyze the behaviour of the uncertain control system.

3. Uncertainty and fuzzy arithmetic

In the literature, the use of the term uncertainty is slightly ambiguous. In order to establish the nomenclature for the ensuing description, the reader is referred to the terminology proposed in (Oberkampf et al., 2004).

On the one hand, we will use the term aleatory uncertainty to describe the inherent variation associated with the physical system or the environment under consideration. These sources of uncertainty can be represented as randomly distributed quantities, usually in terms of probability distribution functions. Typical examples of this kind of uncertainty are manufacturing tolerances, environmental effects, properties of non-uniform materials or any other identifiable disturbances. On the other hand, epistemic uncertainty derives from some level of ignorance of the system or the environment in any activity of the modelling process. In this case, its definition stresses the lack of knowledge as the origin of this uncertainty. Thus, unlike aleatory uncertainty, a mathematical representation of epistemic uncertainty has proven to be much more of a challenge since it is subjective and based on some expert opinion to a certain extent. Typical examples of epistemic uncertainties are some models for boundary conditions, simplified models for joints, models for material damping or unpredictable model changes due to ageing, loading, etcetera.

Uncertainty propagation in dynamic systems has been a very frequent topic in the literature, which has been tackled from two different points of view (De Gersem et al., 2005): *probabilistic* and *possibilistic* approaches. Probabilistic approaches, such as the well-known Monte Carlo Simulation method, investigate the influence of aleatory uncertainties, this method being particularly suitable for finite element models with certain uncertainties. Possibilistic approaches are complementary to probabilistic approaches, since not only are they able to describe problems of aleatory uncertainties to a certain extent, yet without statistical interpretation, but they can also handle problems where incomplete information (epistemic uncertainty) is available. We consider that computationally expensive "brute-force" probabilistic methods are not worthwhile in most cases, where an intuitive worst-case scenario provides enough information. Thus, a possibilistic method in terms of fuzzy arithmetic will be the tool that we develop and propose in order to simulate and analyze uncertainty propagation in control systems.

Fuzzy arithmetic has been used by various researchers as a technique for propagating uncertainty or variability through complex engineering models. The origins of this approach can be found in the theory of Fuzzy Sets (Zadeh, 1965). In contrast to the classical set theory, the elements of a fuzzy set are assigned a degree of membership to the set, which is referred to as the membership level μ. The core of the set is defined as the subset of elements for which $\mu = 1$, whilst the support is the subset for which $\mu > 0$. A fuzzy number is a fuzzy set that is convex and normal, and whose membership function is piecewise continuous.

The issue of performing mathematical operations on fuzzy numbers instead of on conventional numbers can be a challenge rather than a trivial problem. In fact, the Fuzzy Arithmetic processes are usually performed by decomposing the fuzzy numbers into a number of intervals given by the α-cuts at the α-levels μ_i, $(i = 0, 1, \ldots, m)$ with

$$\mu_i = \frac{i}{m} \tag{8}$$

Then, a interval analysis via interval arithmetic can be carried out separately to each membership level μ_i.

For monotonic problems this process may be trivial, since the maxima or minima of the inputs will lead to the maxima or minima for the output. Conversely, for non-monotonic problems this is no longer the case (Sims et al., 2010). In addition, the Standard Fuzzy Arithmetic may become problematic and lead to different results for the same problem depending on the form in which the solution procedure is applied, as can be seen in the examples gathered in (Hanss, 2002). In short, the application of Standard Fuzzy Arithmetic usually leads to overestimate results to a lesser or greater extent and alternative methods must be employed.

The Transformation Method, introduced in (Hanss, 2002), represents a special implementation of Fuzzy Arithmetic that avoids the undesired overestimation which usually arises when Fuzzy Arithmetic is reduced to interval computation. A later efficient implementation of this method was carried out in (Klimke, 2003), taking advantage of the matrix computing environment of MATLAB and providing enhanced features such as fast processing of discretized fuzzy numbers through multi-dimensional arrays, elimination of recurring permutations, automatic decomposition of models, treatment of single occurrences of variables through interval arithmetic and a monotonicity test based on automatic differentiation. Nevertheless, we have to note that the fuzzy parameters are restricted to convex fuzzy numbers when using the Transformation Method.

Specially relevant for an efficient implementation of the Transformation Method is the elimination of recurring permutations. The decomposition scheme of this method sometimes produces recurring points which in the end generate recurring permutations. By removing these recurring permutations from the evaluation procedure one could save a very valuable computation time. Indeed, we could even try to reuse as many points for different α-cuts as possible by selecting only inner points which have already occurred in a higher-level α-cut. For symmetric triangular membership functions, the obtained discretization is identical to the original formulation, but for other arbitrarily shaped membership functions, the distribution of the points is less regular, but of similar density (see Figure 1). However, for the same number of α-cuts, the less regular distribution of the inner points results in less accurate results compared to the original formulation.

The number of permutations r by using this efficient implementation of the Transformation Method is given by the following equation

$$r = m^n + (m+1)^n \tag{9}$$

where $m+1$ is the number of α-cuts and n is the number of fuzzy parameters. As proven in (Klimke, 2003), the new scheme provides a valuable improvement in terms of computational cost unless the number of α-cuts is too large compared to the number of fuzzy inputs. If that was the case, one could disregard the removing of recurring permutations in favour of more accurate results.

4. Fuzzy Finite Element procedure in MATLAB

The fuzzy theory has led to the development of Fuzzy Finite Element methods as that described in (De Gersem et al., 2005; De Munck et al., 2008; Moens & Vandepitte, 2005) for analyzing the propagation of uncertainties in the Frequency Response Functions of a dynamic system. When using this methodology, the uncertainties in the model parameters can be taken into account by fuzzy numbers with their shape obtained from experimental data or assumed from expert knowledge. Then, the numerical procedure for the implementation of these Fuzzy Finite Element methods consists of a sequence of Interval Finite Element procedures based on a general strategy for computing the fuzzy result from operations on fuzzy operands, i.e. the α-sublevel or α-cuts technique.

Figure 1 clarifies this procedure. This technique subdivides the membership range into a number of α-cuts. At each level, the intersection with the membership function of the input uncertainties results in an interval. Based on these input intervals for all uncertain parameters, an interval analysis can be performed obtaining the interval of the output variables at the considered α-cut. Strictly speaking, the interval analysis for a specific α-cut consists in running all the finite elements calculations corresponding to all the possible permutations among input variables at said level and choosing the lower and upper bound of the required output

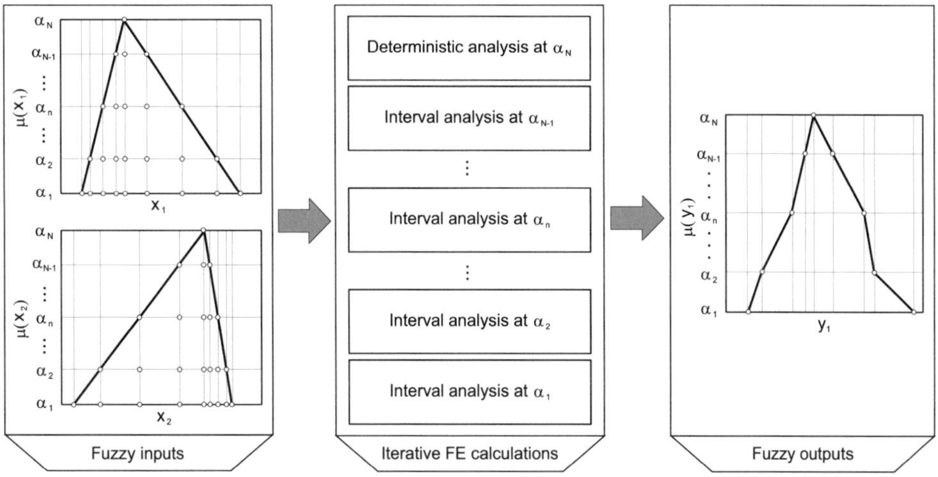

Fig. 1. Scheme of the numerical procedure to perform a Fuzzy Finite Element analysis using four α-cuts.

variables. Note that if $\mu = 1$, the interval analysis degenerates into the deterministic analysis. Finally, the membership functions of the required output variables are assembled from the interval results at all sublevels.

The Fuzzy Finite Element analysis is based on the results of a previous deterministic design of the control system. The control engineer must set the control parameters and gains of the regulator in order to accomplish all the features required for the active damping in terms of both stability and performance. After this process, which is usually easier and faster than other complex control techniques such as those derived from H_∞ control, the Fuzzy Finite Element analysis will simulate the behaviour of the control system when some parameters are considered uncertain. This method is not a robust designing technique but a possibilistic method which tests whether the deterministic design is robust enough to keep the closed loop behaviour of the structure inside the allowable bounds for its stability and performance features.

The set of calculations which are carried out at each permutation of input values is compound of these steps:

Step 1: Finite Element calculations via the *OpenFEM Toolbox*

Step 2: Closed loop simulation of the control system via the *Control System Toolbox*

Step 3: Analysis of stability and performance via fuzzy variables such as stability margins or active damping.

The method chosen for carrying out the interval fuzzy arithmetics was the efficient implementation of the Transformation Method proposed in (Klimke, 2003). Nevertheless, we have included some modifications which will be introduced in the ensuing.

The first modification lies in the fact that Klimke's MATLAB script is made under the assumption that the fuzzy output is the result of evaluating an analytical expression. In our case, we need to replace the evaluation of such analytical function (*inline* class) with a list of MATLAB commands which develops the aforementioned steps. This also allows us to include the possibility of achieving several fuzzy outputs instead of only one. The second modification was not necessary but it endows the method with enhance capabilities. It consists on using *cell* class arrays instead of *double* class arrays to define the fuzzy outputs, so an extra field may

be included where information about each iteration is stored (for instance, the exact value of the fuzzy inputs at each permutation). Figures 2 and 3 show the MATLAB implementation of the efficient Transformation Method after modifying the Klimke's implementation. Note that the MATLAB implementation of the external function in Figure 3 only shows an example corresponding to the evaluation of a test function. In our case, this function would contain all the required commands which carry out the three foregoing calculating steps.
In order to prove the validity of our modified version of the Klimke's Transformation Method, a comparative fuzzy analysis was run. We took as a reference one example found in (Klimke, 2003) where the test function $f(x_1, x_2) = \cos(\pi x_1)x_2$ is subjected to the triangular fuzzy inputs

```
function [fzr]=gtrmrecur_modif(varargin)
% Angel L. Morales, 2011.
% FZR=GTRMRECUR_MODIF(FZ1,FZ2,...,FZN) calls the general transformation
% method implemented by Klimke in 2003 with extended capabilities.
% The function allows N fuzzy numbers in alpha-cut representation.
% An accompanying function called GTRMRECUR_EXTERNAL_FCN is required.
fzin=varargin;
n = nargin;
m = size(fzin{1},1) - 1;
indices.subs = {};
indices.type = '()';
fzr = cell(m+1,2);
for k = 1:2
t = (floor((m+2-k)/2)+rem(m+2-k,2))*2-2+k;
for i = 1:n
c = reshape(fzin{i}(end+1-k:-2:1,:)',t+2-k,1);
c = c(3-k:end);
repvec = t*ones(1,n);
repvec(i) = 1;
x{i} = repmat(shiftdim(c,1-i),repvec);
end
s = k;
z_cell_matrix=gtrmrecur_external_fcn(x);
for j = m+2-k:-2:1
indices.subs(1:n) = {1:s};
w = reshape(subsref(z_cell_matrix,indices),s^n,1);
wc = zeros(size(w));
for cont=1:length(wc) wc(cont)=w{cont}{2}; end;
[none,pos_min]=min(wc); fzr{j,1} = w{pos_min};
[none,pos_max]=max(wc); fzr{j,2} = w{pos_max};
s = s + 2;
end
end
for j = m:-1:1
if fzr{j+1,1}{2}>=fzr{j,1}{2}; fzr{j,1}=fzr{j,1}; else fzr{j,1}=fzr{j+1,1}; end
if fzr{j+1,2}{2}>=fzr{j,2}{2}; fzr{j,2}=fzr{j+1,2}; else fzr{j,2}=fzr{j,2}; end
end
```

Fig. 2. MATLAB implementation of the efficient Transformation Method after modifying Klimke's script.

```
function [z_cell_matrix]=gtrmrecur_external_fcn(x)
% Angel L. Morales, 2011.
% Z_CELL_MATRIX=GTRMRECUR_EXTERNAL_FCN(FZ1,FZ2,...,FZN) calls the function
% which executes the commands in order to obtain the fuzzy output.
% It is called during the execution of FZR=GTRMRECUR_MODIF(FZ1,FZ2,...,FZN)
func = inline('cos(pi.*x1).*x2');
x_vector=cell(size(x));
for cont=1:length(x)
    x_vector{cont} = reshape(x{cont},numel(x{cont}),1);
end
iterations=length(x_vector{1});
z_cell=cell(1,2); z_cell_array=cell(1,iterations);
for iteration=1:iterations
    x1=double(x_vector{1}(iteration));
    x2=double(x_vector{2}(iteration));
    z_cell{1}=[x1 x2];
    z_cell{2}=feval(func,x_vector{1}(iteration),x_vector{2}(iteration));
    z_cell_array{iteration}=z_cell;
end
z_cell_matrix=reshape(z_cell_array,size(x{1}));
```

Fig. 3. Example of the MATLAB function called by the modified Transformation Method which contains the commands for the obtention of the fuzzy output

$\tilde{p}_1 = \langle 2.5, 2.5, 2.5 \rangle_{\text{TFN}}$ and $\tilde{p}_2 = \langle 3, 2, 2 \rangle_{\text{TFN}}$, in accordance to the nomenclature proposed in (Dubois & Prade, 1980). The fuzzy output obtained with the modified version clearly matched the results obtained with the original version. Nevertheless, an unavoidable loss of computational efficiency arose.

Our modified version results more time-consuming because of the different way in which the simulated function is handled, as it can be seen in Table 1. In the original version, the *inline* class analytical expression can be executed only once with the array containing all the required permutations of fuzzy inputs at a time. In the modified version, the expression is evaluated separately at each permutation as it would be the case when a control system is simulated with several MATLAB commands. The elapsed time during these operations is called t_{fcn}. As far as the obtention of the fuzzy output as a *cell* array instead of as a *double* array, this fact does not add any noticeable increase of computational cost but it does lead to heavier variables and higher memory requirements. The elapsed time during these operations is called t_{max}. In all the cases, the loss of efficiency is acceptable with regard to the benefits they provide, specially considering that the elapsed time in any finite element simulation may be on the order of seconds and it has much more restrictive memory requirements.

5. A case study of uncertainty propagation

Consider an aluminium plate in free conditions, the dimensions and material properties of which are detailed in Table 2. The finite element model of this plate was carried out by means of the *OpenFEM Toolbox* of MATLAB (Balmes et al., 2009). After defining the mesh, the matrices of mass (M) and stiffness (K) which define the undamped model were obtained. The eigenvalue problem can then be solved, the natural frequencies and mode shapes being shown in Figure 4. The damping matrix (C) is constructed considering a structural damping of $\xi_i = 0.6\%$ in all the modes.

The piezoelectric actuator and sensor, the properties of which are detailed in Table 3, are collocated in the centre of the plate. As described in (Dosch et al., 1992; Sims et al., 2005), the piezoelectric actuator and sensor may be modelled as a beam which provides bending moments at its ends and measures a voltage proportional to the difference of slope of its ends. Due to collocation, the localization vectors of actuator (L_u) and sensor (L_y) are identical and equal to

$$L_u^{\mathrm{T}} = L_y^{\mathrm{T}} = (0, \ldots, -1, 0, \ldots, 1, 0, \ldots, 0) \tag{10}$$

	Original	Modified
t_{tot} (s)	0.047	0.344
t_{tot} (%)	100.00	100.00
t_{fcn} (s)	0.016	0.313
t_{fcn} (%)	34.04	90.99
t_{max} (s)	0.000	0.000
t_{max} (%)	0.000	0.000
t_{oth} (s)	0.031	0.031
t_{oth} (%)	65.96	9.01
Weight (bytes)	336	8568

Table 1. Efficiency comparison between the original and the modified Klimke's implementation. The total time (t_{tot}), the time for evaluating the analytical expression (t_{fcn}), the time for calculating the maxima and minima of the output fuzzy number (t_{max}) and the time for other calculations (t_{oth}) are shown. The weight means the size in bytes of the output fuzzy variable.

Width (*mm*)	300.00
Length (*mm*)	500.00
Thickness (*mm*)	3.00
Young's modulus (GPa)	72.00
Poisson's coefficient	0.30
Density (kg/m^3)	2700.00
Structural damping (%)	0.60

Table 2. Geometries and material properties of the plate.

Width (*mm*)	40
Length (*mm*)	100
Thickness (*mm*)	0.250
d_{33} (m/V)	$0.30{\cdot}10^{-9}$
d_{31} (m/V)	$-0.15{\cdot}10^{-9}$
e_{31} (N/Vm)	-7.5
k_{33}	0.7
Young's modulus (GPa)	50
Maximum traction (MPa)	80
Maximum compression (MPa)	600
Maximum electric Field (V/mm)	2000
Density (kg/m^3)	7600
Maximum strain	Brittle
Maximum temperature (C)	80°C - 150°C

Table 3. Geometries and material properties of the piezoelectric (Preumont, 2002).

where the non-zero values are placed in the position corresponding to the active rotational degree of freedom of the nodes in which the piezoelectric is located.

As described in the Section 2.2, a Positive Position Feedback control strategy designed with the *Control System Toolbox* of MATLAB is to be used. Figure 5 presents the root locus of the control system after tuning the second order filter parameters (ξ_f and ω_f) so that the first flexible mode of vibration become actively damped. After the tuning process ($\xi_f = 0.9$ and $\omega_f = 900$ rad/s), the next step consists of selecting the control gain which most approaches

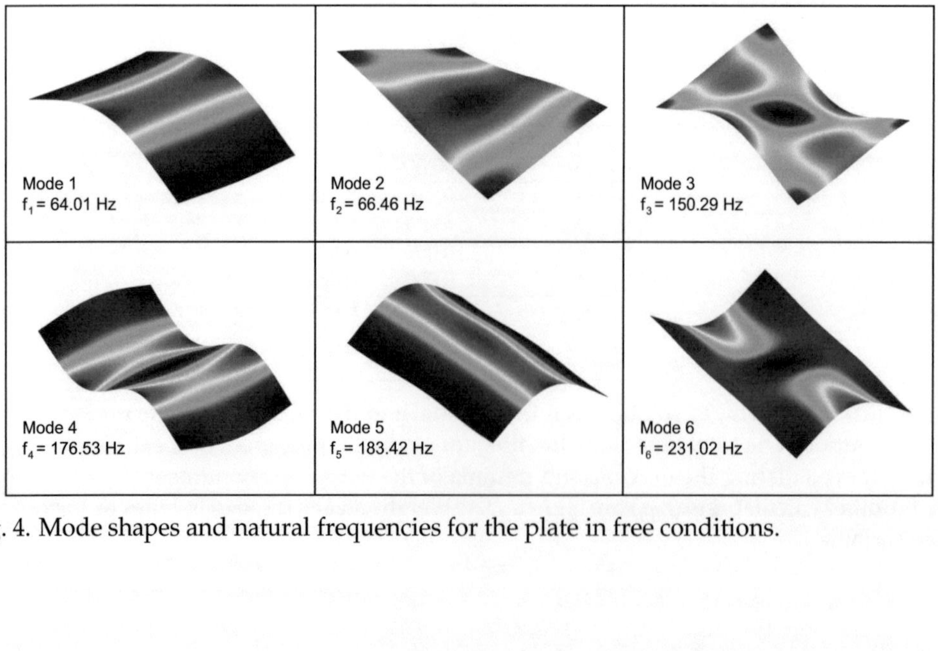

Fig. 4. Mode shapes and natural frequencies for the plate in free conditions.

the maximum damping of the first vibration mode ($\xi_{1,\max}$). In this particular case, a gain of $g = 0.200$ entails a selected damping coefficient of $\xi_{1,\text{sel}} = 88.30\%$. Figure 5 also shows the characteristic stability limit of the Positive Position Feedback control systems and the fact that only the first and the fifth modal shapes seem to be controllable in the view of the wide loops going from the poles to the zeros (Preumont, 2002).

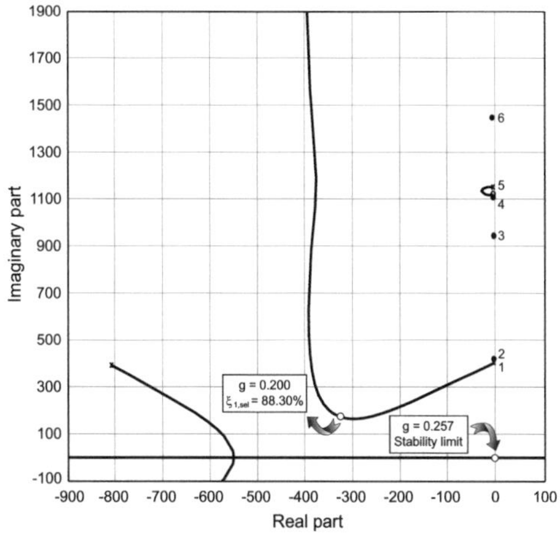

Fig. 5. Root locus of the control system after tuning the second order filter parameters to the first flexible mode of vibration ($\xi_f = 0.9$ and $\omega_f = 900$ rad/s).

In the proposed case study the collocated pair of actuator and sensor are subjected to uncertainty. More precisely, the position of the centre of both the actuator and sensor are considered to be uncertain parameters. Additionally, another source of uncertainty corresponding to the structural damping of the plate is included as this is known to be uncertain in practice. Thus, we have a total of five different fuzzy numbers: $\tilde{x}_a$ (position "x" of the centre of the actuator), $\tilde{y}_a$ (position "y" of the centre of the actuator), $\tilde{x}_s$ (position "x" of the centre of the sensor), $\tilde{y}_s$ (position "y" of the centre of the sensor) and $\tilde{\xi}$ (structural damping). The membership functions of these fuzzy parameters, assuming that they are both symmetric and triangular, can be seen in Figure 6.
After applying the Fuzzy Finite Element algorithm described in Section 4 one can obtain several fuzzy outputs which describe the stability and performance of the control system. In fact, it is possible to choose those variables which better fit the effects which one is interested in. In this particular case, the following are calculated:

$\tilde{G}$ Gain margin.

$\tilde{P}$ Phase margin.

$\tilde{\xi}_{1,\max}$ Maximum damping coefficient of the first mode.

$\tilde{\xi}_{1,\text{sel}}$ Selected damping coefficient of the first mode.

The gain margin $\tilde{G}$ is the increase in the system gain when the phase is -180 that will result in a marginally stable system with intersection of the $-1 + j0$ point on the Nyquist diagram. The phase margin $\tilde{P}$ is the amount phase shift of the system at unity magnitude that will result in a marginally stable system with intersection of the $-1 + j0$ point on the Nyquist diagram. The maximum damping coefficient $\tilde{\xi}_{1,\max}$ is the highest damping achievable in the first mode loop independently of the selected gain, whilst the selected damping coefficient $\tilde{\xi}_{1,\text{sel}}$ is the

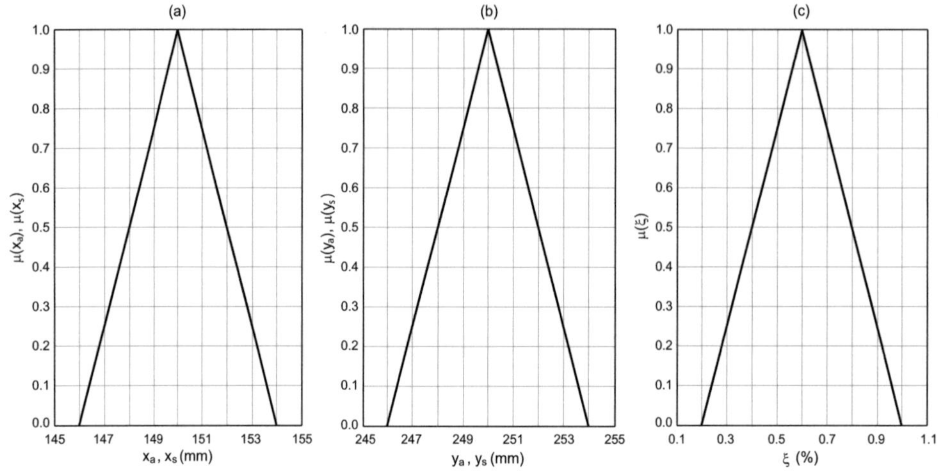

Fig. 6. Membership functions of the input fuzzy numbers: (a) coordinates of the centre of the actuator ($\tilde{x}_a$ and $\tilde{x}_s$), (b) coordinates of the centre of the sensor ($\tilde{y}_a$ and $\tilde{y}_s$) and (c) structural damping of the plate ($\tilde{\xi}$).

damping that the control systems provides at the value of gain selected in the deterministic case. Clearly, the gain and phase margins can be used to quantify controller stability, whilst the damping ratios serve to quantify performance and reliability.
The membership functions of these variables are shown in Figure 7. We observe that the uncertainty considered may lead to a both better and worse behaviour of the control system in comparison to the considered deterministic situation.
Another possibility for obtaining a global view of the whole control system lies in plotting its root locus for different α-sublevels or α-cuts. In particular, we show in Figure 8 the root locus for two different values of the membership. Although the fourth mode has not been

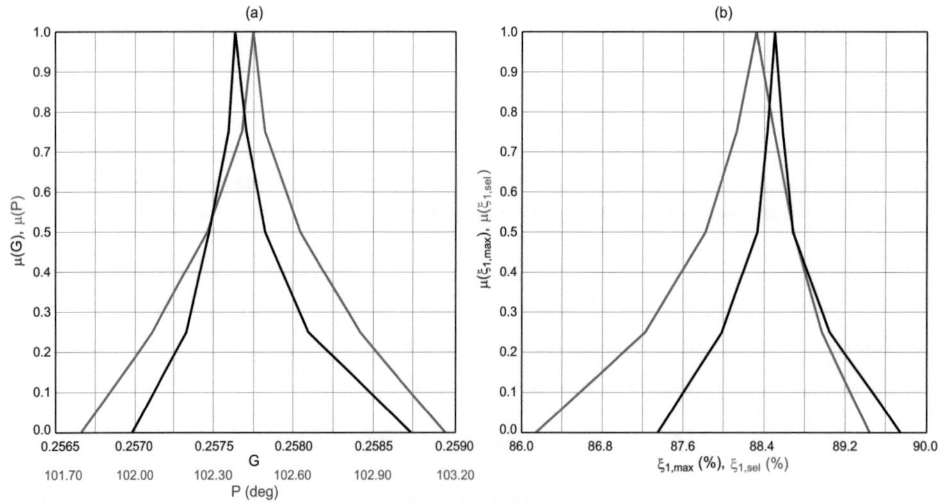

Fig. 7. Membership function of the output fuzzy numbers: (a) stability indicators ($\tilde{G}$ in black color and $\tilde{P}$ in gray color) and (b) performance indicators ($\tilde{\xi}_{1,max}$ in black color and $\tilde{\xi}_{1,sel}$ in gray color).

specifically analyzed via fuzzy variables, we can note that its zero crosses the imaginary axis and becomes unstable for some values of the gain. Note that zeros are essentially related to mode shapes of the structure, which tend to be more sensitive to the parameter uncertainty than the natural frequencies. This fact warns us that a higher gain level may lead to instability of the fourth mode when actively damping the first, which can be detected easily by means of including new fuzzy variables in the analysis such as the maximum real part of the closed loop poles.

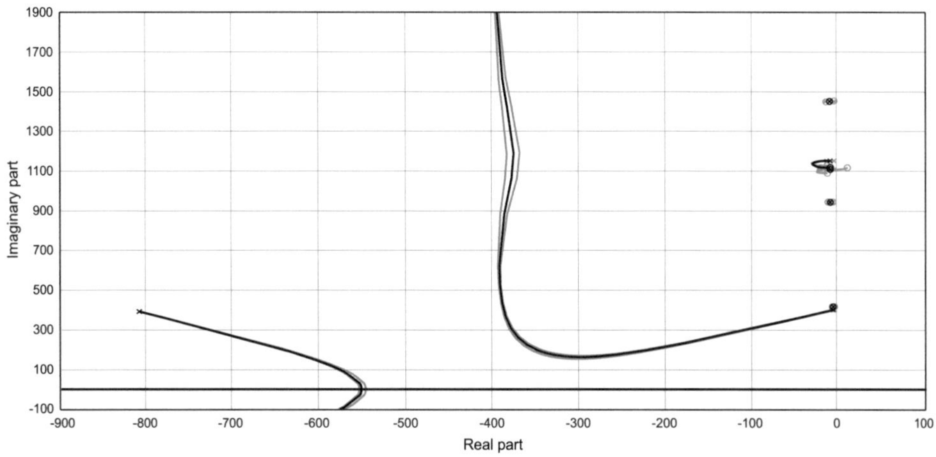

Fig. 8. Root locus of the control system for two different α-cuts: $\mu = 1$ (black) and $\mu = 0$ (grey).

6. Conclusion

In this chapter we have shown the suitability of the matrix computing environment MATLAB to solve control problems of structures via finite element analysis and root locus design and how these two issues have been blended and integrated into a Fuzzy Finite Element methodology for the analysis and simulation of uncertain control of structures.
The Fuzzy Finite Element procedure has been described. The approach relies on the α-cut technique which subdivides the membership range into a number of α-levels. The fuzzy arithmetic is based upon an efficient implementation in MATLAB code for the Transformation Method. This implementation has been modified and improved with some enhanced features. This methodology has been shown to be applicable to a realistic case study related to structural control using a Positive Position Feedback technique and piezoelectric actuators and sensors. In the light of the obtained results, the proposed procedure may prove useful to other analysis involving any other control technique or uncertainty source. In addition, the efficient implementation obtained due to MATLAB programming allows us to achieve high accuracy results together with low computational costs.
Finally, further research may be carried out in this topic. Firstly, a more efficient implementation of the Transformation Method can be found when using *cell* arrays instead of *double* arrays or when considering multiple fuzzy outputs. Secondly, the Transformation Method also allows a sort of sensitivity analysis which should be included in the MATLAB implementation in order to endow our method with extended capabilities. Thirdly, and in-depth comparison between this possibilistic methodology and the robust H_∞ optimal control theory must be carried out in order to identify more precisely the situations in which one method stand out from the other.

7. Acknowledgment

The authors are grateful for the support received from the "Ministerio de Educación" of the Spanish government through the "Programa Nacional de Movilidad de Recursos Humanos del Plan Nacional de I-D+i 2008-2011" and from the EPSRC through grant reference EP/D078601/1.

8. References

Balmes, E., Bianchi, J.-P. & Leclére, J.-M. (2009). *Structural Dynamics Toolbox for use with MATLAB: User's guide.*

De Gersem, H., Moens, D., Desmet, W. & Vandepitte, D. (2005). A fuzzy finite element procedure for the calculation of uncertain frequency response functions of damped structures: Part 2 - numerical case studies, *Journal of Sound and Vibration* 288: 463–486.

De Munck, M., Moens, D., Desmet, W. & Vandepitte, D. (2008). A response surface based optimisation algorithm for the calculation of fuzzy envelope frfs of models with uncertain properties, *Computers & Structures* 86: 1080–1092.

Dosch, J. J., Daniel, D. J. & Garcia, E. (1992). A self-sensing piezoelectric actuator for collocated control, *Journal of Intelligent Material Systems and Structures* 3: 166–185.

Dubois, D. & Prade, H. M. (1980). *Fuzzy sets and systems : theory and applications*, Mathematics in science and engineering, Academic Press, New York.

Gu, D.-W., Petkov, P. H. & Konstantinov, M. M. (2005). *Robust control design with MATLAB*, Springer, London.

Hanss, M. (2002). The transformation method for the simulation and analysis of systems with uncertain parameters, *Fuzzy Sets and Systems* 130: 277–289.

Klimke, A. (2003). An efficient implementation of the transformation method of fuzzy arithmetic, (IANS), extended preprint 2003/009, *Technical report*, University of Stuttgart.

Moens, D. & Vandepitte, D. (2005). A fuzzy finite element procedure for the calculation of uncertain frequency-response functions of damped structures: Part 1 - procedure, *Journal of Sound and Vibration* 288: 431–462.

Oberkampf, W. L., Helton, J. C., Joslyn, C. A., Wojtkiewicz, S. F. & Ferson, S. (2004). Challenge problems: uncertainty in system response given uncertain parameters, *Reliability Engineering & System Safety* 85: 11–19.

OpenFEM (2011).
URL: *http://support.sdtools.com/gf/project/openfem*

Preumont, A. (2002). *Vibration control of active structures: An introduction*, Kluwer Academic, Dordrecht.

Sims, N. D., Bayly, P. V. & Young, K. A. (2005). Piezoelectric sensors and actuators for milling tool stability lobes, *Journal of Sound and Vibration* 281: 743–762.

Sims, N. D., Manson, G. & Mann, B. (2010). Fuzzy stability analysis of regenerative chatter in milling, *Journal of Sound and Vibration* 329: 1025–1041.

Zadeh, L. A. (1965). Fuzzy sets, *Information and Control* 8: 338–353.

Zames, G. (1981). Feedback and optimal sensitivity: Model reference transformations, multiplicative seminorms and approximate inverses, *IEEE Transactions on Automatic Control* 26: 301–320.

Zames, G. & Francis, B. A. (1983). Feedback, minimax sensitivity and optimal robustness, *IEEE Transactions on Automatic Control* 28: 585–601.

Part 4

Modelling, Identification and Simulation

16

Visual and Thermal Image Fusion for UAV Based Target Tracking

K. Senthil Kumar[1], G. Kavitha[2],
R. Subramanian[3] and G. Ramesh[4]
[1]*Division of Avionics, Department of Aerospace Engineering,*
Madras Institute of Technology, Anna University,
[2]*Department of Electronics and Communication Engineering,*
Madras Institute of Technology, Anna University
[3]*Division of Avionics, Department of Aerospace Engineering,*
Madras Institute of Technology, Anna University
[4]*National Aerospace Laboratories (NAL) Bangalore,*
India

1. Introduction

Unmanned aerial vehicles (UAVs) are aircrafts which have the capability of flight without an onboard pilot. These vehicles are remotely controlled, semi-autonomous, autonomous, or have a combination of these capabilities. UAV's has its applications in a whole lot of domains. Image processing applications with specific importance to surveillance and reconnaissance is of immense interest.

UAVs are equipped with imaging sensor platform, which operates remotely controlled, semi-autonomously or autonomously, without a pilot sitting in the vehicle. The platform may have a small or medium size still-video or video camera, thermal or infrared camera systems, airborne light detection and ranging (LIDAR) system, or a combination thereof. All these different kinds of cameras are an effective sensor tool which is portable, light weight and airborne in a platform on the UAV.

Thermal images have a valuable advantage over the visual images. Thermal images do not depend on the illumination, the output is the projection of thermal sensors of the emissions of heat of the objects. This unique merit gives rise for effective segmentation of objects. Ultimately, surveillance measure using an UAV gets improved.

With the development of new imaging sensors arises the need of a meaningful combination of all employed imaging sources. Image fusion of visual and thermal sensing outputs adds a new dimension in making the target tracking more reliable. Target tracking at instances of smoke, fog, cloudy conditions gets improved. With conditions of same background colour perception of target unnoticed getting eliminated with thermal image inclusion, image fusion gives complementary information. A holistic system which represents the combined fused data is perceived at the control level of the UAV's.

2. Thermal imaging

Thermography which uses black body radiation law makes it to have information gathering without visible illumination. Thermal imaging cameras detect radiation in the infrared (IR) range of the electromagnetic spectrum (3-6 μm and 8–14 μm).

The charge coupled device (CCD) and complementary metal oxide semiconductor (CMOS) sensors are used for visible light cameras. These can detect only the non thermal part of the infrared spectrum called near-infrared (NIR). On the other hand, thermal imaging cameras make use specialized focal plane arrays (FPAs) that respond to longer wavelengths (mid- and long-wavelength infrared).

There is also a difference between how far one can see with a cooled and with an uncooled thermal imaging camera. Cooled camera systems are more expensive, but generally have a longer range than uncooled systems under many conditions. Extremely long range thermal imaging applications are best served by cooled camera systems. This is particularly true in the midwave band in humid atmospheric conditions.

The heat radiation is focused onto special receptors in the camera which convert it into a format which is displayed on a monitor in monochrome which is recognisable by the human eye. The objects emitting the greatest intensity of heat are usually presented as the darkest (black) in the greyscale, i.e. known as 'black-hot'. Many cameras have a function whereby the functionality can be switched from 'blackhot' to 'white-hot' and back again at the operator's wish. Probably the greatest 'enemy' of thermal imaging is extended rainfall since that has the effect of cooling all inanimate objects and severely reducing contrast.

Thermal imaging makes it possible of real time target tracking. Detection of targets in dark and low light conditions can be done. All weather operation and dull, dirty and dangerous (DDD) roles are possible.

Thermal imaging cameras produce a clear image in the darkest of nights, in light fog and smoke and in the most diverse weather conditions. There has also been an increased interest in thermal imaging for all kinds of security applications, from long-range surveillance at border crossings, truck and shipping container inspection, to the monitoring of high-security installations such as nuclear power stations, airports, and dams. But thermal imaging has a lot more to offer than just a night vision solution for security applications.

Car manufacturers are integrating night vision modules for driver vision enhancement into cars. By helping drivers to see at night, accidents can be avoided. Boats and yachts are being equipped with thermal imaging cameras for night time navigation and other maritime applications like man overboard searches.

Often the thermal imager is just a small part of the complete system as in an UAS, so it needs to be as small, light and inexpensive as possible. Low-cost thermal imager is used as a pilot's night vision enhancement. It helps pilots by enhancing the ability to see terrain and other aircraft at long ranges, even in total darkness, light fog, dust and smoke. Thermal imaging is a technology that enables detection of people and objects in total darkness and in very diverse weather conditions.

A typical application for thermal imaging is border security, where most threats occur at night. Thermal imaging allows the aircraft to fly in total darkness and detect targets through smoke. The same aircraft can also be used to detect such things as forest fires. Areas which are hotter than the surroundings can indicate the start of a fire and can clearly be seen on a thermal image.

3. Image segmentation

Segmentation is the key and the first step to automatic target recognition, which will directly affect the accuracy of the following work. As a result, the division methods and its precision degree are essential. Infrared heat wave image is different from the visible light images. It reflects the distribution of the object surface temperature and latent characteristics of material form.

The infrared heat radiation, due to the imperfections of the system, will bring a variety of noise in the imaging process. The noise of complex distribution of infrared images makes the signal to noise ratio lower than visible light images.

3.1 2D OTSU algorithm

The two dimensional Otsu algorithm is given as follows. Suppose an image pixel size is M × N, gray-scale of the image ranges from 0 to L-1. The neighborhood average gray g (m, n) of the coordinate definition (m, n) pixel point is as follows:

$$g\,(m,n) = \frac{1}{kxk}\sum_{i=-(k-1)/2}^{(k-1)/2}\sum_{j=-(k-1)/2}^{(k-1)/2} f(m+i, n+j) \tag{1}$$

Calculating the average neighbourhood gray of each pixel point, a gray binary group (i, j) may form. We use C_{ij} *to* represent the occurrence frequency of (i, j). Then the probability P_{ij} of vector (i, j) may be determined by the formula:

$$P_{ij} = \frac{Cij}{M\,X\,N} \tag{2}$$

Here, $0 \leq I, j < L$, and $\sum_{i=0}^{L-1}\sum_{j=0}^{L-1} P_{ij} = 1$.

Assuming the existence of two classes C_0 and C_1 in Two dimensional form, the histogram represents their respective goals and background, and with two different probability density distribution function. If making use of two-dimensional histogram threshold vector (s, t) to segment the image (of which $0 \leq s, t < L$), then the probability of two classes are respectively:

The probability of background occurrence is:

$$\omega_0 = P(C_0) = \sum_{i=0}^{s}\sum_{j=0}^{t} P_{ij} = \omega_0\,(s,t) \tag{3}$$

The probability of object occurrence is:

$$\omega_1 = P(C_1) = \sum_{i=s+1}^{L-1}\sum_{j=t+1}^{L-1} P_{ij} = \omega_1\,(s,t) \tag{4}$$

The definition of dispersion matrix:

$$\sigma B = \omega 0\,[(\mu 0-\mu\tau)(\mu 0-\mu\tau)T] + \omega 1\,[(\mu 1-\mu\tau)(\mu 1-\mu\tau)T] \tag{5}$$

When the track of the above-mentioned dispersion matrix gets the maximum, the corresponding threshold of segmentation is the optimal threshold (S, T), namely:

$$tr(\sigma_B\,(S,T)) = max_{0\leq s,t<L}\,\{tr(\sigma_B\,(S,T))\} \tag{6}$$

We know that 2-D thermal images with noise segmented by Otsu way may get better results compared to one dimensional threshold segmentation methods. However, the computation cost gets huge, which is because the determination of the optimal threshold need to travel all the s and t, of which $0 \leq s, t < L$. That is to say, the more gray scale value of images is, the longer choice time of the threshold is.

The segmentation of various thermal images is illustrated here. The segmentation results can be made more efficient in identification of targets and optimized by a number of methods. These segmentation results are used in fused image target tracking. One such method will be determining optimum threshold using histogram analysis. The method of using chaos based genetic algorithm makes the process time lower. The chaos based genetic algorithm uses Otsu algorithm as fitness function and proceeds for segmentation.
The so-called chaos refers to the uncertainty in the system appearing in seemingly without rules. From the mathematical sense, for determined series initial values, it is possible to predict the long-term behaviour of the system, even know its past behaviour and state by the power system. It is a unique phenomenon of non-linear systems. Chaos has randomicity, ergodicity and regularity. Based on these characteristics of chaos, using chaotic variables to optimize search is no doubt better than random search. Logistic map is the most basic chaotic map. The chaos equation of the Logistic definition can be described as follows:

$$x_{(n+1)} = u\, x_n\, (1 - x_n) \ ; \quad 0 < u \leq 4 \tag{7}$$

x_n lies between 0 and 1. n varies from 0,1,2, etc.

Fig. 1. Thermal Image

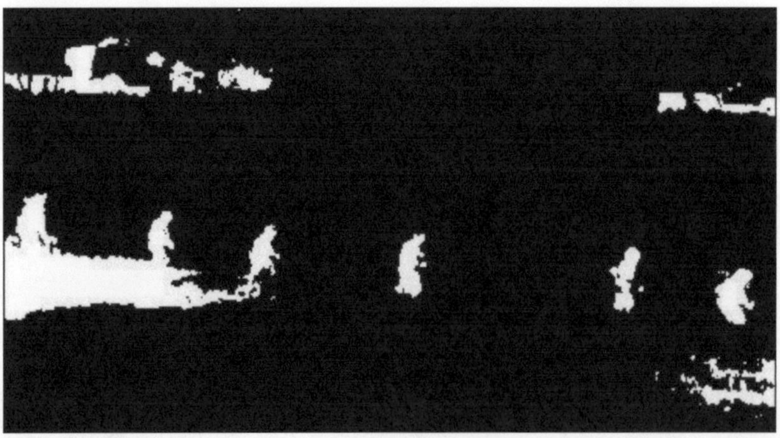

Fig. 2. Segmented Image

When u = 4, the system is the chaos state of the biggest ergodicity. Genetic algorithm is a kind of random search algorithm drawn from natural selection and natural genetic mechanisms of biology, which is particularly well suited to deal with the complex and nonlinear problems that traditional search methods are difficult to resolve.

Fig. 3. Thermal Image

Fig. 4. Segmented Image

The segmentation results are shown in Fig. 1 to Fig. 4 with the segmented image of the thermal image.

4. Image fusion process

Image fusion is the process by which two or more images are combined into a single image retaining the important features from each of the original images. The fusion of images is often required for images acquired from different instrument modalities or capture techniques of the same scene or objects. Important applications of the fusion of images include medical imaging, microscopic imaging, remote sensing, computer vision, and robotics. Fusion techniques include the simplest method of pixel averaging to more complicated methods such as principal component analysis (PCA) and wavelet transform (WT) based fusion.

Image fusion is the process of relevant information extraction from two or more images. The resulting image will encompass more information than any of the given input images. A multi sensor, multi temporal and multi view information techniques are required which overcome the limitations of using single senor information. The benefits of image fusion are extended range of operation, extended spatial and temporal resolution and coverage, reduced uncertainty, higher accuracy, reliability and compact representation.

Various kinds of image fusion for visual, Infrared and Synthetic Aperture Radar (SAR) images exist. Some of the primitive fusion process algorithms also have disadvantages. Direct fusion method makes the image blurred. The pixel based image fusion is computationally complex for large and high resolution images. The image averaging method produces a reduced contrast of information. The requirement is thus a novel and efficient information fusion process. Image fusion has a significant role of recognition of targets and objects. Target identification, localisation, filtering and data association forms an important application of the fusion process. Thus an effective surveillance and reconnaissance system can be formed.

There is information which is redundant and at the same time complementary too. The following summarize several approaches to the pixel level fusion of spatially registered input images. A generic categorization of image fusion methods in the following:

- Linear Superposition, Nonlinear Methods, Expectation Maximisation, Image Pyramids, Wavelet Transform, Generic Multiresolution Fusion Scheme, Optimization Approaches, Artificial Neural Networks, Fuzzy Techniques

Some of the prominent applications of image fusion are:

- Concealed Weapon Detection, Night Time Surveillance, Automatic Landing System, Digital Camera Applications, Medical Diagnosis, Defect Inspection and Remote Sensing

4.1 Wavelet transform

A signal analysis method similar to image pyramids is the discrete wavelet transform. The main difference is that while image pyramids lead to an over complete set of transform coefficients, the wavelet transform results in a nonredundant image representation. The discrete two dimensional wavelet transform is computed by the recursive application of low pass and high pass filters in each direction of the input image (i.e. rows and columns) followed by sub sampling.

These basis functions or baby wavelets are obtained from a single prototype wavelet called the mother wavelet, by dilations or contractions (scaling) and translations (shifts). They have advantages over traditional Fourier methods in analyzing physical situations where the signal contains discontinuities and sharp spikes.

Image fusion process is achieved by multiresolution decomposition at fourth level. The multiwavelet decomposition coefficients of the input images are appropriately merged and a new fixed image is obtained by reconstructing the fused multiwavelet coefficients. The theory of multiwavelets is also based on the idea of multiresolution analysis (MRA) as shown in Fig. 5. During a single level of decomposition using a scalar wavelet transform, the two-dimensional (2-D) image data is replaced with four blocks corresponding to the subbands representing either low-pass or high-pass filtering in each direction.

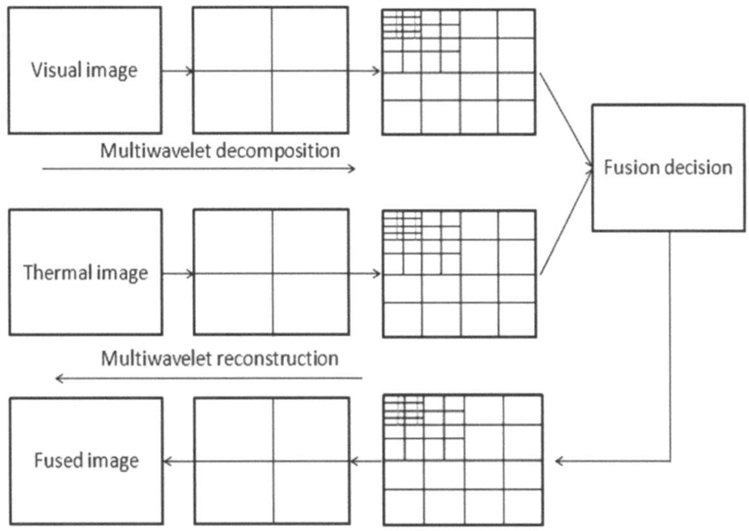

Fig. 5. Wavelet Multi Resolution Analysis

The Haar wavelet is a certain sequence of rescaled "square-shaped" functions which together form a wavelet family or basis. Wavelet analysis is similar to Fourier analysis in that it allows a target function over an interval to be represented in terms of an orthonormal function basis. The Haar wavelet is also the simplest possible wavelet.

4.2 FIS based image fusion

Neural Network and Fuzzy Logic approach can be used for sensor fusion. Such a sensor fusion could belong to a class of sensor fusion in which case the features could be input and decision could be output. The system can be trained from the input data obtained from the sensors.

The basic concept is to associate the given sensory inputs with some decision outputs. The following algorithm for pixel level image fusion using Fuzzy Logic illustrate the process of defining membership functions and rules for the image fusion process using FIS (Fuzzy Inference System) editor of Fuzzy Logic toolbox in MATLAB. The process flow of the process is as follows:

1. The visual and thermal image forms the inputs for the fusion system. The inputs must be with the same field of view.
2. With a gray level conversion applied, the two images are transformed to a column form.
3. The number and type of membership functions for both the input images are given to the FIS. The rule base for FIS decides how the output fused image should be.
4. The fused image is converted back to matrix format from column form.

The fuzzy system considered here is Mamdani type and its' FIS model in MATLAB is shown in Fig. 6. The Mamdani rule base is a crisp model of a system, i.e. it takes crisp inputs and produces crisp outputs. It does this with the use of user-defined fuzzy rules on user-defined fuzzy variables.

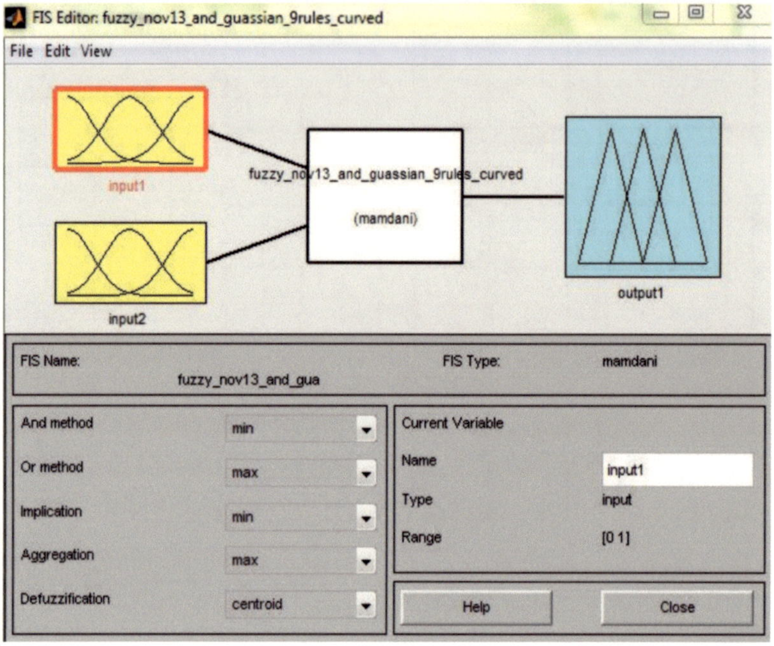

Fig. 6. FIS Model

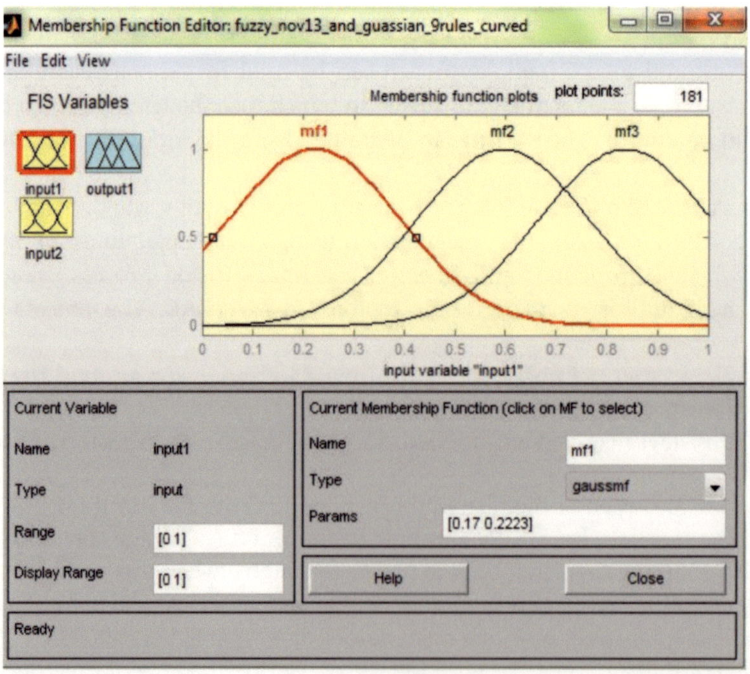

Fig. 7. FIS Membership Function

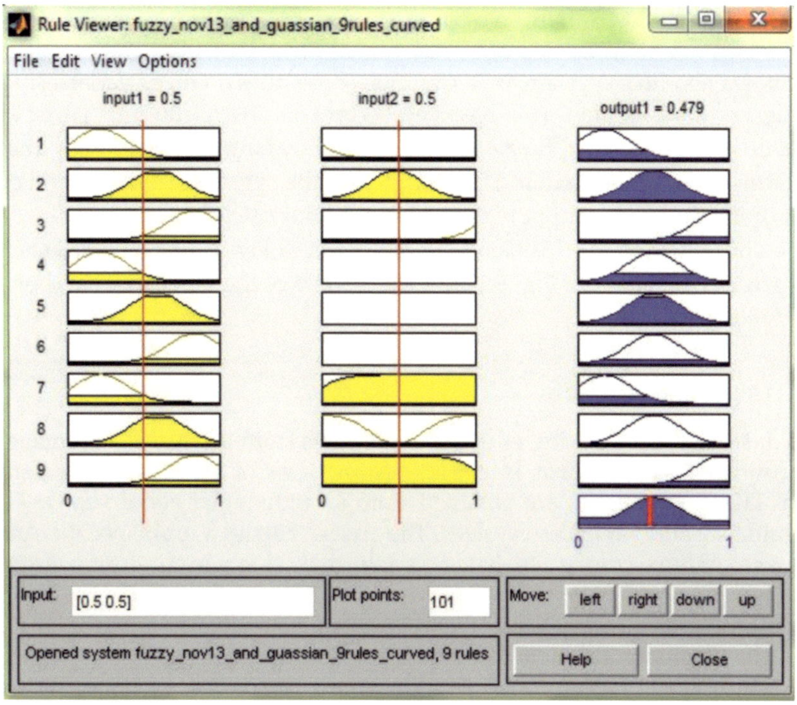

Fig. 8. Rule Base of FIS

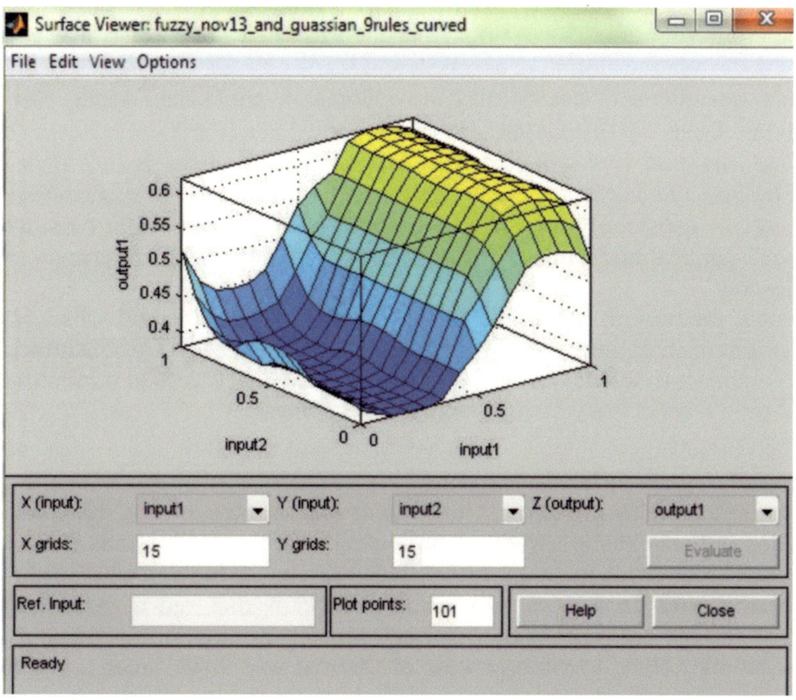

Fig. 9. Surface View of FIS

The idea behind using a Mamdani rule base to model crisp system behavior is that the rules for many systems can be easily described in terms of fuzzy variables. Thus we can effectively model a complex non-linear system, with common-sense rules on fuzzy variables.
The operation of the Mamdani rule base can be broken down into four parts: 1) mapping each of the crisp inputs into a fuzzy variable (fuzzification), 2) determining the output of each rule given its fuzzy antecedents, 3) determining the aggregate output of all of the fuzzy rules; 4) mapping the fuzzy output to crisp output (defuzzification).
The membership function used is Guassian as shown in Fig. 7. The rule base is formed for the fusion process as shown in Fig. 8. The surface view of the two inputs and one output is represented in Fig. 9.

5. Target tracking of objects

Automatic detection and tracking of interested targets from a sequence of images obtained from a reconnaissance platform is an interesting area of research for defence related application. The video images are obtained from an unmanned aerial vehicle (UAV) with on-board guidance and navigation system. The aircraft carries a multispectral camera which acquires images of the territory and sends the information to a ground control station (GCS) in real time.
During flight, the pilot in the ground control station may identify a region of interest as a target. This identification can be click and target type or an intelligent perception type.
The target which appears on a small window could be tracked by engaging track mode. Optical flow is an approximation of the local image motion based upon local derivatives in a given sequence of images. That is, in 2D it specifies how much each image pixel moves between adjacent images while in 3D in specifies how much each volume voxel moves between adjacent volumes. The 2D image sequences used are formed under perspective projection via the relative motion of a camera and scene objects.
The differential methods for determining the optical flow are Lucas-Kanade, Horn-Schunck, Buxton-Buxton, Black-Jepson and variational methods.
Lucas–Kanade method is a widely used differential method for optical flow estimation developed by Bruce D. Lucas and Takeo Kanade. The assumption in this method is that the flow is essentially constant in a local neighbourhood of the pixel under consideration, and solves the basic optical flow equations for all the pixels in that neighbourhood, by the least squares criterion.
Horn–Schunck method of estimating optical flow is a global method which introduces a global constraint of smoothness to solve the aperture problem. The Horn-Schunck algorithm assumes smoothness in the flow over the whole image. Thus, it tries to minimize distortions in flow and prefers solutions which show more smoothness.

5.1 Tracking of objects in fused images

A brief representation of the process used is as represented in Fig. 10. The visual and thermal video is first obtained from an airborne camera. The cameras used must be of acceptable resolution with good preprocessing features. A high resolution, light weight, rugged, portable, stabilized platform sensing element is required to be mounted on the airframe. The images are preprocessed for ego-sensory motion, atmospheric disturbances and inherent noise. Then a fusion process of thermal and visual images is adapted. The algorithms for such a fusion process would involve processing of information separately and then fusing the data. The other way is to fuse and process the data available.

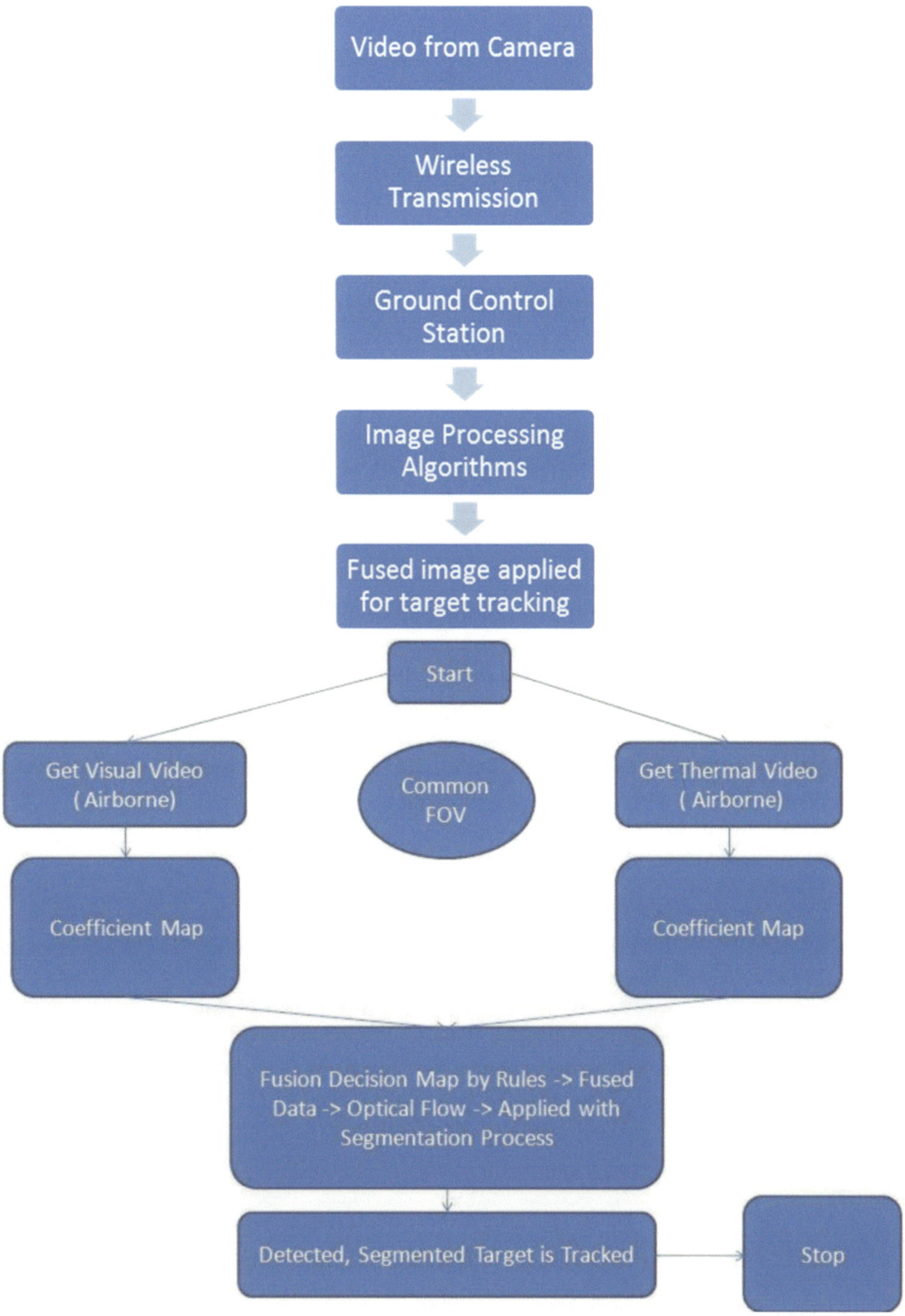

Fig. 10. Process Flow

The transmission of information from on board real time processing and display of all required data are done in the ground station. The control interaction with UAV is done by wireless communication transfer.

The video file obtained from the camera is loaded as an avi file. It is processed in MATLAB. It aids in real time and efficient implementation of the algorithm. The video is processed for detection of targets in a sequence of frames. The target detection and localisation process commences from applying the frames to an optical flow pattern which generates vectors. The target detection is done with respect to feature matching and extraction from the initial frame. The target which is the region of interest is separated out effectively. By using this novel technique, an optimized search process for an effective segmented image with less noise effects when compared to other algorithms is obtained. The targets are thus effectively located and segmented. The output frames are integrated to form a video file. Then effective tracking algorithms are applied for the process. Filtering and the required data association for the output obtained are subsequently done. The inputs needed for processing include that of two images (Visual and thermal) for image fusion. The steps involved are:

1. The airborne video is obtained from the UAV with
   a. A visual and thermal camera onboard the UAV.
   b. Wireless transmission of video to ground control station.
2. The inputs needed are two videos (visual and thermal) which are split into images with respect to frames. The factors to be considered are:
   a. Two videos are to be of same resolution and frame rate.
   b. Two images are to be considered with the same field of view (FOV).
3. Segmentation process is applied to the images and the targets are segmented.
4. For the fusion process:
   a. Consider two images at a time.
   b. Apply wavelet based image fusion with Haar transform with four level decomposition of the image.
   c. An inverse transform is applied to get back the fused image.
5. For tracking algorithm:
   a. The tracking algorithm is implemented in SIMULINK in MATLAB. The fused images are stitched to form a video of the same frame rate.
   b. The fused image is applied to an optical flow technique. The optical flow technique is based on Horn-Schunck method.
   c. Further segmentation accompanied with thresholding principles is applied for the output obtained after computing optical flow.
   d. Blob detection principles accompany the process for spotting the targets in the frame of concern. Thus the targets are given a rectangular boundary of identification.

6. Results

Image fusion results based on wavelet transform are discussed. Two images (Visual and thermal) are taken as shown in Fig. 11 and Fig. 12.

The visual image gives a realistic human sensing view. The thermal image identifies the target with the temperature difference coming into the picture with objects possessing different emissivity values.

Fig. 11. Visual Image

Fig. 12. Thermal Image

The fused image is given as Fig. 13. The fusion process is applied for a concealed weapon detection process. The results for such an application are given below in Fig. 14 to Fig. 15. The visual and thermal images are fused and the fused image gives combined information in one representation.

Fig. 13. Fused Image

Fig. 14. Thermal Image

Fig. 15. Fused Image

The thermal images clearly give the information about concealed weapons. The fused image gives both the RGB based information present in visual image and the concealed weapon information present in thermal image. The fused image is thus capable of giving enhanced detection capabilities.

6.1 Target tracking results

For target tracking, the database of thermal and visual images is considered. The video obtained is converted to a series of frames. Each thermal and visual image is fused and at the end the fused images are combined to form a video which is given for target tracking process.

One such visual and thermal image from the sequence of frames is shown in Fig. 16 and Fig. 17. The fused image obtained as a result of wavelet transform using Haar wavelet is shown in Fig. 18.

Fig. 16. Visual Image

Fig. 17. Thermal Image

Fig. 18. Fused Image

The target tracking results including segmentation, optical flow and identification of targets in their corresponding frame are shown in Fig. 19, Fig. 20 and Fig. 21.
For the four sample frames considered, the segmentation results and tracking results are illustrated. The segmentation shows that of humans being segmented according to the threshold values.

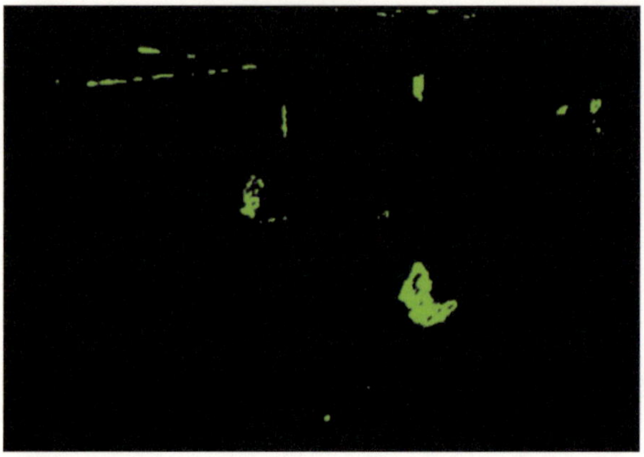

Fig. 19. Segmented Image

Fig. 20. Optical Flow Detection

The optical flow which is found out from the images gives the movement of the humans which is being tracked and given a rectangular representation.

Fig. 21. Target Detected Image

The following results correspond to taking the thermal images alone and doing target tracking. The target tracking for aerial aircrafts' motion is shown in Fig. 22 and Fig. 23. These images correspond to the optical flow and the target detection from a real time video sequence. The target tracking for identification of humans is given in Fig. 24. The targets are tracked with respect to the movement of objects identified with optical flow. In this frame, an airborne flight is being tracked. This aids to the visual perception other than usage of RADAR.

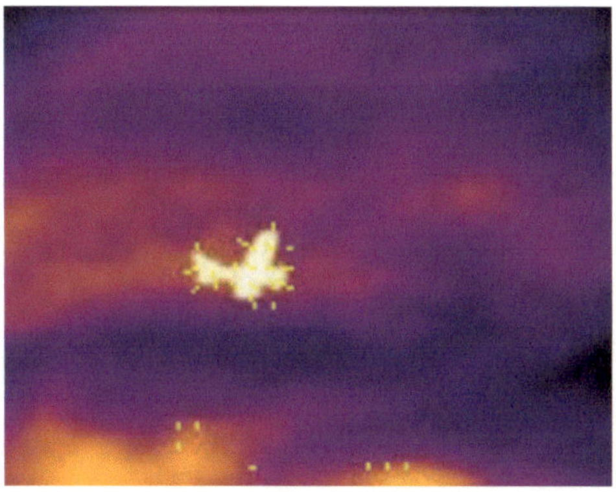

Fig. 22. Optical Flow Detection

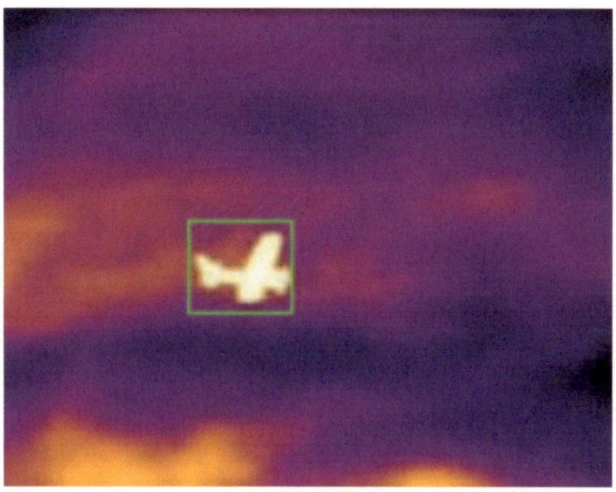

Fig. 23. Target Detected Image

Further sample results for tracking of objects in thermal video is shown in Fig. 24. This is an airborne thermal video which is tracked for vehicles and humans if present. The ego sensory motion is present in this kind of a dynamic moving platform. They have to be compensated for a stabilized video and for the tracking process has to be improved for a multiple target tracking environment.

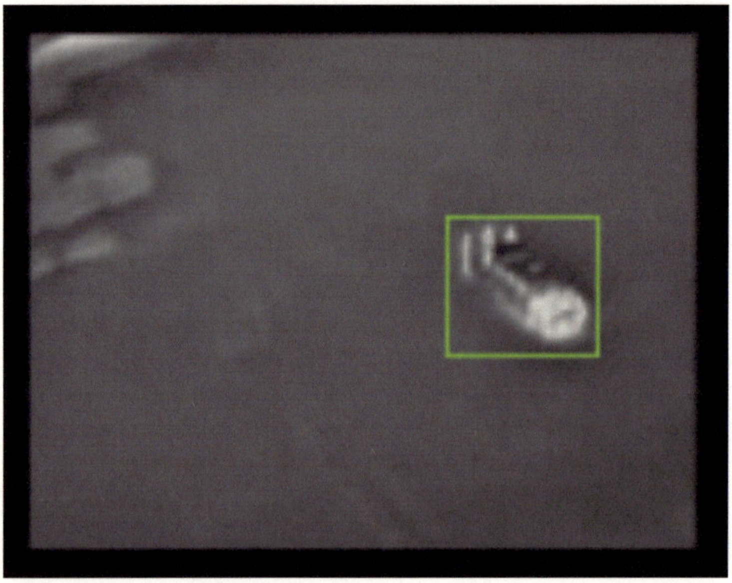

Fig. 24. Target Detection in Aerial Image

7. Conclusion

The airborne images obtained from an UAV are analysed in ground control station. By using the thermal images, all weather and night operation are possible. Visual and thermal image fusion is done and the fused image is given for target tracking.

This system has the benefit of enhanced target tracking application wherein only visual or thermal target tracking would not provide sufficient efficiency. Thus the image fusion process augments information leading to an improved system as a whole. The overall system incorporates segmentation, fusion and target tracking principles.

8. Acknowledgements

The authors are grateful to **The Vice Chancellor**, Anna University and **The Dean,** Madras Institute of Technology, Anna University for providing organizational facilities for carrying out this research work at Madras Institute of Technology. We would like to express our sincere thanks & gratitude to **The Director NAL** for providing sufficient funds for successful completion this sponsored research work. We also express special thanks to V.S.Chandrasekhar, B.P.Shasidhara and K.V.Srinivasan, Scientists, Aeronautical Development Establishment(ADE), DRDO, Bangalore. for their inspiration and encouragement. We would like to convey our thanks and wishes to all the **Avionics students.**

9. References

Y.Chena and C.Han, "Night-time Pedestrian Detection by Visual-Infrared Video Fusion," Proceedings of 7th World congress on Intelligent Control and Automation, China, 2008.

Anjali Malviya and S. G. Bhirud, "Visual Infrared Video Fusion for Night Vision using Background Estimation", Journal of Computing, Vol.2, April 2010.

Alex Leykin, Yang Ran and Riad Hammoud, "Thermal-Visible Video Fusion for Moving Target Tracking and Pedestrian Classification", IEEE Conference on Computer Vision and Pattern Recognition, Minneapolis, 2007.

Zhang Jin-Yu, Chen Yan and Huang Xian-Xiang, "IR Thermal Image Segmentation Based on Enhanced Genetic Algorithms and Two-Dimensional Classes Square Error", Second International Conference on Information and Computing Science, 2009.

Yi Wang, Aldo Camargo, Ronald Fevig, Florent Martel and Richard.R.Schultz, "Image Mosaicking from Uncooled Thermal IR Video Captured by a Small UAV", Proceedings of the IEEE Southwest Symposium on Image Analysis and Interpretation, 2008.

Daniel Olmeda, Arturo de la Escalera and Jos M Armingol, "Detection and Tracking of Pedestrians in Infrared Images", International Conference on Signals, Circuits and Systems, 2009.

Wai Kit Wong, Poi Ngee Tan, Chu Kiong Loo and Way Soong Lim, "An Effective Surveillance System Using Thermal Camera", International Conference on Signal Acquisition and Processing, 2009.

H.Wang, J.Peng and W.Wu, "Fusion algorithm for multisensory images based on discrete multiwavelet transform", Vision, Image and Signal Processing, Proceedings of the IEEE, Vol.149, no.5, 2002.

H.B.Mitchell, Image Fusion: Theories, Techniques and Applications, Springer, 2010. www.imagefusion.org

Wai Kit Wong, Hong Liang Lim, Chu Kiong Loo and Way Soong Lim, "Home alone faint detection surveillance system using thermal camera", Second International Conference on Computer Research and Development, Kuala Lumpur, 2010.

Ju Han and Bir Bhanu, "Fusion of color and infrared video for moving human detection," ACM Portal, Pattern Recognition, pp 1771-1784.

17

Research of Fuzzy-Systems of Automatic Frequency and Phase Control on Basis of MATLAB

Vladimir Gostev
State University of Information and Communication Technologies
Ukraine

1. Introduction

Systems of phase auto fine tuning (phase locked loop - PLL-system) are one of the most widespread functional knots of various electronic systems. A phase-locked loop (PLL) is a closed-loop feedback control system that generates and outputs a signal in relation to frequency and phase of an input "reference" signal. They are used in digital networks for synchronization of some exact setting generators on the reference generator, in frequency synthesizers for multichannel communication systems with frequency consolidation where the grid of carrier frequencies for division of channels is required, for example, in broadcasting and TV, in schemes of restoration bearing and clock frequencies in synchronous communication systems, as discriminators for demodulation is frequency - and phase-modulated bearing, as voice-frequency decoders in telephone switchboards for decoding of figures from accepted voice-frequency combinations. In the given chapter fuzzy-systems of frequency and phase auto fine tuning (PLL-system with the digital fuzzy controllers working on the basis of fuzzy logic) are investigated. Research of fuzzy-systems PLL is spent by mathematical modeling with use of the interactive environment for scientific and engineering calculations MATLAB and a powerful tool of modelling and research of control systems with feedback Simulink.

2.1 Fuzzy-systems of Phase Locked Loop –PLL

Let's consider widely used system of the PLL frequency control which function diagram is resulted on fig. 2.1.

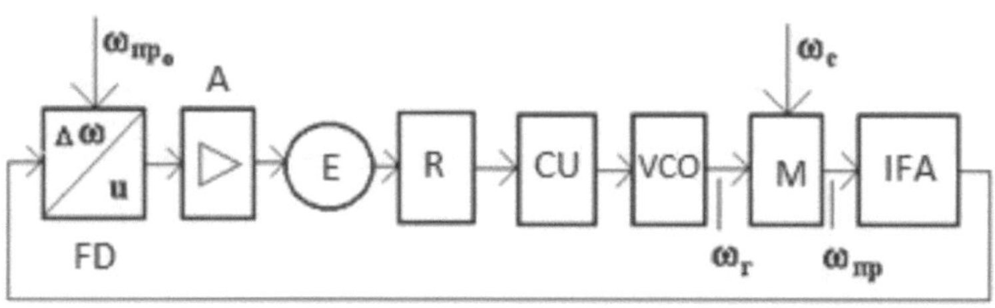

Fig. 2.1. System of the PLL frequency control.

A open-ended circuit of system is consists of serial connection of frequency discriminator FD, an amplifier A, an engine E with a reducer R, a controlling unit CU, a voltage-controlled oscillator VCO, a mixer M and intermediate - frequency amplifier IFA. System operation detail is described in [1]. A frequency discriminator can be presented by the series connection of a device of comparing, nonlinearity $K(\omega)$ and the low-pass filter LPF. An elementary low-pass filter is described by transfer function $G_F(s) = K_F(T_F s + 1)^{-1} = k/(s+b)$, where $k = K_F / T_F$, $b = 1/T_F$, K_F - gain factor T_F - a constant of time of the filter on the output of discriminator. We accept $\omega_{np_0} = const$ and $\omega_c = const$. Inertial properties of intensive elements can be neglected. An engine is used as an integrating element for giving to system astaticism the first order that allows to reduce a dynamic error. It is possible to use the electronic integrator instead of the electromechanical engine. Therefore transfer function of control object may be written down in a type $G_0(s) = \alpha[s(s+a)]^{-1}$, where $a = 1/T_G$, T_G - constant of time of the generator with a controlling unit.
The block diagram of system of the PLL frequency control in interactive system MATLAB we will present in a kind fig. 2.2. For maintenance of demanded dynamics of system it is used Fuzzy controller or PID-controller.
A curve $K(\omega)$ is called the static discrimination characteristic. The fluctuation component on an output of discriminator is described by spectral density S_n and dependence $S_n(\omega)$ is called of fluctuation characteristic of discriminator. At simulation fluctuation component can considered as voltage $V(t)$ - random disturbance applied to the output of the discriminator. A mathematical model of nonlinearity $K(\omega)$ we are describing expression

$$K(\omega) = K_d \omega \exp\{-\frac{\omega^2}{\Delta^2}\} \tag{2.1}$$

where K_d - a conversion coefficient of the discriminator, and Δ - a half-width of the discrimination characteristic, determines resolution capacity of the discriminator, $\omega \equiv \Delta\omega_{np}$ - detuning concerning nominal intermediate frequency $\omega_{np_0} = const$. Graphically a nonlinearity $K(\omega)$ at $\omega \equiv e$ is presented at the fig. 2.3

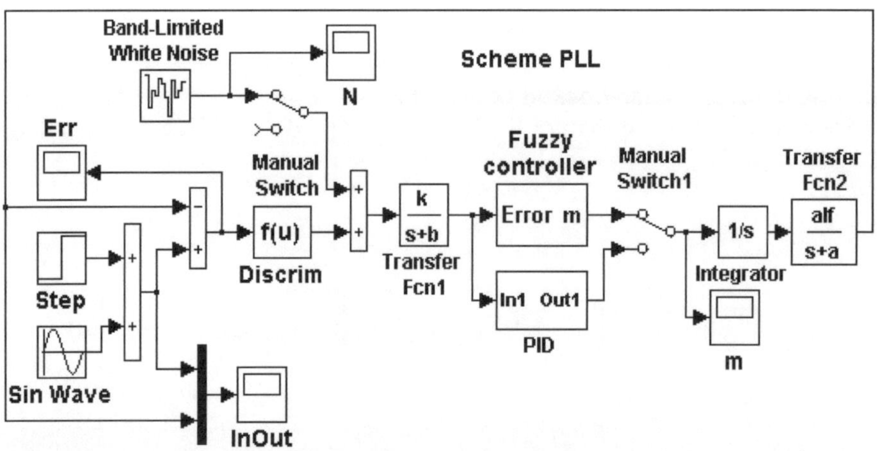

Fig. 2.2. The block diagram of system of the PLL frequency control.

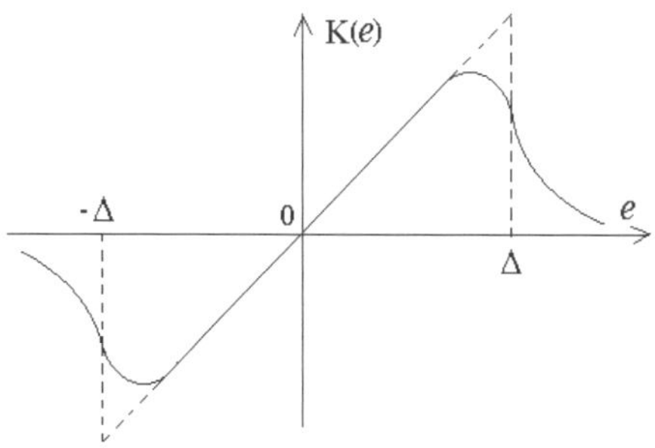

Fig. 2.3. A nonlinearity $K(\omega)$ at $\omega \equiv e$

It should be emphasized, that on an output of the unit of nonlinearity on the block diagram the mismatch error is defined as $K[\omega(t)] \equiv K[e(t)]$. The mismatch error on the input a frequency discriminator is defined as $\omega(t) \equiv e(t)$.
At the description of the discrimination characteristic represented on fig. 2.3, usually used approximation in a type

$$K(e) = K_d e \exp(-ae^2). \tag{2.2}$$

For determine the parameter a at the given half-width of the discrimination characteristic Δ area, bounded by a branch of function (2.2), which is defined as

$$K_d \int_0^{\infty} e \exp(-ae^2) de = \frac{K_d}{2a},$$

replace an area of a right triangle (fig. 2.3) with length of legs Δ and $K_d\Delta$ which is defined as $K_d\Delta^2 / 2$.
From here we have $a = 1/\Delta^2$ also expression (2.2) at $\omega \equiv e$ it will be transformed to expression (2.1).
A frequency discriminator FD (see fig. 2.1) in a figure 2.2 is presented by the comparing circuit from the adder and characteristic of discrimination Discrim -- $K(\omega)$. A low-pass filter LPF is described by link TransferFcn1 with transfer function $G_F(s)$. The object of control - an integrator and the clock oscillator with a controlling unit - with transfer function $G_0(s)$ is presented by links Integrator and Transfer Fcn2.
The digital fuzzy controller (Fuzzy controller on fig. 2.2) is fulfilled under the block diagram with the identical triangular membership function erected in degree and consists of the block of the shaper of sizes A (t) and B (t), the block of comparing of sizes A and B and calculation u_c and the block of normalization variable [2]. The mismatch error $\theta(t)$ from an output of a low-pass filter arrives on a analog-digital converter (AD converter) (Zero-Order Hold), included at the input of a fuzzy controller . A quantization step of AD converter h =0,01s. At the output of a fuzzy controller is included the digital to analog converter (Zero-Order Hold1).
For simplification of normalization (recalculation of values of signals in values of elements of universal set) ranges of change input and output signals (parameters of a fuzzy controller) we is accepting by symmetric:

$$\theta_{max} = -\theta_{min};\ \dot{\theta}_{max} = -\dot{\theta}_{min};\ \ddot{\theta}_{max} = -\ddot{\theta}_{min};\ m_{max} = -m_{min}.$$

Then recalculation of values of signals in values of elements of universal set perform according to the formulas

$$\left.\begin{aligned} u_1^* &= (\theta^* + A_m)/(2A_m); \\ u_2^* &= (\dot{\theta}^* + B_m)/(2B_m); \\ u_3^* &= (\ddot{\theta}^* + C_m)/(2C_m). \end{aligned}\right\} .$$

Values of ranges ($\mathrm{Am} = \theta_{max} = -\theta_{min}$; $\mathrm{Bm} = \dot{\theta}_{max} = -\dot{\theta}_{min}$; $\mathrm{Cm} = \ddot{\theta}_{max} = -\ddot{\theta}_{min}$; $\mathrm{Dm} = m_{max} = -m_{min}$) at adjustment of a fuzzy controller steal up either manually, or automatically by the decision of the optimization task.
If studying of system (see fig. 2.2) the method of mathematical simulation selection following parameters:

$$k = 1; a = 10\,c^{-1}; b = 12{,}5\,c^{-1}; c = 1;\ a = \mathrm{alf} = 15;\ \Delta = 1; K_d = 1.$$

The system was studied when exposed on input an equivalent harmonic signal

$$u(t) = 1 + 0{,}5\sin 2\pi Ft\,,$$

with carrier frequency $F = 0{,}1Hz$.
The adjustment of a fuzzy controller is carried out by criterion of a minimum of a dynamic error. Is received following optimal parameters of a fuzzy controller :

$$\mathrm{Am} = \theta_{max} = 0{,}05;\ \mathrm{Bm} = \dot{\theta}_{max} = 0{,}4;\ \mathrm{Cm} = \ddot{\theta}_{max} = 10;\ \mathrm{Dm} = m_{max} = 150\,.$$

Processes in system of the PLL frequency control (see fig. 2.2) with a fuzzy controller are shown on fig.2.4 where $u(t)$ - an input action, $x(t)$ - an output a system (see fig. 2.4,a), $e(t) \equiv \mathrm{Err}$ – a mismatch error on a discriminator input (see fig. 2.4, b), $m(t)$ - an output of a fuzzy controller (see fig. 2.4, c).
The maximum dynamic error (except for initial burst at the moment of signal capture) does not exceed 0,7 % from amplitude of a sinusoid.
At the fig. 2.4, d transition is presented process of system of the PLL frequency control - response to unit step action. The system fulfills input influence in time, not exceeding 0,16 s, without overshoot.
Thus, the digital fuzzy controller provides not only greater accuracy castings input influence, but and high system performance by an step action.
It should be noted that the research system with the above parameters, without the regulator shows that the system lacks stability.
The system (see fig. 2.2) with a digital fuzzy controller it is researched also in the presence of a stationary white noise (Band-Limited White Noise) on a frequency discriminator output. Implementation of a white noise $v(t)$ is shown at the fig. 2.5, *a*. A mismatch error on an input of the slope detector $e(t)$ and an output of a fuzzy controller $m(t)$ thus are casual processes (see fig. 2.5, b and c).

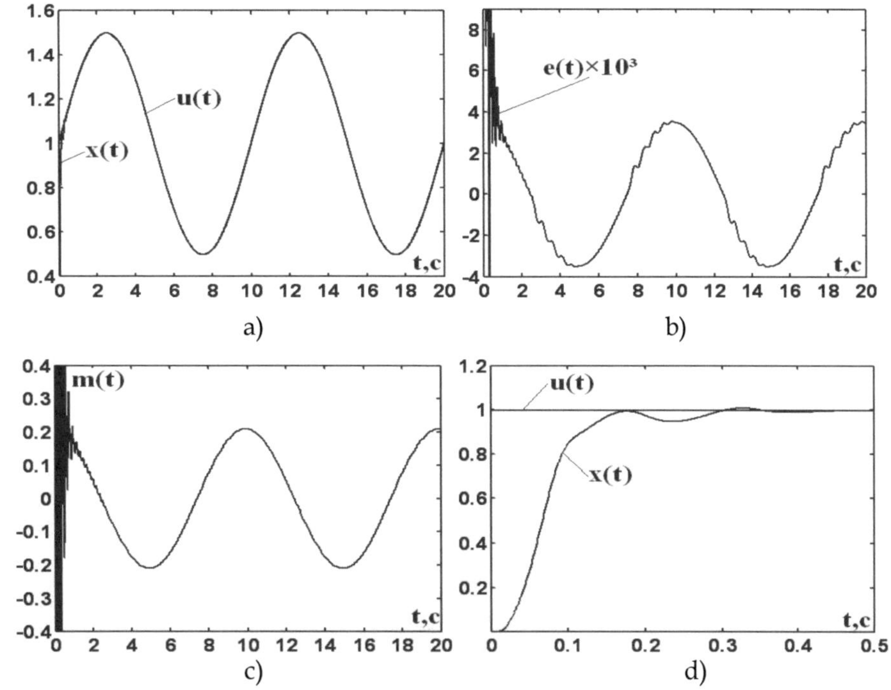

Fig. 2.4. Processes in system of PLL frequency control.

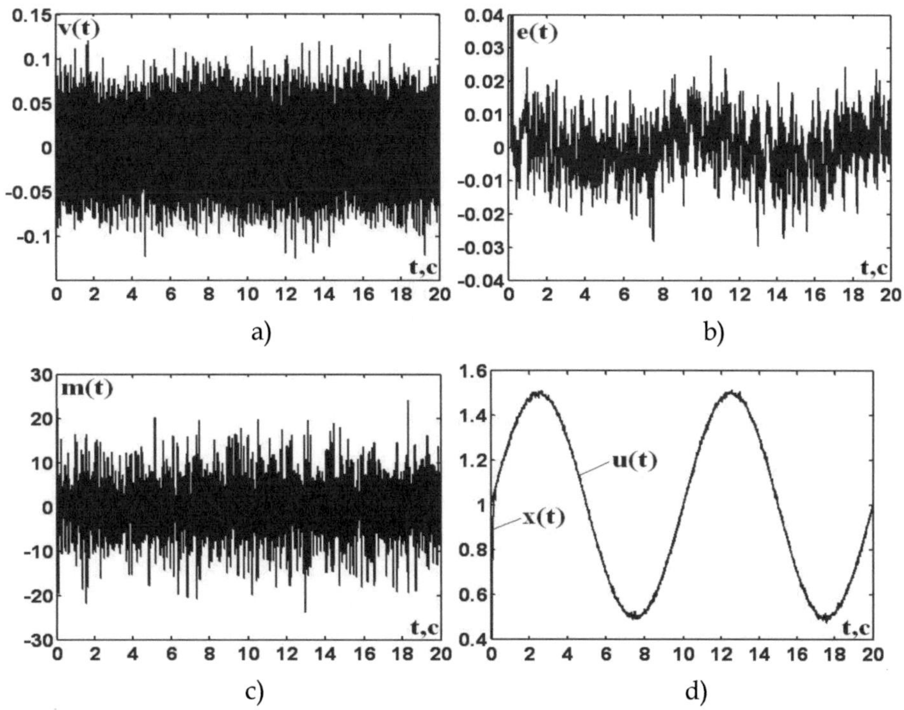

Fig. 2.5. Processes in system in the presence of a stationary white noise

Researches of system in the presence of a stationary white noise show that noise of such intensity (see fig. 2.5 a,) slightly influences a system output $x(t)$ (see fig. 2.5,d), however error of system increases (we compare fig. 2.4, b and 2.5b), therefore at small input influences (at small frequency deviations of the generator from set) noise on a frequency detector output will make the considerable impact on a dynamic error of system.

System (see fig.2.2) was also studied by using a more simple fuzzy controller. Parameter *a* in the fuzzy controller is chosen to be 0.2, and ranges of variation of input and output variables left unchanged: $\mathrm{Am} = 0{,}05;\ \mathrm{Bm} = 0{,}4;\ \mathrm{Cm} = 10;\ \mathrm{Dm} = 150$.

Processes in system (see fig. 2.2) with a fuzzy controller where $u(t)$ - an input , $x(t)$ - an output of system (fig.2.6,a), $e(t) \equiv \mathrm{Err}$ - a mismatch error on a discriminator input (fig.2.6,b). $x(t)$ and $m(t)$ - response to a unit jump of the input signal $u(t)$ respectively, at the system output and the output of fuzzy controller (see fig.2.6,c,d).

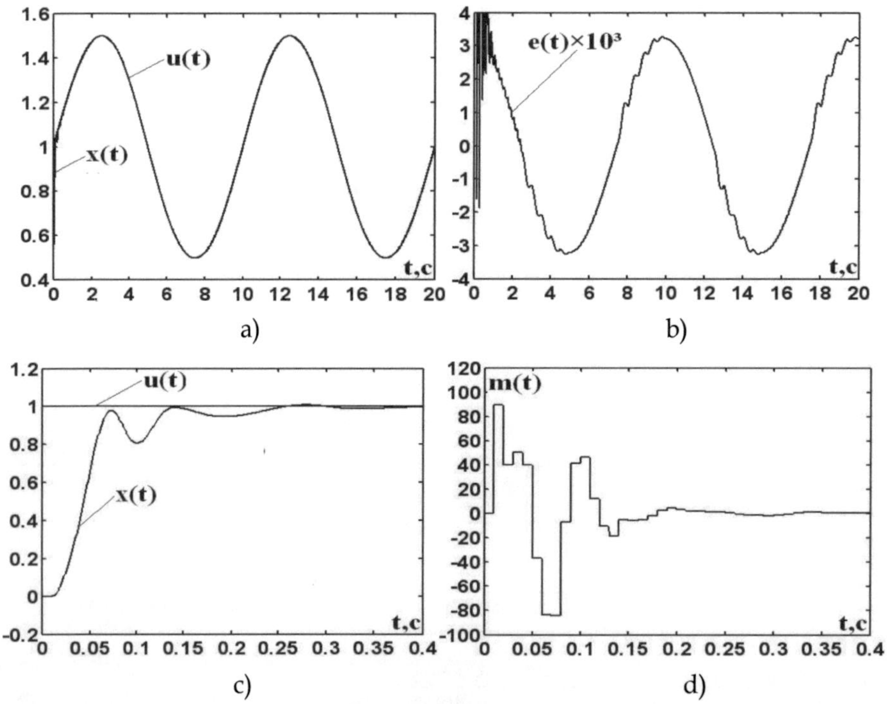

Fig. 2.6. Processes in system with a fuzzy controller

The maximum dynamic error (except for initial burst at the moment of signal capture) does not exceed 0,64 % from amplitude of a sinusoid. The system fulfills input influence in time, not exceeding 0,13s, without overshoot.

Of interest to examine the processes in the system (see Fig.2.2), by using instead of a fuzzy controller of the traditional PID controller. The block diagram of digital PID controller shown in fig.2.2. The transfer function of the regulator

$$W(z) = G_1 + G_2 \frac{z+1}{z-1} + G_3 \frac{z-1}{z},$$

where $G_1 = K$, $G_2 = \frac{K_i h_0}{2}$, $G_3 = \frac{K_d}{h_0}$, h_0 - digitization step.

As a result of tuning of PID-controller at the indicated higher parameters of the system and input an equivalent harmonic signal $u(t) = 1 + 0{,}5\sin 2\pi Ft$, with carrier frequency $F = 0{,}1Hz$, is received following optimal parameters of a PID-controller, at the h_0 =0.01s: $G_1 = 171{,}2$; $G_2 = 0{,}48$; $G_3 = 1800$.

Processes in system (see fig. 2.2) with a PID-controller are shown at the fig. 2.7 where $u(t)$ - an input action, $x(t)$ - an output a system (see fig. 2.7, a), $e(t) \equiv \mathrm{Err}$ - a mismatch error on a discriminator input (see fig. 2.7,b). $m(t)$ - an output of a fuzzy controller (see fig. 2.7,c). The maximum dynamic error on system of the of the PLL frequency control with a PID-controller (except for initial burst at the moment of signal capture) does not exceed 2,4 % from amplitude of a sinusoid. The maximum dynamic error on system of the PLL frequency control with a PID-controller in 3,5 times more than the maximum dynamic error in system of the PLL frequency control with a fuzzy controller and in 3,75 times with a fuzzy controller.

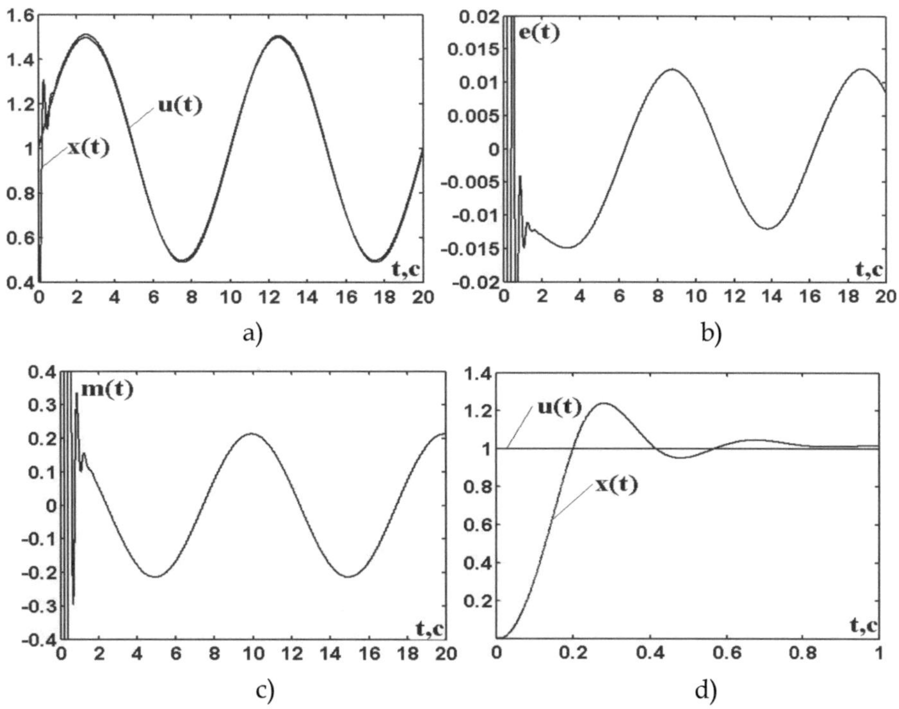

Fig. 2.7. Processes in system with a PID-controller

At the fig. 2.4, d transition is presented process of system with a PID-controller - response to unit step action. The transitional process - the oscillating with the overshoot of more than 20%. The system fulfills input influence in time, exceeding 0,4 s. The regulation time in system of the PLL frequency control with the PID-controller approximately in 2,5 times is more than regulation time in system with a fuzzy controller and in 3 times with an simple fuzzy controller.

Thus, the fuzzy controllers provide accuracy fulfills of input influences and high-speed performance of system of the PLL frequency control it is much better, then the PID-controller.

The system (see fig. 2.2) with a digital PID-controller it is researched also in the presence of a stationary white noise (Band-Limited White Noise) on a frequency discriminator output. Implementation of a white noise $v(t)$ is shown at the fig. 2.8,*a*.

Researches of system in the presence of a stationary white noise show that noise of such intensity (see fig. 2.8 a,) slightly influences a system output $x(t)$ (see fig. 2.5,d) however error of system increases (we compare fig. 2.7, b and 2.8b) therefore at small input influences (at small frequency deviations of the generator from set) noise on a frequency detector output will make the considerable impact on a dynamic error of system.

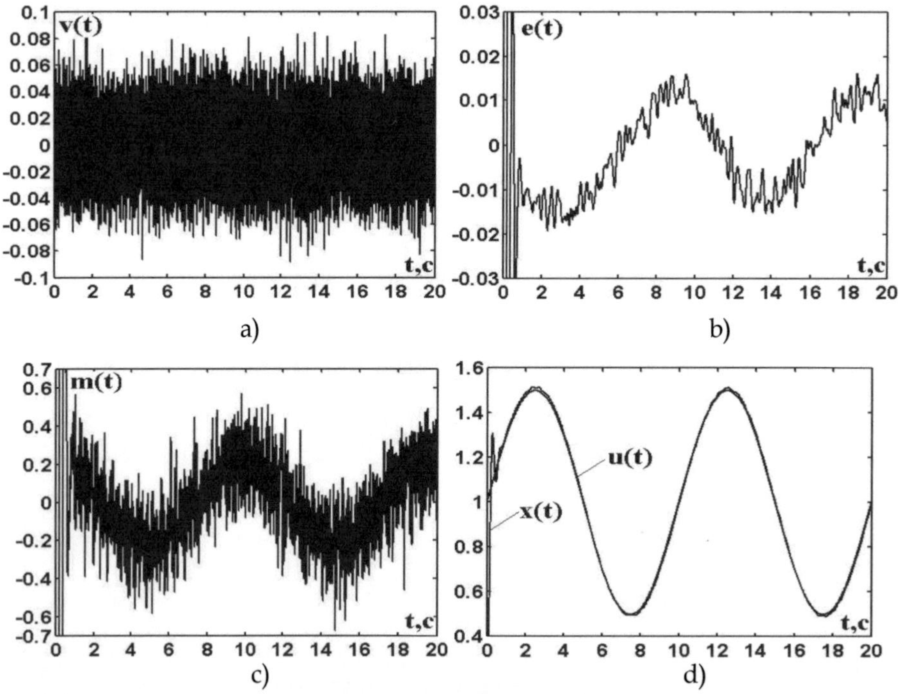

Fig. 2.8. Processes in system in the presence of a stationary white noise

Let's consider a mathematical model (block diagram) of system of the of the PLL frequency control in interactive system MATLAB (see fig. 2.9), with the low-pass filter of the second order which has transfer function in a numerical type

$$G(s) = \frac{k}{a_0 s^2 + a_1 s + 1} = \frac{0,008}{0,008 s^2 + 0,18 s + 1}.$$

A frequency discriminator FD at the fig. 2.9 is presented by the comparator circuit on the adder and the discrimination characteristic (Discrim)

$$K(e) = K_d e \exp\{-\frac{e^2}{\Delta^2}\} = e \exp\{-\frac{e^2}{0,64}\},$$

where conversion coefficient of the discriminator K_d =1, and the half-width of the discrimination characteristic defining resolution capability of the discriminator, Δ =0,8.
The object of control - the integrator and the without inertia clock generator - with transfer function $G_0(s) = alf / s$, $alf = 25$, is presented by link Transfer Fcn1.

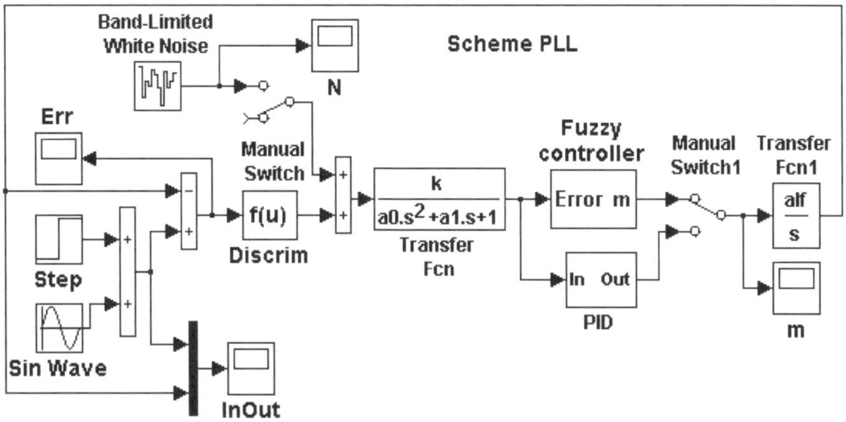

Fig. 2.9. The block diagram of system of the PLL frequency control

In system is used the elementary digital fuzzy controller (Fuzzy controller at the fig. 2.9) is fulfilled under the block diagram. The controller consists of the block of the shaper of sizes A (t) and B (t), the block of comparing of sizes A and B and calculation u_c and the block of normalization output variable[2].
The mismatch error $\theta(t)$ from an output of a low-pass filter arrives on a analog-digital converter (AD converter) (Zero-Order Hold), included at the input of a fuzzy controller. A quantization step of AD converter h =0,01s. On an output of a fuzzy controller is included the digital/analog converter DAC (Zero-OrderHold1).
For simplification of normalization (recalculation of values of signals in values of elements of universal set) ranges of change input and output signals (parameters of a fuzzy controller) we is accepting by symmetric:

$$\theta_{\max} = -\theta_{\min};\ \dot{\theta}_{\max} = -\dot{\theta}_{\min};\ \ddot{\theta}_{\max} = -\ddot{\theta}_{\min};\ m_{\max} = -m_{\min}.$$

Then recalculation of values of signals in values of elements of universal set perform according to the formulas

$$\left.\begin{aligned} u_1^* &= (\theta^* + A_m) / (2A_m); \\ u_2^* &= (\dot{\theta}^* + B_m) / (2B_m); \\ u_3^* &= (\ddot{\theta}^* + C_m) / (2C_m). \end{aligned}\right\}.$$

Values of ranges ($\mathrm{Am} = \theta_{\max} = -\theta_{\min}$; $\mathrm{Bm} = \dot{\theta}_{\max} = -\dot{\theta}_{\min}$; $\mathrm{Cm} = \ddot{\theta}_{\max} = -\ddot{\theta}_{\min}$; $\mathrm{Dm} = m_{\max} = -m_{\min}$) at adjustment of a fuzzy controller steal up either manually, or automatically by the decision of the optimization task.

The system was studied when exposed on input an equivalent harmonic signal

$$u(t) = 1 + 0{,}5\sin 2\pi F t\ ,$$

with carrier frequency $F = 0{,}1Hz$.
The adjustment of a fuzzy controller is carried out by criterion of a minimum of a dynamic error. Is received following optimal parameters of a fuzzy controller:

$$\text{Am} = \theta_{\max} = 0{,}05;\ \ \text{Bm} = \dot{\theta}_{\max} = 0{,}4;\ \ \text{Cm} = \ddot{\theta}_{\max} = 10;\ \text{Dm} = m_{\max} = 150\ .$$

Processes in system of the of the PLL frequency control (see fig. 2.9) with a fuzzy controller are shown on fig. 2.10 where $u(t)$ - an input action, $x(t)$ - an output a system (see fig. 2.10 a,), $e(t) \equiv \text{Err}$ - a mismatch error on a discriminator input (see fig. 2.10,b). $m(t)$ - an output of a fuzzy controller (see fig. 2.10,c).

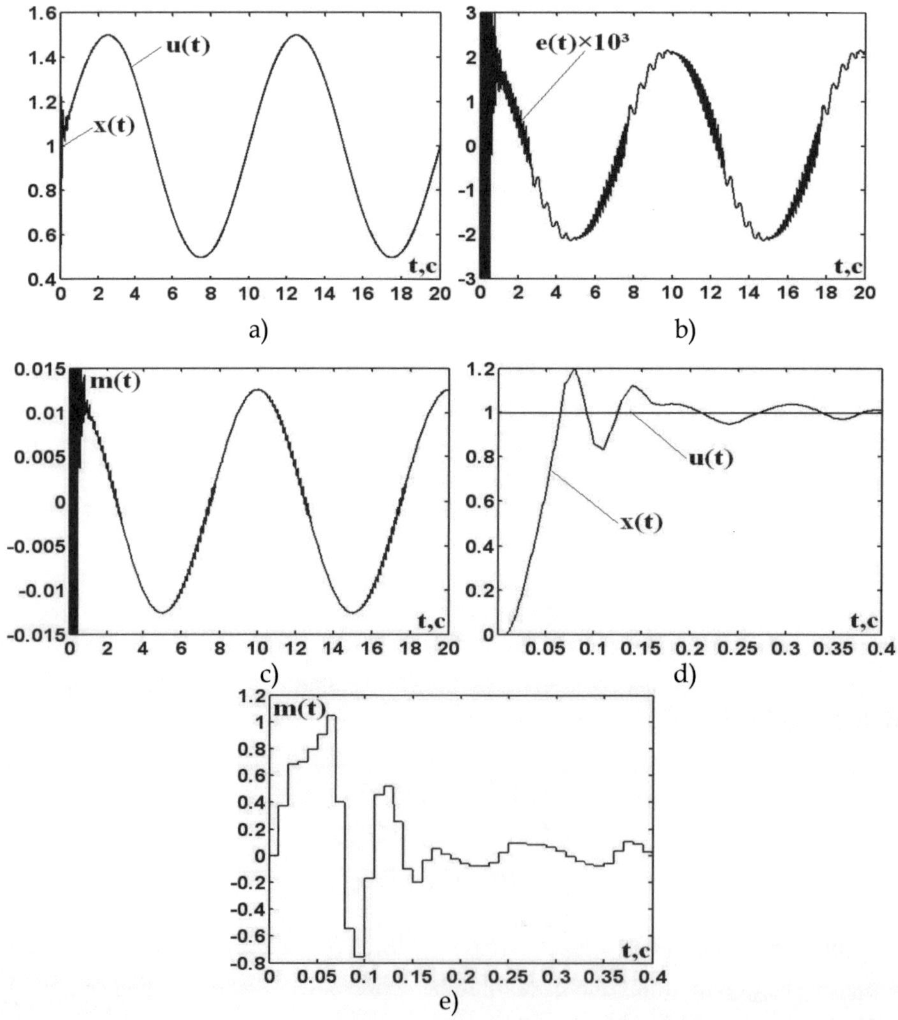

Fig. 2.10. Processes in system

The maximum dynamic error (except for initial burst at the moment of signal capture) does not exceed 0,4 % from amplitude of a sinusoid.
At fig. 2.10,d,e are presented reactions to unit step of input signal $u(t)$ respectively, at the output of system $x(t)$ and at the output of a fuzzy controller $m(t)$. The transition process – the oscillation, which the overshoot of more then 20%. The system fulfills input influence in time, not exceeding 0,25 s.
At usage in system (fig. 2.9 see) a digital PID- controller it is received following results.
Tuning of PID-controller at the indicated higher parameters of the system and input an equivalent harmonic signal $u(t) = 1 + 0,5\sin 2\pi Ft$, with carrier frequency $F = 0,1Hz$, is received following earlier optimal parameters of a PID-controller, at the h_0 =0.01s: $G_1 = 171,2;\ G_2 = 0,48;\ G_3 = 1800$.
Therefore processes in system (see fig. 2.9) with a digital PID-controler same what are shown at the fig. 2.7.
The maximum dynamic error in system of the of the PLL frequency control with the PID-controller (except for initial burst at the moment of signal capture) does not exceed 2,4 % from amplitude of a sinusoid. Transfer process - oscillatory, with overshoot more than 20 %. The system fulfills input influence for time exceeding 0,4 with. The maximum dynamic error in system of the of the PLL frequency control (fig. 2.9) with the PID-controller in 6 times more the maximum dynamic error in system of the of the PLL frequency control with a fuzzy controller see, and regulation time in system of the of the PLL frequency control with the PID- controller approximately in 1,6 times is more than regulation time in system with a fuzzy controller.
Thus, the fuzzy controller is provided with accuracy of working off of input influences and high-speed performance of system of the frequency self-tuning it is much better, than the PID-controller.

2.2 Fuzzy systems of clock synchronization

Systems of clock synchronization CS found a wide circulation in various areas of technique, in particular on digital networks and transmission systems of information DTSI. The modern development of technique demands requires the CS to meet the new higher quality of indicators.
At the fig. 2.11 shows a typical function diagram of CS DTSI. Diagram includes leading and slave clock oscillator - LCO and SCO accordingly; the input device of regenerator - IDR; the extractor of clock synchro signal (ECS); a solver - S; a phase detector – PD; a low-pass filter LPF; a manager -M; a communication line - a CL.

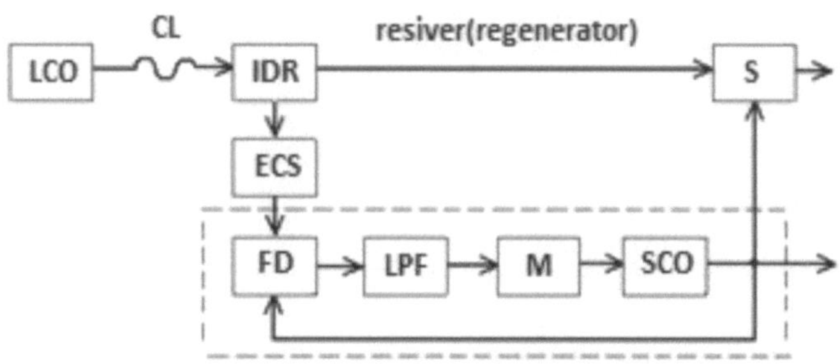

Fig. 2.11. System of clock synchronization

Clock synchronization of digital signals of telecommunication DST is a process of establishment and maintaining the required phase relations between the significant moments of a digital signal of telecommunication DST and a clock synchro signal. Thus, into the decision of the task of clock synchronization include: 1) formation of the clock synchro signal solver of the receiver or a regenerator; 2) "binding" of a phase of the specified synchro signal to a phase of the significant moments DST, accepted from a communication line; 3) monitoring of the given phase relationship between the timing signal accepted from a communication line and a synchro signal submitted on solver of the receiver; 4) framing of controlling influence in the presence of an error at violation of the specified phase relationship; 5) base service of a phase error according to the worked out control action.
The solution of these problem is possible, first of all, creation of system of automatic control of a phase of a clock synchronize of the receiver or regenerator DST. Clearly that inphase operation of the transmitter and receiver DST is inconceivable without presence synhro information (upsetting control of system of automatic control). Clock synchro signal are worked out by clock oscillator CO. Consequently, it is necessary to carry out generating of a clock synchro signal on transmission and on reception that in turn causes of presence TG on transmission and on reception. Thus, the first stage of solving the problem of clock synchronization in practice is implemented by presence TG in a regenerator or a receiving part of the equipment DST, and clock synchronization can be shown to synchronization CO, i.e. process of establishment and maintenance of demanded phase relationships between clock synchro signal two or several CO. Thus CO of transmitter is leading, he works out *setting action*; and CO the receiver or a regenerator - slave, the phase of his synchro signal is a measured variable of automatic system of PLL of a phase. This circumstance is an important feature of the synchronization system , which becomes a telemechanical system.

Setting action - a phase of a clock synhro signal of leader CO in the general case, due to random distortions when moving the synhro signal from the transmitter to the receiver, instability of generating of pulses by leader CO, and other is unknown function of time, i.e. $\varphi_{TG}(t) = \text{var}$. This position gives the grounds to classify system of clock synchronization as follow-up systems of automatics, and at $\varphi_{TG}(t) = const -$ as stabilizing systems.

Basic element of system of clock synchronization is the system PLL which is selected by a dotted line for fig. 2.11

In phase-locked loop systems the coordination of phases of two oscillations is carried out - the current phase of controlled oscillations is set up under a current phase of setting oscillations so that ideally the phase difference of these oscillations saves constant value. As persistence of a phase difference is possible only at equality of oscillation frequencies in PLL systems frequency of controlled oscillations ideally is installed to equal frequency of setting oscillations. This property of PLL systems defines their double assignment - as systems of self-locked of frequency and as systems of self-locked of a phase.

In the first case the immediate aim of application of system is establishment of demanded correspondence between frequencies of two oscillations, and in the second - establishment of demanded correspondence between phases of two oscillations.

The phase-locked systems which immediate aim is establishment of demanded correspondence between frequencies of two oscillations, received a title of phase-locked loop systems of frequency control (PLL frequency control).

If the immediate purpose of functioning of system is the coordination of phases of two oscillations it name the same as also all class of considered systems - the phase-locked loop system (PLL).

Distinction of titles reflects only distinction in immediate mission and does not mean distinctions in principles of actions. Principles of action of systems PLL OF and PLL are identical.

System PLL defines accuracy and high-speed performance of all system of clock synchronization. Object of control in system PLL is the clock VCO which taking into its inertial can be described transfer function

$$G(s) = \alpha[s(s+a)]^{-1}$$

(If an output variable of the generator is the phase of oscillations), or transfer function

$$G(s) = \alpha / (s+a)$$

(If an output variable of the generator is oscillation frequency),
where $\alpha = K_G / T$, $a = 1/T$, K_G - transmission factor, $rad/(s \cdot V)$, $T-$ time constant VCO. Assuming , that the VCO is without inertial element of system PLL, its transfer function can be defined as

$$G(s) = \alpha / s$$

(If an output variable of the generator is the phase of oscillations), or the transfer function

$$G(s) = \alpha$$

(If an output variable of the generator is oscillation frequency), where $\alpha = K_G$, K_G - transmission factor VCO, $rad/(s \cdot V)$.

The mathematical model of the phase detector can be present series connection of the device of comparing, non linearity $K(\varphi)$ and low-pass filter LPF. The simplest LPF is described by the transfer function

$$G_F(s) = K_F / (T_F s + 1) = k / (s + b),$$

where $k = K_F / T_F$, $b = 1/T_F$, K_F – an amplification factor, T_F – the constant of the filter phase detector.

Curve $K(\varphi)$ is called the static discrimination characteristic. Mathematical model of the nonlinearity of the type "discrimination feature" can be described by

$$K(\varphi) = K_d \sin\varphi ,$$

where K_d - gain of phase detector, $\varphi(t) \equiv e(t)$ - a mismatch error on an input of phase detector, or expression at the "linear discrimination characteristic

$$K(\varphi) = \begin{cases} K_d\varphi \text{ at } -\Delta \le \varphi \le \Delta, \\ 0 \text{ at } \quad |\varphi| \rangle \Delta. \end{cases}$$

Usually the half-width Δ "linear" discrimination characteristic of phase detector is equal $\pi/2$, π or 2π.

Discrimination characteristic of phase-frequency detector can be described by the expression

$$K(\varphi)=\begin{cases} K_0 & \text{at } \varphi \langle -2\pi, \\ -K_d\varphi & \text{at } -2\pi \le \varphi \le 2\pi, \\ K_0 & \text{at } \varphi \rangle\, 2\pi. \end{cases}$$

Let's consider a block diagram (a mathematical model) of system of the PLL presented in interactive system MATLAB, in fig.2.12 [3,4]. To ensure the dynamics of the system using fuzzy and PID-controllers (Fuzzy controller and PID at the fig.2.12).

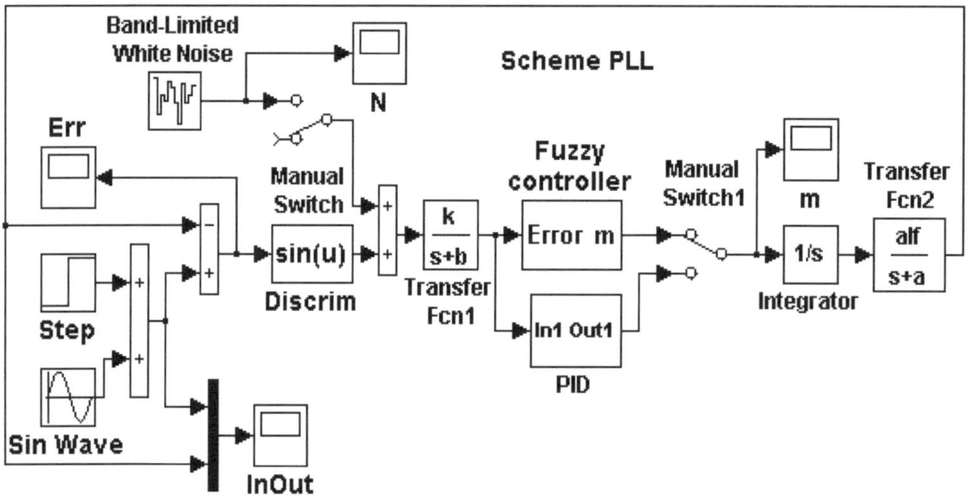

Fig. 2.12. System of the PLL.

Phase detector FD (see fig. 2.11) in fig.2.12 is presented by the compare circuit on the adder and discrimination characteristic Discrim - $K(\varphi)=K_d \sin\varphi$. The low-pas filter LPF is described by link Transfer Fcn1 with transfer function $G_F(s)$. The clock generator with transfer function $G(s)$ is described by links Integrator and Transfer Fcn2.
The digital fuzzy controller (fuzzy controller at the fig. 2.12) is fulfilled under the block diagram, with the identical triangular membership function erected in degree and consists of the block of the shaper of sizes A (t) and B (t), the block of comparing of sizes A and B and calculation u_c and the block of normalization output variable[2]. The mismatch error $\theta(t)$ from an output of a low-pass filter arrives on a analog-digital converter (AD converter) (Zero-Order Hold), included at the input of a fuzzy controller . A quantization step of AD converter h =0,01s. On an output of a fuzzy controller is included the digital/analog converter (Zero-Order Hold1).
For simplification of normalization (recalculation of values of signals in values of elements of universal set) ranges of change input and output signals (parameters of a fuzzy controller) we is accepting by symmetric:

$$\theta_{\max}=-\theta_{\min};\ \dot{\theta}_{\max}=-\dot{\theta}_{\min};\ \ddot{\theta}_{\max}=-\ddot{\theta}_{\min};\ m_{\max}=-m_{\min}.$$

Then recalculation of values of signals in values of elements of universal set perform according to the formulas

$$\left.\begin{aligned} u_1^* &= (\theta^* + A_m)/(2A_m); \\ u_2^* &= (\dot{\theta}^* + B_m)/(2B_m); \\ u_3^* &= (\ddot{\theta}^* + C_m)/(2C_m). \end{aligned}\right\} .$$

Values of ranges ($\mathrm{Am} = \theta_{\max} = -\theta_{\min}$; $\mathrm{Bm} = \dot{\theta}_{\max} = -\dot{\theta}_{\min}$; $\mathrm{Cm} = \ddot{\theta}_{\max} = -\ddot{\theta}_{\min}$; $\mathrm{Dm} = m_{\max} = -m_{\min}$) at adjustment of a fuzzy controller steal up either manually, or automatically by the decision of the optimization task.

Let's notice that mathematical models of systems at the fig. 2.12 and fig. 2.2 differ only discrimination characteristics, therefore at identical parameters of other elements it is necessary to expect identical or close results at research of these systems. If studying of system (see fig. 2.12) the method of mathematical simulation selection following parameters: $k = 1; a = 10\,c^{-1}; b = 12{,}5\,c^{-1}; c = 1;\ a = \mathrm{alf} = 15$. The system was studied when exposed on input an equivalent harmonic signal $u(t) = 1 + 0{,}5\sin 2\pi Ft$ with carrier frequency $F = 0{,}1Hz$.

The adjustment of a fuzzy controller is carried out by criterion of a minimum of a dynamic error. Is received following optimal parameters of a fuzzy controller: $\mathrm{Am} = 0{,}05;\ \mathrm{Bm} = 0{,}4;$ $\mathrm{Cm} = 10;\ \mathrm{Dm} = 150$.

Processes in system (see fig. 2.12) are shown at the fig. 2.13 where $u(t)$ - an input action, $x(t)$ - an output a system (see fig. 2.13,a), $e(t) \equiv \mathrm{Err}$ - a mismatch error on a discriminator input (see fig. 2.13). $m(t)$ - an output of a fuzzy controller (see fig. 2.13c,). The maximum dynamic error (except for initial burst at the moment of signal capture) does not exceed 0,7 % from amplitude of a sinusoid. At the fig. 2.13,d transition is presented process of system - response to unit step action. The system fulfills input influence in time, not exceeding 0,22s, with overshoot not more than 10%.

Thus, the fuzzy controllers provide accuracy fulfills of input influences, but and high-speed performance of system at the jump action. It should be noted that the study of the system without the controller shows, that the system does not have the stability.

The system (see fig. 2.12) with a fuzzy controller it is researched also in the presence of a stationary white noise (Band-Limited White Noise) on an output of frequency discriminator [5]. Implementation of a white noise $v(t)$ is shown at the fig. 2.14,*a*. A mismatch error on an input of the slope detector $e(t)$ and an output of a fuzzy controller $m(t)$ thus are casual processes (see fig. 2.14, b and c). Researches of system in the presence of a stationary white noise show that noise of such intensity slightly influences a system output $x(t)$ (see fig. 2.14 d) however error of system increases (we compare fig. 2.4b and 2.5b) therefore at small input influences (at small frequency deviations of the generator from set) noise on a detector output will make the considerable impact on a dynamic error of system.

It is of interest to consider the processes in the system of PLL (see fig.2.12)if using instead of the fuzzy controller the PID-controller [6]. The transfer function of the digital PID (PID on fig.2.12) controller

$$W(z) = G_1 + G_2\frac{z+1}{z-1} + G_3\frac{z-1}{z},$$

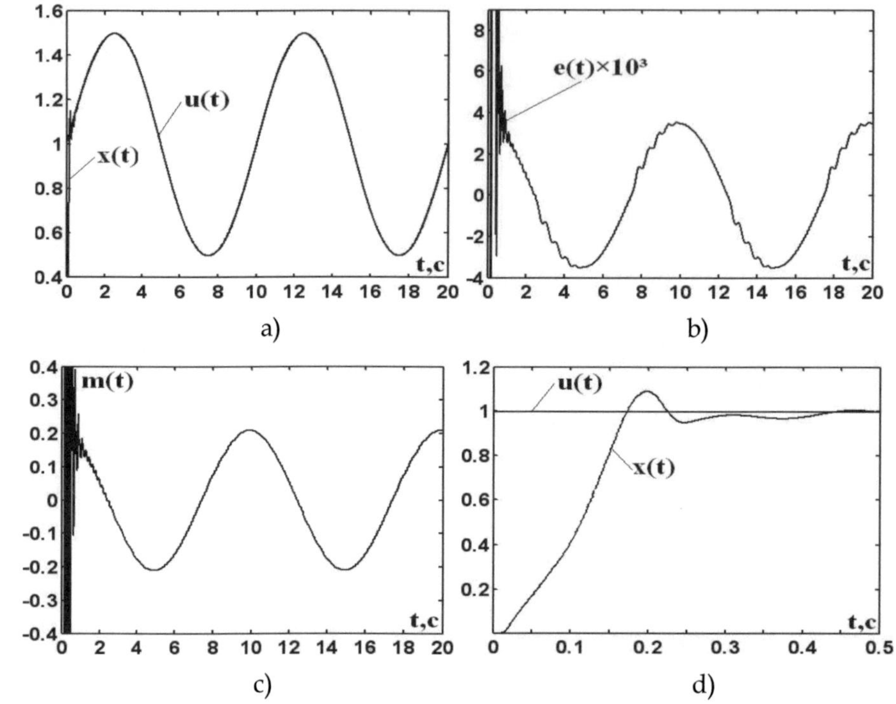

Fig. 2.13. Processes in system

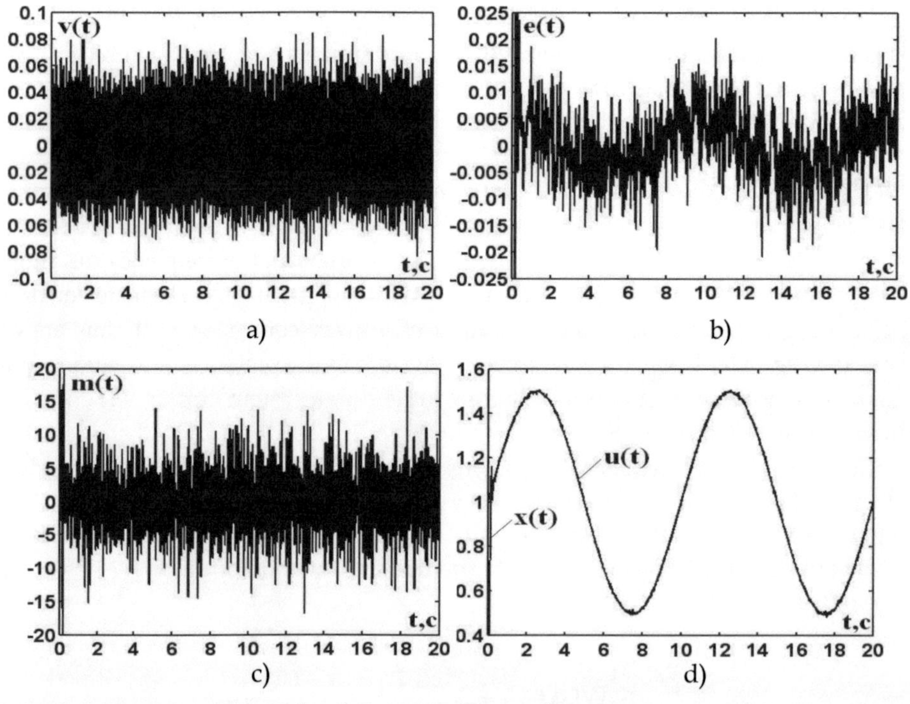

Fig. 2.14. Processes in system with a fuzzy controller in the presence of a stationary white noise

where $G_1 = K$, $G_2 = \frac{K_i h_0}{2}$, $G_3 = \frac{K_d}{h_0}$, h_0 - a digitization step.

As a result of tuning a controller at the indicated higher parameters of the system and input an equivalent harmonic signal is received following optimal parameters of a PID - controller, at the h_0 =0.01c: $G_1 = 130$; $G_2 = 0{,}48$; $G_3 = 2000$. Processes in system (see fig. 2.12) with a PID-controller are shown on fig. 2.15 where $u(t)$ - an input action, $x(t)$ - an output a system (see fig. 2.15,a), $e(t) \equiv \text{Err}$ - a mismatch error on a discriminator input (see fig. 2.15,b). $m(t)$ - an output of a fuzzy controller (see fig. 2.15,c).

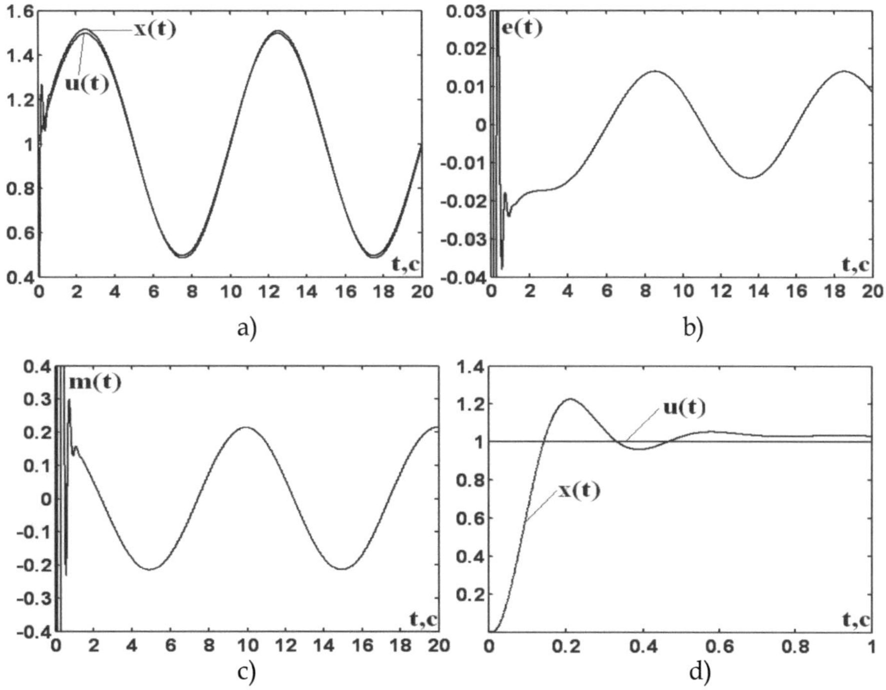

Fig. 2.15. Processes in system with a PID-controller

The maximum dynamic error in system of PLL with a PID - controller (except for initial burst at the moment of signal capture) attains of 2,8% from amplitude of a sinusoid. The maximum dynamic error in system of PLL with a PID-controller in 4 times more than the maximum dynamic error in system of PLL with a fuzzy controller.

On fig. 2.15,d transition is presented process of system with a PID-controller - response to unit step action. The transitional process - the oscillating with the overshoot of more than 20%. The system fulfills input influence in time, exceeding 0,31 s. The overshoot in system of PLL with the PID-controller in 2 times, and the regulation time in 1,4 times more than the appropriate parameters in system of PLL with a fuzzy controller.

When reducing the dynamic error in the PLL with PID-controller increases the overshoot and control time, and decrease in these parameters of the transition process increases dynamic error.

Thus, the fuzzy controllers provide accuracy fulfills of input influences, and high-speed performance of system PLL much better, then PID-controller.

The system (see fig. 2.12) with a PID-controller it is researched also in the presence of a stationary white noise (Band-Limited White Noise) on an output of discriminator. Implementation of a white noise $v(t)$ is shown at the fig. 2.16,*a*. A mismatch error on an input of the detector $e(t)$ and an output of a fuzzy controller $m(t)$ thus are casual processes (see fig. 2.16,b and c). Researches of system in the presence of a stationary white noise show that noise of such intensity slightly influences a system output $x(t)$ (see fig. 2.16,d) however error of system increases (we compare fig. 2.15,b and 2.16,c) therefore at small input influences (at small frequency deviations of the generator from set) noise on a frequency detector output will make the considerable impact on a dynamic error of system.

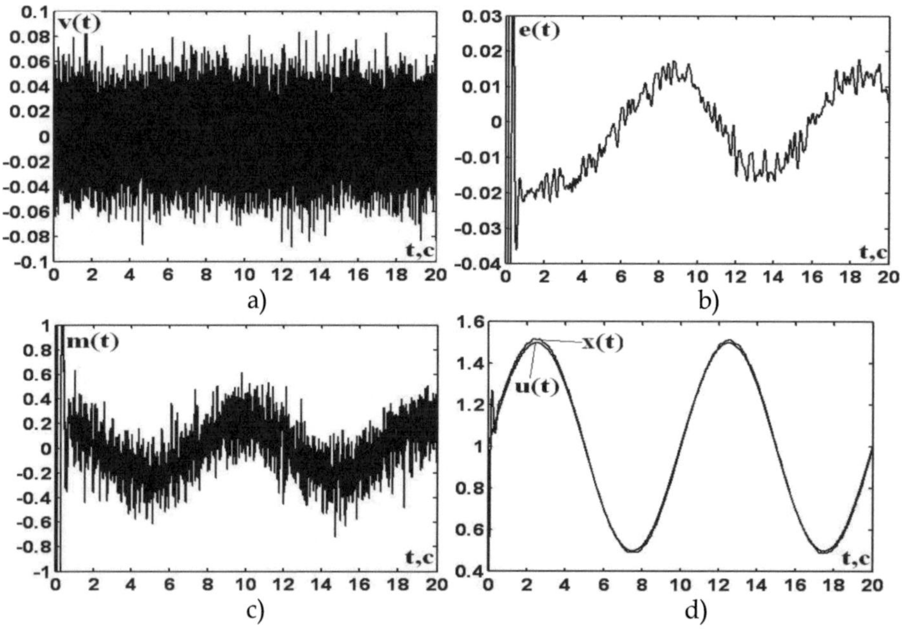

Fig. 2.16. Processes in system in the presence of a stationary white noise

Let's consider the system of the PLL of oscillator with a digital fuzzy controller. One of the main elements of the PLL oscillator is an analog phase detector, the static discrimination characteristic which can be written down in a kind

$$U_{FD} = K_{FD} \cos\varphi \tag{2.3}$$

where K_{FD} - the constant coefficient equal to the maximum value of voltage on an output of the detector, φ - difference in phase fluctuation (one of which is the reference) of the same frequency, field by to the first and second inputs of the detector (when equality the frequencies of two oscillation, the phase difference of these oscillations is constant).
When you change the frequency of input signal, the phase difference become a function of time:

$$\varphi(t) = \varphi_n + 2\pi \int \Delta f(t)dt \tag{2.4}$$

where φ_n - starting value of phase difference at the moment $t=0$, when $\Delta f = f_1 - f_2 = 0$.
Taking into account expressions (2.3) and (2.4) block diagram of a phase detector with variable frequency f_1 and f_2 input signal will have the form shown at the fig.2.17 [7].

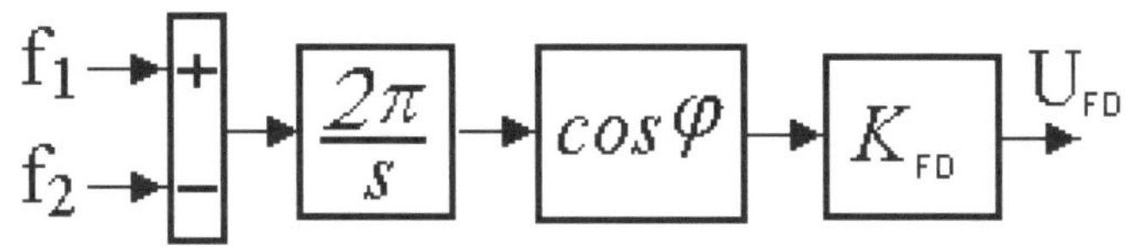

Fig. 2.17. Block diagram of a phase detector

Based on the structural scheme of the phase detector, taking into account the inertia of the filter at the output of the detector and the control element at the input of the oscillator (the filter at the output of the detector and the control element is usually described aperiodic links) can make a mathematical model of system of the PLL frequency control.
The mathematical model system of PLL with a digital fuzzy controller, compiled using the interactive system MATLAB, presented at the fig.2.18. Filter at the output of the digital phase detector and an controlling element of the generator describe the transfer functions:

$$G_1(s) = k/(s+b) = 10/(s+12{,}5),\ G_2(s) = alf/(s+a) = 3/(s+20).$$

The digital fuzzy controller (Fuzzy controller at the fig. 2.18) is fulfilled under the block diagram, with the identical triangular membership function erected in degree and consists of the block of the shaper of sizes A (t) and B (t) (block 1 collected by the diagram), the block of comparing of sizes A and B and calculation u_c (block 2 collected by the diagram) and the block of normalization output variable (block 3 collected by the diagram)[2].

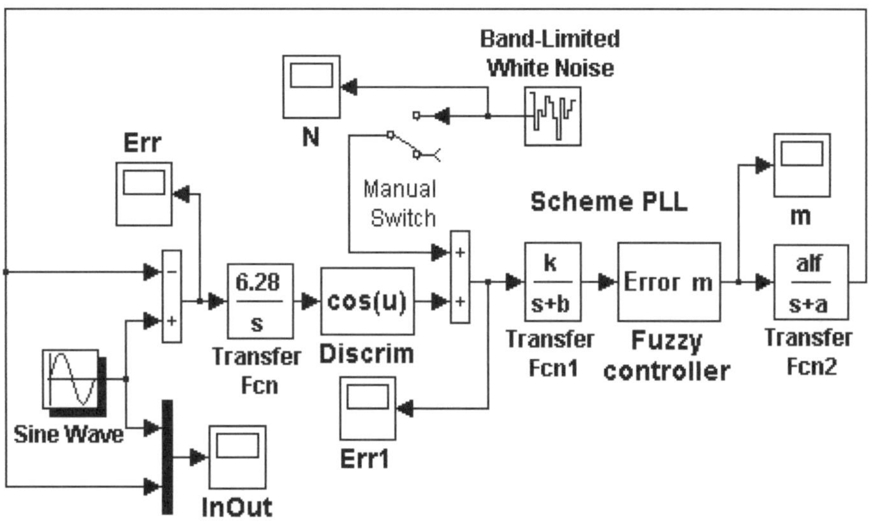

Fig. 2.18. System of the PLL frequency control.

The digitization step is chosen 0,001s. Values of ranges ($\mathrm{Am} = \theta_{\max} = -\theta_{\min}$; $\mathrm{Bm} = \dot{\theta}_{\max} = -\dot{\theta}_{\min}$; $\mathrm{Cm} = \ddot{\theta}_{\max} = -\ddot{\theta}_{\min}$; $\mathrm{Dm} = m_{\max} = -m_{\min}$) at adjustment of a fuzzy controller steal up either manually, or automatically by the decision of the optimization task. At research of the system we will accept, that the difference of frequencies of two fluctuations changes under the sinusoidal law: $\Delta f = 0{,}2\sin(\pi/5)$ or $\Delta f = 0{,}2\sin(\pi/10)$ (i.e. the maximum deviation of frequency of the generator operated pressure, from the set reaches $\pm 20\%$). System of PLL should compensate a deviation of frequency of the generator, therefore an fuzzy controller it is necessary to adjust on the minimum current error of a mismatch in system. As a result of adjustment it is received following optimum parameters of an fuzzy controller:

Am=0,03; Bm=0.5; Cm=10; Dm=20; c=1.

Processes in system (see fig.2.18) at setting action $0{,}2\sin(\pi/5)$ are presented at the fig.2.19, at setting action $0{,}2\sin(\pi/10)$ at the fig. 2.20. In figure $e(t)$ - the error of a mismatch on frequency on an input of the phase detector, $\theta(t)$ – the error of a mismatch on frequency on an output of the phase detector , $m(t)$ - operating pressure on an output of an fuzzy controller, $u(t)$ and $x(t)$ - an input and output of the system accordingly.
Independently of the frequency of input signal the transition process in the system finished for 3 s. Maximum dynamic mismatch error of frequency at the input of the phase detector at the input action $0{,}2\sin(\pi/5)$ does not exceed $2{,}8\cdot 10^{-3}$ (1,4% of the amplitude of the input action), and for input action $0{,}2\sin(\pi/10)$ is approximately $1{,}4\cdot 10^{-3}$ (0,7% of the amplitude of the input).

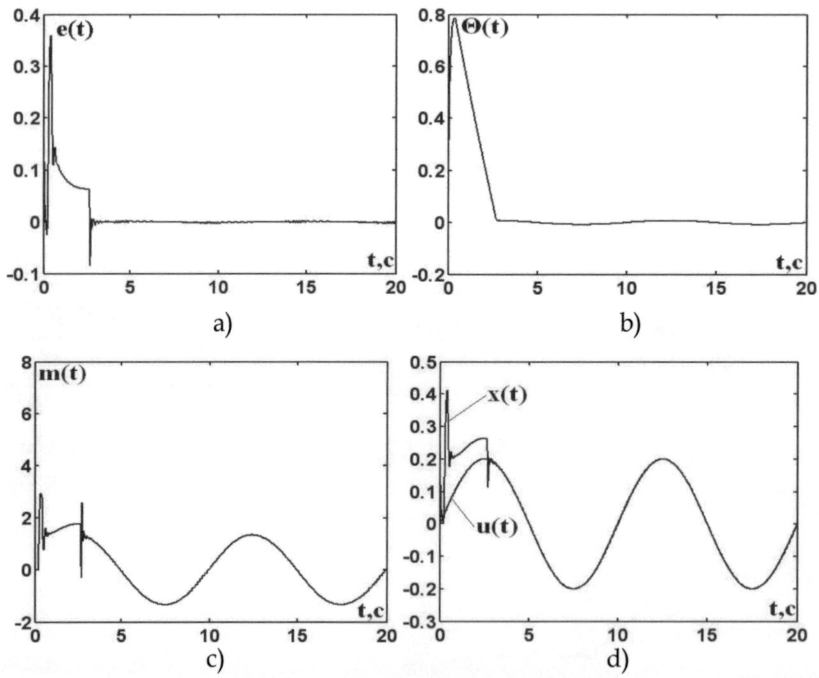

Fig. 2.19. Processes in system at setting action $0{,}2\sin(\pi/5)$

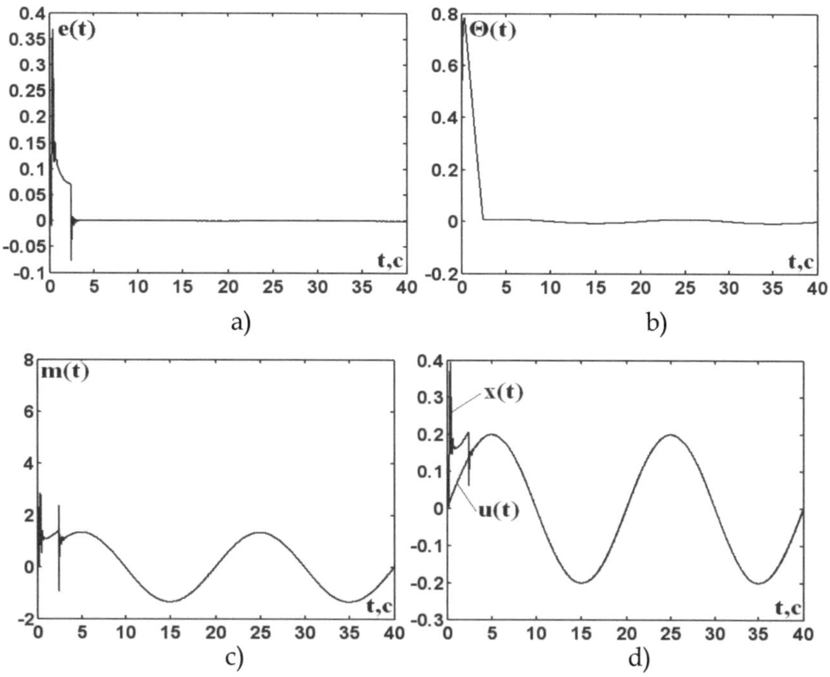

Fig. 2.20. Processes in system at setting action $0{,}2\sin(\pi / 10)$

As show researches of system (see fig. 2.18), a fuzzy controller allows to increase the accuracy of system PLL practically by two order in comparison with system without a controller.

Research of system PLL, accuracy of tracking which defines a synthesized fuzzy controller, on the basis of a mathematical apparatus of interactive system MATLAB allows to define simply enough one of system key parameters - a strip of dynamic tracking.

The strip of dynamic tracing of system PLL is the greatest offset of frequency of an entry basic signal concerning nominal frequency of oscillations of the voltage-controlled oscillator VCO. In this strip slave devise of synchronization should remain in a mode of tracing irrespective of speed of change of entry frequency in all range of frequencies. In other words, in a strip of dynamic tracing system PLL can track arbitrarily fast changes of the input frequency, including spasmodic changes of frequency at the input of system.

The strip of dynamic tracing of system PLL at research of mathematical model of system PLL in interactive system MATLAB is defined simply enough, namely, submitting step signals on input of system PLL it is necessary to find the value of jump of an input signal at which there is a tracing failure (i.e. at which the system ceases to fulfil jump of an input signal). For researched system transients action (responses to jumps of an input signal) are shown at the fig. 2.21. Disruption of tracking occurs when the amplitude of jump A=0,67. This value also defines a strip of dynamic tracking.

It is necessary to mark that at sinusoidal input action (at the set speed of change of input frequency) tracing failure occurs at certain amplitude of the sinusoidal effect, and the amplitude at which there is a tracing failure in this case will be more than at spasmodic change of an input signal. For researched system processes (responses to input action

$A\sin(\pi / 10)$ at various amplitudes A an input signal) are shown at the fig. 2.22. Disruption of tracking occurs when the amplitude A=0,78.

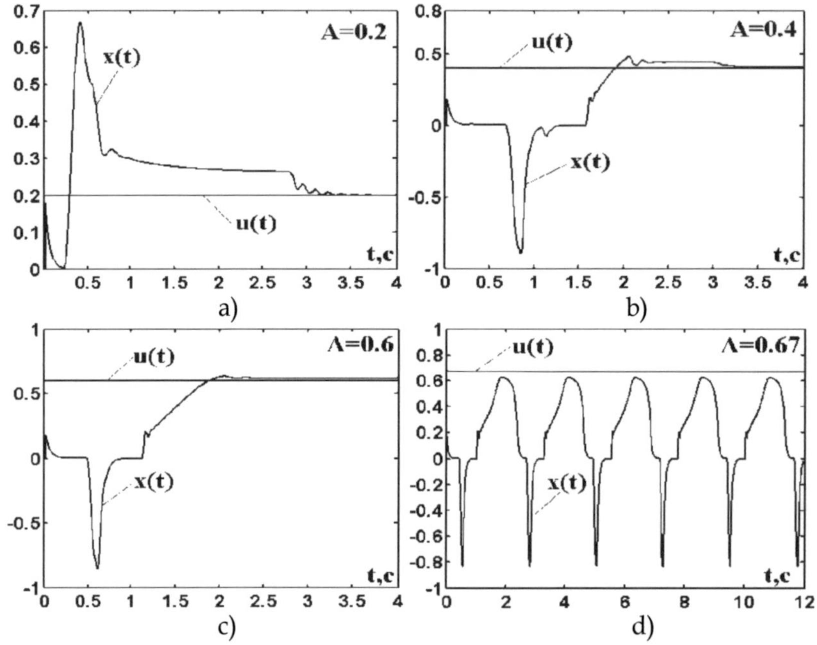

Fig. 2.21. Disruption of tracking occurs when the amplitude of jump A=0,67.

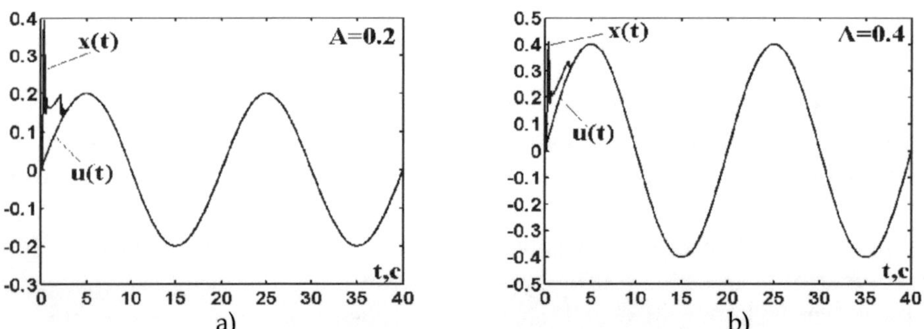

Fig. 2.22. Responses to input action $A\sin(\pi / 10)$ at various amplitudes A an input signal.

Disruption of tracking occurs when the amplitude A=0,78.
Consider the fuzzy system PLL generator with a digital phase detector [8]. Version execution a diagram of a phase detector is shown in fig.2.23 a.

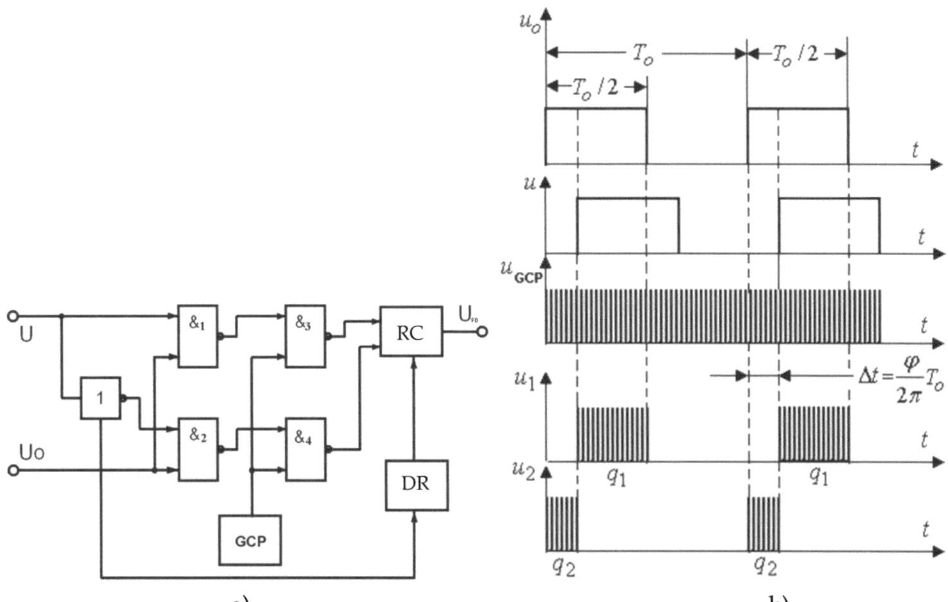

Fig. 2.23. Execution a diagram and principle of operation of a phase detector

The principle of operation of digital phase detector can be explained as follows [7]. At the input of detector come the reference u_0 and u input signals, that are previously transformed into meander shape (see. Fig .2.23,b). The positive half-cycle - logical unit, negative - logical zero. We suppose that the periods of both signals are identical and equal T_o, and the phase difference is equal φ. The counting pulses u_{GCP} from the generator counting pulses arrive on an input of 1 reverse counter RC only at coincidence in time of input reference signal and for an input 2 in the presence of reference and absence input signals. At the end of each period, the next number at the output of down reversible counter is equal to the difference between the numbers q_1 and q_2 (see fig.2.23,b) is remembered and the reverse counter is nullified by the device of reset DR.

$K_{FD} = \dfrac{T_o}{2T_c}$ -a constant rate, is equal to the maximum number on the output of the reversible counter of digital phase detector, T_o- period of reference signal, T_c- period of counting pulses, φ - difference in phase fluctuation (one of which is the reference) of the same frequency, field by to the first and second inputs of the detector (when equality the frequencies of two oscillation, the phase difference of these oscillations is constant). Sampling interval at phase sample and hold devise is defined as $\delta\varphi = 2\pi \dfrac{T_c}{T_o}$. A phase shift φ corresponds to a time shift $\Delta t = \dfrac{\varphi}{2\pi} T_o$.

The static discrimination characteristic of the digital phase detector (see fig. 2.24,a) can be represented as the shaper of function, give at on specific intervals

$$Q_{FD}(\varphi)=\begin{cases}\frac{2}{\pi}K_{FD}(\frac{\pi}{2}-\varphi) & \text{at } 0\le\varphi\le\pi; \\ \frac{2}{\pi}K_{FD}(\varphi-\frac{3\pi}{2}) & \text{at } \pi\le\varphi\le 2\pi,\end{cases} \tag{2.5}$$

And continued periodically on intervals $2k\pi\le\varphi\le 2(k+1)\pi,\ k=1,2,3...,$ and device of sampling-storage DSS (clamp).

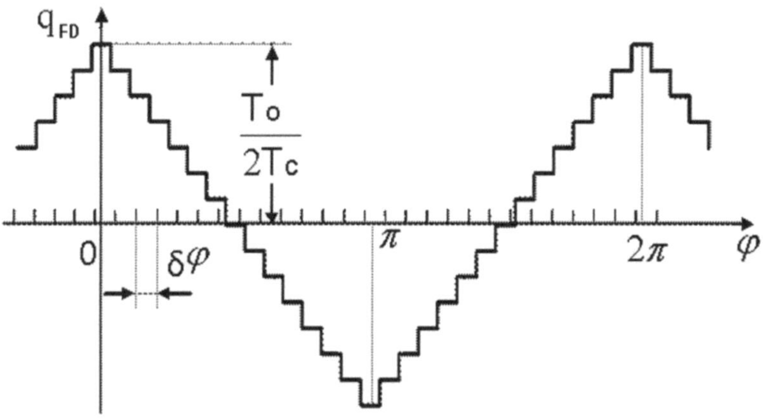

a)

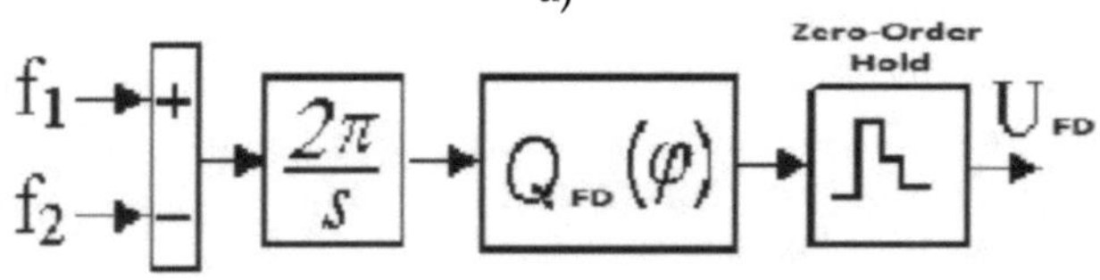

b)

Fig. 2.24. The static discrimination characteristic and block diagram of the digital phase detector

Using the Fourier series expansion is extended periodically at the intervals $2k\pi\le\varphi\le 2(k+1)\pi,\ k=1,2,3...,$ of the functions $Q_{FD}(\varphi)$ we obtain expression in the form

$$Q_{FD}(\varphi)=\frac{8}{\pi^2}K_{FD}[\cos\varphi+\frac{\cos 3\varphi}{9}+\frac{\cos 5\varphi}{25}+\frac{\cos 7\varphi}{49}+...]. \tag{2.6}$$

As practice shows, for determination of a mathematical model of the static discrimination characteristic of the digital phase detector is sufficient to the first three terms of Fourier series.

When you change the frequencies of input signals, the phase difference becomes a function of time (see the formula (2.4)). Taking into account expressions (2.4), (2.6) and the clamp the block diagram of a digital phase detector under varying frequencies f_1 i f_2 of input signals will have the form, shown at the fig. 2.24,b.

At the output of clamp can be activated a filter for smooth the pulsations, for example, a simple analog filter with a transfer function of an aperiodic link $G_1(s) = k / (s + b)$.
On the basis of the block diagram of the numeral phase detector taking into account inertance of the filter on the output of a detector and a controlling unit on the input of oscillator (a controlling unit is usually also described as an aperiodic link) can be make a mathematical model of system of the PLL frequency control.
The mathematical model of system of PLL with the digital fuzzy controller and digital phase detector, compiled using of interactive system MATLAB, is presented on fig. 2.25.

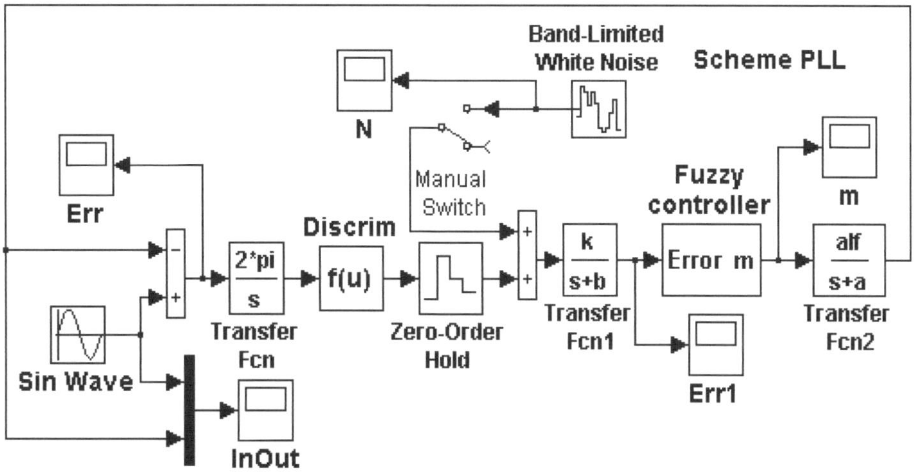

Fig. 2.25. The mathematical model of system of PLL with the digital fuzzy controller and digital phase detector

Filter at the output of the digital phase detector and an controlling element of the generator describe the transfer function:

$$G_1(s) = k / (s + b) = 10 / (s + 12{,}5)\,,\; G_2(s) = alf\ / (s + a) = 3 / (s + 20)\,.$$

The digital fuzzy controller (Fuzzy controller at the fig. 2.25) is fulfilled under the block diagram, with the identical triangular membership function erected in degree and consists of the block of the shaper of sizes A (t) and B (t), the block of comparing of sizes A and B and calculation u_c and the block of normalization output variable[2]. The digitization step is chosen 0,001s. Values of ranges $\mathrm{Am} = \theta_{\max} = -\theta_{\min}$; $\mathrm{Bm} = \dot{\theta}_{\max} = -\dot{\theta}_{\min}$; $\mathrm{Cm} = \ddot{\theta}_{\max} = -\ddot{\theta}_{\min}$; $\mathrm{Dm} = m_{\max} = -m_{\min}$ at adjustment of a fuzzy controller steal up either manually, or automatically by the decision of the optimization task.
At research of the system we will accept, that the difference of frequencies of two fluctuations changes under the sinusoidal law: $\Delta f = 0{,}2\sin(\pi / 5)$ (i.e. the maximum deviation of frequency of the generator from the set reaches $\pm 20\%$). System of PLL should compensate a deviation of frequency of the generator, therefore a fuzzy controller it is necessary to adjust on the minimum current error of a mismatch in system. As a result of adjustment it is received following optimum parameters of a fuzzy controller, c=1: Am=0,08; Bm=2.5; Cm=50; Dm=100.

Processes in system (see fig.2.25) at setting action $0,2\sin(\pi / 5)$ are presented at the fig.2.26.

In the figures $e(t)$ - a mismatch error in frequency at the input of digital phase detector (a) and its steady form in the dynamic mode (b), $\theta(t)$ - error at the output of phase detector– input of fuzzy controller (c) and its steady form in the dynamic mode (d), $m(t)$ - an operating pressure on an output of an fuzzy controller,(e), $u(t)$ and $x(t)$ - an input and output of the system (see fig.2.26) accordingly (f).

Transition process in the system ends in a time not exceeding 0.6sec.The maximum dynamic error of a mismatch on frequency on an input of the phase detector on setting action $0,2\sin(\pi / 5)$ does not exceed $4 \cdot 10^{-3}$. Research shows the system (see fig.2.25), the fuzzy controller can increase the accuracy of the PLL system is almost two orders of magnitude compared to the system without controller.

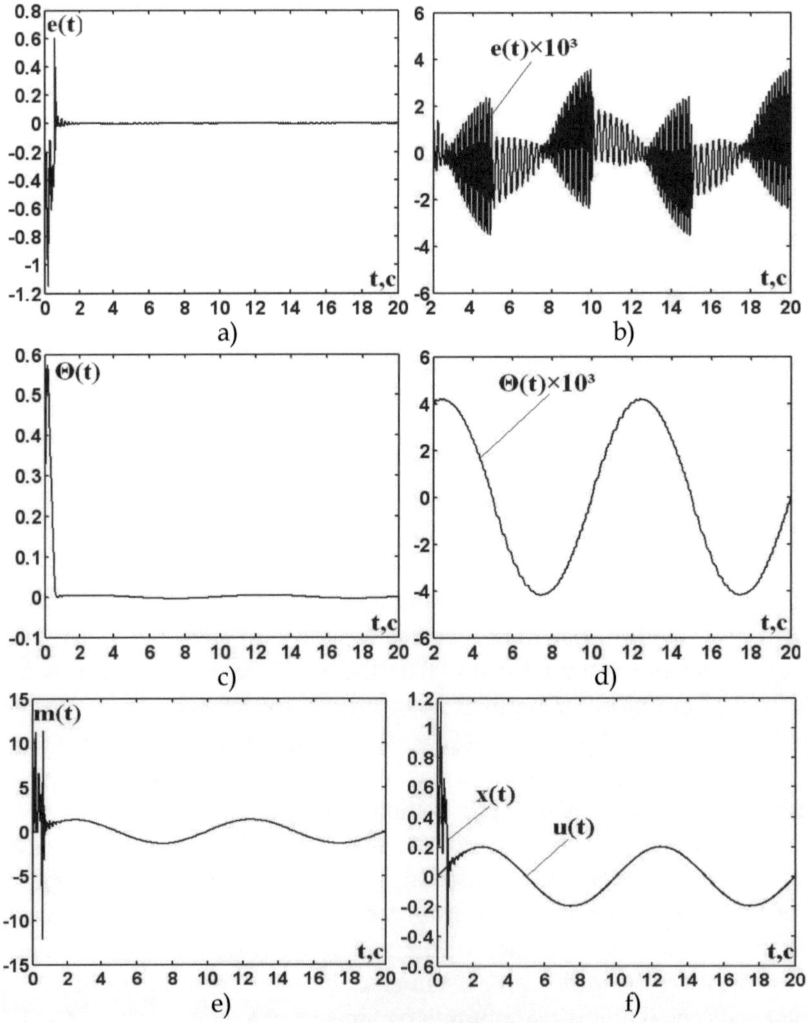

Fig. 2.26. Processes in system at setting action $0,2\sin(\pi / 5)$

Application of fuzzy controllers in PLL appropriate. Since the fuzzy controller is a digital correction device, it can be successfully applied in the digital PLL.

2.3 Combined fuzzy-system of PLL

The mathematical model of combined system of PLL with the digital fuzzy controller, made with use of interactive system MATLAB, is presented on fig.2.27.

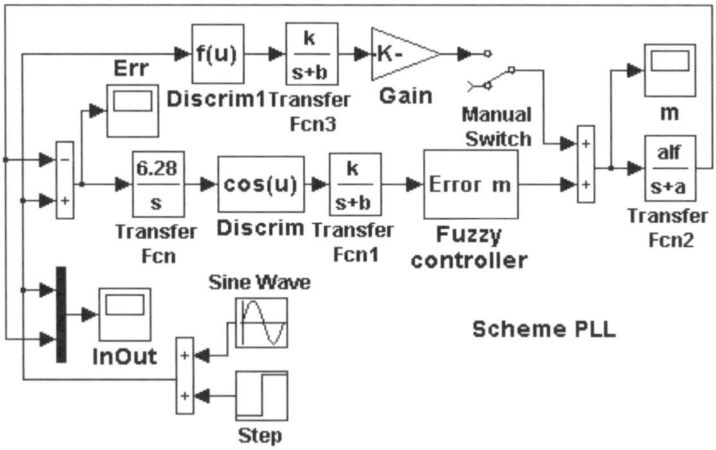

Fig. 2.27. The mathematical model of combined system of PLL with the digital fuzzy controller

Automatic control system name combined (or system with the combined control) when in the law of control except an error, derivatives and integrals from an error, additional communications on setting action or/and on revolting action are entered.

The basic system in detail considered earlier [fig. 2.18], consists of the phase detector which block diagram is resulted on fig. 2.17 and is presented by the comparison device, an integrating link with factor 2π (Transfer Fcn), the discrimination characteristic cosφ (Discrim) and the low-pass filter on an output of the detector with transfer function $G_1(s) = k/(s+b)$ (Transfer Fcn1), an fuzzy controller (Fuzzy controller), the generator operated pressure, with transfer function $G_2(s) = alf/(s+a)$ (Transfer Fcn2), and an individual negative feedback.

Filter at the output of the detector and an operating element of the generator have the transfer functions in a numerical kind: $G_1(s) = k/(s+b) = 10/(s+12{,}5)$; $G_2(s) = alf/(s+a) = 3/(s+20)$.

The digital fuzzy controller with the identical triangular membership functions erected in degree (Fuzzy controller at the fig.2.27) is executed under the basic scheme. The fuzzy controller consists of the block of the shaper of sizes A (t)and B (t), the block of comparison of sizes A (t)and B (t) and calculation u_c and the block of normalization output variable[2] The digitization step is chosen 0,001s. Values of ranges ($\mathrm{Am} = \theta_{max} = -\theta_{min}$; $\mathrm{Bm} = \dot{\theta}_{max} = -\dot{\theta}_{min}$; $\mathrm{Cm} = \ddot{\theta}_{max} = -\ddot{\theta}_{min}$; $\mathrm{Dm} = m_{max} = -m_{min}$) get out at controller adjustment. Additional coupling on setting action includes following elements: the frequency discriminator with the discrimination characteristic (Discrim1)

$$K(e) = K_d e \exp\{-\frac{e^2}{\Delta^2}\},$$

where $K_d = 1$ and $\Delta = 1$, and the filter of the bottom frequencies with transfer function $G_3(s) = k/(s+b)$ (Transfer Fcn3), and the amplifier (Gain) with changeable factor of strengthening.

From consideration of mathematical model of combined system of PLL with a digital fuzzy controller it is visible, that it is impossible to carry out the transfer function of additional coupling equal to return transfer function of generator $1/G_2(s) = (s+a)/alf = (s+20)/3$, i.e. it is impossible to carry out absolute invariancy of system from setting action, but it is possible to reduce a dynamic error of system by selection of transmission factor of amplifier Gain (to reach ε -invariancy).

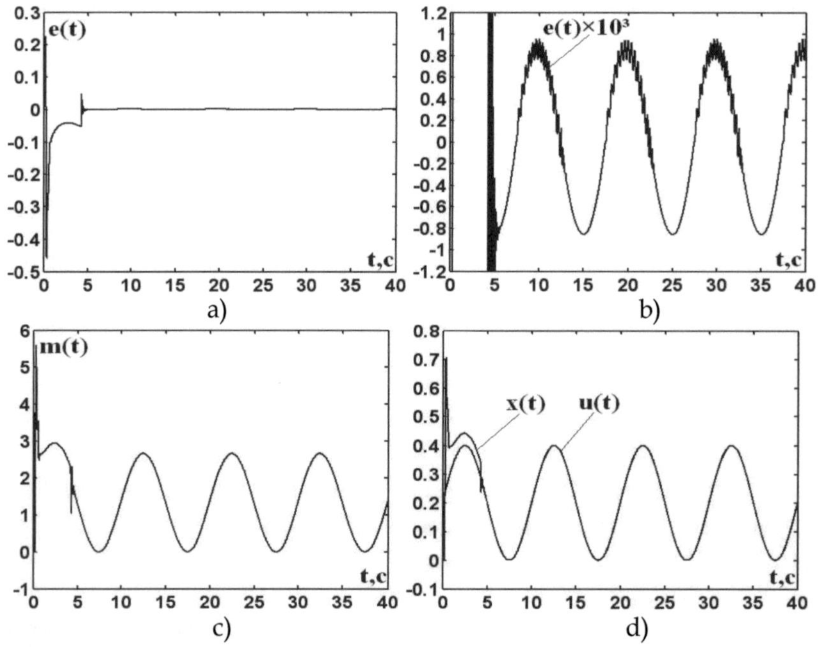

Fig. 2.28. Processes in system at setting action $0,2[1+\sin(\pi/5)]$ (at the disconnected coupling on setting action)

At research of the combined system we will accept, that the difference of frequencies of two fluctuations changes under the sinusoidal law: $\Delta f = 0,2[1+\sin(\pi/5)]$ (i.e. the maximum deviation of frequency of the generator operated pressure, from the set reaches 40%). System of PLL should compensate a deviation of frequency of the generator, therefore an fuzzy controller it is necessary to adjust on the minimum current error of a mismatch in system. As a result of adjustment it is received following optimum parameters of fuzzy controller:

Am=0,03; Bm=0.5; Cm=10; Dm=20; c=1.

Optimum factor of strengthening of amplifier Gain K=7,3.

Processes in system (see fig.2.27) at setting action $0,2[1+\sin(\pi/5)]$ are presented at the fig.2.28 (at the disconnected coupling on setting action) and at the fig. 2.29 (at the included coupling on setting action). In drawings: a) and b) $e(t)$ - a dynamic error of a mismatch on frequency on an input of the phase detector in the transitive and established modes, c) $m(t)$ - operating pressure on an output of an fuzzy controller, d) $u(t)$ and $x(t)$ - an input and output of the system accordingly.

The maximum dynamic error of a mismatch on frequency on an input of the phase detector in system of PLL at the disconnected coupling on setting action $0,2[1+\sin(\pi/5)]$ in the established dynamic mode makes size $9,8\cdot10^{-4}$, and the maximum dynamic error of a mismatch on frequency on an input of the phase detector in system of PLL at the included coupling on setting action $0,2[1+\sin(\pi/5)]$ in the established dynamic mode makes size $3,6\cdot10^{-4}$. Transient time (time of capture of an input signal) in system at the disconnected coupling on setting action makes 4,3 seconds, and in system at the included coupling on setting action 2,5 seconds

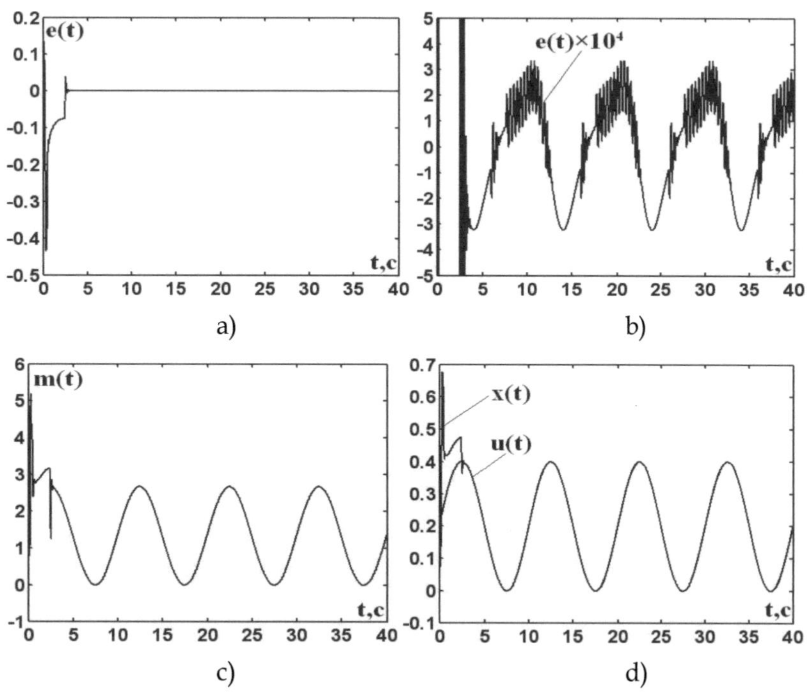

Fig. 2.29. Processes in system at setting action $0,2[1+\sin(\pi/5)]$ (at the included coupling on setting action)

Research combined (with additional coupling on setting action) system of PLL with a digital fuzzy controller by method of mathematical modeling has shown, that additional coupling on setting action reduces the established dynamic error in 2,7 times, and time of capture of an input signal in 1,7 times, in comparison with these indicators in system without coupling on setting action.

Ever more reduce the steady dynamic error can be achieved if in additional coupling on setting action to enter ideal forcing link with transfer function $G(Ts+1)$, where $T=1/a$, and in the factor G should enter k factor and additional adjusting factor K.
The combined system of PLL with the digital fuzzy controller and forcing link shown in Fig.2.30.

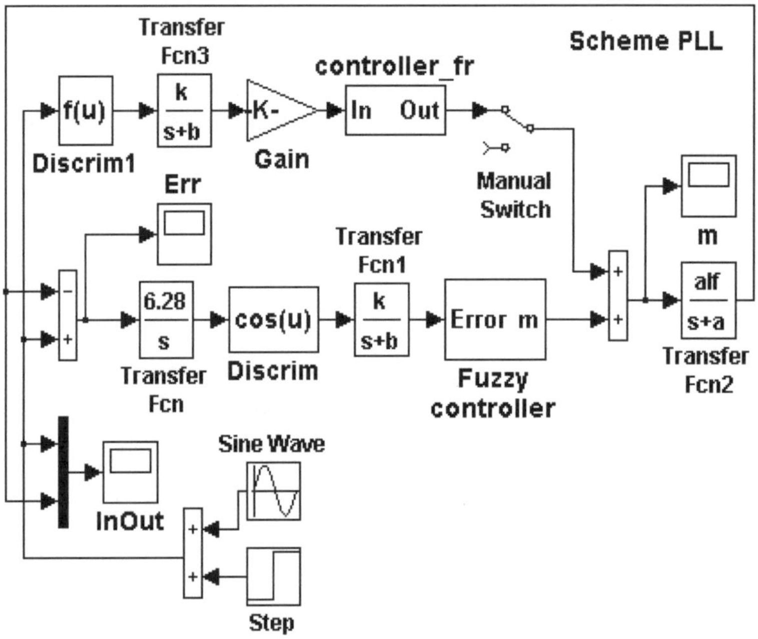

Fig. 2.30. The combined system of PLL with the digital fuzzy controller and forcing link

In this system a digital ideal forcing link (controller _fr) realizes expression (using the first difference from a signal arriving on its input):

$$U_{out}(n)=k\{U_{in}(n)+T[U_{in}(n)-U_{in}(n-1)]/h\}.$$

The scheme of a digital ideal forcing link is resulted on fig. 2.31 (only this link the system on fig. 2.30 differs from the system shown on fig. 2.27). At research of the combined system we will accept, that the difference of frequencies of two fluctuations changes under the sinusoidal law: $\Delta f=0{,}2[1+\sin(\pi/5)]$ (i.e. the maximum deviation of frequency of the generator, from the set reaches 40%).

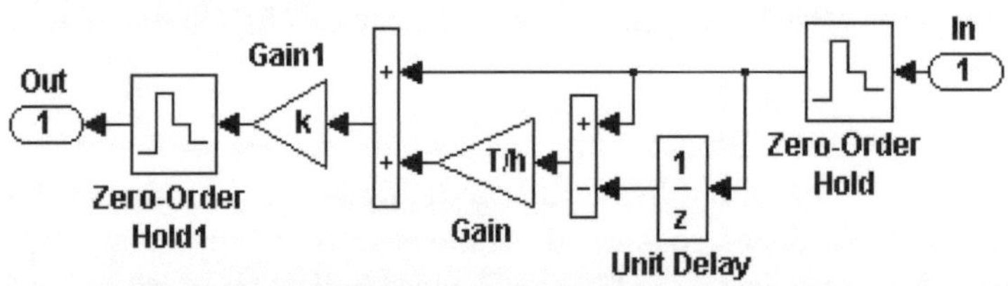

Fig. 2.31. The scheme of a digital ideal forcing link

System of PLL should compensate a deviation of frequency of the generator, therefore a fuzzy controller it is necessary to adjust on the minimum current error of a mismatch in system. As a result of adjustment it is received the same optimum parameters of an fuzzy controller, as in the system shown on fig.2.27: Am=0,03; Bm=0.5; Cm=10; Dm=20; c=1. But the optimum amplification factor of amplifier Gain will be another: K=0,82.

Processes in system (see fig.2.30) at setting action $0,2[1+\sin(\pi / 5)]$ are presented on fig.2.32 (at the disconnected coupling on setting action) and on fig. 2.33 (at the included coupling on setting action). In drawings: a) and b) $e(t)$ - a dynamic error of a mismatch on frequency on an input of the phase detector in the transitive and established modes, c) $m(t)$ - operating pressure on an output of an fuzzy controller, d) $u(t)$ and $x(t)$ - an input and output of the system accordingly.

The maximum dynamic error of a mismatch on frequency on an input of the phase detector in system of PLL at the disconnected coupling on setting action $0,2[1+\sin(\pi / 5)]$ in the established dynamic mode makes size $9,8 \cdot 10^{-4}$, and the maximum dynamic error of a mismatch on frequency on an input of the phase detector in system of PLL at the included coupling on setting action $0,2[1+\sin(\pi / 5)]$ in the established dynamic mode makes size $2,5 \cdot 10^{-4}$.

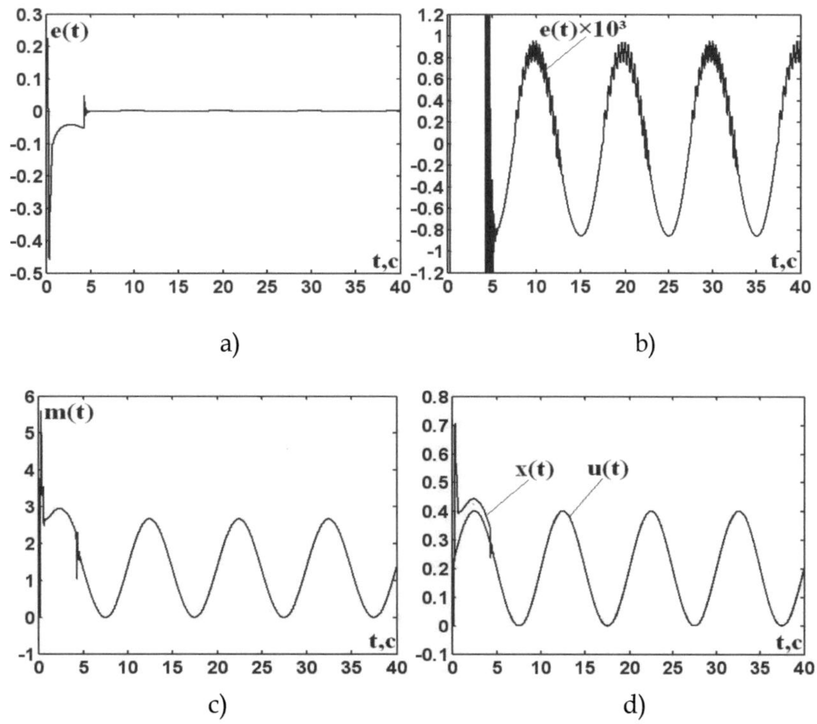

Fig. 2.32. Processes in system at setting action $0,2[1+\sin(\pi / 5)]$ (at the disconnected coupling on setting action)

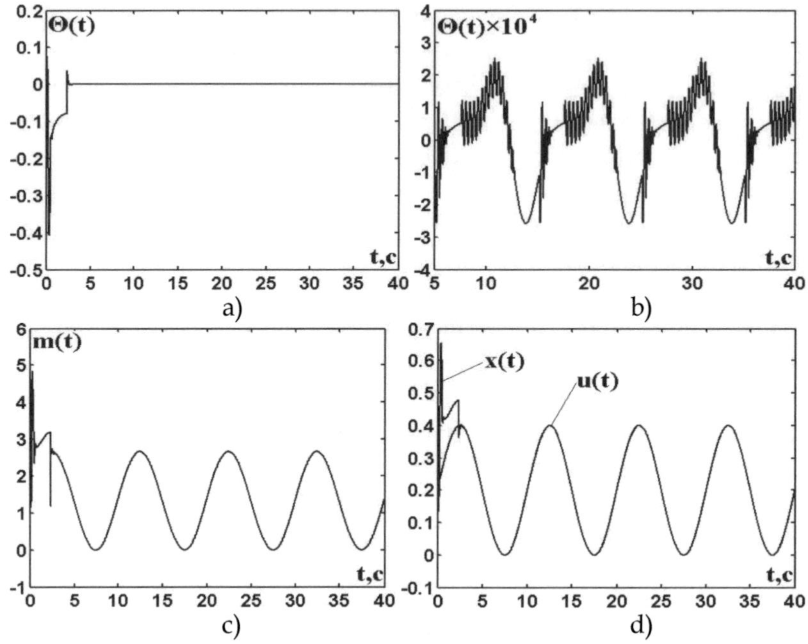

Fig. 2.33. Processes in system at setting action $0{,}2[1+\sin(\pi / 5)]$ (at the included coupling on setting action)

Transient time (time of capture of an input signal) in system at the disconnected coupling on setting action makes 4,3 seconds, and in system at the included coupling on setting action 2,4 seconds.

Thus, in system of PLL with the digital fuzzy controller and a digital ideal forcing link additional communication on setting action reduces the established dynamic error in 3,9 times, and time of capture of an input signal in 1,79 times, in comparison with these indicators in system without communication on setting influence.

2.4 System of PLL with the phase-frequency discriminators

The phase-frequency discriminator has the specific characteristic which can be presented a non-linear element of type "saturation" (see fig. 2.34, a,b) that allows to work in broad range of frequencies.

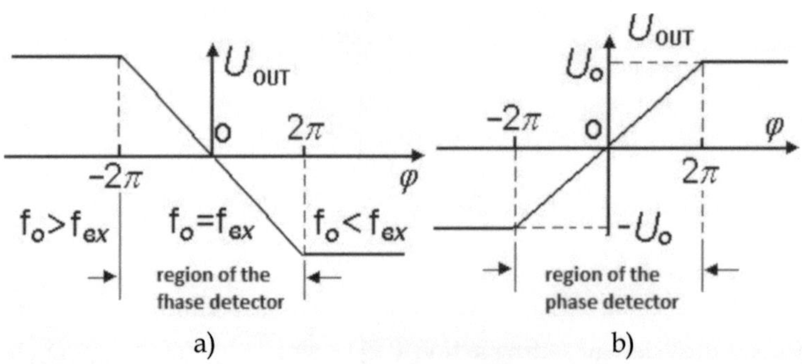

Fig. 2.34. The characteristic of the phase-frequency discriminator

Discrimination characteristic phase-frequency discriminator (see Fig.2.34, a) can be described by

$$K(\varphi)=\begin{cases} 2\pi K_d & \text{at } \varphi < -2\pi, \\ -K_d\varphi & \text{at } -2\pi \le \varphi \le 2\pi, \\ -2\pi K_d & \text{at } \varphi > 2\pi. \end{cases}$$

In interactive system MATLAB the diagram of discriminator with the characteristic presented at the fig. 2.34,a it is possible to present as the connections of three block (see fig. 2.35): the switch (Switch), the inverter (Gain) and the saturation block (Saturation). At the positive signal of an error on a discriminator input (in block Switch parameter Threshold =0.000001) closed a upper contact of switch and the is formed a plot of characteristic $\varphi \ge 0$, at the negative signal of an error on input discriminator is closed bottom contact and formed a plot of characteristic $\varphi \le 0$. Levels of restrictions in a block of saturation (Saturation) are $\pm 2\pi K_d$.

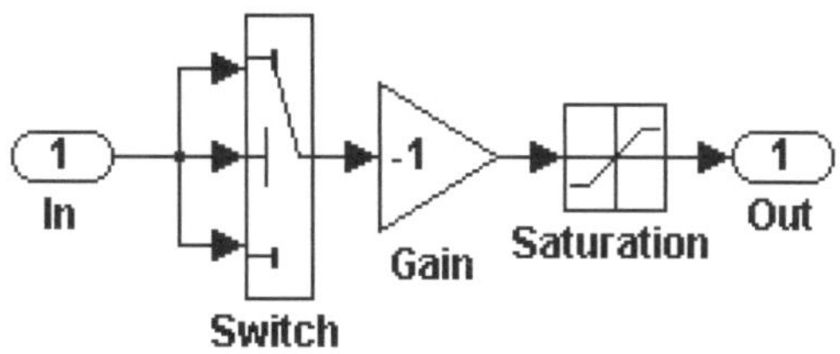

Fig. 2.35. Diagram of discriminator with the characteristic presented at the fig. 2.34,a

Discrimination characteristic phase-frequency discriminator (see fig.2.34, b) can be described by

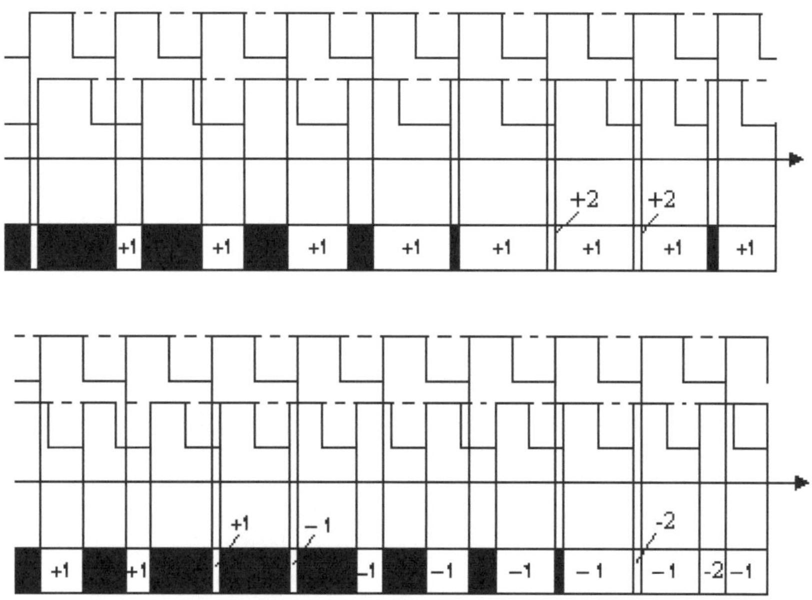

Fig. 2.36. Operating principle of phase-frequency discriminator

$$K(\varphi)=\begin{cases} -U_o \ \text{at} \ \varphi < -2\pi, \\ \dfrac{U_o}{2\pi}\phi \ \text{at} \ -2\pi \le \varphi \le 2\pi, \\ U_o \ \text{at} \ \varphi > 2\pi. \end{cases}$$

In an interactive system MATLAB the diagram of discriminator with the characteristic presented on fig 2.34,b can present only a block saturation (Saturation).
Phase-frequency discriminator with a characteristic shown in fig.2.34, b, is a machine that has five states (-2, -1, 0, +1, +2), and switchable on a leading edge of the reference signal and feedback signal. Reference signal adds to the state machine unit and the feedback signal on the contrary, subtracts. Operating principle of phase-frequency discriminator is shown at the fig.2.36 (darkened color is shown zero state machine).
At fig.2.37 shows the model on which to explore the two systems having the same phase-frequency discriminator (Discrim1), made under the scheme fig.2.35, and the same voltage-controlled oscillator (TransferFcn1), with a transfer function $G(s)=alf\,/\,s$. Transfer coefficient VCO $alf = K_G = 104$ rad / ($s \cdot V$).

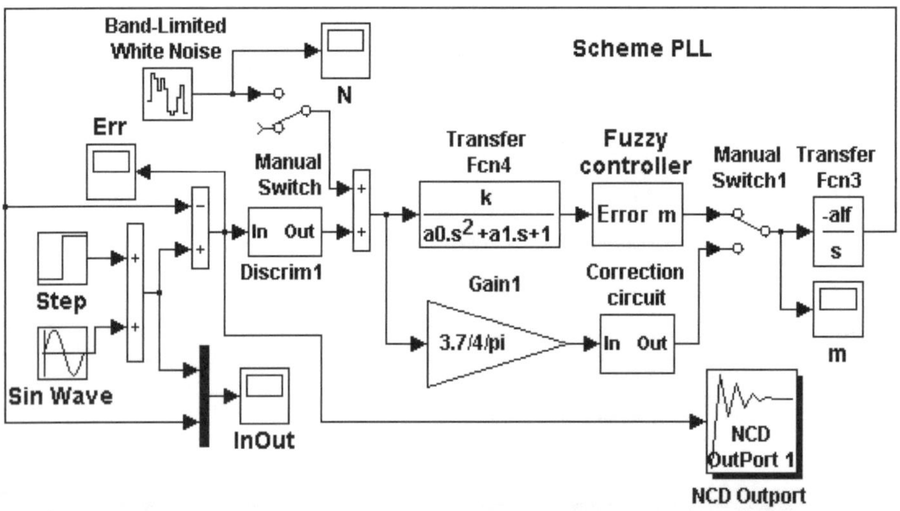

Fig. 2.37. System of PLL with phase-frequency discriminator

With the closure of a switch ManualSwitch1 in the down position simulated the system of PLL. The block diagram of this system, except for blocks Discrim1 and Transfer Fcn1 (is simulating the discriminator and VCO), have two additional blocks: Gain (transfer factor of detector K_{Fd} =3,7/(4π) V/rad) and block Correction circuit (an active filter with an operational amplifier). The transfer function of filter

$$F(s) \cong \frac{\tau_2 s+1}{\tau_1 s(\tau_3 s+1)} = \frac{3330(s+4,55)}{s(s+100)}.$$

System with active filter on the operational amplifier was studied when exposed to on input of an equivalent harmonic signal $u(t)=10+5\sin 2\pi Ft$ with carrier frequency $F=0,1Hz$.

The processes in the system of the PLL frequency control with active filter Correction circuit(see fig.2.37) are shown in fig.2.38 where $u(t)$ - an input action, $x(t)$ -an output system (see fig.2.38,a), $e(t) \equiv \text{Err}$ - a mismatch error on the input of the discriminator (see fig.2.38, b). $m(t)$ - a filter output (see fig.2.38,c). At fig.2.38, shows reaction system on step input $u(t) = 10$.

The results show that the system of the PLL frequency control with active filter Correction circuit has a very high exactness working off entrance influence: a dynamic mismatch error for a given harmonic signal is $4,2 \cdot 10^{-4}$ or 0.082% of the amplitude of input sine impact. System performance is also very high. Settling time is approximately equal to 0.06, but the transient process is oscillatory, with overshoot almost 60% .

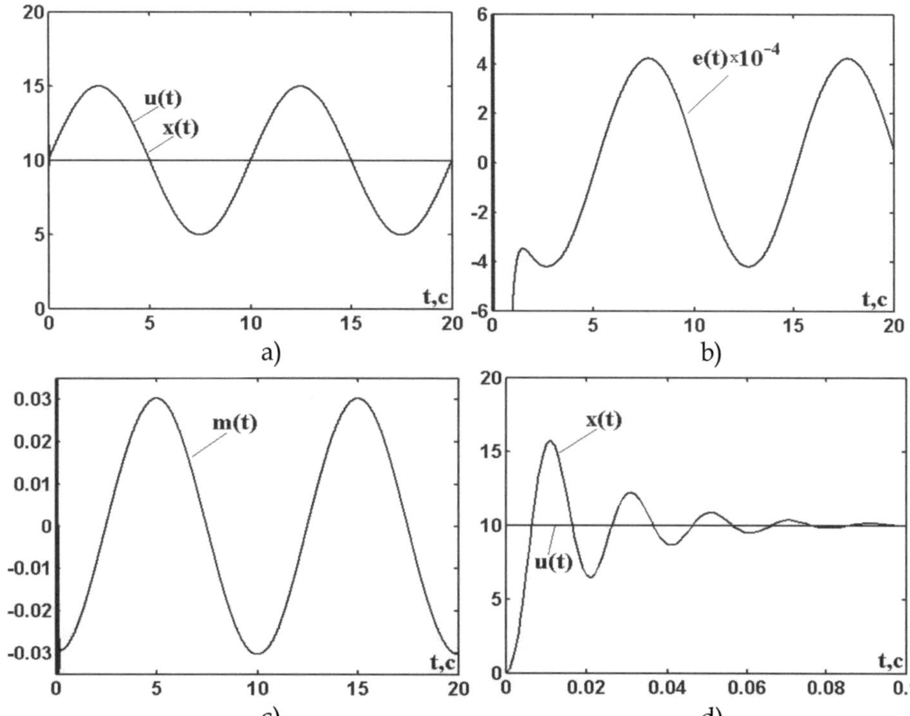

Fig. 2.38. The processes in the system of the PLL frequency control with active filter

With the closure of a switch ManualSwitch1 in the upper position simulated the system of PLL with a low -pass filter LPF pass second and digital fuzzy controller (Fuzzy controller at the fig.2.37) which is executed by the block diagram. The controller consists of the block of the shaper of sizes A (t) and B (t), the block of comparing of sizes A and B and calculation u_c and the block of normalization output variable (block 3 collected by the diagram)[2]. The filter has the transfer function

$$F(s) = \frac{k}{a_0 s^2 + a_1 s + 1} = \frac{0,002}{0,008s^2 + 0,18s + 1},$$

which can also be written as

$$F(s) = \frac{0,25}{s^2 + 22,5s + 125} = \frac{0,25}{(s+10)(s+12,5)}.$$

The mismatch error $\theta(t)$ from an output of a low-pass filter arrives on a analog-digital converter (AD converter) (Zero-Order Hold), included at the input of a fuzzy controller . A quantization step of AD converter h =0,01s. On an output of a fuzzy controller is included the digital/analog converter (Zero-OrderHold1).

For simplification of normalization (recalculation of values of signals in values of elements of universal set) ranges of change input and output signals (parameters of a fuzzy controller) we is accepting by symmetric:

$$\theta_{\max} = -\theta_{\min}; \ \dot{\theta}_{\max} = -\dot{\theta}_{\min}; \ \ddot{\theta}_{\max} = -\ddot{\theta}_{\min}; \ m_{\max} = -m_{\min}.$$

Then recalculation of values of signals in values of elements of universal set perform according to the formulas [2]

$$\left.\begin{aligned} u_1^* &= (\theta^* + A_m) / (2A_m); \\ u_2^* &= (\dot{\theta}^* + B_m) / (2B_m); \\ u_3^* &= (\ddot{\theta}^* + C_m) / (2C_m). \end{aligned}\right\}.$$

Values of ranges ($\mathrm{Am} = \theta_{\max} = -\theta_{\min}$; $\mathrm{Bm} = \dot{\theta}_{\max} = -\dot{\theta}_{\min}$; $\mathrm{Cm} = \ddot{\theta}_{\max} = -\ddot{\theta}_{\min}$; $\mathrm{Dm} = m_{\max} = -m_{\min}$) at adjustment of a fuzzy controller steal up either manually, or automatically by the decision of the optimization task. The system of PLL with a low pass filter LPF and a digital fuzzy controller was investigated when exposed at input an equivalent harmonic signal $u(t) = 10 + 5\sin 2\pi Ft$ with carrier frequency $F = 0,1Hz$.

The adjustment of a fuzzy controller is carried out by criterion of a minimum of a dynamic error. Is received following optimal parameters of fuzzy controller :

$$\mathrm{Am} = 0,0174; \ \mathrm{Bm} = 0,2458; \ \mathrm{Cm} = 4,6607; \ \mathrm{Dm} = 249,89.$$

When setting up a fuzzy controller in an interactive system MATLAB we using a block NCD (Nonlinear Control Design), which implements the method of dynamic optimization for the design of control systems. This tool is designed for use with Simulink, automatically adjusts a system parameters (in the system fig.2.37 adjusted parameters of the fuzzy controller, Am, Bm, Cm, Dm,), based on certain constraints on the temporal characteristics (time of regulating and overshoot for reaction to a step action and limits for the dynamic mismatch error).

The processes in the system of the PLL frequency control with low pass filter LPF and the digital fuzzy controller (see fig.2.37) are shown in Fig.2.39 where $u(t)$ - a input action, $x(t)$ - a system output (see fig.2.39, a) $e(t) \equiv \mathrm{Err}$ –a mismatch error at the input of the discriminator (see fig.2.39, b), $m(t)$ - an output of fuzzy controller (see fig.2.39, c).

The maximum dynamic error (except for initial burst at the moment of signal capture) does not exceed $4,2 \cdot 10^{-3}$ or 0,82% from amplitude of a sinusoid.

At fig.2.39, d shows the system response to a step action $u(t) = 10$ on the output of system $x(t)$ and the output a fuzzy controller $m(t)$. Transient process have overshoot 3,4%. The system fulfills input action in a time not exceeding 0,16 sec.

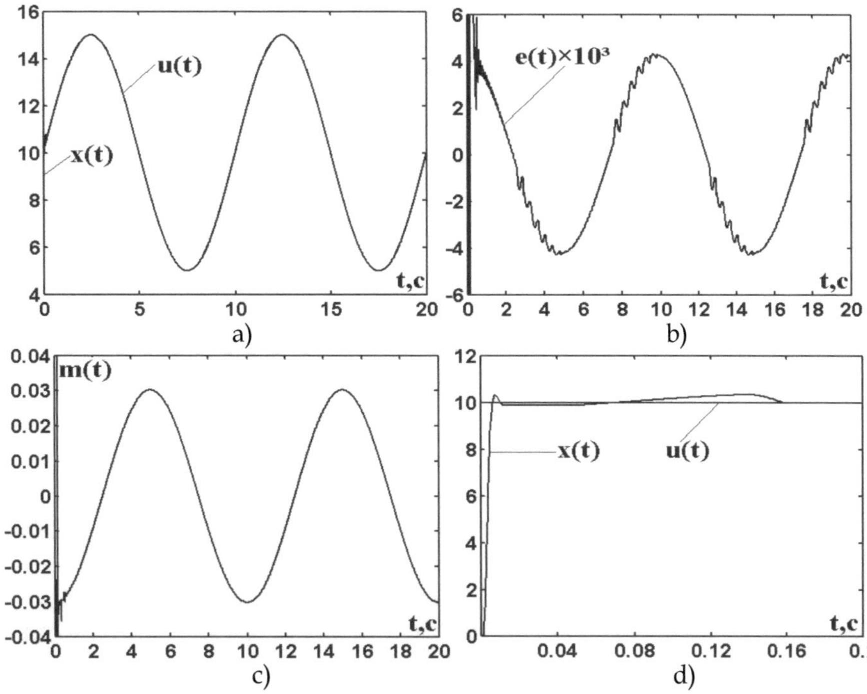

Fig. 2.39. The processes in the system of the PLL frequency control with low pass filter LPF and the fuzzy controller

We remark that the PLL with a low pass filter LPF, but without the digital fuzzy controller, has no stability.

Thus, can conclude that the PLL with a low pass filter LPF and the digital fuzzy controller has a bad quality indicators than the PLL with an active filter on the operational amplifier, but has transient process (overshoot).

Now consider the operation of these systems in the presence of internal noise. In this case, the switch Manual Switch on Fig.2.37 is closed in the upper position, which corresponds to the filing of the noise signal - a stationary white noise (Band-Limited White Noise) on the output phase-frequency detector (Discrim1). Noise signal n (t) represented on Fig.2.40. Amplitude of the noise emissions of approximately 1% of the input signal.

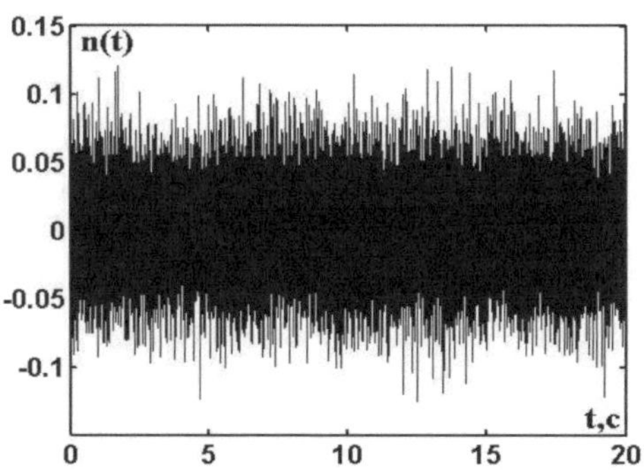

Fig. 2.40. Noise signal on the output phase-frequency detector

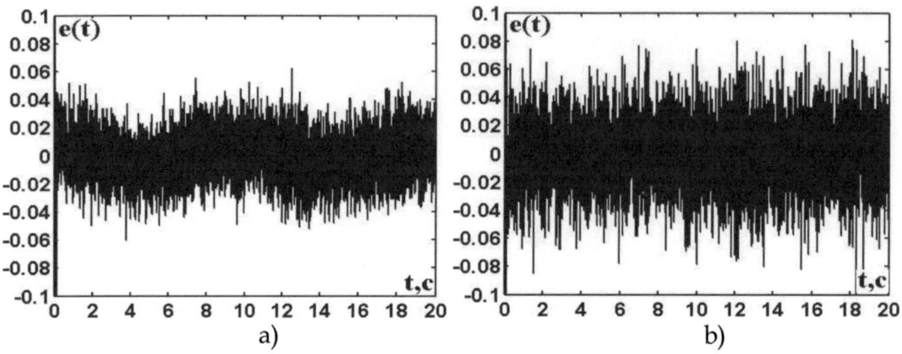

Fig. 2.41. Mismatch errors on the input of phase-frequency discriminator

At fig.2.41 are presented mismatch errors on the input of phase-frequency discriminator at the presence of stationary white noise at the output of the discriminator in the system of a phase-frequency locked loop with low pass filter LPF and the digital fuzzy controller Fuzzy controller (see fig.2.41 a) and in the system of the PLL frequency control with active filter Correction circuit (see Fig.2.41, b).

As seen from the oscillograms the system of system of the PLL frequency control with a low pass filter LPF and a digital fuzzy controller Fuzzy controller has less mismatch error at the input phase-frequency discriminator in the presence of stationary white noise than the system phase-frequency locked loop with active filter Correction circuit.

2.5 Servomechanism of synchronous and in-phase rotation shaft part of drive from the alternating reference voltage

The mathematical model of servomechanism in an interactive system MATLAB is presented in fig.2.42.

The mathematical model of the phase detector is represented serial connection of comparison device, the nonlinearity (Discrim) $K(\varphi) = K_d \sin\varphi$, where K_d - coefficient of conversion of the phase detector, and $\varphi(t) \equiv e(t)$ - a mismatch error on a phase detector input, and the low-pass filter LPF (Transfer Fcn).

Transfer function of a low-pass filter LPF (Transfer Fcn)[2] is

$$G_1(s) = \frac{a}{s+a} = \frac{12,5}{s+12,5}, \quad \mathrm{a} = 1/\tau, \quad \tau = RC = 0,08 \text{ s}.$$

Transfer function of the amplifier of power-modulator P-M (Transfer Fcn1)[2]

$$G_2(s) = \frac{K}{s+a_1} = \frac{500}{s+100}, \quad a_1 = 1/T_y, \; T_y = 0,01 \text{ s}.$$

Transfer function of engine EE (Zero-Pole)[2]

$$G_3(s) = \frac{\alpha}{s(s+b)} = \frac{90}{s(s+10)},$$

where $b = 1/T_{db}; \; T_{db} = 0,1\,c; \; \alpha = Kdb/T_{db}; \; Kdb = 9\ rad/(V \cdot s)$

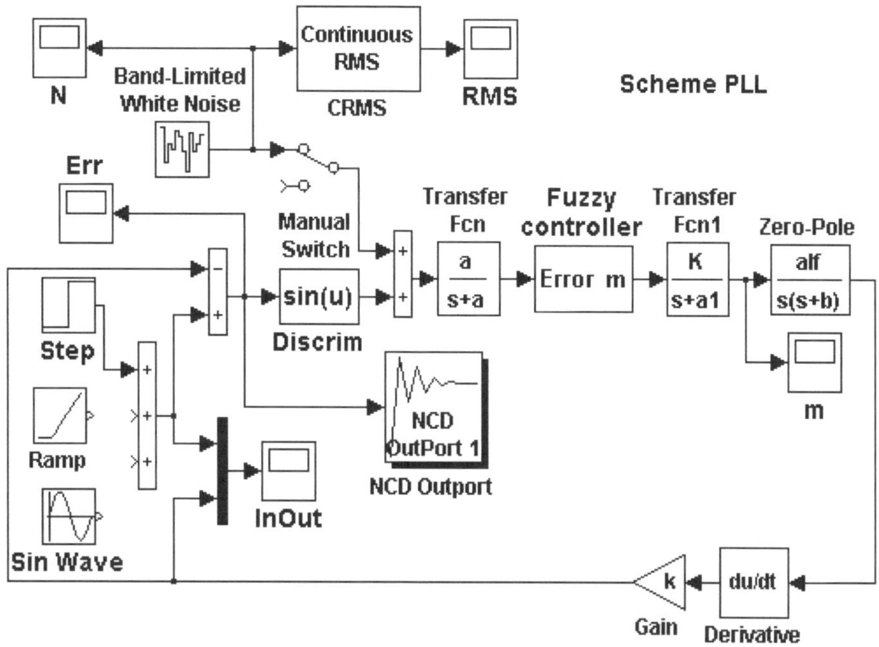

Fig. 2.42. The mathematical model of servomechanism

Transfer function of the tacho-generator (Gane + Derivation)[2]

$$G_4(s) = ks\ ,\ k = 0{,}03\ V \cdot s\,/\,rad.$$

At adjustment of a fuzzy controller in interactive system MATLAB we use unit NCD (Nonlinear Control Design) which implements a method of dynamic optimization for designing of management systems.

The system is researched at typical influences on an input: input: 1.single jump, 2.the equivalent of a harmonic signal $u(t) = 0{,}5\sin 2\pi Ft$ with carrying frequency $F = 0{,}1Hz$ and 3. a linear signal Ramp $u(t) = t$.

Adjustment of a fuzzy controller is carried out by criterion of a minimum of a dynamic error at the equivalent harmonic signal without influence of noise on a phase detector output (contacts of switch are closed in the lower position). Receive the following optimal parameters of fuzzy controller: Am=0,072; Bm=0,168; Cm=1,579; Dm=61,798.

Processes in servomechanism (fig. 2.42 see) with a fuzzy controller without influence of noise on a phase detector output (contacts of switch Manual Switch are closed in the lower position) are shown on fig. 2.43 at an single jump of an input signal, on fig. 2.44 at influence of the equivalent harmonic signal $u(t) = 0{,}5\sin 2\pi F$, with carrying frequency $F = 0{,}1Hz$ and on fig. 2.45 at of the linear signal $u(t) = t$. In pictures $u(t)$ – input influence, $x(t)$ – a system output, $e(t) \equiv \mathrm{Err}$ – a mismatch error on a discriminator input, $m(t)$ - a signal on an engine input.

At an single jump of an input signal transient phenomenon has overshoot of 13 % and ends at time 2,8 (see fig. 2.43). The installed dynamic error is equal to zero. At action of a harmonic signal the maximum dynamic error (except for the release initial at the moment of signal capture) does not exceed 0,5% from amplitude of a sinusoid (see fig. 2.44). At action of the linear signal $u(t) = t$ transient phenomenon comes to an end in time, not exceeding 2c, and the installed dynamic error is close to zero (approximately $2 \cdot 10^{-4}$). Therefore the signal output practically repeats input action (fig. 2.45 see).

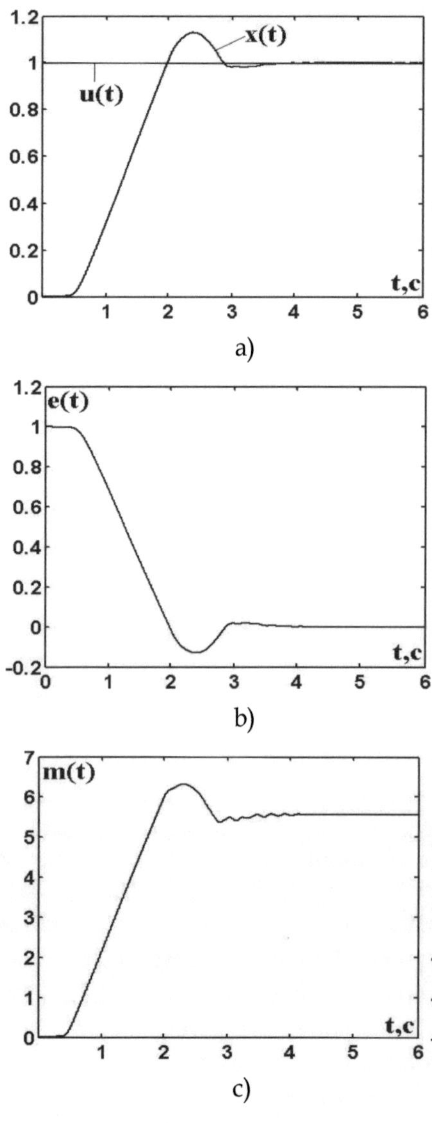

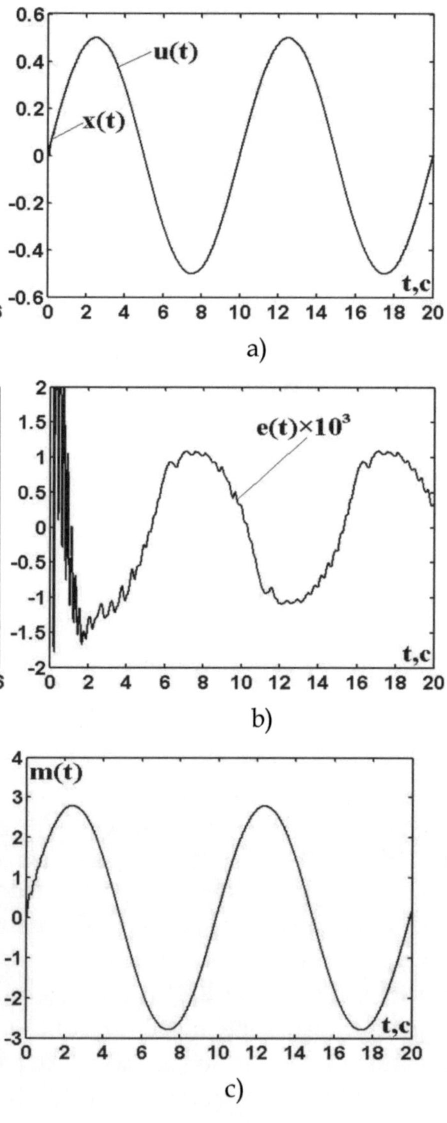

Fig. 2.43. Processes in servomechanis at an single jump

Fig. 2.44. Processes in servomechanism at the equivalent harmonic signal

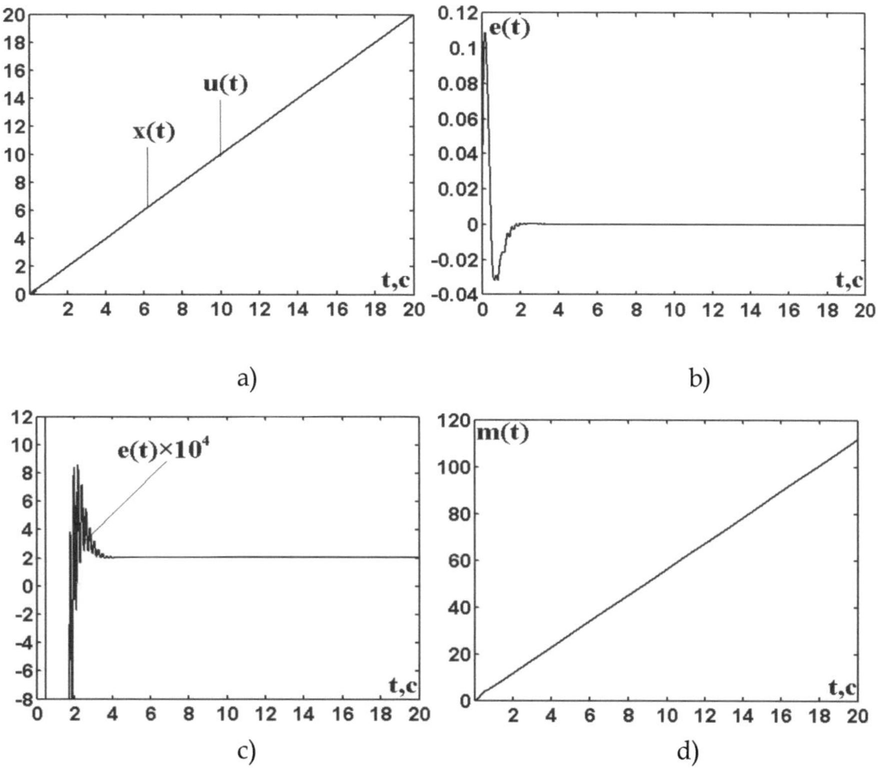

Fig. 2.45. Processes in servomechanism at the linear action

Adjustment of a fuzzy controller by criterion of a minimum of a dynamic error at action of noise on a phase detector output (contacts of switch Manual Switch are closed in the upper position) is enough difficult. The noise signal n (t) - a stationary white noise (Band-Limited White Noise) on a phase detector output (Discrim) is presented on fig. 2.46,a. Current value of a root from root-mean-square of a noise signal (root mean squared value) calculated in unit CRMS is shown at the fig. 2.46b

Instead of fuzzy controller FC (Fuzzy Controller), is executed under the basic scheme, with identical triangular functions of an accessory in the presence of a noise signal on an output of the phase detector for obtaining of a smaller dynamic error in system it is expedient to use fuzzy controller (Fuzzy Controller), fulfilled on the schematic circuit with identical exponential membership functions. For the purpose of an exception (or the considerable decrease) a dynamic error at tracking controlling action, on an output of a fuzzy controller two integrators for giving to a closed circuit of follow-up system astaticism the second order are included.

At system adjustment, except selection of values of ranges Am, Bm, Cm, Dm and parameter c of exponential membership functions in a fuzzy controller, it was required to optimize coefficient k of the tacho-generator of an alternating current. At adjustment of a fuzzy controller in interactive system MATLAB is used unit NCD (Nonlinear Control Design) and received the following optimal parameters of system:

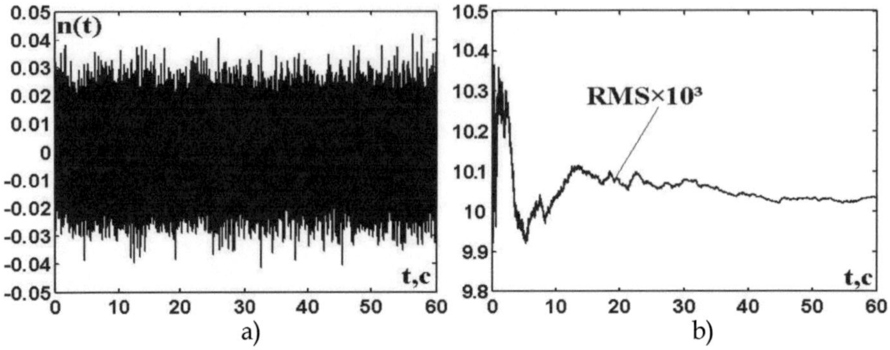

Fig. 2.46. Noise signal

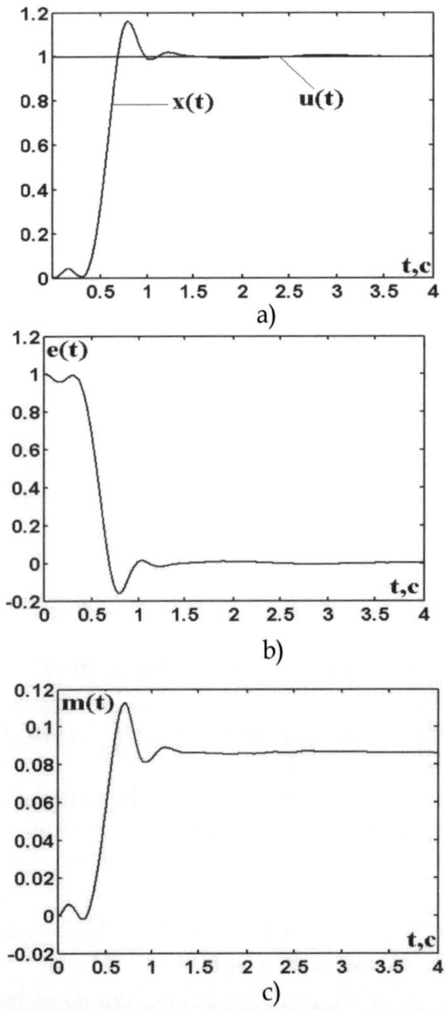

Fig. 2.47. Processes in system at the unit step

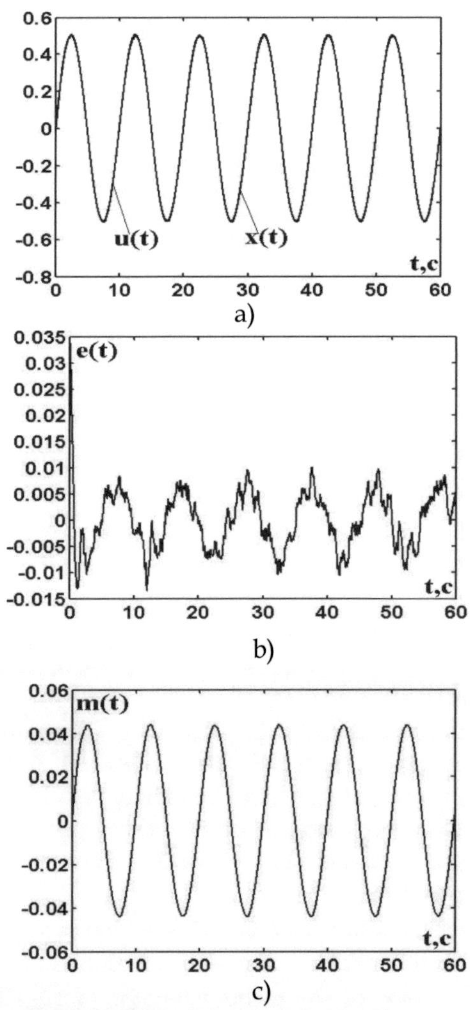

Fig. 2.48. Processes in system at the equivalent harmonic signal

h=0,01; Am=3,9822; Bm=8,6779; Cm=86,357; Dm=116.,64; c=0,19476;

a=12,5;a1=100;K=500; alf=90;b=10;k=1,2865.

Processes in servomechanism (fig. 2.42 see) with a fuzzy controller at influence of noise on a phase detector output (contacts of switch Manual Switch are closed in the upper position) are shown on fig. 2.47 at an unit step of an input signal, on fig. 2.48 at action of the equivalent harmonic signal $u(t) = 0,5\sin 2\pi F$, with carrying frequency $F = 0,1Hz$ and on fig. 2.49 at action of the linear signal $u(t) = t$. In figure $u(t)$ - an input action, $x(t)$ - a system output, $e(t) \equiv \text{Err}$ - a mismatch error on input of a discriminator, $m(t)$ - a signal on an input of engine.
At an single jump of an input signal transient phenomenon has overshoot of 16% and comes to an end during 0,93 s (fig. 2.47 see). The installed dynamic error is equal to zero. At action of a harmonic signal the maximum dynamic error (except for initial burst at the moment of signal capture) does not exceed 1,5% from amplitude of a sinusoid (fig. 2.48 see).
At action of the linear signal $u(t) = t$ transient phenomenon ends at time, not exceeding 1,2 s, and the installed dynamic error does not exceed $8 \cdot 10^{-3}$. The signal output practically repeats input action (fig. 2.49 see).

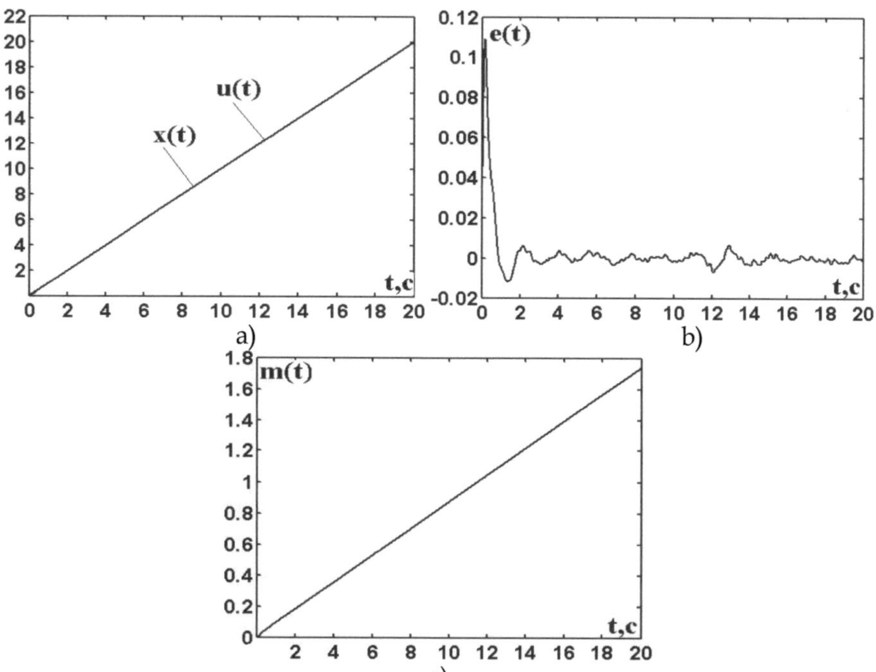

Fig. 2.49. Processes in system at the linear action

3. References

[1] Klepper Dzh., Frenk Dzh. A phase-and frequency-locked frequency. - M.: Energiya, 1977. - 440 s.

[2] Gostev V.I., Skurtov S.N. Fuzzy systems frequency and phase auto-tuning: monograph. - Nezhin: OOO "Vidavnictvo -Aspekt-Poligraf", 2010. 388 p.
[3] Gostev V.I. Fuzzy-system phase-locked loop oscillator // Zviyazok. - 2008. - № 4.
[4] Gostev V.I., Baranov A.A. Storchak K.P. The system clock with a digital fuzzy controller // Zviyazok. - 2007. - № 3 (71). - S.51-54.
[5] Gostev V.I., Kunah N.I., Drobik A.V., Nevol'ko V.A. Investigation of processes in the systems and phase locked loop in the presence of internal noise // Naukovi zapiski Ukrains'kogo naukovo-doslidnogo institutu zvyazku. Naukovo-virobnichii zbirnik. - 2008. - №6(8). p. 51-54
[6] Gostev V.I., Krihoveckii G.Ya., Storchak K.P. The system clock with a digital PID controller with random phase changes of the input // Visnik Derzhavnogo universitetu Informacyino-komunikacyinih tehnologyi. - 2007.- Spec. vip., p. 72-75
[7] Vagapov V.B., Burlyai I.Yu., Ryumshin N.A. Theory of electronic tracking systems. - K.: Tehnika, 2002. - 284 p.
[8] Gostev V.I. Fuzzy-system phase-locked loop oscillator with a digital phase detector // Zviyazok. - 2008. - № 5-6 (81-82). - p. 68-72.

18

Automotive Sketch Processing in C++ with MATLAB Graphic Library

Qiang Li
Jilin University
P. R. China

1. Introduction

The purpose of automotive sketch processing is to separate the sketch into patches and extract the useful information and apply it to assist 2D to 3D transformation. How to extract the useful information depends on what the resources are, what kinds of information are needed, and what methods are applied. In sketches, the information may be extracted from features such as the geometry features, shading, colours and lighting. Geometry features are the most important because they contain the information to identify and distinguish between forms. For example, edges can be used to determine the shapes, and areas can be used to match the size.

This chapter introduces a way to make the automotive sketches ready for 2D to 3D transformation. Three aspects of problems are discussed including the pre-processing of sketches outside computer, the processing of pre-processed sketches inside computer, and the extraction of features. Some of sketch processing algorithms are implemented in C++ using the MATLAB image processing toolbox, Graphic Library and Math Library. Some have been developed from scratch. The work describe in this chapter is concerned with the production of a feasible routine, from the point of view of application, which is capable of dealing with the real world characteristics of automotive sketches. There is no established method which provides a suitable starting point for the transformation of real automotive sketches. The combined algorithms, which are discussed in this chapter, have been found to be useful.

2. A glimpse of the 23D system

A brief set of requirements, from a usability point of view, for 2D to 3D tool can be summaried as follow:

- Can deal with 2D sketches and 3D models.
- Intuitive, simplified and robust.
- Flexible and expandable.
- Compatible with other CAD and CAM systems.

Following the above requirements, a prototype of 2D to 3D system, called "23D", has been implemented to support the novel method of transforming 2D automotive sketches quickly into 3D surface models.

2.1 The development environment

The main development language is Microsoft Visual C++® (Ladd, 1996; Seed, 1996; Smith, 1997; Schildt, 1998) with OpenGL® (Kilgard, 1996; Wright & Sweet, 1996; Fosner, 1997; Silverio et al., 1997; Chin et al., 1998; Segal & Akeley, 2001), MATLAB® C/C++ Math and Graphics Libraries (MathWorks, 2001). The basic functions and some algorithms are implemented based on the Open Geometry (Glaeser & Stachel, 1999), MATLAB optimisation toolbox (MathWorks, 2000), spline toolbox, and image processing toolbox (MathWorks, 2001), Image Analysis Pro (IaePro) (Matthews, 2002) and Microsoft VisSDK (The Vision Technology Group, 2000).

2.2 Multiple working modes

The system needs to deal with 2D sketches and 3D surface models, and transformationfrom 2D to 3D as well. Therefore, the working modes should be easily exchanged between 2D and 3D. In the system, the multiple working modes have been implemented for 2D and 3D manipulations. It is easy to switch the modes, see Fig. 1. 2D sketch is considered as the background in 3D space. Therefore, the 2D working mode is that the background plane containing the sketch is displayed without the 3D models, see Fig. 1a; the 3D working mode is that the 3D models are displayed without the background, see Fig. 1b; and the mixed working mode is that both the 3D models and the 2D background are displayed at the same time, see Fig. 1c. The 2D sketch background is not affected by any 3D manipulations.

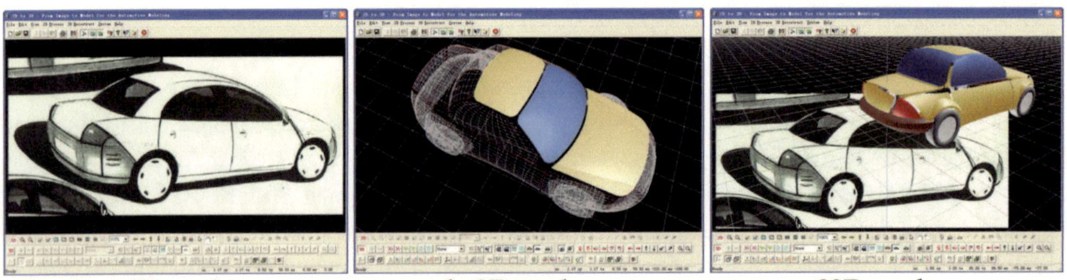

a. 2D mode b. 3D mode c. 23D mode

Fig. 1. Three working modes

3. The pre-processing of a sketch

The sketches are not realistic images. The forms and shadings may contain many inconsistencies compared with a true projection of a possible real object. In addition, the reverse transformations from 2D to 3D are rather complicated and contain possible ambiguities, in that a 2D shape may represent many possible shapes in 3D. Therefore, some assumptions have to be made in order to simplify the problem. The fundamental assumptions made here include:

- The scanned sketches will be pre-processed to reduce the inconsistencies in them. The end result of the pre-processing will be that boundaries are complete and are all closed contours or silhouettes. Any key lines will be clear and without ambiguities so as to give enough information for further processing. With these conditions satisfied, the sketch can be separated into patches which can be represented by parametric models.

- Shadings of sketches may be ignored initially, since many techniques of the representations in sketches are not realistic and exact. To derive meaning from them requires psychological interpretation of the intention of the designer, which is beyond the scope of this project.
- Any side, front, rear or top view of automotive model in the sketches is considered to be orthographic projection, others such as front or rear ¾ perspective views are considered to be perspective projection.
- Minor details are ignored and allowing concentration on the major ones which establish the essential 3D geometry. It is possible that these could be restored after the basic form has been determined, perhaps using parts from a parts library.
- There is a limit to the exaggeration of forms in a sketch that can be used. Designers often do use exaggerated geometry to achieve a desired mood. If translated into 3-D, the resultant model will also contain exaggerated geometry.
- No attempt is made to correct ambiguities of the reverse transformation automatically. These functions are best left for user intervention. The user is likely to be the stylist, who is in a good position to judge which of a number of possibilities best represents the intended vehicle.

As known, not all the sketches are suitable for 3D modelling by the 23D system, but many do contain the required characteristics. There are many different styles in automotive sketching, according to the stylist's personal practice. The information contained varies at the different conceptual design stages, and is not exactly correct in geometry shape and projection, because the sketches are not real-world images. Humans can easily interpret the shape through adding additional information, in the form of prior knowledge of automotive forms to the sketches and ignoring the faults according to this knowledge. However, the computer is not as agile as the human. It must have available enough information to create the shape, which can come from various sources. One approach is to establish a powerful knowledge database to support the object recognition; another approach is to add the information before image processing. The former needs larger investment and longer time to train the computer, and the later needs less investment and is easy to realize. Two examples of the use of an original sketch as a basis for two well established edge detection algorithms are shown in Fig. 2c and 2d. The results show that they are difficult to be interpreted, even by a human. If the results are to be interpretable by a computer program, significantly more sophisticated processing will be required. Therefore, it is necessary and feasible to establish some input requirements for the sketches that will be used for 3D modelling by the method proposed in 23D system, and will form the requirements for the pre-processing stage. The requirements are relative. The more powerful the pre-processing method is, the lower the requirements for the interpretive program are. The original sketches are drawn by stylist, as shown in Fig. 2a and 2e. The results after pre-processing are shown in Fig. 2b and 2f.

The aim of the pre-processing of sketches is to allow the requirements for the interpretive program to be met by a greater variety of original sketches. Essentially, the pre-processing emphasises useful features in the sketches and eliminates useless ones. According to the analysis of Tingyong Pan (Pan, 2002), the form-lines and form-shadings should be enhanced and kept, and the non-form-lines and non-form-shadings should be ignored. The vehicle components should be simplified in details and ambiguities removed. One of the important requirements is that the input sketches should have completed and closed contours or silhouettes. Any key form-lines should be clear to give enough information to the further processing. For example, the original sketches (Fig. 2a and 2e) leave some missing and unclear contours or silhouettes to give an imaginary space. These should be redrawn by stylists, see the sketches in Fig. 2b and 2f. All the silhouettes are closed and clear. Some details are ignored such as small lights, highlights, and shadings. The shading information can be separated from the contour or silhouette information. If the shading information is important and near realistic, and is within the closed contours, it can be kept. Otherwise, it should be ignored or further processed to a suitable form. The shadows of the vehicles are deleted, and the completed silhouettes of wheels are added, which are very important for the determination of the 3D coordinates. Side elevations, front and rear ¾ perspective views are the best starting point for system processing.

a. The original sketch b. The pre-processed sketch

(Both sketches by courtesy of Tingyong Pan)

c. Canny method d. Sobel method

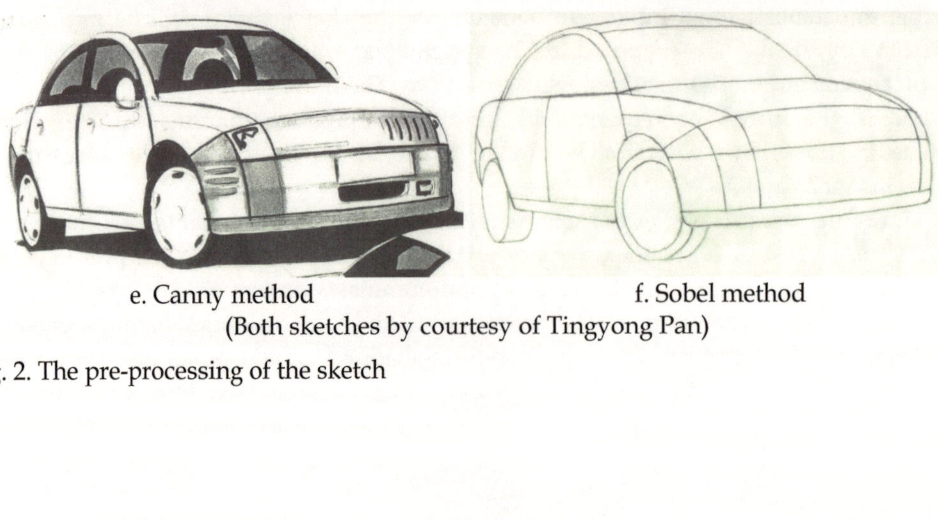

e. Canny method f. Sobel method

(Both sketches by courtesy of Tingyong Pan)

Fig. 2. The pre-processing of the sketch

It is also important to produce pre-processed sketches with simple patches, which can be represented using existing parametric models.
Because the features extracted from sketches are currently pixel-based in order to keep the balance between the speed of processing and the precision of calculation, the suitable size of input sketches should be carefully considered.

4. Sketch processing

Even though the sketches have been pre-processed before scanning, they also need to be subject to further image processing before transforming them into 3D. Some basic functions - such as the adjustment of lightness, hue, and saturation, the exchange from colour to grey scale and B&W, the erasure of unnecessary areas in the sketch, the separation of form from non-form line and shading - are used before edge detection and segmentation. To decrease the size of the dataset and smooth the boundaries, B-spline or NURBS curve fitting to the outlines are applied. These form-lines are disassembled into spline segments and are used to build up the patches, which represent the whole surface model.
The original sketches (if applicable) or pre-processed sketches still need to be processed further in order to obtain a sketch with single pixel edges and closed boundaries, and this sketch is separated into patches for the downstream processes. Therefore, it is necessary to investigate a set of efficient image processing algorithms for this application.

4.1 Image mode selection

There are many modes for the different purposes of raster image processing including colour and non-colour ones. Some typical colour modes such as RGB (red, green and blue), HSV (hue, saturation and value), HLS (hue, lightness and saturation), and CYMK (cyan, yellow, magenta and black) have been described in the books (Foley et al., 1996; Salomon, 1999). The Adobe Photoshop 6.0 supports colour modes such as RGB, CYMK, Lab (lightness, green-red axis and blue-yellow axis), Indexed Colour, and HSB (hue, saturation and brightness), and non-colour modes such as Greyscale, Multi-channel, Bitmap and Duotone.
There are four modes for image displaying and processing supported by the 23D system: RGB colour, 256 greyscale, 16 greyscale, and black and white (B&W). The internal format is RGBA colour; therefore the modes can be changed reversibly. The algorithms of greyscale are different. For example, the Image Analysis Explorer Pro (IaePro) supports three methods to obtain a greyscale as follows.

$$A_{ij} = \begin{cases} 0.2125R_{ij} + 0.7154G_{ij} + 0.0721B_{ij} & \text{Greyscale BT709} \\ 0.299R_{ij} + 0.587G_{ij} + 0.114B_{ij} & \text{Greyscale Y} \\ 0.5R_{ij} + 0.419G_{ij} + 0.081B_{ij} & \text{Greyscale RMY} \end{cases} \quad (1)$$

However, for simplification, the transformation from RGB to 256 greyscale used here is an average algorithm of the colour RGB values (Jain, 1995, pp. 281).

$$A1_{ij}\Big|_{\substack{i=0,\cdots,BmpBgr\_w-1 \\ j=0,\cdots,BmpBgr\_h-1}} = \frac{1}{3}(R_{ij} + G_{ij} + B_{ij}) \quad (2)$$

Where $A1_{ij}$ is the greyscale value of a point in image including three components R_{ij}, G_{ij} and B_{ij}; *BmpBgr_w* and *BmpBgr_h* are the width and the height of sketch in pixels, respectively. In B&W mode, the two levels are obtained from a point between 0 and 255 to bisect the whole range. A similar function is used in Adobe Photoshop 6.0 (Adobe, 2000).

$$A2_{ij}\Big|_{\substack{i=0,\cdots,BmpBgr\_w-1\\ j=0,\cdots,BmpBgr\_h-1}} = \begin{bmatrix}0\\1\end{bmatrix} = \begin{bmatrix}0\\255\end{bmatrix} \begin{array}{l} 0 \le A1_{ij} < D_L \\ D_L \le A1_{ij} \le 255 \end{array} \tag{3}$$

Where $A2_{ij}$ is determined by $A1_{ij}$, and D_L is a threshold to determine a dividing level. The default of D_L is 192, and can be adjusted. The change from 256 greyscale to 16 greyscale is obtained according to the average rule. A coding scheme proposed in 23D system is that the values of 16 intervals are increased through adding the value 17 for smoothness and keeping it spanning to the two ends (0 and 255).
An example is shown in Fig. 3 for the four modes of processing allowed by the system.

a. RGB colour b. 256 greyscale

c. 16 greyscale d. B&W with a threshold of 192

(Colour sketch by courtesy of geocities.com)

Fig. 3. The four display modes of the system

$$A3_{ij}\Big|_{\substack{i=0,\cdots,BmpBgr\_w-1\\ j=0,\cdots,BmpBgr\_h-1}} = \begin{bmatrix} 0\\1\\2\\3\\4\\5\\6\\7\\8\\9\\10\\11\\12\\13\\14\\15 \end{bmatrix} = \begin{bmatrix} 0\\17\\34\\51\\68\\85\\102\\119\\136\\153\\170\\187\\204\\221\\238\\255 \end{bmatrix} \begin{matrix} 0 \le A1_{ij} < 16\\ 16 \le A1_{ij} < 32\\ 32 \le A1_{ij} < 48\\ 48 \le A1_{ij} < 64\\ 64 \le A1_{ij} < 80\\ 80 \le A1_{ij} < 96\\ 96 \le A1_{ij} < 112\\ 112 \le A1_{ij} < 128\\ 128 \le A1_{ij} < 144\\ 144 \le A1_{ij} < 160\\ 160 \le A1_{ij} < 176\\ 176 \le A1_{ij} < 192\\ 192 \le A1_{ij} < 208\\ 208 \le A1_{ij} < 224\\ 224 \le A1_{ij} < 240\\ 240 \le A1_{ij} \le 255 \end{matrix} \tag{4}$$

4.2 Brightness and contrast adjustment

The adjustments of brightness and contrast supply the basic means of image enhancement, which compensate for the losses caused by imperfect scanning methods. The algorithm from MATLAB (MathWorks, 2001) *imadjust* function was used to control the values of RGB components directly. The brightness f_b can be adjusted as follows.

$$f_b = \begin{cases} f_{b0}(255-b)/100 & t \ge b \\ f_{b0}(255-t)/100 & t < b \end{cases} \Big\} \; f_{b0} \ge 0 \quad f_b \in [0,255] \\ \begin{cases} f_{b0}t/100 & t \ge b \\ f_{b0}b/100 & t < b \end{cases} \Big\} \; f_{b0} < 0 \tag{5}$$

Where f_{b0} is the original value of brightness; t and b are the top and the bottom values of brightness. They are adjusted by f_b, $t = t + f_b$ and $b = b + f_b$; h and l are the highest and the lowest values among the values of RGB. The differences are defined as $dx = h - l$, $dy = t - b$. They are limited within 0~255.

$$\begin{cases} h = l + (255-b)dx/dy, t = 255 & t > 255 \\ h = l - bdx/dy, t = 0 & t < 0 \\ l = h - tdx/dy, b = 0 & b < 0 \\ l = h - (t-255)dx/dy, b = 255 & b > 255 \end{cases} \tag{6}$$

If the original value $f_{c0} \ge 0$, the contrast f_c can be adjusted as

$$f_c = f_{c0}dx / 200 \qquad f_c \in [0,255] \tag{7}$$

Then h and l should be adjusted as $h = h - f_c$ and $l = l + f_c$. Otherwise, the image is not enhanced. The boundaries should be adjusted again.

$$\begin{cases} h = x_0 + 0.5dy / k & y_1 \geq t \\ h = 255; t = y_1 & y_1 < t \\ l = x_0 - 0.5dy / k & y_2 \leq b \\ l = 0; b = y_2 & y_2 > b \end{cases} \quad \text{where} \quad \begin{cases} k = tg[arctg(dy / dx)(100 + f_c)] \\ x_0 = 0.5(h + l), y_0 = 0.5(t + b) \\ y_1 = y_0 + k(255 - x_0) \\ y_2 = y_0 - kx_0 \end{cases} \tag{8}$$

The Gamma value f_γ is adjusted according to the original value $f_{\gamma 0}$ as follow.

$$f_\gamma = \left(f_{\gamma 0} / 5\right)^{1.2} \qquad f_\gamma \in [1,10] \tag{9}$$

Therefore, the RGB values of each pixel can be calculated as follow.

$$\begin{bmatrix} R_{ij} \\ G_{ij} \\ B_{ij} \end{bmatrix} = \begin{bmatrix} b + (t - b)\left(C_\gamma\right)^{(R_{ij} - l)/(h - l)} \\ b + (t - b)\left(C_\gamma\right)^{(G_{ij} - l)/(h - l)} \\ b + (t - b)\left(C_\gamma\right)^{(B_{ij} - l)/(h - l)} \end{bmatrix} \qquad \begin{matrix} i = 0, \cdots, BmpBgr\_w - 1 \\ j = 0, \cdots, BmpBgr\_h - 1 \end{matrix} \tag{10}$$

The dialog window and examples are shown in Fig. 4. The range of the sliders is ± 100.

4.3 Edge detection

Many algorithms for edge detection have been developed for different image resources. Because the sketches are not the real-world images and can be pre-processed before imported into the system, the edge detection is just a simple routine to quickly find the necessary points for the further processing. Therefore some basic and common algorithms are implemented into the system including *Sobel, Prewitt, Roberts, Canny, Zerocross, Direct* and *Sobel+*. The system was built using the MATLAB C++ Math Library and the Graphics Library (MathWorks, 2000). The dialog window is shown in Fig.5, which is similar to the MATLAB find edges function.

Some examples are shown in Fig. 6 and Fig. 7. In most cases, the algorithms from the MATLAB edge functions can give good results for original sketches, shown in Fig. 6. However, they give poor results on pre-processed sketches, shown in Fig. 7b and Fig. 7d. The pre-processed sketches are composed of sets of dense and thick strokes coming from a quick expression of the edges according to the original sketches. Therefore, a hybrid algorithm, *Direct*, is proposed to deal with such styled sketches.

The idea comes from a demo - *Region Labelling of Steel Grains* - in the MATLAB image processing toolbox. Two binary images are obtained from pre-processed sketches by using low and high thresholds. The edge points from low threshold image are used to delete the same points from high threshold image. The left edge points from the high threshold image are considered as the edges. In this way minor regions caused by strokes are deleted. The result is shown in Fig. 7c produce from a thick edge image.

a. Original Sketch

b. f_b = -33%

c. f_c = 45%

d. f_b = 34%, f_c = -50%

e. f_Y = 25%

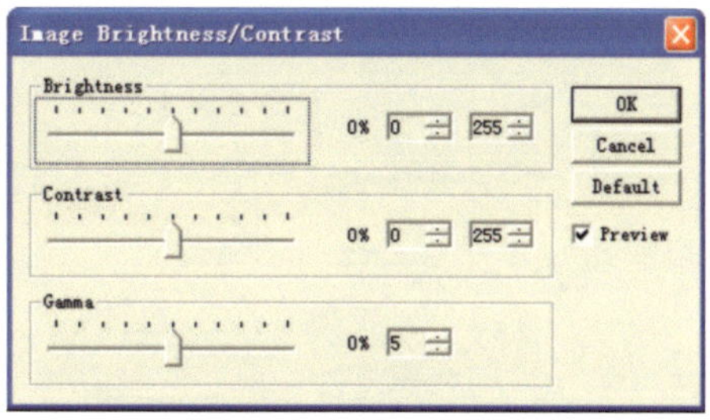

f. The dialog window designed

Fig. 4. The samples of the brightness and contrast adjustment

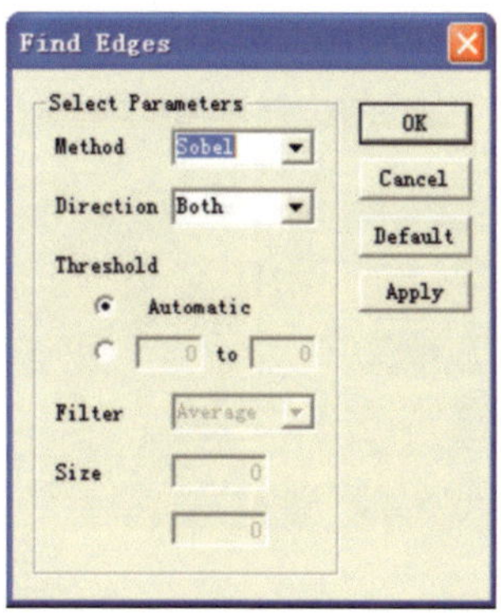

Fig. 5. The dialog window of *Find Edges* function

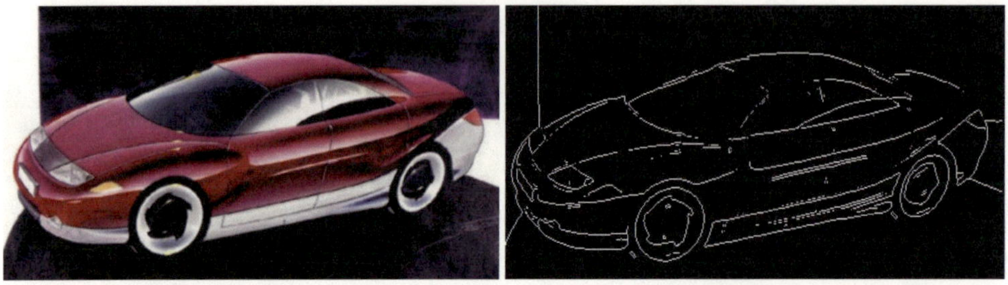

a. Original sketch b. Sobel algorithm, threshold = 0.13

c. Canny algorithm, threshold = 0.15-1.0 d. LoG algorithm, threshold = 0.007

(Original sketch by courtesy of Cor Steenstra, Foresee Car Design)

Fig. 6. Edge detection of the original colour sketch with the different algorithms

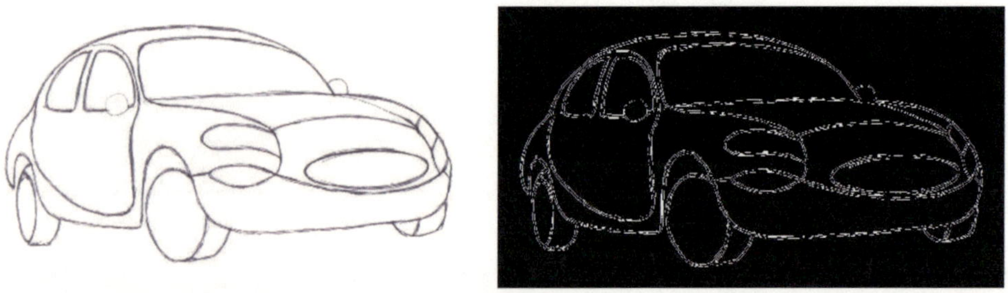

a. Pre-processing sketch b. Roberts algorithm, threshold = 0.1

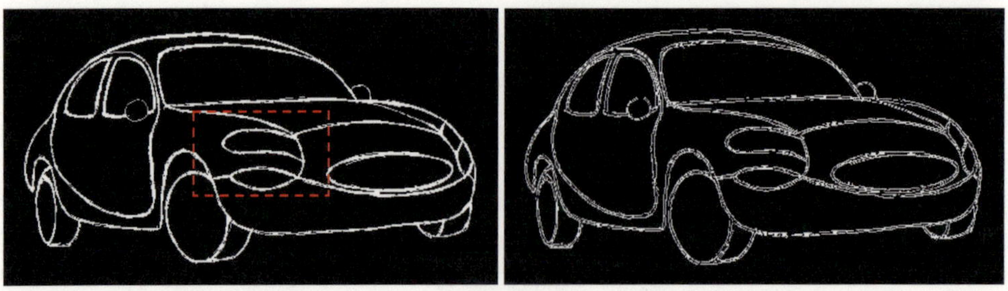

c. Hybrid algorithm d. Sobel+ algorithm

Fig. 7. Edge detection of the pre-processed sketch

To obtain a satisfactory result, it is crucial to select a suitable threshold for edge detection. However, some problems are still left such as thick edges, double edges and broken edges which cause unclosed boundaries, and small 'spurs' or 'prickles'. Therefore, further processing is needed to eliminate these problems.

4.4 Edge morphing

Edge morphing can further refine the image obtained from edge detection. This function is implemented using the MATLAB *bwmorph* function including the method *Bothat, Bridge, Clean, Close, Diag, Dilate, Erode, Fill, Hbreak, Majority, Open, Remove, Shrink, Skel, Spur, Thicken, Thin* and *Tophat*, as shown in Fig. 8. It can apply specific morphological operations to the binary image. Repeated application of these operations may be necessary. *Infinite* means that *Times* are determined by the methods automatically.

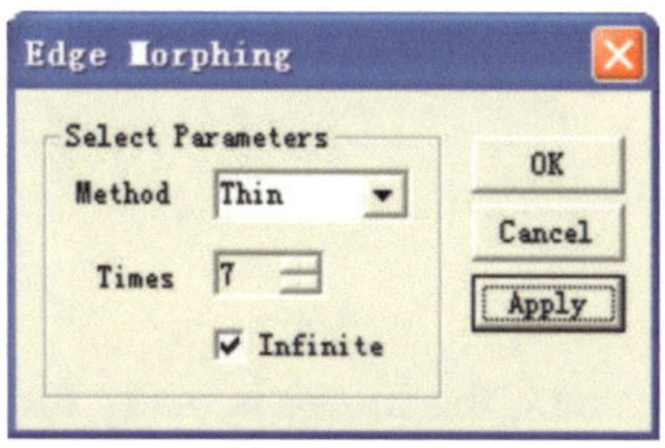

Fig. 8. The dialog window of *Edge Morphing* function

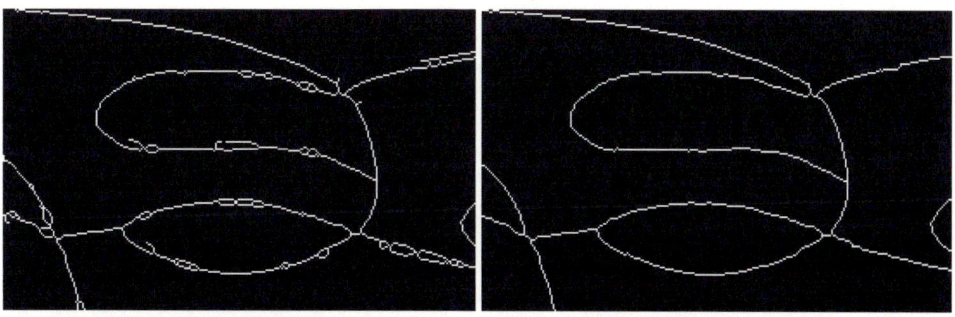

a. Thin operation (Times = 7) b. Debubble algorithm

Fig. 9. Edge thins and debubbles (Please refer to Fig. 7c)

When the edges are not single pixels such as the ones shown in Fig. 7c, edge morphing should be applied. The result after the seven applications of the thin operation is shown in Fig. 9a. The edges become the single pixels, but with some small holes and spurs. This is still not a satisfactory starting point for the transformation. The bubbles and spurs must be eliminated.

4.5 Debubble – a hybrid algorithm

It has not proved to be possible to obtain the required result using a single method. Different hybrid methods have been applied to achieve a good result. Here is a hybrid algorithm proposed in this research to perform an operation of deleting the small holes and spurs, such as shown in Fig. 9a. The algorithm entitled *Debubble,* shown in Fig. 10, applies firstly the *Bwlabel* algorithm in MATLAB to find the small bubbles (holes), which are determined by the bubble size parameter. Once the small bubbles are found, they are filled into solid areas. Then the *Skel* and *Spur* algorithms are applied to obtain the single pixel edges. The actual bubble size is the percentage of the maximum size in pixels, which is compared with the image size in pixels. For example, to obtain the result in Fig. 9b, the actual bubble size is 165, and the image size is 524288 (1024×512). This is just 0.0315% of the image size - very small bubbles! In this case, all the bubbles those are smaller than 165 are deleted. The result shown in Fig. 9b is quite acceptable. Using the *Direct*, *Thin*, and *Debubble* algorithms for the pre-processed sketches can give a good result.

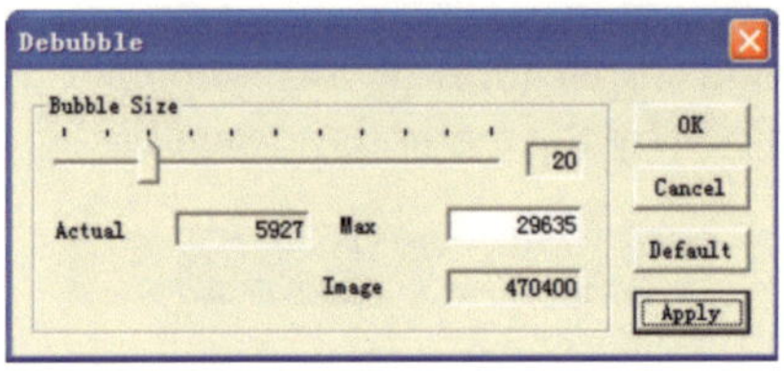

Fig. 10. The dialog window of *Debubble* function

4.6 Edge refinement

Once satisfactory edges are obtained, the image is ready for segmentation. However, there are still anomalies that must be handled. For example, see the case in Fig. 11a, the crossing point of the three patches is not unique. This produces three crossing points. In order to delete this small error, the edge points must be checked and refined.

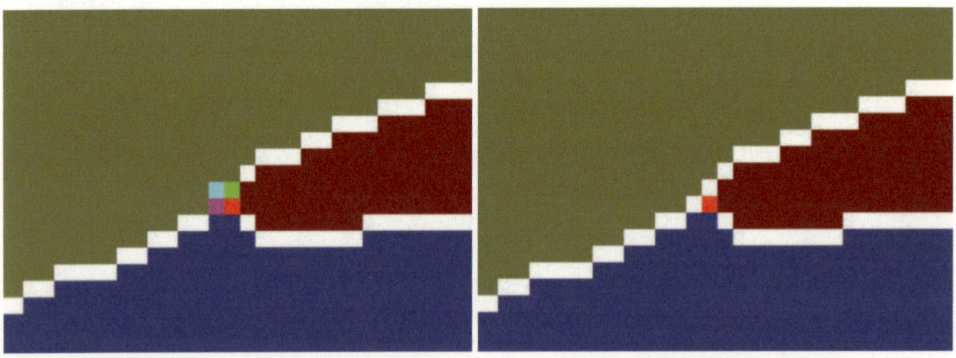

a. Crossing points are not unique b. Unique crossing point

Fig. 11. Crossing point searching

An algorithm is proposed here to perform this operation. It is described as follow:

- Every point is checked in the whole image.
- If it is an edge point, a counter is set with initial value of zero. The point is the current point.
- The eight neighbours of the current point are checked one by one from 0 to 7, see Fig. 12a.
- Once a neighbour point is edge point, the counter is increased by one.
- The current neighbour point is anomaly point, once the counter reaches three within the eight neighbours.

- The last current neighbour is deleted.

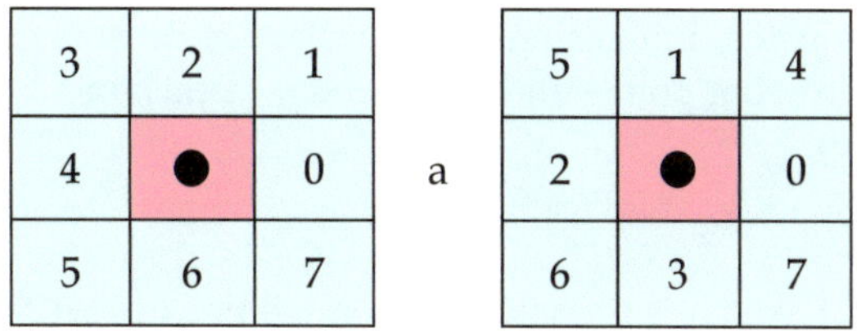

Fig. 12. Eight-neighbour graph

The result is shown in Fig. 11b. Now the three patches share the same single pixel boundaries and have a unique crossing point.

4.7 Patch segmentation with colours

It is easy to separate an image with closed boundaries into patches by applying the MATLAB *Bwlabel* function, and it can then be displayed with the different colour maps. The *Pseudo Colormap* includes *Autumn, Bone, Colorcube, Cool, Copper, Flag, Gray, Hot, HSV, Jet, Lines, Pink, Prism, Spring, Summer, White* and *Winter*, as shown in Fig. 13. The label 0 is assigned to the boundaries between the patches. Label 1 is assigned to the background and used as the silhouette of the whole vehicle. From label 2 onwards, they are assigned to the patches which form the surfaces of the vehicle. After labelling, a pseudo colour map is added for separating the patches. The labelled image is shown in Fig. 14.

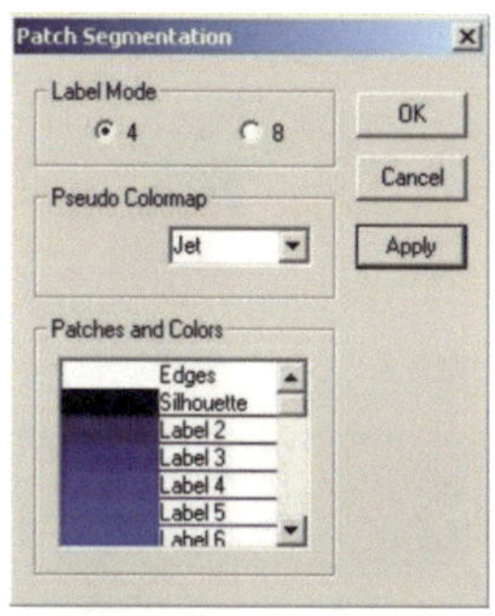

Fig. 13. The dialog window of *Patch Segmentation* function

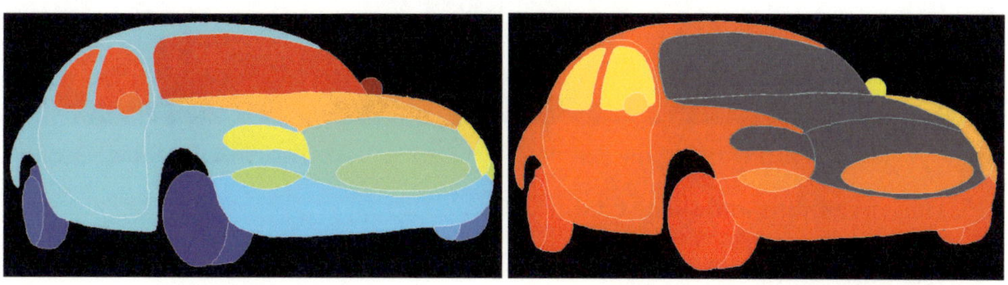

a. Labelled sketch b. Multiple Selection of patches

Fig. 14. The sketch after segmentation

As well as the labelling and colour mapping, some other tasks are performed at the same time, such as finding out the start points of each patch on the boundary and the maximum rectangles containing each patch, initialising the boundary node data and searching all the sequential nodes and the crossing points on the boundary of each patch, and calculating the areas and centres of patches.

4.8 Curve fitting

After the segmentation, the sketch is separated into small patches with zigzag boundaries. In most cases, the shape does not vary largely compared with the original sketch. However, at some corners which contain crossing points, the shape may look strange. The use of spline curve fitting can smooth the zigzag boundaries and provide modification of the shapes if necessary.
The patches are selected by the user, shown in Fig. 15b, for performing the curve fitting. The basic functions are implemented from the MATLAB *Splinetool* function in the spline toolbox [THEM01c]. The similar dialog window, as shown in Fig. 16, was designed. An example is given to demonstrate the curve fitting process, shown in Fig. 15 (refer to the area in Fig. 7c). Comparing the areas from Fig. 15a and Fig. 15d, the boundary of the light is smooth and its shape has been improved.

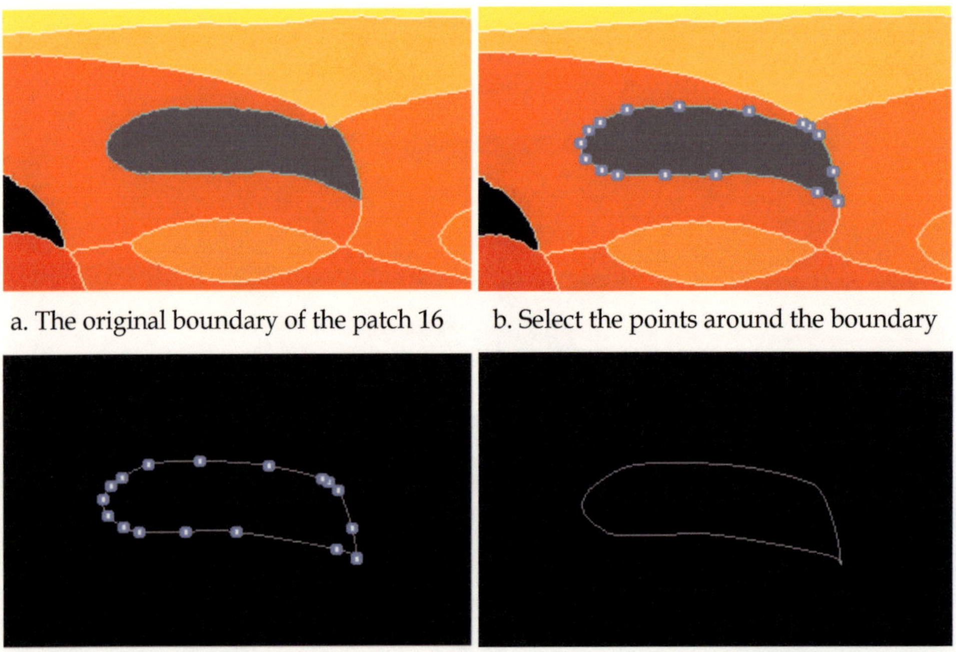

a. The original boundary of the patch 16 b. Select the points around the boundary

c. Curve fitting using the points d. The closed spline

Fig. 15. The curve-fitting and shape modification

5. Feature extraction

The features include the point, curve and patch features extracted from the sketch, which are put into a data structure.

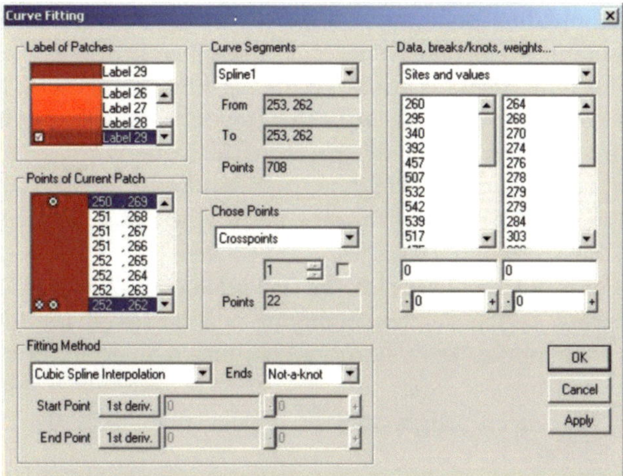

Fig. 16. The dialog window of *Curve Fitting* function

5.1 Data structure for sketch

The points after labelling contain a lot of information for further processing and analysis. Therefore, it is important to establish an efficient data management system. A proposed sketch structure is shown in Fig. 17. The basic unit is a single point, a set of points presents a curve, a close curve or several curves stands for a patch, all the patches make a vehicle.

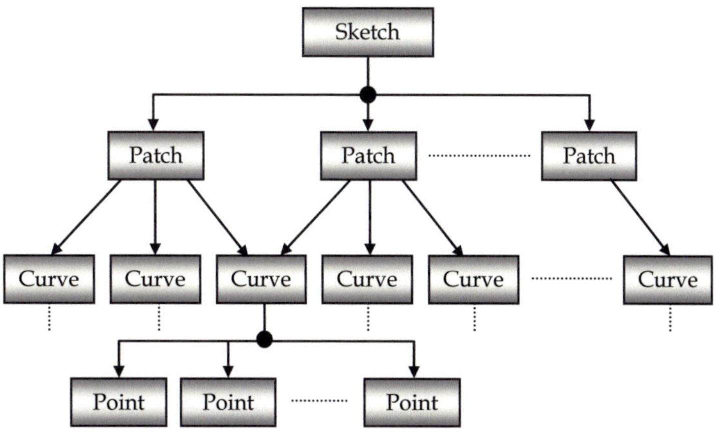

Fig. 17. Sketch data structure

5.2 Point features

After labelling, the sketch becomes a two-dimensional integer array. Zero stands for boundaries as known, but it is necessary to find out which patch it belongs to. They are just the separate edge points with the value of zero at the moment, nothing else. They should be reorganised to useful data.

As the basic unit from data structure, 2D point contains three basic features - the coordinates {x, y}, attributes (crosspoint, selected, breakpoint), and links (previous point, next point).

After labelling, each boundary point has at least two different neighbours. If more than two, the point is a crosspoint. If the point is selected for spline fitting, the selected attribute is true. If the point is used for breaking whole boundary into pieces, the breakpoint attribute is true. The links like a chain join the separated points into a sequential structure. The extraction of point features follows the other feature calculations.
A simple algorithm searching related neighbours is developed as follows

- Assume that the current point is an edge point. The eight neighbours of the current point are checked one by one from 0 to 7, see Fig. 12a.
- Once a neighbour is not an edge point, the first related neighbour is found and saved.
- Carry on searching, any different neighbour will be saved until all neighbours are checked. Return the number of related neighbours and an array containing the different neighbours.
- If the number of related neighbours is greater than two, the current point is a breakpoint.

5.3 Curve features

A set of edge points around a patch make a closed curve. Each closed boundary may have more than one curve segments, i.e., each segment has its own point set. The point sets may be sparse for curve fitting in order to reduce the size of data and obtain a precise representation of the sketch. The following features need to be extracted in a curve:

- Number of points, and the coordinates of each point (values)
- Number of breakpoints if a closed boundary is broken down to several segments.
- The first point and the last point, if the last point is equal to the first point, it is a closed boundary.
- Curve type, either the outer silhouette curve or the internal curve

If using spline fitting to present a curve, the following features need to be extracted.

- Number of selected points for curve fitting
- Fitting method selected.
- End conditions.
- If the point doesn't belong to the original boundary point, a changed tag is given.
- If displaying a spline, a view tag is given.
- If displaying marks on each node, a mark tag is given.

A searching algorithm of boundary curve point setting is based on single pixel has been developed as follows.

- If a point is an edge point and one of its neighbours is the patch, the edge point belongs to the patch.
- The first edge point is the start point of boundary curve, and it becomes the current point, previous point 1 and previous point 2.
- Check the eight neighbours of the current point using the graph in Fig. 12b.
- Once a neighbour point is the edge point and it belongs to the patch, and it is not the previous point 1 and 2, it is a new edge point. Add it to the curve.
- The new edge point becomes the current point. Repeat the same procedure from beginning, until the point is equal to the first point.

In the algorithm, two previous points are used to determine the direction of processing. Using the neighbour graph in Fig. 12b will obtain slightly smoother curves than using the one in Fig. 12a.

5.4 Patch features

Several curve segments are joined together into a closed curve to form a patch. The following features can be extracted.

- The patch serial number, i.e. the label number
- The colour and the title of patch
- If selected for display or processing, a selected tag is given
- The minimum rectangle containing the patch
- The area and centre of the area of patch, the area value is the number of points within the patch. The centre is the sum of coordinates divided by the area.

5.5 Sketch features

When a sketch is separated into patches, the features such as the number of patches and each patch features will be obtained. The neighbourhood will be established. Each patch has the number of neighbours, the shared boundaries with the neighbours. A boundary with one neighbour is the outer silhouette, with two is the inter boundary. The features directly derived from the sketch are shown in Fig. 18.

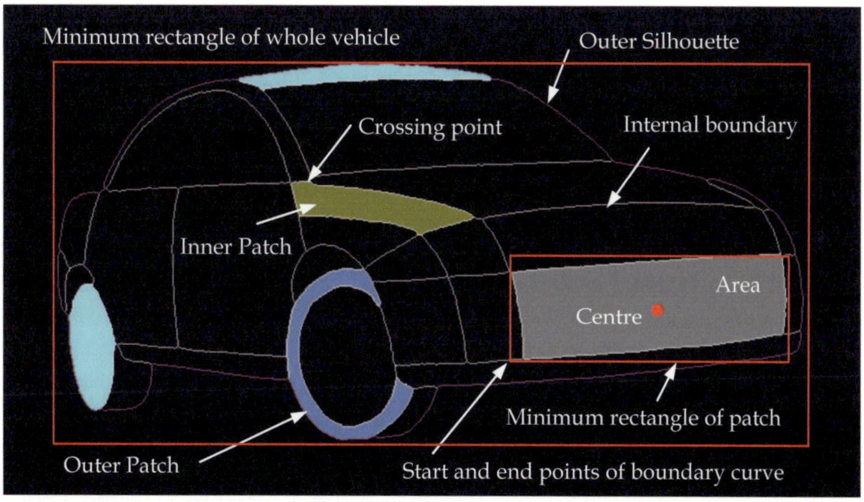

Fig. 18. Features in sketch

Currently, the features directly used for the 2D to 3D transformation are the area and centre of patch. However, more features can be extracted from the points and basic features for further application. It is easy for humans to distinguish where the patch belongs to, what size it is, and where the characteristic points are located. The use of human recognition of patches can help provide a direct and interactive transformation from 2D to 3D, without the need for sophisticated recognition methods. For example, the features such as the position of patch, size and curvature can be used to determine which part of surface it belongs to; the features such as the principal axis of ellipse, size and position can be used for determine the position and tangent points of wheels for coordinate system determination; and features such as symmetric points from breakpoints and the curve between the them, and shading features can be used to determine the curvature of surface, the difference of the areas of 2D patch and its corresponding 3D surface can be used for the adjustment of coordinates. This can all be done in a straightforward manner so long as the patch is correctly identified, which is most readily done by human intervention (although an automated, possibly artificial intelligence based method for this may be feasible, but is outside the scope of this research).

6. Implementation of MATLAB functions

As mentioned above, the 23D system has been implemented the MATLAB functions. Differing from the proposed method of MATLAB implementation, our method was to apply directly the kernel part of their functions. At first, the MATLAB *.m files were converted into *h and *.cpp files of C++. Then, it was to extract the kernel part of the function, and to add them into the 23D system. It was necessary to implement all the related functions. Therefore, no *.dll or *.lib files of MATLAB were used. This method is quite simple and easy to change or enhance the implemented functions.

7. Conclusion

The approach here has been to reduce the problem of pre-processing of the sketch into a number of separate stages, each of which refines or extracts a particular piece of information embodied in the sketch. Some conclusions are summarized below:

- The pre-processing of sketches plays an important role for the input sketches. The more precise the sketches are, the easier the sketch processing is. Pre-processing can be used to translate 'imprecise' sketches to more 'precise' ones, providing a better starting point for the transformation process. This approach allows the system to deal with sketches that have roughly closed boundaries, in turn allowing easier separation into patches.
- For the pre-processed sketches, the related processing algorithms have been investigated in order to obtain the separated patches with single-pixel and closed boundary, which are ready for the 2D to 3D transformation. Facing the specific sketches, some existing or new algorithms and new hybrid algorithms have been proposed.
- Some basic features are extracted from the patches to present points, curves and patches. They are listed below.
  - The boundary points
  - The relationships of the patches
  - The minimum rectangle containing the patches
  - The start and end points for each boundary
  - The areas and geometric centres of the patches
  - The attributes of the points whether they are the selected, break or crossing points

Related searching and calculating algorithms have been also developed. Some features are discussed and may be applied in further research.

- The sketch processing and feature extraction depend on the raster data. Therefore, the method is device dependent. The inherent error is one pixel. Increasing the sketch size can reduce error. But the important issue is the quality of the input sketch. A good sketch will produce significantly better results.
- Curve fitting supplies an additional way to improve the patches. Through the selection and modification of the edge points, the shapes of the patches can be smoothed or even

be changed in some places. This process allows resolution of a further set of imperfections in the original sketch.

- Direct implementation of MATLAB functions is a feasible way to enhance 23D system functions.

8. Acknowledgment

I would like to take this opportunity to express my special thanks to my supervisor, Dr. R. M. Newman, for his invaluable guidance, supports and helps in the research project. Many thanks also go to the other members of the research group, Prof. M. Tovey, C. S. Porter and J. Tabor, for their ideas, supports and helps in the research project, and T. Y. Pan for his exchanging the information, ideas and supports with me.
I am grateful to a number of staffs and students in the MIS, especial in the CTAC, who have discussed with me on my project and have given me lots of support and help, especially to Prof. Keith. J. Burnham, Mrs. A. Todman, and Miss Y. Xie.

9. References

Adobe System Incorporated. (2000). Adobe® Photoshop® 6.0 user guide for Windows® and Macintosh, Adobe System Incorporated, 90024592

Chin, N.; Frazier, C. & Ho, P. (1998). The OpenGL® Graphics System Utility Library. version 1.3, ed. Leech, J.

Foley, J. D.; van Dam, A. & Feiner, S. K. (1996), Computer graphics: principles and practice, 2nd ed. in C, Addison-Wesley Publishing Company, Inc. ISBN 0-201-84840-6

Fosner, R. (1997). OpenGLTM Programming for Windows® 95 and Windows NTTM. Addison-Wesley, ISBN 0-201-40709-4

Glaeser, G. & Stachel, H. (1999). Open Geometry: OpenGL® + Advanced Geometry. Springer-Verlag New York, Inc., ISBN 0-387-98599-9

Kilgard, M. J. (1996). The OpenGL Utility Toolkit (GLUT) Programming Interface. API version 3, Silicon Graphics, Inc.

Ladd, S. R. (1996). C++ Templates and Tools. 2nd ed., M&T Books, ISBN 1-55851-465-1

Matthews, J. (2002). Image Analysis Explorer Pro. version 1.01, http://www.generation5.org/iae.shtml

Pan, T. Y. (2002). Identification of 3D Information from 2D Sketches in Automotive Design, MPhil paper, School of Art and Design, Coventry University

Salomon, D. (1999), Computer graphics and geometric modelling, Springer-Verlag New York, Inc. ISBN 0-387-98682-0

Schildt, H. (1998). C++ from the Ground up. 2nd ed., Osborne/McGraw-Hill, ISBN 0-07-882405-2

Seed, G. H. (1996). An Introduction to Object-oriented Programming in C++: With Applications in Computer Graphics. Springe-Verlag London Ltd., ISBN 3-540-76042-3

Segal, M. & Akeley, K. (2001). The OpenGL® Graphics System: A Specification. version 1.3, ed. Leech, J.

Silverio, C. J.; Fryer, B. & Hartman, J. (1997). OpenGL® Porting Guide. rev. Kempf, R. ed. Cary, C., Silicon Graphics, Inc.

Smith, J. T. (1997). C++ Toolkit for Scientists and Engineers. International Thomson Computer Press, ISBN 1-85032-889-7

The MathWorks, Inc. (2000). MATLAB® C/C++ Graphics Library – The Language of Technical Computing - User's Guide, version 2

The MathWorks, Inc. (2000). MATLAB® C Math Library – The Language of Technical Computing - User's Guide, version 2

The MathWorks, Inc. 2000, "MATLAB® C++ Math Library – The Language of Technical Computing - User's Guide", version 2, The MathWorks, Inc.

The MathWorks, Inc. 2001, "MATLAB® Compiler – The Language of Technical Computing - User's Guide", version 2, The MathWorks, Inc.

The MathWorks Inc. (2001). MATLAB® The Image Processing Toolbox User's Guide, version 3

The MathWorks, Inc. (2001). Spline Toolbox for Use with MATLAB® - User's Guide, version 3.

The Vision Technology Group, Microsoft Research. (2000). The Microsoft Vision SDK. version 1.2, VisSDK@microsoft.com.

Wright, R. S. & Sweet M. (1996). OpenGL Superbible: The Complete Guide to OpenGL Programming for Windows NT and Windows 95. The Waite Group, Inc.

19

Simulation of Rough Surfaces and Analysis of Roughness by MATLAB

F. Gascón[1] and F. Salazar[2]
[1]*Departamento de Física Aplicada II. ETS Arquitectura (US). Avda. Reina Mercedes 2, 41012 Sevilla*
[2]*Departamento de Física Aplicada. ETSI Minas (UPM). C/Ríos Rosas 21, 28003 Madrid*
Spain

1. Introduction

The simulation of physical phenomena in science and engineering has become an important tool because it allows studying a wide range of real problems. On the other hand, it allows resolving problems that, because of its difficulty, it would be not possible to solve by analytical methods. Moreover, simulation is fast and versatile since it permits to vary parameters of the problem easily, allowing analyzing the effect of the modification of them in the response of the system examined.

Simulation requires programming, for which there are many different languages. Each of them has a particular internal structure that distinguishes it from others. Therefore, depending on the problem to be study, it may be advisable to use a specific programming language.

In the scientific-technical context MATLAB has been increasingly used by the great advantages that it offers. For example, the instructions are interpreted and not compiled, the user to enter commands interactively. The data processing is flexible. They can be read and stored in two different formats, ASCII and MATLAB format. ASCII has the advantage that the data and results may be used for other programs. However, MATLAB format may be faster. On the other hand, many functions and libraries of MATLAB are written MATLAB language, enabling the user access to the source files. It is possible to execute instructions of the operating system without exiting the program. Moreover, this language is portable in platforms as Windows or Apple, commonly employed by the researcher. From the point of view of numerical calculation, the use of matrices as basic elements makes it efficient and easy to employ, being also possible to perform graphics of curves and surfaces. Finally, the operations can be performed with simple and intuitive expressions similar to those used in science and engineering.

MATLAB has been used for many applications in general physics, mathematics, optics, electronics, chemistry, biology, medicine, and artificial intelligence, among others. Now we want to employ MATLAB to simulate an optical procedure to measure surface roughness. Thus, the aim of this paper is the determination of the roughness of a surface from the analysis of the speckle pattern obtained in the far field, when the object is illuminated with a monochromatic beam perpendicularly to its surface.

The surface analysis of materials is of great importance, since many technological problems require, previously, the study of the surface state. One of the parameters of any material that changes easily with time is the roughness. Indeed, in many sectors, as civil engineering, architecture, mechanical engineering, etc. materials of different forms and properties are commonly employed, which must meet certain requirements to ensure their use. For this reason, the measurement of some surface parameters, as roughness, must be taking into consideration.

There are different methods for determining roughness. One of the most employed is the profilometer (see next section). However, this paper deals with an optical method based on the speckle interferometry which has some advantages. The methodology is fast, accurate, and does not contact the specimen. Above all this we will talk in the next sections

2. Discretization of the problem. Roughness

A classic device for measuring surface roughness is the mechanical profilometer which is formed by a tiny stylus (with a small ball), and a displacement sensor. The typ moves along a straight line parallel to the surface plane and records the displacements in the perpendicular direction, tracing out the outline of the surface. If the ball has a diameter *bd* it can not be inserted between two grooves whose distance is less than *bd*, being only possible to detect the topographic level with a distance between grooves greater than *bd*.

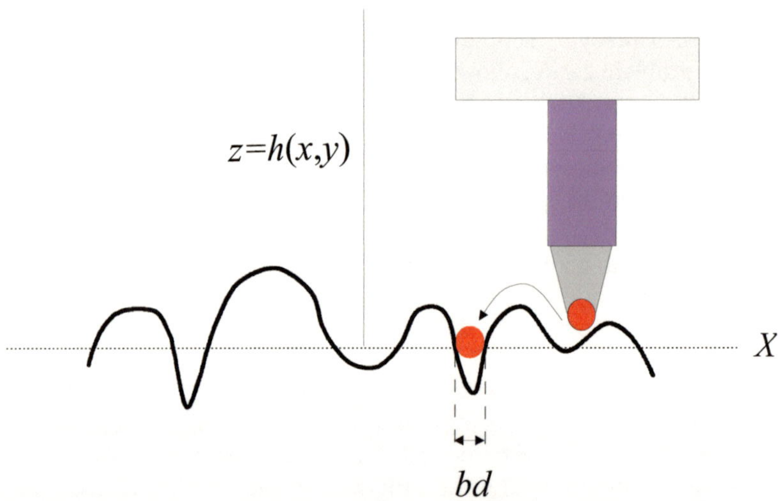

Fig. 1. Classical device for measuring roughness. Observe that when the diameter of the end needle *bd* is greater than the groove, the transducer can not reproduce the high frequencies of the surface outline.

In this article we are interested in using a speckle technique to measure the roughness of a surface. From a didactic viewpoint, the explained idea of the profilometer may be employed to understand the sampling, when a rough surface is simulated by MATLAB.

To start let us suppose a one-dimensional rough surface, and then we extend the results to the case of two variables.

The height of the rough surface can also be measured by sampling. With this aim let us consider a curve $z=h(x)$ as shown in Fig. (2), aligned on the OX axis. For sampling the function $h(x)$ the X co-ordinate axis is divided into intervals of length u measured with respect the origin O resulting in a system of aligned points of co-ordinates 0, u, $2u$, $3u$,... The distance u between two neighbor points, i.e. the sample interval, is called the sampling period and its value is chosen depending of the function to be investigated (in our case the form of the surface). The distance u between two points may be likened to the ball diameter *bd* of the profilometer.

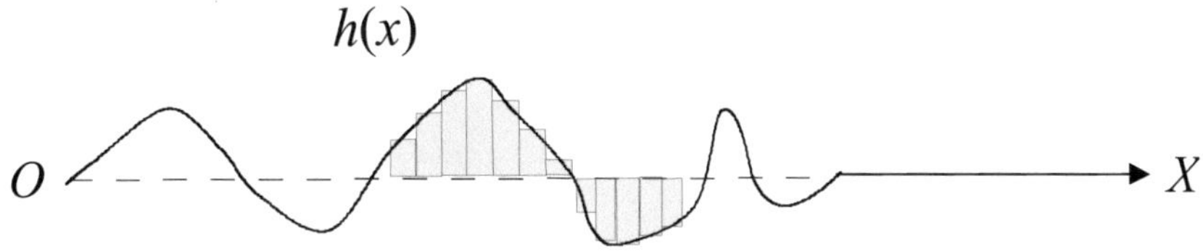

Fig. 2. Rough surface represented by $z=h(x)$. If the sampling period is chosen small, the discrete function $h(xp)$ is very similar to the actual surface.

If N samples are taken, they form a string of N integers for which a value $z_p = h(xp)$ is given. This set of numbers is collecting in a matrix *IF* of dimension $N \times 1$. The range of variation of the index p is 1, 2, 3,..., N, and it represents the element p of the string. Therefore this index p is related with the sampling period as follows: x = 0, u, $2u$, $3u$, ..., $(p\text{-}1)u$. Two neighboring elements of the *IF* matrix contain the values of the surface heights of the grooves of two points on the reference plane separated u meters.
As it will see, when studying the phenomenon of diffraction in the far field, the Fourier transformation must be applied. Therefore, we need to study also the sampling in the frequency domain.
When calculating the finite discrete Fourier transform (DFT) of the *IF* matrix of N elements, a new set of N numbers is obtained which is grouped in another matrix *FO* of dimension $N \times 1$. Due to the Fourier transform is performed from the discrete values of *IF*, the result is also discrete. As a result the distance between two points of the transformed numbers in frequency domain is also quantified. Denoting by v (1,2,...N) the index for the matrix *FO*, the row index represents the harmonic components whose frequencies are α= 0, 1 / (Nu), 2 / (Nu), ..., (v-1) / (Nu). The sampling frequency is defined as $f_s \equiv 1/u$, measured in m^{-1}, and represents the number of measures per unit length. By using this expression, spatial frequency components may also be written in the form α = 0, f_s / N, 2 f_s / N, ..., (v-1) f_s/N.
In general, the matrix element v of *FO* represents the harmonic α_ν in the space of frequencies

$$\alpha_\nu = \frac{(\nu - 1)}{Nu}. \tag{1}$$

Thus there is a correspondence between the index v = 1, 2, 3, ..., N, and the spatial frequency α by means of the factor (f_s/N). Obviously, the sampling process implies that some information about the sampled function is loosed, because no value between two neighboring points is known. However, depending on the physical problem studied, using the Shannon theorem, the sample interval can be modified so that the data be enough for numerical calculus.
Taking into account that the expression obtained for representing a point on the OX-axis has the form $(p\text{-}1)u$, it seems to be appropriate to change to non-dimensional variables. To do so

we divide x for u resulting $(x/u)=(p-1)$, p being 1,2,…,N. This new variable represents the distance from the origin O to an arbitrary point on OX (Fig.3), measured in units of the sampling period u, and the elements of the matrix IF the surface heights at each point. The same idea applies to frequency domain.

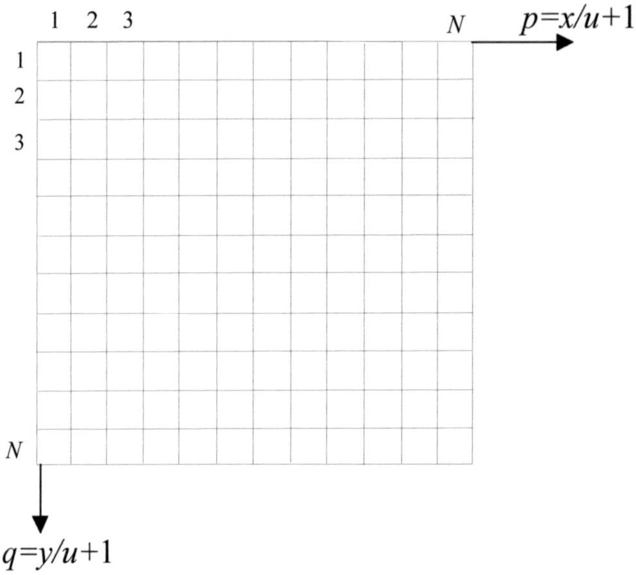

Fig. 3. Reference system without dimensions. The numbers represent the co-ordinates of the matrix elements. At each point (p,q) we assign the corresponding value of the surface height.

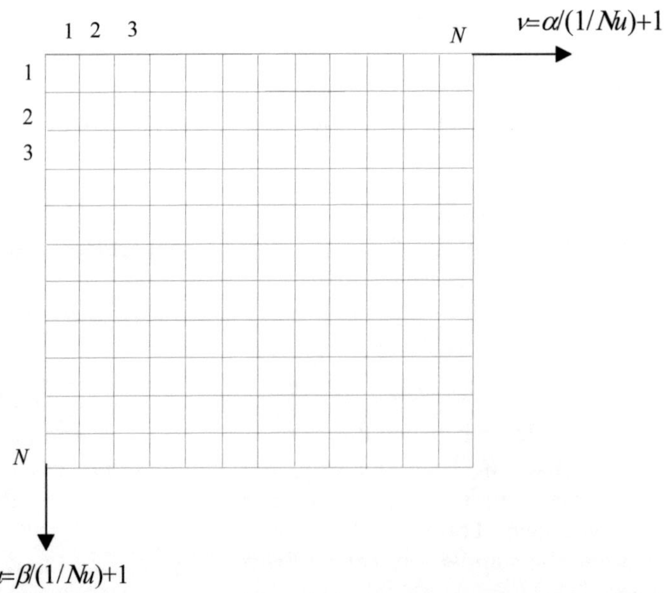

Fig. 4. Space of non-dimensional frequencies. Observe that this grid is initially determined by the matrix IF, then it also has NxN elements

By setting $\alpha(Nu)= \alpha/(1/Nu)$ =(v-1) the spatial frequency α is converted in a dimensionless number representing the basic unities of measurement in this space. Furthermore, $\alpha/(1/Nu)$ is directly the frequency measured in unities of $(1/Nu)$ corresponding to the element v of the matrix *FO* (Fig.4).
When generating a rough surface the components of *IF* are real numbers (Fig.3). However, as we will see, the diffraction of a light beam by a surface can introduce phase factors resulting in complex numbers in the elements of matrix *IF*. In any case the resulting $N\times 1$ string of *IF* and its fast Fourier transform (FFT), are calculated without difficulty with MATLAB. One advantage of the aforementioned procedure is that the sampling distance *u* between two points of *IF* is not directly involved in the numerical calculation, and then it may be considered as a parameter. For this reason the DFT and the FFT of *IF*, i.e. *FO*, is universal respect to the parameter *u*, because the components of *FO* depend only of the non-dimensional elements of the matrix *IF*.
Although with the change of variables introduced the components of *IF* and *FO* are dimensionless, they have physical meaning. In the present study the *p* element of *IF* is a measure of the height of the point at position $x = (p-1)\, u$. *FO* may be interpreted in the same way. So setting any number to the sampling period *u* the values obtained for *FO* show the harmonic amplitudes. For example, giving *u* the arbitrary value 10^{-4} m, and choosing $N = 64$, we have for the first non-zero frequency components, α=156.2, 312.5, 468.8,... m^{-1}.
The above is easily applied to a two-dimensional simulation. For this let us consider two coordinates (x,y) of the system *OXY* (Figs.3,4). For each point of this reference plane is assigned a value which corresponds to the surface height at this point. The data are placed in a two-dimensional array *IF*. If the sampling is done with the same number of samples, say *N*, the dimension of the matrix IF is $N\times N$ (Fig. 3). Two points of coordinates (x_i, y_j) and (x_k, y_l) respectively are separated in the matrix *IF* a distance $((i-j)^2+ (k-l)^2)^{1/2}\, u$, and in dimensionless co-ordinates $((i-j)^2+(k-l)^2)^{1/2}$. In relation to *FO* similar expressions may be obtained, but in frequency space. So the spatial frequencies between two points whose coordinates are (α_h,β_k) and (α_l,β_m) is $((h-k)^2+ (l-m)^2)^{1/2}\, (1/Nu)$ in m^{-1}, and without dimensions $((h-k)^2+ (l-m)^2)^{1/2}$.

3. Fraunhofer diffraction with MATLAB

In this section we are interested in the phenomenon of diffraction of light, given the importance to understand the speckle patterns. With this objective let us use the experimental lay-out depicted in Fig.(5). A collimated monochromatic laser beam LB of wavelength λ is directed to a beam splitter BS, which projects the light perpendicularly on a diffracting rough sample S located on the *OXY* plane. The surface has, in principle, a variable reflectance $R(x,y)$. This means the different scatters that form the surface may have distinct reflection properties. The shape of the radiation beam used determines the geometry and the intensity inside of the illuminated area. If we suppose a beam of homogeneous intensity, its geometry can be expressed easily (in view of the simulation) as an opaque mask *M* placed on the surface, which has the function to define the illuminated area (Fig. 6). Taking into consideration the most cases studied in optics, we will choose a circular mask of diameter *D*. An observation screen is placed parallel to the diffracting surface at a distance of *z* from its plane. The points on the observation plane are specified by means of its x', y' coordinates, with respect to an $O'X'Y'$ coordinate system (on the CCD camera).

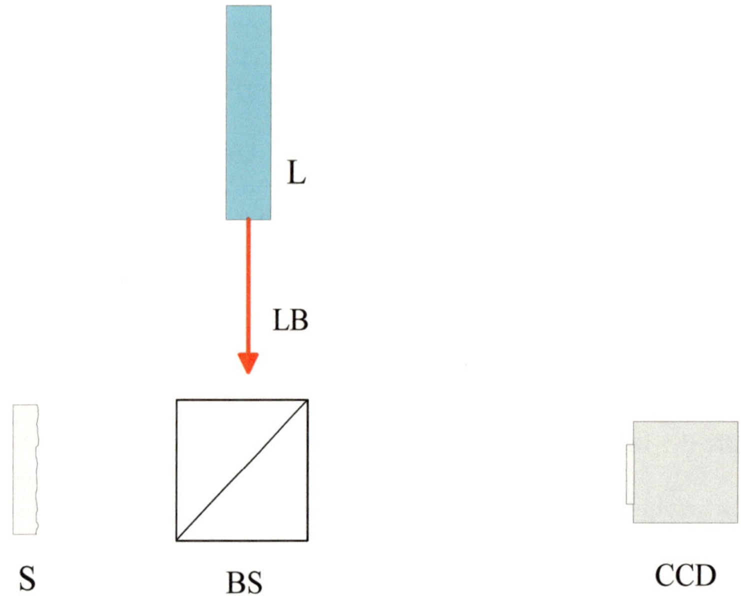

Fig. 5. Experimental set-up. L, laser; LB, laser beam; S, rough sample; BS, beam splitter; CCD camera.

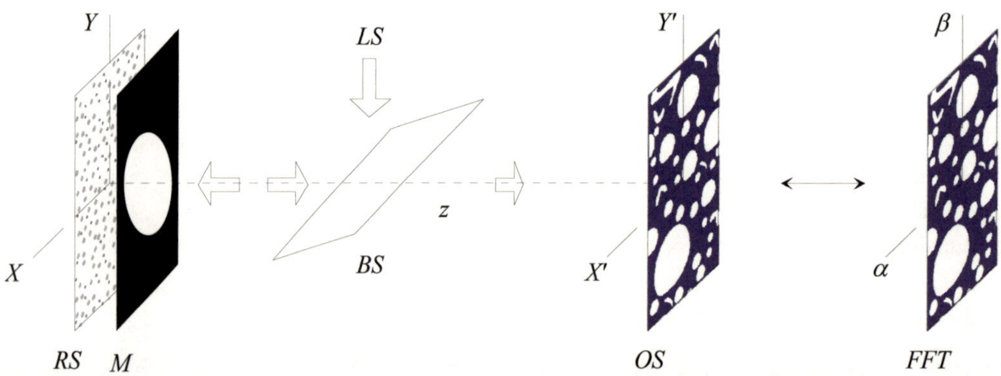

Fig. 6. Steps employed for simulating the rough surface, the aperture, and the speckle pattern. *RS*, rough surface; *M*, mask; *BS*, beam splitter; *FO*, matrix which elements represent the Fourier transform of the reflectance *R*(x,y) on the $OX'Y'$ reference system. The intensity $OS = |FO|^2$ can be interpreted also as an angular spectrum (α, β).

Supposing that the scalar diffraction theory applies, the Fresnel-Kirchhoff integral and the theories of Rayleigh-Sommerfeld can be used. However, the calculation of the diffraction pattern through these theories is not always easy to carry out. Sometimes the procedure may be simplified under certain conditions of the problem. So if the linear dimensions of the aperture (mask in our case) is much greater than the wavelength, i.e. $D >> \lambda$, and the distance *z* between the surface and the observation plane is great enough, the paraxial theories apply. In this case, the mathematical expression for the diffracted field depends on the specific dependence between D and z. When expanding the phase term in the Fresnell-Kirchhoff integral is not possible to neglect the quadratic terms that appear we speaks of Fresnel diffraction. On the contrary, if these terms can not be tacked into consideration we have Fraunhofer diffraction. These approximations are the most important cases in the field of the classical optics.

A possible quantitative criterion to be employed in order to use the Fraunhofer approximation, or that of Fresnel, is based on taking a circle of diameter D, which only includes the regions of interest (in the present case the hole of the mask). Let r be the distance from a point on the diffracting surface to the observation point. Let ρ be the distance from the centre of the circle to a point inside its circle. If $2\pi r/\lambda$ varies linearly with ρ, the diffraction is called Fraunhofer diffraction; if the variation has non-linear terms of magnitude comparable with $\pi/2$, the diffraction is said Fresnel diffraction. Therefore, for Fraunhofer diffraction we obtain $z \gg D^2/(4\lambda)$. In short, the diffracting area must be greater than λ and the observation of the intensity pattern must be carried out from a large distance with respect to the scatter surface. In other circumstances, i.e. if the distance z does not fulfil the conditions needed, non-paraxial terms of the phase must be included in the integrand of the Fresnell-Kirchhoff integral (higher expansion coefficients).

Fraunhofer diffraction is related with the Fourier transform which takes an angular spectrum of the reflectance (or transmittance) to be considered. From a physical point of view it is equivalent to observe the phenomenon in the far field (another possibility is to employ a lens and locate the observation plane on its back focal plane). This angular spectrum means that the Fraunhofer diffraction gives the behaviour of the field amplitude for the directions in space. If we use two variables, the amplitude of the diffracted field done through the Fourier transform depends on α and β, which are related with the directions $\left(\theta_x, \theta_y\right)$ through the following expressions

$$\alpha = \frac{\cos\theta_x}{\lambda}, \beta = \frac{\cos\theta_y}{\lambda}. \tag{2}$$

As we will see in the following section, the proposed method for measuring roughness is developed under the supposition that the conditions of the Fraunhofer diffraction apply. Therefore, this case must be translated to the context of MATLAB.

With this aim, the basic results of the preceding section should used. The elements fo_{ij} of the matrix FO belonging to a row or column represent the complex amplitude of two harmonics separated $1/(Nu)$. Therefore the first angular direction is $\theta_x = \cos^{-1}\left(\left(\nu-1\right)\left(\lambda f_s/N\right)\right)_{\nu=1} = \frac{\pi}{2}$, which corresponds to the frequency $\alpha = 0$ and the direction for the least coefficient of FO is $\theta_x = \cos^{-1}[(N-1)\lambda f_s/N]$ corresponding to the higher frequency $\alpha = (N-1) f_s/N$. In the case of non-dimensional variables we can use for the two axes $Nu \cos \theta_x/\lambda$, and $Nu \cos\theta_y/\lambda$, respectively. If the diffraction pattern is observed on a plane screen a distance z from the diffusing surface, the spatial frequencies may be related with points on that plane. For small angles θ it can be written:

$$\alpha = \frac{\cos\theta_x}{\lambda} \approx \frac{x'}{\lambda z}, \tag{3}$$

and

$$\beta = \frac{\cos\theta_y}{\lambda} \approx \frac{y'}{\lambda z}.$$

Due to the properties of the Fourier transform, the FFT of the reflectance will contain *N/2* of positive frequencies, and *N/2* negative, whose zero spatial frequency occurs at ν =1. In the FFT, the independent variable is the frequency, and in the representation with positive and negative frequencies its maximum value will be $f_s/2$. Based on a reflectance matrix of *NxN* elements located at the *XOY* axes associated, practically centred in the middle, we calculate *FO* by means of the FFT, obtaining another matrix from the centre of which the amplitude of the null frequency harmonic component is indicated.
The intensity registered over a direction (α,β) is found by computing the square modulus of the Fourier transform (FT) of the scattering surface delimited by the mask *M*, after centring the FFT by means of the command C(i,j)=(-1)$^{(i+j)}$.

4. Speckle pattern generation

When a laser beam illuminates a rough surface at scale of the wavelength, the diffraction pattern consists of a random distribution of intensity called speckle. The apparition of speckle may be understood by the fact that the coherent waves falling on the rough surface travel a different optical path from the diffusing surface to the observation point. When the object is rough, the reflectance is a random function on the aperture, and then the corresponding optical paths for the different scatters vary rapidly. As a result, the intensity on the observation screen (or space) also varies very quickly from one point to another of its surroundings, giving brilliant and dark spots irregular in shape.
A model of diffusing and non-absorbent surface is proposed, in which the height of the scatters with respect to a reference plane are supposed as a random variable, and with a gaussian probability density function. A surface of these characteristics is, for example, a metal which is not well polished. We suppose that the rough surface is illuminated by a collimated light beam perpendicularly to its plane resulting in a speckle pattern which is calculated by means of the FFT (Fig. 7).
Due to that optical path δ followed by the different points of the wavefront is not the same, consequently, neither is the phase $2\pi\delta/\lambda$. As we have to count the return path, the path length and height *h(x,y)* of the surface referred to the plane *z*=0 are related by the expression $4\pi h(x,y)/\lambda$. Thus, the reflectance will be proportional to the exponential of this phase factor, adopting the form

$$R(x,y) = R_0(x,y)\exp\left(\frac{4\pi i}{\lambda}h(x,y)\right), \quad (4)$$

where $R_0(x,y)$ is the reflection coefficient of the surface, and $(4\pi i h(x,y)/\lambda)$ is the phase. In the simulation presented in this paper we choose $R_0(x,y)$=1.
By measuring the random height *h(x,y)* of the sampled points (Fig.8), it would be possible to construct the reflectance matrix of $N \times N$ elements. Following the nomenclature of the

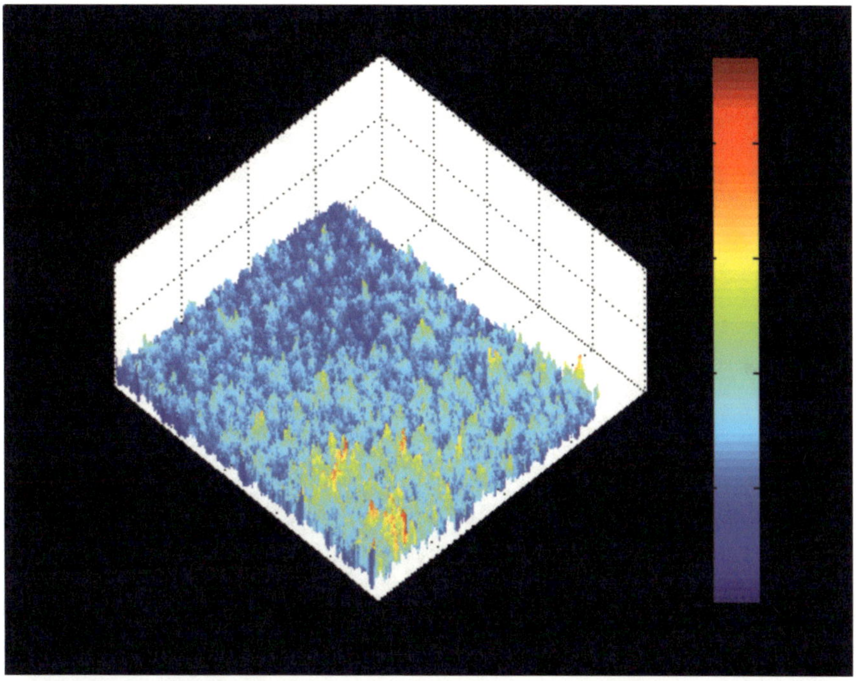

Fig. 7. Three dimensional representation of the intensity of a speckle pattern captured by a CCD camera in the laboratory. The values of the intensity over the OZ axis are in the interval [0,255].

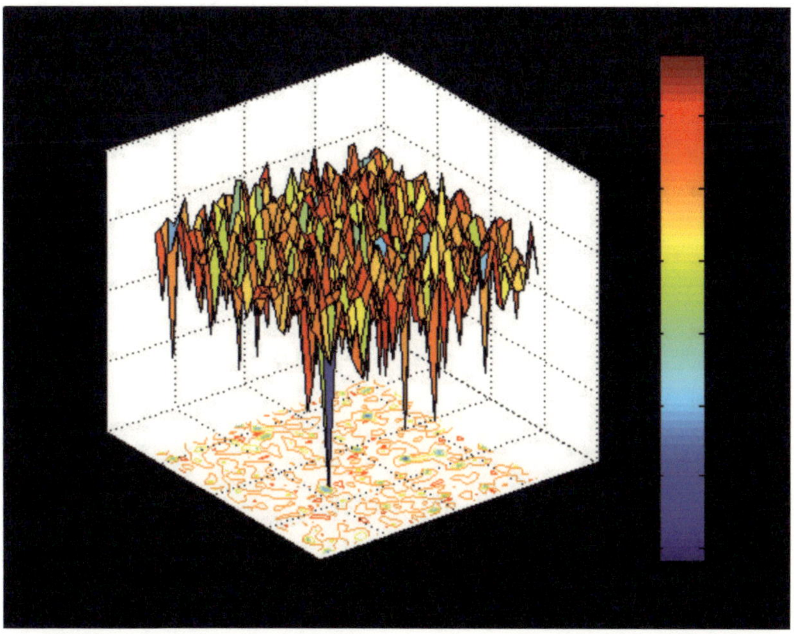

Fig. 8. Rough surface generated by MATLAB. The plane of the figure (OXY) depicts a plot of the surface contour.

preceding section we call this array the *IF* matrix (Fig.9). The elements of *IF* contain the complex reflectance $R(x,y)$ corresponding to each point of the surface, which are separated from their neighbors a distance equal to the sampling period u. The area of the delimiting mask will be represented by points outside a circle with zero reflectance.

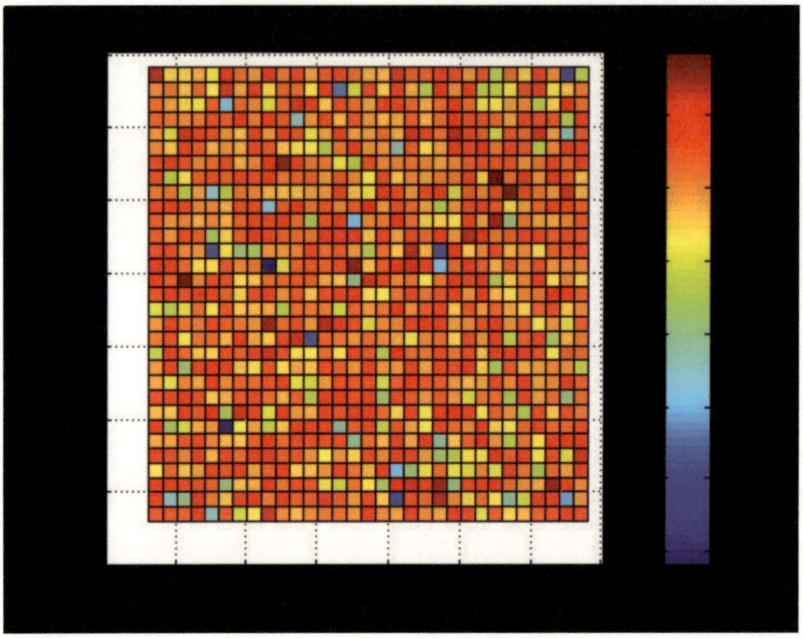

Fig. 9. View of the grid chosen on the *OXY* reference plane for N=64. The colours represent the surface heights at each point (pixel).

Following the same way as in preceding paragraphs, we employ the ratio h/λ as a non-dimensional variable, which will be very useful when changing the wavelength. In the model this variable is equal to a constant multiplied by a random number, which will provide information on the roughness in the simulation. We will call in the program this constant *RU* and it represents a roughness modulating factor. Random numbers with Gaussian distribution are generated in MATLAB by the command *randn*. The mathematical expression for reflectance is

$$R(x,y) = R_0(x,y)\exp\left(\frac{4\pi i}{\lambda}RU\big(rndn(N)\big)\right), \quad (5)$$

where

$$\frac{h}{\lambda} = RU \times randn(N), \quad (6)$$

and the phase

$$\frac{\delta}{\lambda} = 4\pi \times RU \times randn(N). \quad (7)$$

Thus, an element of *RUrandn* is a number equal to an optical path measured in wavelengths. For example, an *RU*=1 and a *randn*=2 give rise max(*RU*randn)=2, which indicates a maximum path difference of 2λ, that is to say, a groove on the reflecting surface with depth equal to λ. However with the same *randn*, but with the modulating factor equal to 0.1, the roughness would be a tenth part. Hence the *RU* factor represents the roughness measured in wavelengths.

To account the transversal geometry of the incident laser beam on the surface, the rough surface is delimited by means of a round mask of diameter *D* (geometry could be different; see section 7.2). The diameter *D* must be greater than the wavelength and the sampling period u. On the other hand it is supposed that the number of sampled points inside the diameter *D* is large enough, in order be sure that the statistics applies.

Once that the characteristics of the surface and beam are defined, the diffraction pattern is obtained by means of the FFT of the reflectance matrix *IF*. The registered intensity of the diffracted light by the rough surface is proportional to the square modulus of the diffracted amplitude, e.g. $|FO|^2$.

5. Definitions of roughness

In this section we try to adapt some definitions of roughness to our specific problem. We start the quantitative definition of the average roughness R_a from the mean surface level, as the average absolute value of the height, for all the points along a straight line (remember the profilometer). Then in a circular matrix of diameter *D* inside the *IF*, corresponds $\pi BD^2/4$ elements. Therefore, the roughness of the sample may be expressed by the following formulae

$$R_a = \frac{4\sum\limits_{BD}|h(x,y)|}{\pi BD}, \tag{8}$$

where the sum is extended to the sampled points within the circle of diameter *BD*. As previously, if we transform this Eq.(8) to non-dimensional variables, we get

$$\frac{R_a}{\lambda} = \frac{4\sum\limits_{BD}\left|\frac{h(x,y)}{\lambda}\right|}{\pi BD} = \frac{4\cdot RU}{\pi BD}\sum_{BD}|randn(N)|. \tag{9}$$

The number of elements *G* within the beam of diameter *D* (*BD*) is less than the $N\times N$ elements of *IF*. Say *L* the length of the square side where the surface is defined. In any case $BD = \chi L$, χ being a constant $(\chi \le 1)$, then it holds

$$G = \frac{1}{4}\pi\chi^2(N\times N), \tag{10}$$

whose maximum value is 0.8, approximately $(\chi = 1)$. If *N* and *BD* are large enough, and surface heights are randomly distributed, the *G* values are representative and R_a can be calculated using *G* elements.

Similarly, the roughness R_q (root mean square) could be expressed as function of *BD*. In fact, considering the usual definition of this parameter, the following formulae may be written

$$R_q = 2.\sqrt{\frac{\sum_{BD}|h(x,y)|^2}{\pi BD}}, \tag{11}$$

and its non-dimensional value

$$\frac{R_q}{\lambda} = \sqrt{\frac{4\sum_{BD}\left|\frac{h(x,y)}{\lambda}\right|^2}{\pi BD}} = 2 \cdot RU\sqrt{\frac{\sum_{BD}|randn(N)|^2}{\pi BD}}. \tag{12}$$

6. Programming using MATLAB

We will see that the simulated specklegram corresponding to the diffraction of a monochromatic radiation by a rough surface is altered by the roughness of the object within a certain range, which depends on the wavelength of the beam used. Therefore, by analyzing some characteristics of the intensity pattern it would be possible to measure roughness.

To understand the idea let us suppose a flat surface, well polished, delimited by an aperture (mask). If a beam strikes on the surface, the delimiting aperture diffracts it resulting in an intensity pattern that depends on the geometry of the obstacle. Now if the surface is scratched, the intensity registered changes, although the aperture maintains its geometry. In both cases the autoconvolution of the intensity is different, which means that the roughness produced on the surface is the cause of the change. Therefore, the convolution of the diffraction pattern could be indicative of the degree of surface polish.

To test the hypothesis, first we constructed a computer model of a rough surface, and second we simulate the diffraction of a collimated monochromatic beam by this surface. The resulting random intensity, that is, the speckle, is stored in a matrix (*FO*) and its autoconvolution (*CO*) is performed. Once all data of *CO* are obtained, the functional relationship of the maximum value of the autoconvolution and its relation with the roughness is analyzed.

The program consists of the following steps:

1. Begin by setting the number of samples *N* along each axis.
2. The matrix *IF* is constructed by using the command RAN = *randn* (*N*).
3. The diameter of the laser beam *BD* is specified, measured in number of array elements.
4. A value to the *RU* is assigned.
5. The *BS* array is constructed. The mask is 0 outside the circle and 1 inside.
6. The matrix RURAN = RU * RAN is introduced, representing the surface heights for each pixel on the area *N*x*N*.
7. The matrix *hs* is defined as *hs* = RURAN.*BS. It represents the height of the points inside the circle (mask *M*).
8. The reflectance matrix is obtained. Its expression is *ts* = exp (4πi RURAN).
9. The array *FO* is calculated, which is the FFT of *ts*.
10. The intensity of the diffraction pattern is determined, $FIDI = |FO|^2$.

11. The autoconvolution CO of FIDI, and its maximum *COV* is computed.
12. In order to manipulate the data more easily, the logarithm of *COV* is given (log(*COV*)).

The detailed program may be found in appendix A

7. Computer results

7.1 Circular beam

Figures 10 shows the results of numerical calculations performed with a PC. In order to the numerical calculations are easy to obtain the data were N = 64, BD = 6, RU = 0, 0.1, 0.2, 0.3 0.4 0.5. The successive rows of the figure refer to these values of roughness, respectively. The first column of the figure corresponds to the surface height along the diameter of the illuminated area. The second column represents the intensity of the diffraction pattern, FIDI, and the third one shows the autoconvolution, *CO*.

For beginning a surface without roughness was chosen. The first row shows the area under study for a perfect mirror, illuminated by a circular beam of diameter BD = 6. The calculated diffraction pattern shows the classical Airy disc corresponding to diffraction by a hole. With the proposed values N = 64 and BD = 6 is N/BD = 64/6, and as $D = BDu$, gives $Nu = 64D/6$. The analysis of Figure 4 shows that the first minimum of the Airy disc in the frequency space is 24, approximately. From Fig 1 it follows

$$\alpha_\nu = \frac{\cos\theta}{\lambda} = \frac{(\nu - 1)}{Nu} \approx \frac{(12-1)}{64u} = \frac{11}{64u} = 0.17\frac{1}{u}.$$

On the other hand, the first minimum given in the theory of diffraction by a circular hole is

$$\alpha_\nu = \frac{\cos\theta}{\lambda} \approx 1.22\frac{1}{Du} = 1.22\frac{1}{6u} = 0.20\frac{1}{u}.$$

Both results agree and differ in a small amount. The difference can be attributed to the small number of values chosen.

The second row refers to the same mirror, but not completely polished, and with a coefficient RU = 0.1. The profile shows small heights and valleys. The Airy disk is a little blurred, and not as clear as in the previous case. In the third row RU = 0.2 the central disk appears deformed and a speckleled. In the fourth and fifth rows the figure is quit different with respect to the first one, and the speckles are on all the pattern. In the last row only speckle may be seen, and no traces of the Airy disk are present. When the roughness is RU = 0.5 (bottom row) yields a rough surface with high grooves. The intensity is formed by irregular random spots being unknown directly the form of the mask, e.g. the symmetrical intensity circle of the Airy function. In summary, diffraction by a specular surface delimited by an aperture produces an intensity pattern concentrated around the direction of the reflected beam, but if the roughness is increasing, the light is diffracted producing speckle which structure is random.

The third figure of each row (third column) corresponds to autoconvolución (*CO*), which has a maximum at the center (*COV*). In effect, the values for the logarithm of *COV* are, respectively: log*COV*(RU=0.0) = 7.78, log*COV*(RU=0.1) = 7.10, log*COV*(*RU*=0.2) = 6.86, log*COV*(RU=0.3)=6.90, log*COV*(*RU*=0.4)= 6.88, and log*COV*(*RU*=0.5)=6.91. In this calculus the logarithm of the autoconvolution hass been used because the maximum value of *CO* is very large. Employing log(*COV*), the data are easier to manipulate.

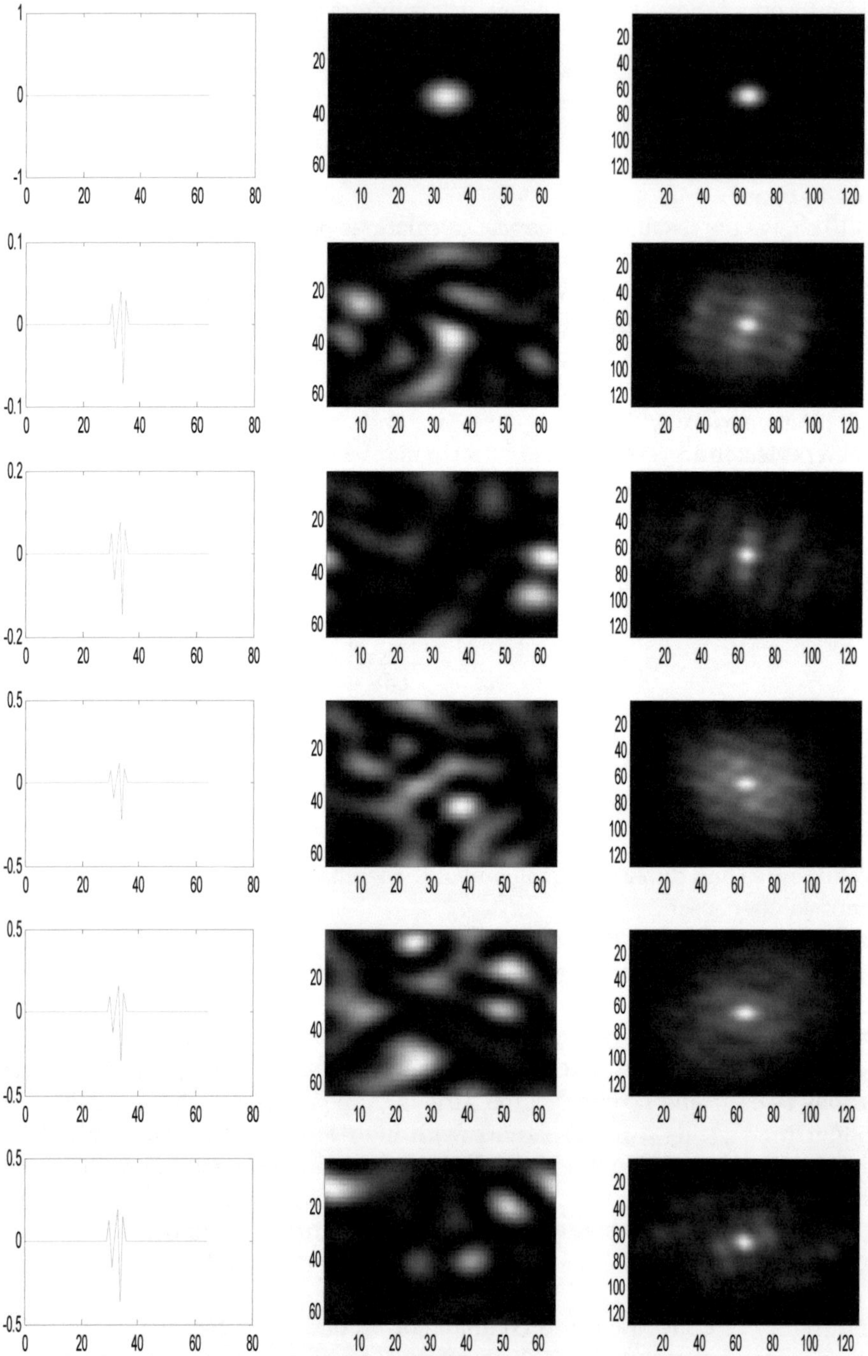

Fig. 10. Computer results for $N = 64$, $BD = 6$, $RU = 0, 0.1, 0.2, 0.3\ 0.4\ 0.5$. The first column shows the roughness along the illuminated area. The second represents the intensity of the diffraction pattern, *FIDI*, and the third column is the autoconvolution, CO. The rows correspond to the different values of *RU*.

These results show that the values of their maxima are not the same. On the contrary, the maximum value for each one depends on the surface roughness. For this reason it seems suitable to employ the maximum value of the autoconvolution of the speckle pattern, as a possible procedure for measuring the roughness of a surface, if the roughness is smaller than the wavelength of light used in the experiment.

At the same time, *COV* depends on the diameter of the beam used (*BD*) also. To see the effect in the autoconvolution when the wide of the laser is changed, we computed log*COV* with *N* and *D* for two different number of data and diameters. For example if *N*= 64, and *BD* = 32, it yields

$$\log COV = 12.0, 11.7, 10.7, 9.8, 9.7, 9.7,$$

whereas with *N* = 128 and *BD* = 32

$$\log COV = 12.6, 12.3, 11.3, 10.4, 10.3, 10.3\,.$$

Therefore the maximum reached by the autoconvolution depends on the number of samples *N* and the beam diameter *BD*.

This result is reasonable if we bear in mind the definition of autoconvolution. In fact, convolution may be regarded as the overlapping area between two functions (in this case the same function) when one is reversed and moves on the other. The result depends on the wide and height of the functions involved. Therefore, if the diameter of the beam changes the autoconvolution modifies its value too.

With the aim to apply this result to laboratory experiments, it seems necessary to have more values of the autoconvolution in other circumstances. In he same way as explained, the following table provide useful data of the log*COV*, for *N*=512 when the diameter *D* ranges from 2^3 to 2^{3+m} (m=1,2,...5). The detailed results for this calculation can be seen in the appendix B.

D\RU	0.0	0.1	0.2	0.3	0.4	0.5
8	10.233	9.231	9.148	9.185	9.078	9.128
18	12.036	10.867	10.35	10.351	10.348	10.368
32	13.810	12.558	11.536	11.546	11.548	11.542
64	15.607	14.294	12.734	12.736	12.740	12.742
128	17.412	16.037	13.945	13.938	13.941	13.937
256	19.216	17.838	15.149	15.141	15.145	15.142
512	21.257	19.881	16.428	16.347	16.347	16.349

Table 1. Values of the autoconvolution log(*COV*) for different diameters and roughness parameters. The results in yellow do not give information since they are very similar.

From these results may be inferred that if the area of the illuminated surface is known, measuring experimentally the autoconvolution of the speckle pattern, it would be possible measuring the roughness of this surface. To conduct laboratory experiments would be necessary to build larger tables with more values, for different incident beam intensities.

By examining the calculations it also follows that for values of *RU* close to zero, the difference between log*COV*, corresponding to a *BD*, and a diameter corresponding to half value, is approximately constant and equal to 2, i.e.

$\log COV' - \log COV = 2 \qquad => COV'/COV = 10^2,$

and, in general,

$$\frac{COV(N')}{COV(N)} = 10^{\left(\frac{N'}{N}\right)}. \tag{13}$$

This property will be important for ulterior calculations.

7.2 Square mask

In the preceding developing calculations, a circular geometry for the beam was supposed. However, other possibilities may occur. For instance, when a laser ray is directed onto a sample under an angle of incidence θ, the effective area intersected by the beam has a quasi-elliptical form. Although an elliptical mask is easy to simulate with MATLAB, this paragraph deals with the study of the effect of employing a square aperture. This approximation simplifies the program, since there is no need the beam diameter datum. Moreover, from the point of view of the results, it has little influence in the final values when comparing these values with those obtained for an elliptical mask.
The simulation gives the results of log(*COV*) for *RU* = 0.0, 0.1, ... 0.5, and *N* = 16, 32, 64, 128, 256, 512, that appear in the following table:

N\RU	0.0	0.1	0.2	0.3	0.4	0.5
16	9.63	9.24	8.08	7.52	7.59	7.57
32	12.04	11.72	10.73	9.49	9.33	9.34
64	14.45	14.10	13.05	11.47	11.14	11.14
128	16.86	16.51	15.48	13.81	12.95	12.95
256	19.27	18.92	17.89	16.19	14.80	14.75
512	21.67	21.33	20.30	18.57	16.68	16.56

Table 2. Values of the autoconvolution log(*COV*) for different data and roughness parameter *RU*. The results in green do not give information.

Figure 11 represents the values of the attached table II. These curves show the dependence of log(*COV*) with the roughness for different values of *N*, provide that the roughness is less than 0.4. Therefore, the trend is maintained even if the aperture is different. From the figure it follows that, except for values marked in green on the table, the dependence of log*COV* with roughness is approximately parabolic, and can be approximated by the equation

$$\log COV = a + b \times RU^2. \tag{14}$$

As in section 7.1., the difference of the log(*COV*) for consecutive values of *RU*, follows certain regularity. In fact, if the values of log(*COV*) for *RU*=0 are examined (see figure 11), we observe that for adjacent values of this variable, the differences between two consecutive points (corresponding to double *N*) are: 2.41, 2.41,2.41, 2.41, 2.40. Taking into consideration these differences, the following mathematical relationship is verified:

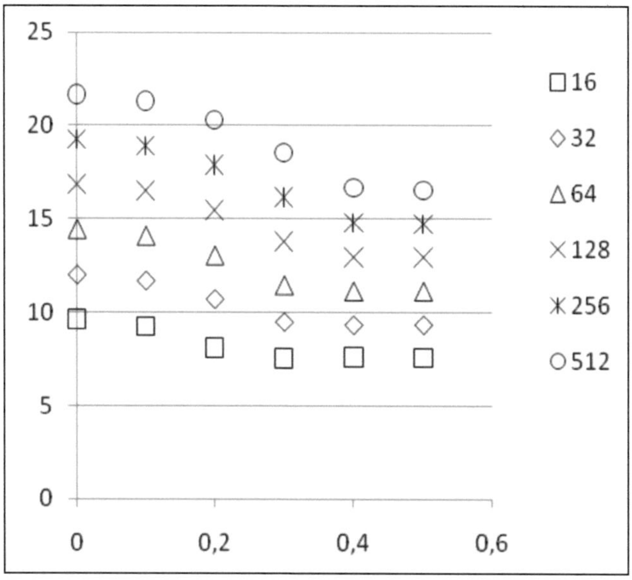

Fig. 11. Values of log(*COV*) for roughness *RU* = 0.0, 0.1, ... 0.5.

$$\log COV' - \log COV = 2.41 \;\Rightarrow\; \frac{COV'}{COV} = 10^{2.41} = 257 \approx 2^8 \quad \forall N'/N \approx 2\,. \tag{15}$$

Table 3 below relates the difference of logarithms with the ratio N'/N.

N′/N	1	2	4	8	.....	2ⁿ
logCOV′-logCOV	0	2.41	2×2.41	3×2.41	.....	n×2.41

Table 3. Logarithmic difference for *RU*=0

From these values it yields,

$$\frac{N'}{N} = 2^n \;\Rightarrow\; n = \frac{\log(N'/N)}{\log 2}, \tag{16}$$

therefore,

$$\log COV' - \log COV = 2.41\frac{\log(N'/N)}{\log 2} \;\Rightarrow\; \log\frac{COV'}{COV} =$$

$$\log(N'/N)^{2.41/\log 2} = \log(N'/N)^{7.999} \approx \log(N'/N)^8$$

$$\Rightarrow\; \frac{COV'}{COV} = (N'/N)^{2.41/\log 2} \;\Rightarrow\; \frac{COV'}{N'^{2.41/\log 2}} = \frac{COV}{N^{2.41/\log 2}} \equiv k \;\Rightarrow\; COV = kN^{2.41/\log 2} \approx kN^8,$$

where *k* is a constant. From the definition of *k* it follows that

$$\log k = \log COV - \frac{2.41}{\log 2}\log N\,. \tag{17}$$

Applying this formula for $N = 64$ we have

$$\log k = 14.45 - \frac{2.41}{\log 2}\log 64 = -0.01000 \quad \Rightarrow \quad k = 0.9772\,, \tag{18}$$

therefore,

$$\log COV = -0.01 + \frac{2.41}{\log 2}\log N = -0.01 + 8.006\log N\,. \tag{19}$$

Using this result to the values of N: 32, 64, 256, 512 (RU=0), we btain for log(COV): 12.04, 14.45, 16.86, 19.27, and 21.68, respectively. These results agree with those of the table II.
A more general fit for log(COV) considering and RU can be found, provided that $RU \le 0.4$:

$$\log COV = -0.01000 + 8.006\log N + b \times RU^2\,. \tag{20}$$

To determine the value of b, we choose, for example, N=128 and RU=0.2, which yields

$$15.48 = -0.01000 + 8.006\log 128 + b \times 0.2^2 \quad \Rightarrow \quad b = -34.50 \tag{21}$$

$$\Rightarrow \quad \log COV = -0.01000 + 8.006\log N - 34.50RU^2 \approx 8.006\log N - 34.50RU^2\,.$$

Solving the unknown in Eq. (20) we have

$$RU = \sqrt{\frac{1}{34.5}\log\left(\frac{N^8}{COV}\right)}\,. \tag{22}$$

The advantage of this formula is that it allows calculating the value of the roughness for each N and D.
To verify the accuracy of these results, we introduce some values of roughness and number of samples in Eq.(20).
For RU=0.1, N=32:

$$\log COV = 8.006\log 32 - 34.50 \times 0.1^2 = 11.70\,.$$

For RU =0.1, N =512:

$$\log COV = 8.006\log 512 - 34.50 \times 0.1^2 = 21.35\,.$$

For RU =0.3, N =32:

$$\log COV = 8.006\log 32 - 34.50 \times 0.3^2 = 8.95\,.$$

For RU =0.3, N =512:

$$\log COV = 8.006\log 512 - 34.50 \times 0.3^2 = 18.59\,.$$

It may be seen that the differences between these values calculated with the formula (20) and those displayed in table II are equal to or less than 0.02, except for the case N = 32, RU = 0.3, which is 0.15. But as in this case the value of the table does not correspond to the difference of logarithms (marked in green), it follows that the equation obtained is suitable for the specified intervals.

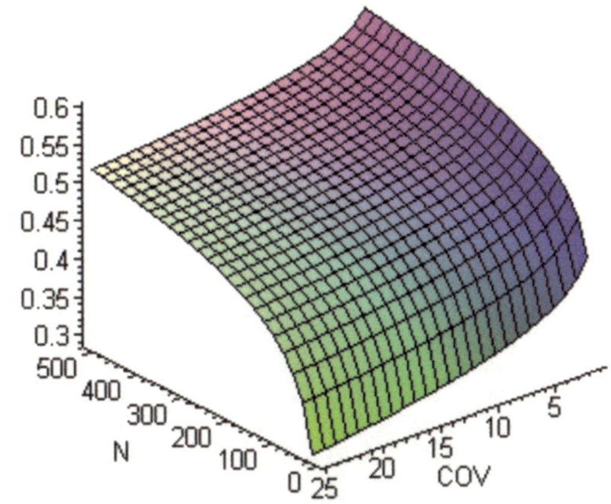

Fig. 12. Values of *RU* (from 0.0 to 0.5) as a function of *N* and *COV* (Eq.(22)).

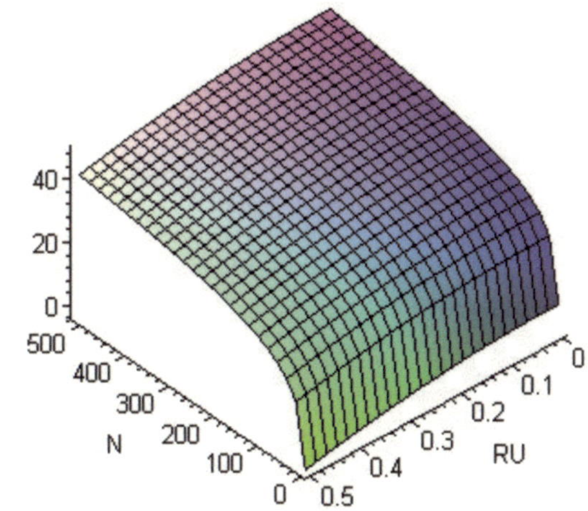

Fig. 13. Thissurface represents the function log(COV) for differerent values of N and *RU* (Eq.(21)).

8. Apendix A

```
L=.......?
BD=.....?

RAN=randn(L);
colormap(gray)

RU1=0
RU2=0.1
RU3=0.2
RU4=0.3
RU5=0.4
RU6=0.5

 for i=1:L
  for j=1:L
   if (BD/2)^2<=((i-.5-L/2)^2+(j-.5-L/2)^2)
```

```
  BS(i,j)=0;
  else
  BS(i,j)=(-1)^(i+j);
  end
  end
 end

RURAN1=RU1*RAN;
 h1=RURAN1.*BS;
 C1=h1(L/2,:);
 ts1=BS.*exp(4i*pi*RURAN1);
 FO1=fft2(ts1);
 FIDI1=(abs(FO1)).*(abs(FO1));
 CO1=conv2(FIDI1,fliplr(flipud(FIDI1)));
 COV1=conv2(FIDI1,fliplr(flipud(FIDI1)),'valid')
LCOV1=log10(COV1)
 RURAN2=RU2*RAN;
 h2=RURAN2.*BS;
 C2=h2(L/2,:);
 ts2=BS.*exp(4i*pi*RURAN2);
 FO2=fft2(ts2);
 FIDI2=(abs(FO2)).*(abs(FO2));
 CO2=conv2(FIDI2,fliplr(flipud(FIDI2)));
 COV2=conv2(FIDI2,fliplr(flipud(FIDI2)),'valid')
LCOV2=log10(COV2)
 RURAN3=RU3*RAN;
 h3=RURAN3.*BS;
 C3=h3(L/2,:);
 ts3=BS.*exp(4i*pi*RURAN3);
 FO3=fft2(ts3);
 FIDI3=(abs(FO3)).*(abs(FO3));
 CO3=conv2(FIDI3,fliplr(flipud(FIDI3)));
 COV3=conv2(FIDI3,fliplr(flipud(FIDI3)),'valid')
LCOV3=log10(COV3)
 RURAN4=RU4*RAN;
 h4=RURAN4.*BS;
 C4=h4(L/2,:);
 ts4=BS.*exp(4i*pi*RURAN4);
 FO4=fft2(ts4);
 FIDI4=(abs(FO4)).*(abs(FO4));
 CO4=conv2(FIDI4,fliplr(flipud(FIDI4)));
 COV4=conv2(FIDI4,fliplr(flipud(FIDI4)),'valid')
LCOV4=log10(COV4)

RURAN5=RU5*RAN;
 h5=RURAN5.*BS;
 C5=h5(L/2,:);
 ts5=BS.*exp(4i*pi*RURAN5);
 FO5=fft2(ts5);
 FIDI5=(abs(FO5)).*(abs(FO5));
 CO5=conv2(FIDI5,fliplr(flipud(FIDI5)));
```

```
 COV5=conv2(FIDI5,fliplr(flipud(FIDI5)),'valid')
LCOV5=log10(COV5)

RURAN6=RU6*RAN;
 h6=RURAN6.*BS;
 C6=h6(L/2,:);
 ts6=BS.*exp(4i*pi*RURAN6);
 FO6=fft2(ts6);
 FIDI6=(abs(FO6)).*(abs(FO6));
 CO6=conv2(FIDI6,fliplr(flipud(FIDI6)));
 COV6=conv2(FIDI6,fliplr(flipud(FIDI6)),'valid')
LCOV6=log10(COV6)

subplot(6,3,1)
plot(C1)
subplot(6,3,2)
imagesc(FIDI1)
subplot(6,3,3)
imagesc(CO1)
subplot(6,3,4)
plot(C2)
subplot(6,3,5)
imagesc(FIDI2)
subplot(6,3,6)
imagesc(CO2)
subplot(6,3,7)
plot(C3)
subplot(6,3,8)
imagesc(FIDI3)
subplot(6,3,9)
imagesc(CO3)
subplot(6,3,10)
plot(C4)
subplot(6,3,11)
imagesc(FIDI4)
subplot(6,3,12)
imagesc(CO4)

subplot(6,3,13)
plot(C5)
subplot(6,3,14)
imagesc(FIDI5)
subplot(6,3,15)
imagesc(CO5)

subplot(6,3,16)
plot(C6)
subplot(6,3,17)
imagesc(FIDI6)
subplot(6,3,18)
imagesc(CO6)

return
```

9. Apendix B

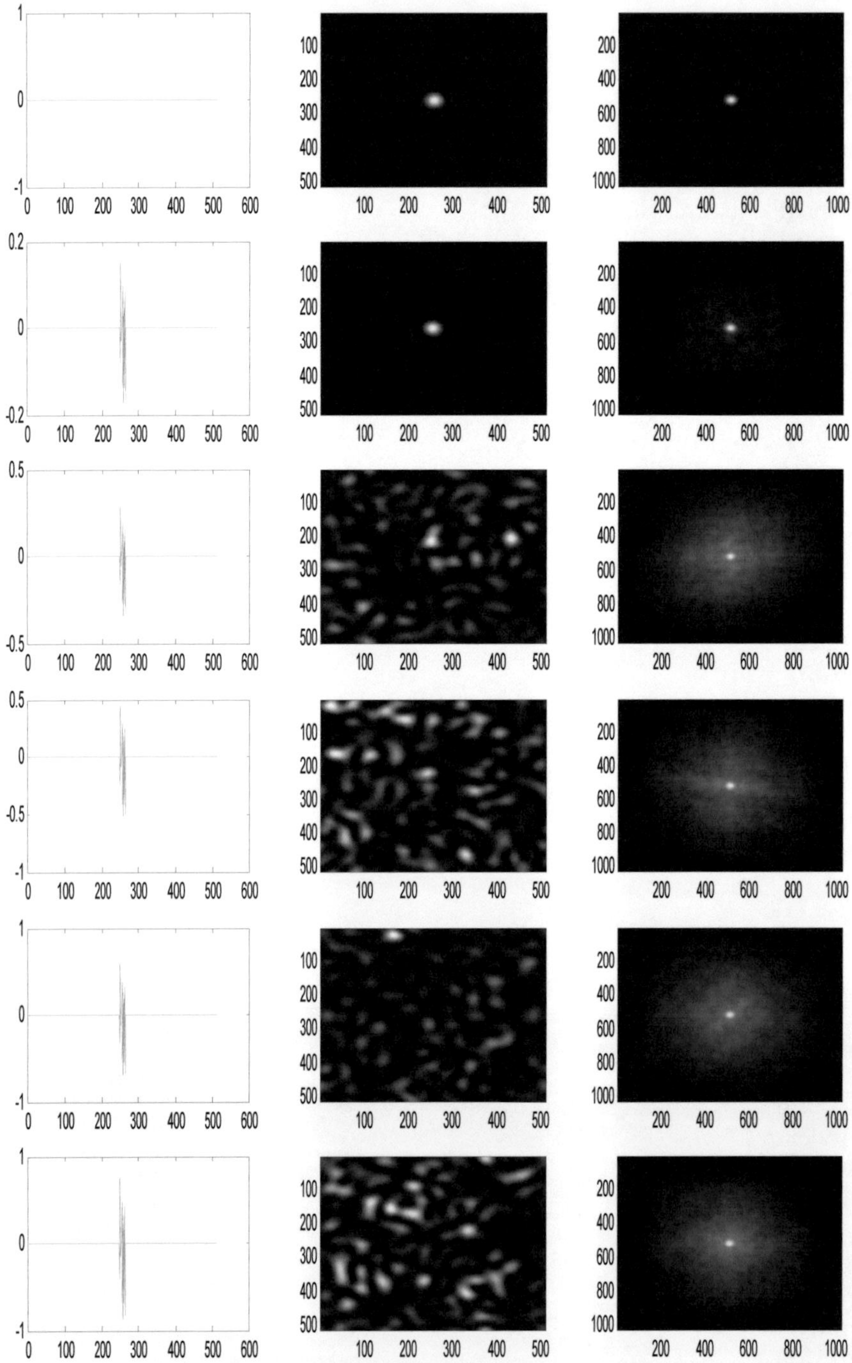

Fig. 14. N=500; D=8; RU= 0.0, 0.1, 0.2, 0.3, 0.4, 0.5. (a) Surface height along the diameter. (b) Diffraction pattern. (c) Autoconvolution.

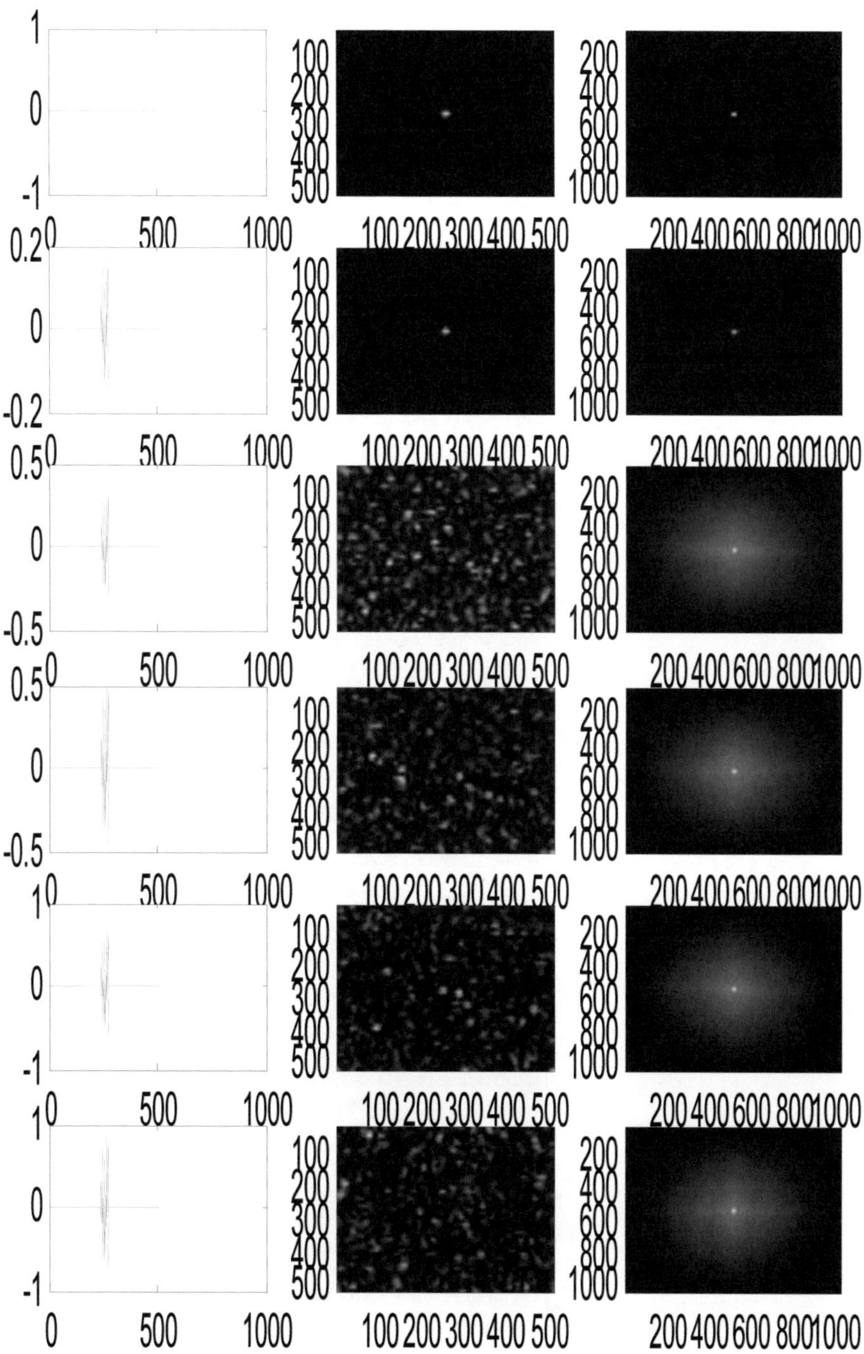

Fig. 15. N=500; D=16; RU= 0.0, 0.1, 0.2, 0.3, 0.4, 0.5. (a) Surface height along the diameter. (b) Speckle pattern. (c) Autoconvolution.

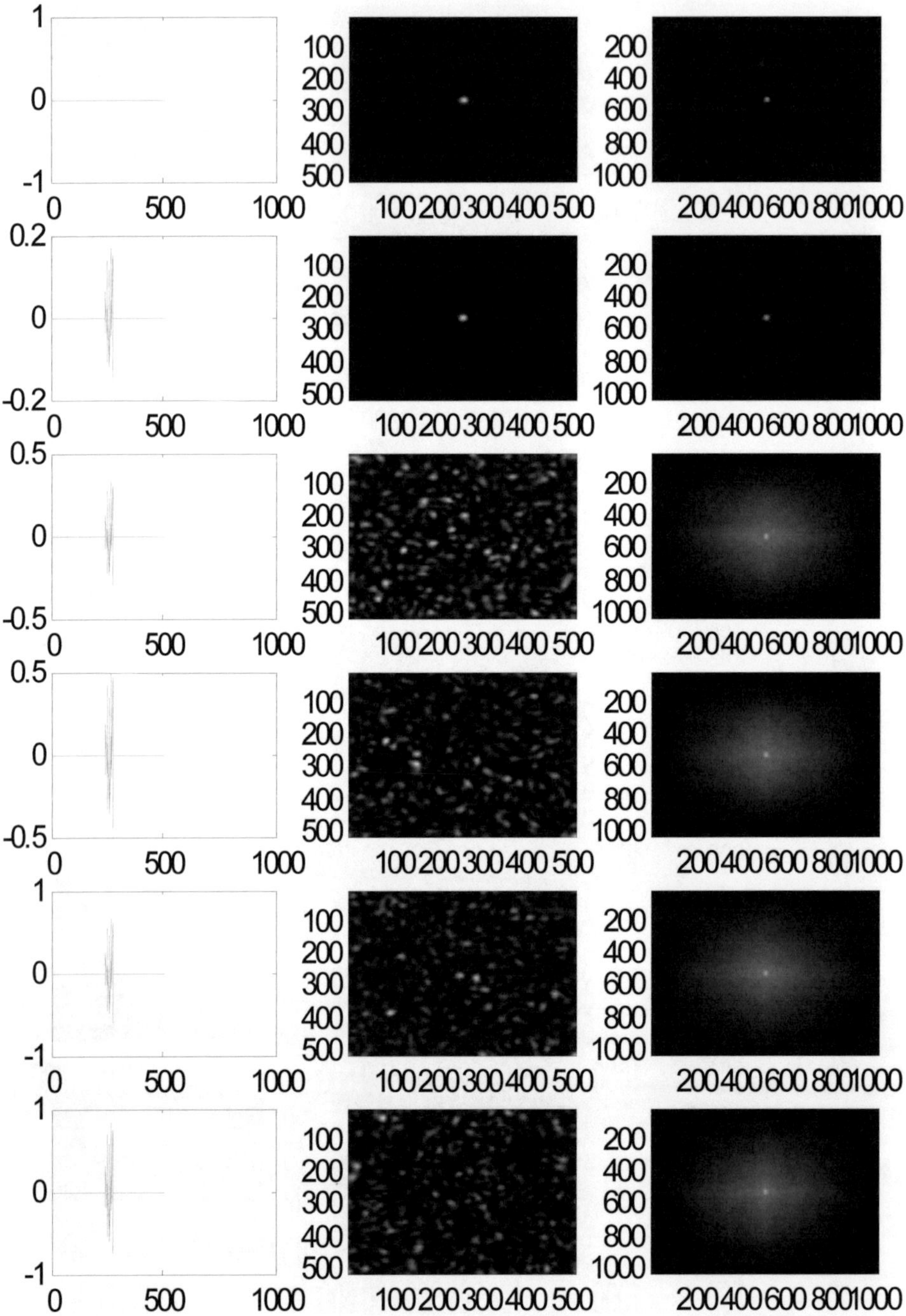

Fig. 16. *N*=500; *D*=32; *RU*= 0.0, 0.1, 0.2, 0.3, 0.4, 0.5. (a) Surface height along the diameter. (b) Speckle pattern. (c) Autoconvolution.

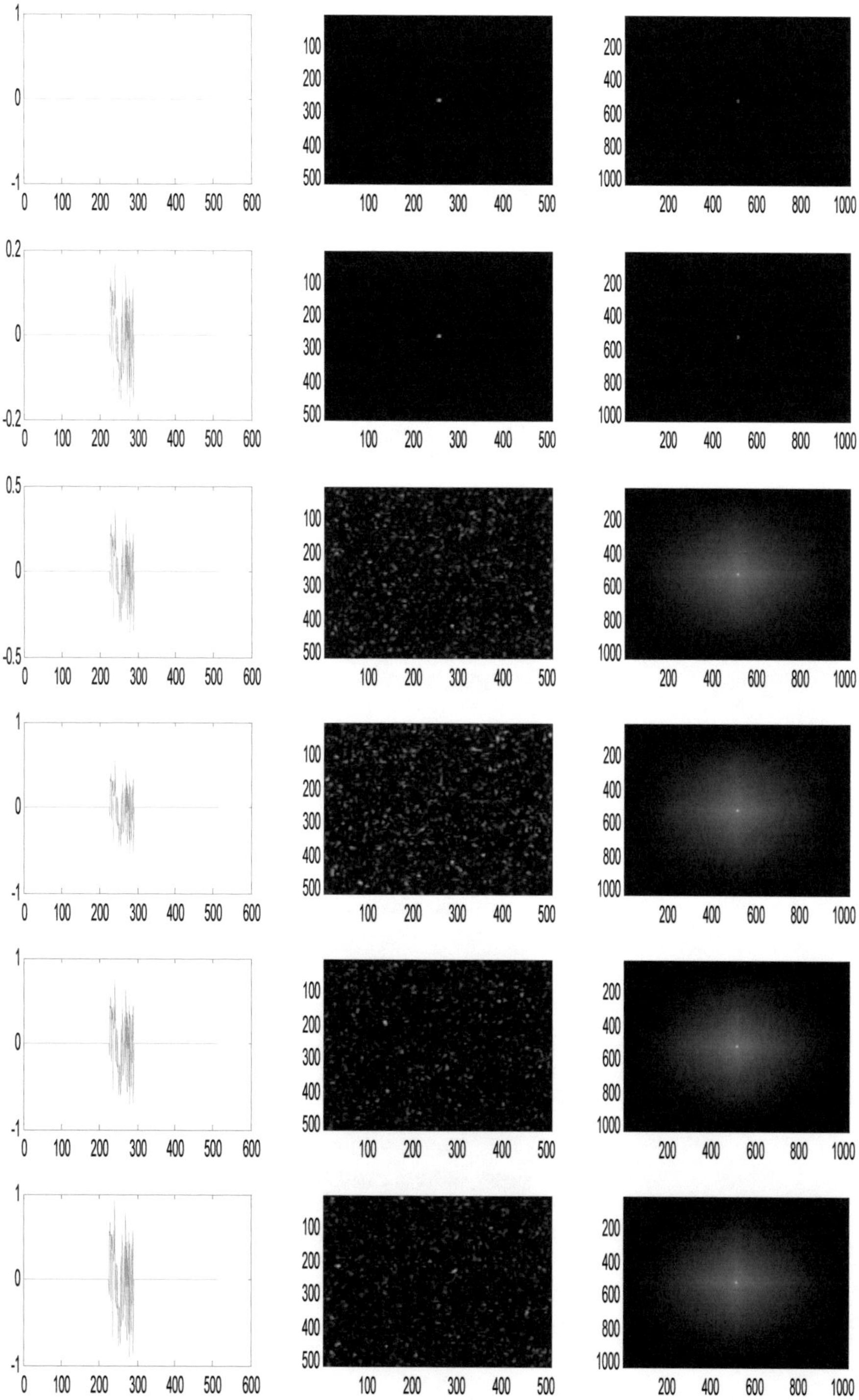

Fig. 17. *N*=500; *D*=64; *RU*= 0.0, 0.1, 0.2, 0.3, 0.4, 0.5. (a) Surface height along the diameter. (b) Speckle pattern. (c) Autoconvolution.

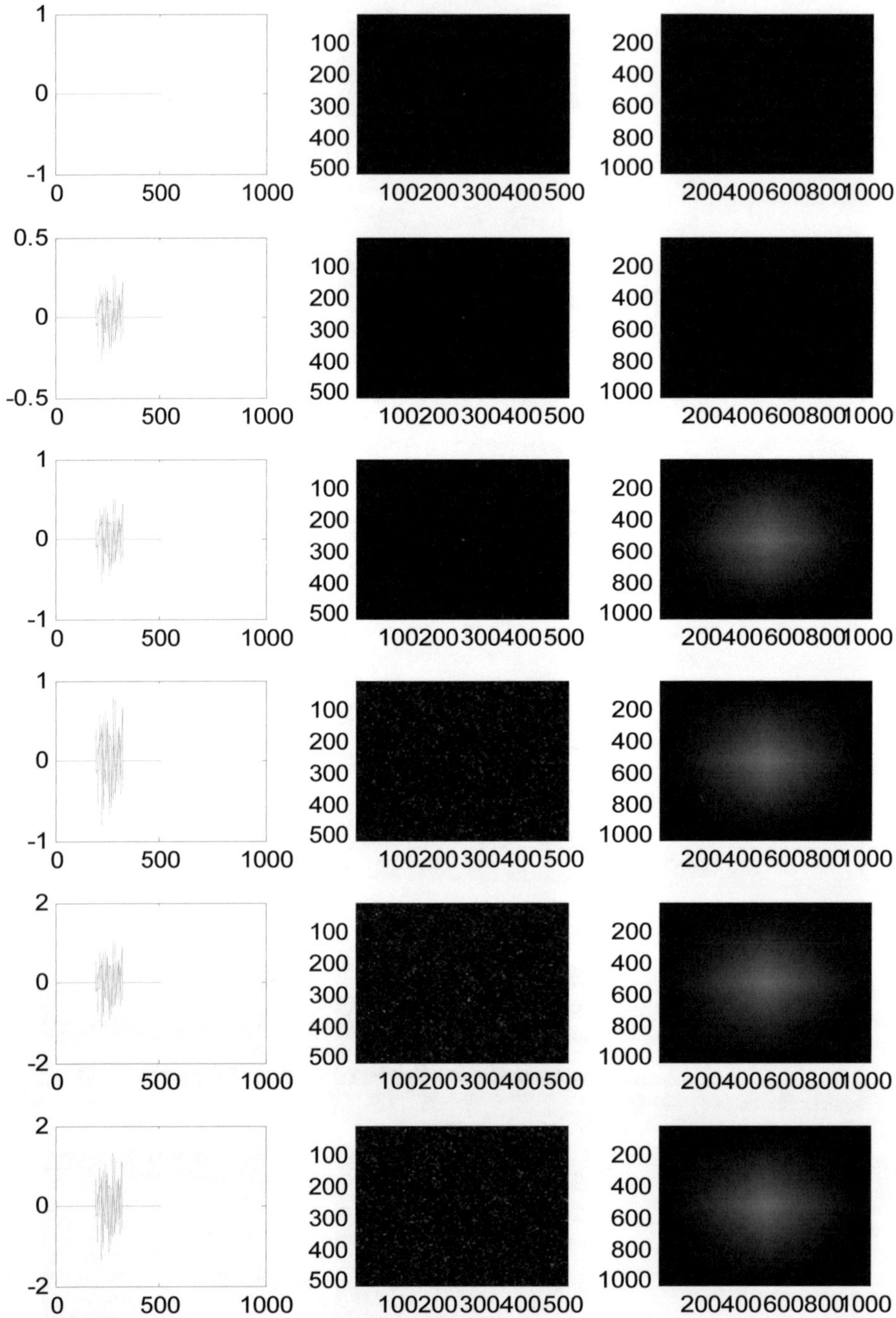

Fig. 18. N=500; D=128; RU= 0.0, 0.1, 0.2, 0.3, 0.4, 0.5. (a) Surface height along the diameter. (b) Speckle pattern. (c) Autoconvolution.

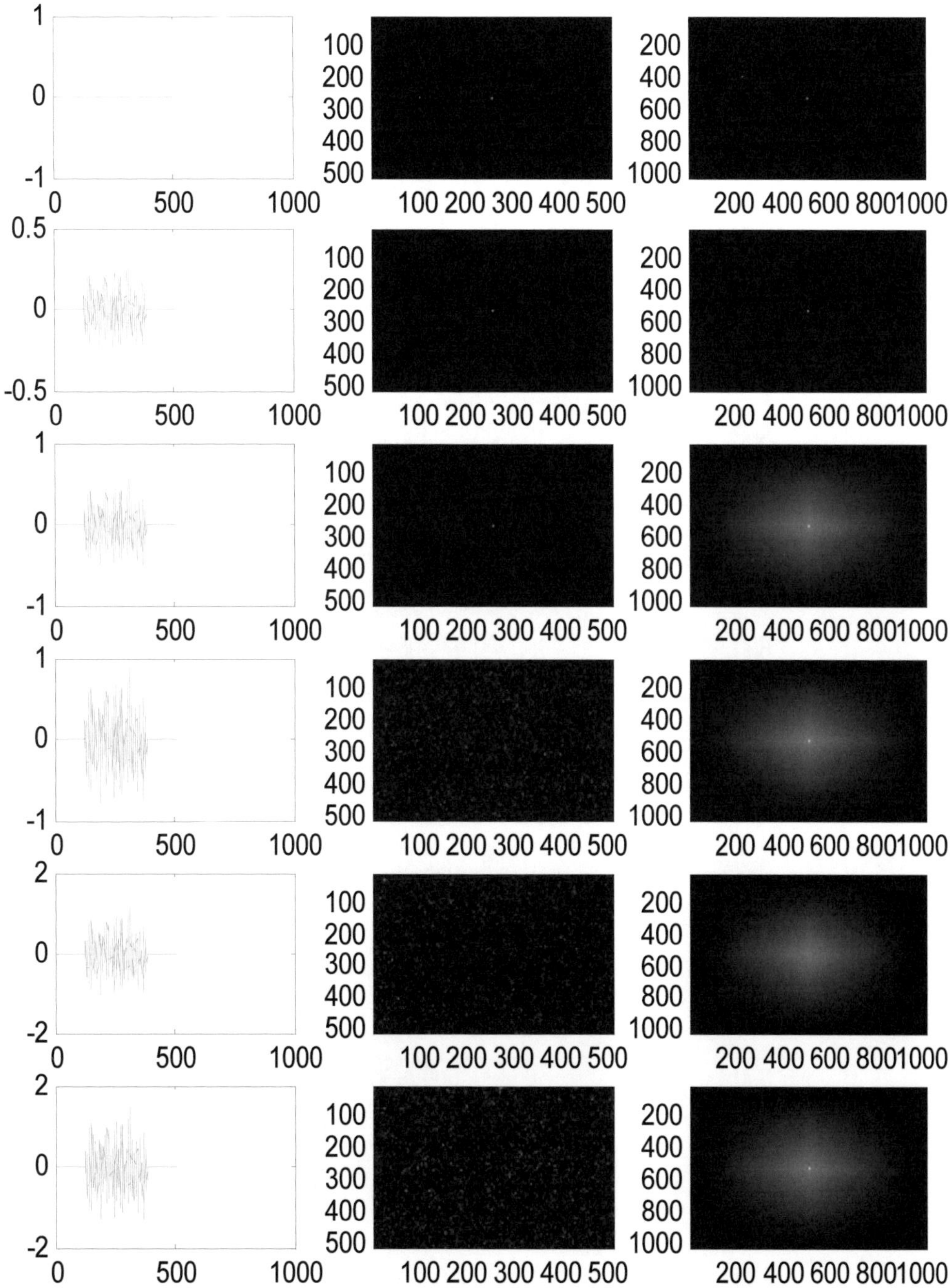

Fig. 19. *N*=500; *D*=256; *RU*= 0.0, 0.1, 0.2, 0.3, 0.4, 0.5. (a) Surface height along the diameter. (b) Speckle pattern. (c) Autoconvolution.

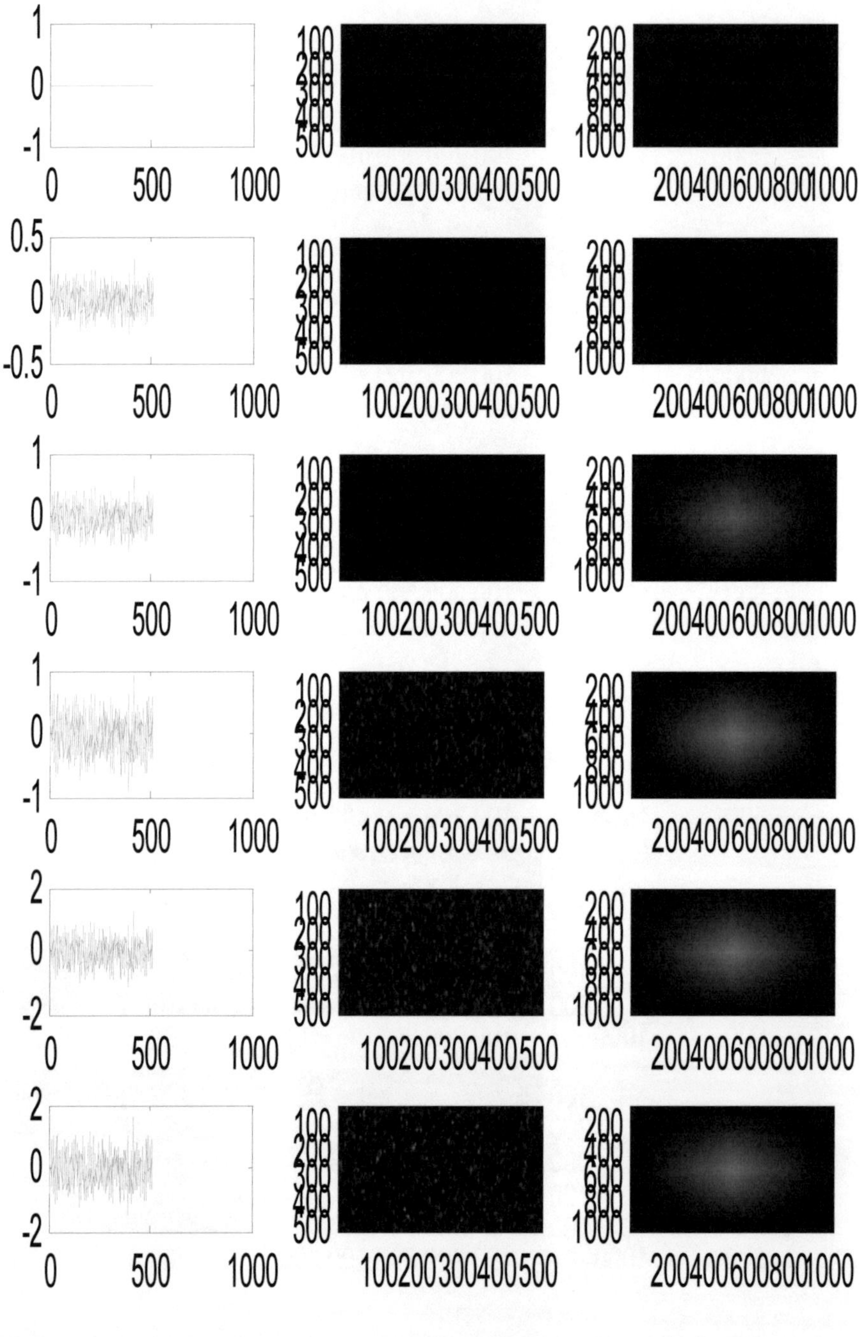

Fig. 20. N=500; D=500; RU= 0.0, 0.1, 0.2, 0.3, 0.4, 0.5. (a) Surface height along the diameter. (b) Speckle pattern. (c) Autoconvolution.

10. References

Born, M; Wolf, E; (1999) Principles Optics, Cambridge University Press. pp. 412-484.

Etter, D.M.; (1997) Engineering problem solving with MATLAB. Prentice-Hall.

Gascón, F.; Salazar, F.; (2006) A simple method to simulate diffraction and speckle patterns with a PC, *Optik*, Vol. 117, pp. 49-57.

Gascón, F.; Salazar, F.; (2008) Numerical computation of in-plane displacements and their detection in the near field by double-exposure objective speckle photography, *Opt. Commun.*, Vol. 281, pp- 6097-6106.

Glio, M.; Musazzi, S.; Perini, U.; Surface measurement by means of speckle wavelength decorrelation", *Opt. Commun.* Vol. 28, 1979, pp. 166-170.

Goodman, J.W.; (1975) Dependence of image speckle contrast on surface roughness. *Opt. Commun*, Vol. 14, pp. 324-327.

Huntley, J.M.; (1989) Speckle photography fringe analysis: assessment of current algorithms, *Appl. Opt.* Vol. 28, pp. 4316-4322. (See references therein).

Kreis, T.; (2005) Handbook of Holographic Interferometry. Wiley-VCH, Weinheim, Ch.1, 2.

Lehmann, P.; Patzelt, S.; Schöne, A.; (1997) Surface roughness measurement by means of polychromatic speckle elongation. *Appl. Opt.* Vol. 36, pp. 2188-2197.

Leonhardt, K.; Tiziani, H.J.; (1982) Removing ambiguities in surface roughness measurement. *Optica Acta*, Vol. 29, pp. 493-499

Lipson, S.G.; Lipson, H.; (1995) Tannhauser: Optical Physics. Cambridge University Press, Cambridge, p.162.

Patzelt, S.; Horn, F; Goch, (2006) G; Fast integral optical roughness measurement of specular reflecting surfaces in the nanometer range. *XVIII Imeko World Congress*, Rio de Janeiro, Brazil.

Persson, U.; (2006) Surface roughness measurement on machined surfaces using angular speckle correlation. J. Mater. *Process. Tech.*, Vol. 180, pp. 233-238.

Pearson, U.; (1993) Measurement of surface roughness on rough machined surfaces using spectral speckle correlation and image analysis. *Wear*, Vol. 160, pp. 221-225.

Pérez Quintián, F., Rebollo, M.A; Nogert, E.N.; Landau M. R.; Gaggioli, N.G.; (1996) Relationship between speckle correlation and refraction index variations: applications for roughness measurements", *Opt. Eng*. Vol 35, , pp. 1175-1178.

Ruffing, B.; (1986) Application of speckle-correlation methods to surface-roughness measurement: a theoretical study, *J. Opt. Soc. Am. A*, vol. 3, pp. 1297-1304.

Ruffing, B.; (1987) Non-contacting roughness measurement of technical surfaces by speckle-correlation method. Doctoral Thesis. University of Karlsruhe. (In german)

Spagnolo, G.S.; Paoletti, D.; (1996) Digital speckle correlation for on-line real-time measurement. *Opt. Commun.* Vol. 132, pp. 24-28.

Stratton, J.A.: (1961) Théorie de l'électromagnétisme, Dunod, Paris. p. 531

Tay, C. J.; Toh, S. L.; Shang, H. M.; Zhang, J.; (1995) Whole-field determination of surface roughness by speckle correlation. *Appl. Opt*, vol. 34, pp. 2324-2335.

Xiaomei, Xu.; (2009) Non-contact Surface Roughness Measurement Based on Laser Technology and Neural Network. *Proc. IEEE*, International Conference on Mechatronics and Automation. Changchun, China.

Yamaguchi, I.; Kobayashi, K.; Yaroslavsky, L.; (2004) Measurement of surface roughness by speckle correlation. *Opt. Eng.*, Vol. 43, pp. 2753-2761.

Yoshimura, T.; Kato, K.; Nakagawa, K.; (1990) Surface-roughness dependence of the intensity correlation function under speckle-pattern illumination, *J. Opt. Soc. Am. A*, Vol. 7, pp. 2254-2259.

Zhao, Gao; Xuezeng, Zhao; (2008) On-Line Surface Roughness Measurement Based on Specular Intensity Component of Speckle Patterns. *Proc. IEEE* 2008, International Conference on Information and Automation. Zhangjiajie, China.

20

MATLAB in Biomodeling

Cristina-Maria Dabu
CRIFST – Romanian Academy
Romania

1. Introduction

Mathematical modeling and computer simulations are widespread instruments used for biological systems study.

Matlab and Simulink are powerful, high-level programming language which offer the opportunity to apply the principles of linear systems theory in the analysis of biological systems; the opportunity to develop adequate computer simulation techniques and algorithms in order to model dynamic responses of physiological systems, and to collect and analyze data and to visualize the results information for the simulation processes

2. Systemic modeling in biosciences

Models are extremely useful in understanding how the neuronal cell stores, computes, integrates and transmit the information necessary for the survival of the organism. Computer assisted models permit also to create a variety of test scenarios that would be too difficult, expensive or dangerous to allow to happen in reality.

The main goal in modeling and simulation in the area of Biosciences is to develop integrative models and simulation which allow the dynamic representation of signaling and metabolic networks in the neuronal cell as open systems with distinct input and output ports and specific response mechanisms. The systemic approach in the actual researches in the field of biomodeling aim to fit together the different level at which complex biological systems are working, from genes through cells, organs to the whole organism (Noble, 2002). The majority of biological and physiological control systems are nonlinear and the control is often accomplished parametrically.

Biological systems are hierarchical systems, characterized by:

1. Each level has unique language, concepts or principles;
2. Each level is an integration of items from a lower level; discoveries or descriptions at i^{-th} tlevel aid understanding of phenomena at i+1 level;
3. Relationship between levels is not symmetrical;

In fig.1. is presented the algorithm used for developing biological systemic and mathematical models. Control systems theory, applied in the neuronal modeling, is used to analyze the dynamic properties of the neuronal metabolic and signaling pathways and to understand the role of feedback loops in the reaction networks. The essence of this approach lies in the dynamics of the system and cannot be described merely by enumerating the components of the system. In the systemic approach, the neuronal cell is considered an open system with distinct input and output ports and specific response mechanisms.

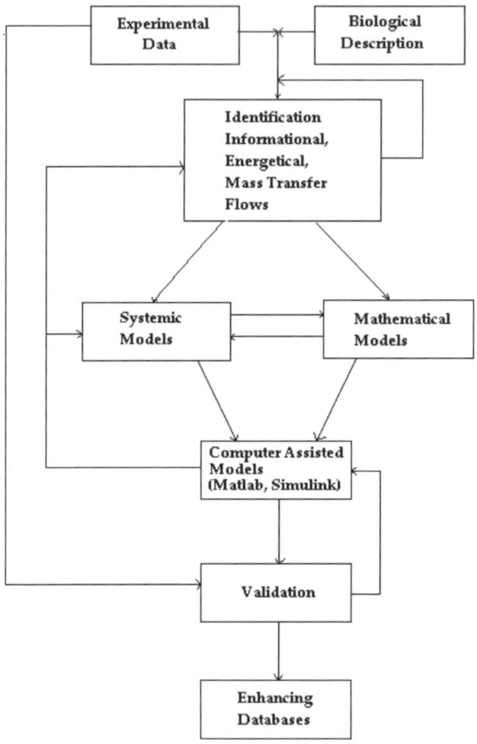

Fig. 1. The algorithm for developing systemic and mathematical models in neurobiology

Biological systems are adaptive systems, stable, equipped with control mechanisms (feedback) extremely fine (Heinrich, 1996). In fig.2 we have considered a model rule to regulate processes within the neuron, a model that, in various forms, otherwise we will find all subprocesses in regulating cell.

In the neuronal cell, extracellular and intracellular stimuli are captured and measured by specialized receptor structures located in the cytoplasm and in the cell membrane. Stimuli are represented by various substances that circulate in the body (hormones, oxygen ions, different protein structures), environmental factors (radiation, temperature variations, etc.) and electrical impulses from adjacent cells. Based on these stimuli, and coded programs to DNA, control mechanisms (feedback) provides nerve cell adaptation to environmental conditions. They aim to develop cell responses to stimuli coming from the external environment and internal, depending on the deviation e(t) measured between the model output (encoded at the genetic level) $y_M(t)$ and output biosystem (neuronal cell) y(t).

$$\varepsilon(t) = y_M(t) - y(t) \tag{1.1}$$

Under ideal operating conditions for the neuronal cell $\varepsilon(t) \rightarrow 0$

Where:
u(t) = input size
r(t) = size reference
y(t) = output size
p(t) = disturbance

Models about the mechanisms of neuron refers to adaptive changes in cell metabolism, compared with the extracellular environment. In the presence of enzymes, synthesized as a result of chemical reactions, substances taken from the cell improper turns feeding their cell substance. Exchange with the outside is permanent and will work antientropic cell, because it will prevent their growth through disruption of entropy.

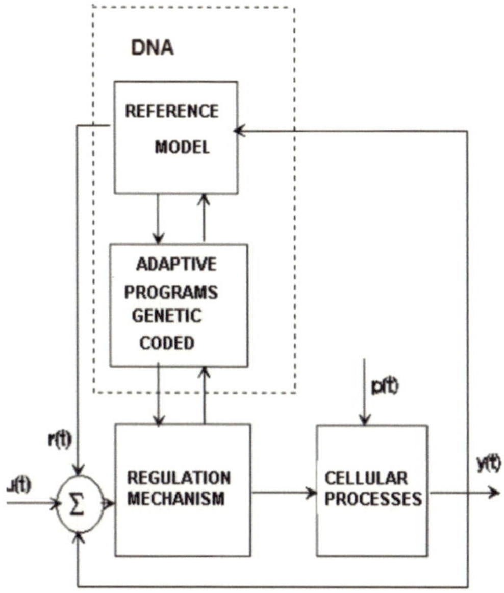

Fig. 2. The systemic model for the regulation processes in the neuronal cell

3. Neuronal cell processes modeling

3.1 The systemic and mathematical models of protein synthesis in the neuronal cell

From the systems theory viewpoint, the neuronal cell is an open system with distinct input and output ports and specific response mechanisms. Signaling action through the pathways result in different categories of cellular responses like ionic channel opening or closing, neuronal differentiation or neuronal cell death. The dynamical models of signaling pathways are nonlinear and the analysis of their behavior in challenging request specific algorithms.

In a first approximation, the protein synthesis process at neuronal level may be modeled like a open three-compartmental system (fig.3.)

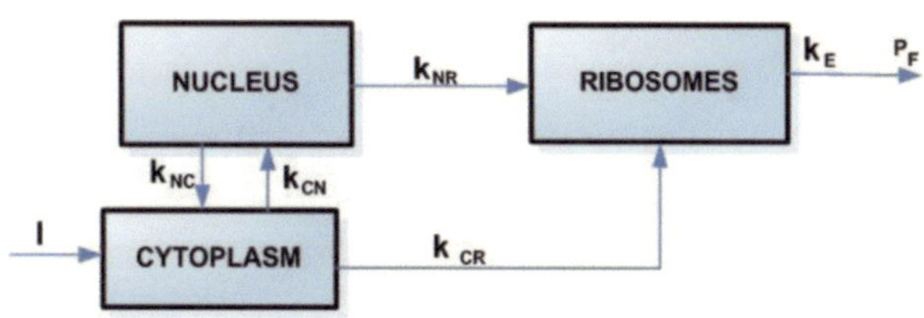

Fig. 3. The three-compartmental model for the protein synthesis process

The equilibrium equations which are describing the system are:

$$\frac{d}{dt}q_N(t) = (-k_{NC} + k_{CN})q_C - k_{NR}q_R \quad (2.1.1)$$

$$\frac{d}{dt}q_C(t) = (k_{NC} - k_{CN})q_N - k_{CR}q_R + i(t) \quad (2.1.2)$$

$$\frac{d}{dt}q_R(t) = k_{NR}q_N - k_{CR}q_C - k_e P_f(t) \quad (2.1.3)$$

Passing in the matrix form, we have:

$$\frac{d\bar{q}}{dt} = A\bar{q} \quad (2.1.8)$$

$$\begin{pmatrix} q_N(t) \\ q_C(t) \\ q_R(t) \end{pmatrix} = \bar{q} \qquad \frac{d}{dt}\begin{pmatrix} q_N(t) \\ q_C(t) \\ q_R(t) \end{pmatrix} = \frac{d\bar{q}}{dt} \qquad \begin{pmatrix} 0 \\ I(t) \\ -k_e P_f(t) \end{pmatrix} = \bar{b} \quad (2.1.5)$$

$$\begin{pmatrix} 0 & (-k_{NC} + k_{CN}) & -k_{NR} \\ -(-k_{NC} + k_{CN}) & 0 & -k_{CR} \\ k_{NR} & k_{CR} & 0 \end{pmatrix} = A \quad (2.1.6)$$

Using the substitutions (2.5) and (2.6) we get the next afine equation:

$$\frac{d\bar{q}}{dt} = A\bar{q} + \bar{b} \quad (2.1.7)$$

With the initial condition: $\bar{q}(t_0) = \overline{q_0}$

In order to solving this equation, we have firste to determinate the solution of the homogenous equation:

$$\frac{d\bar{q}}{dt} = A\bar{q} \quad (2.1.8)$$

The General solution of such an equation is:

$$\bar{q}(t) = Ce^{A(t-t_0)}, A \in M_{3,3}(R) \quad (2.1.9)$$

where:

$$e^{A(t-t_0)} = \sum_{n \geq 0} \frac{A^n (t-t_0)}{n!} \quad (2.1.10)$$

The proper values of matrix A, used in the study of the protein synthesis process stability are:

$$
\begin{aligned}
\lambda_1 &= 0 \\
\lambda_2 &= i\sqrt{k_{CR}^2 + k_{CN}^2 + k_{NR}^2} \\
\lambda_3 &= i\sqrt{k_{CR}^2 + k_{CN}^2 + k_{NR}^2}
\end{aligned}
\tag{2.1.11}
$$

The main biochemical process in the protein synthesis is the formation of the peptide bound. The necessary information for the synthesis of a protein is stored at the specific structural gene level coded as purines and pyrimidine bases of DNA molecule structure. To each amino acid is corresponding a characteristic group of three bases, called codon, the total number of specific combinations being 64. Through a process of transcription, the code is transferred in the form of an m_{RNA} molecule, synthesized in the nucleus and then transferred into the cytoplasm. The RNA molecule acts on the ribosomes, in the initiation stage of synthesis process. During the transcription process, each sequence of DNA is copied into a corresponding sequence on the m_{RNA}.

The RNA synthesized in the neuronal cell nucleus is transferred through the nuclear pores in the cytoplasm in two forms: m_{RNA} and t_{RNA}, each of the two macromolecular structures fulfilling specific roles in the synthesis the proteins. Also, in the cytoplasm of amino acid activation occurs in the presence of ATP, under the influence of specific amino-synthase, resulting in an amino-AMP synthetase complex. In this specific t_{RNA}, also synthesized by the DNA transcription synthase is released, forming amino acid-activated t_{RNA} complex.

Amino acids activated and coupled with t_{RNA}, reach the ribosomes structures where protein synthesis takes place in three phases:

- initiation phase
- elongation phase
- termination phase

In the protein synthesis process are implied:

- DNA
- Amino acids
- Ribosomal RNA (r_{RNA})
- Messenger RNA, formed the nucleus (m_{RNA})
- Cytoplasmic transfer RNA (t_{RNA})
- Enzyme activation of amino acids (amino t_{RNA}-synthase)
- Initiation Factors
- Transfer Factors
- Termination factors

The initiation phase

The protein synthesis process is triggered under the influence of initiation factors existing in the cytoplasm, and, especially, the m_{RNA}, which contains an initiation codon Uracil-Guanine-Adenine (UGA), which is fixed on the 40S ribosomal subunit. On the initiation codon is fixing the initiation t_{RNA}, which is containing the initiation anticodons (sequence complementary codon UGA) and carries the emtionina. The t_{RNA} initiation is carried at the P-site P-peptidyl from the 60S subunit (Haulica, 1997).

The elongation phase

On the codone that follows the initaiting one, is fixing itself the corresponding t_{RNA} which is bringing the first aminoacid from the proteic sequence, and positioning itself on an second site (A) from the 60S subunit. When two t_{RNA} molecules are fixed on the ribosome, is acting a ribosomal transpeptidase which is transferring the formilmetioninic residue from the P site t_{RNA} on the A site t_{RNA}, forming a dipeptidil-t_{RNA} is. Then, through a phenomenon of translocation, during which the ribosome dipeptidil-t_{RNA} is and moving in opposite directions on the distance of a codon, dipeptidil reach the site of P-t_{RNA}, and the site of, remained open, it's loaded with fixed t_{RNA} the second amino acid sequence. By repeating the process, to add new amino acids, in accordance with the code sent. The process described is carried out based on energy supplied by ATP and GTP, and elongation of existing factors in the cytoplasm (Haulica, 1997).

The terminal phase

Is triggered by m_{RNA} termination codon (UGA or UAA), reached the site of the codon A. t_{RNA} is not fixed, but protein termination. At this point, unlink transpeptidase peptide chain composed of the last t_{RNA}. Peptide passes into the cytoplasm, being separated into ribosomal subunits (Haulica, 1997).

Based on bio-physiological processes described above, we have developed the following model for the systemic process of protein synthesis in the neuronal cell (fig.4), where:

DNA = deoxyribonucleic acid

m_{RNA} = messenger ribonucleic acid

t_{RNA} = transfer ribonucleic acid

r_{RNA} = ribosomal ribonucleic acid

In the cytoplasm, the conservation equations for t_{RNA} and m_{RNA} mass will be:

$$\frac{dM_{RNA_t}}{dt} = Q_{RNA_{tP}} + Q_{RNA_{tL}} - Q_{RNA_{tD}} - Q_{RNA_{tAMP}} \tag{2.1.12}$$

$$\frac{dM_{RNA_m}}{dt} = Q_{RNA_{mp}} + Q_{RNA_{mL}} - Q_{RNA_{mD}} - Q_{RNA_{mR}} \tag{2.1.13}$$

Where:

M_{RNAm}, M_{RNAt} = mass of m_{RNA}, respectively mass of t_{RNA};

Q_{RNAmP}, Q_{RNAtP} = m_{RNA} flows, respectively t_{RNA} flows, coming from the nucleus into the cytoplasm through nuclear pores;

Q_{RNAmL}, Q_{RNAtL} = m_{RNA} flows, and that t_{RNA}, which are in free state in the cytoplasm;

Q_{RNAmD}, Q_{RNAtD} = m_{RNA} flows, and that t_{RNA}, degraded citosolic nuclease;

Q_{RNAmR} = flow mRNA, ribosomal binding sites linked in t_{RNA};

$Q_{RNAtAMP}$ = = flow, which combined with amino-AMP-synthetase complex, forming a complex amino acid-activated tRNA (Dabu, 2001)

When the cell is in rest, we have:

$$\frac{dM_{RNA_m}}{dt} = 0 \tag{2.1.14}$$

$$0 = Q_{RNA_{m_P}} + Q_{RNA_{m_L}} - Q_{RNA_{m_D}} - Q_{RNA_{m_R}} \tag{2.1.15}$$

$$\frac{dM_{RNA_t}}{dt} = 0 \tag{2.1.16}$$

$$0 = Q_{RNA_{t_P}} + Q_{RNA_{t_L}} - Q_{RNA_{t_D}} - Q_{ARN_{tAMP}} \tag{2.1.17}$$

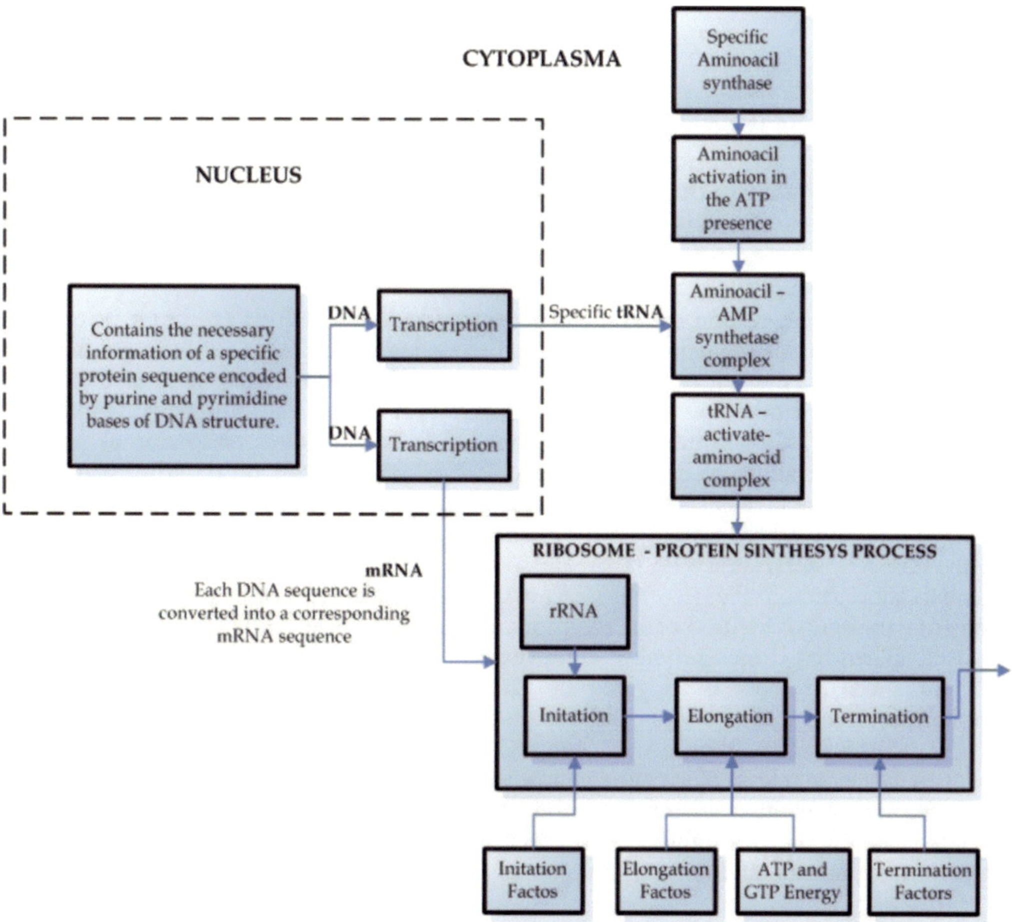

Fig. 4. The multi-compartmental model of protein synthesis process in the neuronal cell

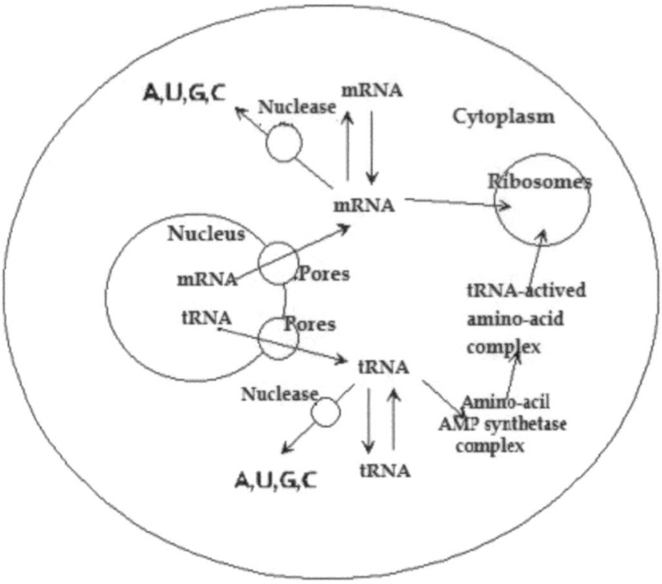

Fig. 5. Chart status for tRNA and mRNA in the neuronal cell

3.2 Modeling the behavior of Ca^{2+} ions as second messengers

The dynamical model for the Ca^{2+} regulation is nonlinear and the analysis of this process behavior request specific algorithms and tools. MatLab and Simulink offer adequate tools and algorithms for modeling these kind of processes.

In a neuronal cell in resting state, Ca^{2+} concentration is maintained at values below 10^{-7} mol/l, because the existing balance between influx and efflux of Ca^{2+}. Ca^{2+} influxes that may come from outside the cell by IL-type channels, the ISA, the messengers I, or G protein receptor complex or other messengers (cAMP, cGMP, IP4). Another source is the influx of Ca^{2+} stores in cell Ca^{2+} bound in the mitochondria or reticulum endo (sarco) plasma. Increasing concentrations of free cytoplasmic Ca^{2+} is compensated (in the idle state of the cell) by effluxes equivalent achievement either to exter (pump ATPase Ca^{2+} receptor-operated and how other messengers II system and antiport third Na^+/Ca^{2+}) or to deposits (by the Ca^{2+} ATPase) (Haulica 1997).

Cell activation through the occurrence of an action potential (AP) or through the coupling action of a messenger I with specific receptors, stimulates the Ca^{2+} influx and mobilization of deposits. When the concentration of cytoplasmic free Ca^{2+} exceeds the threshold value of 10^{-5} mol/l, cell response is triggered by Ca^{2+} as second messenger. Depending on the receptors involved in the process and the path followed, cell responses may get different aspects: the degradation of cAMP and cGMP, the formation of cGMP and cAMP, glycogenolysis, the release of synaptic neuromediators, protein synthesis, etc.

The effects of activation of other second messengers, Ca^{2+}-CaM complex, modulatory activated creates the possibility of two or more lines of receptor-activated intracellular signaling a significant effect on the final pool of the cell response (Rousset et al. 2003)

3.2.1 Modeling the behavior of neuronal Ca^{2+} when cell is in rest

When the cell is at rest, free cytoplasmic Ca^{2+} concentration is maintained at values below 10^{-7} mol/l, and the system is described by the following equation (Dabu, 2001):

$$\begin{cases} \dfrac{d[Ca_L^{2+}]}{dt} = Q_{Ca^{2+}I_L} + Q_{Ca^{2+}I_{SA}} + Q_{Ca^{2+}Msg_I} + Q_{Ca^{2+}G} + Q_{Ca^{2+}Mit} + Q_{Ca^{2+}RE} - \\ \qquad - Q_{Ca^{2+}EATP} - Q_{Ca^{2+}LATP} \end{cases} \tag{2.2.1}$$

Where:
$[Ca^{2+}{}_L]$ = concentration of free Ca^{2+} in nerve cell cytoplasm in a state of rest;
$Q_{Ca^{2+}IL}$ = influx of extracellular Ca^{2+} ion channels IL;
$Q_{Ca^{2+}ISA}$ = influx of extracellular free Ca^{2+} ion channels ISA;
$Q_{Ca^{2+}MsgI}$ = free extracellular Ca^{2+} influx through messengers I.
$Q_{Ca^{2+}G}$ = free extracellular Ca^{2+} influx through G protein;
$Q_{Ca^{2+}Mit}$ = flow freely from the mitochondrial Ca^{2+} deposits
$Q_{Ca^{2+}RE}$ = free flow of Ca^{2+} from the endoplasmic reticulum;
$Q_{Ca^{2+}EATP}$ = efflux by intracellular free Ca^{2+} ATPase pump;
$Q_{Ca^{2+}LATP}$ = intracellular free Ca^{2+} flux through the ATPase of caught and stored Ca^{2+} in mitochondria

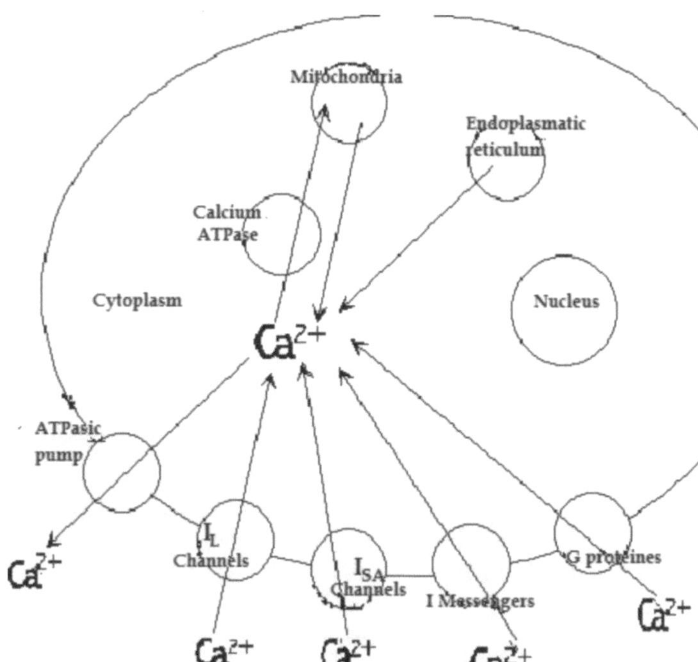

Fig. 6. The states chart for Ca^{2+} inside the neuronal cell in rest state

3.2.2 The cellular response modeling

Ca^{2+} acts as a messenger II in activating the cellular response when the neuronal cell is activated either by the occurrence of an action potentialor after coupling a messenger I with a specific receptor and the concentration of Ca^{2+} free in the cytoplasm exceeds the threshold value of about 10^{-5} mol/l. At the occurrence of an action potential in the neuronal cell as result of releasing the synaptic mediator in the synaptic space, the membrane depolarization at terminal button level stopes the penetration of Na^+ from outside the cell and generate the increasing of Ca^{2+} influx inside the cell.

The ions penetrate from the extracellular environment through two kinds of channels:

1. voltage-dependent Na^+ channels opened by action potential
2. voltage-dependent ionic channels, which are opened with a certain delay.

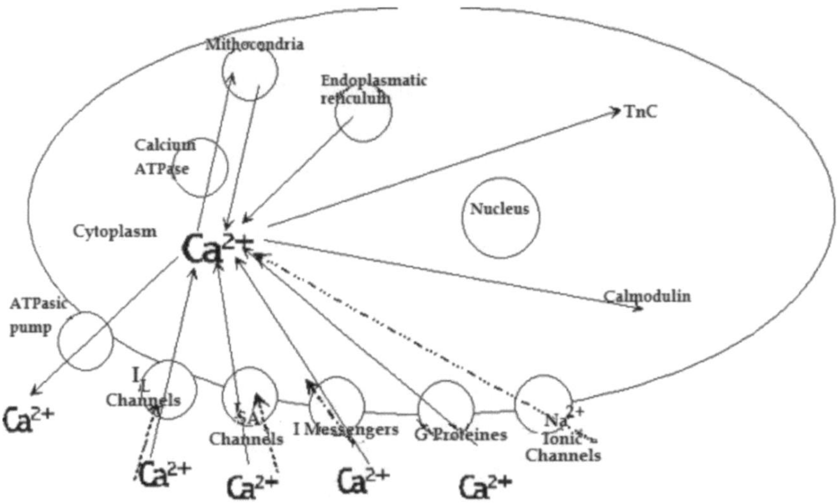

Fig. 7. States diagram for the free Ca^{2+} as cell reponse initiator in the activated neuronal cell cytoplasm

$$\begin{cases} \frac{d[Ca_L^{2+}]}{dt} = Q_{Ca^{2+}I_L} + Q_{Ca^{2+}I_{SA}} + Q_{Ca^{2+}Msg_I} + Q_{Ca^{2+}G} + Q_{Ca^{2+}Mit} + Q_{Ca^{2+}RE} + \\ \quad + Q_{Ca^{2+}Na^+} - Q_{Ca^{2+}EATP} - Q_{Ca^{2+}LATP} - Q_{Ca^{2+}Cmd} - Q_{Ca^{2+}TnC} \\ \frac{d[Ca_L^{2+}}{dt} \geq 0{,}99 * 10^{-5} \end{cases} \quad (2.2.2)$$

Where:

$[Ca^{2+}{}_L]$ = free concentration of the nerve cell cytoplasm in rest state;

$Q_{Ca^{2+}IL}$ = influx of extracellular Ca^{2+} ion channels IL;

$Q_{Ca^{2+}ISA}$ = influx of extracellular free Ca^{2+} ion channels ISA;

$Q_{Ca^{2+}MsgI}$ = free extracellular Ca^{2+} influx through Messengers I channels.

$Q_{Ca^{2+}G}$ = free extracellular Ca^{2+} influx through G protein channels;

$Q_{Ca^{2+}Mit}$ = flow freely from the mitochondrial Ca^{2+} deposits

$Q_{Ca^{2+}RE}$ = free flow of Ca^{2+} from the endoplasmic reticulum;

$Q_{Ca^{2+}EATP}$ = efflux by intracellular free Ca^{2+} ATPase pump;

$Q_{Ca^{2+}LATP}$ = intracellular free Ca^{2+} flux through the Ca^{2+} ATPase of captured and stored in mitochondria Ca^{2+};

$Q_{Ca^{2+}Na^+}$ = Ca^{2+} influx through voltage-dependent Na^+ channels opened by action potential

$Q_{Ca^{2+}Cmd}$ = free flow of cytoplasmic Ca^{2+} which combines with Calmodulin

$Q_{Ca^{2+}TnC}$ = free flow of cytoplasmic Ca^{2+}, which combine with TnC

In order to developing the model in SIMULINK, in order to describe the behavior of intracellular Ca^{2+} as messenger II, the following things were considered:

- description of the biological process
- analysis of a great number of lab tests regarding the behavior of Ca^{2+} , including:

The models that were built are characterized by the fact that, for input data that is similar (from the point of view of equivalence with the real world) to measurable input data for the real system in laboratory conditions, the output data, from point of view of values and evolution in time, was very close to the experimental data obtained from the lab tests.

Also, the obtained models have been verified, to establish their validity and adjustments were made where it was required, for a higher fidelity of the models.

The models were developed with MATLAB 4.2 for Windows and SIMULINK 1.3. In their development, the following were considered:

1. Intracellular Ca^{2+} is one of the most important messengers II, having a decisive role in secretion, motility, intermediary metabolism, cellular division, and cell death;
2. Intracellular Ca^{2+} concentration is very important in information processing at neuronal level;
3. The mechanisms for regulation of Ca^{2+} distribution within a neuronal cell include mainly non-linear processes, whose kinetics depends both on time and space
4. Not all the sub-systems that contribute to the regulation of intracellular Ca^{2+} concentration operate at the same rate. Some are rapid systems, while others are slow systems, with delays and idle periods;
5. Research demonstrated the existence of more Ca^{2+} transport sub-systems at neuronal level: mitochondrial sub-system, endo(sarco)plasmatic reticulum sub-system, ionic channels transportation, Ca^{2+} ATPases transportation and transport through Na^{+}/Ca^{2+} ion exchangers
6. Laboratory tests carried out on mouse hippocampus cells demonstrated that, following and action potential, intracellular Ca^{2+} concentration could reach the value of 1mM, while, at rest, intracellular Ca^{2+} concentration is about 0.1 mM. Laboratory tests analysis, performed with the FURA-2 system have shown that the induction of an intracellular depolarization, following 10-20 action potentials, increases the level of intracellular Ca^{2+} concentration within soma and proximal apical dendrites from 0.02-0.05 mM to 0.1-0.2 mM. The time required for the concentration level to come back to the initial value was about 100 ns. Other similar Laboratory tests analyzes have shown that the level of intracellular Ca^{2+} concentration could increase by 400-500% as a response to an electric pulse applied for 500 ms, with a comeback to the initial value period of 5 s.
7. Fluctuation of the Ca^{2+} concentration at cell level depends on:
   - the volume of the substance where the process takes place;
   - local diffusion coefficient
   - geometry of the elements and structures analyzed (Dabu,2008)

In figures 8 and 11 are presented the Simulink models for the regulation of the Ca^{2+} in the neuronal cell in rest state and activated state of the cell. The input ports are the input ionic channels and receptor sites from the neuronal membrane where signaling molecules initiate coupled sets of chemical reactions within the cellular space The output ports are the output ionic channels and the specific binding sites from the neuronal membrane where the signaling molecules are binding and initiate bio-chemical reactions outside the cell.

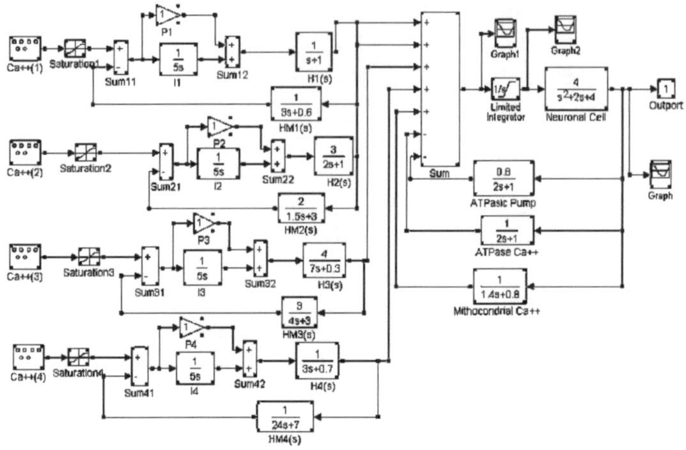

Fig. 8. The Simulink model for the regulation of the Ca^{2+} in the rest state of the neuronal cell

The results of the simulations are Presented in figures 9 and 10

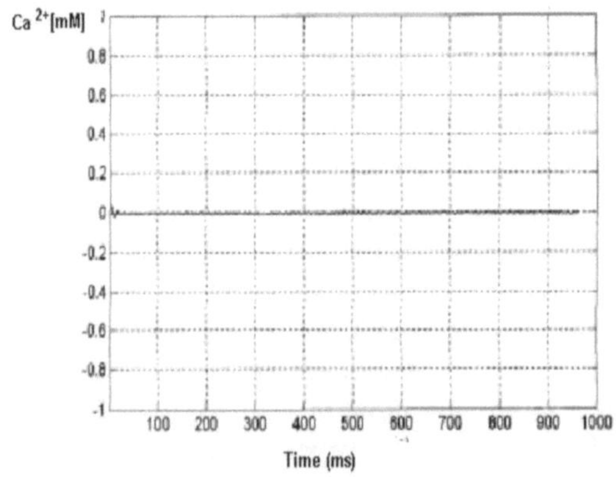

Fig. 9. Simulation results with low variation of Ca^{2+} concentration

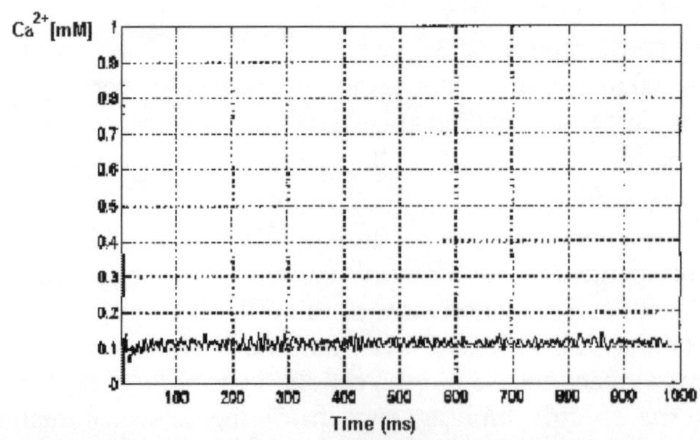

Fig. 10. Simulation results with higher variation of Ca^{2+} concentration

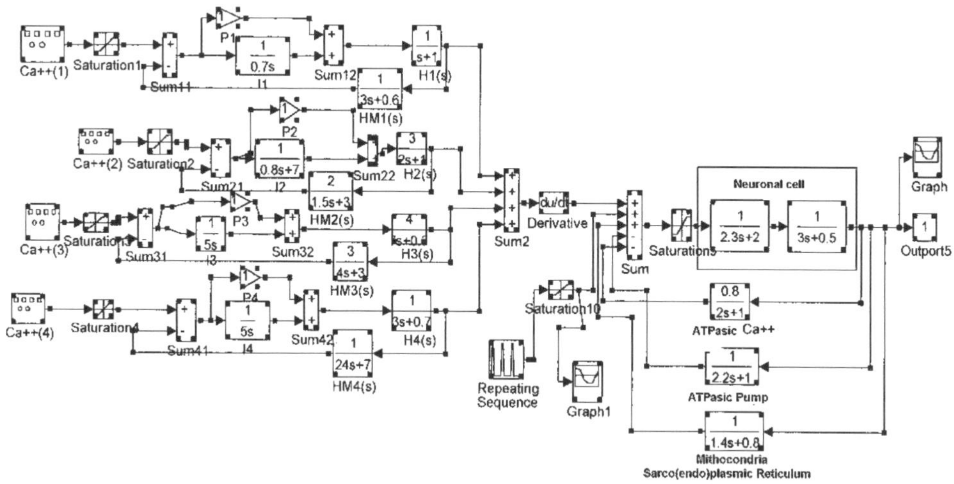

Fig. 11.The Simulink model for the regulation of the Ca^{2+} in the activate state of the cell

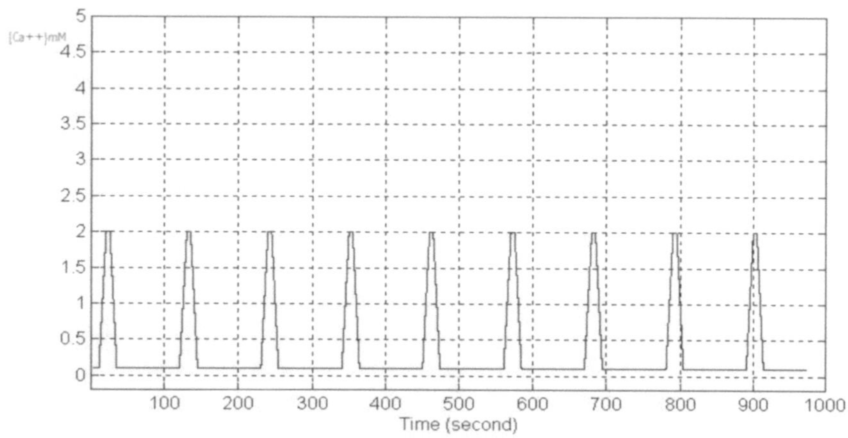

Fig. 12. Simulation for the activate neuronal cell

4. Matlab and simulink in computer assisted modeling and systemic approach for aerobic bioremediation

The aerobic bioremediation treatment process technology use special bacteria blends engineered in order to biodegrade the organic contamination (fig. 13) into harmless carbon dioxide and water, to derive energy, with no potential environmental impacts, as compared to conventional burning methods. Some of the carbon is used by bacteria as "food" to derive new carbohydrates, proteins and nucleic acids for growth. One bacteria category is initializing the process, and other bacteria families are continuing the process (figure 2). The absence of one bacteria species from the bacteria blend is diminishing the purifying capacity of the whole system .

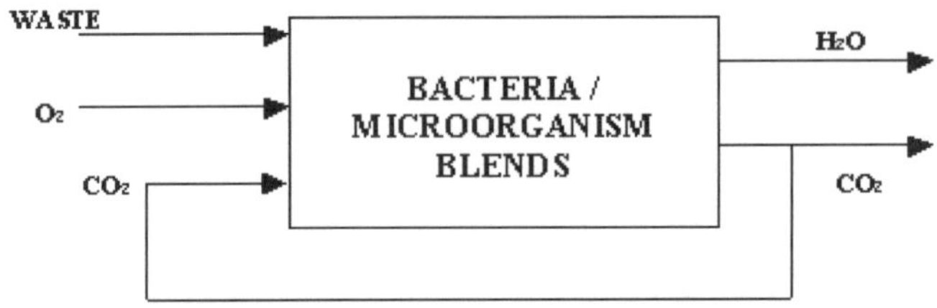

Fig. 13. The systemic model for aerobic bioremediation

For bioremediation to be effective, microorganisms must enzymatically attack the pollutants and convert them to harmless products. As bioremediation can be effective only where environmental conditions permit microbial growth and activity, its application often involves the manipulation of environmental parameters to allow microbial growth and degradation to proceed at a faster rate. The most used procedures for environmental parameters manipulation are: biosparging, bioventing, the use of oxygen releasing compounds; pure oxygen injection, hydrogen peroxide infiltration, ozone injection. All these procedure add in the contaminated area supplemental supply of oxygen which becomes available to aerobic, hydrocarbon-degrading bacteria. Like other technologies, bioremediation has its limitations. Some contaminants, such as chlorinated organic or high aromatic hydrocarbons, are resistant to microbial attack. They are degraded either slowly or not at all, hence it is not easy to predict the rates of clean-up for a bioremediation exercise. There are no rules to predict if a contaminant can be degraded (Rockne et al., 2000).

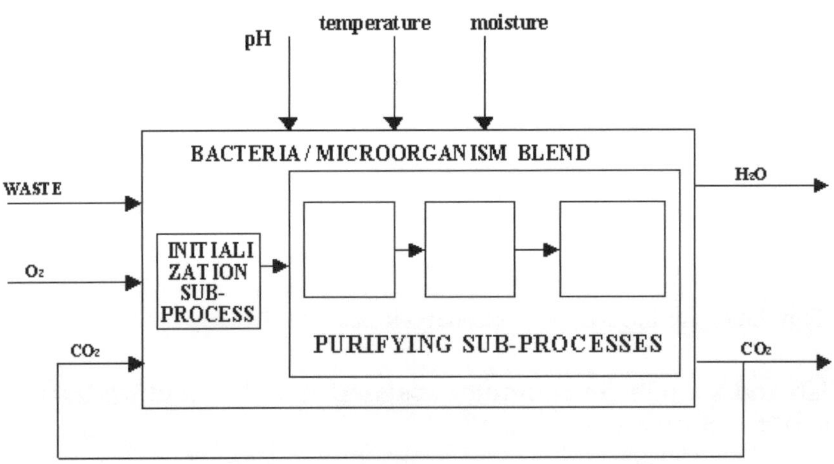

Fig. 14. The compartmental systemic model for aerobic bioremediation

Microbial growth and activity are readily affected by pH, temperature, and moisture. Temperature affects biochemical reactions rates, and the rates of many of them double for each 10°C rise in temperature. Above a certain temperature, however, the cells die. Available water is essential for all the living organisms, and irrigation is needed to achieve the optimal moisture level. The amount of available oxygen will determine whether the system is aerobic or anaerobic (fig.14)

Biomodeling using Simulink and Matlab can provide important answers regarding the mechanisms of biodegradation reactions and the evolution of degenerative capabilities in bacteria/microorganisms. They are usefully to predict the outcome of the bioprocesses and to evaluate the time and the costs of the intervention, it is necessary to create and use systemic and computer assisted mathematical models to describe the bioremediation processes (Dabu 2004).

For developing such models, it is necessary to look down the following steps:

1. Establishing the scope of the required treatment;
2. Identifying the inputs and outputs of the system;
3. Identifying the environmental parameters which affect the process and the corresponding sub-processes (bioavailability, penetration or uptake of the compounds trough the cell envelope, flow and transport, biochemical reactions, release of products);
4. Identifying the inhibitory and activator effects of different compounds or microorganism classes;
5. Identifying the compartmental systemic model of the process.
6. Identifying the transfer functions which are describing every compartment of the model and the transfer function for the entire model (Dabu & Nicu 1998, Dabu 2004).

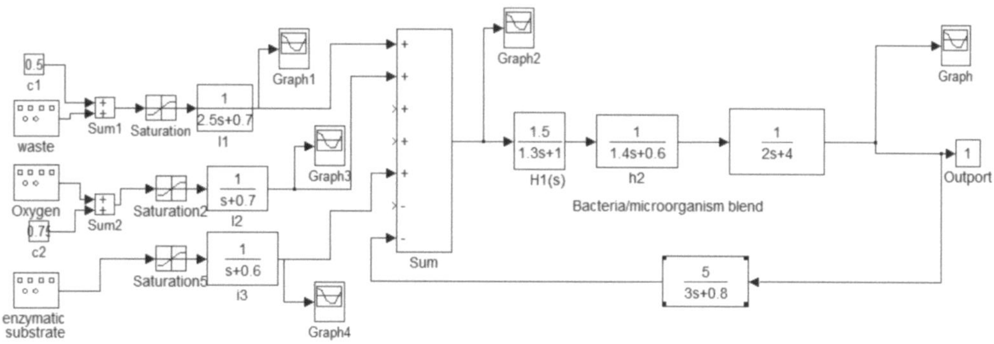

Fig. 15. The Simulink model for an anaerobic bioremediation process

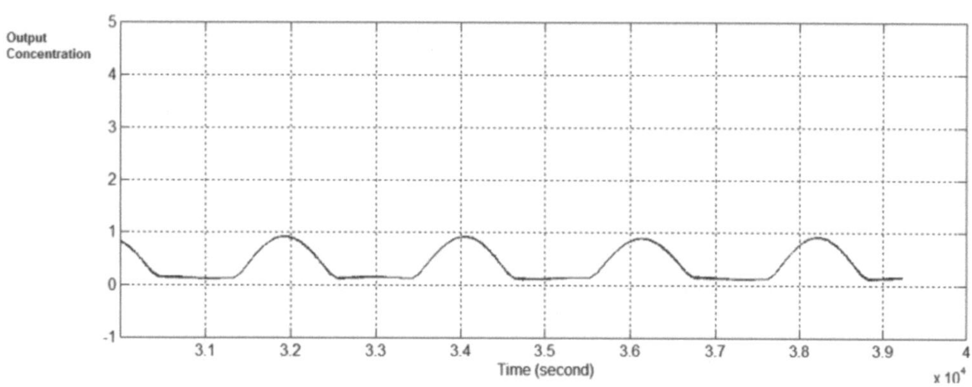

Fig. 16. The simulation output

5. References

B. N. Anderson & R. D. B. N. Anderson & R. D. Henkler. (2000). Monitoring and Control of Field Bioremediation. Biotechnology 2000:Proceedings of the 11th International Biotechnology Symposium & 18th DECHEMA Annual Meeting on Biotechnology, Berlin. Section VI, Environmental Biotechnology, pp. 403-407

Cristina - Maria Dabu, M. D. Nicu, "Environmental Biotechnologies and their Implications in Ecological Problems", Modern Biotechnologies and the Environment Protection, 1998, 130-135;

Dabu C.M. Contributions about mathematical and computer aided modeling of neuronal structures applied in radiobiology, "Politehnica" University of Bucharest, 2001, pp 5-15

Dr. Cristina -Maria Dabu,. Environmental Biotechnologies and the environment quality A.G.I.R. Bulletin, no. 4, 2004, 85-88;

Dabu C.M. Computational Models end e-Science, Dr. Eng. Cristina - Maria Dabu, E_COMM_LINE 2005 Volume, 2005, pp351-355

Jiri Dambrosky, Computer modelling of microbial hydrolytic dehalogenation, Pure &Appl. Chem., vol.70, No.7, 1998, 1375-1383;

Gonzalez Perez P.P, Modelling intracellular signalling networks using behaviour-based systems and the blackboard architecture, Universidad Nacional Autónoma de México, pp.1

Haulica, I., Fiziologie umama, Editia a II -a, Ed. Medicala , Bucuresti, 1997, pp 45-99

Heinrich, R. & Schuster, S. 1996 The regulation of cellular systems. New York: Chapman & Hall

Rockne, K. J., J. C. Chee-Sanford, R. A. Sanford, B. Hedlund, J. T. Staley, S. E. Strand (2000) Anaerobic naphthalene degradation by microbial pure cultures under nitrate-reducing conditions. Applied Environmental Microbiology. 66 (4), 1595-1601.

Matthieu Rousset, Thierry Cens, Sophie Gavarini, Andreas Jeromin, Pierre Charnet, Down-regulation of Voltage-gated Ca2_ Channels by Neuronal Calcium Sensor-1 Is _ Subunit-specific, The Journal of Biological Chemistry, Vol. 278, No. 9, Issue of February 28, pp. 7019-7026, 2003

Noble, D. 2002 Modeling the heart—from genes to cells to the whole organ. Science 295, 1678–1682. (doi:10.1126/science.1069881)

Shreedhar Maskey, Andreja Jonoski, Dimitri P. Solomatine, Groundwater Remediation Strategy Using Global Optimization Algorithms, Jourmal of Water Resources Planning and Management, 2002, 431-440;

M. Vidali, Bioremediation. An overview, IUPAC, Pure and Applied Chemistry 73, 2001, 1163–1172

21

Non Linear Algorithm for Automatic Image Processing Applications in FPGAs

Emerson Carlos Pedrino[1], Valentin Obac Roda[2] and Jose Hiroki Saito[1,3]
[1]Federal University of Sao Carlos, Department of Computer Science
[2]Federal University of Rio Grande do Norte, Department of Electrical Engineering
[3]Faculty of Campo Limpo Paulista
Brazil

1. Introduction

Mathematical morphology supplies powerful tools for low-level image analysis. The design of morphological operators for a given application is not a trivial one. For some problems in low level image processing the best result is achieved applying to the image an ordered sequence of morphological operators, that can be done manually, but is not easy and not always leads to the best solution. Genetic programming (GP) is a branch of evolutionary computing, and it is consolidating as a promising method for applications of digital image processing. The main objective of genetic programming is to discover how computers can learn to solve problems without being programmed for that. In the search for a practical automatic solution for low level image processing using mathematical morphology and genetic programming we present in this chapter a Matlab algorithm used for this purpose. Two sample images feed the Matlab application, the first one the original image with all defects, the second one the goal image where the defects of the original image were corrected. If we want to find the mathematical morphology operators that implement a certain filter that removes specific noise from the image, we supply a noisy image and an image were the noise was removed. The second image can be obtained from the noisy image applying an image manipulation program. After the parameters are supplied to the Matlab algorithm, the developed program starts to search for the sequence of morphological operators that leads to the best solution. The program works iteratively, and at each iteration compares the result of the morphological operations applied to the image set with the previous ones. To quantify how good is the solution at each iteration the resulting image is compared with the reference image using the mean absolute error (MAE) of the pixels. The best solution of the process is the image from a certain set whose error is less than a reference error indicated to the function. Using this methodology it was possible to solve a number of low level image processing problems, including edge detection, noise removal, separation of text from figures, with an error less than 0.5%, most of the time. Examples are presented along the text to clarify the use of the proposed algorithm. In addition, the sequence of operators obtained by the Matlab procedure was used to reconfigure an hardware architecture implemented in FPGAs to process images with the generated instructions in real time.

2. Theoretical background

In this section it will be presented a brief review of the theoretical background needed to understand the concepts used in the development of the current work. Firstly, it will be presented the theoretical basis of mathematical morphology followed by the fundamentals ideas of the genetic programming approach.

2.1 Mathematical morphology

Morphological image processing is a nonlinear branch in image processing developed by Matheron and Serra in the 1960´s, based on geometry, and on the mathematical theory of order (Dougherty, 1992; Serra, 1982; Weeks, 1996; Soille, 1999; Sonka et al., 1993; Facon, 1996). Morphological image processing has proved to be a powerful tool for binary and grayscale image computer vision processing tasks, such as edge detection, noise suppression, skeletonization, segmentation, pattern recognition, and enhancement. Initial applications of morphological processing were biomedical and geological image analysis problems. In the 1980´s, extensions of classical mathematical morphology and connections to other fields were developed by several research groups worldwide along various directions, including: computer vision problems, multi scale image processing, statistical analysis, and optimal design of morphological filters, to name just a few (Pedrino et al., 2010). The basic operations in mathematical morphology are the dilation and the erosion, and these operations can be described by logical and arithmetic operators. Dilation and erosion morphological operators can be represented respectively by the sum and subtraction of Minkowski sets (Dougherty, 1992):

$$A \oplus B = \cup \{B + a \mid a \in A\} \tag{1}$$

$$A \ominus -B = \cap \{A + b \mid b \in B\} \tag{2}$$

In Equation (1), A is the original binary image, B is the structuring element of the morphological operation, and B+a is the B displacement by a. Therefore, the dilation operation is obtained by the union of all B displacements in relation to the valid A elements. In Equation (2), -B is the 180º rotation of B in relation to its origin. Therefore, the erosion operation corresponds to intersection of the A displacements by the valid points of -B. According to Equation (1), the dilation operation will expand an image, and the erosion operation will shrink it. These operations are fundamental to morphological processing, and many of the existing morphological algorithms are based on these two primitives operations. These ideas can be extended to gray level image processing using maximum and minimum operators, too (Gonzalez & Woods, 2008). Many applications examples can be found in that text. In addition, color is known to play a significant role in human visual perception. The application of mathematical morphology to color images is difficult due to the vector nature of the color data. Mathematical Morphology is based on the application of lattice theory to spatial structures (Angulo & Serra, 2005). The definition of morphological operators needs a totally ordered complete lattice structure. A lattice is a partially ordered set in which any two elements have at least an upper bound (supremum) and a greatest lower bound (infimum). The supremum and the infimum are represented by the symbols $\vee$ and $\wedge$, respectively. Thus, a lattice is complete if every subset of the lattice has a single supremum and a single infimum. The application of mathematical morphology to color images is difficult due to the vector nature of the color data. The extension of concepts from grayscale morphology to color morphology must first choose an appropriate color ordering, a color space that determines the way in which colors are represented, and an infimum, and a supremum operator in the selected color space should also be defined. There are several techniques for ordering vectors. The two main approaches are marginal ordering and vector ordering. In the marginal ordering, each component P of a pixel is ordered independently, and the operations are applied to each channel; unfortunately, this procedure has some drawbacks, e.g., producing new colors that are not contained in the original image and may be unacceptable in applications that use color for object recognition. The vector ordering method for morphological processing is more advisable. Only one processing over the three dimensional data is performed using this method. There are several ways of establishing the order, e.g., ordering by one component, canonical ordering, ordering by distance and lexicographical ordering (Chanussot & Lambert, 1998). Once these orders are defined, then the morphological operators are defined in the classical way (Pedrino, 2010).

2.2 Genetic programming

Genetic programming (GP) is a technique for automatic programming nowadays and may provide a better context for the automatic generation of morphological procedures. GP is a branch of evolutionary computation and artificial intelligence, based on concepts of genetics and Darwin's principle of natural selection to genetically breed and evolve computer programs to solve problems (Koza, 1992). Genetic Programming is the extension of the genetic algorithms (Holland, 1975) into the space of programs. That is, the objects that constitute the population are not fixed-length character strings that encode possible solutions to a certain problem. They are programs (expressed as parse trees) that are the candidate solutions to the problem. There are few applications of GP for the automatic construction of morphological operators. According to Koza, in GP, populations of many computer programs are genetically bred by means of the Darwinian principle of survival and reproduction of the fittest individual in a population. In this approach, GP starts with an initial population of computer programs generated randomly, in which each program is represented by functions and terminals (operands) appropriate to a certain problem domain. Each chromosome (computer program) in the population is measured in terms of its fitness measure. This measure indicates how well a particular individual performs in a particular problem environment. The nature of the fitness depends on the problem at hand. A new offspring population of chromosomes is generated based on the current population using the Darwinian principle of reproduction and survival of the fittest, as seen before. In addition, the genetic crossover operator is used, too. The reproduction operator can copy, in proportion to a fitness, a chromosome (computer program) from current population into the new population. The crossover operator can produce new offspring computer programs from two parental chromosomes based on their fitness. Typically, the programs are of different sizes and shapes. After these process, a new population of individuals is generated and the old one is deleted. This process is repeated for many generations until a desired result can be obtained.

3. Developed system

The developed system for automatic construction of morphological operators uses a genetic programming algorithm that operates with two images from a certain image set, an input image, and an image containing only features of interest which should be extracted from the input image. The genetic procedure looks in the space of mathematical morphology operators for sequences that allow extracting the features of interest from the original image. The operators are predefined procedures from a database that work with any kind of structuring elements having different shapes and sizes. It is also possible to include new operators in the database when necessary. The program output is a tree based structure containing the best individual of the final population. The genetic algorithm parameters are supplied by the user using a text user interface. The main parameters are: tree depth, number of chromosomes, number of generations, crossover rate, mutation rate, and certain kinds of operators suited to a particular problem. The mean absolute error (MAE) was used as a fitness measure. The cost function using the MAE was calculated as follows:

$$d(a,b)=\sum_i\sum_j |(a(i,j)-b(i,j)|/XY \tag{3}$$

In Equation (3), 'a' is the resulting image evaluated by a particular chromosome (program), and 'b' is the goal image with the same size as 'a', and '(i,j)' is the pixel coordinate. The programs are encoded as tree structure chromosome. The main steps of the proposed algorithm are illustrated in Figure 1. In the Figure, the index 'i' refers to an individual in the population. The reprodution rate is 'pr', the crossover rate is 'pc', and the mutation rate is 'pm'. The goal image can be created using an editor program. As Figure 1 shows, initially the genetic parameters are selected by the user, along with a couple of sample images that represent the problem to be solved. Then, the genetic procedure generates a random population of computer programs (chromosomes), according to the user specifications. A fitness value is assigned to each program, after the operations of reproduction, crossover and mutation, a new population of individuals is generated. The described evolutionary process is repeated by many generations and can be stopped according to a stop condition. The mutation operator, that was not previously discussed, simply generates an individual belonging to the space of solutions of the problem and connects it to a random point of a particular randomly chosen chromosome. Such operation is performed with a given probability.

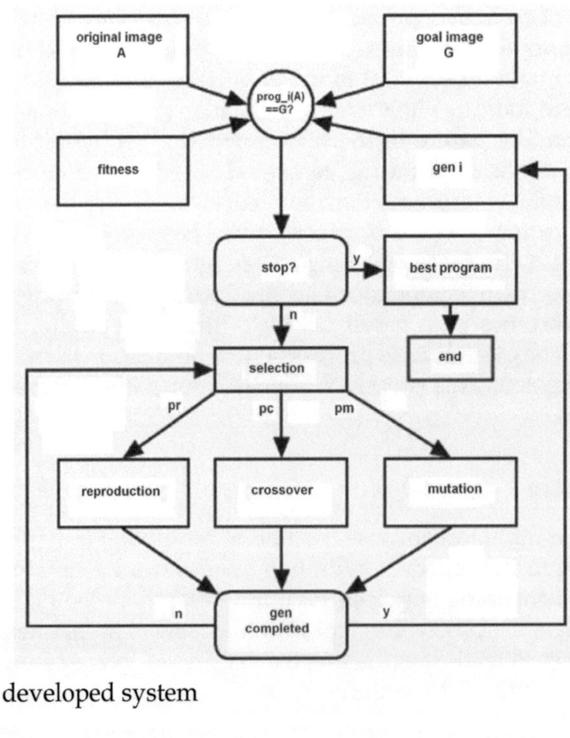

Fig. 1. Flowchart of developed system

The process of evaluating a given depth four chromosome of the population of individuals is shown in Figure 2. 'Img_in' corresponds to the input image, 'ero' and 'dil' instructions corresponds to the erosion and dilation operations respectively. The argument 'end_n' matches an address of a table containing all combinations of structuring element for a given problem. Both the instructions, and the arguments are found in an intelligent manner when a pair of input images are presented to the genetic procedure. It can be seen in Figure 2 that initially the input image is eroded, followed by two dilations and the resulting image is eroded again. All the morphological operators in the example use the same structuring element pointed by 'end_n'.

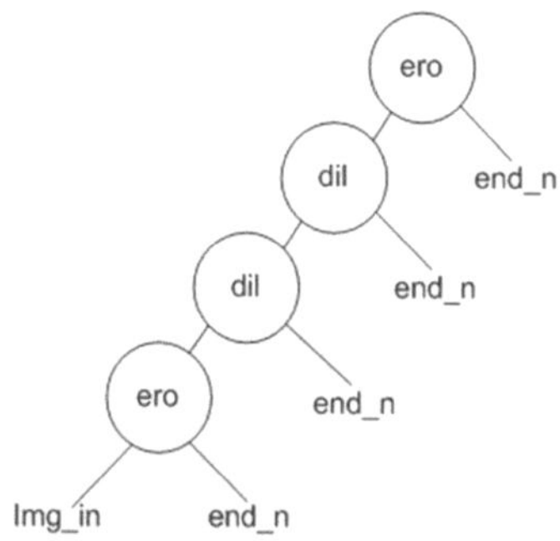

Fig. 2. Example of a chromosome representing a morphological filter and its arguments

The tournament selection method was the one chosen to be used in this work (Koza, 1992). The training set, used to extract the pair of images used in the presented method, was obtained using samples of synthetic images of various resolutions. For each resolution the maximum depth size for each chromosome tree and the error calculation functions were changed. The training will be further detailed in Section 3.1. As follows, the Matlab developed algorithm is presented along with some examples. In all the examples binary images were used, however, the method can be extended to handle any type of image.

3.1 Matlab algorithm

The Matlab algorithm for binary images mathematical morphology automatic processing developed in this work is presented as follows.

```
% - Developed Algorithm
% - pop: Initial Population
% - nc: number of chromosomes
% - cr: randomly generated chromosome
% - cr_col: columns of cr
% - num_instr: number of instructions
% - profd: maximum tree depth
% - arg: pointer to the table of arguments
pop=pop_init(nc,cr,cr_col,num_instr,profd,arg);
% - ger: generations
% - ng: number of generations
% - ct_aux: auxiliary cost
ger=0;
ct_aux=inf;
while (ger<=ng)
```

```
        % - ct_gn: costs from generation 'n'
        % - img_org: input image
        % - img_obj: goal image
        % - instr: instruction table
        ct_gn=cost(nc,pop,img_org,img_obj,instr,profd);
        % - elt: best program of generation 'n'
        % - ct_min: cost of best program
        [elt,ct_min]=elit_indv(pop,ct_gn);
        % - Elitism
        % - sol: best program found
        if (ct_min < ct_aux)
          ct_aux=ct_min;
          sol=elt;
        end
        % err: tolerated error
        if (ct_aux<=err)
          break;
        end
        % - Crossover
        % - pop_g: new population
        % - tx_cs: crossover rate
        tx_cs_conv=(-10*tx_cs/100)+10;

        pop_g=crossover(tx_cs_conv,pop,nc,img_org,img_obj,instr
,profd,sol);
        % - Mutation
        tx_mt_conv=(-10*tx_mt/100)+10;
        pop=mutation(pop_g,num_instr,profd,nc,tx_mt_conv,arg);
        ger=ger+1;
end
```

According to the previous code, the function *pop_init* is responsible for generating randomly, using user provided parameters, the initial population of individuals. The parameters are described as follows.

- nc: number of chromosomes (programs);
- cr: initial chromosome user created;
- cr_col: number of columns of cr;
- num_instr: instruction number;
- profd: maximum depth tree tolerated;
- arg: pointers vector for the arguments table;

The implementation of the algorithm *pop_init* function is shown as follows. This function uses another function called *ger_cr* to generate chromosomes randomly.

```
function p_i=pop_init(nc,cr,cr_col,num_instr,profd,arg)
% Initial Population of Individuals
pop(1,1:cr_col)=cr;
for i=2:nc
        cr=gera_cr(num_instr,profd,arg);
        pop(i,:)=cr;
end
p_i=pop;
```

```
function cr=ger_cr(num_instr,profd,arg)
cr=zeros(1,profd*4);
[~,num_arg]=size(arg);
for i=1:4:profd*4
    aleat=round(rand*(num_instr-1));
    cr(i)=aleat;
    aleat=round(rand*(num_arg-1))+1;
    cr(i+1)=aleat;
    aleat=round(rand*(num_arg-1))+1;
    cr(i+2)=aleat;
    aleat=round(rand*(num_arg-1))+1;
    cr(i+3)=aleat;
end
```

The cost function is responsible for calculating the cost of each chromosome in current population of individuals. Internally, it uses two other functions, *build_op* and *comp*, the first one is responsible for building the program, according to the tree structure shown previously, and the second is responsible for calculating the fitness of chromosomes. Below, the code part related to the *cost* and *build_op* functions is presented. Following, the function *comp* is presented, too. The main parameters used for each function are the following.

- nc: number of chromosomes;
- pop: current population;
- img_org: input image;
- img_obj: goal image;
- instr: instructions vector;
- profd: maximum depth allowed to each chromosome.

The *build_op* function is responsible for the construction of each individual, using functions and arguments provided by the user through the instructions vector and by the table of arguments. The input image is applied to each program generated automatically and the *comp* function tests whether the object pixels and the image background pixels correspond to the pixels of the object and background of the goal image, thereby creating a vector containing all the costs associated to each program obtained in the present generation.

```
function c=cost(nc,pop,img_org,img_obj,instr,profd)
% - It Evaluates the Cost of Each Individual from the Current
Population
c=ones(1,nc);
for i=1:nc
    sample=build_op(instr,pop(i,:),profd,img_org);
    c(i)=comp(amostra_c,img_obj);
end
```

```
function op = build_op(instr,cr,profd,img)
% - It Builds a Program
%   to be Applied to the
%   Input Image
op=eval([char(instr(cr(1)+1)),'(','img',',',num2str(cr(2)),',
',num2str(cr(3)),',',num2str(cr(4)),')']);
```

```
aux_op=op;
% - Building
for i=5:4:profd*4
        op=eval([char(instr(cr(i)+1)),'(','aux_op',',',num2str(
cr(i+1)),',' ,num2str(cr(i+2)),',',num2str(cr(i+3)),')']);
        aux_op=op;
end


function comp_ab = comp(a,b)
% - It Compares two images (a and b)
TP=0.005;
FN=0.005;
TN=0.005;
FP=0.005;
[lin,col]=size(a);
for i=1:lin
    for j=1:col
       if b(i,j) && a(i,j)
            TP=TP+1;
       else
            if b(i,j) && ~a(i,j)
                FP=FP+1;
            else if ~b(i,j) && ~a(i,j)
                    TN=TN+1;
                else
                    if ~b(i,j) && a(i,j)
                        FN=FN+1;
                    end
                end
            end
       end
    end
end
SV=TP/(TP+FN);
SP=TN/(TN+FP);
comp_ab=1-(sqrt((1-SP)^2+(1-SV)^2))/sqrt(2);
comp_ab=1-comp_ab;
```

The *elit_indv* function returns the best current generation chromosome, the elite, and their associated cost; its parameters are the following.

- pop: current population;
- ct_gn: vector cost for the current population;

The implementation of the *elit_indv* function is shown as follows.

```
function [elt,ct_min]=elite_indv(pop,ct)
% Best Individual
[ct_min,ind]= min(ct);
elt=pop(ind,:);
```

The next function implemented was the genetic crossing (crossover), which can be seen below. Its main parameters are:

- tx_cs: crossing rate, between 0 and 1 (0 - 100%);
- pop: current population;
- nc: number of chromosomes;
- img_org: input image;
- img_obj: goal image;
- instr: instructions vector;
- profd: maximum depth allowed for each chromosome;
- sol: best chromosome (program) found so far.

The crossing is performed between two trees in the population of individuals, selected according to a given probability, user specified. The crossing method used is similar to the one implemented by Koza (Koza, 1992).

```
function
pop_g=crossover(tx_cs,pop,nc,img_org,img_obj,instr,profd,sol)
% - Crossover.
pop_g=pop;
pop_g(1,:)=sol;
pop_indv_at=2;
while (pop_indv_at<=nc)
    rd_c=round(rand*nc+.5);
    p1=pop(rd_c,:);
    rd_c=round(rand*nc+.5);
    p2=pop(rd_c,:);
    rd_c=round(rand*nc+.5);
    p3=pop(rd_c,:);
    px=[p1;p2;p3];
    % - Tournament selection.
    ct_gn=custo(3,px,img_org,img_obj,instr,profd);
    [elt,~]=elite_indv(px,ct_gn);
    % father
    p=elt;
    [~,ind_p2]=sort(ct_gn);
    % mother
    m=px(ind_p2(2),:);
    rd_num=rand*10;
    if (rd_num>tx_cs)
        ind_imp=1:4:profd*4;
        [~,c_ind_imp]=size(ind_imp);
        ind_p=ind_imp(round(rand*(c_ind_imp)+0.5));
        ind_m=ind_imp(round(rand*(c_ind_imp)+0.5));
        gen_p=p(ind_p);
        gen_m=m(ind_m);
        p(ind_p)=gen_m;
        m(ind_m)=gen_p;
        aux=round(rand*(3)+0.5);
        crt_p=ind_p+aux;
        crt_m=ind_m+aux;
        gen_p=p(crt_p:ind_p+3);
        gen_m=m(crt_m:ind_m+3);
        p(crt_p:ind_p+3)=gen_m;
```

```
            m(crt_m:ind_m+3)=gen_p;
            pop_g(pop_indv_at,:)=p;
            pop_indv_at=pop_indv_at+1;
            if (~rem(nc,2))
                pop_g(pop_indv_at,:)=m;
                pop_indv_at=pop_indv_at+1;
            end
        else
            pop_g(pop_indv_at,:)=p;
            pop_indv_at=pop_indv_at+1;
            if (~rem(nc,2))
                pop_g(pop_indv_at,:)=m;
                pop_indv_at=pop_indv_at+1;
            end
        end
    end
```

- The mutation function swaps parts of the selected programs, according to a given probability, with parts of programs belonging to the space of solutions of a given problem; its parameters are shown as follows.
- pop: current population;
- num_instr: number of instructions;
- profd: maximum depth allowed for each chromosome;
- nc: number of chromosomes;
- tx_mt: mutation rate, between 0 and 1 (0 - 100%);
- arg: pointers vector for the argument table.

```
function pop_g=mutation(pop,num_instr,profd,nc,tx_mt,arg)
% Mutation.
[~,num_arg]=size(arg);
pop_g=pop;
for i=1:nc
    for j=1:4:profd*4
        rd_num=rand*10;
        if (rd_num>tx_mt)
            rd=round(rand*(num_instr-1));
            pop_g(i,j)=rd;
        end
        rd_num=rand*10;
        if (rd_num>tx_mt)
            rd=round(rand*(num_arg-1))+1;
            pop_g(i,j+1)=rd;
        end
        rd_num=rand*10;
        if (rd_num>tx_mt)
            rd=round(rand*(num_arg-1))+1;
            pop_g(i,j+2)=rd;
        end
        rd_num=rand*10;
        if (rd_num>tx_mt)
            rd=round(rand*(num_arg-1))+1;
```

```
                pop_g(i,j+3)=rd;
            end
        end
    end
```

3.2 Application examples

In this subsection some application examples, using the algorithm described in the previous subsection, are presented. All examples are for binary images and use equations 1 and 2 shown in subsection 2.1. A synthetic image containing four objects with different shapes was generated for implementation of the examples. The training set consisted of three samples with different resolutions for each picture object. In addition, they were used three different maximum allowed sizes for each tree size, representing the chromosomes. Also, in each case the algorithm was run three times. In the first example, it was tried to find a combination of morphological filters and logical operators to recognize the star present in the input image (Figure 3). In this figure it is possible to see the desired image and the training process. The error found for this example was zero. Other training pairs were used through the training set also resulting in errors very close to zero. For this example the following genetic parameters and arguments were used.

ng=50,
nc=500,
tx_cs=90%,
tx_mt=10%,
arg=[1 2 3 4 5 6 7 8],
tb_arg=[0 0 0;0 0 1;0 1 0;0 1 1;1 0 0;1 0 1;1 1 0; 1 1 1].

The 'arg' vector pointers to 'tb_arg' that corresponds to the table of structuring elements used in the morphological operations. The instructions vector used in this example was the following:

instr={'nop' 'dil' 'ero' 'or1' 'and1' 'sto1' 'cpl'},

were:
nop means no operation;
dil corresponds to a dilation through the structuring elements contained in *tb_arg;*
ero corresponds to an erosion through the structuring elements contained in *tb_arg;*
or1 is equivalent to a logical OR operation;
and1 is equivalent to a logical AND operation;
sto1 corresponds to a storage operator of the current results in a temporary memory variable;
cpl is equivalent to a logical NOT operation.

"5 4 2 4 2 7 5 2 3 5 3 6 3 2 2 8 4 4 5 6 6 6 7
2 1 2 4 5 2 4 4 4 6 6 3 7 4 6 3 6 2 7 5 7 4 4 7
7 3 7 3 2 4 6 7 3 5 2 4 5 2 2 3 6 4 5 7 2 4 7 5
1 3 2 7 3 5 5 5 7 6 6 6 1 1 2 8 8 2 5 7 6 6 5 5
8 0 6 6 5 1 6 5 2 6 1 2 2 6 4 3 3 1 5 2 7 2 7 2
4 6 6 2 3 4 5 1 2"

Figure 4 shows the algorithm generated to recognize the star presented in the input image. The arguments are pointers to the arguments table containing the structuring elements

for the morphological operators. The generated machine code, in decimal, for the given example considering the architecture cited in this work can be seen as follows.
The above code is transferred to a FPGA dedicated processor architecture. The FPGA processor processes in real time the images from a video camera with the objective of determining the shapes intended, according to the training algorithm. The addresses for the arguments table containing the structuring elements are shown in bold characters, thus the three arguments will point to three rows of the table forming a structuring element of size 3x3, equivalent to the size used in implementing each stage of the above architecture. Using this approach it is possible to build 512 different shapes structuring elements. The numbers representing the functions are pointers to the instruction vector 'instr', whose index starts at zero, and are not represented in bold characters. Thus, for example, code 1 **6 5 2** corresponds to the instruction dil (img, [1 0 1, 1 0 0, 0 0 1]), which is a dilation of 'img' by the structuring element shown as argument. The image 'img' is obtained from the result of the previous instruction by a pipeline process, and so on.

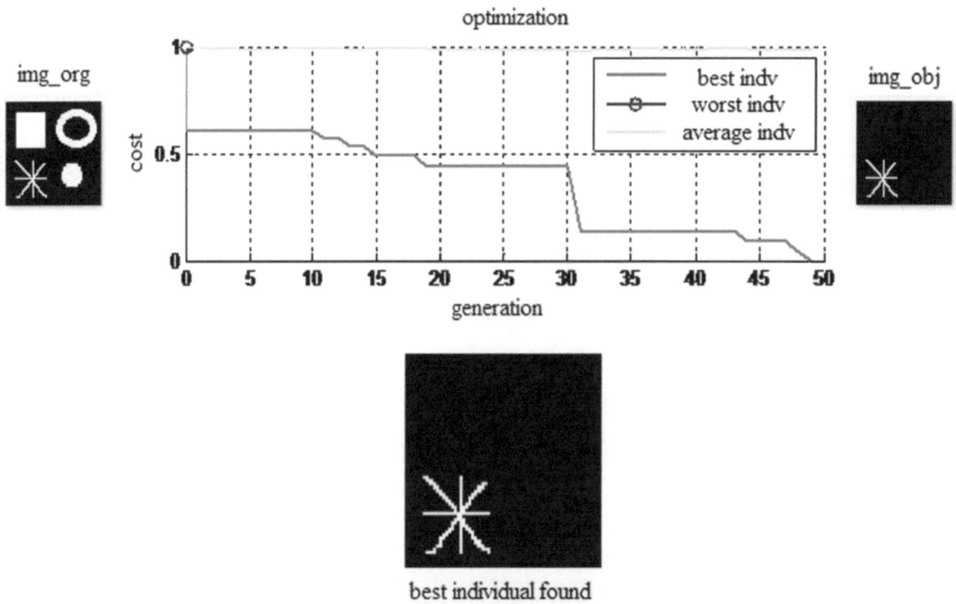

Fig. 3. Example of an automatic filter construction for recognizing the star present in the input image

Another application example obtained by the developed system, was the decomposition of an any shape structuring element in smaller size 3x3 structuring elements. For this example we used the same parameters of the previous example. The training process for the evolutionary system of the given problem is illustrated in Figure 5. A binary 17x17 size object, not decomposed by the algorithm proposed by Park and Chin (Park & Chin, 1995), could be decomposed by the proposed methodology. The process converged after iteration 300, and the error obtained was zero. The following opcode was generated for the addressed problem.

"0 7 2 5 0 1 2 4 0 5 1 2",

where the zeros correspond to successive dilations of the input image by the following structuring elements.

[1 1 0;0 0 1;1 0 0], [0 0 0;0 0 1;0 1 1], e [1 0 0;0 0 0;0 0 1]

After successive dilations of a central point by the above structuring elements, it was possible to find the object shown in Figure 5.

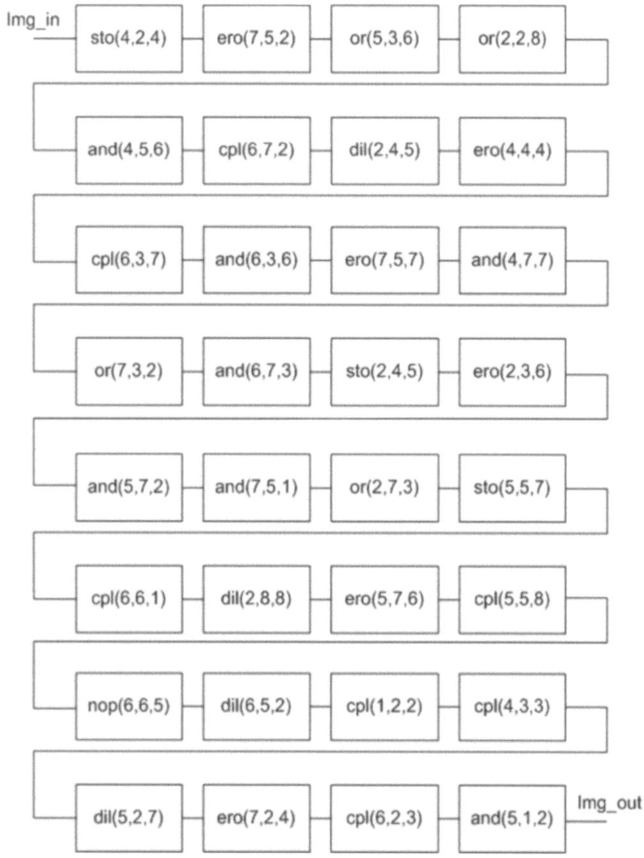

Fig. 4. Algorithm generated for the automatic pattern recognition filter construction problem shown in Figure 3

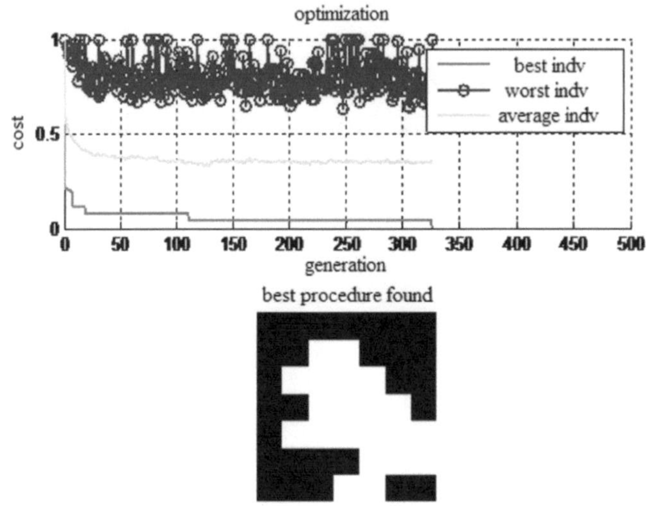

Fig. 5. Example of decomposition of a 17x17 structuring element

As mentioned earlier in this chapter, the results obtained by the aforesaid system were used to set up a FPGA implemented architecture, whose block diagram is shown in Figure 6. The architecture has several reconfigurable pipeline stages that can deal with 3x3 structuring elements. The concatenation of several stages allows operations with larger size structuring elements, whose shape can also be flexible.

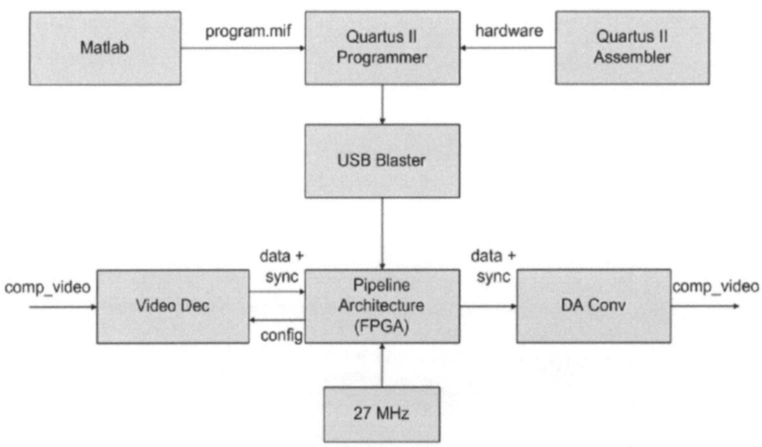

Fig. 6. Architecture used to process the programs generated by the proposed system (Pedrino et al., 2010)

4. Conclusion

The construction of a Matlab algorithm using a methodology for automatic construction of morphological and logical operators by the use of genetic programming was presented in this chapter. When presenting pairs of images to the system from a training set, a set of instructions and arguments for a given problem and appropriate genetic parameters, an evolutionary process builds a sequence of nonlinear image operators that given an input image produces an output image as close as possible to the goal image provided. The algorithm generated in this work was also used to configure a pipeline processing architecture in FPGA, capable of processing images in real time, with the images provided by a CCD video camera. Examples were shown in the text in order to demonstrate the feasibility of the developed methodology for automatic construction of image processing algorithms. The task of designing an imaging processing sequence of operators is not so trivial, so the proposed methodology might be very helpful as an aid for the expert in this situation.

5. Acknowledgments

Emerson C. Pedrino is grateful to the "Fundação de Amparo a Pesquisa do Estado de São Paulo" for the financial support of this work, thoughout the project, proc. 2009/17736-4. The authors are also grateful to the Departament of Computer Science/University Federal de São Carlos, Faculty of Campo Limpo Paulista, and to the Department of Electrical Engineering/UFRN.

6. References

Dougherty, E. R. (1992). *An Introduction to Morphological Image Processing*, SPIE, Bellingham, Wash, USA

Serra, J. (1982). *Image Analysis and Mathematical Morphology*, Academic Press, San Diego, Calif, USA

Weeks Jr., A. R. (1996). *Fundamentals of Electronic Image Processing*, SPIE, Bellingham, Wash, USA

Soille, P. (1999). *Morphological Image Analysis, Principles and Applications*, Springer, Berlin, Germany

Sonka, M., Hlavac, V. & Boyle, R. (1993). *Image Processing, Analysis and Machine Vision*, Chapman & Hall, Boca Raton, Fla, USA

Facon, J. (1996). *Morfologia Matemática: Teoria e Exemplos*, Editora Universitária da Pontifícia Universidade Católica do Paraná, Prado Velho, Brazil (In portuguese)

Pedrino, E. C., Roda, V. O. & Saito, J. H. (2010). A Genetic Programming Approach to Reconfigure a Morphological Image Processing Architecture. *International Journal of Reconfigurable Computing*, Vol.2011, pp. 712494-712503

Gonzalez, R. C. & Woods, R. E. (2008). *Digital Image Processing*. Prentice Hall, Upper Saddle River, NJ

Angulo, J. & Serra, J. (2005). Morphological Coding of Color Images by Vector Connected Filters, In: *Centre de Morphologie Mathématique*, Ecole des Mines de Paris, Paris, France

Chanussot, J. & Lambert, P. (1998). Total ordering based on space filling curves for multivalued morphology, In: *Proceedings of the 4th International Symposium on Mathematical Morphology and Its Applications*, 51–58

Koza, J. (1992). *Genetic Programming*, MIT Press, Cambridge, Mass, USA

Holland, J. (1975). *Adaptation in Natural and Artificial Systems*, MIT Press, Cambridge, Mass, USA

Park, H. & Chin, R. T. Decomposition of arbitrarily shaped morphological structuring elements, *IEEE Trans. Pattern Anal. Mach. Intell.*, Vol.17, No1, pp. 2-15

22

Using MATLAB to Compute Heat Transfer in Free Form Extrusion

Sidonie Costa, Fernando Duarte and José A. Covas
University of Minho
Portugal

1. Introduction

Rapid Prototyping (RP) is a group of techniques used to quickly fabricate a scale model of a part or assembly using three-dimensional computer aided design (CAD) data (Marsan, Dutta, 2000). A large number of RP technologies have been developed to manufacture polymer, metal, or ceramic parts, without any mould, namely Stereolithography (SL), Laminated Object Manufacturing (LOM), Selected Laser Sintering (SLS), Ink-jet Printing (3DP) and Fused Deposition Modeling (FDM).

In Fused Deposition Modelling (developed by Stratasys Inc in U.S.A.), a plastic or wax filament is fed through a nozzle and deposited onto the support (Pérez, 2002; Ahn, 2002; Ziemian & Crawn, 2001) as a series of 2D slices of a 3D part. The nozzle moves in the X-Y plane to create one slice of the part. Then, the support moves vertically (Z direction) so that the nozzle deposits a new layer on top of the previous one. Since the filament is extruded as a melt, the newly deposited material fuses with the last deposited material.

Free Form Extrusion (FFE) is a variant of FDM (Figure 1), where the material is melted and deposited by an extruder & die (Agarwala, Jamalabad, Langrana, Safari, Whalen & Danthord, 1996; Bellini, Shor & Guceri, 2005). FFE enables the use of a wide variety of polymer systems (e.g., filled compounds, polymer blends, composites, nanocomposites, foams), thus yielding parts with superior performance. Moreover, the adoption of co-extrusion or sequential extrusion techniques confers the possibility to combine different materials for specific properties, such as soft/hard zones or transparent/opaque effects.

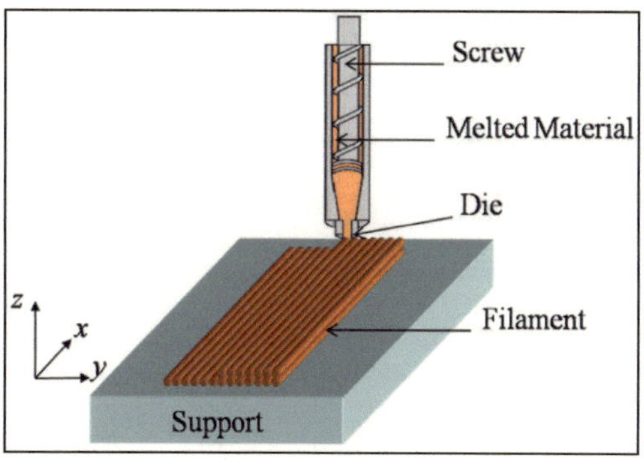

Fig. 1. Free Form Extrusion (FFE).

Due to their characteristics - layer by layer construction using melted materials - FDM and FFE may originate parts with two defects: i) excessive filament deformation upon cooling can jeopardize the final dimensional accuracy, ii) poor bonding between adjacent filaments reduces the mechanical resistance. Deformation and bonding are mainly controlled by the heat transfer, i. e., adequate bonding requires that the filaments remain sufficiently hot during enough time to ensure adhesion and, simultaneously, to cool down fast enough to avoid excessive deformation due to gravity (and weight of the filaments above them). Therefore, it is important to know the evolution in time of the filaments temperature and to understand how it is affected by the major process variables. Rodriguez (Rodriguez, 1999) studied the cooling of five elliptical filaments stacked vertically using via finite element methods and later found a 2D analytical solution for rectangular cross-sections (Thomas & Rodriguez, 2000). Yardimci and Guceri (Yardimci & S.I. Guceri, 1996) developed a more general 2D heat transfer analysis, also using finite element methods. Li and co-workers (Li, Sun, Bellehumeur & Gu, 2003; Sun, Rizvi, Bellehumeur & Gu, 2004) developed an analytical 1D transient heat transfer model for a single filament, using the Lumped Capacity method. Although good agreement with experimental results was reported, the model cannot be used for a sequence of filaments, as thermal contacts are ignored.

The present work expands the above efforts, by proposing a transient heat transfer analysis of filament deposition that includes the physical contacts between any filament and its neighbours or supporting table. The analytical analysis for one filament is first discussed, yielding an expression for the evolution of temperature with deposition time. Then, a MatLab code is developed to compute the temperature evolution for the various filaments required to build one part. The usefulness of the results is illustrated with two case studies.

2. Heat transfer modelling

During the construction of a part by FDM or FFE, all the filaments are subjected to the same heat transfer mechanism but with different boundary conditions, depending on the part geometry and deposition sequence (Figure 2).

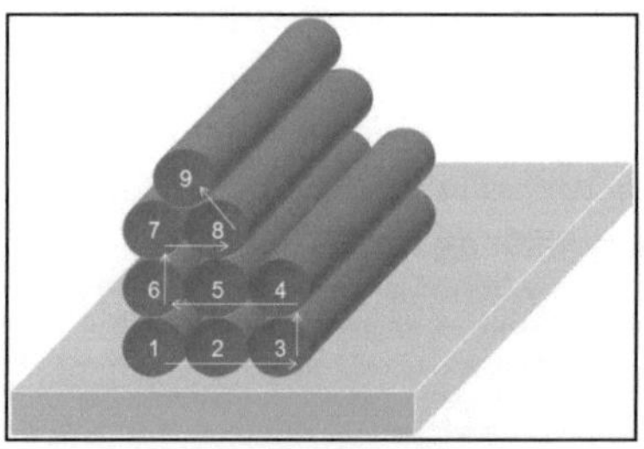

Fig. 2. Example of a sequence of filaments deposition.

Consider that N is the total number of deposited filaments and that $T_r(x,t)$ is the temperature at length x of the *r-th* filament ($r \in \{1,\ldots,N\}$) at instant t. The energy balance for an element dx of the *r-th* filament writes as:

$$\left\{\begin{array}{l} Energy\ in\ at\ one\ face - Heat\ loss\ by\ convection\ with\ surroundings \\ -Heat\ loss\ by\ conduction\ with\ adjacent\ filaments\ or\ with\ support \end{array}\right. =$$

$$= Change\ \text{in}\ internal\ energy + Energy\ out\ at\ opposite\ face$$

This can be expressed as a differential equation. After some assumptions and simplifications (Costa, Duarte & Covas, 2008):

$$\frac{\partial T_r}{\partial t} = -\frac{P}{\rho\, CA}\left(h_{conv}\left(1-\sum_{i=1}^{n} a_{r_i}\lambda_i\right)(T_r - T_E) + \sum_{i=1}^{n} h_i a_{r_i}\lambda_i\left(T_r - T_{r_i}\right)\right) \tag{1}$$

where P is filament perimeter, ρ is density, C is heat capacity, A is area of the filament cross-section, h_{conv} is heat transfer coefficient, n is number of contacts with adjacent filaments or with the support, λ_i is fraction of P that in contact with an adjacent filament, T_E is environment temperature, h_i is thermal contact conductance for contact i ($i \in \{1,...,n\}$) and T_{r_i} is temperature of the adjacent filament or support at contact i ($r_i \in \{1,...,N+1\}$, $r_i \neq r$, $T_1,\ldots, T_N$ are temperatures of filaments, T_{N+1} is support temperature). In this expression, variables a_{r_i} are defined as (see Figure 3):

$$a_{r_i} = \begin{cases} 1 & \text{if the } r-th \text{ filament has the } i-th \text{ contact} \\ 0 & \text{otherwise} \end{cases}, \forall i \in \{1,...,n\}, \forall r \in \{1,...,N\} \tag{2}$$

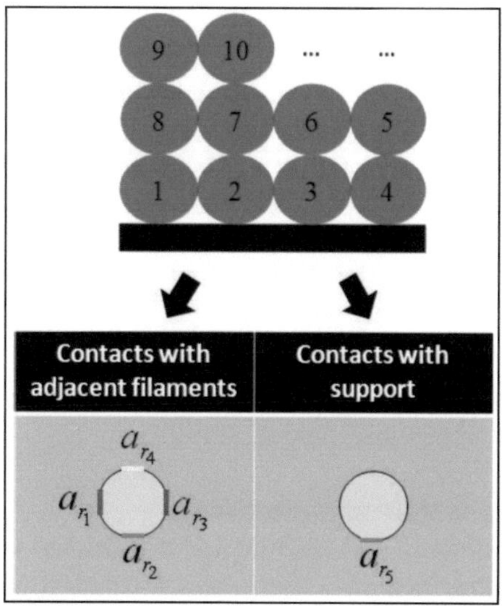

Fig. 3. Contact areas of a filament (n = 5).

Considering that:

$$\begin{cases} b\left(a_{r_1},...,a_{r_n}\right) = h_{conv}\left(1-\sum_{i=1}^{n} a_{r_i}\lambda_i\right) + \sum_{i=1}^{n} a_{r_i} h_i \lambda_i \\ Q\left(a_{r_1},...,a_{r_n}\right) = \dfrac{h_{conv}\left(1-\sum_{i=1}^{n} a_{r_i}\lambda_i\right)T_E + \sum_{i=1}^{n} a_{r_i} h_i \lambda_i T_{r_i}}{b\left(a_{r_1},...,a_{r_n}\right)} \end{cases} \tag{3}$$

equation (1) can be re-written as:

$$\frac{\rho VC}{PL\ b\left(a_{r_1},...,a_{r_n}\right)}\frac{\partial T_r(t)}{\partial t}+T_r(t)=Q\left(a_{r_1},...,a_{r_n}\right) \tag{4}$$

Since the coefficients are constants, the characteristic polynomial method can be used to yield the solution:

$$T_r(t)=\left(T_{r0}-Q\left(a_{r_1},...,a_{r_n}\right)\right)\ e^{\frac{-PL\ b\left(a_{r_1},...,a_{r_n}\right)}{\rho VC}(t-t_r)}+Q\left(a_{r_1},...,a_{r_n}\right) \tag{5}$$

In this expression, t_r is the instant at which the *r-th* filament starts to cool down or contact with another filament and $T_{r0}=T_r(t_r)$ is the temperature of the filament at instant t_r. Taking k as thermal conductivity, the Biot number can be defined (Bejan, 1993):

$$Bi=\frac{A}{P}\frac{b\left(a_{r_1},...,a_{r_n}\right)}{k} \tag{6}$$

When Bi is lower than 0.1, the filaments are thermally thin, i.e., thermal gradients throughout the cross section can be neglected. In this case, Eq. (5) becomes:

$$Bi\le 0.1\Rightarrow T_r(t)=\left(T_{r0}-Q\left(a_{r_1},...,a_{r_n}\right)\right)\ e^{\frac{-PL\ b\left(a_{r_1},...,a_{r_n}\right)}{\rho VC}(t-t_r)}+Q\left(a_{r_1},...,a_{r_n}\right) \tag{7}$$

3. Computer modelling

Equations (5) and (7) quantify the temperature of a single filament fragment along the deposition time. In practice, consecutive filament fragments are deposited during the manufacture of a part. Thus, it is convenient to generalize the computations to obtain the temperature evolution of each filament fragment at any point x of the part, for different deposition techniques and 3D configuration structures.

3.1 Generalizing the heat transfer computations

Up-dating the thermal conditions: The boundary conditions must be up-dated as the deposition develops. The code activates the physical contacts and redefines the boundary conditions for a specific filament position, time and deposition sequence. For all the filaments, three variables need to be up-dated:

- time t_r (TCV-1): instant at which the *r-th* filament starts cooling down, or enters in contact with another filament;
- temperature T_{r0} (TCV-2): temperature at t_r;
- -vector a_{ri} (TCV-3): in Eq. (3), sets in the contacts for the *r-th* filament ($i\in\{1,...,n\}$, where n is the number of contacts).

Simultaneous computation of the filaments temperature: During deposition, some filaments are reheated when new contacts with hotter filaments arise; simultaneously, the latter cool down due to the same contacts. This implies the simultaneous computation of the filaments temperature via an iterative procedure. The convergence error was set at $\varepsilon = 10^{-3}$, as a good compromise between accuracy and the computation time.

Deposition sequence: The deposition sequence defines the thermal conditions TCV-1, TCV-2 and TCV-3. Three possibilities were taken in: unidirectional and aligned filaments, unidirectional and skewed filaments, perpendicular filaments (see Figure 4). In all cases, the filaments are deposited continuously under constant speed (no interruptions occur between successive layers).
Some parts with some geometrical features may require the use of a support material, to be removed after manufacture. This possibility is considered in the algorithm for unidirectional and aligned filaments.

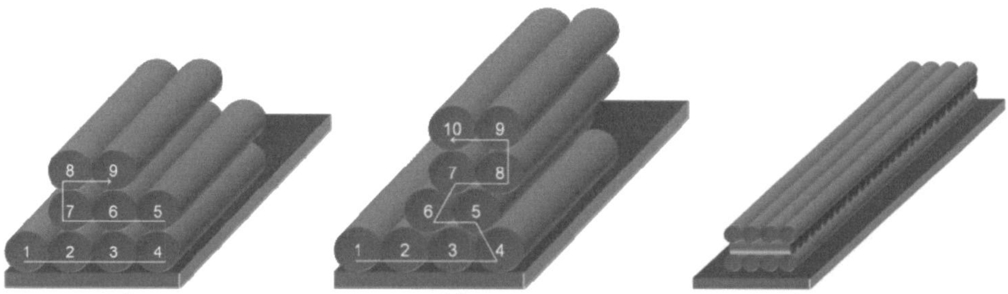

a) b) c)

Fig. 4. Deposition sequences: a) unidirectional and aligned filaments; b) unidirectional and skewed filaments; c) perpendicular filaments.

3.2 Computing the temperatures

The computational flowchart is presented in Figure 5 and a MatLab code was generated. In order to visualize the results using another software (Excel, Tecplot...), a document in *txt* format is generated after the computations, that includes all the temperature results along deposition time.

4. MatLab code for one filament layer

In order to illustrate how the MatLab code "*FFE.m*" was implemented, the segment dealing with the temperature along the deposition time for the first layer of filaments, using one or two distinct materials, is presented here. The code has the same logic and structure for the remaining layers.

4.1 Input variables

Two arguments need to be introduced in this MatLab function:

- A matrix representing the deposition sequence, containing *m* rows and *n* columns, for the number of layers and maximum number of filaments in a layer, respectively. Each cell is attributed a value of 0, 1, or 2 for the absence of a filament, the presence of a filament of material A or of a filament of material B, respectively. An example is given in Figure 6.
- The vertical cross section of the part (along the filament length) where the user wishes to know the temperature evolution with time.

The code includes one initial section where all the variables are defined (Figure 7), namely environment and extrusion temperatures, material properties, process conditions, etc. The dimensions of all matrixes used are also defined.

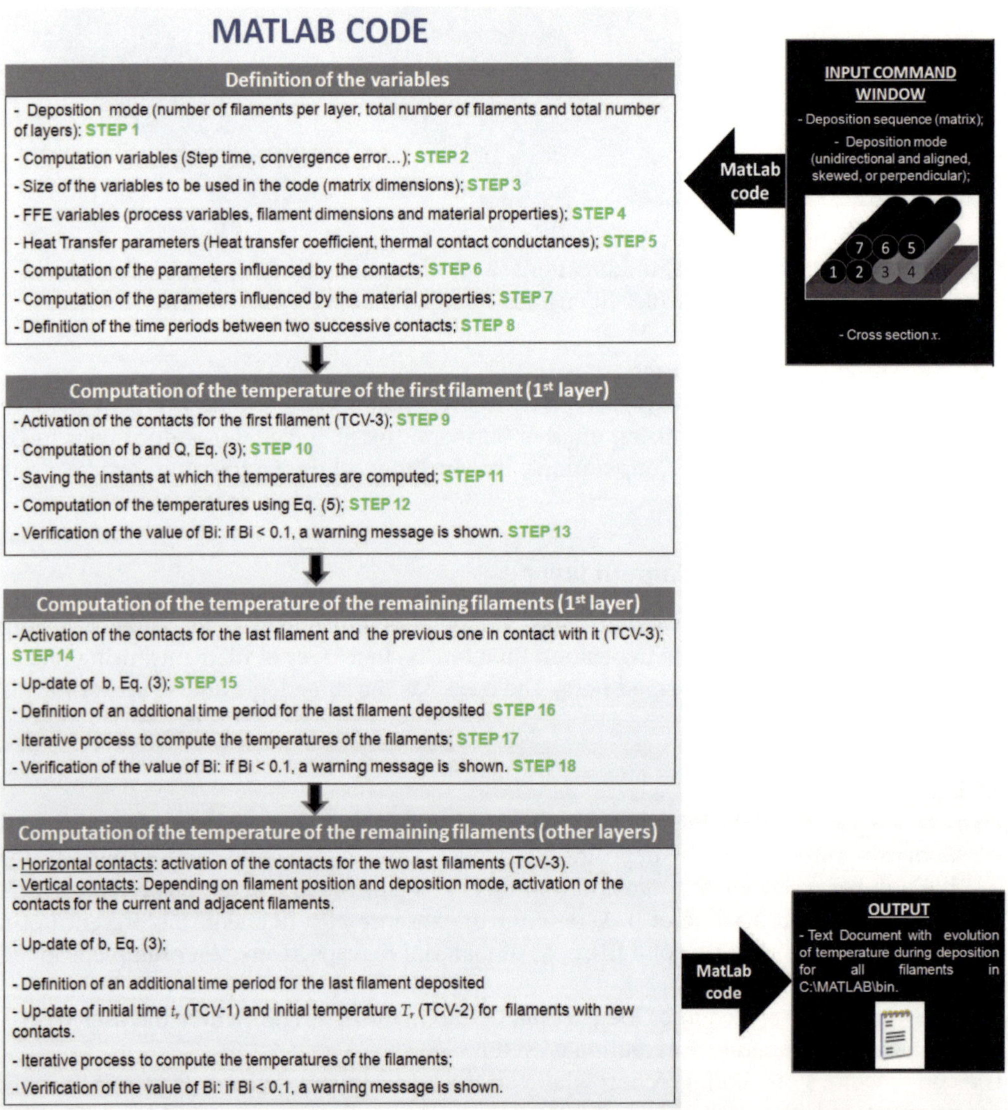

Fig. 5. General procedure to compute all the temperatures.

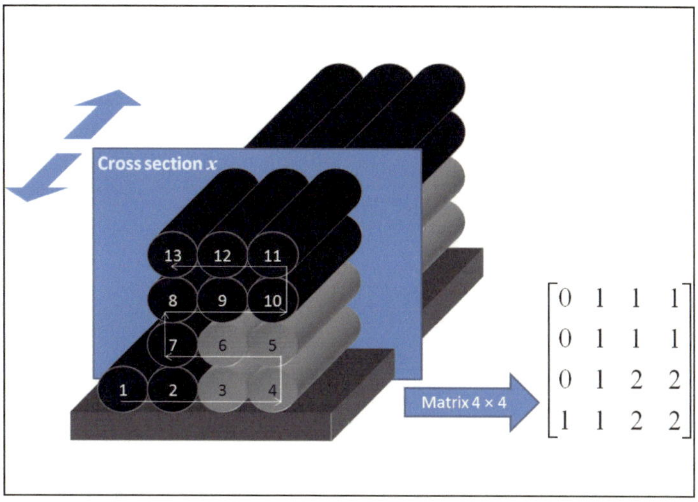

Fig. 6. Example of deposition sequence and corresponding input matrix.

```
function FFE(matrix,x)

%_____________________________________ STEP 1 _____________________________________
%Definition of the vector that contains the number of total filaments in each layer
matrix_lin = size(matrix,1);
matrix_col = size(matrix,2);
vector = zeros(matrix_lin,2);
contar = 0;
for i = matrix_lin:-1:1
   contar = contar + 1;
   for j = 1:matrix_col
      if matrix(i,j) ~= 0
         vector(contar,1) = vector(contar,1) + 1;
      end
   end
end
%Number of layers
m = length(vector(:,1));
%Number of filaments
n = 0;
for j = 1:m
   if m == 1
      n = vector(1,1);
   else
      if vector(j,2) <= 1
         n = n + vector(j,1);
      end
   end
end

%_____________________________________ STEP 2 _____________________________________
%Computation variables
passo = 0.05;         %Step time
temp_mais = 15;       %Additional time computation after construction of the part
erro = 0.001;         %Convergence error
```

```
%________________________________________ STEP 3 ________________________________________
%Definition of the size of the variables
h = zeros(1,5); lambda = zeros(1,5); a = zeros(n,5); T = zeros (n,5);
vec_b = zeros(n,5); vec_Q = zeros(n,5); b = zeros(1,n); Q = zeros(1,n);
T_begin = zeros(1,n); dif = zeros(1,n); Biot = zeros(1,n); save_T = zeros(1,n);
old_T = zeros(1,n); save_lim = zeros(1,n); viz = zeros(11,n);


%________________________________________ STEP 4 ________________________________________


%Process Variables
T_L = 270;          %Extrusion temperature (°C)
T_E = 70;           %Temperature of the envelope (°C)
v = 0.02;           %Velocity of the extrusion head (m/sec)
for lin = 1:n       %Temperature of support (°C)
   T(lin,1) = T_E;
end

%Filament dimensions
w = 0.0003;             %Layer Thickness (meters)
L = 0.02;               %Length of the filament (meters)
area = pi * (w/2)^2;    %Area of the cross section of filament (meters^2)
per = pi * w;           %Perimeter of the cross section of filament (meters)
vol = area*L;           %Volume of the filament
A_p = per*L;            %Superficial area of the filament

% Material Properties

%Thermal conductivity (W/m.K)
conductivity(1) = 0.1768; % material A
conductivity(2) = 0.5;    % material B
%Density (kg/m^3)
ro(1) = 1050;             % material A
ro(2) = 1500;             % material B
%Specific heat (J/kg.K)
C(1) = 2019.7;            % material A
C(2) = 2500.7;            % material B

%________________________________________ STEP 5 ________________________________________
% Heat transfer coefficient (lost of heat by natural convection)
h_conv = 45;

%Thermal contact conductances between
h(1,1) = 200;           % filament and left adjacent filament
h(1,2) = 200;           % filament and down adjacent filament
h(1,3) = 200;           % filament and right adjacent filament
h(1,4) = 200;           % filament and top adjacent filament
h(1,5) = 10;            % filament and support

%Fraction of perimeter contact between
lambda(1,1) = 0.2;      % filament and left adjacent filament
lambda(1,2) = 0.25;     % filament and down adjacent filament
lambda(1,3) = 0.2;      % filament and right adjacent filament
lambda(1,4) = 0.25;     % filament and top adjacent filament
lambda(1,5) = 0.25;         % filament and support
```

Fig. 7. Definition of the variables.

The parameters used in Equation (5) and those necessary to compute variables b and Q (in Eq. (3)) must also be defined. Finally, the time increment between two consecutive contacts is calculated taking into consideration the type of deposition sequence (Figure 8).

```
% ___________________________________ STEP 6 ___________________________________
%Definition of the parameters influenced by the contacts
for col = 1:5
   for lin = 1:n
      vec_b(lin,col) = h(1,col)*lambda(1,col);
      vec_Q(lin,col) = vec_b(lin,col)*T(lin,col);
   end
end
```

```
% ___________________________________ STEP 7 ___________________________________
%Definition of the parameters influenced by the material properties
contar = 0;
number_filament = 0;
for i = matrix_lin:-1:1
   contar = contar + 1;
   if isodd(contar) == 1
      for j = 1:matrix_col
         if matrix(i,j) ~= 0
            number_filament = number_filament + 1;
            escalar(number_filament) = -per/(ro(matrix(i,j))*area*C(matrix(i,j)));
            esc(number_filament) = h_conv/(ro(matrix(i,j))*L*C(matrix(i,j)));
            kt(number_filament) =  conductivity(matrix(i,j));
         end
      end
   else
      for j = matrix_col:-1:1
         if matrix(i,j) ~= 0
            number_filament = number_filament + 1;
            escalar(number_filament) = -per/(ro(matrix(i,j))*area*C(matrix(i,j)));
            esc(number_filament) = h_conv/(ro(matrix(i,j))*L*C(matrix(i,j)));
            kt(number_filament) =  conductivity(matrix(i,j));
         end
      end
   end
end

% ___________________________________ STEP 8 ___________________________________
%Definition of the periods of time between two successive contacts
for i = 1:(n+2)
   if isodd(i) == 1
      limite(i,1) = (i*L-x)/v;
      limite(i,2) = (i*L+x)/v;
   else
      limite(i,1) = limite(i-1,2);
      limite(i,2) = ((i+1)*L-x)/v;
   end
end
for road = 1:n
   linha = 0;
   for i = 0:passo:limite(n,2)
      linha = linha + 1;
      temp(linha,road) = T_L;
   end
end
```

Fig. 8. Definition of the parameters to be used for the computation of temperatures and time between two consecutive contacts.

4.2 Computation of the temperatures for the first filament of the first layer

Computation of the temperatures starts with the activation of the contact between the first filament and the support. Parameters *b* and *Q* (equation (3)) are calculated (Figure 9).

The temperatures are computed at each time increment; confirmation of the value of Biot number (Eq. (6)) is also made: if greater than 0.1, the code devolves a warning message (Figure 10).

```
for layer = 1:m
   if layer == 1
      for num = 1:vector(layer,1)
         if num == 1
%_______________________________ STEP 9 _______________________________
            a(num,5) = 1;      %Activation of the contact with support

%_______________________________ STEP 10 ______________________________
           %Definition of the variables b and Q defined in equation Eq. 7
            b(num) = h_conv*(1-lambda*a(num,:)') + vec_b(num,:)*a(num,:)';
            Q(num) = (h_conv*(1-lambda*a(num,:)')*T_E +
vec_Q(num,:)*a(num,:)')/b(num);
```

Fig. 9. Activation of the contacts and computation of *b* and *Q* for the first filament.

```
%_______________________________ STEP 11 ______________________________
            p = 0;
            for t = 0:passo:limite(num,1)
               p = p+1; abcissa(p) = t;
            end

%_______________________________ STEP 12 ______________________________
           %Computation of the temperatures of the first filament
            for t = (limite(num,1)+passo):passo:limite_final
               p = p+1; abcissa(p) = t;
               temp(p,num)=(T_L-Q(num))*exp(escalar(num)*b(num)*(t-limite(num,1)))
               +Q(num);
            end
           %Saving the last temperature of the period time of cooling down
            T_begin(num) = temp(p,num);

%_______________________________ STEP 13 ______________________________
            %Verification of the value of Biot Number
            Biot(num) = (vol/A_p)*(b(num)/kt(num));
            if Biot(num)>=0.1
               'WARNING! We cannot use a Lumped System'
            End
```

Fig. 10. Computation of the temperatures for the first filament and verification of the value of the Biot number.

4.3 Computation of the temperatures for the remaining filaments of the first layer

Before proceeding to the remaining filaments of the first layer, the lateral and support contacts for each filament being deposited must be defined, as well as for the previous one. Consequently, the variable *b* in expression Eq. (3) is up-dated (Figure 11).

At this point, only the lateral and support contacts must be defined, since only the first layer is being computed. For the remaining layers, other contacts (such as the vertical ones) must be considered. Once each filament is deposited, the code checks whether the part has been completed. If so, it remains in the same conditions during a pre-defined time, in order to reach the equilibrium temperature (Figure 12).

```
%_______________________________________ STEP 14 _______________________________________
      else
         %Activation of the contacts
         a(num-1,3) = 1; a(num,1) = 1; a(num,5) = 1;

%_______________________________________ STEP 15 _______________________________________
         %Up-dating of the variable b
         for j = 1:num
            b(j) = h_conv*(1-lambda*a(j,:)') + vec_b(j,:)*a(j,:)';
         end
```

Fig. 11. Activation of the contacts for the current and previous filaments and up-dating of variable *b*.

```
%_______________________________________ STEP 16 _______________________________________
         if m == 1
            if num == vector(layer,1)
               limite_final = limite(num,2) + temp_mais;
            else
               limite_final = limite(num,2);
            end
         else
            limite_final = limite(num,2);
         end
```

Fig. 12. Definition of an additional time for the last filament.

Finally, the temperatures of the remaining filaments are computed. At each time increment, the temperatures of the adjacent filaments are saved and parameter Q (Eq. (3) is up-dated. The value of the Biot number is checked before the deposition of a new filament (Figure 13).

```
         for t = (limite(num,1)+passo):passo:limite_final
            p = p+1; abcissa(p) = t;
            last = p-1;
            for j = 1:num
               save_T(j) = temp(last,j);
            end

%_______________________________________ STEP 17 _______________________________________
            %Iterative process
            for q = 1:100000

              %Saving contacts and temperatures of adjacent filaments
               for j = 1:num
                  if j == 1
                     T(j,3) = save_T(j+1);
                     viz(3,j) = j+1;
                  end
                  if j > 1 & j < num
                     T(j,1) = save_T(j-1);
                     viz(1,j) = j-1;
                     T(j,3) = save_T(j+1);
                     viz(3,j) = j+1;
                  end
                  if j == num
                     T(j,1) = save_T(j-1);
                     viz(1,j) = j-1;
                  end
                  for k = 1:5
                     if T(j,k) ~= 0 & k ~= 5
```

```
                    vec_Q(j,k) = vec_b(j,k)*T(j,k);
                 end
              end

              %Up-dating of the variable Q
              Q(j) = (h_conv*(1-lambda*a(j,:)')*T_E +
vec_Q(j,:)*a(j,:)')/b(j);
              old_T(j) = save_T(j);
           end
          %Computation of the temperatures
           if num == 2
              save_T(1) = (T_begin(1)-Q(1))*exp(escalar(1)*b(1)*
                          (t-limite(1,1)))+Q(1);
              save_T(2) = (T_L-Q(2))*exp(escalar(2)*b(2)*(t-
limite(1,1)))+Q(2);
              save_lim(1,1) = limite(num,1);
              save_lim(1,2) = limite(num,1);
           else
              for j=1:num-2
                 save_T(j) = (T_begin(j)-Q(1))*exp(escalar(j)*b(j)*
                          (t-save_limite(1,j)))+Q(j);
              end
              save_T(num-1) = (T_begin(num-1)-Q(num-1))*
                    exp(escalar(num-1)*b(num-1)*(t-limite(num,1)))+Q(num-
1);
              save_T(num) = (T_L-Q(num))*
                    exp(escalar(num)*b(num)*(t-limite(num,1)))+ Q(num);
              save_lim(1,num-1) = limite(num,1);
              save_lim(1,num) = limite(num,1);
           end
           for j = 1:num
              dif(j) = abs(save_T(j)-old_T(j));
           end
           try = 1;
           stop = 0;
           for j = 1:num
              if dif(try) < erro
                 try = try+1;
              end
              if try == num+1;
                 stop = 1;
              end
           end
           if stop == 1
              for j = 1:num
                 temp(p,j) = save_T(j);
              end
              break;
           end
        end
     end
     T_begin(num) = temp(p,num);
     %End of iterative process

%________________________________ STEP 18 ________________________________
     %Verification of the Biot Number
     for j=1:num
        Biot(j) = (vol/A_p)*(b(j)/kt(j));
        if Biot(j)>=0.1
           'WARNING! We can not use a Lumped System'
           j
           Biot(j)
        end
     end
  end
end
```

```
    end
end
```

Fig. 13. Computation of the temperature of the filaments of the first layer and verification of the Biot number.

5. Results

In order to demonstrate the usefulness of the code developed, two case studies will be discussed. The first deals with a part constructed with two distinct materials, while the second illustrates the role of the deposition sequence.

5.1 Case study 1

Consider the small part with the geometry presented in Figure 14, to be manufactured under the processing conditions summarized in Table 1.

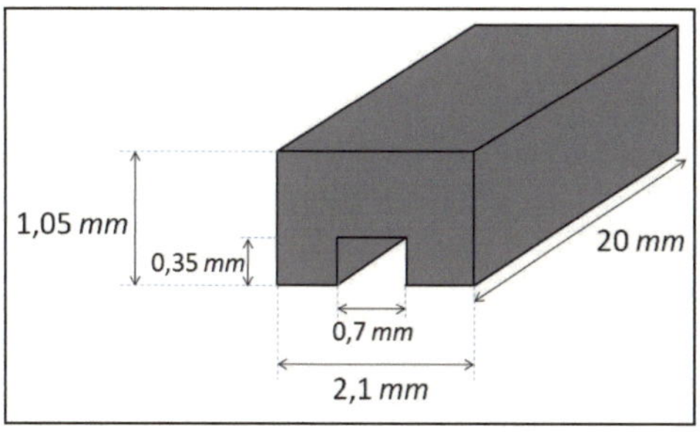

Fig. 14. Geometry of the part.

Property	Value
Extrusion temperature (°C)	270
Environment temperature (°C)	70
Extrusion velocity (m/s)	0.025
Filament length (m)	0.02
Cross section x (m)	0.01
Geometric form of cross section	circle
Cross section diameter (m)	0.00035
Contact ratio	88%
Heat transfer coefficient (convection) (W/m^2°C)	60
Thermal contact conductance with filaments (W/m^2°C)	180
Thermal contact conductance with support (W/m^2°C)	10
Thermal conductivity (W/m°C) materials A / B	0.1768 / 0.5
Specific heat (J/kg°C) materials A / B	2019.7 / 2500.7
Density materials A / B	1.05 / 1.5

Table 1. Processing conditions

The production of this part requires the use of a support material. Figure 15 shows the deposition sequence and corresponding material matrix, while Figure 16 presents the evolution of temperature of every filament with deposition time. As expected, once a new filament is deposited, the temperature of the preceding adjacent filaments increases and their rate of cooling decreases.

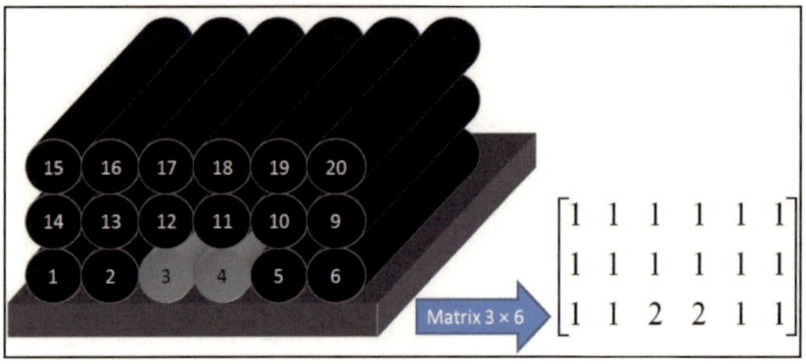

Fig. 15. Filaments deposition sequence and corresponding material matrix.

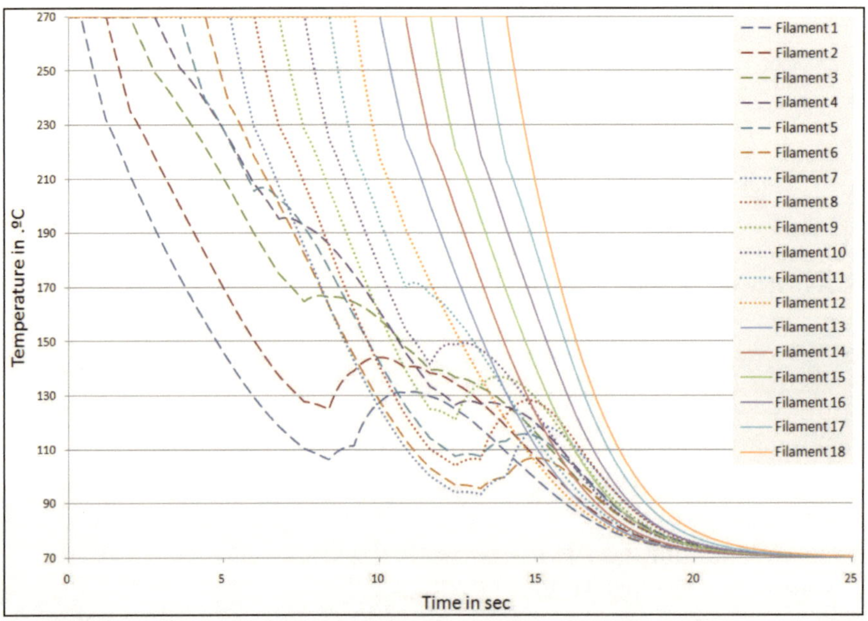

Fig. 16. Temperature evolution with time (at x = 0.01 m), for the deposition sequence illustrated in Figure 15.

5.2 Case study 2

Consider now the parallelepipedic part depicted in Figure 17, to be built using unidirectional and aligned and perpendicular sequences, respectively, under the processing conditions summarized in Table 2.

Figures 18 and 19 depict the deposition sequence and corresponding temperatures (this required an additional part of the code together with the use of the Tecplot software). At each time increment, a 1 mm or a 0.35 mm filament portion was deposited, for unidirectional and aligned and perpendicular filaments, respectively. This lower value is related with the lower contact area arising from this deposition mode. Consequently, the total computation time was circa 7 minutes for unidirectional and aligned deposition and more than two and a half hours for perpendicular filaments for a conventional portable PC. As the manufacture is completed (t = 14.4 sec), the average part temperature is approximately 120 °C or 90 °C depending on the deposition mode. This information is relevant for practical purposes, such as evaluating the quality of the adhesion between adjacent filaments, or the extent of deformation.

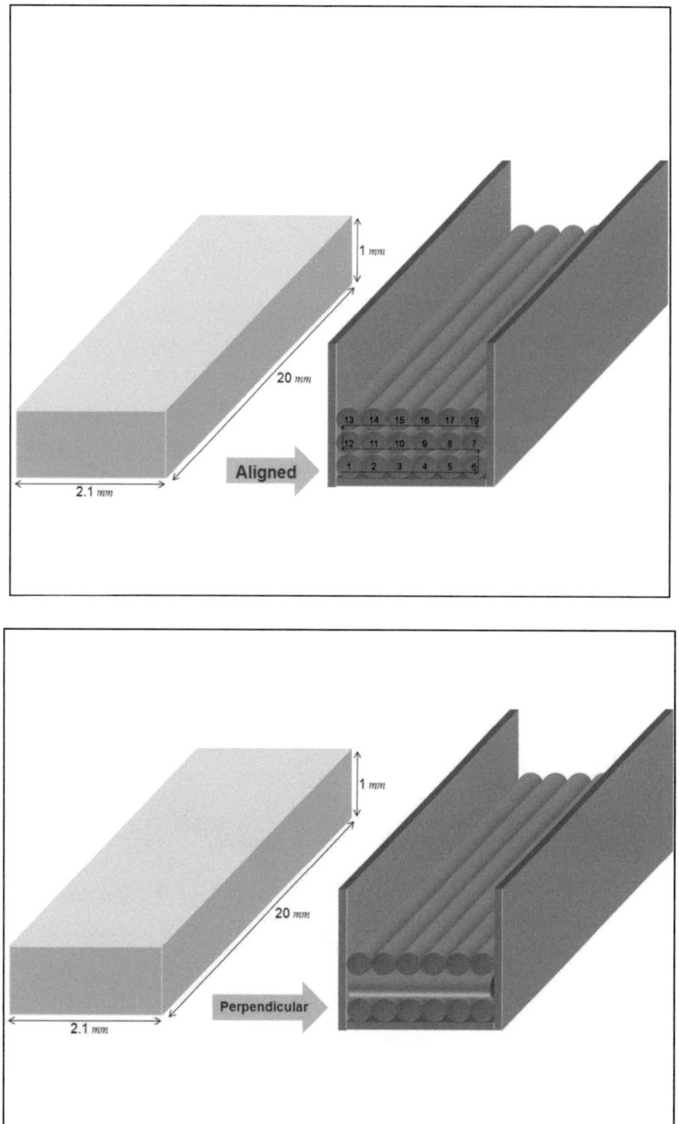

Fig. 17. Geometry of the part and corresponding deposition sequence: top: unidirectional and aligned; bottom: perpendicular.

Property	Value
Extrusion temperature (°C)	270
Environment temperature (°C)	70
Extrusion velocity (m/s)	0.025
Filament length (m)	0.02
Geometric form of cross section	circle
Cross section diameter (m)	0.00035
Contact ratio	88%
Heat transfer coefficient (convection) (W/m²°C)	70
Thermal contact conductance with filaments (W/m²°C)	200
Thermal contact conductance with support (W/m²°C)	15
Thermal conductivity (W/m°C)	0.1768
Specific heat (J/kg°C)	2019.7
Density	1.05

Table 2. Processing conditions

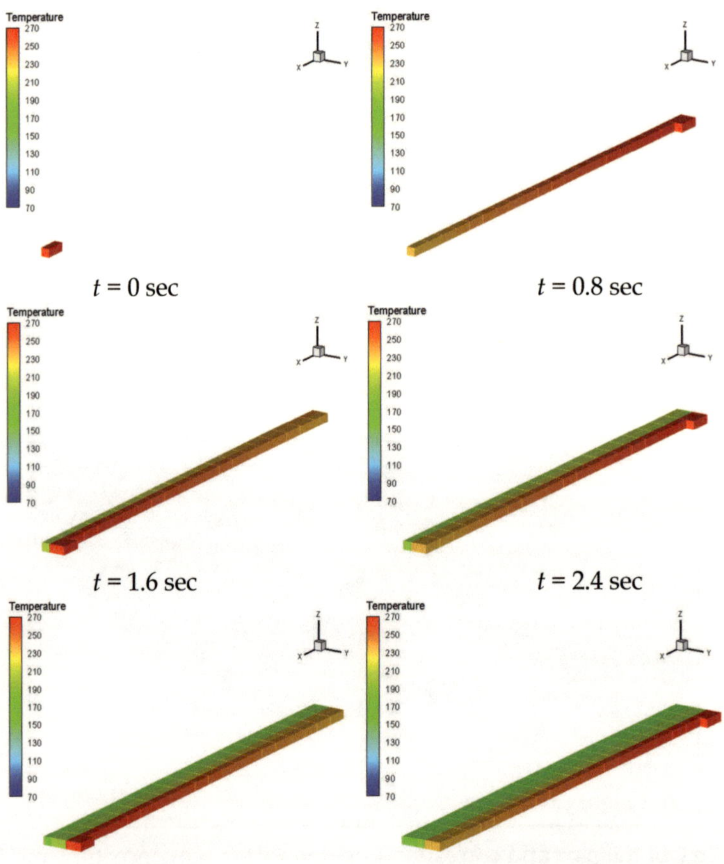

$t = 0$ sec $t = 0.8$ sec

$t = 1.6$ sec $t = 2.4$ sec

$t = 3.2$ sec $t = 4$ sec

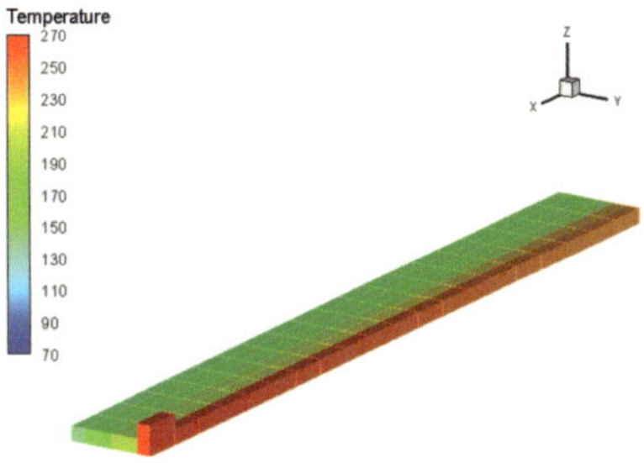

$t = 4.8$ sec

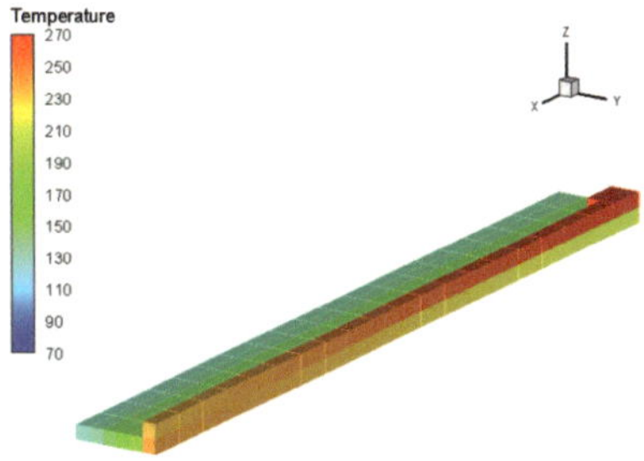

$t = 5.6$ sec

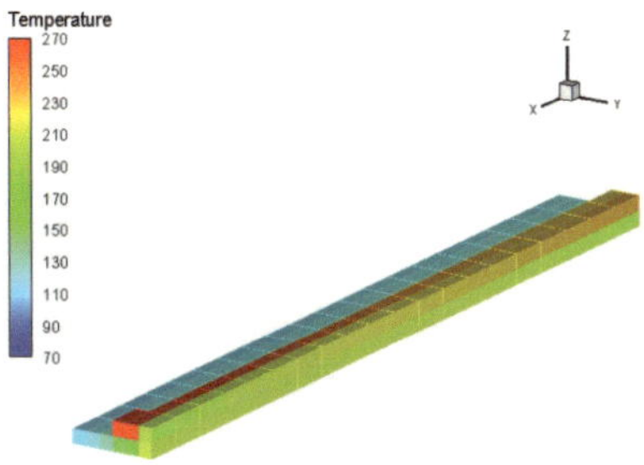

$t = 6.4$ sec

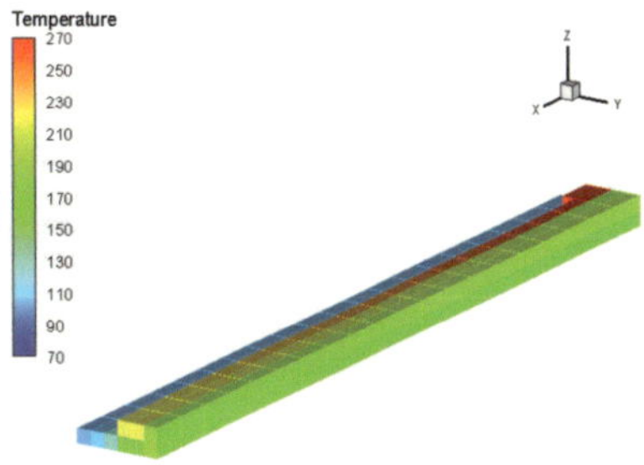

$t = 7.2$ sec

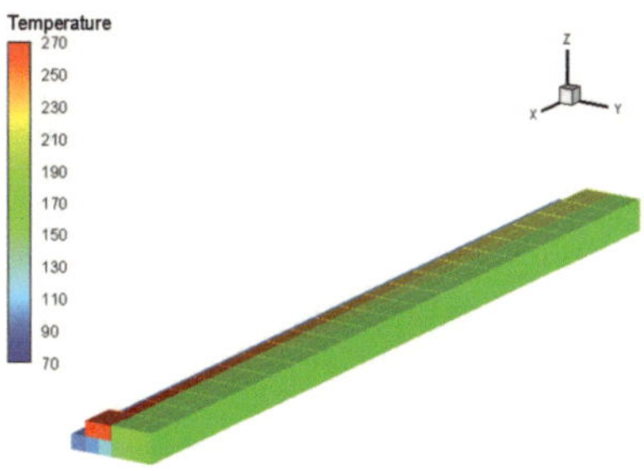

$t = 8$ sec

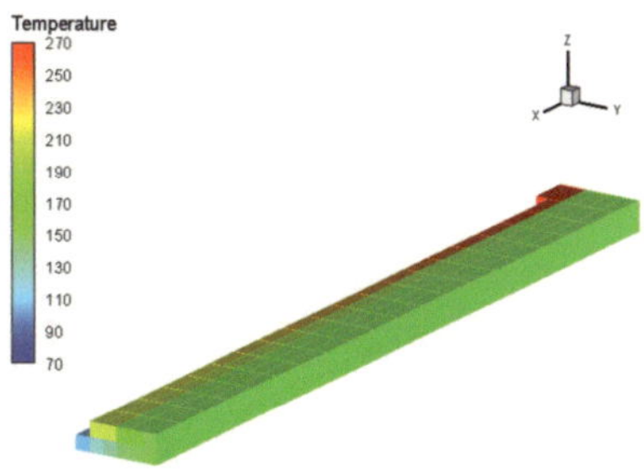

$t = 8.8$ sec

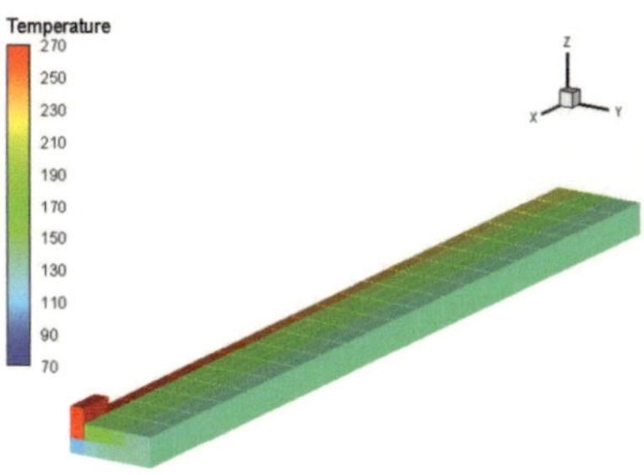

$t = 9.6$ sec

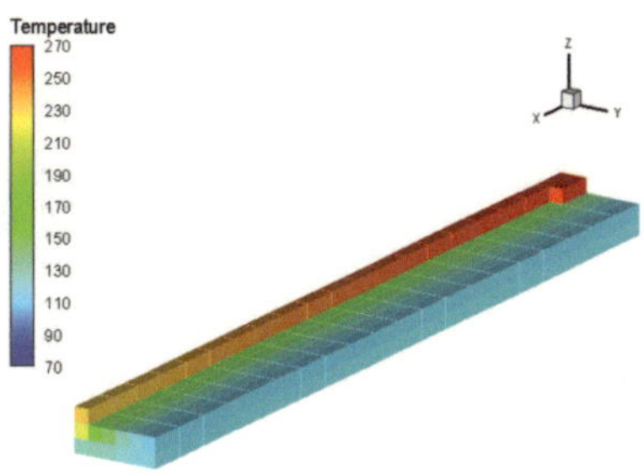

$t = 10.4$ sec

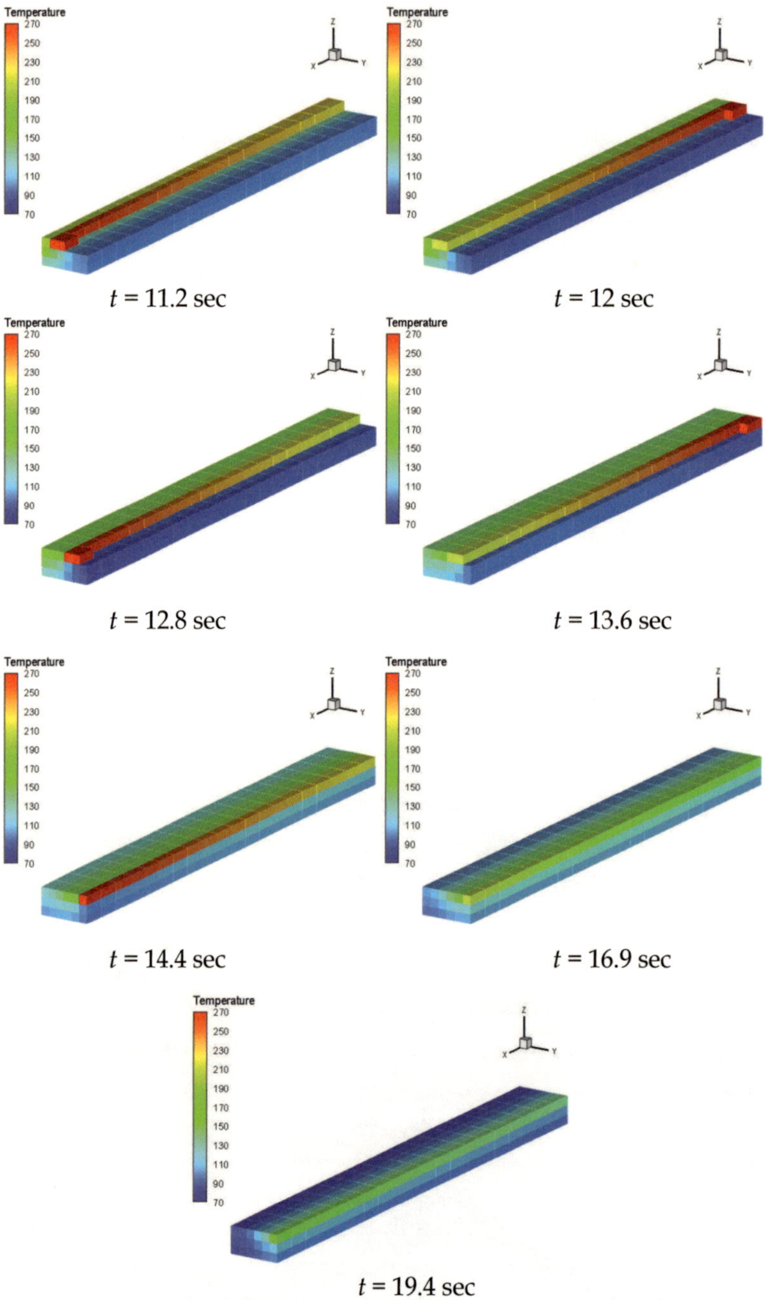

Fig. 18. Deposition sequence of the part of Figure 17 (unidirectional and aligned filaments).

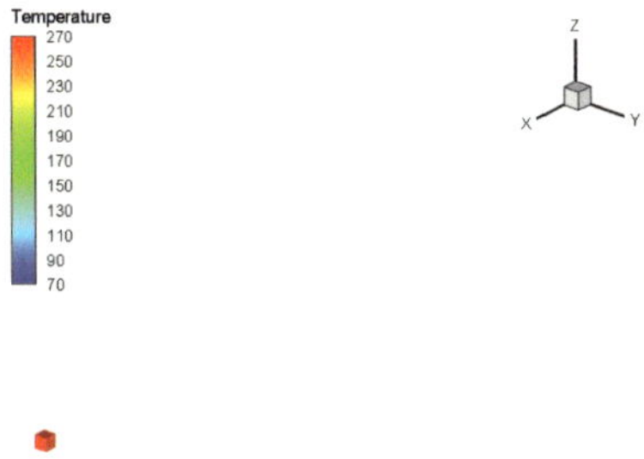

$t = 0$ sec

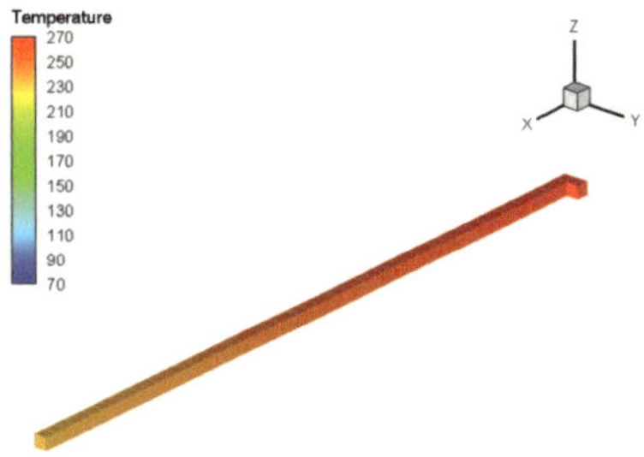

$t = 0.8$ sec

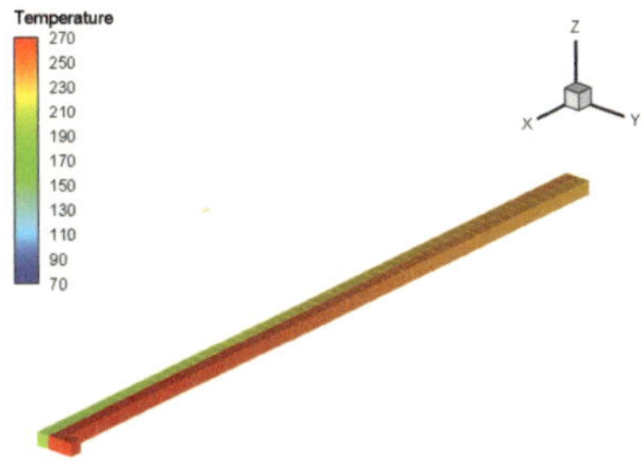

$t = 1.6$ sec

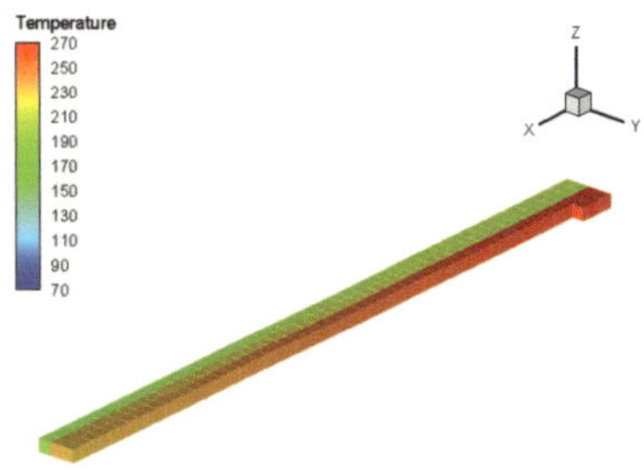

$t = 2.4$ sec

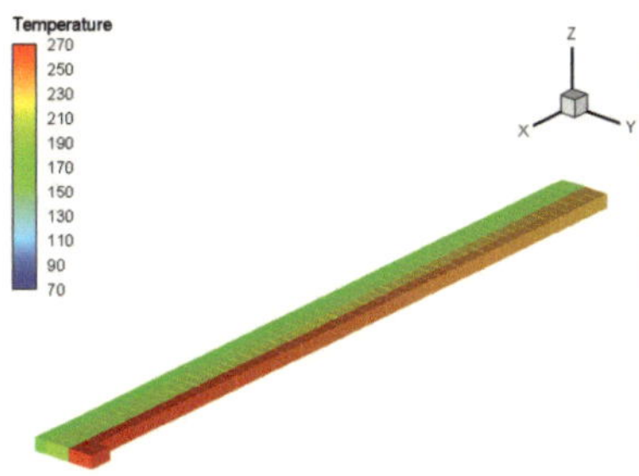

$t = 3.2$ sec

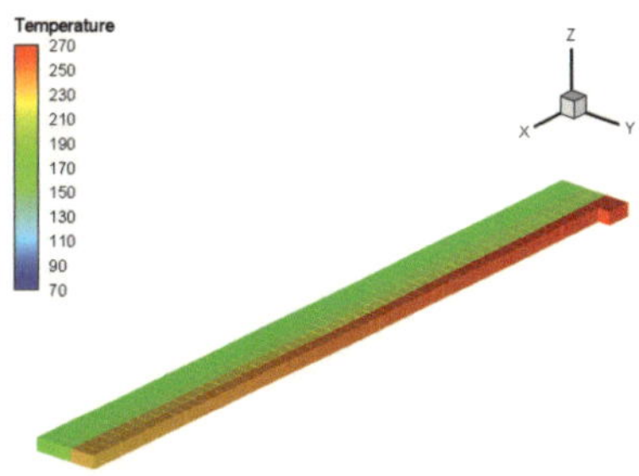

$t = 4$ sec

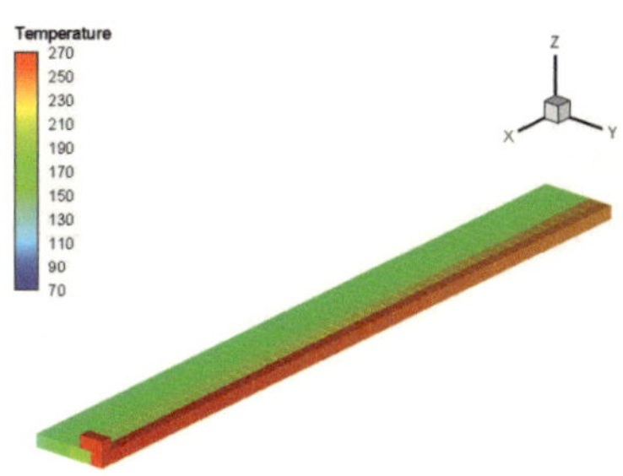

$t = 4.8$ sec

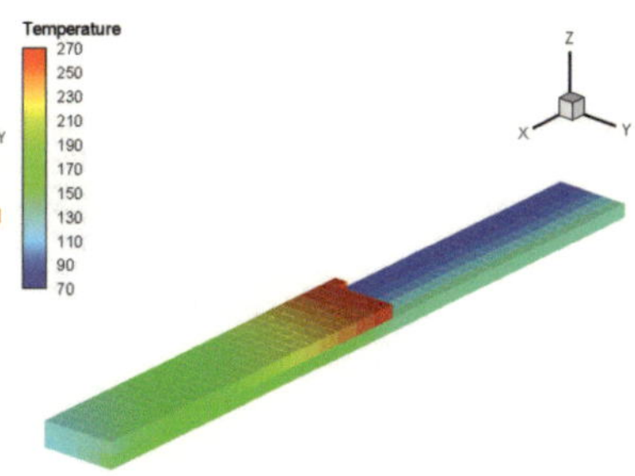

$t = 7.4$ sec

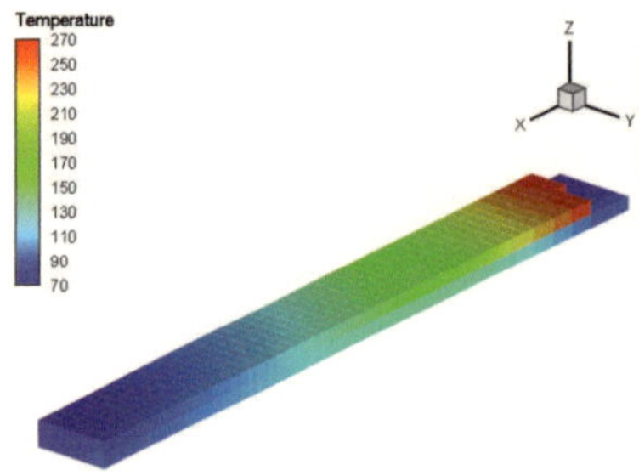

t = 9.6 sec

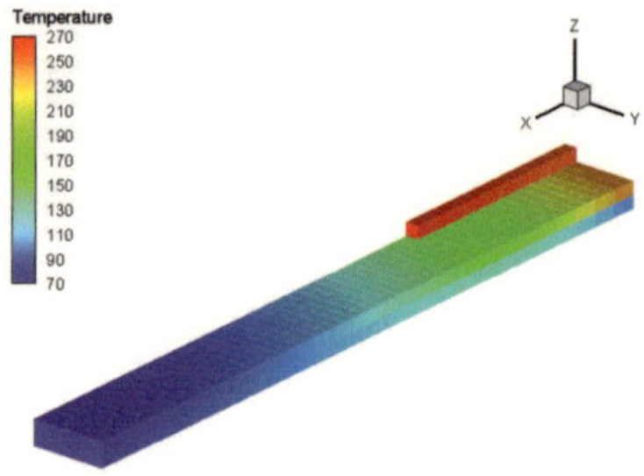

t = 9.9 sec

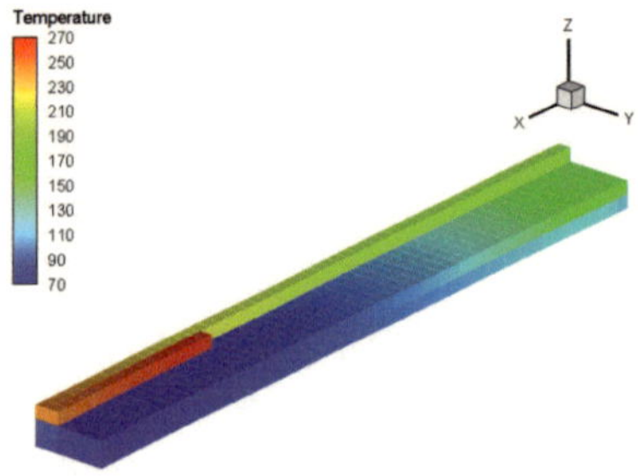

t = 10.7 sec

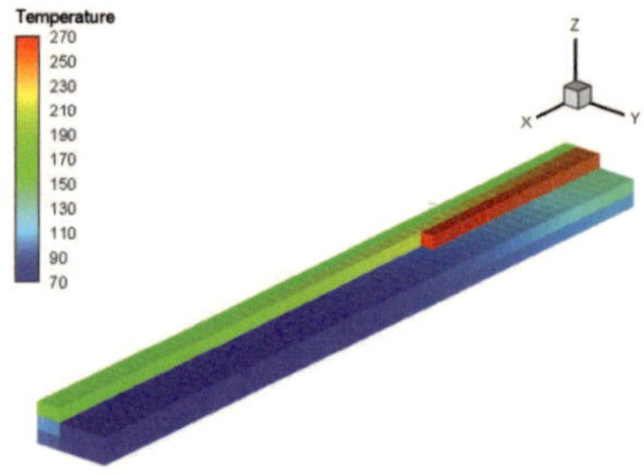

t = 11.5 sec

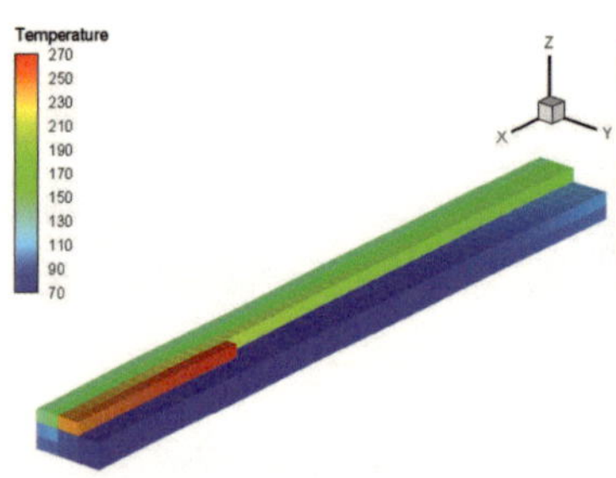

t = 12.3 sec

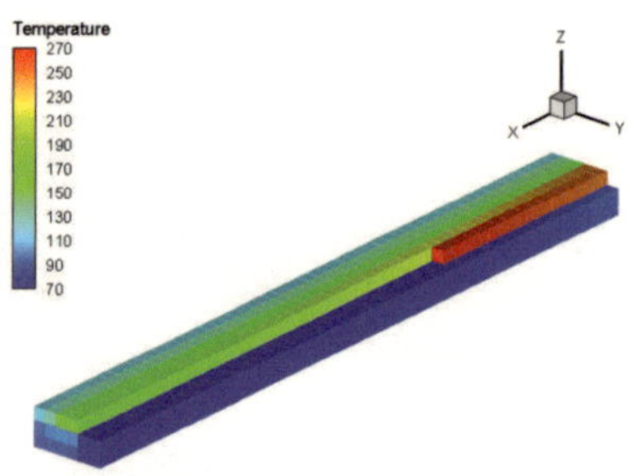

t = 13.1 sec

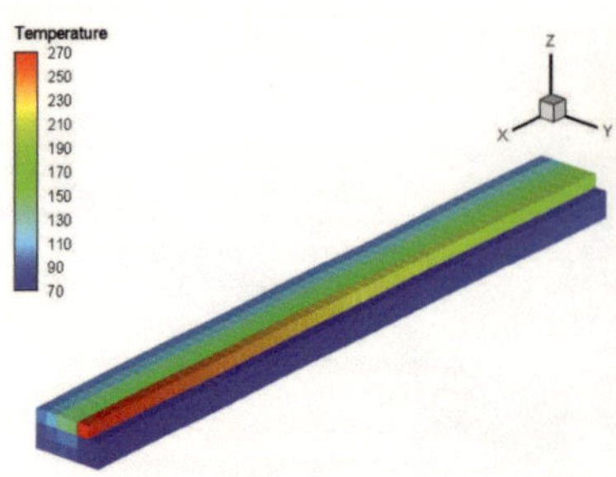

t = 13.6 sec

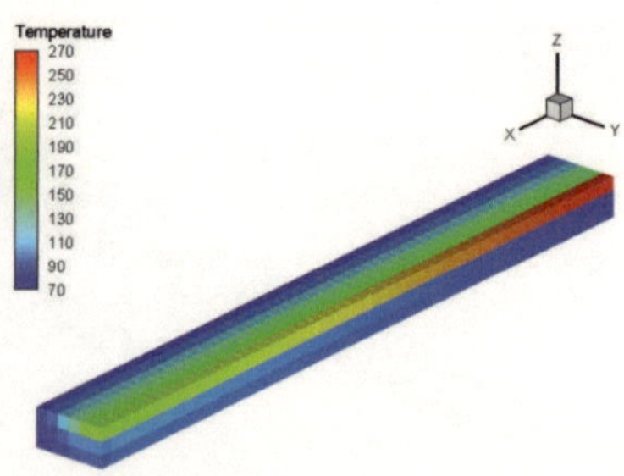

t = 14.4 sec

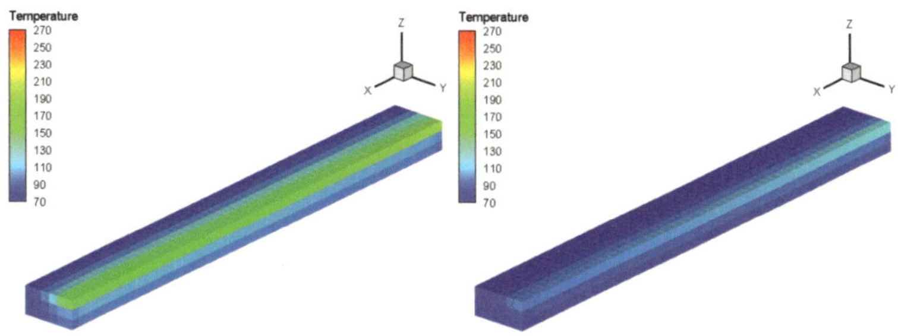

t = 16.9 sec t = 19.4 sec

Fig. 19. Deposition sequence of the part of Figure 17 (perpendicular filaments).

6. Conclusion

In Free Form Extrusion, FFE, a molten filament is deposited sequentially to produce a 3D part without a mould. This layer by layer construction technique may create problems of adhesion between adjacent filaments, or create dimensional accuracy problems due to excessive deformation of the filaments, if the processing conditions are not adequately set. This chapter presented a MatLab code for modelling the heat transfer in FFE, aiming at determining the temperature evolution of each filament during the deposition stage. Two case studies illustrated the use of the programme.

7. References

Rodriguez, J. F. (1999). *Modelling the mechanical behaviour of fused deposition acrylonitrile-butadiene-styrene polymer components*, Ph.D. Dissertation, Department of Aerospace and Mechanical Engineering, University of Notre Dame, Notre Dame, USA

Thomas, J. P. & Rodríguez, J. F. (2000). *Modeling the fracture strength between fused deposition extruded roads*, Solid Freeform Fabrication Symposium Proceeding, Austin.

Yardimci, M. A. & Guceri, S. I. (1996). *Conceptual framework for the thermal process modelling of fused deposition*, Rapid Prototyping Journal, 2, 26-31.

Li, L.; Sun, Q.; Bellehumeur, C. & Gu, P. (2003). *Modeling of bond formation in FDM process*, Trans. NAMRI/SME, 8, 613-620.

Sun, Q.; Rizvi, G.C.; Bellehumeur, C. & Gu, T. P. (2004). *Experimental study and modeling of bond formation between ABS filaments in the FDM process*, Proc. SPE ANTEC'2004.

Costa, S.; Duarte, F. & Covas, J. A. (2008). *Towards modelling of Free Form Extrusion: analytical solution of transient heat transfer*, Esaform 2008, Lyon, France.

Bejan, A. (1993). *Heat Transfer*, John Wiley & Sons, Inc., New York.

Marsan, A.; Dutta, D. (2000). *A review of process planning techniques in layered manufacturing*, Rapid Prototyping Journal, Vol.6, No.1, pp. 18-35, ISSN 1355-2546.

Pérez, C. J. L. (2002). *Analysis of the surface roughness and dimensional accuracy capability of fused deposition modelling processes*, International Journal of Production Research, Vol.40, Issue 12, pp. 2865 - 2881, ISSN 1366-588X.

Ahn, S. H. (2002). *Anisotropic material properties of fused deposition modeling ABS*, Rapid Prototyping Journal, Vol.8, No.4, pp. 248–257, ISSN 1355-2546.

Ziemian, C. W. & Crawn, P. M. (2001). *Computer aided decision support for fused deposition modeling*, Rapid Prototyping Journal, Vol.7, No.3, pp. 138-147, ISSN 1355-2546.

Agarwala, M. K.; Jamalabad, V. R.; Langrana, N. A.; Safari, A.; Whalen, P. J. & Danthord, S. C. (1996). *Structural quality of parts processed by fused deposition*, Rapid Prototyping Journal, Vol.2, No.4, pp. 4-19, ISSN 1355-2546.

Bellini, A.; Shor, L. & Guceri, S. (2005). *New developments in fused deposition modeling of ceramics*, Rapid Prototyping Journal, Vol.11, No.4, pp. 214-220, ISSN 1355-25.

Part 5

Image Processing

23

MATLAB as a Tool in Nuclear Medicine Image Processing

Maria Lyra, Agapi Ploussi and Antonios Georgantzoglou
Radiation Physics Unit, A' Radiology Department, University of Athens
Greece

1. Introduction

Advanced techniques of image processing and analysis find widespread use in medicine. In medical applications, image data are used to gather details regarding the process of patient imaging whether it is a disease process or a physiological process. Information provided by medical images has become a vital part of today's patient care.

The images generated in medical applications are complex and vary notably from application to application. Nuclear medicine images show characteristic information about the physiological properties of the structures-organs. In order to have high quality medical images for reliable diagnosis, the processing of image is necessary. The scope of image processing and analysis applied to medical applications is to improve the quality of the acquired image and extract quantitative information from medical image data in an efficient and accurate way.

MatLab (**Mat**rix **Lab**oratory) is a high performance interactive software package for scientific and engineering computation developed by MathWorks (Mathworks Inc., 2009). MatLab allows matrix computation, implementation of algorithms, simulation, plotting of functions and data, signal and image processing by the Image Processing Toolbox. It enables quantitative analysis and visualisation of nuclear medical images of several modalities, such as Single Photon Emission Computed Tomography (SPECT), Positron Emission Tomography (PET) or a hybrid system (SPECT/CT) where a Computed Tomography system (CT) is incorporated to the SPECT system. The Image Processing Toolbox (Mathworks Inc., 2009) is a comprehensive set of reference-standard algorithms and graphical tools for image processing, analysis, visualisation and algorithm development. It offers the possibility to restore noisy or degraded images, enhance images for improved intelligibility, extract features, analyse shapes and textures, and register two images. Thus, it includes all the functions that MatLab utilises in order to perform any sophisticated analysis needed after the acquisition of an image. Most toolbox functions are written in open MatLab language offering the opportunity to the user to inspect the algorithms, to modify the source code and create custom functions (Wilson et al., 2003, Perutka, 2010).

This chapter emphasises on the utility of MatLab in nuclear medicine images' processing. It includes theoretical background as well as examples. After an introduction to the imaging techniques in nuclear medicine and the quality of nuclear medicine images, this chapter proceeds to a study about image processing in nuclear medicine through MatLab. Image processing techniques presented in this chapter include organ contouring, interpolation, filtering, segmentation, background activity removal, registration and volume quantification. A section about DICOM image data processing using MatLab is also presented as this type of image is widely used in nuclear medicine.

2. Nuclear medicine imaging

Nuclear Medicine is the section of science that utilises the properties of radiopharmaceuticals in order to derive clinical information of the human physiology and biochemistry. According to the examination needed for each patient, a radionuclide is attached to a pharmaceutical (tracer) and the whole complex is then delivered to the patient intravenously or by swallowing or even by inhalation. The radiopharmaceutical follows its physiological pathway and it is concentrated on specific organs and tissues for short periods of time. Then, the patient is positioned under a nuclear medicine equipment which can detect the radiation emitted by the human body resulting in images of the biodistribution of the radiopharmaceutical.

In Nuclear Medicine, there are two main methods of patient imaging, the imaging with Planar Imaging, Dynamic Imaging or SPECT and the PET. During the last decade, hybrid systems have been developed integrating the CT technique with either SPECT or PET resulting in SPECT/CT and PET/CT respectively. This chapter will concentrate on the implementation of MatLab code in gamma camera planar imaging, SPECT and SPECT/CT methods.

The gamma camera is composed of a collimator, a scintillator crystal usually made of NaI (or CsI), the photomultiplier tubes, the electronic circuits and a computer equipped with the suitable software to depict the nuclear medicine examinations. In planar imaging, the patient, having being delivered with the suitable radiopharmaceutical, is sited under the gamma camera head. The gamma camera head remains stable at a fixed position over the patient for a certain period of time, acquiring counts (disintegrations). These will constitute the radiopharmaceutical distribution image. The counts measured in a specific planar projection originate from the whole thickness of patient (Wernick & Aarsvold, 2004).

In SPECT, the gamma camera head rotates around the patient remaining at well defined angles and acquiring counts for specific periods of time per angle. What makes SPECT a valuable tool in nuclear medicine is the fact that information in the three dimensions of the patient can be collected in a number of slices with a finite known volume (in voxels). Thus, SPECT technique is used to display the radiopharmaceutical distribution in a single slice removing the contribution from the overlying and underlying tissues.

In order to obtain the most accurate quantitative data from SPECT images, two issues that have to be resolved are the attenuation correction and the Compton scattering that the photons are undergone until reach and interact with the slice of interest tissues. As an examining organ has certain dimensions, each slice along the axis of the gamma camera has different distance from the detector. Thus, each photon experiences different attenuation. These two phenomena usually lead to distortion of the measured activity concentration (Wernick & Aarsvold, 2004). The acquired data are processed in order to correct and compensate the undesired effect of these physical phenomena. The projection data of each slice constitute the sinogram. As a result, a series of sinograms is the files acquired. However, this kind of files needs reconstruction in order to get an image with diagnostic value. The most known reconstruction methods are the Filtered Back-Projection (FBP) and the Iterative methods.

Attenuation correction is resolved by using the constant linear attenuation coefficient (μ) method or using the transmission source method. In the first one, the distance that each photon has travelled is calculated based on the patient geometry and the exponential reduction of their intensity. Then, considering the human body as a uniform object, an attenuation map is implemented in the reconstructed image. The latter method utilises a transmission source which scans the patient. This depicts each pixel or voxel of the patient with a specific μ producing an attenuation coefficient map. Finally, the attenuation map is implemented on the image resulting in a more accurate diagnosis.

The second issue of scatter correction can be resolved by the electronics of the gamma camera and the filtering process during reconstruction. When a photon undergoes scattering, its energy reduces. So, a well defined function can accept for imaging photons with energy at a certain narrow energy window around the central photopeak of the γ-emission.

A hybrid SPECT/CT scanner is capable of implementing both a CT scan and a SPECT scan or it can be used for each of these scans separately. Using the CT scan, the anatomy of a specific patient area can be imaged while the SPECT scan can depict the physiology of this area. Then, the registration of the two images drives at an image of advanced diagnostic value. Moreover, the CT data is used for the implementation of attenuation correction. (Delbeke et al., 2006)

The range of nuclear medicine examinations is fairly wide. It includes, among others, patients' studies, as myocardium perfusion by ^{99m}Tc-Tetrofosmin or ^{99m}Tc-Sestamibi, striatum imaging in brain by ^{123}I-Ioflupane (DaTSCAN), renal parenchyma imaging by ^{99m}Tc-De-Methylo-Sulfo-Acid (DMSA) and ^{99m}Tc-Methylo-Di-Phosphonate (MDP) for bone scintigraphy. Fundamental image analysis methods of myocardium, brain, kidneys, thyroid, lungs and oncological (e.g. neuroblastoma) nuclear medicine studies include regions' properties, boundary analysis, curvature analysis or line and circle detection.

Image processing serves in reconstruction of images acquired using SPECT techniques, in improvement of the quality of images for viewing and in preparation of images for quantitative results.

Data of the mentioned examinations are used in the following applications of MatLab algorithms to make the image processing and analysis in nuclear medicine clear and show the MatLab utility for these studies.

2.1 Image quality in nuclear medicine

Image quality plays an important role in nuclear medicine imaging as the goal is a reliable image of the projected organ to be provided, for accurate diagnosis or therapy. The physical characteristics that are used to describe image quality are (1) contrast, (2) spatial resolution and (3) noise.

Image contrast is the difference in intensity corresponding to different concentration of activity in the patient. For high diagnostic accuracy, nuclear medicine images must be of high contrast. The image contrast is principally affected by the radiopharmaceutical that is used for imaging and the scattered radiation. In general, it is desirable to use a radiopharmaceutical which has a high uptake within the target organ.

Spatial resolution is defined as the ability of the imaging modality to reproduce the details of a nonuniform radioactive distribution. The spatial resolution is separated into intrinsic resolution (scintillator, photomultiplier tubes and electronic circuit) and system resolution (collimator, scintillator, photomultiplier tubes and electronic circuit). The intrinsic resolution depends on the thickness of scintillation crystal while the system resolution depends mainly on the distance from the emitting source to collimator. The resolution of a gamma camera is limited by several factors. Some of these are the patient motion, the statistical fluctuation in the distribution of visible photons detected and the collimators geometry (Wernick & Aarsvold, 2004).

Noise refers to any unwanted information that prevents the accurate imaging of an object. Noise is the major factor in the degradation of image quality. Image noise may be divided into random and structured noise. Random noise (also referred as statistical noise) is the result of statistical variations in the counts being detected. The image noise is proportional to $N^{1/2}$ where N is the number of detected photons per pixel. Therefore, as the number of counts increases the noise level reduces. Image noise is usually analysed in terms of signal-to-noise-ratio (SNR). SNR is equal to $N/ N^{1/2}$. If the SNR is high, the diagnostic information of an image is appreciated regardless of the noise level. Structured noise is derived from non-uniformities in the scintillation camera and overlying structures in patient body.

2.2 Complex topics

In the previous section, several issues arising from the need of achieving the best image quality have to be resolved. Sometimes, the whole procedure becomes really hard to be completed. Some concepts in image processing and analysis are theory-intensive and may be difficult for medical professionals to comprehend.

Apart from that, each manufacturer uses different software environment for the application of reconstruction and presentation of the images. This drives at a lack of a standard pattern based on which a physician can compare or parallel two images acquired and reconstructed by nuclear imaging systems of different vendors. This is a node on which MatLab can meet a wide acceptance and utilisation.

These complex topics can be analysed and resolved using MatLab algorithms to turn up the most effective techniques to emerge information through medical imaging.

3. Image analysis and processing in nuclear medicine

In the last several decades, medical imaging systems have advanced in a dynamic progress. There have been substantial improvements in characteristics such as sensitivity, resolution, and acquisition speed. New techniques have been introduced and, more specifically, analogue images have been substituted by digital ones. As a result, issues related to the digital images' quality have emerged.

The quality of acquired images is degraded by both physical factors, such as Compton scattering and photon attenuation, and system parameters, such as intrinsic and extrinsic spatial resolution of the gamma camera system. These factors result in blurred and noisy images. Most times, the blurred images present artefacts that may lead to a fault diagnosis. In order the images to gain a diagnostic value for the physician, it is compulsory to follow a specific series of processing.

Image processing is a set of techniques in which the data from an image are analysed and processed using algorithms and tools to enhance certain image information that is more useful to human interpretation (Nailon, 2010). The processing of an image permits the

extraction of useful parameters and increases the possibility of detection of small lesions more accurately.
Image processing in nuclear medicine serves three major purposes: a) the reconstruction of the images acquired with tomographic (SPECT) techniques, b) the quality improvement of the image for viewing in terms of contrast, uniformity and spatial resolution and, c) the preparation of the image in order to extract useful diagnostic qualitative and quantitative information.

3.1 Digital images

In all modern nuclear medicine imaging systems, the images are displayed as an array of discrete picture elements (pixels) in two dimensions (2D) and are referred as digital images. Each pixel in a digital image has an intensity value and a location address (Fig. 1). In a nuclear medicine image the pixel value shows the number of counts recorded in it. The benefit of a digital image compared to the analogue one is that data from a digital image are available for further computer processing.

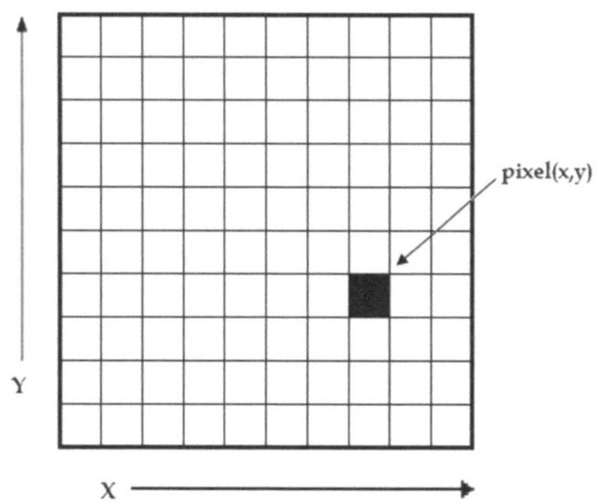

Fig. 1. A digital image is a 2D array of pixels. Each pixel is characterised by its (x, y) coordinates and its value.

Digital images are characterised by matrix size, pixel depth and resolution. The matrix size is determined from the number of the columns (m) and the number of rows (n) of the image matrix (m×n). The size of a matrix is selected by the operator. Generally, as the matrix dimension increases the resolution is getting better (Gonzalez et al., 2009). Nuclear medicine images matrices are, nowadays, ranged from 64×64 to 1024×1024 pixels.
Pixel or bit depth refers to the number of bits per pixel that represent the colour levels of each pixel in an image. Each pixel can take 2^k different values, where k is the bit depth of the image. This means that for an 8-bit image, each pixel can have from 1 to 2^8 (=256) different colour levels (grey-scale levels). Nuclear medicine images are frequently represented as 8- or 16- bit images.
The term resolution of the image refers to the number of pixels per unit length of the image. In digital images the spatial resolution depends on pixel size. The pixel size is calculated by the Field of View (FoV) divided by the number of pixels across the matrix. For a standard FoV, an increase of the matrix size decreases the pixel size and the ability to see details is improved.

3.2 Types of digital images – MatLab

MatLab offers simple functions that can read images of many file formats and supports a number of colour maps. Depending on file type and colour space, the returned matrix is either a 2D matrix of intensity values (greyscale images) or a 3D matrix of RGB values. Nuclear medicine images are grey scale or true colour images (RGB that is Red, Green and Blue).

The image types supported from the Image Processing Toolbox are listed below:

- Binary Images. In these, pixels can only take 0 or 1 value, black or white.
- Greyscale or intensity images. The image data in a greyscale image represent intensity or brightness. The integers' value is within the range of [0… 2^{k-1}], where k is the bit depth of the image. For a typical greyscale image each pixel can represented by 8 bits and intensity values are in the range of [0…255], where 0 corresponds to black and 255 to white.
- True color or RGB. In these, an image can be displayed using three matrices, each one corresponding to each of red-green-blue colour. If in an RGB image each component uses 8 bits, then the total number of bits required for each pixel is 3×8=24 and the range of each individual colour component is [0…255].
- Indexed images. Indexed images consist of a 2D matrix together with an m×3 colour map (m= the number of the columns in image matrix). Each row of map specifies the red, green, and blue components of a single colour. An indexed image uses direct mapping of pixel values to colour map values. The colour of each image pixel is determined by using the corresponding value of matrix as an index into map.

The greyscale image is the most convenient and preferable type utilised in nuclear medicine image processing. When colouring depiction is needed, the RGB one should be used and processed. The indexed type images should be converted to any of the two other types in order to be processed. The functions used for image type conversion are: `rgb2gray`, `ind2rgb`, `ind2gray` and reversely. Any image can be also transformed to binary one using the command: `im2bw`. Moreover, in any image, the function `impixelinfo` can be used in order to detect any pixel value. The user can move the mouse cursor inside the image and the down left corner appears the pixel identity (x, y) as well as the (RGB) values. The pixel range of the image can be displayed by the command `imdisplayrange`.

3.3 MatLab image tool

The Image Tool is a simple and user-friendly toolkit which can contribute to a quick image processing and analysis without writing a code and use MatLab language. These properties makes it a very useful tool when deep analysis is not the ultimate goal but quick processing for better view is desirable.

The Image Tool opens by simply writing the command `imtool` in the main function window. Then a new window opens and the next step is loading an image. In the menu, there are many functions already installed in order to use it as simple image processing software. The tools include image information appearance, image zooming in and out, panning, adjustment of the window level and width, adjustment of contrast, cropping, distance measurement, conversion of the image to a pixel matrix and colour map choices (grey scale, bone colour, hot regions among others). These are the most common functions likely to be performed in the initial processing approach. Moreover, the user can make some further manipulations such as 3D rotation to respective 3D images and plotting of pixel data.

3.4 Image processing techniques - MatLab

Image processing techniques include all the possible tools used to change or analyse an image according to individuals' needs. This subchapter presents the most widely performed image processing techniques that are applicable to nuclear medicine images. The examples used are mostly come from nuclear medicine renal studies, as kidneys' planar images and SPECT slices are simple objects to show the application of image processing MatLab tools.

3.4.1 Contrast enhancement

One of the very first image processing issues is the contrast enhancement. The acquired image does not usually present the desired object contrast. The improvement of contrast is absolutely needed as the organ shape, boundaries and internal functionality can be better depicted. In addition, organ delineation can be achieved in many cases without removing the background activity.

The command that implements contrast processing is the `imadjust`. Using this, the contrast in an image can be enhanced or degraded if needed. Moreover, a very useful result can be the inversion of colours, especially in greyscale images, where an object of interest can be efficiently outlined. The general function that implements contrast enhancement is the following:

```
J = imadjust(I,[low_in high_in],[low_out high_out],gamma);
```

while the function for colour inversion is the following:

```
J = imadjust(I,[0 1],[1 0],gamma); or J = imcomplement(I);
```

suppose that J, is the new image, I, is the initial image and gamma factor depicts the shape of the curve that describes the relationship between the values of I and J. If the gamma factor is omitted, it is considered to be 1.

3.4.2 Organ contour

In many nuclear medicine images, the organs' boundaries are presented unclear due to low resolution or presence of high percentage of noise.

In order to draw the contour of an organ in a nuclear medicine image, the command `imcontour` is used. In addition, a variable `n` defines the number of equally spaced contours required. This variable is strongly related with the intensity of counts. For higher `n` values, the lines are drawn with smaller spaces in between and depict different streaks of intensity. The type of line contouring can be specified as well. For example, when a contour of 5 level contours, drawn with solid line, is the desirable outcome, the whole function is:

Example 1I = imread('kindeys.jpg');

```
figure, imshow(I)

J = imcontour(I,5,'-');

Figure, imshow(J)
```

where J and I stands for the final and the initial image respectively and the symbol ('-') stands for the solid line drawing. An example of the initial image, the contour with n=15 and n=5 respectively, follows.

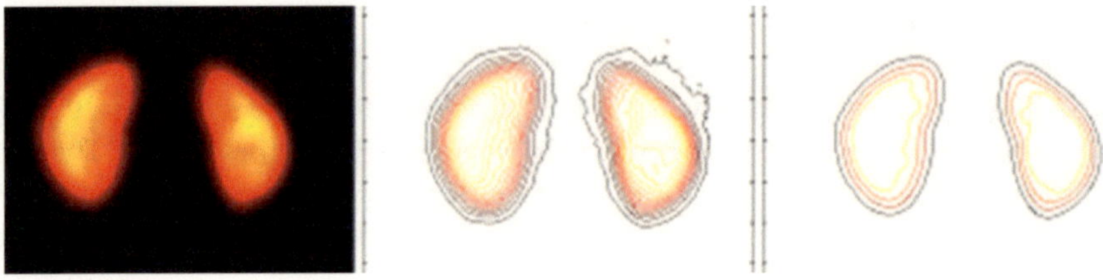

Fig. 2. (a) Original image depicting kidneys, (b) organs contoured with n = 15, (c) organs contoured with n = 5.

3.4.3 Image interpolation

Interpolation is a topic that has been widely used in image processing. It constitutes of the most common procedure in order to resample an image, to generate a new image based on the pattern of an existing one. Moreover, re-sampling is usually required in medical image processing in order to enhance the image quality or to retrieve lost information after compression of an image (Lehmann et al., 1999).

Interpreting the interpolation process, the user is provided with several options. These options include the resizing of an image according to a defined scaling factor, the choice of the interpolation type and the choice of low-pass filter.

The general command that performs image resizing is `imresize`. However, the way that the whole function has to be written depends heavily on the characteristics of the new image. The size of the image can be defined as a scaling factor of the existing image or by exact number of pixels in rows and columns. Concerning the interpolation types usually used in nuclear medicine, these are the following: a) nearest-neighbour interpolation (`'nearest'`), where the output pixel obtains the value of the pixel that the point falls within, without considering other pixels, b) bilinear interpolation (`'bilinear'`), where the output pixel obtains a weighted average value of the nearest 2x2 pixels, c) cubic interpolation (`'bicubic'`), where the output pixel obtains a weighted average value of the nearest 4x4 pixels (Lehmann et al., 1999).

When an image has to resize in a new one, with specified scaling factor and method, then the function Implementing that, is the following:

```
NewImage = imresize(Image, scale, method);
```

For example, for a given image I, the new image J shrunk twice of the initial one, using the bilinear interpolation method, the function will be:

```
J = imresize(I, 0.5, 'bilinear');
```

This way of image resizing contributes to the conversion of image information during any such process, a fact that is valuable in the precision of a measurement. Bilinear interpolation is often used to zoom into a 2D image or for rendering, for display purposes. Apart from the previous methods, the cubic convolution method can be applied to 3D images.

3.4.4 Image filtering

The factors that degrade the quality of nuclear medicine images result in blurred and noisy images with poor resolution. One of the most important factors that greatly affect the quality of clinical nuclear medicine images is image filtering. Image filtering is a mathematical processing for noise removal and resolution recovery. The goal of the filtering is to compensate for loss of detail in an image while reducing noise. Filters suppressed noise as well as deblurred and sharpened the image. In this way, filters can greatly improve the image resolution and limit the degradation of the image.

An image can be filtered either in the frequency or in the spatial domain. In the first case the initial data is Fourier transformed, multiplied with the appropriate filter and then taking the inverse Fourier transform, re-transformed into the spatial domain. The basics steps of filtering in the frequency domain are illustrated in Fig. 3.

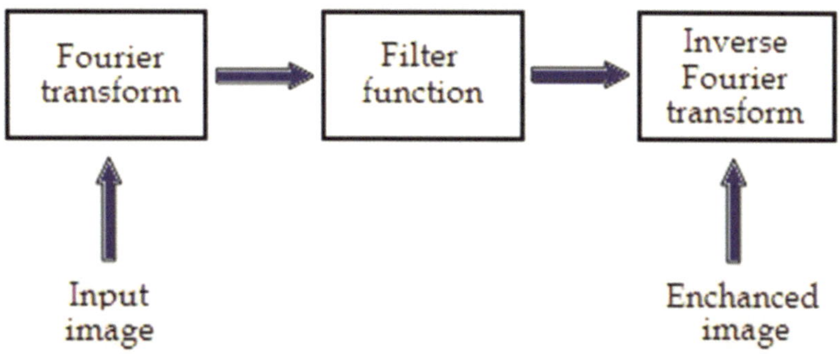

Fig. 3. Basics steps of frequency domain filtering.

The filtering in the spatial domain demands a filter mask (it is also referred as kernel or convolution filter). The filter mask is a matrix of odd usually size which is applied directly on the original data of the image. The mask is centred on each pixel of the initial image. For each position of the mask the pixel values of the image is multiplied by the corresponding values of the mask. The products of these multiplications are then added and the value of the central pixel of the original image is replaced by the sum. This must be repeated for every pixel in the image. The procedure is described schematically in Fig. 4.

If the filter, by which the new pixel value was calculated, is a linear function of the entire pixel values in the filter mask (e.g. the sum of products), then the filter is called linear. If the output pixel is not a linear weighted combination of the input pixel of the image then the filtered is called non-linear.

According to the range of frequencies they allow to pass through filters can be classified as low pass or high pass. Low pass filters allow the low frequencies to be retained unaltered and block the high frequencies. Low pass filtering removes noise and smooth the image but at the same time blur the image as it does not preserve the edges. High pass filters sharpness the edges of the image (areas in an image where the signal changes rapidly) and enhance object edge information. A severe disadvantage of high pass filtering is the amplification of statistical noise present in the measured counts.

The next section is referred to three of the most common filters used by MatLab: the mean, median and Gaussian filter.

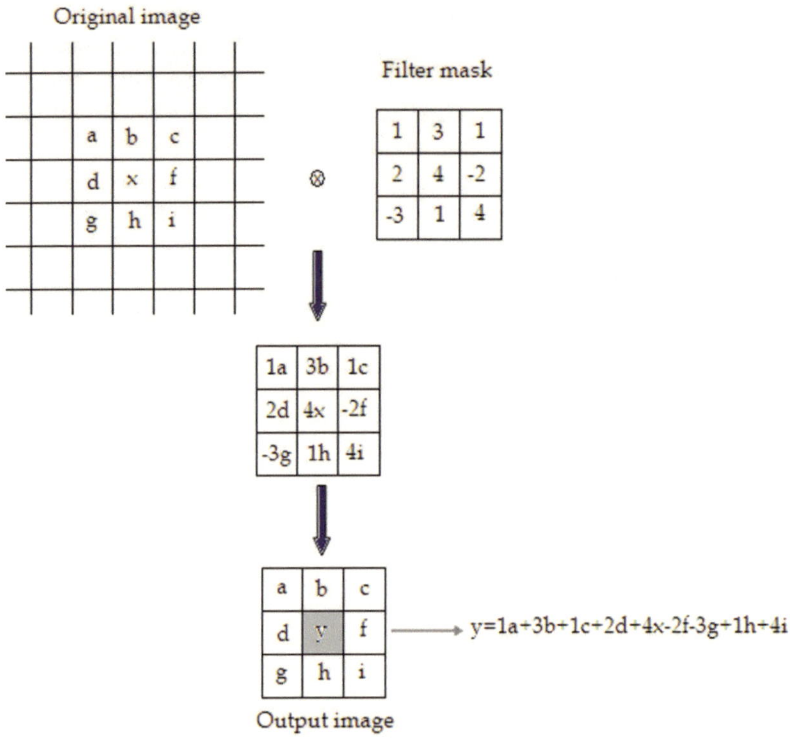

Fig. 4. Illustration of filtering process in spatial domain.

3.4.4.1 Mean filter

Mean filter is the simplest low pass linear filter. It is implemented by replacing each pixel value with the average value of its neighbourhood. Mean filter can be considered as a convolution filter. The smoothing effect depends on the kernel size. As the kernel size increases, the smoothing effect increases too. Usually a 3×3 (or larger) kernel filter is used. An example of a single 3×3 kernel is shown in the Fig. 5.

a	b	c
d	e	f
g	h	i

$$\longrightarrow \frac{1}{9}(a+b+c+d+e+f+g+h+i)$$

Fig. 5. Filtering approach of mean filter.

The Fig.5 depicts that by using the mean filter, the central pixel value would be changed from "e" to " (a+b+c+d+e+f+g+h+i) 1/9".

3.4.4.2 Median filter

Median filter is a non linear filter. Median filtering is done by replacing the central pixel with the median of all the pixels value in the current neighbourhood.
A median filter is a useful tool for impulse noise reduction (Toprak & Göller, 2006). The impulse noise (it is also known as salt and paper noise) appears as black or (/and) white

pixels randomly distributed all over the image. In other words, impulse noise corresponds to pixels with extremely high or low values. Median filters have the advantage to preserve edges without blurring the image in contrast to smoothing filters.

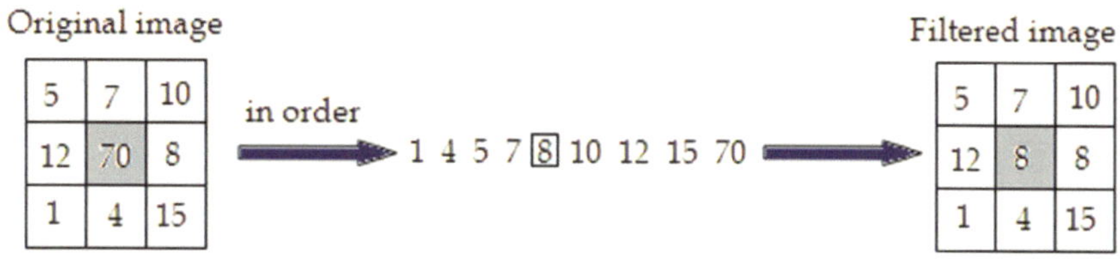

Fig. 6. Filtering approach of Median Filter.

3.4.4.3 Gaussian filter

Gaussian filter is a linear low pass filter. A Gaussian filter mask has the form of a bell-shaped curve with a high point in the centre and symmetrically tapering sections to either side (Fig.7). Application of the Gaussian filter produces, for each pixel in the image, a weighted average such that central pixel contributes more significantly to the result than pixels at the mask edges (O'Gorman et al., 2008). The weights are computed according to the Gaussian function (Eq.1):

$$f(x) = \frac{1}{\sigma\sqrt{2\pi}} e^{-(x-\mu)^2 / (2\sigma^2)} \tag{1}$$

where μ, is the mean and σ, the standard deviation.

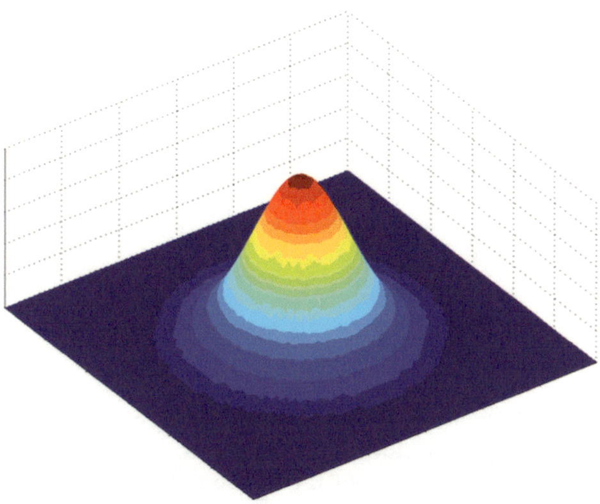

Fig. 7. A 2D Gaussian function.

The degree of smoothing depends on the standard deviation. The larger the standard deviation, the smoother the image is depicted. The Gaussian filter is very effective in the reduction of impulse and Gaussian noise. Gaussian noise is caused by random variations in the intensity and has a distribution that follows the Gaussian curve.

3.5 Filtering in MatLab

In MatLab, using Image Processing Toolbox we can design and implemented filters for image data. For linear filtering, MatLab provides the `fspecial` command to generate some predefined common 2D filters.

```
h=fspecial(filtername, parameters)
```

The `filtername` is one of the average, disk, gaussian, laplacian, log, motion, prewitt, sobel and unsharp filters; that is the `parameters` related to the specific filters that are used each time. Filters are applied to 2D images using the function `filter2` with the syntax:

```
Y = filter2(h,X)
```

The function `filter2` filters the data in matrix X with the filter `h.` For multidimensional images the function `imfilter` is used.

```
B = imfilter(A,h)
```

This function filters the multidimensional array A with the multidimensional filter h. `imfilter` function is more general than `filter2` function. For nonlinear filtering in MatLab the function `nlfilter` is applied, requiring three arguments: the input image, the size of the filter and the function to be used.

```
B = nlfilter(A, [m n], fun)
```

Example 2

The following example describes the commands' package that can be used for the application of the mean (average) filter in a SPECT slice for different convolution kernel sizes (for 3×3, 9×9, 25×25 average filter).

```
h=fspecial('average', [3 3]);
b=imfilter(a,h);
figure, imshow(b);
i=fspecial('average', [9 9]);
c=imfilter(b,h);
figure, imshow(c);
j=fspecial('average', [25 25]);
d=imfilter(c,h);
figure, imshow(d);
```

Figure 8 presents different implementations of the mean filter on a kidneys image with filters 3x3, 9x9, 15x15, 20x20 and 25x25.
As it can be easily noticed, the mean filter balances and smoothes the image, flattening the differences. The filtered images do not present edges at the same extent as in the original one. For larger kernel size, the blurring of the image is more intense. Image smoothening can be used in several areas of nuclear medicine and can serve in different points of view of the examined organ.

Example 3

In this example we will try to remove impulse noise from a SPECT slice, for example in a renal study. For this reason we mix the image with impulse noise (salt and pepper). The image has a 512×512 matrix size and grey levels between 0 and 255. The most suitable filter for removing impulse noise is the median filter. Because it is a nonlinear filter, the command `nlfilter` is now used.

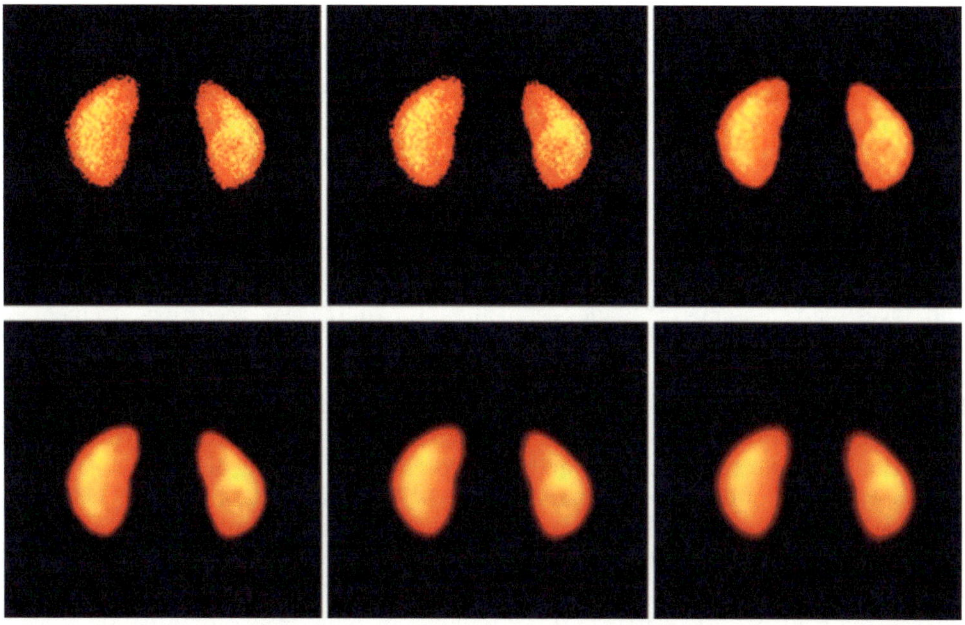

Fig. 8. Mean filter applied on kidneys image (a) Original image, (b) average filter 3x3, (c) average filter 9x9, (d) average filter 15x15, (e) average filter 20x20 and, (f) average filter 25x25 *[(a) to (f) from left to right].*

```
I = imread('kidneys.tif');
figure, imshow(I);
J = imnoise(I,'salt & pepper',0.05);
figure, imshow(J);
fun = @(x) median(x(:));
K = nlfilter(J,[3 3],fun);
figure, imshow(K);
```

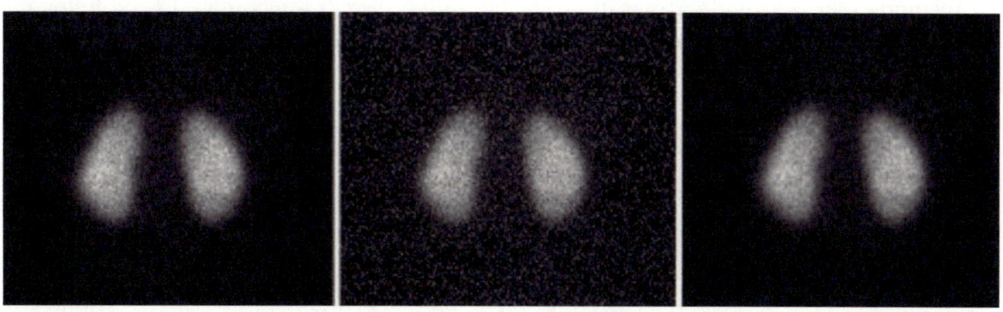

Fig. 9. Impulse noise elimination by median filter. (a) Original image (b) the image with impulse noise (c) the image on which the noise is suppressed with the median filter. *[(a) to (c) from left to right]*

Example 3 can be very useful in the nuclear medicine examinations of parenchymatous organs (liver, lungs, thyroid or kidneys) as it consists of a simple enough method for the reduction of noise which interferes in the image due to the construction of electronic circuits.

3.6 Image segmentation

The image segmentation describes the process through which an image is divided into constituent parts, regions or objects in order to isolate and study separately areas of special interest. This process assists in detecting critical parts of a nuclear medicine image that are not easily displayed in the original image.

The process of segmentation has been developed based on lots of intentions such as delineating an object in a gradient image, defining the region of interest or separating convex components in distance-transformed images. Attention should be spent in order to avoid 'over-segmentation' or 'under-segmentation'. In nuclear medicine, segmentation techniques are used to detect the extent of a tissue, an organ, a tumour inside an image, the boundaries of structures in cases that these are ambiguous and the areas that radiopharmaceutical concentrate in a greater extent. Thus, the segmentation process serves in assisting the implementation of other procedures; in other words, it constitutes the fundamental step of some basic medical image processing (Behnaz et al., 2010).

There are two ways of image segmentation: a) based on the discontinuities and, b) based on the similarities of structures inside an image. In nuclear medicine images, the discontinuity segmentation type finds more applications. This type depends on the detection of discontinuities or else, edges, inside the image using a threshold. The implementation of threshold helps in two main issues: i) the removal of unnecessary information from the image (background activity) and, ii) the appearance of details not easily detected.

The edge detection uses the command `edge`. In addition, a threshold is applied in order to detect edges above defined grey-scale intensity. Also, different methods of edge detection can be applied according to the filter each of them utilises. The most useful methods in nuclear medicine are the 'Sobel', 'Prewitt', 'Roberts', 'Canny' as well as 'Laplacian of Gaussian'. It is noted that the image is immediately transformed into a binary image and edges are detected. The general function used for the edge detection is the following:

```
[BW] = edge (image, 'method', threshold)
```

Where [BW] is the new binary image produced, image is the initial one; 'method' refers to the method of edge detection and 'threshold' to the threshold applied. In nuclear medicine, the methods that find wide application are the *sorbel*, *prewitt* and *canny*. In the following example, the *canny* method is applied in order to detect edges in an image.

Example 4

```
I = imread('kidneys.jpg');
figure, imshow(I)
J = edge(I,'canny', 0.048);
figure, imshow(J)
```

Another application of segmentation in nuclear medicine is the use of gradient magnitude. The original image is loaded. Then, the edge detection method of *sobel* is applied in accordance with a gradient magnitude which gives higher regions with higher grey-scale intensity. Finally, the foreground details are highlighted and segmented image of the kidneys is produced. The whole code for that procedure is described below.

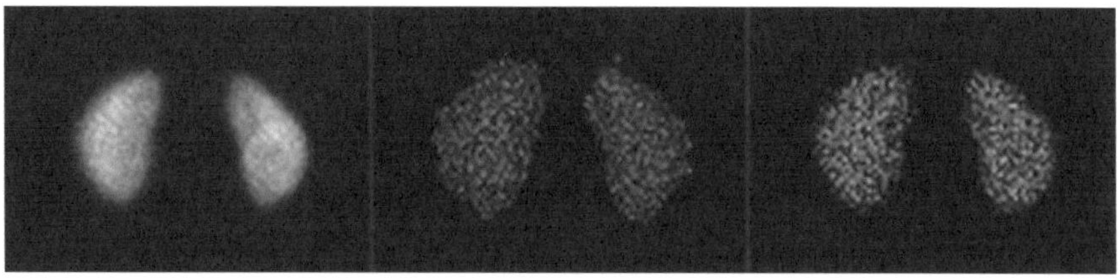

Fig. 10. Edge detection (a) Original kidneys image, (b) edge detection with *canny* method and threshold 0.2667, (c) edge detection with *prewitt* method and threshold 0.038. *[(a) to (c) from left to right]*

Example 5

```
I = imread('kidneys.jpg');
Figure, imshow(I)
hy = fspecial('sobel');
hx = hy';
Iy = imfilter(double(I), hy, 'replicate');
Ix = imfilter(double(I), hx, 'replicate');
gradmag = sqrt(Ix.^2 + Iy.^2);
figure, imshow(gradmag,[])
se = strel('disk', 20);
K = imopen(I, se);
figure, imshow(K)
```

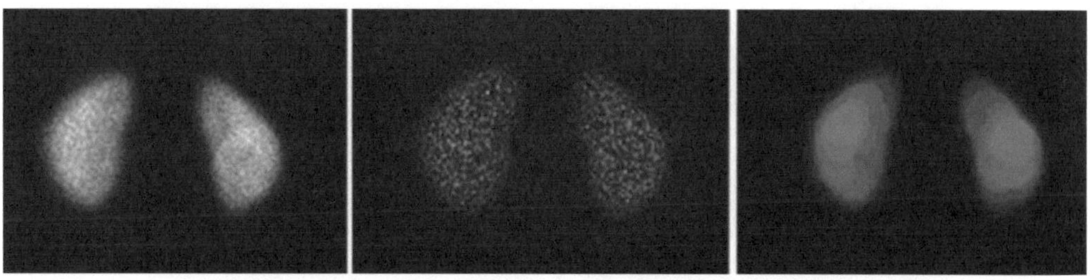

Fig. 11. Gradient Magnitude process: (a) Original image, (b) image after implementation of filter and gradient magnitude, (c) image after masking of foreground objects *[(a) to (c) from left to right]*

In the final image, the outline of the organs is depicted. The area inside the kidney has been separated into larger parts with grey-scale intensity weighted and decided from the closest 20 pixels in a circular region. In the areas of kidney that have higher activity concentrated, more than one layer of circular regions have been added presenting a final lighter region.

3.7 Background activity removal

One of the first steps to be completed in the medical image processing is removing the background activity. This procedure is based on image segmentation as in order to achieve the background activity removal, the organs' boundaries are first defined. The steps in this procedure are the following: i) the image is read, ii) the image is appeared, iii) a grey level threshold is decided by MatLab, iv) the image is transformed into binary image in order to isolate the two kidneys, v) the binary image is multiplied by the initial one, vi) the final image is appeared, vii) the colour can change (or not) according to individuals' needs. The following example of kidneys image describes the process.

Example 6

```
I = imread('kidneys.jpg');
figure, imshow(I)                                            (fig.12a)
graythresh(I) and the value of the threshold is calculated: ans = 0.2667
I2 = im2bw(I, 0.2667)                                        (fig.12b)
I3 = immultiply(I2, I)
imshow(I3)                                                   (fig.12c)
colormap(hot)                                                (fig.12d)
```

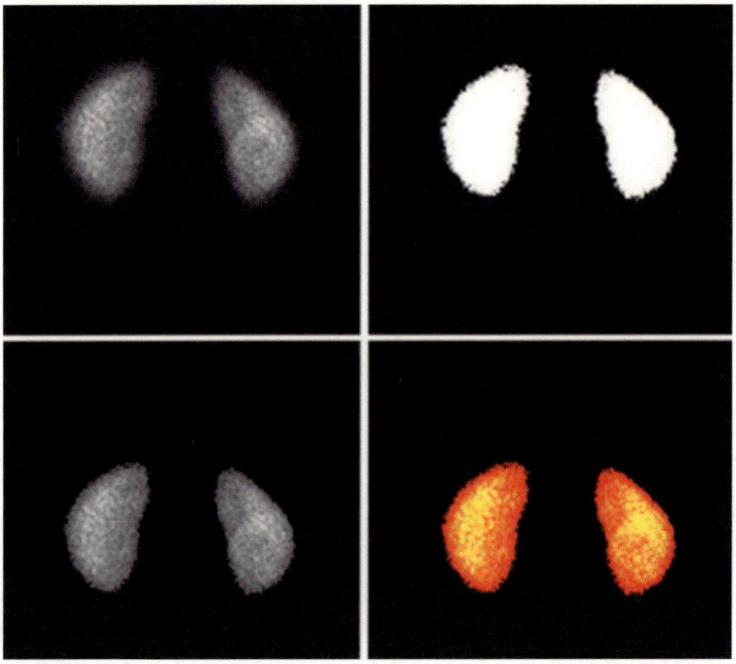

Fig. 12. Background subtraction: (a) Original image, (b) segmented binary image after thresholding depicting only sharp organ boundaries, (c) image after background removal, (d) change of colour to nuclear medicine pattern. [*(a) to (d) from left to right*]

3.8 Image registration

Image registration is used for aligning two images of the same object into a common coordinate system presenting the fused image. The one image is usually referred as reference and the other as sensed (or referred). Image registration is a spatial transform. The images can be acquired from different angles, at different times, by different or same modalities. A typical example of the use of image registration from different modalities in nuclear medicine is the combination of SPECT and CT images (SPECT/CT) or PET and CT (PET/CT). Image registration is used mainly for two reasons: i) to obtain enhanced information and details from the image for more accurate diagnosis or therapy (Li & Miller, 2010) and, ii) to compare patient's data (Zitova & Flusser, 2003). MatLab can be used in order to perform such a process. The whole procedure shall follow a specific order.

The first step of the procedure includes the image acquisition. After that, each image is reconstructed separately. Any filters needed are applied as well as enhancements in brightness and contrast. The process of filter application has been described in a previous section. The next step includes the foundation of a spatial transformation between the two images, the one of SPECT and the other of CT. The key figure in this step concerns about the alignment of the two images. A spatial transformation modifies the spatial relationship between the pixels of an image relocating them to new positions in a new image. There are several types of spatial transformation including the affine, the projective the box and the composite (Delbeke et al., 2006). The final step in image registration is the overlapping of the two images allowing a suitable level of transparency. A new image is created containing information from both pictures from which, the first has been produced. The whole procedure can be described with a set of commands which is user customised as different registration function packages can be constructed for different uses.

3.9 Intensity volume and 3-D visualisation

Volume visualisation in nuclear medicine consists of a method for extracting information from volumetric data utilising and processing a nuclear medicine image (Lyra et al., 2010b). In MatLab, this can be achieved by constructing a 3D surface plot which uses the pixel identities for (x, y) axes and the pixel value is transformed into surface plot height and, consequently, colour. Apart from that, 3D voxel images can be constructed; SPECT projections are acquired, iso-contours are depicted on them including a number of voxels and, finally all of them can be added in order to create the desirable volume image. (Lyra et al., 2010a).

Volume rendering - very often used in 3D SPECT images - is an example of efficient coding in MatLab. Inputs to the function are the original 3D array, the position angle, zoom or focus of the acquired projections. The volume rendering used in 3D myocardium, kidneys, thyroid, lungs and liver studies, took zoom and angles of 5.6 degrees, a focal length in pixels depending of the organs' size. The size of the re-projection is the same as the main size of input image (e.g. 128x128 for the 128x128x256 input image). The volume rendering by MatLab is slow enough but similar to other codes' volume rendering. An example image of myocardial 3-D voxel visualisation follows (Fig. 13):

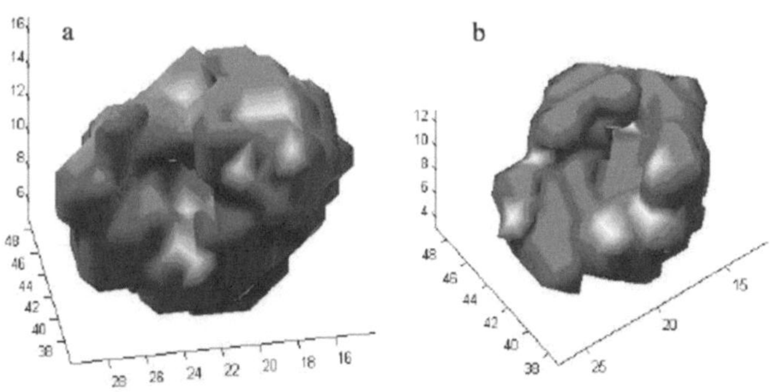

Fig. 13. 3D myocardial voxel visualisation; the image does not depicts the real volume but the voxelised one (Lyra et al 2010a).

4. MatLab mesh plot

MatLab is unique in data analysis in neurological imaging. We used MatLab and the functions of Image Processing Toolbox, to extract 3D basal ganglia activity measurements in dopamine transporters DaTSCAN scintigraphy. It can be easily run in an ordinary computer with Windows software, provides reproducible - user independent - results allowing better follow-up control comparing to the semi-quantitative evaluation of tracer uptake in basal ganglia.

The surface plot or the mesh plot can be used in order to extract information about the consistency of an organ or the loss of functionality. In order to construct a surface plot from a striatum image, the series of images that include the highest level of information was selected (Lyra et al 2010b) (Fig. 14):

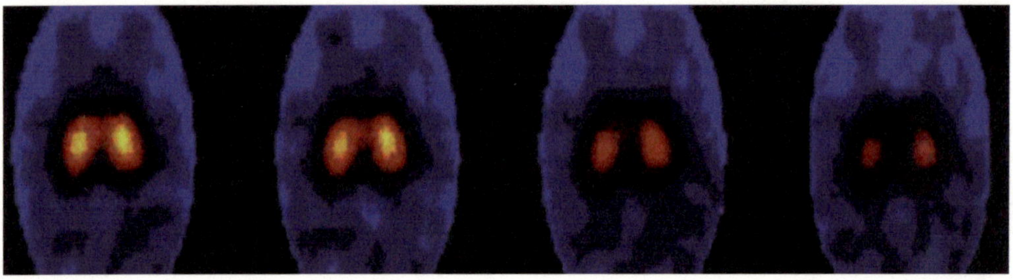

Fig. 14. A Series of central 123I-DaTSCAN SPECT imaging slices of I-123/Ioflupane; uptake is highest in middle 4 slices, and these were summarized for region of interest analysis (Lyra et al 2010b).

After the selection, ROI analysis was performed in order to concentrate on the area of interest which is the middle site of the image. The area of interest was selected and a package of functions was implemented.

Example 7

```
I = imread('striatum.jpg');
figure, imshow(I)
[x,y] = size(I);
X = 1:x;
Y = 1:y;
[xx,yy] = meshgrid(Y,x);
J = im2double(I);
figure, surf(xx,yy,J);
shading interp
view(-40,60)
```

The whole procedure was, finally, resulted in the surface plot that is presented in the Fig. 15.

A point of interest could be that although the images that were used to construct the surface plot were small and blurred, the final plot is clear and gives a lot of information regarding the activity concentration in these two lobes. The angle of view can be defined by the user giving the opportunity to inspect the whole plot from any point of view.

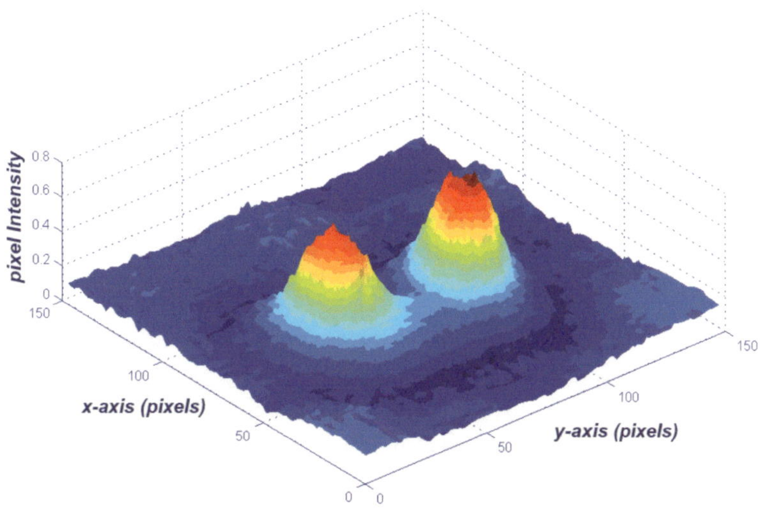

Fig. 15. Surface Plot of pixel intensity; x and y axes represent the pixels identities while the z axis represents the pixel intensity.

5. DICOM image processing using MatLab

The digital medical image processing started with the development of a standard for transferring digital images in order to enable users to retrieve images and related information from different modalities with a standardised way that is identical for all imaging modalities. In 1993, a new image format was established by National Electrical Manufacturers Association (NEMA). The Digital Imaging and Communication in Medicine (DICOM) standard allows the communication between equipment from different modalities and vendors facilitating the management of digital images. The DICOM standard defines a set of common rules for the exchange, storage and transmission of digital medical images with their accompanying information (Bidgood & Horii, 1992).
A DICOM file consists of the data header (so called metadata) and the DICOM image data set. The header includes image related information such as image type, study, modality,

matrix dimensions, number of stored bits, patient's name. The image data follow the header and contains 3D information of the geometry (Bankman, 2000). The DICOM files have a .dcm extension.

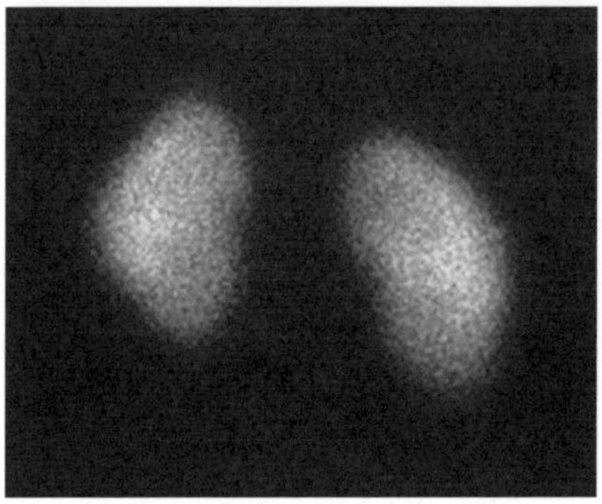

Fig. 16. Posterior image of kidneys in a DICOM format.

In nuclear medicine, the most common and supported format for storing 3D data using DICOM is to partition the volume (as myocardium or kidneys) into slices and to save each slice as a simple DICOM image. The slices can be distinguished either by a number coding in the file name or by specific DICOM tags.
MatLab supports DICOM files and is a very useful tool in the processing of DICOM images. An example of reading and writing metadata and image data of a DICOM file using MatLab is given in the next section. Let us consider a planar projection from a kidneys scan study for a 10-month-old boy as the DICOM image (Fig. 16).
The specific DICOM image is a greyscale image. Assuming "kidneys" is the name of the DICOM image we want to read, in order to read the image data from the DICOM file use the command `dicomread` in the following function.

```
I = dicomread('kidneys.dcm');
```

To read metadata from a DICOM file, use the `dicominfo` command. The latter returns the information in a MatLab structure where every field contains a specific piece of DICOM metadata. For the same DICOM image as previously,

```
info = dicominfo('kidneys.dcm')
```

A package of information appears in the command window including all the details that accompany a DICOM image. This is a great advantage of this image format in comparison to jpeg or tiff formats as the images retain all the information whereas the jpeg or tiff ones lose a great majority of it. For the specific image, the following information appears:

```
info =
Filename: 'kidneys.dcm'
FileModDate: '17-Feb-2011 14:04:18'
FileSize: 128000
Format: 'DICOM'
FormatVersion: 3
Width: 256
Height: 256
BitDepth: 16
```

```
ColorType: 'grayscale'
FileMetaInformationGroupLength: 212
FileMetaInformationVersion: [2x1 uint8]
MediaStorageSOPClassUID: '1.2.840.10008.5.1.4.1.1.7'
MediaStorageSOPInstanceUID: [1x57 char]
TransferSyntaxUID: '1.2.840.10008.1.2.1'
ImplementationClassUID: '1.2.840.113619.6.184'
ImplementationVersionName: 'Xeleris 2.1220'
SourceApplicationEntityTitle: 'XELERIS-6400'.
```

The rest of the information has been omitted as there is a huge amount of details. To view the image data imported from a DICOM file, use one of the toolbox image display functions `imshow` or `imtool`.

```
imshow(I,'DisplayRange',[]);
```

Similarly, an anterior planar image of thyroid gland can be imported and displayed in a DICOM format by using the toolbox image display function

```
imshow(K,'DisplayRange',[]);
```

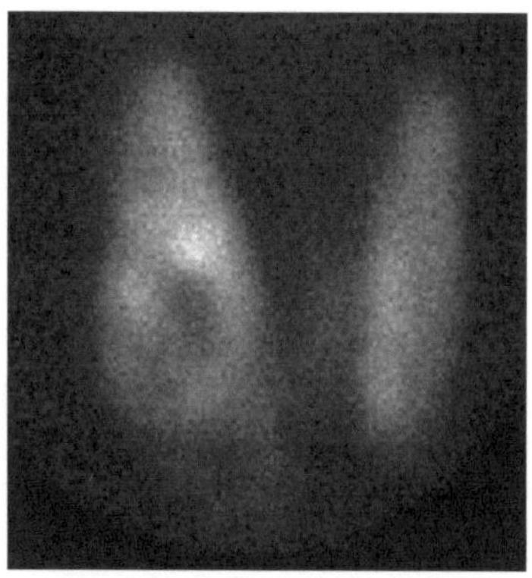

Fig. 17. Anterior planar image of thyroid gland in a DICOM format.

The image loaded can be now modified and processed in any desirable way. Many times, words or letters that describe the slice or projection appear within the image. These can be deleted and a new image without letters is created. To modify or write image data or metadata to a file in DICOM format, use the `dicomwrite` function. The following commands write the images `I` or `K` to the DICOM file `kidneys_file.dcm` and the DICOM file `thyroid_file.dcm`

```
dicomwrite(I, .dcm'), dicomwrite(K, .dcm')
```

On a DICOM format image any filtering, segmentation and background removing can be applied to get the final image and extract the most possible information useful in Diagnosis. In Fig.18 a DICOM format planar image of thyroid gland is imported and displayed (a) and further processed (b) by Gaussian filter and background removing.

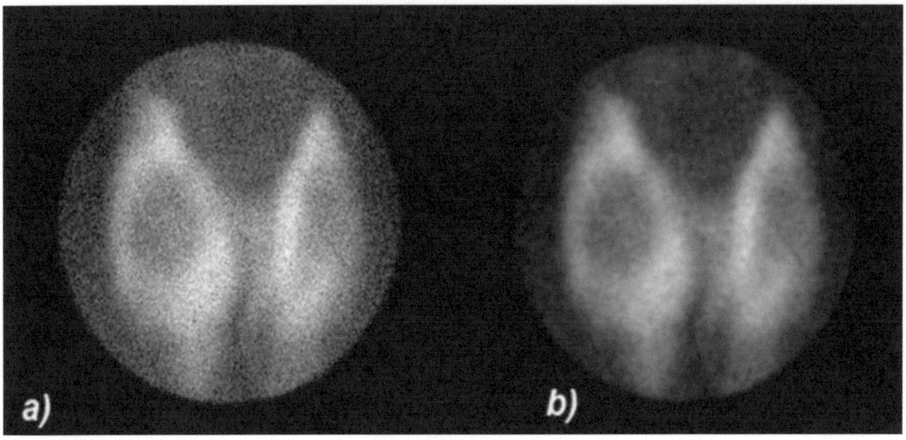

Fig. 18. (a) Thyroid gland DICOM image and (b) Gaussian filter and background removing are applied on the same image

The `dicomwrite` function is very useful too, in the case that we have to partition a volume into slices and to storage each slice as a simple DICOM image for further processing and analysis.

6. Conclusion

Image processing and analysis applied to nuclear medicine images for diagnosis, improve the acquired image qualitatively as well as offer quantitative information data useful in patient's therapy and care. Advanced techniques of image processing and analysis find widespread use in nuclear medicine. MatLab and Image Processing Toolbox enable both quantitative analysis and visualization of Nuclear Medicine images acquired as planar or angle projected images to reconstruct tomographic (SPECT, PET) slices and 3D volume surface rendering images.

7. Acknowledgment

The authors would like to acknowledge Ms Maria Gavrilelli, Medical Physicist, MSc from "Medical Imaging" Athens Paediatric Nuclear Medicine Center, Athens, Greece, for her medical images contribution.

8. References

Bankman, I. (2000). *Handbook of Medical Imaging*, Academic Press, ISSN 0-12-077790-8, United States of America

Bidgood, D. & Horii, S. (1992). Introduction to the ACR-NEMA DICOM standard. *RadioGraphics*, Vol. 12, (May 1992), pp. (345-355)

Delbeke, D.; Coleman, R.E.; Guiberteau M.J.; Brown, M.L.; Royal, H.D.; Siegel, B.A.; Townsend, D.W.; Berland, L.L.; Parker, J.A.; Zubal, G. & Cronin, V. (2006). Procedure Guideline for SPECT/CT Imaging 1.0. *The Journal of Nuclear Medicine*, Vol. 47, No. 7, (July 2006), pp. (1227-1234).

Gonzalez, R.; Woods, R., & Eddins, S. (2009) *Digital Image Processing using MATLAB*, (second edition), Gatesmark Publishing, ISBN 9780982085400, United States of America

Lehmann, T.M.; Gönner, C. & Spitzer, K. (1999). Survey: Interpolation Methods in Medical Image Processing. *IEEE Transactions on Medical Imaging*, Vol.18, No.11, (November 1999), pp. (1049-1075), ISSN S0278-0062(99)10280-5

Lyra, M.; Sotiropoulos, M.; Lagopati, N. & Gavrilleli, M. (2010a). Quantification of Myocardial Perfusion in 3D SPECT images - Stress/Rest volume differences, Imaging Systems and Techniques (IST), 2010 IEEE International Conference on 1-2 July 2010, pp 31 - 35, Thessaloniki, DOI: 10.1109/IST.2010.5548486

Lyra, M.; Striligas, J.; Gavrilleli, M. & Lagopati, N. (2010b). Volume Quantification of I-123 DaTSCAN Imaging by MatLab for the Differentiation and Grading of Parkinsonism and Essential Tremor, *International Conference on Science and Social Research*, Kuala Lumpur, Malaysia, December 5-7, 2010. http://edas.info/p8295

Li, G. & Miller, R.W. (2010). Volumetric Image Registration of Multi-modality Images of CT, MRI and PET, Biomedical Imaging, Youxin Mao (Ed.), ISBN: 978-953-307-071-1, InTech, Available from:
http://www.intechopen.com/articles/show/title/volumetric-image-registration-of-multi-modality-images-of-ct-mri-and-pet

O' Gorman, L.; Sammon, M. & Seul M. (2008). *Practicals Algorithms for image analysis*, (second edition), Cambridge University Press, 978-0-521-88411-2, United States of America

Nailon, W.H. (2010). Texture Analysis Methods for Medical Image Characterisation, Biomedical Imaging, Youxin Mao (Ed.), ISBN: 978-953-307-071-1, InTech, Available from:
http://www.intechopen.com/articles/show/title/texture-analysis-methods-for-medical-image-characterisation

MathWorks Inc. (2009) *MATLAB User's Guide*. The MathWorks Inc., United States of America

Perutka K. (2010). Tips and Tricks for Programming in Matlab, Matlab - Modelling, Programming and Simulations, Emilson Pereira Leite (Ed.), ISBN: 978-953-307-125-1, InTech, Available from: http://www.intechopen.com/articles/show/title/tips-and-tricks-for-programming-in-matlab

Toprak, A. & Guler, I. (2006). Suppression of Impulse Noise in Medical Images with the Use of Fuzzy Adaptive Median Filter. *Journal of Medical Systems*, Vol. 30, (November 2006), pp. (465-471)

Wernick, M. & Aarsvold, J. (2004). *Emission Tomography: The Fundamentals of PET and SPECT*, Elsevier Academic Press, ISBN 0-12-744482-3, China

Wilson, H.B.; Turcotte, L.H. & Halpern, D. (2003). *Advanced Mathematics and Mechanics Applications Using MATLAB* (third edition), Chapman & Hall/CRC, ISBN 1-58488-262-X, United States of America

Zitova, B. & Flusser J. (2003). Image Registration methods: a survey. *Image and Vision Computing*. Vol 21, (June 2003), pp. (977-1000)

24

Selected Methods of Image Analysis in Optical Coherence Tomography

Robert Koprowski and Zygmunt Wróbel
University of Silesia, Faculty of Computer Science and Materials Science
Institute of Computer Science, Department of Biomedical Computer Systems
Poland

1. Introduction

OCT is a new technique of picturing that uses uninvasional and contactless optical method based on interferometry of partially compact light for receiving sections images of human eyes in vivo. It allows picturing structural changes caused by eyes diseases, mapping thickness of retina and analyses shield of optical nerve and coats of nerve fibers. OCT has been developed since 1995 when it was initiated by measurement of intraocular distance by A.F. Frechera (Fercher el at., 1995) in years 2002-2004 the quick growth of quality and speed of eye picturing acquisition was observed but particularly in 2003 linear picturing and 2004 fast picturing with high resolution –Fig. 1. (Leitgeb el at., 2004; Ozcan el at., 2007; Bauma B. E. & Tearney, 2002).

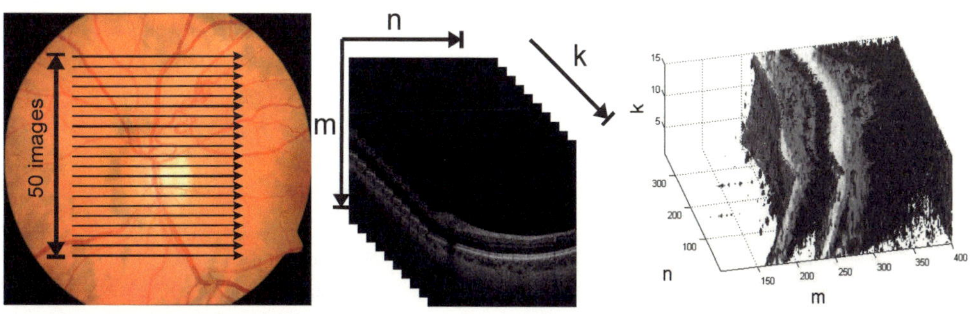

Fig. 1. The comparison of normal optic nerve head images with differential optical coherence tomography (OCT) technologies M×N×K=740×800×50

In work have been won input images L_{GRAY} in number near 1000 from optical tomograph SOCT Copernicus in the following parameters: wave length of light source: 840nm, width of spectrum: 50nm, pivotal resolution width (longitudinal): 6μm, traverse resolution: 12-18 μm of tomograph window: 2mm, speed of measurement: 25 000 scans in k pivot per second, maximum width of scanning: 10mm, maximum number of punctual scans in k pivot falling to n pivot: 10 500, become write down in gray levels about resolution M×N×K=740×800×50 where for each pixel falls to 8 bits.

The next part of considerations will be concerned with methods of analysis and processing of images automatically appointing layers borders visible on fig. 2 like: RPE - Retinal

Pigment Epithelium, OPL - Outer plexiform layer, IS/OS - Boundary between the inner and outer segments of the photoreceptors.

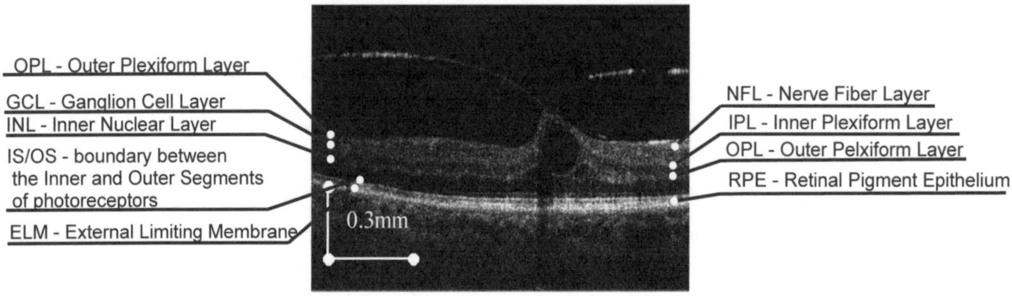

Fig. 2. Section scheme of individual layers along with marked characteristic gauged areas - image taken from SOCT Copernicus.

These considerations will be concerned with analysis of images sequences that have been already archived. Therefore, the possibilities of interference with the OCT device's apparatus will not be considered for increasing range of brightness level. Data from images sequence will not be taken into account, either - each image is analyzed independently. The source of acquiring given images assigned for analyses described by algorithms is free, i.e. any OCT device which allows to receive 2D image about minimum resolution 300×400 pixels.

The need of thickness analysis of individual layers RPE, IS/OS, NFL or OPL results from necessity of quantitative assessment but not qualitative, e.g. disease progression or efficiency of therapy, e.g. diabetes or Birdshot Chorioretinopathy.

Four methods of individual visible layers analyses will be discussed on Fig. 2 namely:

- Method of modified active contour - ACM. This method is based on basic information acquired from image like for example: the lightest RPE layer which will be identified in first period and on its base the remaining layers analysis will be carried out as OPL or IS/OS method of modified active contour for implemented line.
- The wandering small part method in discovering Canny edge - CCA. This method relies on preliminary edge detection using Canny detector and next continuity of lines correction on ends and conducting their connection with remaining ones (Canny, 1986; Koprowski & Wróbel, 2008).
- Random method of contour analysis - RAC. Points that start marking the edges are chosen at random during the preliminary image period, next the correction of their numbers is carried out in order for the remaining numbers, that come up to certain expectations, to become the first points of the lines appointed with the wandering small part method (Koprowski & Wróbel, 2009).
- Method based on hierarchic approach - HAC . There is preliminary identification of main layers like OPL or RPE on the smallest resolution and then the remaining layers are identified like IS/OS and the layers reconnaissance accuracy is gradually improved OPL and RPE (Koprowski & Wróbel, 2009).

2. Present state of knowledge - results acquired with known algorithms

Among results acquired with known algorithms there is in this chapter the description of the results:

- Acquired by other authors
- Acquired by authors of this work which have not brought satisfactory results in this application.

2.1 Results acquired for algorithms processed by authors not bringing desired results for OCT images

Among these results there have been methods which have not given satisfactory results as:

1. Method using Hough transform (Gonzalez & Woods, 1992). This method in this case did not give satisfactory results because the wanted layers on OCT image can change thickness and in general case can not be continuous. Additionally, the radius of curvature describing border of layers can be changed in wide ranges (Koprowski & Wróbel, 2009). It happens for example in shield of optical nerve (Costa el at., 2006) where individual OPL layers , RPE or IS/OS they are much worse visible (Klinder el at., 2009). Certain improvement of this method would be area analysis in which individual areas (with given width) would be brought closer by the lines. However, in this case emerges their mutual connections problem and problem of computational complexity.
2. Method of active contour in its typical version also does not produce desired results (Liang el at., 2006). At automatic selection of starting points using for example, method of Canny contour discovering or Gabor's filters (Gonzalez & Woods, 1992) only borders between the layers with the greatest contrast are discovered - RPE. In other cases, for the others layers, the method does not produce the expected results unless it is applied interactively with the user. Because the considerations in this work are applied only to fully automatic methods, the above method cannot be taken into account because of the mentioned interaction with the user. The method after the modifications introduced by the authors will be presented later in the algorithm ACM and CCA.
3. Method of texture analysis. In this case individual OPL layers, RPE or IS/OS are similar in case of texture which almost by definition disqualifies the described method. Despite this fact, the methods of texture analysis can be successfully used for emitting the wanted object from background (vitreous body). For example, for other type of images the methods have been successfully used in segmentation (Farsiu el at., 2008).
4. Also, methods of extended objects analyses (Koprowski el at., 2005) do not find application here because of the possibility of great size change in both the very object and its thickness and also the possibility of the object's division into two or more parts.

Methods suggested below in the work and processed by the authors (Koprowski el at., 2005, 2008, 2009) are a modification of the already mentioned known methods of analyses and processing of images and they are also new algorithms protected by copyright.

2.2 Results acquired by other authors

According to the best of author's knowledge there are no known algorithms analyses of eyes retina taking into account discovering the mentioned borders OPL, RPE or IS/OS including shield of optical nerve. Approaches suggested and introduced in (Chinn el at., 1997) or (Drexler el at., 2003) work only for typical cases in which the degree of pathology is insignificantly small. Applications used and enclosed for OCT device for example Copernicus also do not work successfully. In case of greater pathology, layers identified automatically are not continuous or they are not identified in a correct manner. The erroneus action that occurs often is incorrect connection of the identified layers and erroneous identifying of optical nerve shield. Additionally, the realized applications added to such a device like Copernicus or Stratus they are protected by copyright and rigorous form of algorithm is not rendered accessible outside. It results in the inability to estimate quantitatively the results and their accuracy in comparison with the author approaches suggested in this work.

Despite it, there is a whole big group of methods working correctly for simple cases where in OCT images there are well identified (with sufficient contrast) individual layers. They are the methods processed in LabVieW or in C++ (for example Bauma B. E. & Tearney, 2002) the processed results were also published in user manual Copernicus (Optopol) or in one of the chapters (Barry, 205). In this last position of literature (Farsiu el at., 2008) one of the few applications that analize individually further discussed OPL or RPE layers completely automatically is presented. It seems that OCT image analysis of eye is similar to the analysis of skin, or even coat material of a tennis ball (Thrane, 2001) however, the specificity of approach lies in variability in thickness of layers, individual variability of individual cases. In such cases of thickness changes of individual RPE, IS/OS, NFL or OPL layers, their mutual positions can be so big that typical algorithms work incorrectly. Obviously, there is coordinately a whole remaining group of methods interacting with user in which the user indicates representative or marks of segmentation area, giving off of layer and the implemented algorithm using, for example, the method of area expansion segmentates the marked area (Klinder el at., 2009), or fractal analisys. Algorithms for which correct results were acquired even for images of big radius of pathology distortion that work fully automatically are presented in next chapters in the form of block schemes. Detailed description of individual steps of discussed algorithms and their property like for example sensitivity to parameters change is discussed in given publications (Koprowski el at., 2005, 2008, 2009).

On this basis, taking into account also medical premises and taken attempts introduced below, four algorithms of analyses and processing of images of eye retina layers OCT were suggested.

3. The description of the suggested and compared algorithms

The algorithms presented below are both, known from the literature and modified by the authors and also new ones. Individual layers are marked in Cartesian coordinate match like RPE-y_{RPE}, IS/OS - $y_{IS/OS}$ layer. To avoid the conflict in designation, in chosen cases overhead index indicating algorithm type (ACM, CCA, RAC or HAC) - for example $y_{RPE}^{(CCA)}$ was added.

3.1 Preliminary processing of image

Preliminary processing of image is common for all discussed methods ACM (Koprowski & Wróbel, 2009), CCA -(Koprowski & Wróbel, 2008), RAC (Koprowski el at., 2005) or HAC (Koprowski & Wróbel, 2009). Preliminary algorithms of processing of images include filtration with median filter of square mask sized about 21×21 for elimination of hum and slight artefacts introduced by measuring match in the course of acquisition of image. Selection of size of mask has been carried arbitrarily on base of image resolution M×N=740×800 and width of interests layers(OPL, RPE or IS/OS). Obviously, it must be mentioned here that there are many others methods belonging to filtration in preliminary

processing of image like for example adaptation filters, spatially adaptive wavelet filter (Adler et al., 2004; Gnanadurai & Sadasivam, 2005) or fuzzy-based wavelet.
The second element of processing of preliminary image was normalization from minimum-maximum partition of image pixels brightness for full partition from 0 for 1. This procedure is aimed at the expansion of pixel brightness range for image on which the quality of visible object is degraded for different reasons.
So transformed images L_{MED} (after filtration of median filter and normalization) were subjected to analysis with available algorithms and algorithms suggested by authors (ACM, CCA, RAC, HAC).

3.2 Description of ACM algorithm

The ACM method - active modified contour, it is based on basic information acquired from image like for example the plainest RPE layer which will be identified in the first period and on its base the analysis of the remaining layers like OPL or IS/OS will be carried out (Akiba et al., 2003; Choma el at., 2003). The picture 3 presents structure of unit algorithm (block scheme) in which chosen blocks (layer analysis OPL, IS/OS, ELM) can work independently.

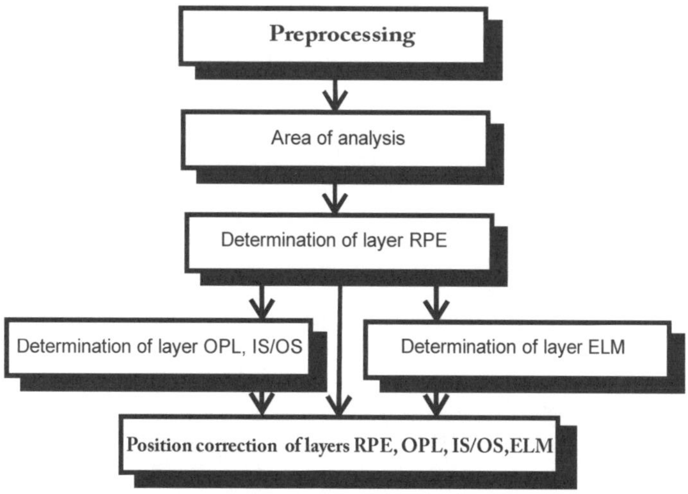

Fig. 3. Block scheme of algorithm

The block scheme introduced in picture 3 divides the work of the whole ACM algorithm into four phases::

- Preliminary processing – filtration with median filter and normalization were described in the former subchapter.
- Appointing of RPE layer site and next using modified active contour method assigning remaining OPL or IS/OS layers.
- Appointment of external border of ELM retina site.
- Correction of the received layers in relation to the area of analysis - taking into account quality of areas of introduced objects.

After preliminary process of image processing (filtration and normalization receiving L_{MED}) L_{GRAY} image analysis was started by analyzing the place of maximum for next columns of images matrixes. If we mark lines and columns of the image matrixes by m and n new $L_{BIN}^{(ACM)}$ image includes value "1" in places where pixels are brighter in given column by

90% for this column maximum taking a stand brightness. In the remaining places there is value "0". On this base calculating of the center sites of longest section for each image column $L_{BIN}^{(ACM)}$ receiving course y_R was carried out (Fig. 2).

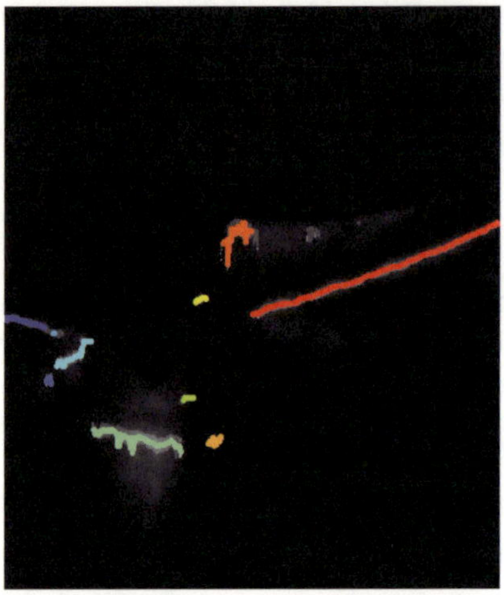

Fig. 4. The sum of $L_{BIN}^{(ACM)}$ image in 50% weight and 50% L_{MED} and drawn y_R course (y_{RS}),

Fig. 5. Functions of 3th row y_{RS} (k_1,k_2) for any possible couples of concentrations

Course of y_R function is further subjected to the operation of concentrations analyses by k-means method acquiring $y_{RS}^{(k)}$ for each k-concentration. Next the operation of approxymation through polynomial of 3 row ($y_{RS}^{(k1,k2)}$) of each couple $y_{RS}^{(k1)}$ and $y_{RS}^{(k2)}$ for $k_1 \neq k_2$ is performed. All polynomial functions $y_{RS}^{(k1,k2)}$ received for all possible pairs of concentration (k_1, k_2) are shown in Fig. 2-3. For each function y_R a number of points is appointed contained in partition ±15 pixels. Next the pair (k_1,k_2) is appointed for which number of point contained in partition ±15 pixels is maximum at chosen $y_{RS}^{(k1*,k2*)}$ in simplification further called y_{RPE} function. Result is shown in Fig. 2-3 by white line (course of $y_{RPE}^{(ACM)}$). ELM and IS/OS borders were appointed on the basis of course $y_{RPE}^{(ACM)}$.

Algorithms in both cases were very approximated for each other and they concerned in biggest fragment method of modified active contour (exact differences between suggested method and classic method of active contour is shown in Gonzalez & Woods 1992). According to the introduced visual scheme in Fig. 5 values of medians in areas over and below of analysis pixel in blocks about sizes $p_{yu}\times(p_{xl}+p_{xp}+1)$ for method of active contour are appointed.

Next the value of their remainder is calculated and written down in matrix ΔS in following form:

$$\Delta S = \begin{array}{r|cccc} \cdots & & & \cdots & \\ 4 & \Delta_{S,4,1} & \Delta_{S,4,2} & \Delta_{S,4,3} & \Delta_{S,4,4} \\ 3 & \Delta_{S,3,1} & \Delta_{S,3,2} & \Delta_{S,3,3} & \Delta_{S,3,4} \\ 2 & \Delta_{S,2,1} & \Delta_{S,2,2} & \Delta_{S,2,3} & \Delta_{S,2,4} \\ 1 & \Delta_{S,1,1} & \Delta_{S,1,2} & \Delta_{S,1,3} & \Delta_{S,1,4} \\ 0 & \Delta_{S,0,1} & \Delta_{S,0,2} & \Delta_{S,0,3} & \Delta_{S,0,4} \; \cdots \\ -1 & \Delta_{S,-1,1} & \Delta_{S,-1,2} & \Delta_{S,-1,3} & \Delta_{S,-1,4} \\ -2 & \Delta_{S,-2,1} & \Delta_{S,-2,2} & \Delta_{S,-2,3} & \Delta_{S,-2,4} \\ -3 & \Delta_{S,-3,1} & \Delta_{S,-3,2} & \Delta_{S,-3,3} & \Delta_{S,-3,4} \\ -4 & \Delta_{S,-4,1} & \Delta_{S,-4,2} & \Delta_{S,-4,3} & \Delta_{S,-4,4} \\ \cdots & & & \cdots & \end{array} \tag{1}$$

Where ΔS=med(Lu)-med(Ld) for Lu and Ld that are areas of the size properly $p_{yu}\times(p_{xl}+p_{xp}+1)$ and $p_{yd}\times(p_{xl}+p_{xp}+1)$ and

p_{yu} - value of Lu line,
p_{yd} - value of Ld line,
p_u - partition of relocation pixel and areas Lu i Ld for top,
p_d - partition of relocation pixel and areas Lu i Ld to bottom,
p_{xl} - number of column on the left of the analyzed pixel,
p_{xp} - number of column on the right of the analyzed pixel,
p_{ly} - distance in pivot oy respect $y_{RPE}^{(ACM)}$
p_{xud} - distance between neighbor pixels in pivot oy,
med – medians.

After creating ΔS matrix about size $(p_u+p_d+1)\times N$ sorting is performed for next columns begining from biggest values of remainders between Lu and Ld areas. Next the analysis of individual values for the following columns so that the pxud remainder does not surpass the assumed level is performed. For 1000 pieces of test images this value was established at the level of 2. The remaining parameters like pyu and pyd influence the sensitivity of the method and p_u and p_d are the range of searching possible pixels sites. By increasing p_{yu} and pyd values, time of calculations is increased. Searching for the new values of sites points of $y_{IS/OS}^{(ACM)}$ layer is started from course $y_{RPE}^{(ACM)}$. Points of initial $y_{IS/OS}^{(ACM)}$ layer emerge from slip by pIy in attitude of $y_{RPE}^{(ACM)}$ course.

New sites are appointed in partition from $y_{IS/OS}^{(ACM)}-p_{yu}$ to $y_{IS/OS}^{(ACM)}+p_{yd}$.

The received $y_{IS/OS}^{(ACM)}$, $y_{RPE}^{(ACM)}$, $y_{ELM}^{(ACM)}$ course (layers) must additionally grant the following conditions from premises subsequent of eye structure (these conditions will be served in Cartesian coordinate match) (Hausler & Lindner, 1998):

- $y_{RPE}^{(ACM)} < y_{IS/OS}^{(ACM)} < y_{ELM}^{(ACM)}$ for each x,
- $y_{ELM}^{(ACM)} - y_{RPE}^{(ACM)} \approx 0.1$ mm -being the initial value starting work of active contour method (Ko el at., 2005),
- $y_{ELM}^{(ACM)} - y_{IS/OS}^{(ACM)} \approx$ od 0 do 1 mm for different x (Yun el at., 2004).

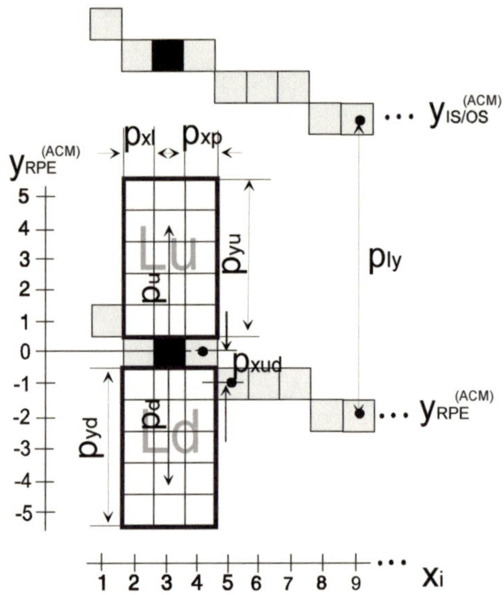

Fig. 6. Scheme of visual values scaling difference of brightness method

Appling this restriction, correct results for automatic achieved RPE, IS/OS or ELM layer finding has been achieved (Fig. 7).

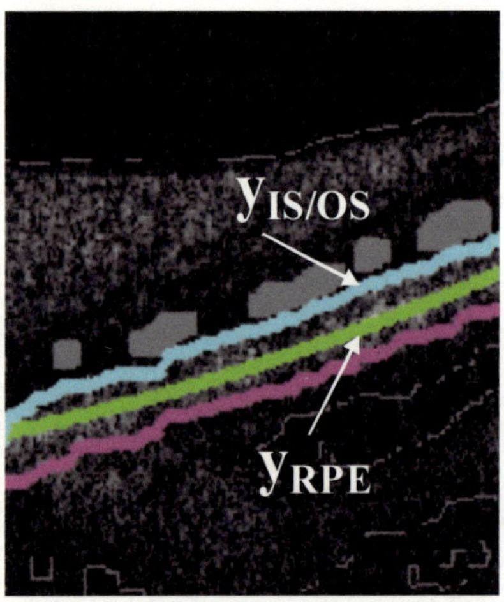

Fig. 7. Accommodation of function course $y_{IS/OS}^{(ACM)}$ and $y_{RPE}^{(ACM)}$.

3.3 Description of CCA algorithm

Method of small part wandering about in discovering Canny edge - CCA relies on preliminary detection of edge using Canny detector and next corrections of lines continuity on ends and performing the connection with the remaining ones- Fig. 8.

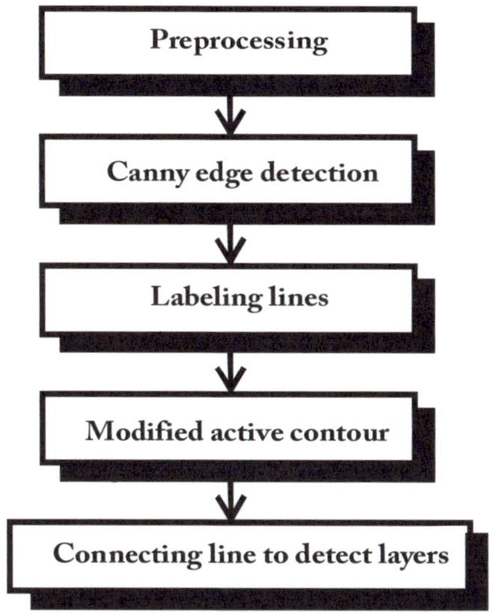

Fig. 8. Block scheme of CCA algorithm

The first period of the used CCA method is discovering edge with assistance of Canny method (Canny, 1986) on L_{MED} image. For so emerged binary $L_{BIN}^{(CCA)}$ the operation of labeling was conducted where each concentration (about value "1") owns label et=1,2,...,Et-1,Et. Next, for each label et labeling is conducted giving each concentration (line) label. Received image $L_{IND}^{(CCA)}$ is shown in pseudocolors on Fig. 7.

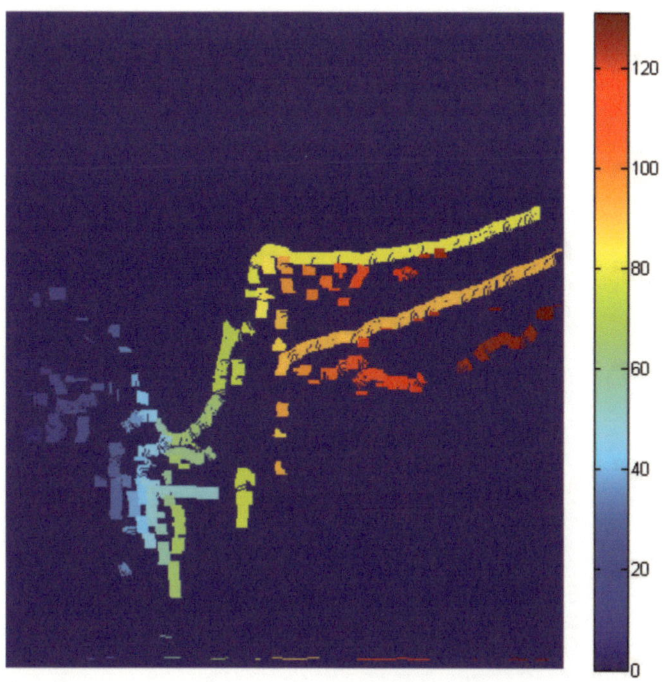

Fig. 9. $L_{IND}^{(CCA)}$ Image in pseudocolors (label Et=131)

Fig. 9 shows values of labels for the next line of $L_{IND}^{(CCA)}$ image. Each continuous line of edge visible on $L_{IND}^{(CCA)}$ image (Fig. 9) for labels e_t=1,2,...,E_t-1,E_t has been transformed for form k=1,2,3,…,K-1,K points ($x_{et,k}$ $y_{et,k}$) in Cartesian match of coordinates. Method of modified active contour has been employed for each "stretch" of edge in both directions. For this purpose for two first pairs of coordinates of first edge ($x_{1,1}$,$y_{1,1}$) and ($x_{1,2}$,$y_{1,2}$) and two last ones ($x_{1,K-1}$,$y_{1,K-1}$) and ($x_{1,K}$,$y_{1,K}$) a straight line has been appointed going through these points, that is according to visual drawing below (Fig. 10):

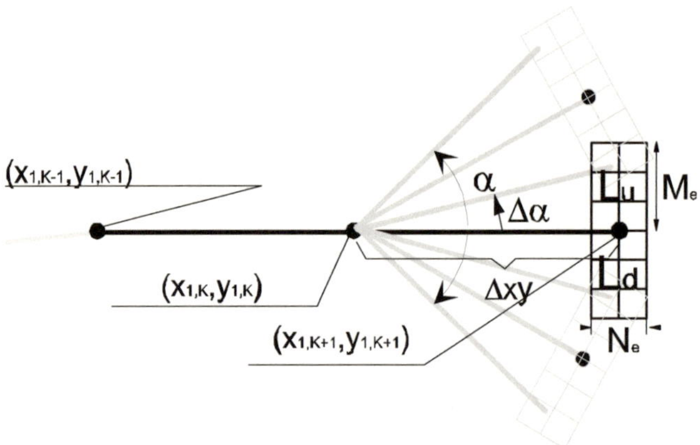

Fig. 10. Graphic interpretation of modified active contour method for appointment of next point beginning from points positions ($x_{1,K-1}$,$y_{1,K-1}$) and ($x_{1,K}$,$y_{1,K}$) for establishing new point (pixel) ($x_{1,K+1}$,$y_{1,K+1}$). For simplification angle of depression of final points of edges was established at β=0°.

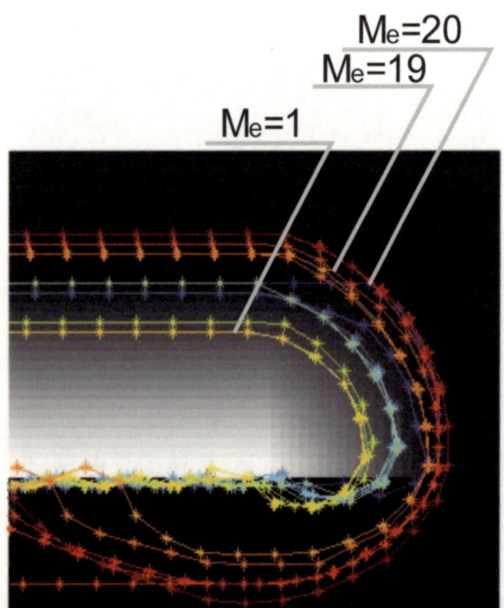

Fig. 11. Artificial image and fragment of modified active contour operation for α=40, $\Delta\alpha$=1, Δxy=N_e=4, M_e changed in range (1,20)

Fig. 11 presents the ideas of method of active contour where beginning from points position $(x_{1,K-1},y_{1,K-1})$ and $(x_{1,K},y_{1,K})$ straight line going through them is established with an angle of depression β_1 and in distance Δxy appointing of the position of new point $(x_{1,K+1},y_{1,K+1})$ for different potential positions (in angle partition $\beta_1(1)\pm\alpha$ through $\Delta\alpha$). The choice of proper position of contour point acquired through adding next points for existing edge is acquired on base of analyses of average values from areas Lu and Ld about size $M_e \times N_e$ (Fig. 3-8). α angle for which the best adjustment for the analyzed point $(x_{1,K+1},y_{1,K+1})$ exists is the one for which the remainder in average values between areas Lu and Ld is the biggest.

As it happens, the suggested method of modified active contour has very curious properties. The parameters of this algorithm are as follows:

α - Angle in which range the best adjusting for the given criterion is searched,

$\Delta\alpha$ - Accuracy with which we search for the best adjusting,

Δxy - the distance between the present and the next searched point of active contour $(x_{1,K+1},y_{1,K+1})$, $(x_{1,K+2},y_{1,K+2})$ and so on,

Me - Height of analyzed Lu and Ld area

Ne - Width of analyzed Lu and Ld area

On the base of the above-mentioned findings and realized measurements (Koprowski & Wróbel, 2009) values of parameters of active contour on α=45, $\Delta\alpha$=1, Δxy=1, Me=11, Ne=11 were established. Iterations for individual et edges of active contour method have been interrupted, then if one of the following situations happened:

The possible number of iterations has been surpassed - established arbitrary for 1000,

For this point the condition of remainder in average values between areas Lu and Ld has not been granted

At least two points own the same coordinates - it precludes to looping of algorithm.

For parameters established this way, the results have been acquired that are presented below Fig. 10, Fig. 11).

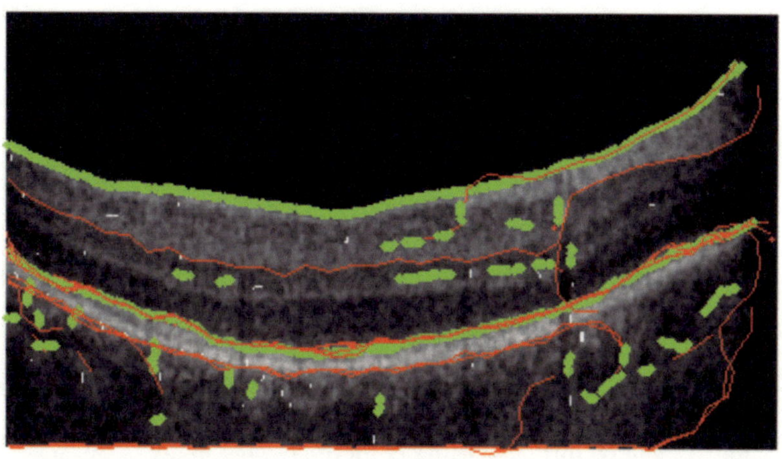

Fig. 12. Operation of modified active contour on real image for α=40, $\Delta\alpha$=1, Δxy=Ne=11, Me =10. The green line marks the contour acquired with Canny method, the red line marks next points of active contour method.

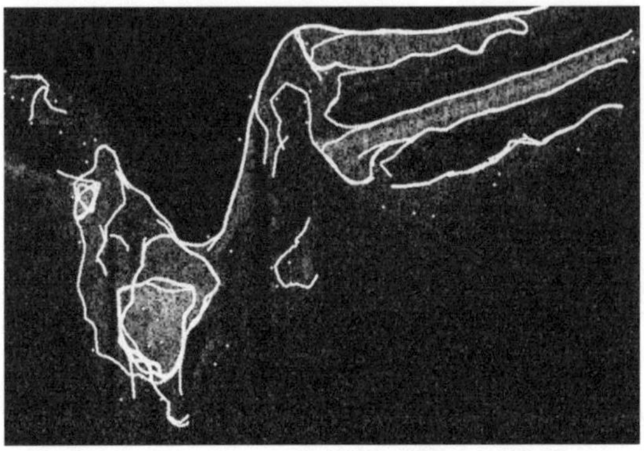

Fig. 13. Operation of modified active contour after the described correction on real image for α=40, $\Delta\alpha$=1, Δxy=Ne=11, Me =11

As shown on drawings above (Fig. 10, Fig. 11) the suggested method discovers correctly individual layers on OCT image of an eye.

3.4 Random method of contour analysis – RAC

Points starting the operation of the algorithm - RAC are chosen at random in the preliminary period (Koprowski & Wróbel, 2009). Next, the correction of their number is performed, so that the remaining ones, granting proper conditions become the first points for the appointed RPE, IS/OS, NFL or OPL layers. This line become stretched further by method of modified active contour introduced in description of CCA algorithm (Fig. 14).

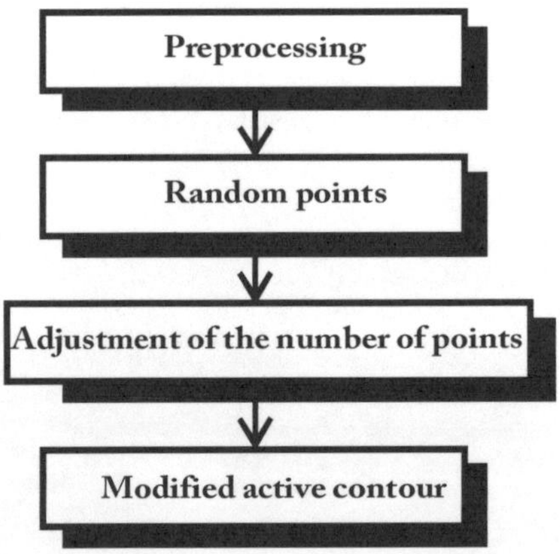

Fig. 14. Block scheme of RAC algorithm

It has already been mentioned that preliminary position of starting points was chosen at random. random values from monotonous partition were acquired (0,1) for each of new points of image matrixes - Lo (about resolution of L_{MED} image there is.: M×N). For Lo image pixels created this way (random) binarization with threshold pr is carried out . Each new pixel with value "1" will be further starting point $o^*_{i,j}$ (where index "i" means next starting point however, "j" means next points created on its base). This way, by selecting value of threshold pr in range (0.1) we influence the number of starting points. In the next period, the position of starting points is modified in the assigned H area of the sizes M_H×N_H. The modification relies on correction of point position $o^*_{i,1}$ with coordinates ($x^*_{i,1}$, $y^*_{i,1}$) to new coordinates ($x_{i,1}$, $y_{i,1}$) where possibly relocation is in range $x_{i,1}= x^*_{i,1}\pm(N_H)/2$ and $y_{i,1}= y^*_{i,1}\pm(M_H)/2$. Change of coordinates follows in area $\pm(M_H)/2$ and $\pm(N_H)/2$ in which the biggest value is achieved in remainder between pixels in eight- neighbor match. Next the correction of repeating points is performed- this which have the same coordinates are deleted.

For assigning layers on OCT image the component of contour were later indicated in meaning of his fragments subjected later to modification and processing in the following manner. For each $o^*_{i,1}$ point chosen at random with coordinates ($x^*_{i,1}$, $y^*_{i,1}$) iteration process is performed relying on searching of next $o_{i,2}$, $o_{i,3}$, $o_{i,4}$, $o_{i,5}$ points and so on, according to dependence described in CCA algorithm (Fig. 8).

In the described case of iteration appointment contour component becomes essential introduction of limitation range (next parameters) which includes:

- j_{MAX} - maximum number of iterations - limitation whose purpose is to eliminate algorithm looping if every time, points $o_{i,j}$ will be appointed with different locations and contour will have for example spiral form.
- Stopping the iteration process if it will be discovered that $x_{i,j}=x_{i,j+1}$ and $y_{i,j}=y_{i,j+1}$. This situation happens most often if Lu and Ld areas are of a similar size as area H or are bigger (about sizes $M_H\times N_H$). As for the random choosing and correcting starting points, here might also appear the situation that after the correction there will be $x_{i,j}=x_{i,j+1}$ and $y_{i,j}=y_{i,j+1}$
- Stopping the iteration process if $y_{i,j}>M_M$ or $x_{i,j}>N_M$ or in cases where the indicated $o_{i,j}$ point will be outside the picture.
- Stopping the iteration process if still better matching point in respect does not grant condition admissible $\Delta\alpha$ (allowable curvature contour).

At this stage, components of the outline for the given parameters are obtained. These parameters include:

Size of h_x and h_y mask is strictly related to resolution of image and size of identified area accepted for $M_M\times N_M = 864\times1024$ on $M_H\times N_H=23\times23$

p_r - threshold responsible for the number of starting points - changed practically in range 0-0.1,

j_{MAX} - maximum admissible number of iterations - established arbitrarily at 100,

$\Delta\alpha$ - partition of angle established in partition 10-70°,

$M_H\times N_H$ -size of correction area, square area, converted in range $M_H\times N_H=5\times5$ to $M_H\times N_H=25\times25$

$\Delta\alpha$ - admissible maximum change of angle between the folowing points of contour established in partition 10-70°.

The analyzing the acquired values it must be noticed that stopping the iteration process happens only when $x_{i,j}=x_{i,j+1}$ and $y_{i,j}=y_{i,j+1}$ (as it was said earlier). Or then only if points $o_{i,j}$ and $o_{i,j+1}$ have the same position. This condition does not concern oi,j points which have the same coordinates but for different "i", that is the ones that emerged in definite point of iterations from different initial points. Easing of this condition leads to generation overlap on the elements of contour which must be analyzed.

As it has been presented above, the performed iteration process can cause overlapping of $o_{i,j}$ points with the same coordinates ($x_{i,j}$, $y_{i,j}$) emerged from different initial oi,1points. This property is used for ultimate appointment of contour layers on OCT image.

In a general case, it can happen that despite relatively small values of the accepted p_r threshold, the randomly chosen $o_{i,1}$ starting point is placed beyond the edge of object. Then, the next iterations can join it with the remaining part. In such a case the deletion process of outstanding branch is performed - alike for lopping off of branch in frameworking (Gonzalez & Woods, 1992).
Exemplary results showed on Fig. 15 are acquired for real OCT image for p_r=0.02, $\Delta\alpha$=80°, M_H×N_H=35×35.

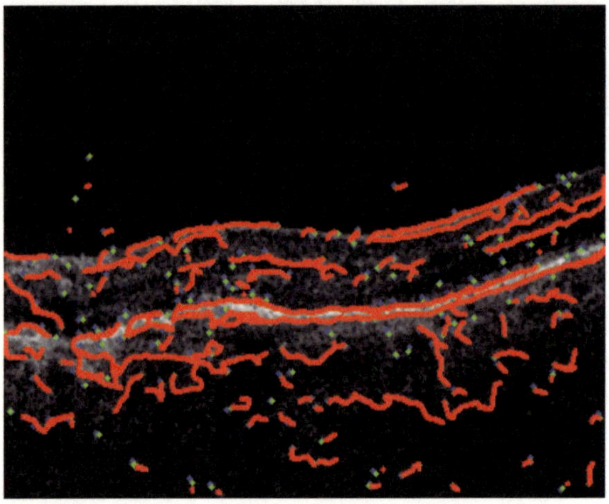

Fig. 15. Exemplary results acquired for real image OCT for p_r=0.02, $\Delta\alpha$=80°, M_H×N_H=35×35.

Fig. 1 - correctly indicated contour components are visible and other fragments of contour which from the point of view of limitation are not deleted. However, on the other hand number of available parameters and its form allow enough liberty in their selection in order to get desired results. In majority of cases, obtaining the intentional form of contour is possible for one established M_H×N_H value. However, it can turn out that the use of hierarchic approach is required for which M_H×N_H size will be decreased, thanks to which greater accuracy of the suggested method will be acquired and it will introduce weight (hierarchies) of importance of individual contours.

3.5 Method based on hierarchic approach – HAC

The method based on hierarchic approach - HAC (Koprowski & Wróbel, 2009).The main NFL or RPE layers are initially identified on image of the smallest resolutions and next remaining layers are identified like for example IS/OS and accuracy reconnaissance of NFL and RPE layers (Fig. 3-2) is gradually increased.
From foundation, described algorithm should give satisfactory results mainly from part of criterion operation speed. The described methods (algorithms) are characterized by big accuracy of account, however, they are not sufficiently fast (it is hard to get analysis speed of single 2D image in time not surpassing 10ms or 50 ms on processor PII 1.33 GHz). Thus, decrease of L_{MED} image resolution was suggested about near 50% for such value of pixels number in rows and columns (with M×N=740×800) which is power of value "2" there is M×N=256×512 (L_{MED2}) applying further decomposition for L_{D16} image (where symbol "D" - means decomposition and symbol "16" means block size for which it has been received). Any exit (output) image pixel after decomposition has value equal median from area (block) of 16×16 size entrance (input) image according to Fig. 17.

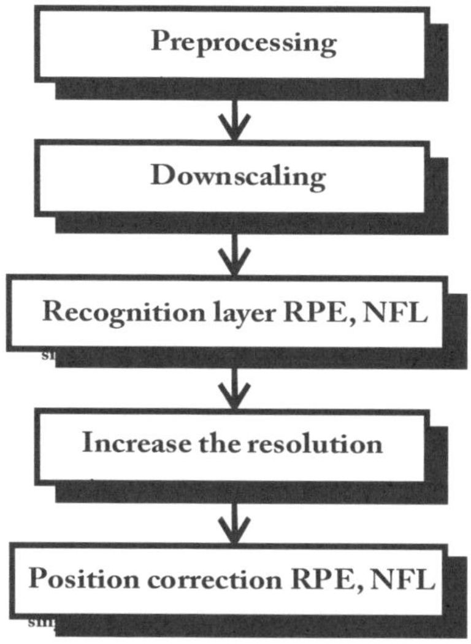

Fig. 16. Block scheme of HAC algorithm

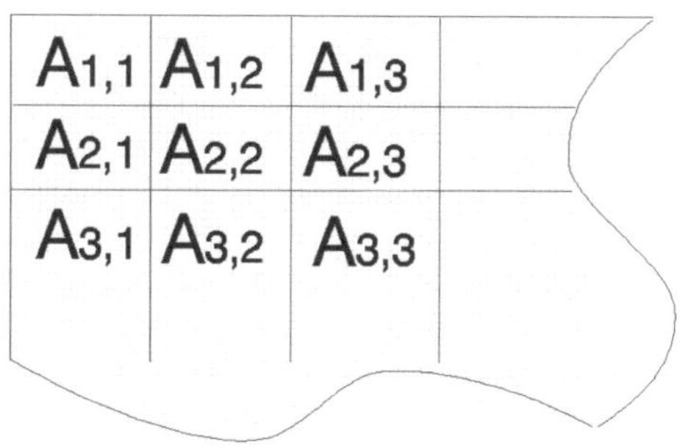

Fig. 17. Location of blocks na obrazie L_{MED2}

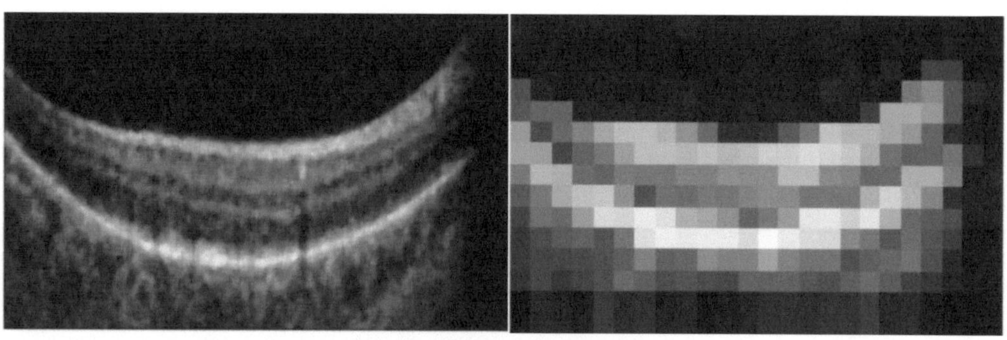

Fig. 18. Image before and after decomposition - L_{MED2} i L_{D16}

Exemplary L_{D16} result and input L_{MED2} image are shown on Fig. 18. L_{D16} Image will be subjected to the operation of appointment of pixel positions with maximum value for each column. Applying this thresholding method by maximum value in rows, in 99% of cases only one maximum value in column is received.

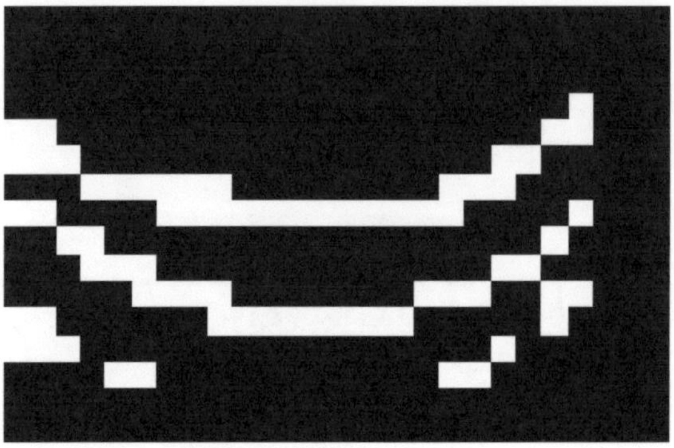

Fig. 19. Exemplary L_{DB16} image

In order to appoint position of NFL and RPE borders precisely, the use one more L_{DB16} image was essential. This image is a binary image with white pixels placed in places for which remainder between neighbor pixels in vertical tis greater than assigned pr threshold - accepted in range (0, 0.2). In result, the cooridnates of points border locations $y_{NFL}^{(HAC)}$ and $y_{RPE}^{(HAC)}$ are received as locations of values "1" in L_{DB16} image for which $y_{NFL}^{(HAC)}(x) \leq y_{RPE}^{(HAC)}(x)$. This relative simple approach gives unbelieveably satisfactory results. This method for selection of pr threshold on level 0.01 gives satisfactory results in nearly 70% of images in not compound cases (that is, the ones which are not images with visible pathology or shield of optical nerve). Unfortunately, for the remaining 30% of cases, selection of p_r threshold in accepted borders does not decrease the emerging errors (Fig. 19).
The correction of erroneous reconnaissance of $y_{NFL}^{(HAC)}$ and $y_{RPE}^{(HAC)}$ layers is important because for this approach these errors will be copied (In presented further hierarchic approach) for next exact approximations. After correction taking into consideration number of white pixels for individual L_{DM16} image columns, and mutual situating taking into consideration NFL and RPE layers position, presented correction gives for above-mentioned images class efficiency at the level of 99% of cases. Despite the accepted limitations, this method brings erroneous results for initial columns of image (with hierarchic approach definition) unfortunately, these errors are copied further.
The cause of erroneous reconnaissance of layers locations is the difficulty in distinguishing proper layers in case of discovering three "line", three points in given column in which position is changed in admissible range for individual x.

3.6 Decrease of decomposition area

Relatively simple period of processing of tomographyc image with particular consideration of speed of operation is escalation of accuracy and the same decrease of $A_{m,n}$ area's size (Fig. 17) - block on L_{MED} image. It was assumed that $A_{m,n}$ areas will be decreased in sequence to 1×1 size by a half in each iteration. Decrease of $A_{m,n}$ area is equivalent with next period execution of NFL and RPE line position approximation.
Increase of accuracy (precision) position of NFL and RPE lines indicated in former iteration is tied with two periods:

- Coordinate condensing (x,y) in meaning of indirect appointment (in center of point (x,y) put exactly) using method of linear interpolation.
- Change of position of the condensed points so that they bring closer the wanted borders in a better way.

If first part is intuitive and it leads to resampling process, the second requires exact explanations.The second period relies on adjusting individual point to wanted layer. Because in ox axis the image is from definition already decomposed and pixel brightness in the analyzed image is similar to median value of the primary image, properly in window A (Fig.17) modification of RPE and NFL point position follows in vertical axis only. Analysis of individual RPE and NFL points is independent in meaning of addiction from the position of point in line.

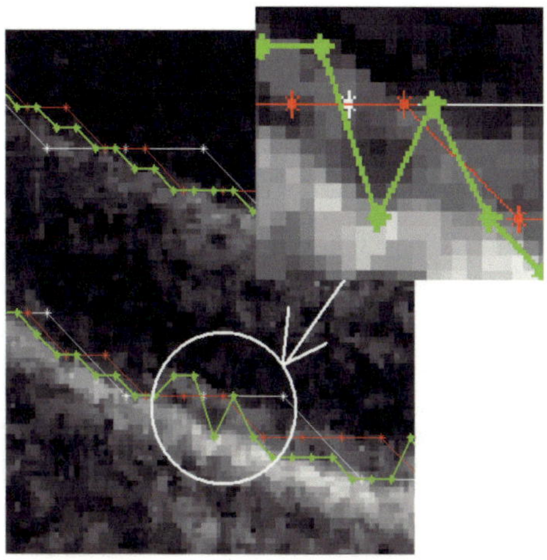

Fig. 20. Results of the processes of adjusting for two iterations. White color marks input RPE points and red and green color mark next approximations.

Each RPE point remaining from the previous iteration and new arising from the interpolation, are in various stages of the algorithm matched to RPE layer with ever greater precision. Change of the position of $y_{RPE}^{(HAC)}$ point (x) is in the range $\pm p_u$ where range of variation is not dependent on the scale of considerations (size of A area) and follows closely the distance between the NFL and RPE. For blocks A of size 16 × 16 to 1 × 1 p_u is constant and is 2. This value was adopted on the basis of the typical average for examined hundreds of L_{GRAY} images the distance between the NFL and RPE of about 32 pixels which means that the decomposition into A blocks of size 16×16 are two pixels so p_u=2. In this regard, ± 2 is looking for maximum L_{DM} image and it adopts a new position of RPE NFL point. This way the process of RPE or NFL is more similar to the actual conduct of the analyzed layer. Results obtained from the fit shown in Fig. 3-6. The white color shows the input RPE values as input data for this stage of the algorithm and the decomposition on A blocks of size 16 x 16 (L_{DM16} and L_{D16} images), red matching results for A blocks of size 8 x 8 (L_{DM8} and L_{D8} images) and green match results for A blocks of size 4 x 4 (L_{DM4} and L_{D4} images). As shown in Fig. 3-6 further decomposition and the next smaller and smaller A areas and hence higher resolution, image is obtained with greater accuracy at the expense of time (Indeed, increasing the number of analyzed $y_{RPE}^{(HAC)}(x)$, $y_{NFL}^{(HAC)}(x)$ points and their neighborhoods $\pm p_u$).

This method for A size 16 × 16 has large enough properties of the Global Approach to the brightness of pixels that there is no need to introduce at this stage the additional treatment to distinguish between closely spaced layers (that were not previously visible because of image resolutions). By contrast, with the A areas of sizes 4 x 4 other layers are already visible, which should be further analyzed correctly. Increasing accuracy makes IS/OS layer visible which is located near the RPE layer (Fig. 20). Thus, in a circled area there is high fluctuation of position in oy axis of RPE layer. Therefore, a next algorithm step was developed taking into account the partition on RPE and IS/OS layers for appropriate high-resolution. As shown in Fig. 21. presented method copes perfectly with detection of NFL, RPE and IS/OS layers marked appropriately by colors red, blue and green.

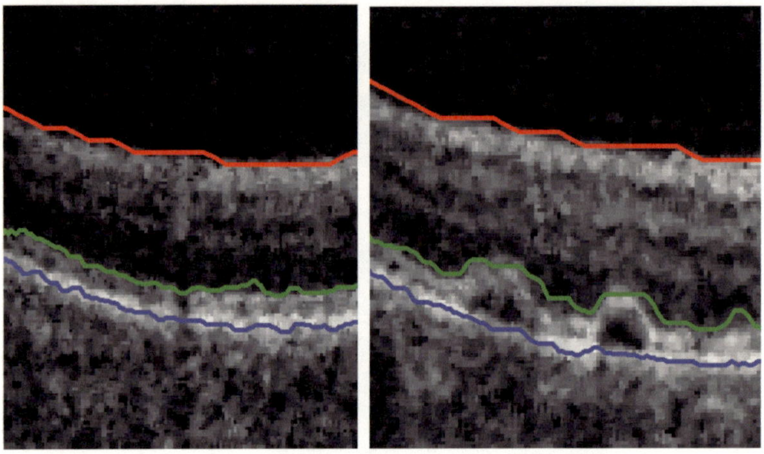

Fig. 21. Fragments of L_{MED} images with drawn NFL course- red, RPE - blue and IS/OS - green

4. Summary

Presented methods ACM, CCA, RAC or HAC give correct results at detection (identifying) RPE, IS/OS, NFL or OPL layers on tomographyc image of eye. Differences in suggested methods are visible only at their comparison of efficiencie for analysis of some hundreds mentioned tomographyc images. Comparing the mentioned methods we must bear in mind accuracy of reconnaissance of layer, reactions of algorithms on pathologies, shields of optical nerves and speed of operation in this case for computer (P4 CPU 3GHz, 2GB RAM).
The following table Tab 1 shows composite comparison of the suggested algorithms and Tab. 2. comparison of result acquired with assistance of the discussed algorithm taking into consideration typical and critical fragments of operations of individual algorithms.

Algorithm/Feature	**ACM**	**CCA**	**RAC**	**HAC**
Total error in the diagnosis of layers	5%	4%	7%	2%
The rate of detection layer RPE - MATLAB	15 s	5s	10s	1s
The rate of detection layer RPE - C++	0.85 s	0.27s	1.2s	50ms

Table 1. Composite comparison of the suggested algorithms

Random. Described method gives correct results at appointment of contour (separation of layers) equal on OCT images and for other images for which classic methods of appointment of contour they not bring results or results do not supply continuous contour. Big influence of hum on the acquired results is one of the algorithm's defects. It results from fact that number of pixels with big value that is the disturbance increases the possibility of choosing at random the starting point in this place and in consequence element contour. Time of account is the second defect which is greater if the number of chosen points is greater /or cause for which next $o_{i,j+1}$ points search has been detained.

Method	A case of wrong diagnosis - due to the nature of the method	Sample reconstruction of 3D NFL layers - blue, RPE - red and IS / OS - green
ACM	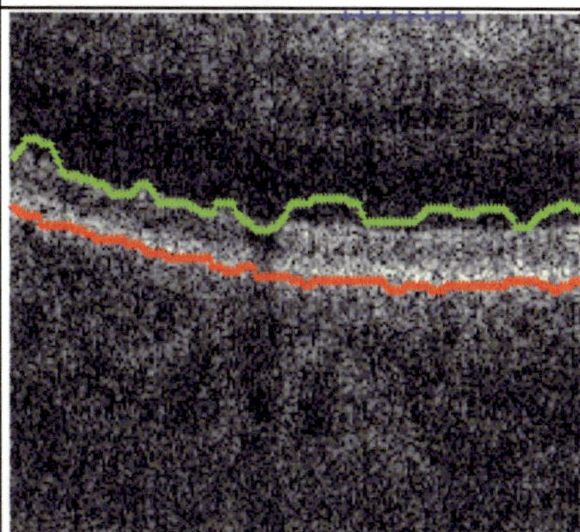	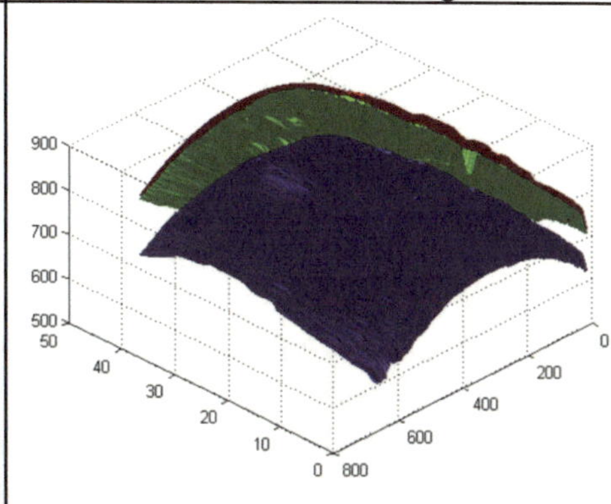
CCA	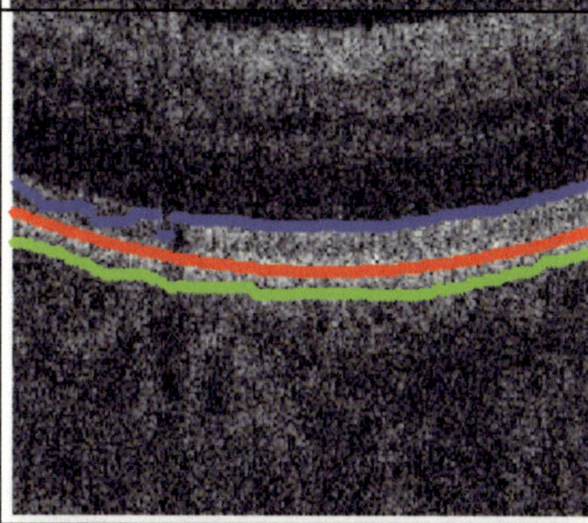	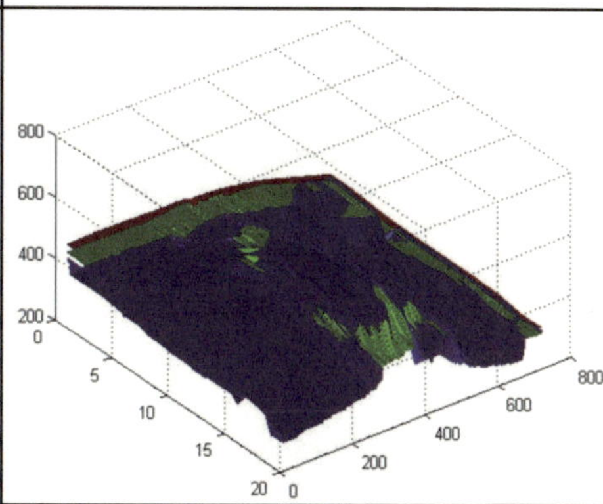
RAC	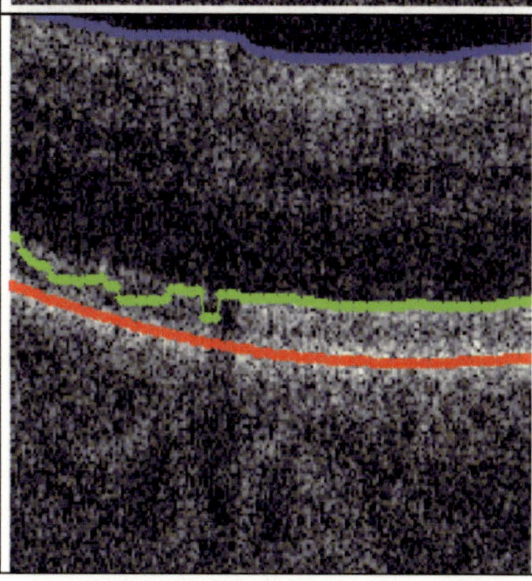	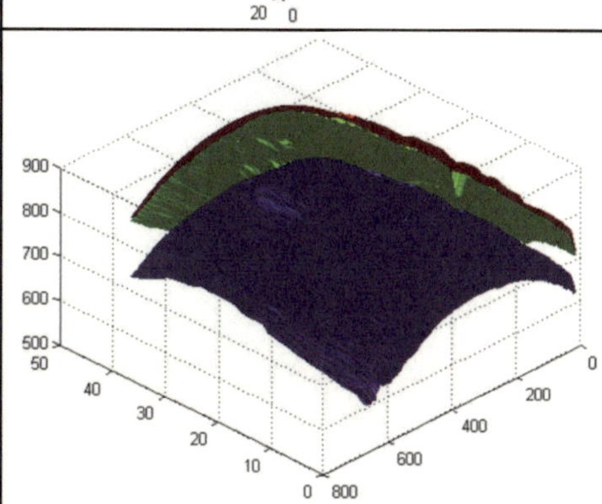

Table 2. Comparison of the results obtained by the described algorithms

Hierarhic. Presented algorithm discovers NFL, RPE and IS/OS layers in time for 50ms on computer with processor 2.5GHz Intel Core 2 Quad. Performed measurement of time was measured as value of average analysis 700 images dividing individual images on A blocks (Fig. 3-3) about sizes 16×16, 8×8, 4×4, 2×2. It is possible to decrease this time by modifying number of approximation blocks and simultaneously boosting identification error of position of layer - results shown in a table below.

Summary of the various stages of analysis time algorithm presented in the table above clearly indicates that the first phase of the longest pre – stage processing image where the dominant importance (in terms of execution time) has a filtration of median filter and the final stage of determining the exact location of the RPE and IS/OS layers. The exact breakdown of RPE and IS / OS, in fact involves an analysis of and the correction of the position of credits primarily RPE and IS / OS in all columns for the most accurate image zoom (due to the small distance between the RPE and IS / OS is not possible to carry out this division in the previous approximations). The reduction in computation time can therefore occur only by increasing the layer thickness of measurement error. And so, for example, for analysis in the first approximation for a size 32 × 32 and then 16 × 16 thick errors arising in the first stage and reproduced in subsequent. For the approximations for A of size 16 × 16 and then 8×8, 4×4, 2×2 and 1×1 the highest accuracy is achieved but the calculation time increases approximately twice.

A key element that crowns the results obtained from the proposed algorithm is a 3D reconstruction based on the sequence of $L_M^{(i)}$ images. The sequence of images and more precisely the location sequence of $NFL^{(i)}(n)$, $RPE^{(i)}(n)$ and $IS/OS^{(i)}(n)$ layers based 3D reconstruction tompgraphyc image. For example a sequence of 50 images and the resolution of one $L_M(i)$ image on level M×N=256×512 is obtained through the 3D image composed of three layers of the NFL, RPE and IS/OS of size 50 × 512. The results shown in (Koprowski & Wróbel, 2008),for example the reconstruction of the original image (without the treatment described above) based on the pixel brightness - reconstruction performed using the algorithm described above based on the $NFL_{(i)}(n)$, $RPE^{(i)}(n)$ and $IS/OS^{(i)}(n)$ information.

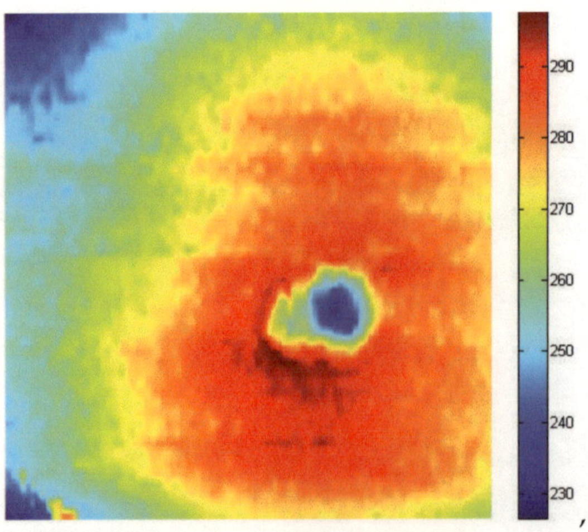

Fig. 22. Spatial location layers RPE

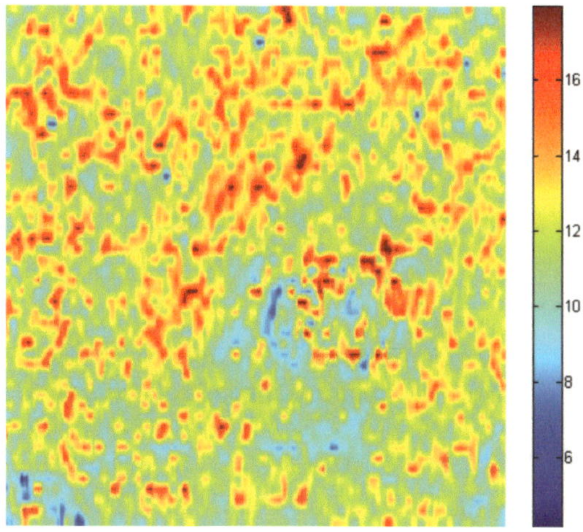

Fig. 23. Layer thickness IS/OS-RPE

It is clearly apparent from the layers of the ability to automatically determine locations of thickest positions or the thinnest between any points.

5. References

Adler D. C., Ko T. H., & Fujimoto J. G., "Speckle reduction in optical coherence tomography images by use of a spatially adaptive wavelet filter," Opt. Lett. 29, 2878–2880 (2004).

Akiba, M., Chan, K. P. & Tanno, N., Full-field optical coherence tomography by twodimensional heterodyne detection with a pair of CCD cameras. Optics Letters, 2003. 28(10): p. 816-18.

Barry C.: Optical Ccoherence tomography for retinal imaging dissertation, De promotor: Prof. Dr. T.G. van Leeuwen, De copromotor: Prof. Dr. J.F. de Boer 2005

Bauma B. E. & Tearney G. J.: Handbook of Opticall Coherence Thomography, MarcelDekker 2002

Canny J.: A Computational Approach to Edge Detection, IEEE Transactions on Pattern Analysis and Machine Intelligence, Vol. 8, No. 6, Nov. 1986.

Chinn, S. R. & Swanson, E. A. e Fujimoto, J. G., Optical coherence tomography using a frequency-tunable optical source. Optics Letters, 1997. 22(5): p. 340-342.

Choma MA, Sarunic MV, Yang C & Izatt JA. Sensitivity advantage of swept source and Fourier domain optical coherence tomography. Opt Express 2003 11:2183–9.

Costa, R. A., Skaf, M., et al., Retinal assessment using optical coherence tomography. Progress in Retinal and Eye Research, 2006. 25(3): p. 325-353.

Drexler W, Sattmann H, Hermann B, et al. Enhanced visualization of macular pathology with the use of ultrahigh-resolution optical coherence tomography. Arch Ophthalmol 2003;121:695–706. [PubMed: 12742848]

Farsiu S, Chiu SJ, Izatt JA. & Toth CA. Fast detection and segmentation of drusen in retinal optical coherence tomography images. Proceedings of Photonics West, San Jose, CA, February 2008; 68440D1-12 and Proc. SPIE, Vol. 6844, 68440D (2008);

Fercher AF, Hitzenberger CK, Kamp G. & Elzaiat SY. Measurement of intraocular distances by backscattering spectral interferometry. Opt Commun 1995;117:43–8.

Gnanadurai D. & Sadasivam V., "Undecimated wavelet based speckle reduction for SAR images," Pattern Recognition Letters, 26, 793-800 (2005).

Gonzalez R. & Woods R.: Digital Image Processing, Addison-Wesley Publishing Company, 1992, Chap. 4.

Hausler G. & Lindner MW. Coherence radar and spectral radar-new tools for dermatological diagnosis. J Biomed Opt 1998;3:21–31.

Klinder T., Ostermann J., Ehm M., Franz A., Kneser R. & Lorenz C., Automated model-based vertebra detection, identification, and segmentation, Medical Image Analysis 13 (2009) 471–482

Ko, T. H., Fujimoto, J. G., et al., Comparison of ultrahigh- and standard-resolution optical coherence tomography for imaging macular pathology. Ophthalmology, 2005. 112(11): p. 1922-1935.

Koprowski R., Izdebska-Straszak G., Wróbel Z. & Adamek B. The cell structures segmentation with using of decision trees. Pattern Recognition and Image Analysis, Vol. 15, No. 3, 2005,

Koprowski R. & Wróbel Z.: Hierarchic Approach in the Analysis of Tomographic Eye ImageAdvances in Soft Computing, Springer Berlin / Heidelberg Volume 57, 2009, p 463-470

Koprowski R. & Wróbel Z.: Identyfication of layers in a tomographic image of an eye based on the Canny edge detection, Conference on Information Technologies in Biomedicine, 2008

Koprowski R. & Wróbel Z.: Layers Recognition in Tomographic Eye Image Based on Random Contour Analysis Advances in Soft Computing, Springer Berlin / Heidelberg Volume 57, 2009, p 471-478

Koprowski R., Wróbel Z.: Determining correspondence in stereovision images of patients with faulty posture Congress on Image and Signal Processing, 2008

Leitgeb, R. A., Drexler, W., et al., Ultrahigh resolution Fourier domain optical coherence tomography. Optics Express, 2004. 12(10): p. 2156-2165.

Liang J, McInerney T. & Terzopoulos D.:United Snakes, Medical Image Analysis, Volume 10, Issue 2, April 2006, Pages 215-233

Ozcan A., Bilenca A., Desjardins A. E., B. E. Bouma B. E., & Tearney G. J., "Speckle reduction in optical coherence tomography images using digital filtering," J. Opt. Soc. Am. A. 24, 1901-1910 (2007).

Thrane L.: Optical Coherence Tomography: Modeling and Applications, Risø National Laboratory, Roskilde, Denmark, May 2001

25

Image Processing for Optical Metrology

Miguel Mora-González, Jesús Muñoz-Maciel, Francisco J. Casillas,
Francisco G. Peña-Lecona, Roger Chiu-Zarate
and Héctor Pérez Ladrón de Guevara
Universidad de Guadalajara, Centro Universitario de los Lagos
México

1. Introduction

Optical measurements offer the desirable characteristics of being noninvasive and nondestructive techniques that are able to analyze in real time objects and phenomena in a remote sense. Science areas that involve optical characterization include physics, biology, chemistry and varied fields of engineering. The use of digital cameras to record objects or a specific phenomenon permits the exploitation of the potential of that the associated images can be processed to determine one or several parameter or characteristics of what is being recorded. These images need to be processed and securely there will be a model associated with the optical metrology that will provide an insight or a comprehensive understanding of the image being analyzed. Matlab® is the suitable platform to implement image processing algorithms due to its ability to perform the whole processing techniques and procedures to analyze and image. At the same time it provides a flexible and a fast programming language for user constructing algorithms. In the present chapter we provide some fundamentals about image acquisition, filtering and processing, and some applications. Some applications are well-know techniques while others offer the state of the art in the field under study. All authors agree that Matlab® is a powerful tool for image processing and optical metrology.
All algorithms and/or sentences used in this chapter are made in such manner so that they work in the Matlab® R2007b platform or superior. Matlab® is a trade mark of Mathworks Inc., from here on we will refer it as Matlab only. Also the Matlab functions and parameters used along the chapter are typed in italics and in apostrophes, respectively.
Algorithms in present chapter are presented in two formats depending on the algorithm extension: 1) Image titles and/or figure captions for low algorithms extension; 2) Subsection ends for larger algorithms.

2. Image processing and acquisition

In the present section, image and processing acquisition principles in Matlab are established.

2.1 Image acquisition

Image acquisition is the initial stage in every vision system for human or artificial image data interpretation. Image acquisition is the recording process of a real object, this implies that the vision process totally depends on quality acquisition; this could be an analogical or digital. The analogical acquisition process is a representation of the object with several techniques like designing, painting, photography, and video. In a similar way, digital imaging acquisition is able to represent a real object, however object properties are presented in a discrete form. Every object characteristics are mapped from a real plane to a digital plane where a group of discrete values (i.e 1, 2, 3, …,) represent position, form, color and texture.

2.1.1 Acquisition and digital image representation

Image acquisition process in Matlab can be done by the use of either *imread* or *getsnapshot* functions for stored images or video, respectively. Each function stores the object representation in a discrete *lxmxn* array, where *l* can be related to color data; *m* and *n* indexes represent the image spatial coordinates.
An example of a real image is shown in Figure 1a, and in Figure 1b, the representation in a matrix array of the selected area from the image. Digital images are described as a bi-dimensional $f(x,y)$ function, where x and y represent the spatial coordinates. The f value at the (x,y) position point is proportional to the intensity or gray scale of the image.
In Matlab, a digital image satisfies following conditions: first, spatial and gray scale values must be discrete; and second, intensities are sampling at 8 bits (255 values).

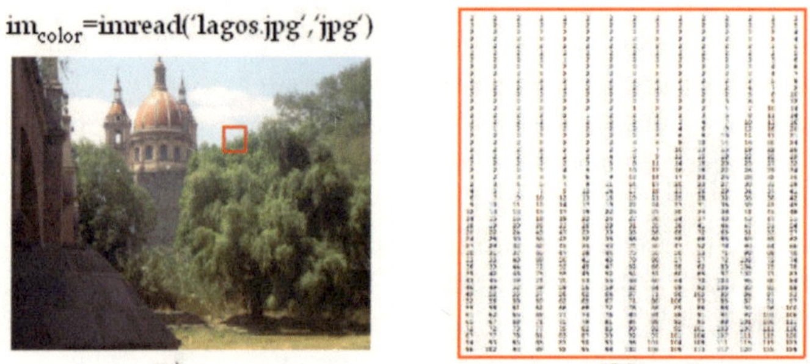

a) b)

Fig. 1. a) real color image, and b) matrix of the green color component of the selected area.

2.1.2 Image discretization

Image discretization is the process of converting an analogical image to a digital image; this process depends on the sampling and quantization stages.
Correspondence between analogical and digital images is given by the number of pixels used. If the number of pixels is enough to satisfy the Nyquist criteria (Oppenheim et al., 1997), the acquired image is a satisfactory representation of the real object observed. Quantization is the process of assigning a color or gray discrete level to each sample.
Therefore, image discretization quality depends on frequency sampling as in quantization levels used. It must be noted that Matlab only reads digital images. Acquisition process can be done with scanners, CCD cameras, etc.

2.2 Thresholding and high contrast image

Frequently, acquired images under real conditions present a background problem. When relevant foreground elements are mixed with low interest background ones. Another problem that hides the desired information is a low contrast image. Therefore, the use of algorithms that deals with can be implemented in order to enhance the images. Equalization, binarization and thresholding algorithm are alternatives that have proved to be successful.

In the following subsection, a method for the conversion of color images into gray levels is presented. Next, by using histogram equalization, a high contrast image from the gray scale levels is obtained. Finally, binarization process by establishing a thresholding is described in order to get a two color image (black (0) and white (255)) from a gray level scale (Poon & Banerjee, 2001).

2.2.1 Histogram

Histogram is the graphical representation of pixels gray values distribution. Images can be classified according to its histogram as high, medium or low contrast images. A low contrast image has a histogram with a low fraction of all possible gray values, around less than 40% of the whole scale. A high contrast image has more than 90% of the gray values.

Color images can also be classified in accordance with its histogram by considering human ocular sensitivity to primary colors. This is given by the first component of the YIQ matrix:

$$Y = 0.299R + 0.587G + 0.114B, \tag{1}$$

Where Y and RGB are the lumma components used in color television systems NTSC (that represents a gray scale in the YIQ space) and the primary components, red, green and blue, respectively. The histogram transformation for a color image is given by the following pixel to pixel operation:

$$T_{gsl}(r_k) = s_k, \tag{2}$$

where r_k and s_k are the original pixel intensities in color and gray scale levels (gsl) respectively. In figure 2 is shown the image obtained by the use of equation (2) and its corresponding histogram, these operations can be done by using the Matlab functions *rgb2gray* and *imhist*.

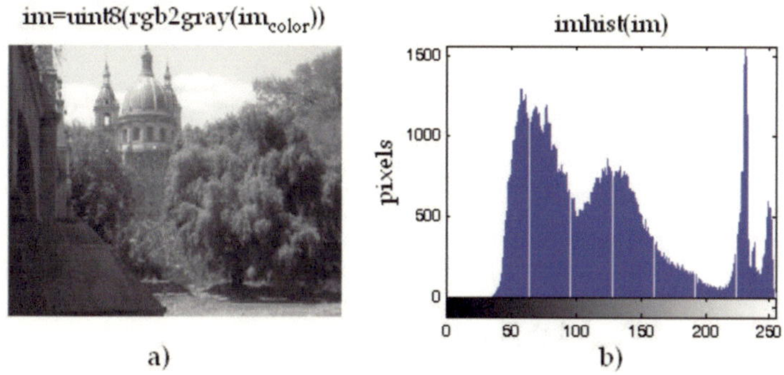

Fig. 2. a) gsl photography, b) histogram.

2.2.2 Histogram equalization

Histogram equalization is the transformation of the intensity values of an image that is typically applied to enhance the contrast of the image. As an example, the contrast of the image of the figure 2a, can be handled by applying histogram equalization and it is shown in figure 3 with its respective histogram, this operation can be done by using the Matlab function *histeq*.

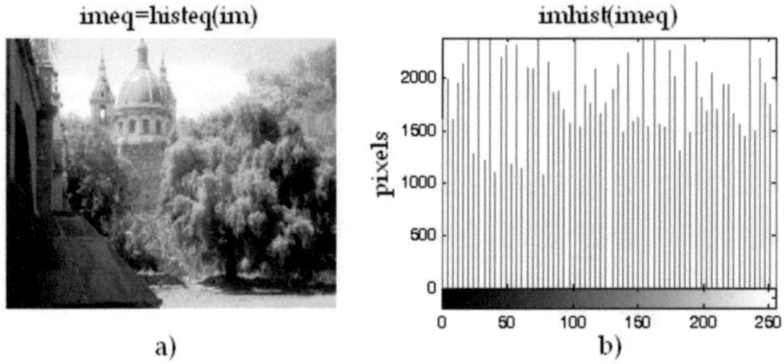

Fig. 3. a) Photography equalization, b) histogram.

In order to get the discrete values in a gsl, the following equation is used

$$T_{eq}(s_k) = \sum_{j=0}^{k} \frac{n_j}{n}(L-1), \tag{3}$$

where k = 0,1,2,..., (L-1), L represents the gray level numbers into an image (255 as an example), n_j is the frequency of appearance of an specific j-th gray level and n is the total number of pixels of the image.

2.2.3 Thresholding by histogram

Thresholding is a non-linear operation for image segmentation that consists in the conversion of a gsl image into a binary image according to a threshold value. This operation is used to separate some regions of the foreground of an image from its background. Thresholding operation can be done by using the Matlab function *graythresh*. Binarization may be considered as an especial case of thresholding as shown in figure 4. The Matlab function that binaries an image is *im2bw*.

Fig. 4. Image binarization by thresholding.

2.3 Spatial filtering

In order to reduce noise or enhance some specific characteristics of an image some filters like high-pass, low-pass, band-pass or band-stop are used. These filters can be applied in the frequency domain (section 2.4) or in the spatial domain. Spatial domain filtering is described in this section. Filtering operations are directly applied to the image (pixel to pixel). The mathematical functions applied in the spatial domain are well known as convolution, and are described by (Mora-González et al., 2008)

$$f(x,y) * g(x,y) = \sum_{m=-\frac{M+1}{2}}^{\frac{M+1}{2}} \sum_{n=-\frac{N+1}{2}}^{\frac{N+1}{2}} f(m,n)g(x-m,y-n), \tag{4}$$

where *f*, *g*,(*x*,*y*), (*m*,*n*) and *M*x*N* are the original image, the convolution mask or matrix, the original image coordinates, the coordinates where the convolution is performed, and the size of convolution mask, respectively. Equation (4) is applied by doing a homogeneous scanning with the convolution mask versus the whole image to be convolved. These filters are also known as Finite Impulse Response (FIR) filters because they are applied to a finite section of the spatial domain (In this case the finite section is the image). Equation (4) can be implemented in Matlab by using nested *for* loops, also *conv2*, *fspecial* or *imfilter* functions can be used too. These kinds of filters are dependent of the convolution mask form as is explained in the following two subsections.

2.3.1 Low-pass filters

Low-pass filters applied to images have the purpose of image smoothing, by blurring the edges into the image and lowering the contrast. The main characteristic of a low-pass convolution mask is that all of its elements have positive values. Some commonly used low-pass filters are: averaging, gaussian, quadratic, triangular and trigonometric. These mask are presented in a matrix form like

$$g(m,n) = \frac{1}{\sum_{m=1}^{M}\sum_{n=1}^{N} w_{m,n}} \begin{bmatrix} w_{1,1} & w_{1,2} & \cdots & w_{1,N} \\ w_{2,1} & w_{2,2} & \cdots & w_{2,N} \\ \vdots & \vdots & \ddots & \vdots \\ w_{M,1} & w_{M,2} & \cdots & w_{M,N} \end{bmatrix}, \tag{5}$$

with

$$w = \left\{ \begin{array}{c} A\exp\left(-B\left[\left(m-\frac{M+1}{2}\right)^2+\left(n-\frac{N+1}{2}\right)^2\right]\right), \quad gaussian \\ A\left[1-B\left(m-\frac{M+1}{2}\right)^2-B\left(n-\frac{N+1}{2}\right)^2\right], \quad cuadratic \\ \frac{A}{2}+\frac{A}{4}\cos\left[B\left(m-\frac{M+1}{2}\right)\right]+\frac{A}{4}\cos\left[B\left(n-\frac{N+1}{2}\right)\right], \quad trigonometric \\ A, \quad average \end{array} \right\}, \tag{6}$$

where *A*, *B* and *w* are the amplitude, the width function factor and the weight function of the spatial filter, respectively. In order to determine the effectiveness of the masks of the equations (5) and (6), Magnitude Spectra (MS) are obtained to analyze the low frequencies allowed to pass by the filter and high frequencies attenuation. This is expressed as

$$MS(\omega) = 20\log\left|\Im\{g(m,n)\}\right|, \tag{7}$$

where ω and $\Im$ are the MS frequency component and the Fourier transform operator, respectively.
In figure 5, the MS of the convolution mask from equations (5) and (6) are shown. Spatial gaussian filter behavior is more stable because allows low frequencies to pass and also attenuate middle and high frequencies faster than other filters, as can be observed. The mask for nine elements is shown in table 1. It must be mentioned that the processing time slow down conforming the convolution mask increases. Spatial filtering also has a problem in the image edges, because they cannot be convolved and there are $(M-1)/2$ and $(N-1)/2$ lost information elements in x and y axes, respectively. By using the *fspecial* function, low-pass masks can be generated by applying the '*gaussian*' or '*average*' Matlab parameters.
Another mask types designed for signal processing can be implemented on image processing by a two dimensional extension. In figure 6 it is shown three different low-pass filters applied in the test image.

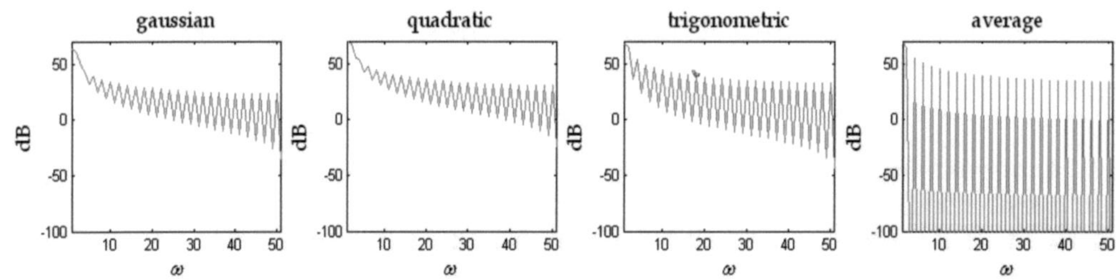

Fig. 5. MS of equations (5) and (6) masks, with A=1, B=1 and w=1. Matlab code representation of equation (7) is: *MS=20*log10(abs(fft(g)))*.

Gaussian	Quadratic	Trigonometric	Average
$\begin{pmatrix} .0449 & .1221 & .0449 \\ .1221 & .3319 & .1221 \\ .0449 & .1221 & .0449 \end{pmatrix}$	$\begin{pmatrix} 0 & .1667 & 0 \\ .1667 & .3333 & .1667 \\ 0 & .1667 & 0 \end{pmatrix}$	$\begin{pmatrix} .1011 & .1161 & .1011 \\ .1161 & .1312 & .1161 \\ .1011 & .1161 & .1011 \end{pmatrix}$	$\frac{1}{9}\begin{pmatrix} 1 & 1 & 1 \\ 1 & 1 & 1 \\ 1 & 1 & 1 \end{pmatrix}$

Table 1. 3x3 convolution masks g for low-pass filters of equations (5) and (6), with A=1, B=1 and w=1.

Fig. 6. Low-pass 3x3 filters examples applied to figure 1a. Matlab parameters used: a) average, b) gaussian and c) disk.

2.3.2 High-pass filters

High frequency components are mostly located in image borders, like fast tone changes and marked details. The main purpose of a high-pass filter is to highlight the image details for skeletonizing, geometrical orientation, contrast enhancement, and revealing hidden characteristics, among many others. One of the most common high-pass spatial filters is the high-boost that consists in an interactive subtraction process between the original image and low-pass filters. The weighting function for a 3x3 matrix is obtained by

$$w = \begin{cases} 9C - \frac{1}{9}, & m = 2, n = 2 \\ -\frac{1}{9}, & m \neq 2, n \neq 2 \end{cases}. \tag{8}$$

The differential filters are another kind of high-pass filters that get its weighting function based on the partial derivates applied to the image. The most usual differential filters are the gradient and laplacian, based on the following equations

$$\left|\nabla(f(x,y))\right| = \sqrt{\left(\frac{\partial f}{\partial x}\right)^2 + \left(\frac{\partial f}{\partial y}\right)^2} \approx \left|\frac{\partial f}{\partial x}\right| + \left|\frac{\partial f}{\partial y}\right|, \quad \textit{gradient magnitude}, \tag{9}$$

and

$$\nabla^2(f(x,y)) = \frac{\partial^2 f}{\partial x^2} + \frac{\partial^2 f}{\partial y^2}, \quad \textit{laplacian}, \tag{10}$$

if the magnitude of the partial derivatives work with a 3x3 mask, then

$$\left|\frac{\partial f}{\partial x}\right| = \frac{1}{\kappa + 2}\left[(w_{1,3} + \kappa \cdot w_{2,3} + w_{3,3}) - (w_{1,1} + \kappa \cdot w_{2,1} + w_{3,1})\right] \tag{11}$$

and

$$\left|\frac{\partial f}{\partial y}\right| = \frac{1}{\kappa + 2}\left[(w_{1,1} + \kappa \cdot w_{1,2} + w_{1,3}) - (w_{3,1} + \kappa \cdot w_{3,2} + w_{3,3})\right]. \tag{12}$$

Other used filters based on gradients are the Sobel, Prewitt and Canny. The Sobel spatial filter uses the central weight constant k=2 (Pratt, 2001). Meanwhile the Pewwit space filter uses k=1. The Canny space filter uses two different thresholds for weak and strong edges detection (Canny, 1986). Table 2 shows the nine elements masks of the most utilized high-pass filters. Figure 7 shows six examples of the application of these functions as high-pass filters to figure 1a. It is observed that the Canny filter is the most powerful edge detector filter.

2.4 Mathematical discrete transforms

Discrete transform analysis has played an important role in digital image processing. Several transform types are applicable to digital image processing, but due to their optical metrology potential applications, Fourier and Radon transforms are presented in this chapter section.

2.4.1 Fourier transform

Discrete Fourier Transform (DFT) represents the change from spatial to frequency domain. In convergent optical systems this transform represents the propagated optical perturbation from exit pupil to the focal point in a single lens arrangement. Equations (13) and (14) represent the DFT pair for the mathematical two dimensional (2D) model (Gonzalez, 2002)

$$\Im\{f(x,y)\} = F(u,v) = \frac{1}{MN}\sum_{x=1}^{M}\sum_{y=1}^{N} f(x,y)\exp\left[-i2\pi\left(\frac{ux}{M}+\frac{vy}{N}\right)\right], \tag{13}$$

Sobel		Prewitt		Gradient		Laplacian
$\left\lvert\frac{\partial f}{\partial x}\right\rvert = \begin{pmatrix}1 & 0 & -1\\ 2 & 0 & -2\\ 1 & 0 & -1\end{pmatrix}$	$\left\lvert\frac{\partial f}{\partial y}\right\rvert = \begin{pmatrix}1 & 2 & 1\\ 0 & 0 & 0\\ -1 & -2 & -1\end{pmatrix}$	$\left\lvert\frac{\partial f}{\partial x}\right\rvert = \begin{pmatrix}1 & 0 & -1\\ 1 & 0 & -1\\ 1 & 0 & -1\end{pmatrix}$	$\left\lvert\frac{\partial f}{\partial y}\right\rvert = \begin{pmatrix}1 & 1 & 1\\ 0 & 0 & 0\\ -1 & -1 & -1\end{pmatrix}$	$\left\lvert\frac{\partial f}{\partial x}\right\rvert = \begin{pmatrix}1 & 1 & -1\\ 1 & -2 & -1\\ 1 & 1 & -1\end{pmatrix}$	$\left\lvert\frac{\partial f}{\partial y}\right\rvert = \begin{pmatrix}1 & 1 & 1\\ 1 & -2 & 1\\ -1 & -1 & -1\end{pmatrix}$	$\begin{pmatrix}0 & 1 & 0\\ 1 & -4 & 1\\ 0 & 1 & 0\end{pmatrix}$

Table 2. Some 3x3 convolution masks g for high-pass differential filters (Bow, 2002).

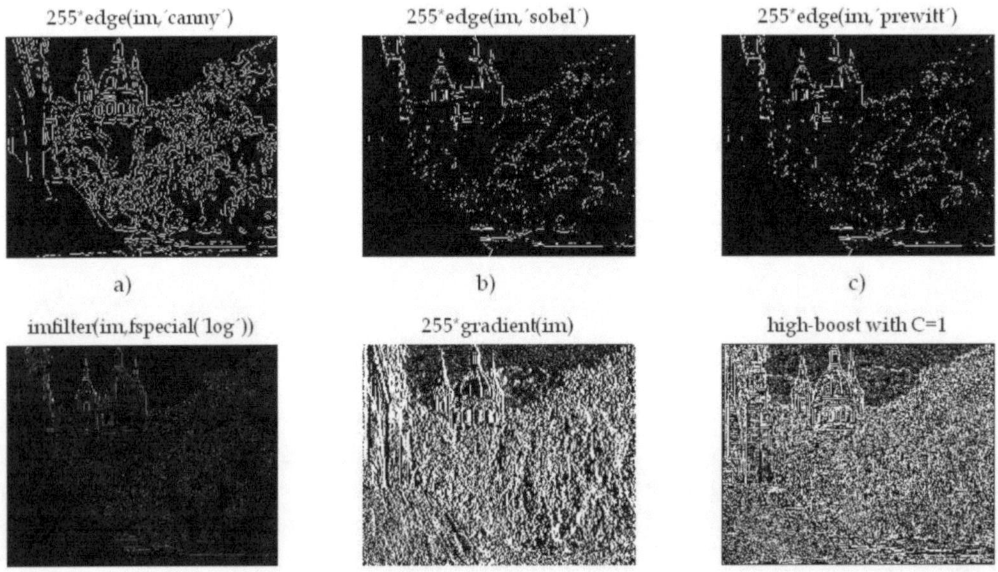

Fig. 7. High-pass 3x3 filters examples applied to figure 1a. Matlab parameters and functions used: a) 'canny', b) 'sobel', c) 'prewitt', d) laplacian with 'log', e) *gradient* and f) high-boost filter.

and

$$\Im^{-1}\{F(u,v)\} = f(x,y) = \sum_{u=1}^{M}\sum_{v=1}^{N} F(u,v)\exp\left[i2\pi\left(\frac{ux}{M}+\frac{vy}{N}\right)\right], \tag{14}$$

where (u,v), MxN and $\Im^{-1}$ are the Fourier space coordinates, the image size, the inverse Fourier transform operator, respectively. Matlab has *fft2* and *ifft2* special functions for equations (13) and (14), respectively, where FFT is the acronyms of Fast Fourier Transform. Other functions of Fourier transforms are *fft, ifft* for one dimension, and *fftshift* for the shifting of the zero-frequency component to spectra center. An important characteristic obtained from the Fourier transform is that it gives the frequencies content of the image. Due to this property, frequency filter design is a very straight forward task. Low frequencies are located into the matrix around the central coordinates, while frequencies gradually increase as are spread out from its center in a radial form. This characteristic is ideal for frequency filtering (low-pass, high-pass, band-pass, and band-stop). The frequency filtering process consists in the multiplication between image Fourier transform with a binary circular mask. Figure 8 shows the filtered Fourier spectra and the resulting filtered images for a high-pass, low-pass, band-pass and band-stop.

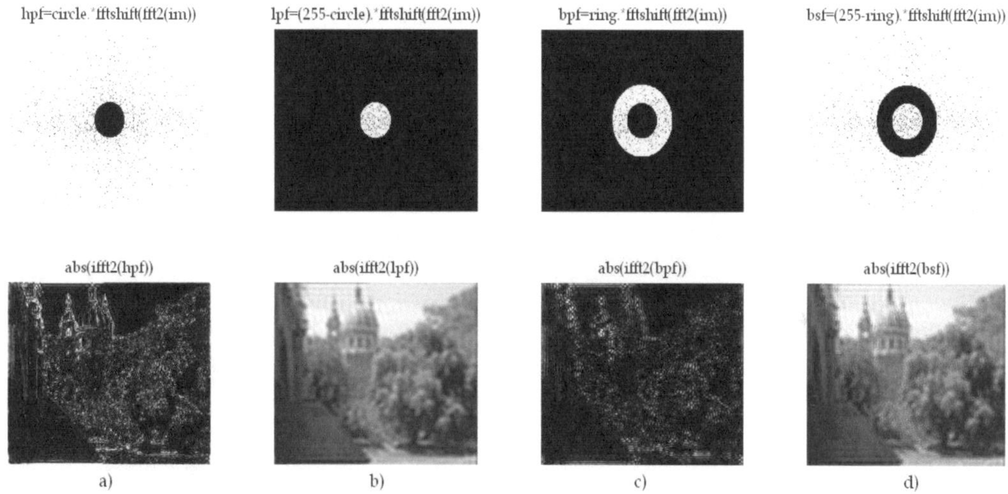

Fig. 8. Fourier filtering applied to figure 1a. a) high-pass, b) low-pass, c) band-pass and d) band-stop. Where, circle and ring are masks of 30 and 60 pixels radii.

2.4.2 Radon transform

Radon transform applied in pattern recognition or digital image processing may be considered as the image's gsl projection over a given angle with respect to x axis. The mathematical model of the Radon transform is (Bracewell, 1995)

$$\Re\{f(x,y)\} = \int_{-\infty}^{\infty}\int_{-\infty}^{\infty} f(x,y)\delta\left(R - x\cos\theta - y\sin\theta\right)dxdt, \quad (15)$$

where $\Re$, δ, R and θ are the Radon transform operator, the Dirac delta function, the distance from the origin to the profile line and the angle of direction of the same line, respectively. Each of these parameters can be observed in figure 9, Q is the origin of the profile line to be obtained (thick blue bold line). Equation (15) is implemented in Matlab with the special function *radon*.

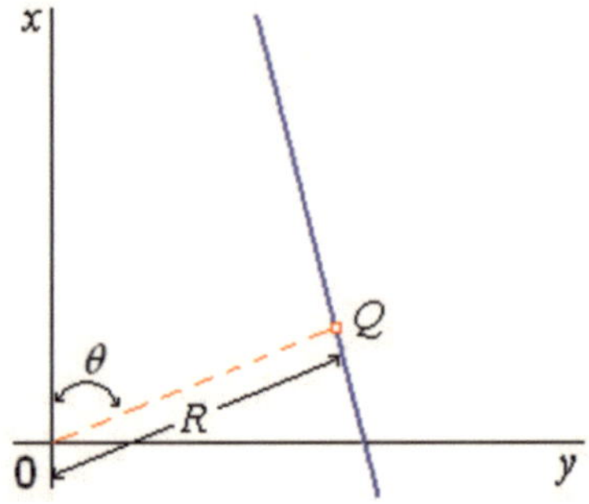

Fig. 9. Radon transform parameters.+

3. Optical metrology fundamentals

Optical metrology is a field of physics that include theoretical and experimental methods to estimate physical parameters using the light wavelength as fundamental scale.

3.1 Optical interferometry

Optical interferometry is based in the light interference phenomenon to determine different physical variables. A typical application is in nondestructive optical testing that requires high accuracy. The interferometer is the optical system used by this technique, which allows by interfering fringes the estimation of deformation components, shapes, strains or vibrations in objects with polished or rough surfaces. According to users' requirements, different configurations of interferometers can be selected to measure displacements components.

3.1.1 Interference

Figure 10 shows the schematic of a common optical arrangement used in interferometry well known as Michelson interferometer. The beam splitter (BS) splits the incident collimated laser light in two wavefronts that propagate in different directions and are reflected by the plane mirrors M1 and M2 respectively, and then they are combined with the same BS to form an interference pattern that can be observed directly on the screen.

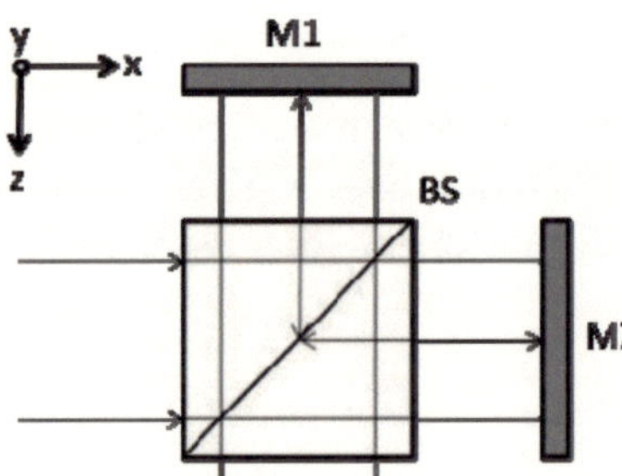

Fig. 10. Michelson interferometer.

The superposition of the two wavefrons at a position (x,y) is expressed by the complex sum:

$$U(x,y) = a_1(x,y)\exp[i\phi_1(x,y)] + a_2(x,y)\exp[i\phi_2(x,y)], \tag{16}$$

where $a_1(x,y)$ and $a_2(x,y)$ are the amplitudes and its respective phases $\phi_1(x,y)$ y $\phi_2(x,y)$. The intensity at a point in the interference pattern is determined with the product of perturbation U multiplied by its complex conjugated U^*, this is

$$I(x,y) = U(x,y) \cdot U^*(x,y), \tag{17}$$

then, the resulting intensity is given by

$$I(x,y) = I_1(x,y) + I_2(x,y) + 2\sqrt{I_1(x,y)I_2(x,y)}\cos[\phi(x,y)], \tag{18}$$

where $I_1(x,y)=a_1^2(x,y)$ and $I_2(x,y)=a_1^2(x,y)$ are the intensities for each wavefront and $\phi(x,y)$ is the phase difference between them, since these propagate along to different paths before the interference.

Due to cosine of equation (18), $I(x,y)$ reaches its maxima when $\phi(x,y)$ corresponds to even multiples of π (constructive interference) and its minima for odd multiples of π (destructive interference) (Gasvik, 2002). In general, optical interferometry is applied to estimate this phase difference, which can arise due to geometrical variations or deformations in a testing object. In figure 11 are shown two synthetic interference patterns when is replaced a mirror: a) with tilt in y and defocus and b) with defocus and coma in the interferometer of figure 10. The phase difference involving the geometrical variations of the mirrors is given by $\phi(x,y)=4\pi\Delta z/\lambda$, where λ is the wavelength of the illumination source and Δz is the shape phase difference introduced by the mirrors.

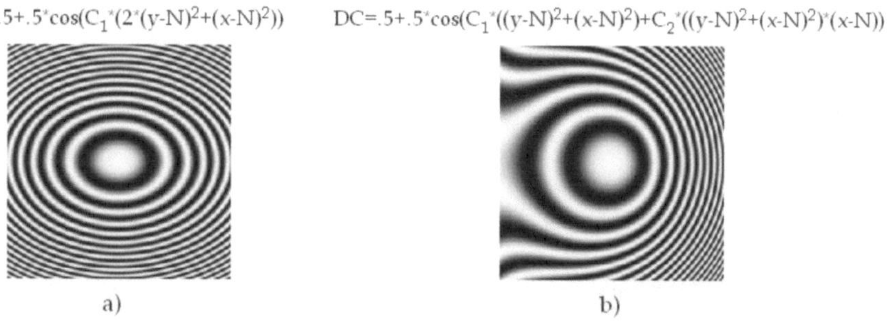

Fig. 11. Fringe patterns of mirrors with: a) tilt in y and defocus, YD; and b) defocus and coma, DC. These wavefronts were generated using nested for loops. For these cases N=128 pixels; C_1=0.01 and C_2= 0.00001 are the numerical parameter of each aberration.

Another way to generate fringe patterns is by replacing a mirror of the interferometer for a testing object with an optically rough surface that experiments a deformation. In this case, the interference fringe pattern is not observed directly on the screen as in the previous described case. The superposition of a wavefront reflected by a rough surface (object beam) with a regular wavefront (reference beam) as the reflected by a plane mirror in the Michelson interferometer causes that I_1, I_2 and ϕ of equation (18) vary fast and randomly, normally obtaining a speckle pattern. In speckle pattern interferometry the fringe patterns are obtained by the correlation of two speckle patterns recorded using a CCD camera placed at the screen position of the interferometer for the object before and after a deformation $\Delta\phi(x,y)$. Assuming $I_i(x,y)$, $I_f(x,y)$ are the intensities of the speckle patterns for the initial no-deformed state and the final deformed state respectively, the fringe patter can be calculated by (Lehmann, 2001)

$$\left|I_f(x,y)-I_i(x,y)\right|, \tag{19}$$

and the phase difference involving the deformation of the object is given by $\Delta\phi(x,y)=4\pi z'/\lambda$, where z′ is the displacement of the object in z direction (Waldner, 2000).

3.1.2 Phase shifting

In order to determine the phase $\phi(x,y)$ from fringe patterns, is applied a procedure well-known as phase shifting. For this procedure can be registered several images introducing a phase difference which experimentally is achieved with a piezoelectric (PZ) that modifies the optical path length of one of the beams. A widely used algorithm to calculate the phase employs four consecutive images shifted by $\pi/2$ (Huntley, 2001)

$$\phi(x,y)=\tan^{-1}\left[\frac{I_d(x,y)-I_b(x,y)}{I_a(x,y)-I_c(x,y)}\right], \tag{20}$$

where $I_a(x,y)$, $I_b(x,y)$, $I_c(x,y)$ and $I_d(x,y)$ are the intensities of the shifted images. Due to the inverse tangent, in this pattern arise an effect of wrapping in a 2π module; moreover can be affected by noise of high frequency in the case of speckle interferograms. If the interest of the user is to explore the reduction of speckle noise and phase unwrapping techniques can consults references (Sirohi, 1993) and (Ghiglia, 1998).
In figure 12 are shown the wrapped phases calculated with equation (20) using the fringe patterns presented in the section.

3.2 Image diffraction

The mathematical representation for a collimated wavefront passing through a convergent optical system until the focal point is given by the Fourier transform, as is observed in figure 13. By setting a diffraction grating in the entrance pupil of a convergent lens, a Fraunhofer diffraction pattern is obtained in the focal point (Goodman, 2005), given by

$$U_o(u,v)=\frac{A\cdot\exp\left[j\frac{\pi}{f\lambda}\left(u^2+v^2\right)\right]}{j\lambda f}\int_{-\infty}^{\infty}\int r(x,y)\cdot\exp\left[-j\frac{2\pi}{f\lambda}(xu+yv)\right]dxdy, \tag{21}$$

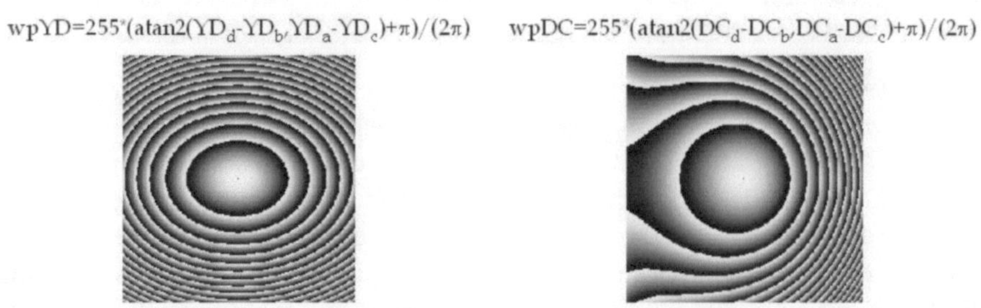

a) b)

Fig. 12. Calculated wrapped phases for: a) tilt in y and defocus, wpYD; and b) defocus and coma, wpDC.

where $U_o(u, v)$, $r(x, y)$, A and λ are the complex amplitude distribution of the field in the back focal plane of the lens, the grating function, the amplitude of the monochromatic plane wave and the illumination wavelength, respectively. The result of equation (21) varies depending on the function of the grating. For our purposes, those functions are binary and sinusoidal.

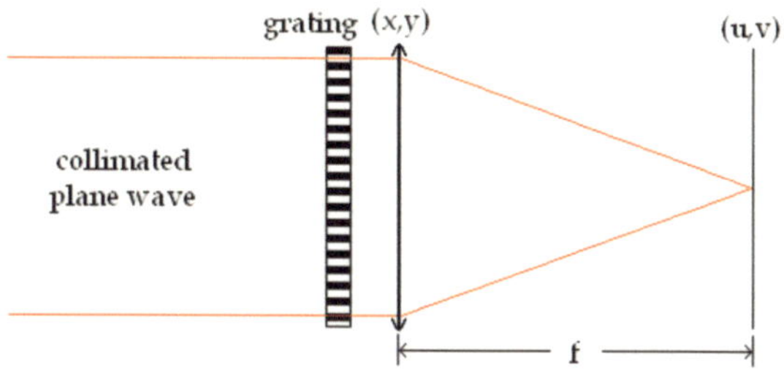

Fig. 13. Diagram for performing the Fourier transform of a grating with a positive lens.

3.2.1 Binary grating

A binary grating can be mathematically represented by a Fourier series expansion of a step function (*fstep*) bounded in the $[0,T]$ interval, see figure 14a. The function is defined by:

$$f_{step}(x,y) = \begin{cases} a, & 0 < y < \frac{T}{2} \\ 0, & \frac{T}{2} \leq y \leq T \end{cases}, \tag{22}$$

and its Fourier series expansion is given by (Tolstov, 1962)

$$r_{bin}(x,y) = \frac{a}{(2\pi)^2} \sum_{m,n=-\infty}^{\infty} \frac{[(-1)^n - 1]}{mn} \exp[i\omega_0(mx + ny)], \tag{23}$$

where T and a are the grating period and the amplitude, respectively. Then the intensity profile at the focal plane is calculated from equations (17) and (21), with $r(x,y)$ as vertical binary grating of equation (23), giving (Mora-González et al., 2009)

$$I_{bin}(u,v) = h_0^2 \sum_{k=-\infty}^{\infty} \left(\frac{\sin\left(k\frac{\pi}{2}\right)}{k\frac{\pi}{2}} \right)^2 \cdot \delta\left[Ku, K\left(v - \frac{k\omega_0}{K}\right)\right], \tag{24}$$

here $h_0 = \frac{2Aa\pi^2}{f\lambda}$ is the zero diffraction order amplitude, $K = \frac{2\pi}{f\lambda}$ is the scale factor at the focal plane and $\omega_0 = \frac{2\pi}{T}$ is the angular frequency. The binary grating intensity profile presents an infinite number of diffraction orders (harmonics) modulated by a sinc function (see figure 14b).

3.2.2 Sinusoidal grating

In order to observe the sinusoidal grating profile, it must be above x axis because negative gsl cannot be observed. The equation proposed for the vertical sinusoidal grating is given by (see figure 14c)

$$r_{\sin}(x,y) = a\left[\tfrac{1}{2} + \tfrac{1}{2}\sin(\omega_0 y)\right]. \tag{25}$$

The intensity profile at the focal plane from equation (21) with $r(x,y)$ as vertical sinusoidal grating of equation (25), giving (Mora-González et al., 2009)

$$I_{\sin}(u,v) = h_1^2\delta\left[Ku, K\left(v + \tfrac{\omega_0}{K}\right)\right] + h_0^2\delta[Ku, Kv] + h_1^2\delta\left[Ku, K\left(v - \tfrac{\omega_0}{K}\right)\right], \tag{26}$$

where $h_1 = \frac{Aa\pi^2}{f\lambda}$ is the ±1 sinusoidal diffraction orders amplitude. The sinusoidal grating intensity profile only presents three diffraction orders (see figure 14d), those harmonics are characteristic of the Fourier transform of sinusoidal functions.

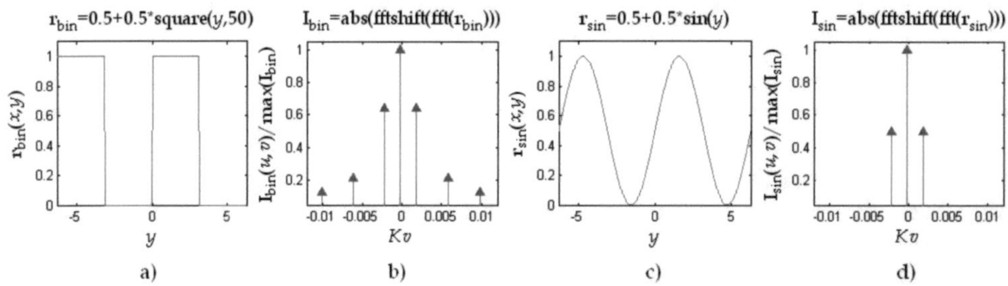

Fig. 14. Functions of a) binary and c) sinusoidal gratings. Fourier spectra of b) binary and d) sinusoidal gratings.

4. Aplications

As shown in previous sections, Digital Image Processing is a useful tool to obtain improved results in Optical Metrology. Applications details are presented in following subsections.

4.1 Fringe analysis

Fringe analysis refers to the process of finding the phase associated to physical variables that are being estimated. A typical case consists in the interpretation of the fringe patterns that can be achieved with phase shifting techniques, when the object under study remains static while three or more frames are acquired when the experiment conditions are free of environmental perturbations. Another case is when the environmental conditions are not met, and then the analysis of a single interferogram is more convenient. In both cases a wrapped phase is obtained before the related continuous phase is assessed.

Phase unwrapping is a numerical technique for retrieving a continuous phase from the calculated phase by using the arctangent (*atan2*) of the sine and cosine functions of the phase. In its simplest form, phase unwrapping consists in the addition or subtraction of a 2π multiple when a discontinuity bigger than π is found between adjacent pixels (Robinson, 1993). This approach however is very sensitive to noise, and is said to be path dependent. It means that any error may propagate along the path followed to phase unwrapping. In this study we will review the least square method (Ghiglia, 1998). Basically, it consists in the integration of the phase gradient by solving a linear equation system employing a numerical technique. Lets assume $\phi^x(x,y)$ and $\phi^y(x,y)$ as the phase differences in the horizontal and vertical directions, respectively. These phases are calculated from the wrapped phase $\phi^w(x,y)$ as follows:

$$\phi^{x}(x,y)=\tan^{-1}\left\{\frac{\sin\left[\phi^{w}(x,y)-\phi^{w}(x-1,y)\right]}{\cos\left[\phi^{w}(x,y)-\phi^{w}(x-1,y)\right]}\right\}p(x,y)p(x-1,y), \tag{27}$$

and

$$\phi^{y}(x,y)=\tan^{-1}\left\{\frac{\sin\left[\phi^{w}(x,y)-\phi^{w}(x,y-1)\right]}{\cos\left[\phi^{w}(x,y)-\phi^{w}(x,y-1)\right]}\right\}p(x,y)p(x,y-1), \tag{28}$$

In the above equations *p(x,y)* is a pupil function equal to one inside of an interferogram field and zero otherwise. A discretized Laplacian equation is then obtained from the phase differences:

$$\begin{aligned}L(x,y)&=\phi^{x}(x+1,y)-\phi^{x}(x,y)+\phi^{y}(x,y+1)-\phi^{y}(x,y)\\&=-4\phi(x,y)+\phi(x+1,y)+\phi(x-1,y)+\phi(x,y+1)+\phi(x,y-1)\end{aligned}. \tag{29}$$

This equation represents a linear equations system that can be solved with iterative algorithms. In particular, is employed an overrelaxation method (SOR) due to it may be easily programmed. The following equation is then iterated until the solution converges:

$$\begin{aligned}&\phi^{k+1}(x,y)=\phi^{k}(x,y)+\\&+\frac{\left[d\phi^{k}(x,y)-\phi(x+1,y)-\phi(x-1,y)-\phi(x,y+1)-\phi(x,y-1)+L(x,y)\right]r}{d},\end{aligned} \tag{30}$$

where, *d=p(x+1,y)+p(x-1,y)+p(x,y+1)+p(x,y-1)*, and *r* is a parameter of the SOR method that must be set between the [1,2] range. Figure 15 shows the wrapped phase ϕ^{w} obtained from the sine and cosine of the phase and the unwrapped phase ϕ. A simple iterative algorithm that unwraps the phase from the discretized Laplacian is given as:

```
Algoritm 1. % Unwraps phase.
while (q<max)%q is the number of iterations (500 for this case)
 q=q+1;
 for i=1:n
  for j=1:m
   if p(i,j)==1
    t=p(i+1,j)+p(i-1,j)+p(i,j+1)+p(i,j-1);
    g(i,j)=g(i,j)-((t*g(i,j)-g(i+1,j)-g(i-1,j)-g(i,j+1)-g(i,j-1)+L(i,j))*1.95/t);%iterated equation
   else
    g(i,j)=0;
end,end,end,end
```

A single interferogram with open fringes may also be analyzed for phase recovering (Creath & Wyant, 1992). Experimentally an open fringe interferogram can be achieved if a tilt term is added to the phase, usually by tilting the reference beam in an interferometer. Equation (18) can be modified in order to include a tilt term in the x direction, this is as follows:

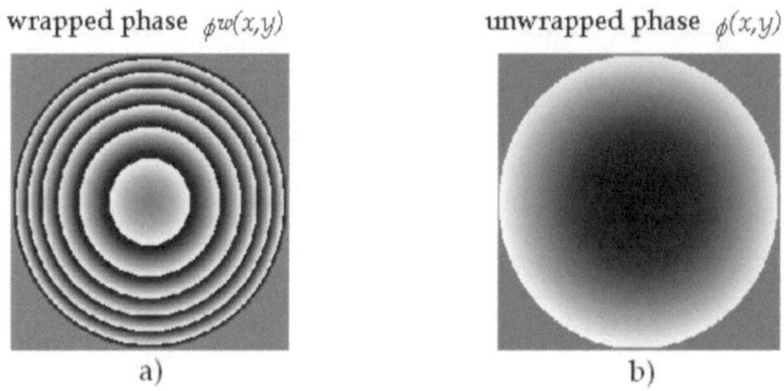

Fig. 15. a) wrapped and b) unwrapped phase.

$$I(x,y) = a(x,y) + b(x,y)\cos\left[\phi(x,y) + 2\pi t x\right] \tag{31}$$

where $a(x,y)=I_1(x,y)+I_2(x,y)$ is known as the background intensity and $b(x,y)=2[I_1(x,y)I_2(x,y)]^{1/2}$ is the modulation or visibility term. The Fourier transform of the expression below can be written as:

$$\tilde{I}(u,v) = \tilde{a}(u,v) + C(u+t,v) + C^*(u-t,v). \tag{32}$$

Then the Fourier spectra of an open fringe interferogram contains three terms, $\tilde{a}(u,v)$ is a narrow peak at the center of the Fourier spectra and $C(u+t,v)$ and $C^*(u-t,v)$ are shifted complex conjugate intensities symmetrically located respect to the origin of the Fourier

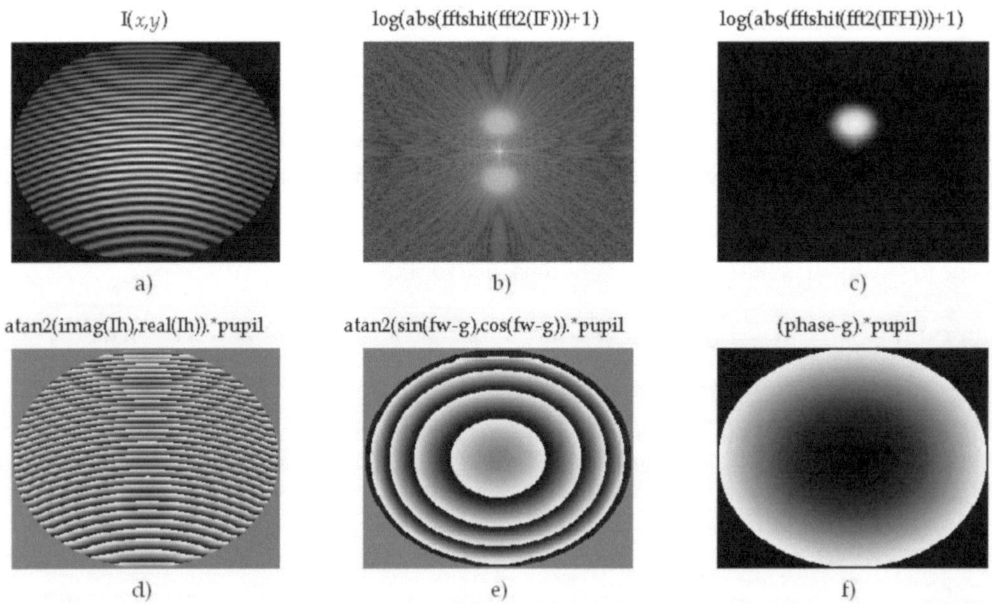

Fig. 16. Process of phase recovery from a single interferogram with closed fringes, as shown in algorithm 2. a) Interferogram, b) Fourier spectrum, c) filtered Fourier spectrum, d) wrapped phase with tilt, e) wrapped phase without tilt, and f) unwrapped continuous phase.

domain (Takeda, 1982). The Fourier procedure to recover the phase consist in isolating either $C(u,v)$ or $C^*(u,v)$. Then the inverse transform is taken in order to retrieve the wrapped phase from the imaginary and real parts of the filtered spectra. The last step, as done with phase shifting procedures, is to apply a phase unwrapping procedure to recover the continuous phase. The complete process of phase recovery from an open fringe interferogram is observed in figure 16.

```
Algoritm 2. % Phase recovery from a single interferogram
for i=1:256
 for j=1:256
  if sqrt((i-128)^2+(j-128)^2)<126 %creates a function pupil
   pupil(i,j)=1;
  else
   pupil(i,j)=0;
  end
  x=(i-128)/128;
  y=(j-128)/128;
  phase(i,j)=2*pi*(4*(x^2+y^2)+16*x);
  g(i,j)=2*pi*16*x;
  back(i,j)=128*exp(-1*(x^2+y^2));
  mod(i,j)=127*exp(-1*(x^2+y^2));
  I(i,j)=(back(i,j)+mod(i,j)*cos(phase(i,j)))*pupil(i,j); % Interferogram with closed fringes
  H(i,j)=exp(-180*((x-0.25)^2+y^2));%Band-Pass filter
  G(i,j)=1-exp(-1000*(x^2+y^2));%High pass filter
end,end
IF=fftshift(fft2(I));%Fourier transform of the interferogram
IFH=IF.*H.*G; %Filtered Fourier transform
Ih=ifft2(fftshift(IFH)); %Inverse Filtered Fourier transform
fw=atan2(imag(Ih),real(Ih)).*pupil;%Wrapped phase with tilt
fw1=atan2(sin(fw-g),cos(fw-g)).*pupil; %Wrapped phase without tilt
phase1=(phase-g).*pupil; %Unwrapped phase
```

4.2 Wavefront deformation analysis

Optical metrology applied for the determination of different physical variables has greatly contributed with the constant advance of technology at a point that it is becoming a powerful measurement alternative for the solution of problems in engineering and sciences.

4.2.1 Deformation analysis using speckle interferometry

In this section, is presented a deformation analysis for the estimation of out-of-plane displacement components in a simulated model of a cantilever made of aluminum with a load applied at its free end. The example corresponds to a typical problem in structural mechanics where the Young´s modulus can be determined from the displacement of the loaded bar made of an isotropic material. The suggested arrangement for the testing in electronic speckle pattern interferometry (ESPI) is shown in figure 17. The laser light beam is divided by the beam splitter BS1. One beam is reflected by a mirror attached to a piezoelectric PZ (PC controlled), and then is expanded to uniformly illuminate at a small angle respect to the normal of the object surface, and the other beam is coupled into an optical fiber to obtain the reference illumination. The light reflected by the object and the reference beam introduced with BS2 interfere on the CCD.

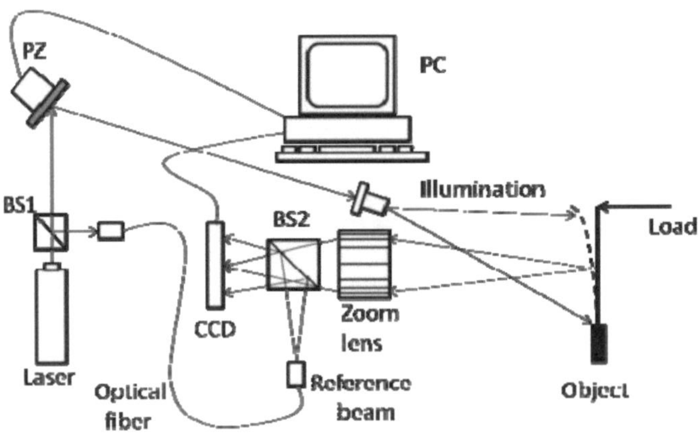

Fig. 17. Electronic speckle pattern interferometer.

The object was simulated by considering the following dimensions: 15 cm length and 3 cm height with a thickness of 0.5 cm. Using the two intensities $I_i(x,y)$, $I_f(x,y)$ of the speckle patterns generated by ESPI arrangement seen in the CCD image plane before and after applying a force of 0.1 N, the correlation fringes using equation (19) is shown in figure 18a and in figure 18b is shown the wrapped phase calculated by equation (20). In figure 18c is shown the filtered and unwrapped phase using a conventional spatial average filter of 3 x 3 pixels and an iterative least-squares algorithm.

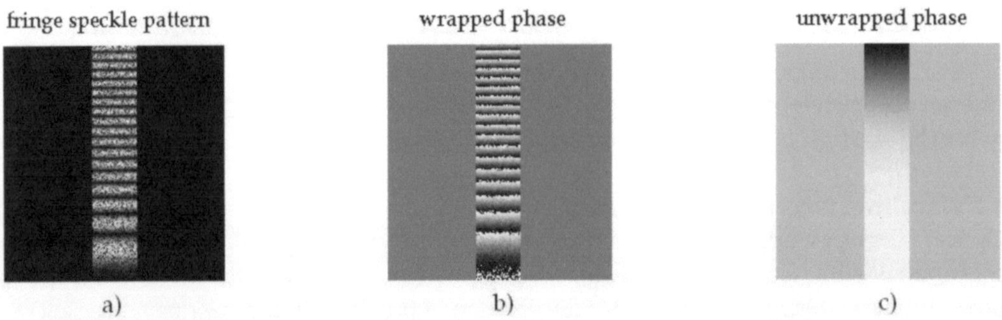

Fig. 18. Deformation analysis of a cantilever with ESPI. a) interference fringe pattern; b) wrapped phase and c) unwrapped phase.

4.3 Wavefront detection

Optical testing using diffraction gratings as wavefront modulators is another alternative to detect wavefront aberrations.

4.3.1 Grating diffraction

Diffraction gratings are optical devices commonly used on physics. There are several gratings types, but as shown in 3.2 section, sinusoidal gratings only diffracts three harmonic modes, due to this property, sinusoidal gratings have been developed by different techniques. According to the method reported by (Mora-González et al., 2009), is possible to generate these gratings by laser printing on acetates. In figure 19, are shown different increment sizes (Δy) of three sine profiles and the corresponding spectra of equations (25) and (26), respectively. It must be pointed that for larger Δy values, the resolution diminishes and more diffraction orders emerge.

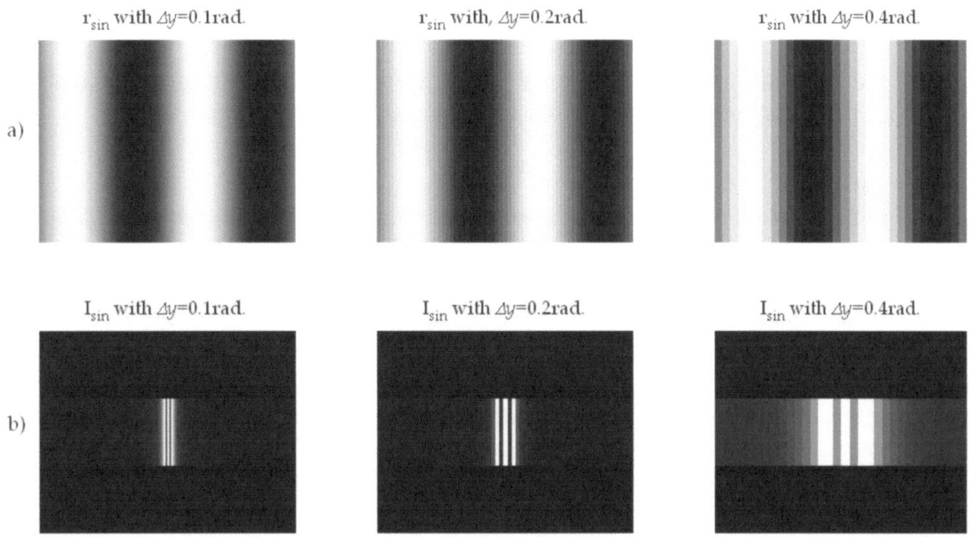

Fig. 19. Sinusoidal gratings generated in Matlab. With a) grating r_{sin}=255*[.5+.5*sin(y)] and b) Fourier spectra I_{sin}=*fftshift*(*fft2*(r_{sin})).

4.3.2 Ronchi test

The Ronchi test is one of the most non invasive optical tests used in optical workshops, due to the simplicity for observing aberrations over the optical surface. The test only needs to propagate a convergent aberrated wavefront through a diffraction grating to obtain a modulated fringe pattern (ronchigram) (Mora-González et al., 2001, 2003, 2011). In figure 20 is shown the typical diagram of the Ronchi test using a collimated illumination system.
In figure 21 are shown the ronchigram before and after circular low-pass filtering and their corresponding wrapped phase calculated with equation (20).

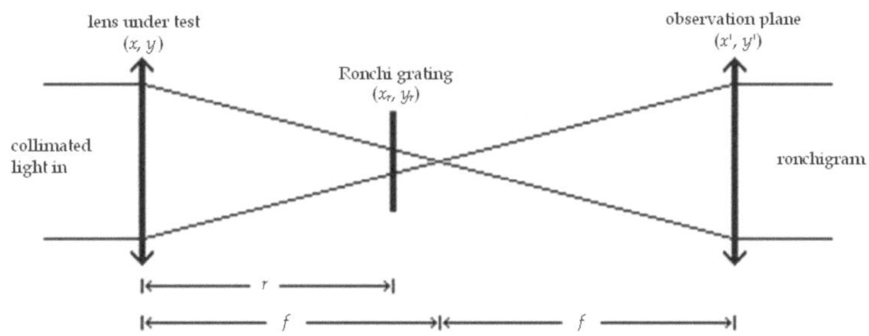

Fig. 20. Collimated light Ronchi test diagram. Where f is the focus of lenses and r is the distance between lens under test and Ronchi grating.

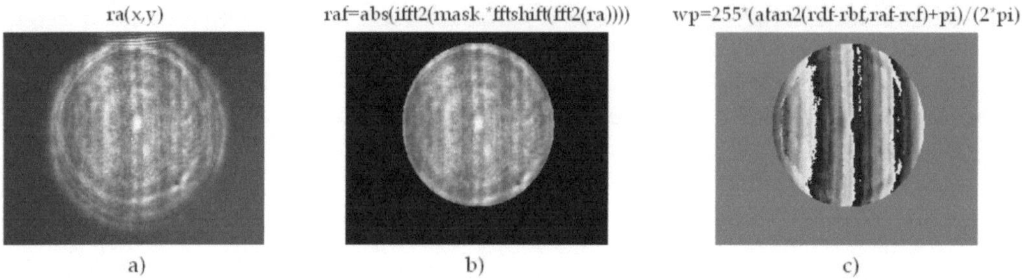

Fig. 21. Ronchi test results. a) ronchigram a: ra(x,y); b) frequency filtered ronchigram a and applied pupil: raf(x,y); and c) wrapped phase of ronchigrams a, b, c and d: wp(x,y).

4.4 Bio-metrology

In the present subsection several functions of Matlab and their applications as blood flow measurement and pattern recognition in fingerprint are shown.

4.4.1 Blood flow measurement

Laser speckle effect is an interference phenomena that is produced when an optical rough surface is illuminated by a laser source that can be observed directly or imaged by using an optical system. The resulting intensity well known as speckle pattern is the result of multiple interferences produced by the roughness of the object under test. The speckle pattern consists in a distribution of brilliant points and dark points.

By assuming ideal conditions like high coherent light source, unique frequency and perfect diffusing surface. It can be proved that the standard deviation of the intensity fluctuations from a speckle pattern is equal to the same that the average of the intensity. Speckle pattern contrast is defined by the relationship between standard deviation (σ) and the averaged intensity (I) (Goodman, 2005):

$$specklecontrast = \frac{\sigma}{\langle I \rangle}. \tag{33}$$

If the illuminated surface is static, the contrast observed in the speckle pattern is maximum, however, if the surface is moving, the speckle patterns changes completely. This phenomenon is known as "decorrelation" and can be observed when light is dispersed by a great number of moving dispersers, i. e. moving particles into a fluid. The decorrelation is used for fluid velocity quantification considering that a speckle pattern photography taken at a finite time is blurred (contrast losing) in flowing areas. Contrast changes depend on fluid velocity and photography exposure time (T). By assuming a Lorentzian velocity distribution, speckle contrast ($\sigma/<I>$) is defined as correlation and exposure time function (τ_c/T).

$$\frac{\sigma}{\langle I \rangle} = \left\{ \frac{\tau_c}{2T} \left[1 - \exp\left(-\frac{2T}{\tau_c} \right) \right] \right\}^{\frac{1}{2}}. \tag{34}$$

Correlation time τ_c is inversely proportional to local velocity of the dispersing particles. The following code calculates a contrast image from a speckle image. Local blood flow velocity can be found from image contrast information and equation (34). Figure 22 shown speckle images before and after processing.

```
Algoritm 3. % Calculation of speckle contrast.
Im2 = imread('speckle_img.bmp'); % load the bmp image file into the memory.
Im2 = im2double(Im2);
windowSize = 5; %define the window size for the filter.
avgFilter = fspecial('average',windowSize); % generate an averaging filter.
stdSpeckle = stdfilt(I,ones(windowSize)); %caculates the local standar deviation of image.
avgSpeckle = imfilter(I,avgFilter,'symmetric'); %calculates the average of each pixel
ctrSpeckle = stdSpeckle./avgSpeckle; %caculates the speckle contrast image
```

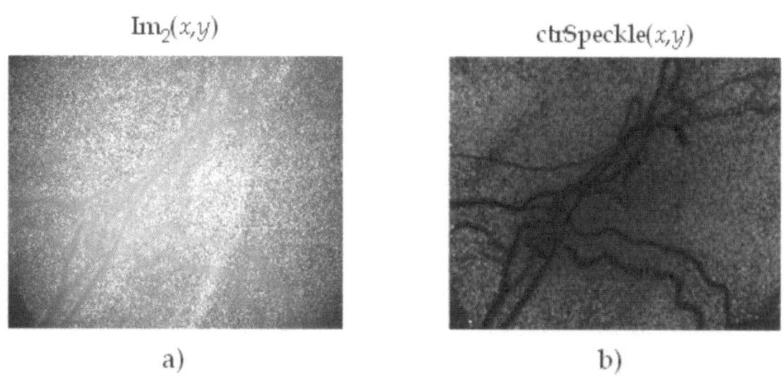

Fig. 22. Blood flow measurement results. a) speckle image of a rat cortex. b) speckle image of contrast after processing with the code of algoritm 3.

4.4.2 Fingerprint measurement

Several applications in pattern recognition are also utilized in optical metrology, finger print parameters measurements is an example. The present subsection shows a new form for fingerprint core determination based in the Radon transform of a fingerprint image, applied in x and y axes directions. The core is located by the interception of the extremes (local minimum and maximum) of the Radon transforms (Mora-González et al., 2010).

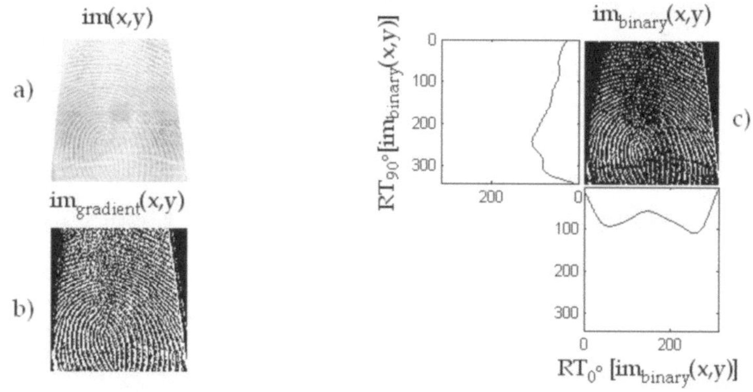

Fig. 23. Images for fingerprint core point detection. a) original fingerprint im(x,y), b) gradient of original fingerprint im_gradient(x,y), and c) binarized gradient im_binary(x,y) and its 0° - 90° Radon transforms.

The process for core finding is very simple. First, a high-pass filter with a gradient type convolution mask is applied to a fingerprint image in order to enhance the contrast. Next the image is skeletonized, and the Radon Transform (RT) is applied in the x and y directions to obtain RT_{90} and RT_0 profiles, respectively. Finally, the noise produced from ridges and rows in the fingerprint is minimized by a least-squares algorithm. The whole process is illustrated in figure 23 by using the following algorithm:

```
Algoritm 4. % Fingerprint analysis.
[im,map]=imread(FileName); %read fingerprint
im=double(im); %change image format
[Nx,Ny]=size(im); %image size
im_gradient=gradient(im); %gradient spatial filter
level = graythresh(im_gradient); %finding the threshold of gradient
for x=1:Nx
 for y=1:Ny
  if (im_gradient(x,y)>15*level) %fingerprint skeletonization
   im_binary(x,y)=1;
  else
   im_binary(x,y)=0;
end,end,end
[RT,xp] = radon(bg,[0 90]); %Radon transform
leastsq_0=polyfit(xp,RT(:,1),21); %21° polynomial adjustment for 0° Radon transform
leastsq_90=polyfit(xp,RT(:,2),21); %21° polynomial adjustment for 90° Radon transform
y_leastsq0=polyval(leastsq_0,xp); %least square approximation of 0° Radon transform
y_leastsq90=polyval(leastsq_90,xp); %least square approximation of 90° Radon transform
```

5. Conclusion

Mathematical fundamentals for Digital Image Processing and their implementation by means of algorithms and Matlab commands were established. It has been demonstrated according to some Optical Metrology applications, the Matlab algorithms efficiency. This confirms that Matlab is a computational powerful tool. However, optical metrology applications are not only limited to the discussed examples in the present chapter. Applications of all the proposed algorithms can be extended without any problem from deformation analysis by another interferometric techniques (Speckle photography, Moiré, etc.) or optical tests (Hartmann, Foucault, etc.), until analysis and pattern recognition in medicine (X-Ray images, tomography, etc.), among other branches of science and engineering.

6. Acknowledgment

The authors wish to express their gratitude for financial support of this project to *Departamento de Ciencias Exactas y Tecnología*, of *Centro Universitario de los Lagos, Universidad de Guadalajara*. The image of figure 22 courtesy of Julio Cesar Ramirez San-Juan, Ph.D (*Instituto Nacional de Astrofísica Óptica y Electrónica*).

7. References

Bow, S.T. (2002). *Pattern Recognition and Image Preprocesing* (2nd Ed.), Marcel Dekker, Inc., ISBN 0-8247-0659-5, New York, USA.

Bracewell, R.N. (1995). *Two-Dimensional Imaging*, Prentice Hall, ISBN 0-13-062621-X, New Jersey, USA.

Canny, J. (1986). A Computational Approach to Edge Detection, *IEEE Trans. on Pattern Analysis and Machine Intelligence*, Vol.PAMI-8, No.6, (November 1986), pp. 679-698, ISSN 0162-8828.

Creath, K.; Schmit, J. and Wyant, J.C. (2007), Optical Metrology of Diffuse Surfaces, In: *Optical Shop Testing, 3th ed.*, Malacara, D., pp. 756-807, John Wiley & Sons, Inc., ISBN 978-0-471-48404-2, Hoboken, New Jersey, USA.

Gasvik, K.J. (2002). *Optical Metrology*, John Wiley & Sons, Ltd., ISBN 0-470-84300-4, Chichester, West Sussex, England.

Ghiglia, D.C., Pritt, M.D. (1998), *Two-Dimensional Phase Unwrapping: Theory Algorithms and Software*, Wiley-Interscience, ISBN 0-471-24935-1, New York, USA.

Gonzalez, R.C. & Woods, R.E. (2002). *Digital Image Procesing* (2nd Ed.), Prentice Hall, ISBN 0-201-18075-8, New Jersey, USA.

Goodman, J.W. (2005). *Introduction to Fourier Optics* (3rd Ed.), Roberts and Company Publishers, ISBN 0-9747077-2-4, Englewood, USA.

Huntley, J. M. (2001), Automated analysis of speckle interferograms, In: *Digital Speckle Patter Interferometry and Related Techniques*, Rastogi, P. K., pp. 59-140, John Wiley & Sons, Ltd., ISBN 0-471-49052-0, Chichester, West Sussex, England.

Lehmann, M. (2001). Speckle Statistics in the Context of Digital Speckle Interferometry, In: *Digital Speckle Patter Interferometry and Related Techniques*, Rastogi, P. K., pp. 1-58, John Wiley & Sons, Ltd., ISBN 0-471-49052-0, Chichester, West Sussex, England.

Mora González, M. & Alcalá Ochoa, N. (2001). The Ronchi test with an LCD grating, *Opt. Comm.*, Vol.191, No.4-6, (May 2001), pp. 203-207, ISSN 0030-4018.

Mora-González, M. & Alcalá Ochoa, N. (2003). Sinusoidal liquid crystal display grating in the Ronchi test, *Opt. Eng.*, Vol.42, No.6, (June 2003), pp. 1725-1729, ISSN 0091-3286.

Mora-González, M.; Casillas-Rodríguez, F.J.; Muñoz-Maciel, J.; Martínez-Romo, J.C.; Luna-Rosas, F.J.; de Luna-Ortega, C.A.; Gómez-Rosas, G. & Peña-Lecona, F.G. (2008). Reducción de ruido digital en señales ECG utilizando filtraje por convolución, *Investigación y Ciencia*, Vol.16, No.040, (September 2008), pp. 26-32, ISSN 1665-4412.

Mora-González, M.; Pérez Ladrón de Guevara, H.; Muñoz-Maciel, J.; Chiu-Zarate, R.; Casillas, F.J.; Gómez-Rosas, G.; Peña-Lecona, F.G. & Vázquez-Flores, Z.M. (2009). Discretization of quasi-sinusoidal diffraction gratings printed on acetates, *Proceedings of SPIE 7th Symposium Optics in Industry*, Vol.7499, 74990C, ISBN 978-0-8194-8067-5, Guadalajara, México, September 2009.

Mora-González, M.; Martínez-Romo, J.C.; Muñoz-Maciel, J.; Sánchez-Díaz, G.; Salinas-Luna, J.; Piza-Dávila, H.I.; Luna-Rosas, F.J. & de Luna-Ortega, C.A. (2010). Radon Transform Algorithm for Fingerprint Core Point Detection. *Lecture Notes in Computer Science*, Vol.6256, No.1, (September 2010), pp. 134-143, ISSN 0302-9743.

Mora-González, M.; Casillas, F.J.; Muñoz-Maciel, J.; Chiu-Zarate, R. & Peña-Lecona, F.G. (2011). The Ronchi test using a liquid crystal display as a phase grating, *Proceedings of SPIE Optical Measurement Systems for Industrial Inspection VII*, Vol.8082 part two, 80823G, ISBN 978-0-8194-8678-3, Münich, Germany, May 2011.

Oppenheim, A.V.; Willsky, A.S. & Nawab, S.H. (1997). *Signasl and Systems, 2nd ed.*, Prentice Hall, Inc., ISBN 0-13-814757-4, New Jersey, USA.

Pratt, W.K. (2001). *Digital Image Processing* (3th Ed.), John Wiley & Sons, Inc., ISBN 0-471-22132-5, New York, USA.

Robinson, D.W. (1993). Phase unwrapping methods, In: *Interferogram Analysis,* Robinson, D.W. and Reid, G.T., pp. 195-229, IOP Publishing, ISBN 0-750-30197-X, Bristol, England.

Sirohi R. S. (1993), *Speckle Metrology,* Marcel Dekker, Inc., ISBN 0-8247-8932-6, New York, USA.

Takeda, M.; Ina, H. & Kobayashi, S. (1982). Fourier-transform method of fringe-pattern analysis for computer-based topography and interferometry, *J. Opt. Soc. Am.*, Vol.72, No.1, (January 1982), pp. 156-160, ISSN 0030-3941.

Tolstov, G.P. (1962). *Fourier Series,* Dover Publications, Inc., ISBN 0-486-63317-9, New York, USA.

Waldner, S. P. (2000). *Quantitative Strain Analysis with Image Shearing Speckle Pattern Interferometry (Shearography),* Doctoral Thesis, Swiss Federal Institute of Technology, Zurich, Swiss.